Sensor Fusion and Its Applications

edited by
Dr. Ciza Thomas

Sensor Fusion and Its Applications
Edited by Dr. Ciza Thomas

CBS, Edition 2016

Published by InTech

Janeza Trdine 9, 51000 Rijeka, Croatia

Publishing Process Manager Jelena Marusic

Technical Editor Goran Bajac

Cover Designer Martina Sirotic

Additional hard copies can be obtained from orders@intechopen.com

Sensor Fusion and Its Applications, Edited by Dr. Ciza Thomas
p. cm.
ISBN 978-953-307-101-5

INTECH
open science | open minds

Contents

Preface

The idea of this book on Sensor fusion and its Applications comes as a response to the immense interest and strong activities in the field of sensor fusion. Sensor fusion represents a topic of interest from both theoretical and practical perspectives.

The technology of sensor fusion combines pieces of information coming from different sources/sensors, resulting in an enhanced overall system performance with respect to separate sensors/sources. Different sensor fusion methods have been developed in order to optimize the overall system output in a variety of applications for which sensor fusion might be useful: sensor networks, security, medical diagnosis, navigation, biometrics, environmental monitoring, remote sensing, measurements, robotics, etc. Variety of techniques, architectures, levels, etc., of sensor fusion enables to bring solutions in various areas of diverse disciplines.

This book aims to explore the latest practices and research works in the area of sensor fusion. The book intends to provide a collection of novel ideas, theories, and solutions related to the research areas in the field of sensor fusion. This book aims to satisfy the needs of researchers, academics, and practitioners working in the field of sensor fusion. This book is a unique, comprehensive, and up-to-date resource for sensor fusion systems designers. This book is appropriate for use as an upper division undergraduate or graduate level text book. It should also be of interest to researchers, who need to process and interpret the sensor data in most scientific and engineering fields.

Initial chapters in this book provide a general overview of sensor fusion. The later chapters focus mostly on the applications of sensor fusion. Much of this work has been published in refereed journals and conference proceedings and these papers have been modified and edited for content and style. With contributions from the world's leading fusion researchers and academicians, this book has 22 chapters covering the fundamental theory and cutting-edge developments that are driving this field.

Several people have made valuable contributions to this book. All researchers who have contributed to this book are kindly acknowledged: without them, this would not have been possible. Jelena Marusic and the rest of the sciyo staff provided technical and editorial assistance that improved the quality of this work.

Editor

Dr. Ciza Thomas
College of Engineering,
Trivandrum
India

1

State Optimal Estimation for Nonstandard Multi-sensor Information Fusion System

Jiongqi Wang and Haiyin Zhou
National University of Defense Technology
China

1. Introduction

In the field of information fusion, state estimation is necessary[1-3]. The traditional state estimation is a process to use statistics principle to estimate the target dynamical (or static) state by using of measuring information including error from single measure system. However, single measure system can't give enough information to satisfy the system requirement for target control, and is bad for the precision and solidity of state estimation. Therefore, developing and researching information fusion estimation theory and method is the only way to obtain state estimation with high precision and solidity.

The traditional estimation method for target state (parameter) can be traced back to the age of Gauss; in 1975, Gauss presented least square estimation (LSE), which is then applied in orbit determination for space target. In the end of 1950s, Kalman presented a linear filter method, which is widely applied in target state estimation and can be taken as the recursion of LSE[4]. At present, these two algorithms are the common algorithms in multi-sensor state fusion estimation, which are respectively called as batch processing fusion algorithm and sequential fusion algorithm.

The classical LSE is unbiased, consistent and effective as well as simple algorithm and easy operation when being applied in standard multi sensor information fusion system (which is the character with linear system state equation and measuring equation, uncorrelated plus noise with zero mean)[5]. However, because of the difference of measuring principle and character of sensor as well as measuring environment, in actual application, some non-standard multi-sensor information fusion systems are often required to be treated, which mainly are as follows:

1) Each system error, mixing error and random disturbed factor as well as each nonlinear factor, uncertain factor (color noise) existing in multi sensor measuring information[6];

2) Uncertain and nonlinear factors existing in multi sensor fusion system model, which is expressed in two aspects: one is much stronger sense, uncertain and nonlinear factors in model structure and another is time-change and uncertain factor in model parameter[7];

3) Relativity between system noise and measuring noise in dynamical system or relativity among sub-filter estimation as well as uncertain for system parameter and unknown covariance information[8-9].

Ignoring the above situations, the optimal estimation results cannot be obtained if still using the traditional batch processing fusion algorithm or sequential fusion algorithm. So to research the optimal fusion estimation algorithm for non standard multi-sensor system with the above situations is very essential and significative[10].

In the next three sections, the research work in this chapter focuses on non-standard multi-sensor information fusion system respectively with nonlinear, uncertain and correlated factor in actual multi-sensor system and then presents the corresponding resolution methods.

Firstly, the modeling method based on semi-parameter modeling is researched to solve state fusion estimation in nonstandard multi-sensor fusion system to eliminate and solve the nonlinear mixing error and uncertain factor existing in multi-sensor information and moreover to realize the optimal fusion estimation for the state.

Secondly, a multi-model fusion estimation methods respectively based on multi-model adaptive estimation and interacting multiple model fusion are researched to deal with nonlinear and time-change factors existing in multi-sensor fusion system and moreover to realize the optimal fusion estimation for the state.

Thirdly, self-adaptive optimal fusion estimation for non-standard multi-sensor dynamical system is researched. Self-adaptive fusion estimation strategy is introduced to solve local dependency and system parameter uncertainty existed in multi-sensor dynamical system and moreover to realize the optimal fusion estimation for the state.

2. Information Fusion Estimation of Nonstandard Multisensor Based on Semi parametric Modeling

From the perspective of parameter modeling, any system models generally consist of two parts: deterministic model (It means that the physical model and the corresponding parameters are determined) and non-deterministic model (It means that the physical models are determined but some parameter uncertainty, or physical models and parameters are not fully identified). In general case, the practical problems of information fusion can be described approximately by means of parametric modeling, then to establish the compact convergence of information processing model. Namely, the part of the systematic error of measurement can be deduced or weaken through the establishment of the classic parametric regression model, but it cannot inhibit mixed errors not caused by parametric modeling and uncertainty errors and other factors. Strictly speaking, the data-processing method of classical parametric regression cannot fundamentally solve the problem of uncertainty factors[11]. Yet it is precisely multi-sensor measurement information in the mixed errors and uncertainties that have a direct impact on the accuracy indicated by the model of multi-sensor fusion system, then in turn will affect the state estimation accuracy to be estimated and computational efficiency. So, it is one of the most important parts to research and resolve such error factors of uncertainty, and to establish a reasonable estimation method under the state fusion estimation.

As for this problem, there are a large number of studies to obtain good results at present. For instance, systematic error parameter model suitable for the engineering background is established to deal with the system error in measurement information. Extended-dimensional vector is employed to directly turn systematic error into the problem of the state fusion estimation under the standard form[12]. However, due to the increase of the number of parameters to be estimated, the treatment not only lowered the integration of estimation accuracy, but also increased the complexity of the computation of the matrix inversion. In addition, robust estimation theory and its research are designed to the problem of the incomplete computing of the abnormal value and the condition of systems affected by the large deviation[13]. A first order Gauss - Markov process is used to analyze and handle the random noise in measurement information. However, most of these treatments and researches are based on artificial experience and strong hypothesis, which are sometimes so contrary to the actual situation that they can doubt the feasibility and credibility of the state fusion estimation.

The main reason for the failure of the solution of the above-mentioned problems is that there is no suitable uncertainty modeling method or a suitable mathematical model to describe the non-linear mixed-error factors in the multi-sensor measurement information[14].

Parts of the linear model (or called) semi-parameter model can be used as a suitable mathematical model to describe the non-linear mixed-error factors in the measurement information [15]. Semi-parametric model have both parametric and non-parametric components. Its advantages are that it focused on the main part of (i.e. the parameter component) the information but without neglecting the role of the interference terms (non-parametric component). Semi-parametric model is a set of tools for solving practical problems with a broad application prospects. On the one hand, it solves problems which are difficult for only parameter model or non-parametric model alone to solve, thus enhancing the adaptability of the model; on the other, it overcome the issue of excessive loss of information by the non-parametric method and describe practical problems closer to the real and made fuller use of the information provided by data to eliminate or weaken the impact of the state fusion estimation accuracy caused by non-linear factors more effectively.

This section attempts to introduce the idea of semi-parametric modeling into the fusion state estimation theory of the non-standard multi-sensor. It establishes non-standard multi-sensor fusion state estimation model based on semi-parametric regression and its corresponding parameters and non-parametric algorithm. At the same time of determining the unknown parameters, it can also distinguish between nonlinear factors and uncertainties or between system error and accidental error so as to enhance the state fusion estimation accuracy.

2.1 State Fusion Estimation Based on Mutual Iteration Semi-parametric Regression

In terms of the optimal state fusion estimation of the multi-sensor fusion system integration, its main jobs are to determine the "measurement information" and the state of mapping relationship to be assessed, to reveal statistical characteristics of measurement errors, and then to reach the result to be consistent with the optimal state fusion of the project scene. The mapping matrix is determined by specific engineering and the model established by the physical background, having a clear expression generally. Therefore, the core task of the multi-sensor consists in the statistical characteristics of the measurement error analysis. But in practice, the differences of sensor measuring principle and its properties often touch upon the existence of the observing system error and the non-standard multi-sensor data fusion system under the influence of nonlinear uncertain elements. Among them, the errors in constant-value system or parameterized system are rather special but conventional system error. For these systems, it is easy to deal with[12]. But in fact, some systematic errors, non-linear uncertainties in particular, which occur in the multi-sensor information fusion system, are difficult to be completely expressed by parameters. In the first place, there are many factors which effect the value-taken of nonlinearity but all of these cannot be considered when establishing mathematical models. Secondly, some relative simple functional relations are chosen to substitute for functional relation between those factors and their parameters, so the established functional model are often said to be the approximate expression of the practical problems, that is to say, there is the existence of the model representation for error. When the error value of the model is a small amount, there is nothing much influence on the result of the assessment of the general state of this system if omitting it. But when the error value of the model is comparatively large, the neglect of it will exert a strong influence and lead to the wrong conclusion. Therefore, we main focused on the refinement issues of the state fusion estimation model under the condition of the non-linear uncertain factors (those non-linear uncertainties which are not parameterized fully), introducing semi-parametric regression analysis to establish non-standard multi-sensor information fusion estimation theory based on semi-parametric regression and its corresponding fusion estimation algorithm.

(1) Semi-parametric Regression Model

Assuming a unified model of linear integration of standard multi-sensor fusion system is:

$$\boldsymbol{Y}^N = \boldsymbol{HX} + v^N$$

Where, Y^N is the observation vector, X the state vector of the fusion to be estimated, v^N observation error, H the mapping matrix between metrical information and the state fusion to be estimated. In this model, v^N is supposed to be white noise of the zero mean. That is to say, except observation error, the observation vector Y^N is completely used as the function of status to be assessed. However, if the model is not accurate, with nonlinear uncertainties, the above formula cannot be strictly established and should be replaced by:

$$\boldsymbol{Y}^N = \boldsymbol{H}^N \boldsymbol{X} + \boldsymbol{S}^N + v^N \tag{2.1}$$

Where, $S^N(t)$ is the amount of model error which describes an unknown function relationship, it is the function of a certain variables t.

Currently, there are three methods for using semi-parametric model to estimate the error with nonlinear factor model in theory, including the estimation of part of the linear model of approximation parameterization, the estimation of part of the linear model of regularization matrix compensation, and part of the two-stage linear model estimation[16]. But the process of its solution implies that the algorithm realization is comparative complex, and that the accuracy of estimation depends on the cognition of characteristics of non-parametric component as well as the choice of basis function. Taking the estimation of part of the linear model of regularization matrix compensation for instance, the programming of key factors like regular matrix and smoothing factor are highly hypothetical, including some elements presumed in advance, furthermore, the solution process is very complex. If there is something error or something that cannot meet the model requirement in the solution of smoothing factor α and regularization matrix R_s, it will directly lead to unsolvable result to the semi-parametric fusion model. Here, we propose an algorithm based on the state fusion estimation of mutual-iteration semi-parametric regression, by the compensation for the error of the non-standard multi-sensor fusion model and the spectrum feature analysis to non-linear uncertainties, through aliasing frequency estimation method of decoupling to define the best fitting model, thus establishing the algorithm between the model compensation for the state fusion estimation model and the state fusion estimation of mutual iteration semi-parametric regression, isolating from non-linear uncertainties and eliminating the influence on its accuracy of the state fusion estimation.

(2) The basis function of nonlinear uncertainties is expressed as a method for decoupling parameter estimation of the aliasing frequency.

According to the signal processing theory, in the actual data processing, model errors and random errors under the influence of the real signal, non-linear uncertainties are often at different frequency ranges. Frequency components which are included in the error of measurement model are higher than the true signal frequency, but lower than random errors, so it can be called sub-low-frequency error[17-18]. It is difficult for classical least squares estimation method to distinguish between non-linear model error and random errors. However, the error characteristics of the measurement model can be extracted from the residual error in multi-sensor observation. Namely, it is possible to improve the state estimation accuracy if model error of residual error (caused mainly by the non-linear uncertainties) can be separated from random noise and the impact of model error deducted in each process of iterative solution.

On consideration that nonlinear factors S in semi-parametric model can be fitted as the following polynomial modulation function forms:

$$S(t) = \sum_{m=0}^{M-1} \left(\sum_{i=0}^{N_m-1} a_i^{(m)} t^i \right) \cdot \exp\{j2\pi f_m t\} \overset{\text{def}}{=} \sum_{m=0}^{M-1} b_m(t) \cdot \exp\{j2\pi f_m t\} \tag{2.2}$$

Where, f_m is the frequency item of non-linear uncertainties, $b_m(t)$ the amplitude envelope of each component signal, $a_k^{(m)}$ polynomial coefficients corresponding to envelope function. From Equation (2.2), $S(t)$ is a multi-component amplitude-harmonic signal. It is complicated to directly use maximum likelihood estimation method to distinguish the frequency parameters of various components and amplitude parameter but apply the combination of matching pursuit and the ESPRIT method of basis pursuit to decouple parameter estimation.

Firstly, recording $y_0(t) = S(t)$, the method of ESPRIT [19] to estimate the characteristic roots closest to the unit circle from $y_0(t)$ is used to estimate frequency of corresponding harmonic components $\hat{\lambda}$. Without loss of generality, if the estimation corresponded to f_0, that is, $\hat{f}_0 = (1/2\pi) \cdot \operatorname{Arg}\{\hat{\lambda}\}$, according to this, the original signal frequency is shifted to frequency to get

$$\tilde{y}_0(t) = y_0(t) \cdot \exp\{-j2\pi \hat{f}_0 t\} \tag{2.3}$$

The baseband signal is obtained from low pass and filter of the shifted signal $\tilde{y}_0(t)$. Namely, it can be used as an estimate of amplitude envelope $b_0(t)$.

Noting: $\hat{b}_0(t) = \mathrm{LPF}[\tilde{y}_0(t)]$, among them, $\mathrm{LPF}[\cdot]$ refers to low-pass filter. The observation model of amplitude envelope is deduced from Formula (2.2):

$$\hat{b}_0(t) = \sum_{i=0}^{N_0-1} a_i^{(0)} t^i + \varepsilon(t) \tag{2.4}$$

The corresponding coefficient $\hat{a}_i^{(0)}$ is estimated by Least Square, which is also used to reconstruct the corresponding signal components.

$$\bar{b}_0(t) = \sum_{i=0}^{N_0-1} \hat{a}_i^{(0)} t^i \cdot \exp\{j2\pi\hat{f}_0 t\}$$

To move forward a step, the reconstruction of the harmonic component of amplitude modulation is subtracted from $y_0(t)$, then we can obtain residual signal:

$$y_1(t) = y_0(t) - \bar{b}_0(t) \tag{2.5}$$

The residual signal is used as a new observing signal to repeat the above processes to get parameter estimates of multi-component signals, that is $\{\hat{f}_k, \hat{a}_i^{(k)}\}$, $i = 0,1,\cdots,N_k - 1,\ k = 0,1,\cdots,M-1$. The stop condition of iterative algorithm can be represented as residual control criterion and the order selection of other models.

(3) Steps of how to calculate mutual iterative state estimation

By means of the basis function to nonlinear uncertainties and the estimation method of decoupling parameter of corresponding aliasing frequency, nonlinear uncertainties can be extracted by fitting method, establishing multi-sensor fusion system model. The optimal fusion estimate of the state $\boldsymbol{X}$ to be estimated can be determined by the mutual iteration method of the following linear and nonlinear factors. If the degree of the Monte-Carlo simulation test is L, the implementation algorithm will be as following.

Step1: For the obtaining multi-sensor fusion system, least squares estimation fusion is used to get $\boldsymbol{X}_j$ in the known observation sequence $Y_{1j}, Y_{2j}, \cdots, Y_{Nj}$ $(j = 1,2,\cdots,L)$;

Setp2: Computing observation residuals $Y'_{1j}, Y'_{2j}, \cdots, Y'_{Nj}$ in multi-sensor fusion system;

Setp3: Examining whether the observation residual family $\{Y'_{i1}, Y'_{i2}, \cdots, Y'_{iL} \mid i = 1,2,\cdots,N\}$ is white noise series, if it is, turn to Step5, if not, turning to Step4;

Step4: With the method for aliasing frequency estimation, nonlinear uncertainties vector $\boldsymbol{S}^N = \{S_1, S_2, \cdots, S_N\}$ can be determined. That is to say, S_i should satisfy the following conditions:

$$\begin{cases} Y'_{i1} = S_i + v_{i1} \\ Y'_{i2} = S_i + v_{i2} \\ \cdots\cdots\cdots \\ Y'_{iL} = S_i + v_{iL} \end{cases}, i = 1, 2, \cdots, N$$

Where, the white noise series is $v_{i1}, v_{i2}, \cdots, v_{iL}$, $Y_{1j}, Y_{2j}, \cdots, Y_{Nj}$ is replaced by $Y_{1j} - S_1, Y_{2j} - S_j, \cdots, Y_{Nj} - S_N$, and then turn to Step1.

Step5: The exported value of $\hat{\boldsymbol{X}} = \frac{1}{L}\sum_{j=1}^{L}\boldsymbol{X}_j$ is the optimal fusion estimate of the state to be estimated.

The above algorithm is all dependent on iteration. We will keep estimating and fitting the value of the nonlinear uncertainty vector S^N. Simultaneously, it is also a process of being close to the true value of a state to be assessed. When approaching the true state values, observation residuals equaled to Gaussian white noise series. This method is in essence an improvement to iterative least squares estimation of Gauss-Newton by the use of two-layer iterative correction. Step4 (a process of fitting nonlinear uncertainties) is a critical part.

2.2 Analysis of Fusion Accuracy

Two theorems will be given in the following. Comparing to the classical least square algorithm, the state fusion estimation accuracy based on mutual iteration semi-parametric regression will be analyzed in theory to draw a corresponding conclusion.

Theorem 2.2: On the condition of nonlinear uncertain factors, the estimation for $\hat{\boldsymbol{X}}$ is $\hat{\boldsymbol{X}}_{\mathrm{BCS}}$ which is called unbiased estimation, and $\hat{\boldsymbol{X}}$ is obtained from the state fusion estimation based on mutual iteration semi-parametric regression, while with classical weighted least squares, the estimate value $\hat{\boldsymbol{X}}_{\mathrm{WLSE}}$ is biased estimate.

Demonstration: Under the influence of factors of the nonlinear uncertain error, the state fusion estimation based on semi-parametric regression from the generalized unified fusion model (2.1) is deduced as:

$$\hat{\boldsymbol{X}}_{\mathrm{BCS}} = \left(\boldsymbol{H}^{\mathrm{T}}\boldsymbol{R}^{-1}\boldsymbol{H}\right)^{-1}\boldsymbol{H}^{\mathrm{T}}\boldsymbol{R}^{-1}(\boldsymbol{Y} - \hat{\boldsymbol{S}}) \tag{2.6}$$

And $\hat{\boldsymbol{S}}$ is function fitted values of nonlinear uncertain error vector, then its expectation is:

$$\mathrm{E}[\hat{\boldsymbol{X}}_{\mathrm{BCS}}] = \mathrm{E}[(\boldsymbol{H}^{\mathrm{T}}\boldsymbol{R}^{-1}\boldsymbol{H})^{-1}\boldsymbol{H}^{\mathrm{T}}\boldsymbol{R}^{-1}(\boldsymbol{Y} - \hat{\boldsymbol{S}})] = (\boldsymbol{H}^{\mathrm{T}}\boldsymbol{R}^{-1}\boldsymbol{H})^{-1}\boldsymbol{H}^{\mathrm{T}}\boldsymbol{R}^{-1}\boldsymbol{H}\boldsymbol{X} = \boldsymbol{X} \tag{2.7}$$

$\hat{\boldsymbol{X}}_{\mathrm{BCS}}$ is the unbiased estimation of $\boldsymbol{X}$. The estimated value $\hat{\boldsymbol{X}}_{\mathrm{WLSE}}$ is computed by the method of weighted least squares estimation fusion. That is:

$$\hat{\boldsymbol{X}}_{\mathrm{WLSE}} = (\boldsymbol{H}^{\mathrm{T}}\boldsymbol{R}^{-1}\boldsymbol{H})^{-1}\boldsymbol{H}^{\mathrm{T}}\boldsymbol{R}^{-1}\boldsymbol{Y} = (\boldsymbol{H}^{\mathrm{T}}\boldsymbol{R}^{-1}\boldsymbol{H})^{-1}\boldsymbol{H}^{\mathrm{T}}\boldsymbol{R}^{-1}(\boldsymbol{H}\boldsymbol{X} + \hat{\boldsymbol{S}}) \tag{2.8}$$

Its expectation is:

$$\mathrm{E}[\hat{\boldsymbol{X}}_{\mathrm{WLSE}}]=\mathrm{E}[(\boldsymbol{H}^{\mathrm{T}}\boldsymbol{R}^{-1}\boldsymbol{H})^{-1}\boldsymbol{H}^{\mathrm{T}}\boldsymbol{R}^{-1}(\boldsymbol{H}\boldsymbol{X}+\hat{\boldsymbol{S}})]=\boldsymbol{X}+(\boldsymbol{H}^{\mathrm{T}}\boldsymbol{R}^{-1}\boldsymbol{H})^{-1}\boldsymbol{H}^{\mathrm{T}}\boldsymbol{R}^{-1}\hat{\boldsymbol{S}} \tag{2.9}$$

The following relationship formula is from Formula (2.6) and (2.8):

$$\hat{\boldsymbol{X}}_{\mathrm{WLSE}}=\hat{\boldsymbol{X}}_{\mathrm{BCS}}+(\boldsymbol{H}^{\mathrm{T}}\boldsymbol{R}^{-1}\boldsymbol{H})^{-1}\boldsymbol{H}^{\mathrm{T}}\boldsymbol{R}^{-1}\hat{\boldsymbol{S}} \tag{2.10}$$

Theorem 2.3: On the condition of nonlinear error factors, the valuation accuracy of $\hat{\boldsymbol{X}}$ which is based on the state fusion estimation of the mutual iteration semi-parametric regression ranked above the valuation accuracy which is based on the method of weighted least squares estimation fusion.

Demonstration: The estimation accuracy of semi-parametric state fusion is supposed to be $\mathrm{Cov}[\hat{\boldsymbol{X}}_{\mathrm{BCS}}]$, so:

$$\mathrm{Cov}[\hat{\boldsymbol{X}}_{\mathrm{BCS}}]=\mathrm{E}[(\hat{\boldsymbol{X}}_{\mathrm{BCS}}-\boldsymbol{X})(\hat{\boldsymbol{X}}_{\mathrm{BCS}}-\boldsymbol{X})^{\mathrm{T}}]=(\boldsymbol{H}^{\mathrm{T}}\boldsymbol{R}^{-1}\boldsymbol{H})^{-1} \tag{2.11}$$

However, the valuation accuracy $\mathrm{Cov}[\hat{\boldsymbol{X}}_{\mathrm{WLSE}}]$ obtained by the method of weighted least squares estimation fusion.

$$\begin{aligned}\mathrm{Cov}[\hat{\boldsymbol{X}}_{\mathrm{WLSE}}]&=\mathrm{E}[(\hat{\boldsymbol{X}}_{\mathrm{WLSE}}-\boldsymbol{X})(\hat{\boldsymbol{X}}_{\mathrm{WLSE}}-\boldsymbol{X})^{\mathrm{T}}]\\&=\mathrm{E}[(\hat{\boldsymbol{X}}_{\mathrm{BCS}}+\boldsymbol{P}-\boldsymbol{X})(\hat{\boldsymbol{X}}_{\mathrm{BCS}}+\boldsymbol{P}-\boldsymbol{X})^{\mathrm{T}}]=(\boldsymbol{H}^{\mathrm{T}}\boldsymbol{R}^{-1}\boldsymbol{H})^{-1}+\boldsymbol{P}^{\mathrm{T}}\boldsymbol{P}\end{aligned} \tag{2.12}$$

Where, $\boldsymbol{P}=(\boldsymbol{H}^{\mathrm{T}}\boldsymbol{R}^{-1}\boldsymbol{H})^{-1}\boldsymbol{H}^{\mathrm{T}}\boldsymbol{R}^{-1}\hat{\boldsymbol{S}}$, obviously $\boldsymbol{P}^{\mathrm{T}}\boldsymbol{P}>0$, the estimation accuracy of $\hat{\boldsymbol{X}}$ based on the state fusion estimation of the mutual iteration semi-parametric regression is superior to the estimation accuracy obtained by the method of weighted least squares estimation fusion.

2.3 Numerical Examples and Analysis

In order to verify these conclusions, the experiment of numerical simulation is conducted on the basis of the method of the state fusion estimation of the mutual iteration semi-parametric.

On consideration of the state fusion estimation of the constant-value $x=10$, the fusion system, which consists of three sensors, is used to the conduction of the state fusion estimation. The measurement equation of non-standard multi-sensor fusion is: $y_i=x+b_i+v_i$, $i=1,2,3$; where v_i noise which is zero mean, and each variance is the Gaussian-noise of $R_1=1, R_2=2$ and $R_3=3$. Simultaneously, non-linear error component $b_i(i=1,2,3)$ is something related to cycle colored noise of the number of Monte-Carlo simulation L, each amplitude is $b_1=0.5, b_2=1$ and $b_3=1.5$. The simulation times $L=100$. The estimate values and estimated variance of the state to be estimated are obtained from the method of the classical least squares estimation and the state fusion estimation of the mutual iteration semi-parametric given in the Table 2.1. Comparing the simulation results by the two methods, the fusion estimation accuracy is relatively low by the use of the least squares due to the influence of nonlinearity error. And it can also be predicted that with the increase of non-linear error factors, the estimation accuracy is bound to reduce more and more. But the method for the state fusion estimation of the mutual iteration semi-parametric can separate white noise series in observation noise from non-linear error factors, canceling its influence to state fusion estimation accuracy by fitting estimates. If there is nonlinearity error, the state estimator, which is obtained by the method for the state fusion estimation of the iteration semi-parametric, will be the optimal estimation of true value.

Fusion Algorithm	State Fusion Estimation	Fusion Estimation Variance
Method of Weighted Least Squares Estimation Fusion.	11.084	1.957
Method of State Fusion Estimation of Iteration Semi-parametric	10.339	1.434

Table 2.1. Comparison of Estimation Result between the two Fusion Algorithms

3. Nonstandard Multisensor Information Fusion Estimate Based on Multi-model Fusion

In recent years, it becomes a hot research topic to establish the parametric / semi-parametric model in the control of a complex nonlinear model, which has also been a great application, but there are so few tactics which are used in actual projects. The main reason for this problem is due to the difficulties of establishing an accurate model for complex non-linear parameters and the uncertainty of the actual system to a degree. These uncertainties sometimes are performed within the system, sometimes manifests in the system outside. The designer can not exactly describe the structure and parameters of the mathematical model of the controlled object in advance within the system. As the influence to the system from external environment, it can be equivalent to be expressed by many disturbances, which are unpredictable but might be deterministic or even random. Furthermore, some other measurement noise logged in the system from the feedback loop of the different measurement, and these random disturbances and noise statistics are always unknown. In this case, for dynamic parameters of the model which is from doing experiments on the process of parametric modeling, it is hard for the accuracy and adaptability expressed by the test model, which is even a known model structure, to estimate parameters and their status in the real-time constraints conditions.

Multi-model fusion processing is a common method for dealing with a complex nonlinear system[20-21], using multi-model to approach dynamic performance of the system, completing real-time adjustment to model parameter and noise parameter which is related to the system, and programming multiple model estimator based on multiple model. This estimator avoided the complexity of the direct model due to the reason that it can achieve better estimation to its accuracy, complex tracking speed and stability. Compared with the single model algorithm, multi-model fusion has the following advantages: it can refine the modeling by appropriate expansion model; it can improve the transient effect effectively; the estimation will be the optimal one in the sense of mean square error after assumptions are met; the algorithm with parallel structure will be conducive to parallel computing.

Obtaining the state optimal fusion estimate is the processing of using multi-model to approach dynamic performance of the system at first, then realizing the disposure of multi-model multi-sensor fusion to the controlled object tracking measurement, This is the problem of the multi-model fusion estimation in essence[22]. The basic idea of it is to map the uncertainty of the parameter space (or model space) to model set. Based on each model parallel estimator, the state estimation of the system is the optimal fusion of estimation obtained by each estimator corresponding to the model. As it is very difficult to analyze this system, one of these methods is to use a linear stochastic control system to denote the original nonlinear system approximately and to employ the treatment of thinking linear regression model to solve the nonlinear problem which should be solved by uncertain control systems [23]. The fusion approach diagram is shown in Fig. 3.1.

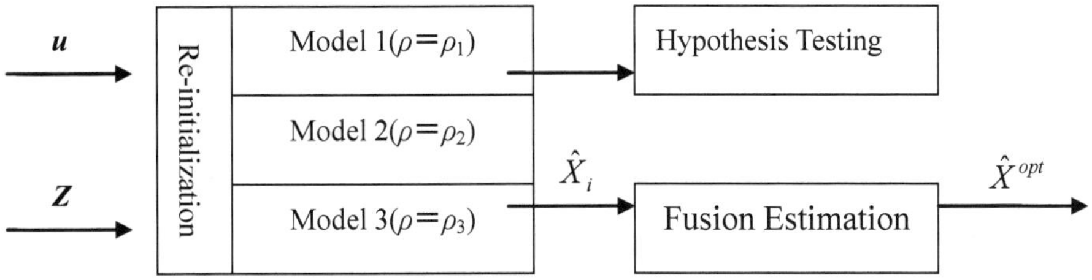

Fig. 3.1. Multi-model Fusion Estimation Approach Principle

Where, since different operational modes of stochastic uncertain systems worked with a group of parallel estimator, the input of each estimator will be the control input u and metrical information Z in a system, while the output of each estimator will be each one based on output residuals and state estimation X_i in a single model. According to the residual information, a hypothesis testing principle is used for programming model weight of an estimator corresponding to each model to reflect the situation that the probability of a model-taken at the determining time in a system. And the overall system state estimation is the weighted average value of the state estimation of each estimator.

3.1 Basic Principles of Multi-model Fusion

The description of multi-model fusion problem can be summed up: if the mathematical model of the object and the disturbance cannot be fully determined, multiple models will be designed as control sequence to approach the process of complex nonlinear time-varying in a system so as to make specified performance approaching as much as possible and keep it best.

The following nonlinear system will be given:

$$\begin{cases} \boldsymbol{X}(k+1) = F(\boldsymbol{X}(k), \boldsymbol{\theta}(k)) \\ \boldsymbol{Z}(k) = G(\boldsymbol{X}(k), \boldsymbol{\theta}(k)) \end{cases} \tag{3.1}$$

Where, $\boldsymbol{X}(k) \in \mathrm{R}^n$ is supposed to be the system state vector, $\boldsymbol{Z}(k) \in \mathrm{R}^m$ being the system output vector, F, G being nonlinear functions, $\boldsymbol{\theta}(k)$ being the vector of uncertain parameters.

(1) Model Design

Without loss of generality, the system output space is supposed to be Υ, then some outputs $Z_1 \leq \cdots \leq Z_N$ can be chosen from Υ and get a corresponding equilibrium $(X_i, \theta_i, Z_i), i = 1, \cdots, N$. The linearization expansion of the system at each equilibrium point can get some linear model $\sum_i$ from the original nonlinear system, and they constituted linear multi-model representation of the original system. Now the parameter $\theta \in \{\theta_1, \theta_2, \cdots, \theta_N\}$ can choose some discrete values. Thus the following model set can be obtained:

$$\Omega = \{M_i \mid i = 1, 2, \cdots, N\} \tag{3.2}$$

Where, M_i is related to the parameter θ. In a broad sense, M_i can express plant model and also feedback matrix of different states and the different local area where the error fall on. Also defined a collection of design-based estimator Ω:

$$\mathrm{E} = \{E_i \mid i = 1, 2, \cdots, N\} \tag{3.3}$$

Where, E_i is supposed to be designed based estimator M_i.

Based on the above analysis, the linear multi-model of the nonlinear systems (3.1) can be described as follows:

$$\begin{cases} \boldsymbol{X}(k+1) = \boldsymbol{\Phi}(\theta_i, k)\boldsymbol{X}(k) + \boldsymbol{C}(\theta_i, k)\boldsymbol{u}(k) + \boldsymbol{\Gamma}(\theta_i, k)w(k) \\ \boldsymbol{Z}_i(k) = \boldsymbol{H}(\theta_i, k)\boldsymbol{X}(k) + v_i(k) \end{cases} \quad i = 1, 2, \cdots, N \tag{3.4}$$

Where, $\boldsymbol{\Phi}(\boldsymbol{\theta}, k), \boldsymbol{C}(\boldsymbol{\theta}, k), \boldsymbol{\Gamma}(\boldsymbol{\theta}, k)$ are the system matrixes, $\boldsymbol{u}(k)$ being the control vector of the system, $\boldsymbol{H}(\boldsymbol{\theta}, k)$ being the mapping matrix, $w(k)$ being the n dimensional system noise sequence, $v(k)$ being the m dimensional system noise sequence. The meanings of other symbol are the same as those in Equation (3.1). Here, the multi-model fusion refers to use some linear stochastic control systems given in Equation (3.4) to solve nonlinear problems in Equation (3.1).

(2) Selection of Estimator

This is the second most important aspect, namely, choosing some estimators that can reasonably describe nonlinear systems to complete the process of the state fusion estimation.

(3) Rules and Model Fusion

In order to generate the global optimal fusion estimation, fusion rules can be fallen into three patterns:

1) Soft Decision or No Decision: At any k moment, global estimates are obtained from the estimation $\hat{\boldsymbol{X}}_{ik}$ $(i = 1, 2, \cdots, N)$ based on all estimators instead of the mandatory use of the estimator to estimate the value. It is claimed to be the mainstream multi-model fusion

method. If the conditional mean of the system state is considered as estimation, global estimates will be the sum of the probability weighted of estimated value of all estimators. That is:

$$\hat{\boldsymbol{X}}_{k|k} = \mathrm{E}\left(\boldsymbol{X}_k \mid \boldsymbol{Z}^k\right) = \sum_{i=1}^{N} \hat{\boldsymbol{X}}_{ik} P(M_{ik} \mid \boldsymbol{Z}^k) \tag{3.5}$$

2) Hard Decision: The approximation of the obtained global estimates is always from the estimated value of some estimators. The principle of selection of these estimators is the model maximum possible matching with the current model and the final state estimation will be mandatory. If only one model is to be selected in all models by maximum probability, consider its estimated value as the global one.

3) Random Decision: Global estimates are determined approximately based on some of the randomly selected sequence of the estimated model. The first fusion mode is the main method of multi-model fusion estimation. With the approximation of the nonlinear system and the improvement for system fault tolerance, the tendency of the multi-model fusion will be: estimating designing real-time adaptive weighted factor and realizing the adaptive control between models.

In reality, according to different model structures and fusion methods, multi-model fusion algorithm can be divided into two categories: (1) fixed multi-model (FMM); (2) interacting multiple model (IMM)[24-25]. The latter is designed for overcoming the shortcomings of the former. It can expand the system to the new mode without changing the structure of the system, but requires some prior information of a probability density function and the condition that the switching between the various models should satisfy the Markov process. Related closely to the fixed structure MM algorithms, there is a virtually ignored question: the performance of MM Estimator is heavily dependent on the use of the model set. There is a dilemma here: more models should be increased to improve the estimation accuracy, but the use of too many models will not only increase computation, but reduce the estimator's performance.

There are two ways out of this dilemma: 1) Designing a better model set (But so far the available theoretical results are still very limited); 2) using the variable model set.

It will be discussed Multi-model Adaptive Estimation (MMAE) and Interactive Multiple Model in Multi-model estimation method in a later paper.

3.2 Multi-model Adaptive Estimation

(1) The Fusion Architecture in MMAE

Multiple model adaptive estimators consisted of a parallel Kalman filter bank and hypothesis testing algorithm. Each library has a special filter system model, the independent vector parameters ($a_i, i = 1, 2, \cdots, N$) are used to describe its inherent Kalman filter model. Each Kalman filter model formed the current system state estimation $\hat{X}_i$ according to the independent unit under its own model and input vector, then using the estimate of the formation of the predictive value of the measurement vector, considering the residual error obtained by subtracting this value to the actual measurement vector Z as the similar levels of instruction between the filter model and the real system model. The smaller the residual error is the more matching between filter model and the real system model. Assuming the residual error is used to calculate the conditional probability p_i in the conditions of the actual measured values and the actual vector parameter a by test algorithm. The conditional probability is used to weigh the correctness of each Kalman filter state estimate. The probability weighted average being from the state estimation, formed the mixed state estimation of the actual system $\hat{X}_{MMAE}$. Multiple model adaptive estimators are shown in Fig. 3.2.

(2) The Filtering Algorithm in MMAE

Step1 Parallel Filtering Equation

The Kalman filter of the $i\ (i = 1, 2, \cdots, N)$ linear model is:

$$\begin{cases} \boldsymbol{X}_i(t_k) = \boldsymbol{\Phi}_i \boldsymbol{X}_i(t_{k-1}) + \boldsymbol{C}_i \boldsymbol{u}(t_{k-1}) + \boldsymbol{\Gamma}_i w_i(t_{k-1}) \\ \boldsymbol{Z}_i(t_k) = \boldsymbol{H}_i \boldsymbol{X}_i(t_k) + v_i(t_k) \end{cases} \tag{3.6}$$

The symbols have the same meaning as those of Formula (3.4). In addition, systematic noise $w_i(t_k)$ and observation noise $v_i(t_k)$ are both zero mean white noise, and for all k, j, satisfying:

$$\left.\begin{aligned} &\mathrm{E}[w_i(t_k)] = 0 \\ &\mathrm{E}[v_i(t_k)] = 0 \\ &\mathrm{E}[w_i(t_k) w_i^T(t_j)] = \boldsymbol{Q}_i \delta_{k,j} \\ &\mathrm{E}[v_i(t_k) v_i^T(t_j)] = \boldsymbol{R}_i \delta_{k,j} \\ &\mathrm{E}[w_i(t_k) v_i^T(t_j)] = 0 \end{aligned}\right\} \tag{3.7}$$

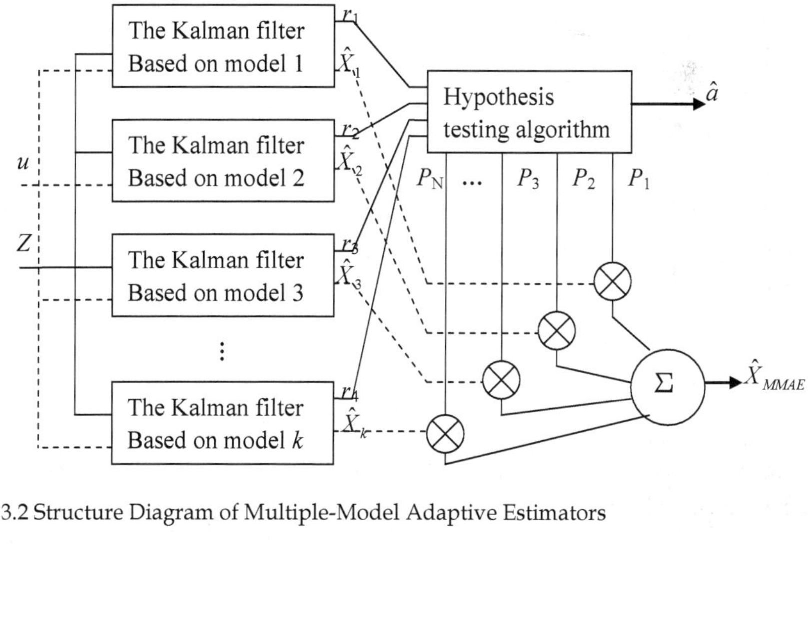

Fig. 3.2 Structure Diagram of Multiple-Model Adaptive Estimators

The Kalman filter algorithm use the above model to determine the optimum time to update the prediction and measurement of Kalman filter state estimation, optimum estimate update equation and state estimation error covariance matrix. Based on Kalman filter model, the update time equation of the Kalman filter state estimation is as follows:

$$\begin{cases} \hat{\boldsymbol{X}}_i(k/k-1) = \boldsymbol{\Phi}_i \hat{\boldsymbol{X}}_i(k-1/k-1) + \boldsymbol{C}_i \boldsymbol{u}(k-1) \\ \hat{\boldsymbol{Z}}_i(k/k-1) = \boldsymbol{H}_i \hat{\boldsymbol{X}}_i(k/k-1) \end{cases} \tag{3.8}$$

The update time equation of the state estimation error covariance matrix is:

$$\boldsymbol{P}_i(k/k-1) = \boldsymbol{\Phi}_i \boldsymbol{P}_i(k-1/k-1)\boldsymbol{\Phi}_i^{\mathrm{T}} + \boldsymbol{\Gamma}_i \boldsymbol{Q}_i \boldsymbol{\Gamma}_i^{\mathrm{T}} \tag{3.9}$$

The Kalman filter state estimation can achieve the measurement update by the following formula:

$$\hat{\boldsymbol{X}}_i(k/k) = \hat{\boldsymbol{X}}_i(k/k-1) + \boldsymbol{K}_i(k)\boldsymbol{r}_i(k) \tag{3.10}$$

And the gain of Kalman is:

$$\boldsymbol{K}_i(k) = \boldsymbol{P}_i(k/k-1)\boldsymbol{H}_i^{\mathrm{T}} \boldsymbol{A}_i(k)^{-1} \tag{3.11}$$

The O-C residual vector referred to the deviation by subtracting the measured value $Z_i(k)$ to the Kalman estimation based on previous measurements $Z_i(k/k-1)$, and that is:

$$\boldsymbol{r}_i(k) = \boldsymbol{Z}_i(k) - \boldsymbol{H}_i \hat{\boldsymbol{X}}_i(k/k-1) \tag{3.12}$$

Its variance matrix is:

$$\boldsymbol{A}_i(k) = \boldsymbol{H}_i \boldsymbol{P}_i(k/k-1)\boldsymbol{H}_i^{\mathrm{T}} + \boldsymbol{R}_i \tag{3.13}$$

And the update equation of the state estimate covariance matrix is:

$$\boldsymbol{P}_i(k/k) = [\mathrm{I} - \boldsymbol{K}_i(k)\boldsymbol{H}_i]\boldsymbol{P}_i(k/k-1) \tag{3.14}$$

Step2 Solving of Model Probability

It can obtain the new residual income of single linear model at any moment through the calculation of each parallel filter system of local filtering equation. At this moment, on the basis of the residual information and a hypothesis test principle, the model probability, corresponding to each estimator model, is designed reflect real-time system model in determining the time to take the possibility of a size. The representation of the probability of two models will be given as:

1) The representation of the model probability based on statistical properties of residuals

It is known to all: If the Single Kalman model and the system model phase are matching, the residual is the Gaussian white noise of the sequence zero-mean, and the variance matrix can be obtained by Formula (3.13). Therefore, the conditional probability density function under the condition of the measured values $\boldsymbol{Z}(t_k)$ of the $i\,(i=1,2,\cdots,N)$ filter model at the kth moment is:

$$f_{\boldsymbol{Z}(t_k)|\boldsymbol{H}_i,\boldsymbol{Z}(t_{k-1})}(\boldsymbol{Z}(t_k) \mid \boldsymbol{H}_i, \boldsymbol{Z}(t_{k-1})) = \frac{1}{(2\pi)^{m/2} \mid \boldsymbol{A}_i \mid^{1/2}} \exp\left\{-\frac{1}{2}\boldsymbol{r}_i^{\mathrm{T}}(k)\boldsymbol{A}_i^{-1}\boldsymbol{r}_i(k)\right\} \tag{3.15}$$

Defining the following objective function:

$$J_i(k) = p(\boldsymbol{\theta}_i \mid \boldsymbol{Z}_k) = p_i(t_k) = \Pr\{\boldsymbol{H} = \boldsymbol{H}_i \mid \boldsymbol{Z}(t_k) = \boldsymbol{Z}_k\} \tag{3.16}$$

And there will be the following recurrence relations:

$$p_i(t_k) = f_{Z(t_k)|H_i,Z(t_{k-1})}(Z(t_k) \mid H_i, Z(t_{k-1})) \cdot p_i(t_{k-1}) \tag{3.17}$$

For the normalized of the above objective function, if:

$$J_i(k) = p_i(t_k) = \frac{f_{Z(t_k)|H_i,Z(t_{k-1})}(Z(t_k) \mid H_i, Z(t_{k-1})) \cdot p_i(t_{k-1})}{\sum_{j=1}^{N} f_{Z(t_k)|H_j,Z(t_{k-1})}(Z(t_k) \mid H_j, Z(t_{k-1})) \cdot p_j(t_{k-1})} \tag{3.18}$$

The representation of the model probability based on statistical properties of residuals will be obtained.

2) The representation of the model probability based on normalized residuals

From the preceding analysis, it shows that O-C residual error $r_i(k)$ meant that the error between the actual output at the k time and the output of the ith model, so the residual can be used directly to define the following performance index function:

$$J_i(k) = \omega(\theta_i \mid Z^k) = \frac{S(k) - r_i^2(k)}{(N-1)S(k)} \tag{3.19}$$

Where, the model weight of the ith estimator will be $S(k) = \sum_{i=1}^{N} r_i^2(k)$, $\omega(\theta_i \mid Z^k)$, which is the weighted value in the actual model. The more accurate the ith estimator is, the smaller the corresponding residuals will be. Therefore, the greater the model weight of the estimator is, the smaller other corresponding models will be.

It does not involve the statistical distribution residuals in this model probabilistic representation, but the calculation is relatively simple.

Step3 Optimal Fusion Estimate

The optimal fusion estimate of the state is the product integration of the local estimates corresponding to local parallel linear model and their corresponding performance index function. That is:

$$\hat{X}_k^{\text{opt}} = \sum_{i=1}^{N} J_i(k) \hat{X}_i(k \mid k) \tag{3.20}$$

There are the following forms in the covariance matrix:

$$P^{\text{opt}}(k \mid k) = \sum_{i=1}^{N} J_i(k) \{ P_i(k/k) + [\hat{X}_i(k \mid k) - \hat{X}_k^{\text{opt}}][\hat{X}_i(k \mid k) - \hat{X}_k^{\text{opt}}]^{\mathrm{T}} \} \tag{3.21}$$

In addition, the estimates of the actual model parameters at the kth moment will be:

$$\hat{\theta}_k^{\text{opt}} = \sum_{i=1}^{N} J_i(k) \theta_i \tag{3.22}$$

3.3 Interacting Multiple Model Algorithm

The American Scholar Blom was the first one who proposed IMM algorithm in 1984. There are the following advantages in the interacting multiple model algorithm. In the first place, IMM is the optimum estimate after the completeness and the exclusive condition are

satisfied in the model. Secondly, IMM can expand the new operation model of the estimated system without changing the structure of the system. Furthermore, the amount of computation in IMM is moderate, having advantages of nonlinear filtering.
(1) The Fusion Architecture of IMM
Assuming a certain system can be described as the following state equation and measurement equation:

$$\begin{cases} X(k+1) = \Phi(k,m(k))X(k) + w(k,m(k)) \\ Z(k) = H(k,m(k))X(k) + v(k,m(k)) \end{cases} \tag{3.23}$$

Where, $X(k)$ is the system state vector, $\Phi(k,m(k))$ being the state transition matrix;

$w(k,m(k))$ is a mean zero, the variance being the Gaussian white noise $Q(k,m(k))$;
$Z(k)$ is the measurement vector, $H(k,m(k))$ being the observation matrix;
$v(k,m(k))$ is a mean zero, the variance being the Gaussian white noise $R(k,m(k))$;
And there is no relation between $w(k,m(k))$ and $v(k,m(k))$.
Where, $m(k)$ means an effective mode at t_k sampling time. At t_k time, the effective representation of m_i is $m_i(k) = \{m(k) = m_i\}$. All possible system mode set is $M = \{m_1, m_2, \cdots, m_N\}$. The systematic pattern sequence is assumed to be first-order Markov Chain, then the transition probability from $m_i(k+1)$ to $m_j(k)$ will be:

$$P\{m_i(k+1) \mid m_j(k)\} = \pi_{ji}, \quad m_i, m_j \in M \tag{3.24}$$

And

$$\sum_{i=1}^{N} \pi_{ji} = 1 \quad j = 1, 2, \cdots, N \tag{3.25}$$

When received measurement information, the actual transition probability between models is the maximum posterior probability based on the above π_{ji} and measurement set $\{Z^k\}$.
The core of the interacting multiple model algorithms can modify the filter's input/output by using the actual transition probability in the above. The schematic figure of inter-influencing multiple model algorithms will be given in Fig. 3.3.

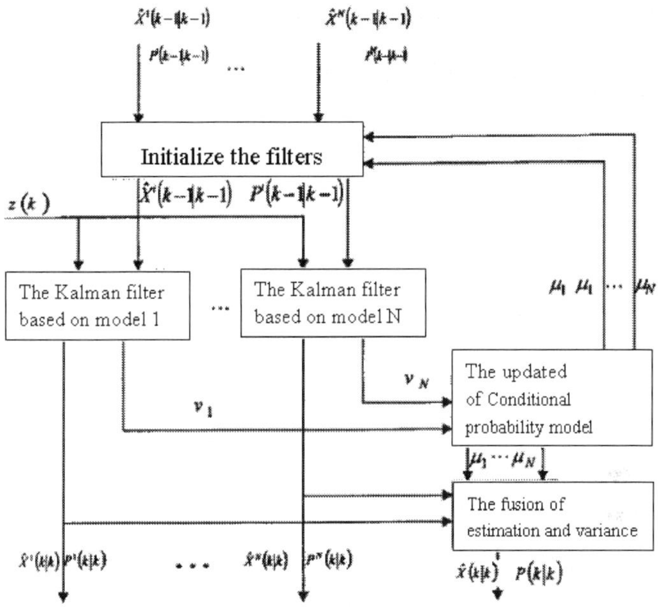

Fig. 3.3 Algorithm Flow of the Interacting Multiple Model

(2) The Filtering Algorithm for IMM

The interacting multiple model expanded the state of the conditional mean along the model space to do the Bayes probability. It is the optimum estimate under the condition of target motion model set covering model and the model of mutual independence. The interacting multiple model algorithm is a recursive algorithm: the model number is supposed to be limited, and each algorithm included 4-step in a cycle: input interaction, filter calculation, the updated for model probability and output interaction.

Step1 Input interaction

Input interaction is the most typical step of the interacting multiple model algorithm, using all state and model conditional probability obtained at last circulation as the computation and input state of each filtering model and the input state error covariance matrix.

That is:

$$\hat{X}_{0i}(k-1\,|\,k-1)=\sum_{j=1}^{N}\hat{X}_{j}(k-1\,|\,k-1)\mu_{j|i}(k-1\,|\,k-1) \tag{3.26}$$

$$P_{0i}(k-1\,|\,k-1)=\sum_{j=1}^{N}\mu_{j|i}(k-1\,|\,k-1)\{P_{j}(k-1\,|\,k-1)+a\cdot a^{T}\} \tag{3.27}$$

And

$$a=[\hat{X}_{j}(k-1\,|\,k-1)-\hat{X}_{0i}(k-1\,|\,k-1)] \tag{3.28}$$

The predicted probability of the model $\mu_{j|i}$ is:

$$\mu_{j|i}(k-1|k-1) = P\{m_j(k-1)|m_i(k), Z^{k-1}\} = \frac{1}{c_i}\pi_{ji}\mu_j(k-1) \tag{3.29}$$

Where

$$c_i = \sum_{j=1}^{N} \pi_{ji}\mu_j(k-1) \tag{3.30}$$

$\mu_i(k)$ means the probability of model m_i at the kth time,

And that is: $\mu_i(k) = P\{m_i(k)|Z^k\}$.

Step2 Filter Calculation

Each filter will do the Kalman filtering after obtaining measurement data collection $Z(k)$ signal. What the filter of each model outputted are the mode estimation, covariance matrix, the residual covariance matrix of the Kalman filter and the updated state vector. Kalman filter equations of the ith model at the kth time will be introduced below.

The state and covariance prediction of the ith model at the kth time is:

$$X_i(k|k-1) = \Phi_i \hat{X}_{0i}(k-1|k-1) \tag{3.31}$$

$$P_i(k|k-1) = \Phi_i P_{0i}(k-1|k-1)\Phi_i^T + Q_i \tag{3.32}$$

The residual vector of the Kalman Filter is the difference between measured values and the Kalman filter estimates of the previous measured values. That is:

$$v_i(k) = Z(k) - H_i \hat{X}_i(k|k-1) \tag{3.33}$$

And $Z(k)$ is the measurement data collection at the kth time.

The residual covariance matrix of the Kalman filter is:

$$S_i(k) = H_i P_i(k|k-1) H_i^T + R_i \tag{3.34}$$

The gain matrix of the Kalman filter is:

$$K_i(k) = P_i(k|k-1) H_i^T S_i^{-1} \tag{3.35}$$

The updated state equation of the Kalman filter is:

$$\hat{X}_i(k|k) = \hat{X}_i(k|k-1) + K_i v_i \tag{3.36}$$

The state covariance updated equation of the Kalman filter is:

$$P_i(k|k) = (I - K_i H_i) P_i(k|k-1) \tag{3.37}$$

Step3 Updated for Model Probability

Model probability provides information for working of a model at any time, which is given by Bayes Theorem. The updated equation of the specific model probability is:

$$\mu_i(k) = P\{m_i(k)|Z^k\} = \frac{1}{c}\Lambda_i(k)\sum_{j=1}^{N}\pi_{ji}\mu_j(k-1) \tag{3.38}$$

Where, $c = P\{Z(k)|Z^{k-1}\} = \sum_{i=1}^{N}\Lambda_i(k)\cdot c_i$

So, $\Lambda_i(k)$ is the likelihood function for model m_i the kth time, the likelihood value will be calculated by the residual error and the updated amount of covariance. That is:

$$\Lambda_i(k) = N[v_i(k):0, S_i(k)] = |2\pi S_i|^{-1/2} \exp\{-\frac{1}{2} v_i^T S_i^{-1} v_i\} \tag{3.39}$$

Step4 Output Fusion

The final state of the output is obtained by weighting and combining all sub-model state estimation, namely, by the product of the state estimation of each model and model probability.

$$\hat{X}(k \mid k) = \sum_{i=1}^{N} \hat{X}_i(k \mid k) \cdot \mu_i(k) \tag{3.40}$$

Simultaneously, the estimated covariance matrix is:

$$P(k \mid k) = \sum_{i=1}^{N} \mu_i(k)\{P_i(k \mid k) + b \cdot b^T\} \tag{3.41}$$

And

$$b = [\hat{X}_i(k \mid k) - \hat{X}(k \mid k)] \tag{3.42}$$

As will be readily seen, when IMM estimation is taking into historical information of mode at the kth time, it also mixes the previous estimated information in the beginning of each circulation to avoid the shortcoming that the complexity of the optimal estimation will present an exponential growth with time. It is the main aspect that can distinguish interacting multiple model algorithm from other non-interacting multiple model estimation.

4. Nonstandard Multi-sensor Information Fusion Based on Local Filtering Estimate Decoupling

The algorithm of the state fusion estimation of dynamic multi-sensor system is related to the fusion structure. There commonly are: centralization, distribution and hybrid[26-27]. Each fusion structure has its own particular advantages and disadvantages. For instance, problems as heavy computational burden and poor tolerance are existed in the centralization, but all the raw sensor measurements are used without loss, so the fusion result is the optimal one. In regard to the distribution, it adopts two-level information processing to use a primary filter and several local filters replace the original single centralized fusion model. In the first stage, each local filter processed the information of each corresponding subsystem measurement in parallel; then in the second stage, the primary filter will filter the local state of each local filter to improve the computational efficiency and error tolerance of the system. However, the distributed fusion estimation always assumes that the local estimates obtained from each sensor are independent of each other and that the local covariance is diagonal to achieve the decoupling of the estimated state of each sensor, which is the basis for the distributed optimal algorithm. In the multi-sensor system, state estimates of the corresponding local filter in each subsystem are often related. In view of the relevant local filter, the distributed fusion filter is needed to transform in order to achieve the global optimal estimates to make the local filtering estimate irrelevant in the actual operation.

The distributed joint filter (FKF, Federal Kalman Filter) was proposed by an American Scholar N.A. Carlson in 1988 concerning with a special form of distributed fusion. It has been considered as a new information fusion method which is only directed towards the synthesis of the estimated information of sub-filter. The sub-filter is also a parallel structure and each filter adopted the Kalman filter algorithm to deal with its own sensor measurements. In order to make the structure of the master filter and the accuracy of the centralized fusion estimation similar, the feature which distinguished the combined filter from the general distributed filter is that the combined filter applied variance upper bound technique and information distribution principle to eliminate the correlation estimates of the sub-filter in each sensor, and distributed the global state estimate information and noise information of the system to each sub-filter without changing the form of sub-filter algorithm. Therefore, it has the advantages of more simple in algorithm, better fault tolerance and easy to implement, etc. When information distribution factor determined the performance of the combined filter, the selection rules became the focus of recent research and debate[28]. Under the present circumstances, it is the main objective and research direction in this field to search for and design "information distribution" which will be simple, effective and self-adaptive.

4.1 Analysis and Decoupling for the Relevance of the Combined Filter

The system description will be given as:

$$\boldsymbol{X}(k+1) = \boldsymbol{\Phi}(k+1,k)\boldsymbol{X}(k) + \boldsymbol{\Gamma}(k+1,k)w(k) \tag{4.1}$$

$$\boldsymbol{Z}_i(k+1) = \boldsymbol{H}_i(k+1)\boldsymbol{X}_i(k+1) + v_i(k+1) \qquad i = 1,2,\cdots,N \tag{4.2}$$

Where, $\boldsymbol{X}(k+1) \in \mathrm{R}^n$ is the system state vector at the $k+1$ time, $\boldsymbol{\Phi}(k+1,k) \in \mathrm{R}^{n \times n}$ being the state transition matrix of the system, $\boldsymbol{\Gamma}(k+1,k)$ being the process noise distribution matrix, $\boldsymbol{Z}_i(k+1) \in \mathrm{R}^m$ $(i = 1,2,\cdots,N)$ being the measurements of the i sensor at the $k+1$ time, and $\boldsymbol{H}_i(k+1)$ being the mapping matrix of the ith sensor at the $\boldsymbol{H}_i(k+1)$ time. Assume $\mathrm{E}[w(k)] = 0$, $\mathrm{E}[w(k)w^{\mathrm{T}}(j)] = \boldsymbol{Q}(k)\delta_{kj}$, $\mathrm{E}[v_i(k)] = 0$, and $\mathrm{E}[v_i(k)v_i^{\mathrm{T}}(j)] = \boldsymbol{R}_i(k)\delta_{kj}$.

Theorem 4.1: In the multi-sensor information fusion system described by Equation (4.1) and (4.2), if local estimates are unrelated, the global optimal fusion estimate of the state $\hat{\boldsymbol{X}}_g$ can have the following general formulas:

$$\begin{cases} \hat{\boldsymbol{X}}_g = \boldsymbol{P}_g \sum\limits_{i=1}^{N} \boldsymbol{P}_i^{-1}\hat{\boldsymbol{X}}_i = \boldsymbol{P}_g\boldsymbol{P}_1^{-1}\hat{\boldsymbol{X}}_1 + \boldsymbol{P}_g\boldsymbol{P}_2^{-1}\hat{\boldsymbol{X}}_2 + \cdots + \boldsymbol{P}_g\boldsymbol{P}_N^{-1}\hat{\boldsymbol{X}}_N \\ \boldsymbol{P}_g = (\sum\limits_{i=1}^{N} \boldsymbol{P}_i^{-1})^{-1} = (\boldsymbol{P}_1^{-1} + \boldsymbol{P}_2^{-1} + \cdots + \boldsymbol{P}_N^{-1})^{-1} \end{cases} \tag{4.3}$$

Where, $\hat{\boldsymbol{X}}_i, \boldsymbol{P}_i$ $i = 1,2,\cdots,N$ are respectively referred as the local estimates of the subsystem and the corresponding estimated covariance matrix.

Supposing $\hat{X}_g(k|k), P_g(k|k)$ are the optimal estimates and the covariance matrix of the combined Kalman filter (the fusion center), $\hat{X}_i(k|k), P_i(k|k)$ being the estimate and the covariance matrix of the i sub-filter, $\hat{X}_m(k|k), P_m(k|k)$ being the estimate and the covariance matrix of the Master Filter, and if there is no feedback from the fusion center to the sub-filter, when the Master Filter completed the fusion process at k time, there will be $\hat{X}_m(k|k)=\hat{X}(k|k)$, $P_m(k|k)=P(k|k)$. The forecast for the main filter will be (Because of no measurements, the Master Filter only had time updates, but no measurement updates.):

$$\begin{cases} \hat{X}_m(k+1|k)=\Phi_k\hat{X}(k|k) \\ P_m(k+1|k)=\Phi(k)P(k|k)\Phi^{\mathrm{T}}(k)+\Gamma(k)Q(k)\Gamma^{\mathrm{T}}(k) \end{cases} \tag{4.4}$$

Where, the meanings of $\Phi(k)$, $\Gamma(k)$ and $Q(k)$ are the same as those above. As the ith sub-filter has both time updates and measurement updates, it should have:

$$\begin{aligned} \hat{X}_i(k+1|k+1) &= \hat{X}_i(k+1|k)+K_i(k+1)(Z_i(k+1)-H_i(k+1)\hat{X}_i(k+1|k)) \\ &= \Phi(k)\hat{X}_i(k|k)+K_i(k+1)(Z_i(k+1)-H_i(k+1)\Phi(k)\hat{X}_i(k|k)) \end{aligned} \tag{4.5}$$

Accordingly,

$$\begin{aligned} &\tilde{X}_i(k+1|k+1)=X(k+1|k+1)-\hat{X}_i(k+1|k+1) \\ &=\Phi(k)X(k|k)+\Gamma(k)w(k)-\Phi(k)\hat{X}_i(k|k) \\ &\quad -K_i(k+1)[H_i(k+1)(\Phi(k)X(k|k)+\Gamma(k)w(k))+v_i(k+1)-H_i(k+1)\Phi(k)\hat{X}_i(k|k)] \\ &=(\mathrm{I}-K_i(k+1)H_i(k+1))\Phi(k)\tilde{X}_i(k|k) \\ &\quad +(\mathrm{I}-K_i(k+1)H_i(k+1))\Gamma(k)w(k)-K_i(k+1)v_i(k+1) \end{aligned} \tag{4.6}$$

Then we can get the covariance of the local sub-filters i and j at the $k+1$ th time:

$$\begin{aligned} &P_{i,j}(k+1)=\mathrm{Cov}(\tilde{X}_i(k+1|k+1),\tilde{X}_j(k+1|k+1)) \\ &=(\mathrm{I}-K_i(k+1)H_i(k+1))\Phi(k)P_{i,j}(k)\Phi^{\mathrm{T}}(k)(\mathrm{I}-K_j(k+1)H_j(k+1))^{\mathrm{T}} \\ &\quad +(\mathrm{I}-K_i(k+1)H_i(k+1))\Gamma(k)Q(k)\Gamma^{\mathrm{T}}(k)(\mathrm{I}-K_j(k+1)H_j(k+1))^{\mathrm{T}} \\ &=(\mathrm{I}-K_i(k+1)H_i(k+1))(\Phi(k)P_{i,j}(k)\Phi^{\mathrm{T}}(k)+\Gamma(k)Q(k)\Gamma^{\mathrm{T}}(k))(\mathrm{I}-K_j(k+1)H_j(k+1))^{\mathrm{T}} \end{aligned} \tag{4.7}$$

There is no measurement in the master filter, so the time updates is also the measurement updates:

$$\begin{cases} \hat{X}_m(k+1|k+1)=\hat{X}_m(k+1|k)=\Phi(k)\hat{X}(k|k) \\ \tilde{X}_m(k+1|k+1)=X(k+1|k+1)-\hat{X}_m(k+1|k+1) \\ \qquad =\Phi(k)X(k|k)+\Gamma(k)w(k)-\Phi(k)\hat{X}(k|k)=\Phi(k)\tilde{X}(k|k)+\Gamma(k)w(k) \end{cases} \tag{4.8}$$

Therefore, the covariance of any sub-filter i and the Master Filter m at the $(k+1)$ th time will be:

$$\begin{aligned}\boldsymbol{P}_{i,m}(k+1) &= \mathrm{Cov}(\tilde{\boldsymbol{X}}_i(k+1\mid k+1), \tilde{\boldsymbol{X}}_m(k+1\mid k+1)) \\ &= (\mathrm{I}-\boldsymbol{K}_i(k+1)\boldsymbol{H}_i(k+1))\boldsymbol{\Phi}(k)\boldsymbol{P}_{i,m}(k)\boldsymbol{\Phi}^{\mathrm{T}}(k) \\ &\quad + (\mathrm{I}-\boldsymbol{K}_i(k+1)\boldsymbol{H}_i(k+1))\boldsymbol{\Gamma}(k)\boldsymbol{Q}(k)\boldsymbol{\Gamma}^{\mathrm{T}}(k)\end{aligned} \tag{4.9}$$

As can be seen, only on the condition of both $\boldsymbol{Q}(k)=0$ and $\boldsymbol{P}_{i,j}(k)=0$, the filtering errors between each sub-filter and the Master Filter at $(k+1)$ time are not related to each other. While in the usual case, both constraint conditions are hard to establish.
In addition, supposing:

$$\begin{aligned}\boldsymbol{B}_i(k+1) &= (\mathrm{I}-\boldsymbol{K}_i(k+1)\boldsymbol{H}_i(k+1))\boldsymbol{\Phi}(k), \boldsymbol{C}_i(k+1) \\ &= (\mathrm{I}-\boldsymbol{K}_i(k+1)\boldsymbol{H}_i(k+1))\boldsymbol{\Gamma}(k), \quad (i=1,2,\cdots,N)\end{aligned} \tag{4.10}$$

And:

$$\begin{aligned}&\begin{bmatrix}\boldsymbol{P}_{1,1}(k+1) & \cdots & \boldsymbol{P}_{1,N}(k+1) & \boldsymbol{P}_{1,m}(k+1) \\ \vdots & \ddots & \vdots & \vdots \\ \boldsymbol{P}_{N,1}(k+1) & \cdots & \boldsymbol{P}_{N,N}(k+1) & \boldsymbol{P}_{N,m}(k+1) \\ \boldsymbol{P}_{m,1}(k+1) & \cdots & \boldsymbol{P}_{m,N}(k+1) & \boldsymbol{P}_{m,m}(k+1)\end{bmatrix} \\
&= \begin{bmatrix}\boldsymbol{B}_1(k+1)\boldsymbol{P}_{1,1}(k)(\boldsymbol{B}_1(k+1))^{\mathrm{T}} & \cdots & \boldsymbol{B}_1(k+1)\boldsymbol{P}_{1,N}(k)(\boldsymbol{B}_N(k+1))^{\mathrm{T}} & \boldsymbol{B}_1(k+1)\boldsymbol{P}_{1,m}(k)\boldsymbol{\Phi}^{\mathrm{T}}(k) \\ \vdots & \ddots & \vdots & \vdots \\ \boldsymbol{B}_N(k+1)\boldsymbol{P}_{N,1}(k)(\boldsymbol{B}_1(k+1))^{\mathrm{T}} & \cdots & \boldsymbol{B}_N(k+1)\boldsymbol{P}_{N,N}(k)(\boldsymbol{B}_N(k+1))^{\mathrm{T}} & \boldsymbol{B}_N(k+1)\boldsymbol{P}_{N,m}(k)\boldsymbol{\Phi}^{\mathrm{T}}(k) \\ \boldsymbol{\Phi}(k)\boldsymbol{P}_{m,1}(k)(\boldsymbol{B}_1(k+1))^{\mathrm{T}} & \cdots & \boldsymbol{\Phi}(k)\boldsymbol{P}_{m,N}(k)(\boldsymbol{B}_N(k+1))^{\mathrm{T}} & \boldsymbol{\Phi}(k)\boldsymbol{P}_m(k)\boldsymbol{\Phi}^{\mathrm{T}}(k)\end{bmatrix} \\
&+ \begin{bmatrix}\boldsymbol{C}_1(k+1)\boldsymbol{Q}(k)(\boldsymbol{C}_1(k+1))^{\mathrm{T}} & \cdots & \boldsymbol{C}_1(k+1)\boldsymbol{Q}(k)(\boldsymbol{C}_N(k+1))^{\mathrm{T}} & \boldsymbol{C}_1(k+1)\boldsymbol{Q}(k)\boldsymbol{\Gamma}^{\mathrm{T}}(k) \\ \vdots & \ddots & \vdots & \vdots \\ \boldsymbol{C}_N(k+1)\boldsymbol{Q}(k)(\boldsymbol{C}_1(k+1))^{\mathrm{T}} & \cdots & \boldsymbol{C}_N(k+1)\boldsymbol{Q}(k)(\boldsymbol{C}_N(k+1))^{\mathrm{T}} & \boldsymbol{C}_N(k+1)\boldsymbol{Q}(k)\boldsymbol{\Gamma}^{\mathrm{T}}(k) \\ \boldsymbol{\Gamma}(k)\boldsymbol{Q}(k)(\boldsymbol{C}_1(k+1))^{\mathrm{T}} & \cdots & \boldsymbol{\Gamma}(k)\boldsymbol{Q}(k)(\boldsymbol{C}_N(k+1))^{\mathrm{T}} & \boldsymbol{\Gamma}(k)\boldsymbol{Q}(k)\boldsymbol{\Gamma}^{\mathrm{T}}(k)\end{bmatrix} \\
&= \begin{bmatrix}\boldsymbol{B}_1(k+1) & \cdots & 0 & 0 \\ \vdots & \ddots & \vdots & \vdots \\ 0 & \cdots & \boldsymbol{B}_N(k+1) & 0 \\ 0 & \cdots & 0 & \boldsymbol{\Phi}(k)\end{bmatrix}\begin{bmatrix}\boldsymbol{P}_{1,1}(k) & \cdots & \boldsymbol{P}_{1,N}(k) & \boldsymbol{P}_{1,m}(k) \\ \vdots & \ddots & \vdots & \vdots \\ \boldsymbol{P}_{N,1}(k) & \cdots & \boldsymbol{P}_{N,N}(k) & \boldsymbol{P}_{N,m}(k) \\ \boldsymbol{P}_{m,1}(k) & \cdots & \boldsymbol{P}_{m,N}(k) & \boldsymbol{P}_{m,m}(k)\end{bmatrix}\begin{bmatrix}\boldsymbol{B}_1^{\mathrm{T}}(k+1) & \cdots & 0 & 0 \\ \vdots & \ddots & \vdots & \vdots \\ 0 & \cdots & \boldsymbol{B}_N^{\mathrm{T}}(k+1) & 0 \\ 0 & \cdots & 0 & \boldsymbol{\Phi}^{\mathrm{T}}(k)\end{bmatrix} \\
&+ \begin{bmatrix}\boldsymbol{C}_1(k+1) & \cdots & 0 & 0 \\ \vdots & \ddots & \vdots & \vdots \\ 0 & \cdots & \boldsymbol{C}_N(k+1) & 0 \\ 0 & \cdots & 0 & \boldsymbol{\Gamma}(k)\end{bmatrix}\begin{bmatrix}\boldsymbol{Q}(k) & \cdots & \boldsymbol{Q}(k) & \boldsymbol{Q}(k) \\ \vdots & \ddots & \vdots & \vdots \\ \boldsymbol{Q}(k) & \cdots & \boldsymbol{Q}(k) & \boldsymbol{Q}(k) \\ \boldsymbol{Q}(k) & \cdots & \boldsymbol{Q}(k) & \boldsymbol{Q}(k)\end{bmatrix}\begin{bmatrix}\boldsymbol{C}_1^{\mathrm{T}}(k+1) & \cdots & 0 & 0 \\ \vdots & \ddots & \vdots & \vdots \\ 0 & \cdots & \boldsymbol{C}_N^{\mathrm{T}}(k+1) & 0 \\ 0 & \cdots & 0 & \boldsymbol{\Gamma}^{\mathrm{T}}(k)\end{bmatrix}\end{aligned} \tag{4.11}$$

As can be seen, due to the influence of the common process noise $w(k)$, even if $\boldsymbol{P}_{i,j}(k)=0$, there cannot get $\boldsymbol{P}_{i,j}(k+1)=0$. At this time, "variance upper-bound" technology can be used to eliminate this correlation. Known by the matrix theory[29], there are upper-bound existed in the phalanx being composed of $\boldsymbol{Q}(k)$ from the Formula (4.11).

$$\begin{bmatrix} \boldsymbol{Q}(k) & \cdots & \boldsymbol{Q}(k) & \boldsymbol{Q}(k) \\ \vdots & \ddots & \vdots & \vdots \\ \boldsymbol{Q}(k) & \cdots & \boldsymbol{Q}(k) & \boldsymbol{Q}(k) \\ \boldsymbol{Q}(k) & \cdots & \boldsymbol{Q}(k) & \boldsymbol{Q}(k) \end{bmatrix} \le \begin{bmatrix} \beta_1^{-1}\boldsymbol{Q}(k) & \cdots & 0 & 0 \\ \vdots & \ddots & \vdots & \vdots \\ 0 & \cdots & \beta_N^{-1}\boldsymbol{Q}(k) & 0 \\ 0 & \cdots & 0 & \beta_m^{-1}\boldsymbol{Q}(k) \end{bmatrix} \tag{4.12}$$

And: $\beta_1+\beta_2+\cdots+\beta_N+\beta_m=1, \quad 0\le\beta_i\le 1$

As can be seen, the positive definite of the upper-bound in Formula (4.12) is stronger than that of original matrix. That is to say, the difference between the upper-bound matrix and the original matrix is positive semi-definite.

A similar upper-bound can also be set in the initial state covariance $\boldsymbol{P}_0$. That is:

$$\begin{bmatrix} \boldsymbol{P}_{1,1}(0) & \cdots & \boldsymbol{P}_{1,N}(0) & \boldsymbol{P}_{1,m}(0) \\ \vdots & \ddots & \vdots & \vdots \\ \boldsymbol{P}_{N,1}(0) & \cdots & \boldsymbol{P}_{N,N}(0) & \boldsymbol{P}_{N,m}(0) \\ \boldsymbol{P}_{m,1}(0) & \cdots & \boldsymbol{P}_{m,N}(0) & \boldsymbol{P}_{m,m}(0) \end{bmatrix} \le \begin{bmatrix} \beta_1^{-1}\boldsymbol{P}_{1,1}(0) & \cdots & 0 & 0 \\ \vdots & \ddots & \vdots & \vdots \\ 0 & \cdots & \beta_N^{-1}\boldsymbol{P}_{N,N}(0) & 0 \\ 0 & \cdots & 0 & \beta_m^{-1}\boldsymbol{P}_{m,m}(0) \end{bmatrix} \tag{4.13}$$

It also can be seen from this, there is no related items in the right side of the Formula (4.13). Namely, if enlarge the initial covariance of the master filter and each sub-filter, the correlation of the initial covariance errors of the mater filter and each sub-filter. Then, it can be known from Formula (4.7) and (4.9).

$$\boldsymbol{P}_{i,j}(k)=0 \quad (i\ne j, i,j=1,2,\cdots,N,m).$$

It can be got the following by substituting Formula (4.12) and (4.13) into Formula (4.11):

$$\begin{bmatrix} P_{1,1}(k+1) & \cdots & P_{1,N}(k+1) & P_{1,m}(k+1) \\ \vdots & \ddots & \vdots & \vdots \\ P_{N,1}(k+1) & \cdots & P_{N,N}(k+1) & P_{N,m}(k+1) \\ P_{m,1}(k+1) & \cdots & P_{m,N}(k+1) & P_{m,m}(k+1) \end{bmatrix}$$

$$\le \begin{bmatrix} B_1(k+1) & \cdots & 0 & 0 \\ \vdots & \ddots & \vdots & \vdots \\ 0 & \cdots & B_N(k+1) & 0 \\ 0 & \cdots & 0 & \Phi(k) \end{bmatrix} \begin{bmatrix} P_{1,1}(k) & \cdots & 0 & 0 \\ \vdots & \ddots & \vdots & \vdots \\ 0 & \cdots & P_{N,N}(k) & 0 \\ 0 & \cdots & 0 & P_{m,m}(k) \end{bmatrix} \begin{bmatrix} B_1^{\mathrm{T}}(k+1) & \cdots & 0 & 0 \\ \vdots & \ddots & \vdots & \vdots \\ 0 & \cdots & B_N^{\mathrm{T}}(k+1) & 0 \\ 0 & \cdots & 0 & \Phi^{\mathrm{T}}(k) \end{bmatrix}$$

$$+ \begin{bmatrix} C_1(k+1) & \cdots & 0 & 0 \\ \vdots & \ddots & \vdots & \vdots \\ 0 & \cdots & C_N(k+1) & 0 \\ 0 & \cdots & 0 & \Gamma(k) \end{bmatrix} \begin{bmatrix} \beta_1^{-1}Q(k) & \cdots & 0 & 0 \\ \vdots & \ddots & \vdots & \vdots \\ 0 & \cdots & \beta_N^{-1}Q(k) & 0 \\ 0 & \cdots & 0 & \beta_m^{-1}Q(k) \end{bmatrix} \begin{bmatrix} C_1^{\mathrm{T}}(k+1) & \cdots & 0 & 0 \\ \vdots & \ddots & \vdots & \vdots \\ 0 & \cdots & C_N^{\mathrm{T}}(k+1) & 0 \\ 0 & \cdots & 0 & \Gamma^{\mathrm{T}}(k) \end{bmatrix} \quad (4.14)$$

If taken the equal sign, that is, achieved the de-correlation of local estimates, on the one hand, the global optimal fusion estimate can be realized by Theorem 4.1 , but on the other, the initial covariance matrix and process noise covariance of the sub-filter themselves can enlarged by β_i^{-1} times. What's more, the filter results of every local filter will not be optimal.

4.2 Structure and Performance Analysis of the Combined Filter

The combined filter is a 2-level filter. The characteristic to distinguish from the traditional distributed filters is the use of information distribution to realize information share of every sub-filter. Information fusion structure of the combined filter is shown in Fig. 4.1.

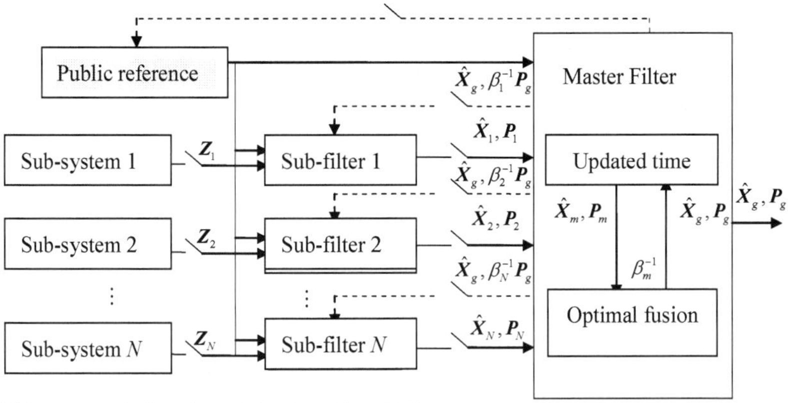

Fig. 4.1 Structure Indication of the Combined Filter

From the filter structure shown in the Fig. 4.1, the fusion process for the combined filter can be divided into the following four steps.

Step1 Given initial value and information distribution: The initial value of the global state in the initial moment is supposed to be $\boldsymbol{X}_0$, the covariance to be $\boldsymbol{Q}_0$, the state estimate vector of the local filter, the system covariance matrix and the state vector covariance matrix separately, respectively to be $\hat{\boldsymbol{X}}_i, \boldsymbol{Q}_i, \boldsymbol{P}_i, \quad i=1,\cdots,N$, and the corresponding master filter to be $\hat{\boldsymbol{X}}_m, \boldsymbol{Q}_m, \boldsymbol{P}_m$ .The information is distributed through the information distribution factor by the following rules in the sub-filter and the master filter.

$$\begin{cases}\boldsymbol{Q}_g^{-1}(k)=\boldsymbol{Q}_1^{-1}(k)+\boldsymbol{Q}_2^{-1}(k)+\cdots+\boldsymbol{Q}_N^{-1}(k)+\boldsymbol{Q}_m^{-1}(k) \quad \boldsymbol{Q}_i^{-1}(k)=\beta_i\boldsymbol{Q}_g^{-1}(k)\\ \boldsymbol{P}_g^{-1}(k|k)=\boldsymbol{P}_1^{-1}(k|k)+\boldsymbol{P}_2^{-1}(k|k)+\cdots+\boldsymbol{P}_N^{-1}(k|k)+\boldsymbol{P}_m^{-1}(k|k) \quad \boldsymbol{P}_i^{-1}(k|k)=\beta_i\boldsymbol{P}_g^{-1}(k|k)\\ \hat{\boldsymbol{X}}_i(k|k)=\hat{\boldsymbol{X}}_g(k|k) \qquad i=1,2,\cdots,N,m\end{cases} \tag{4.15}$$

Where, β_i should meet the requirements of information conservation principles:

$$\beta_1+\beta_2+\cdots+\beta_N+\beta_m=1 \quad 0\le\beta_i\le1$$

Step2 the time to update the information: The process of updating time conducted independently, the updated time algorithm is shown as follows:

$$\begin{cases}\hat{\boldsymbol{X}}_i(k+1|k)=\boldsymbol{\Phi}(k+1|k)\hat{\boldsymbol{X}}_i(k|k) \qquad i=1,2,\cdots,N,m\\ \boldsymbol{P}_i(k+1|k)=\boldsymbol{\Phi}(k+1|k)\boldsymbol{P}_i(k|k)\boldsymbol{\Phi}^{\mathrm{T}}(k+1|k)+\boldsymbol{\Gamma}(k+1|k)\boldsymbol{Q}_i(k)\boldsymbol{\Gamma}^{\mathrm{T}}(k+1|k)\end{cases} \tag{4.16}$$

Step3 Measurement update: As the master filter does not measure, there is no measurement update in the Master Filter. The measurement update only occurs in each local sub-filter, and can work by the following formula:

$$\begin{cases}\boldsymbol{P}_i^{-1}(k+1|k+1)\hat{\boldsymbol{X}}_i(k+1|k+1)=\boldsymbol{P}_i^{-1}(k+1|k)\hat{\boldsymbol{X}}_i(k+1|k)+\boldsymbol{H}_i^{\mathrm{T}}(k+1)\boldsymbol{R}_i^{-1}(k+1)\boldsymbol{Z}_i(k+1)\\ \boldsymbol{P}_i^{-1}(k+1|k+1)=\boldsymbol{P}_i^{-1}(k+1|k)+\boldsymbol{H}_i^{\mathrm{T}}(k+1)\boldsymbol{R}_i^{-1}(k+1)\boldsymbol{H}_i(k+1) \qquad i=1,2,\cdots,N\end{cases} \tag{4.17}$$

Step4 the optimal information fusion: The amount of information of the state equation and the amount of information of the process equation can be apportioned by the information distribution to eliminate the correlation among sub-filters. Then the core algorithm of the combined filter can be fused to the local information of every local filter to get the state optimal estimates.

$$\begin{cases}\hat{\boldsymbol{X}}_g(k|k)=\boldsymbol{P}_g(k|k)\sum_{i=1}^{N,m}\boldsymbol{P}_i^{-1}(k|k)\hat{\boldsymbol{X}}_i(k|k)\\ \boldsymbol{P}_g(k|k)=(\sum_{i=1}^{N,m}\boldsymbol{P}_i^{-1}(k|k))^{-1}=(\boldsymbol{P}_1^{-1}(k|k)+\boldsymbol{P}_2^{-1}(k|k)+\cdots+\boldsymbol{P}_N^{-1}(k|k)+\boldsymbol{P}_m^{-1}(k|k))^{-1}\end{cases} \tag{4.18}$$

It can achieve the goal to complete the workflow of the combined filter after the processes of information distribution, the updated time, the updated measurement and information fusion. Obviously, as the variance upper-bound technique is adopted to remove the correlation between sub-filters and the master filter and between the various sub-filters in the local filter and to enlarge the initial covariance matrix and the process noise covariance of each sub-filter by β_i^{-1} times, the filter results of each local filter will not be optimal. But some information lost by the variance upper-bound technique can be re-synthesized in the final fusion process to get the global optimal solution for the equation.

In the above analysis for the structure of state fusion estimation, it is known that centralized fusion structure is the optimal fusion estimation for the system state in the minimum variance. While in the combined filter, the optimal fusion algorithm is used to deal with local filtering estimate to synthesize global state estimate. Due to the application of variance upper-bound technique, local filtering is turned into being suboptimal, the global filter after its synthesis becomes global optimal, i.e. the fact that the equivalence issue between the combined filtering process and the centralized fusion filtering process. To sum up, as can be seen from the above analysis, the algorithm of combined filtering process is greatly simplified by the use of variance upper-bound technique. It is worth pointing out that the use of variance upper-bound technique made local estimates suboptimum but the global estimate after the fusion of local estimates is optimal, i.e. combined filtering model is equivalent to centralized filtering model in the estimated accuracy.

4.3 Adaptive Determination of Information Distribution Factor

By the analysis of the estimation performance of combined filter, it is known that the information distribution principle not only eliminates the correlation between sub-filters as brought from public baseline information to make the filtering of every sub-filter conducted themselves independently, but also makes global estimates of information fusion optimal. This is also the key technology of the fusion algorithm of combined filter. Despite it is in this case, different information distribution principles can be guaranteed to obtain different structures and different characteristics (fault-tolerance, precision and amount of calculation) of combined filter. Therefore, there have been many research literatures on the selection of information distribution factor of combined filter in recent years. In the traditional structure of the combined filter, when distributed information to the subsystem, their distribution factors are predetermined and kept unchanged to make it difficult to reflect the dynamic nature of subsystem for information fusion. Therefore, it will be the main objective and research direction to find and design the principle of information distribution which will be simple, effective and dynamic fitness, and practical. Its aim is that the overall performance of the combined filter will keep close to the optimal performance of the local system in the filtering process, namely, a large information distribution factors can be existed in high precision sub-system, while smaller factors existed in lower precision sub-system to get smaller to reduce its overall accuracy of estimated loss. Method for determining adaptive information allocation factors can better reflect the diversification of estimation accuracy in subsystem and reduce the impact of the subsystem failure or precision degradation but improve the overall estimation accuracy and the adaptability and fault tolerance of the whole system. But it held contradictory views given in Literature [28] to determine information distribution factor formula as the above held view. It argued that global optimal estimation accuracy had nothing to do with the information distribution factor values when statistical characteristics of noise are known, so there is no need for adaptive determination.

Combined with above findings in the literature, on determining rules for information distribution factor, we should consider from two aspects.
1) Under circumstances of meeting conditions required in Kalman filtering such as exact statistical properties of noise, it is known from filter performance analysis in Section 4.2 that: if the value of the information distribution factor can satisfy information on conservation principles, the combined filter will be the global optimal one. In other words, the global optimal estimation accuracy is unrelated to the value of information distribution factors, which will influence estimation accuracy of a sub-filter yet. As is known in the information distribution process, process information obtained from each sub-filter is $\beta_i \boldsymbol{Q}_g^{-1}$, $\beta_i \boldsymbol{P}_g^{-1}$, Kalman filter can automatically use different weights according to the merits of the quality of information: the smaller the value of β_i is, the lower process message weight will be, so the accuracy of sub-filters is dependent on the accuracy of measuring information; on the contrary, the accuracy of sub-filters is dependent on the accuracy of process information.
2) Under circumstances of not knowing statistical properties of noise or the failure of a subsystem, global estimates obviously loss the optimality and degrade the accuracy, and it is necessary to introduce the determination mode of adaptive information distribution factor. Information distribution factor will be adaptive dynamically determined by the sub-filter accuracy to overcome the loss of accuracy caused by fault subsystem to remain the relatively high accuracy in global estimates. In determining adaptive information distribution factor, it should be considered that less precision sub-filter will allocate factor with smaller information to make the overall output of the combined filtering model had better fusion performance, or to obtain higher estimation accuracy and fault tolerance.
In Kalman filter, the trace of error covariance matrix $\boldsymbol{P}$ includes the corresponding estimate vector or its linear combination of variance. The estimated accuracy can be reflected in filter answered to the estimate vector or its linear combination through the analysis for the trace of $\boldsymbol{P}$. So there will be the following definition:
Definition 4.1: The estimation accuracy of attenuation factor of the i th local filter is:

$$EDOP_i \overset{\Delta}{=} \sqrt{\mathrm{tr}(\boldsymbol{P}_i \boldsymbol{P}_i^{\mathrm{T}})} \tag{4.19}$$

Where, the definition of $EDOP_i$ (Estimation Dilution of Precision) is attenuation factor estimation accuracy, meaning the measurement of estimation error covariance matrix in i local filter, $\mathrm{tr}(\bullet)$ meaning the demand for computing trace function of the matrix.

When introduced attenuation factor estimation accuracy $EDOP_i$, in fact, it is said to use the measurement of norm characterization $\boldsymbol{P}_i$ in $\boldsymbol{P}_i$ matrix: the bigger the matrix norm is, the corresponding estimated covariance matrix will be larger, so the filtering effect is poorer; and vice versa.
According to the definition of attenuation factor estimation accuracy, take the computing formula of information distribution factor in the combined filtering process as follows:

$$\beta_i = \frac{EDOP_i}{EDOP_1 + EDOP_2 + \cdots + EDOP_N + EDOP_m} \tag{4.20}$$

Obviously, β_i can satisfy information on conservation principles and possess a very intuitive physical sense, namely, the line reflects the estimated performance of sub-filters to improve the fusion performance of the global filter by adjusting the proportion of the local estimates information in the global estimates information. Especially when the performance degradation of a subsystem makes its local estimation error covariance matrix such a singular huge increase that its adaptive information distribution can make the combined filter participating of strong robustness and fault tolerance.

5. Summary

The chapter focuses on non-standard multi-sensor information fusion system with each kind of nonlinear, uncertain and correlated factor, which is widely popular in actual application, because of the difference of measuring principle and character of sensor as well as measuring environment.

Aiming at the above non-standard factors, three resolution schemes based on semi-parameter modeling, multi model fusion and self-adaptive estimation are relatively advanced, and moreover, the corresponding fusion estimation model and algorithm are presented.

(1) By introducing semi-parameter regression analysis concept to non-standard multi-sensor state fusion estimation theory, the relational fusion estimation model and parameter-non-parameter solution algorithm are established; the process is to separate model error brought by nonlinear and uncertainty factors with semi-parameter modeling method and then weakens the influence to the state fusion estimation precision; besides, the conclusion is proved in theory that the state estimation obtained in this algorithm is the optimal fusion estimation.

(2) Two multi-model fusion estimation methods respectively based on multi-model adaptive estimation and interacting multiple model fusion are researched to deal with nonlinear and time-change factors existing in multi-sensor fusion system and moreover to realize the optimal fusion estimation for the state.

(3) Self-adaptive fusion estimation strategy is introduced to solve local dependency and system parameter uncertainty existed in multi-sensor dynamical system and moreover to realize the optimal fusion estimation for the state. The fusion model for federal filter and its optimality are researched; the fusion algorithms respectively in relevant or irrelevant for each sub-filter are presented; the structure and algorithm scheme for federal filter are designed; moreover, its estimation performance was also analyzed, which was influenced by information allocation factors greatly. So the selection method of information allocation factors was discussed, in this chapter, which was dynamically and self-adaptively determined according to the eigenvalue square decomposition of the covariance matrix.

6. Reference

Hall L D, Llinas J. Handbook of Multisensor Data Fusion. Bcoa Raton, FL, USA: CRC Press, 2001

Bedworth M, O'Brien J. the Omnibus Model: A New Model of Data Fusion. IEEE Transactions on Aerospace and Electronic System, 2000, 15(4): 30-36

Heintz, F., Doherty, P. A Knowledge Processing Middleware Framework and its Relation to the JDL Data Fusion Model. Proceedings of the 7th International Conference on Information Fusion, 2005, pp: 1592-1599

Llinas J, Waltz E. Multisensor Data Fusion. Norwood, MA: Artech House, 1990

X. R. Li, Yunmin Zhu, Chongzhao Han. Unified Optimal Linear Estimation Fusion-Part I: Unified Models and Fusion Rules. Proc. 2000 International Conf. on Information Fusion, July 2000

Jiongqi Wang, Haiyin Zhou, Deyong Zhao, el. State Optimal Estimation with Nonstandard Multi-sensor Information Fusion. System Engineering and Electronics, 2008, 30(8): 1415-1420

Kennet A, Mayback P S. Multiple Model Adaptive Estimation with Filter Pawning. IEEE Transaction on Aerospace Electron System, 2002, 38(3): 755-768

Bar-shalom, Y., Campo, L. The Effect of The Common Process Noise on the Two-sensor Fused-track Covariance. IEEE Transaction on Aerospace and Electronic Systems, 1986, Vol.22: 803-805

Morariu, V. I, Camps, O. I. Modeling Correspondences for Multi Camera Tracking Using Nonlinear Manifold Learning and Target Dynamics. IEEE Computer Society Conference on Computer Vision and Pattern Recognition, June, 2006, pp: 545-552

Stephen C, Stubberud, Kathleen. A, et al. Data Association for Multisensor Types Using Fuzzy Logic. IEEE Transaction on Instrumentation and Measurement, 2006, 55(6): 2292-2303

Hammerand, D. C. ; Oden, J. T. ; Prudhomme, S. ; Kuczma, M. S. Modeling Error and Adaptivity in Nonlinear Continuum System, NTIS No: DE2001-780285/XAB

Crassidis. J Letal.A. Real-time Error Filter and State Estimator.AIAA-943550.1994:92-102

Flammini, A, Marioli, D. et al. Robust Estimation of Magnetic Barkhausen Noise Based on a Numerical Approach. IEEE Transaction on Instrumentation and Measurement, 2002, 16(8): 1283-1288

Donoho D. L., Elad M. On the Stability of the Basis Pursuit in the Presence of Noise. http: //www-stat.stanford.edu/-donoho/reports.html

Sun H Y, Wu Y. Semi-parametric Regression and Model Refining. Geospatial Information Science, 2002, 4(5): 10-13

Green P.J., Silverman B.W. Nonparametric Regression and Generalized Linear Models. London: CHAPMAN and HALL, 1994

Petros Maragos, FangKuo Sun. Measuring the Fractal Dimension of Signals: Morphological Covers and Iterative Optimization. IEEE Trans. On Signal Processing, 1998(1): 108~121

G, Sugihara, R.M.May. Nonlinear Forecasting as a Way of Distinguishing Chaos From Measurement Error in Time Series, Nature, 1990, 344: 734-741

Roy R, Paulraj A, kailath T. ESPRIT--Estimation of Signal Parameters Via Rotational Invariance Technique. IEEE Transaction Acoustics, Speech, Signal Processing, 1989, 37:984-98

Aufderheide B, Prasad V, Bequettre B W. A Compassion of Fundamental Model-based and Multi Model Predictive Control. Proceeding of IEEE 40th Conference on Decision and Control, 2001: 4863-4868

Aufderheide B, Bequette B W. A Variably Tuned Multiple Model Predictive Controller Based on Minimal Process Knowledge. Proceedings of the IEEE American Control Conference, 2001, 3490-3495

X. Rong Li, Jikov, Vesselin P. A Survey of Maneuvering Target Tracking-Part V: Multiple-Model Methods. Proceeding of SPIE Conference on Signal and Data Proceeding of Small Targets, San Diego, CA, USA, 2003

T.M. Berg, et al. General Decentralized Kalman filters. Proceedings of the American Control Conference, Mayland, June, 1994, pp.2273-2274

Nahin P J, Pokoski Jl. NCTR Plus Sensor Fusion of Equals IFNN. IEEE Transaction on AES, 1980, Vol. AES-16, No.3, pp.320-337

Bar-Shalom Y, Blom H A. The Interacting Multiple Model Algorithm for Systems with Markovian Switching Coefficients. IEEE Transaction on Aut. Con, 1988, AC-33: 780-783

X.Rong Li, Vesselin P. Jilkov. A Survey of Maneuvering Target Tracking-Part I: Dynamic Models. IEEE Transaction on Aerospace and Electronic Systems, 2003, 39(4): 1333-1361

Huimin Chen, Thiaglingam Kirubarjan, Yaakov Bar-Shalom. Track-to-track Fusion Versus Centralized Estimation: Theory and Application. IEEE Transactions on AES, 2003, 39(2): 386-411

F.M.Ham. Observability, Eigenvalues and Kalman Filtering. IEEE Transactions on Aerospace and Electronic Systems, 1982, 19(2): 156-164

Xianda, Zhang. Matrix Analysis and Application. Tsinghua University Press, 2004, Beijing

X. Rong Li. Information Fusion for Estimation and Decision. International Workshop on Data Fusion in 2002, Beijing, China

2

Air traffic trajectories segmentation based on time-series sensor data

José L. Guerrero, Jesús García and José M. Molina
University Carlos III of Madrid
Spain

1. Introduction

ATC is a critical area related with safety, requiring strict validation in real conditions (Kennedy & Gardner, 1998), being this a domain where the amount of data has gone under an exponential growth due to the increase in the number of passengers and flights. This has led to the need of automation processes in order to help the work of human operators (Wickens et al., 1998). These automation procedures can be basically divided into two different basic processes: the required online tracking of the aircraft (along with the decisions required according to this information) and the offline validation of that tracking process (which is usually separated into two sub-processes, segmentation (Guerrero & Garcia, 2008), covering the division of the initial data into a series of different segments, and reconstruction (Pérez et al., 2006, García et al., 2007), which covers the approximation with different models of the segments the trajectory was divided into). The reconstructed trajectories are used for the analysis and evaluation processes over the online tracking results.

This validation assessment of ATC centers is done with recorded datasets (usually named opportunity traffic), used to reconstruct the necessary reference information. The reconstruction process transforms multi-sensor plots to a common coordinates frame and organizes data in trajectories of an individual aircraft. Then, for each trajectory, segments of different modes of flight (MOF) must be identified, each one corresponding to time intervals in which the aircraft is flying in a different type of motion. These segments are a valuable description of real data, providing information to analyze the behavior of target objects (where uniform motion flight and maneuvers are performed, magnitudes, durations, etc). The performance assessment of ATC multisensor/multitarget trackers require this reconstruction analysis based on available air data, in a domain usually named opportunity trajectory reconstruction (OTR), (Garcia et al., 2009).

OTR consists in a batch process where all the available real data from all available sensors is used in order to obtain smoothed trajectories for all the individual aircrafts in the interest area. It requires accurate original-to-reconstructed trajectory's measurements association, bias estimation and correction to align all sensor measures, and also adaptive multisensor smoothing to obtain the final interpolated trajectory. It should be pointed out that it is an off-line batch processing potentially quite different to the usual real time data fusion systems used for ATC, due to the differences in the data processing order and its specific processing techniques, along with different availability of information (the whole trajectory can be used by the algorithms in order to perform the best possible reconstruction).

OTR works as a special multisensor fusion system, aiming to estimate target kinematic state, in which we take advantage of both past and future target position reports (smoothing problem). In ATC domain, the typical sensors providing data for reconstruction are the following:

- Radar data, from primary (PSR), secondary (SSR), and Mode S radars (Shipley, 1971). These measurements have random errors in the order of the hundreds of meters (with a value which increases linearly with distance to radar).
- Multilateration data from Wide Area Multilateration (WAM) sensors (Yang et al., 2002). They have much lower errors (in the order of 5-100 m), also showing a linear relation in its value related to the distance to the sensors positions.
- Automatic dependent surveillance (ADS-B) data (Drouilhet et al., 1996). Its quality is dependent on aircraft equipment, with the general trend to adopt GPS/GNSS, having errors in the order of 5-20 meters.

The complementary nature of these sensor techniques allows a number of benefits (high degree of accuracy, extended coverage, systematic errors estimation and correction, etc), and brings new challenges for the fusion process in order to guarantee an improvement with respect to any of those sensor techniques used alone.

After a preprocessing phase to express all measurements in a common reference frame (the stereographic plane used for visualization), the studied trajectories will have measurements with the following attributes: detection time, stereographic projections of its x and y components, covariance matrix, and real motion model (MM), (which is an attribute only included in simulated trajectories, used for algorithm learning and validation). With these input attributes, we will look for a domain transformation that will allow us to classify our samples into a particular motion model with maximum accuracy, according to the model we are applying.

The movement of an aircraft in the ATC domain can be simplified into a series of basic MM's. The most usually considered ones are uniform, accelerated and turn MM's. The general idea of the proposed algorithm in this chapter is to analyze these models individually and exploit the available information in three consecutive different phases.

The first phase will receive the information in the common reference frame and the analyzed model in order to obtain, as its output data, a set of synthesized attributes which will be handled by a learning algorithm in order to obtain the classification for the different trajectories measurements. These synthesized attributes are based on domain transformations according to the analyzed model by means of local information analysis (their value is based on the definition of segments of measurements from the trajectory).They are obtained for each measurement belonging to the trajectory (in fact, this process can be seen as a data pre-processing for the data mining techniques (Famili et al., 1997)).

The second phase applies data mining techniques (Eibe, 2005) over the synthesized attributes from the previous phase, providing as its output an individual classification for each measurement belonging to the analyzed trajectory. This classification identifies the measurement according to the model introduced in the first phase (determining whether it belongs to that model or not).

The third phase, obtaining the data mining classification as its input, refines this classification according to the knowledge of the possible MM's and their transitions, correcting possible misclassifications, and provides the final classification for each of the trajectory's measurement. This refinement is performed by means of the application of a filter.

Finally, segments are constructed over those classifications (by joining segments with the same classification value). These segments are divided into two different possibilities: those belonging to the analyzed model (which are already a final output of the algorithm) and those which do not belong to it, having to be processed by different models. It must be noted that the number of measurements processed by each model is reduced with each application of this cycle (due to the segments already obtained as a final output) and thus, more detailed models with lower complexity should be applied first. Using the introduced division into three MM's, the proposed order is the following: uniform, accelerated and finally turn model. Figure 1 explains the algorithm's approach:

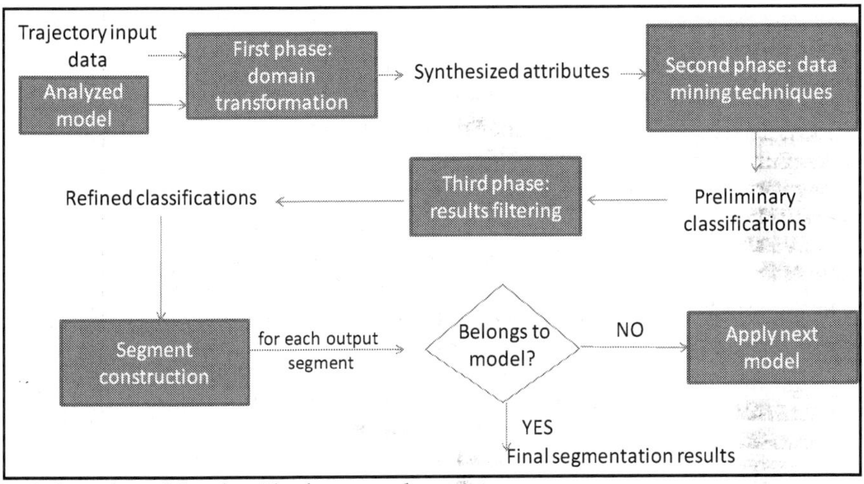

Fig. 1. Overview of the algorithm's approach

The validation of the algorithm is carried out by the generation of a set of test trajectories as representative as possible. This implies not to use exact covariance matrixes, (but estimations of their value), and carefully choosing the shapes of the simulated trajectories. We have based our results on four types of simulated trajectories, each having two different samples. Uniform, turn and accelerated trajectories are a direct validation of our three basic MM's. The fourth trajectory type, racetrack, is a typical situation during landing procedures. The validation is performed, for a fixed model, with the results of its true positives rate (TPR, the rate of measurements correctly classified among all belonging to the model) and false positives rate (FPR, the rate of measurements incorrectly classified among all not belonging the model). This work will show the results of the three consecutive phases using a uniform motion model.

The different sections of this work will be divided with the following organization: the second section will deal with the problem definition, both in general and particularized for the chosen approach. The third section will present in detail the general algorithm, followed by three sections detailing the three phases for that algorithm when the uniform movement model is applied: the fourth section will present the different alternatives for the domain transformation and choose between them the ones included in the final algorithm, the fifth will present some representative machine learning techniques to be applied to obtain the classification results and the sixth the filtering refinement over the previous results will be introduced, leading to the segment synthesis processes. The seventh section will cover the results obtained over the explained phases, determining the used machine learning technique and providing the segmentation results, both numerically and graphically, to provide the reader with easy validation tools over the presented algorithm. Finally a conclusions section based on the presented results is presented.

2. Problem definition

2.1 General problem definition

As we presented in the introduction section, each analyzed trajectory (T^i) is composed of a collection of sensor reports (or measurements), which are defined by the following vector:

$$\vec{x}_j^i = \left(x_j^i, y_j^i, t_j^i, R_j^i\right), j \in \{1, \dots, N^i\} \tag{1}$$

where j is the measurement number, i the trajectory number, N is the number of measurements in a given trajectory, x_j^i, y_j^i are the stereographic projections of the measurement, t_j^i is the detection time and R_j^i is the covariance matrix (representing the error introduced by the measuring device). From this problem definition our objective is to divide our trajectory into a series of segments (B_k^i), according to our estimated MOF. This is performed as an off-line processing (meaning that we may use past and future information from our trajectory). The segmentation problem can be formalized using the following notation:

$$T^i = \bigcup B_k^i \qquad B_k^i = \{x_j^i\} \qquad j \in \{k_{min}, \dots, k_{max}\} \tag{2}$$

In the general definition of this problem these segments are obtained by the comparison with a test model applied over different windows (aggregations) of measurements coming from our trajectory, in order to obtain a fitness value, deciding finally the segmentation operation as a function of that fitness value (Mann et al. 2002), (Garcia et al., 2006).

We may consider the division of offline segmentation algorithms into different approaches: a possible approach is to consider the whole data from the trajectory and the segments obtained as the problem's basic division unit (using a global approach), where the basic operation of the segmentation algorithm is the division of the trajectory into those segments (examples of this approach are the bottom-up and top-down families (Keogh et al., 2003)). In the ATC domain, there have been approaches based on a direct adaptation of online techniques, basically combining the results of forward application of the algorithm (the pure online technique) with its backward application (applying the online technique reversely to the time series according to the measurements detection time) (Garcia et al., 2006). An alternative can be based on the consideration of obtaining a different classification value for each of the trajectory's measurements (along with their local information) and obtaining the segments as a synthesized solution, built upon that classification (basically, by joining those adjacent measures sharing the same MM into a common segment). This approach allows the application of several refinements over the classification results before the final synthesis is performed, and thus is the one explored in the presented solution in this chapter.

2.2 Local approach problem definition

We have presented our problem as an offline processing, meaning that we may use information both from our past and our future. Introducing this fact into our local representation, we will restrict that information to a certain local segment around the measurement which we would like to classify. These intervals are centered on that measurement, but the boundaries for them can be expressed either in number of measurements, (3), or according to their detection time values (4).

$$B(x_m^i) = \{x_j^i\} \quad j \in [m-p, \dots, m, \dots, m+p] \tag{3}$$

$$B(x_m^i) = \{x_j^i\} \quad t_j^i \in \{t_m^i - n, \dots, t_m, \dots, t_m^i + n\} \tag{4}$$

Once we have chosen a window around our current measurement, we will have to apply a function to that segment in order to obtain its transformed value. This general classification function $F(\overrightarrow{x_j^i})$, using measurement boundaries, may be represented with the following formulation:

$$F(\overrightarrow{x_m^i}) = F(\overrightarrow{x_m^i} | T^i) \Rightarrow F(\overrightarrow{x_j^i} | B(x_m^i)) = F_p(\vec{x}_{m-p}^i, \dots, \vec{x}_m^i, \dots, \vec{x}_{m+p}^i) \tag{5}$$

From this formulation of the problem we can already see some of the choices available: how to choose the segments (according to (3) or (4)), which classification function to apply in (5) and how to perform the final segment synthesis. Figure 2 shows an example of the local approach for trajectory segmentation.

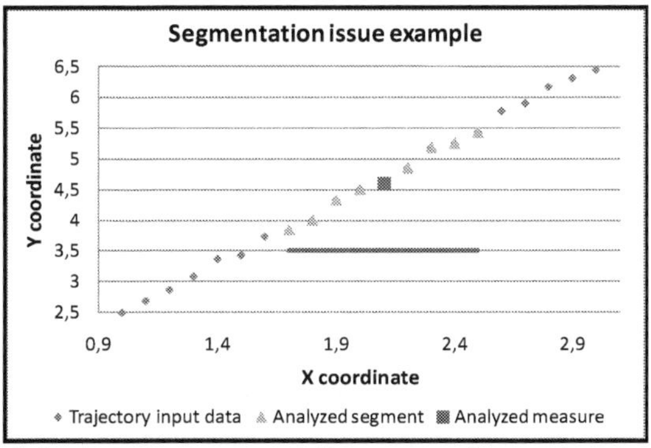

Fig. 2. Local approach for trajectory segmentation approach overview

3. General algorithm proposal

As presented in the introduction section, we will consider three basic MM's and classify our measurements individually according to them (Guerrero & Garcia, 2008). If a measurement is classified as unknown, it will be included in the input data for the next model's analysis. This general algorithm introduces a design criterion based on the introduced concepts of TPR and FPR, respectively equivalent to the type I and type II errors (Allchin, 2001). The design criterion will be to keep a FPR as low as possible, understanding that those measurements already assigned to a wrong model will not be analyzed by the following ones (and thus will remain wrongly classified, leading to a poorer trajectory reconstruction). The proposed order for this analysis of the MM's is the same in which they have been introduced, and the choice is based on how accurately we can represent each of them.

In the local approach problem definition section, the segmentation problem was divided into two different sub-problems: the definition of the $F_p(\overrightarrow{x_m^i})$ function (to perform measurement classification) and a final segment synthesis over that classification.

According to the different phases presented in the introduction section, we will divide the definition of the classification function $F(\overrightarrow{x_j^i})$ into two different tasks: a domain transformation $Dt(\overrightarrow{x_j^i})$ (domain specific, which defines the first phase of our algorithm) and a final classification $Cl(Dt(\overrightarrow{x_j^i}))$ (based on general classification algorithms, represented by the data mining techniques which are introduced in the second phase). The final synthesis over the classification results includes the refinement over that classification introduced by the filtering process and the actual construction of the output segment (third phase of the proposed algorithm).

The introduction of the domain transformation $Dt(\overrightarrow{x_j^i})$ from the initial data in the common reference frame must deal with the following issues: segmentation, (which will cover the decision of using an independent classification for each measurement or to treat segments as an indivisible unit), definition for the boundaries of the segments, which involves segment extension (which analyzes the definition of the segments by number of points or according to their detection time values) and segment resolution (dealing with the choice of the length of those segments, and how it affects our results), domain transformations (the different possible models used in order to obtain an accurate classification in the following phases), and threshold choosing technique (obtaining a value for a threshold in order to pre-classify the measurements in the transformed domain).

The second phase introduces a set of machine learning techniques to try to determine whether each of the measurements belongs to the analyzed model or not, based on the pre-classifications obtained in the first phase. In this second phase we will have to choose a $Cl(Dt(\overrightarrow{x_j^i}))$ technique, along with its configuration parameters, to be included in the algorithm proposal. The considered techniques are decision trees (C4.5, (Quinlan, 1993)) clustering (EM, (Dellaert, 2002)) neural networks (multilayer perceptron, (Gurney, 1997)) and Bayesian nets (Jensen & Graven-Nielsen, 2007) (along with the simplified naive Bayes approach (Rish, 2001)).

Finally, the third phase (segment synthesis) will propose a filter, based on domain knowledge, to reanalyze the trajectory classification results and correct those values which may not follow this knowledge (essentially, based on the required smoothness in MM's

changes). To obtain the final output for the model analysis, the isolated measurements will be joined according to their classification in the final segments of the algorithm.
The formalization of these phases and the subsequent changes performed to the data is presented in the following vectors, representing the input and output data for our three processes:

Input data: $T^i = \left\{\overrightarrow{x_j^i}\right\},\ j\epsilon\{1..N^i\}\quad \vec{x}_j^i = \left(x_j^i, y_j^i, t_j^i, R_j^i\right)$

Domain transformation: $\mathrm{Dt}(\overrightarrow{x_j^i}) \Rightarrow \mathrm{F}(\overrightarrow{x_j^i}|T^i) \Rightarrow \mathrm{F}(\overrightarrow{x_j^i}|B_j^i) = \{\mathrm{Pc}_k^j\},\ k \in \{1..M\}$

Pc_k^j = pre-classification k for measurement j, M = number of pre-classifications included

Classification process: $\mathrm{Cl}(\mathrm{Dt}(\overrightarrow{x_j^i})) = \mathrm{Cl}(\{\mathrm{Pc}_k^j\}) = C_j$

C_j= automatic classification result for measurement j (including filtering refinement)

Final output: $T^i = \bigcup B_k^i \quad B_k^i = \{x_j^i\}\ j \in [k_{min}, k_{max}]$

B_k^i= Final segments obtained by the union process

4. Domain transformation

The first phase of our algorithm covers the process where we must synthesize an attribute from our input data to represent each of the trajectory's measurements in a transformed domain and choose the appropriate thresholds in that domain to effectively differentiate those which belong to our model from those which do not do so.
The following aspects are the key parameters for this phase, presented along with the different alternatives compared for them, (it must be noted that the possibilities compared here are not the only possible ones, but representative examples of different possible approaches):

- ***Transformation function:*** correlation coefficient / Best linear unbiased estimator residue
- ***Segmentation granularity:*** segment study / independent study
- ***Segment extension,*** time / samples, and ***segment resolution,*** length of the segment, using the boundary units imposed by the previous decision
- ***Threshold choosing technique,*** choice of a threshold to classify data in the transformed domain.

Each of these parameters requires an individual validation in order to build the actual final algorithm tested in the experimental section. Each of them will be analyzed in an individual section in order to achieve this task.

4.1 Transformation function analysis

The transformation function decision is probably the most crucial one involving this first phase of our algorithm. The comparison presented tries to determine whether there is a real accuracy increase by introducing noise information (in the form of covariance matrixes). This section compares a correlation coefficient (Meyer, 1970) (a general statistic with no noise information) with a BLUE residue (Kay, 1993) (which introduces the noise in the measuring process). This analysis was originally proposed in (Guerrero & Garcia, 2008). The equations for the CC statistical are the following:

$$CC(x_j|B_k) = \frac{\sigma_{xy}(x_j|B_k)}{\sigma_x(x_j|B_k)\sigma_y(x_j|B_k)} \quad \sigma_x(x_j|B_k) = \sqrt{\frac{\sum_{i=\mathrm{kmin}}^{\mathrm{kmax}}(x_i-\bar{x})^2}{\mathrm{kmax}-\mathrm{kmin}}}$$
$$\sigma_{xy}(x_j|B_k) = \frac{1}{\mathrm{kmax}-\mathrm{kmin}+1}\sum_{i=\mathrm{kmin}}^{kmax}(x_i-\bar{x})(y_i-\bar{y}) \tag{6}$$

In order to use the BLUE residue we need to present a model for the uniform MM, represented in the following equations:

$$\vec{x}_m(k) = \begin{bmatrix} x_m(k) \\ y_m(k) \end{bmatrix} = \begin{bmatrix} 1 & t_k & 0 & 0 \\ 0 & 0 & 1 & t_k \end{bmatrix} \begin{bmatrix} x_0 \\ vx_0 \\ y_0 \\ vy_0 \end{bmatrix} + \begin{bmatrix} n_x(k) \\ n_y(k) \end{bmatrix} = H(t_k)\vec{\theta} + \vec{n}(k) \tag{7}$$

$$\langle\vec{\theta}\rangle = \begin{bmatrix} \langle x_0\rangle \\ \langle vx_0\rangle \\ \langle y_0\rangle \\ \langle vy_0\rangle \end{bmatrix} = \left(\sum_k H(t_k)^T R_k^{-1} H(t_k)\right)^{-1} \sum_k H(t_k)^T R_k^{-1}\overline{x_m}(k) \tag{8}$$

With those values we may calculate the interpolated positions for our two variables and the associated residue:

$$x_{int}(t) = \langle x_0\rangle + \langle vx_0\rangle t \qquad y_{int}(t) = \langle y_0\rangle + \langle vy_0\rangle t \tag{9}$$

$$res(x_j|B_k) = \frac{1}{(kmax-kmin+1)}\sum_{k=kmin}^{k=kmax}\left(x(k)-x_{int}(k)\;\; y(k)-y_{int}(k)\right)\; R_k^{-1}\begin{pmatrix} x(k)-x_{int}(k) \\ y(k)-y_{int}(k) \end{pmatrix} \tag{10}$$

The BLUE residue is presented normalized (the residue divided by the length of the segment in number of measurements), in order to be able to take advantage of its interesting statistical properties, which may be used into the algorithm design, and hence allow us to obtain more accurate results if it is used as our transformation function.

To obtain a classification value from either the CC or the BLUE residue value these values must be compared with a certain threshold. The CC threshold must be a value close, in absolute value, to 1, since that indicates a strong correlation between the variables. The BLUE residue threshold must consider the approximation to a chi-squared function which can be performed over its value (detailed in the threshold choosing technique section). In any case, to compare their results and choose the best technique between them, the threshold can be chosen by means of their TPR and FPR values (choosing manually a threshold which has zero FPR value with the highest possible TPR value).

To facilitate the performance comparison between the two introduced domain transformations, we may resort to ROC curves (Fawcett, 2006), which allow us to compare their behavior by representing their TPR against their FPR. The result of this comparison is shown in figure 3.

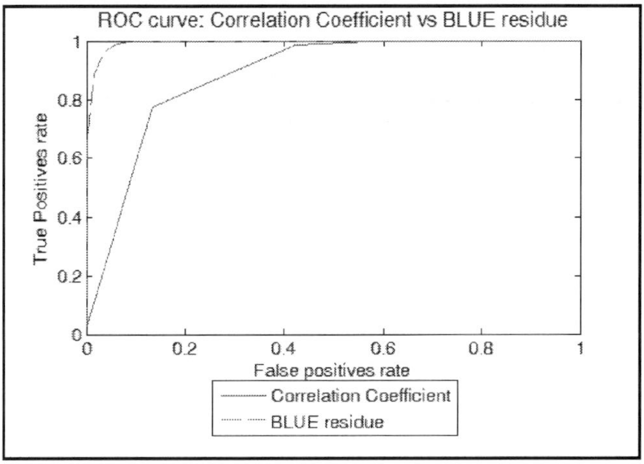

Fig. 3. Comparison between the two presented domain transformations: CC and BLUE residue

The comparison result shows that the introduction of the sensor's noise information is vital for the accuracy of the domain transformation, and thus the BLUE residue is chosen for this task.

4.2 Segmentation granularity analysis

Having chosen the BLUE residue as the domain transformation function, we intend to compare the results obtained with two different approaches, regarding the granularity they apply: the first approach will divide the trajectory into a series of segments of a given size (which may be expressed, as has been presented, in number of measurements of with detection time boundaries), obtain their synthesized value and apply that same value to every measurement belonging to the given segment. On the other hand, we will use the approach presented in the local definition of the problem, that, for every measurement belonging to the trajectory, involves choosing a segment around the given measurement, obtain its surrounding segment and find its transformed value according to that segment (which is applied only to the central measurement of the segment, not to every point belonging to it).

There are a number of considerations regarding this comparison: obviously, the results achieved by the local approach obtaining a different transformed value for each measurement will be more precise than those obtained by its alternative, but it will also involve a greater computational complexity. Considering a segment size of *s_size* and a trajectory with n measurements, the complexity of obtaining a transformed value for each of these measurements is $O(n * s\_size)$ whereas obtaining only a value and applying it to the whole segment is $O(n)$, introducing efficiency factors which we will ignore due to the offline nature of the algorithm.

Another related issue is the restrictions which applying the same transformed value to the whole segment introduces regarding the choice of those segments boundaries. If the transformed value is applied only to the central measurement, we may choose longer of

shorter segments according to the transformation results (this choice will be analysed in the following section), while applying that same transformed value to the whole segments introduces restrictions related to the precision which that length introduces (longer segments may be better to deal with the noise in the measurements, but, at the same time, obtain worse results due to applying the same transformed value to a greater number of measurements).
The ROC curve results for this comparison, using segments composed of thirty-one measurements, are shown in figure 4.

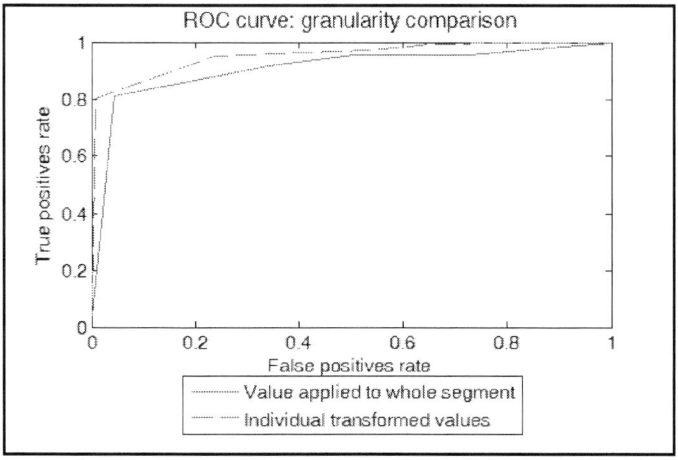

Fig. 4. Comparison between the two presented granularity choices

Given the presented design criterion, which remarks the importance of low FPR values, we may see that individual transformed values perform much better at that range (leftmost side of the figure), leading us, along with the considerations previously exposed, to its choice for the algorithm final implementation.

4.3 Segment definition analysis

The definition of the segments we will analyze involves two different factors: the boundary units used and the length (and its effects on the results) of those segments (respectively referred to as segment extension and segment resolution in this phase's presentation). One of the advantages of building domain-dependent algorithms is the use of information belonging to that domain. In the particular case of the ATC domain, we will have information regarding the lengths of the different possible manoeuvres performed by the aircrafts, and will base our segments in those lengths. This information will usually come in the form of time intervals (for example, the maximum and minimum duration of turn manoeuvres in seconds), but may also come in the form on number of detections in a given zone of interest. Thus, the choice of one or the other (respectively represented in the problem definition section by equations (4) and (3)) will be based on the available information.

With the units given by the available information, Figure 5 shows the effect of different resolutions over a given turn trajectory, along with the results over those resolutions.

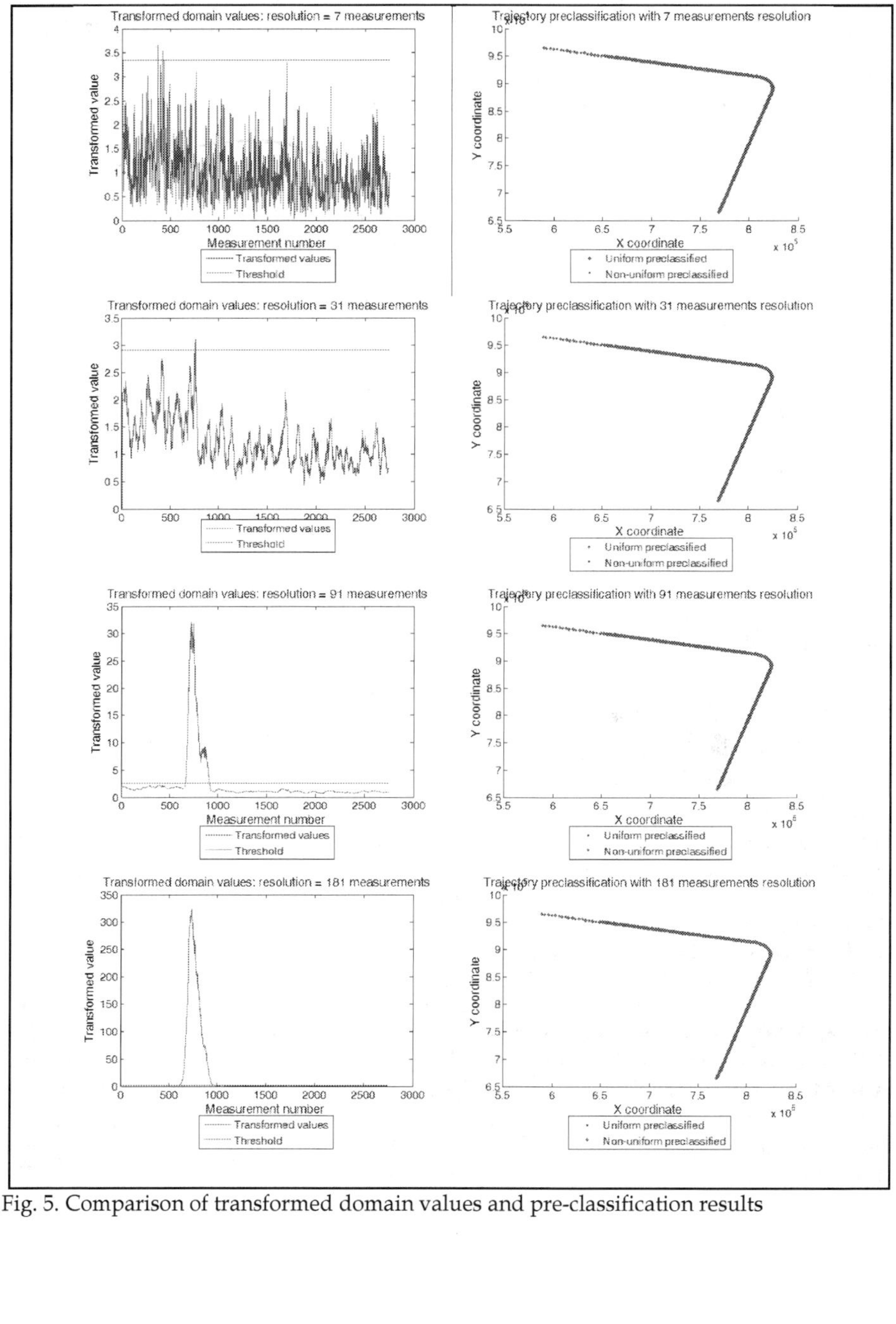

Fig. 5. Comparison of transformed domain values and pre-classification results

Observing the presented results, where the threshold has been calculated according to the procedure explained in the following section, we may determine the resolution effects: short segments exhibit several handicaps: on the one hand, they are more susceptible to the noise effects, and, on the other hand, in some cases, long smooth non-uniform MM segments may be accurately approximated with short uniform segments, causing the algorithm to bypass them (these effects can be seen in the lower resolutions shown in figure 5). Longer segments allow us to treat the noise effects more effectively (with resolution 31 there are already no misclassified measurements during non-uniform segments) and make the identification of non-uniform segments possible, avoiding the possibility of obtaining an accurate approximation of these segments using uniform ones (as can be seen with resolution 91) However, long segments also make the measurements close to a non-uniform MM increase their transformed value (as their surrounding segment starts to get into the non-uniform MM), leading to the fact that more measurements around the non-uniform segments will be pre-classified incorrectly as non-uniform (resolution 181). A different example of the effects of resolution in these pre-classification results may be looked up in (Guerrero et al., 2010).
There is, as we have seen, no clear choice for a single resolution value. Lower resolutions may allow us to obtain more precise results at the beginning and end of non-uniform segments, while higher resolution values are capital to guarantee the detection of those non-uniform segments and the appropriate treatment of the measurements noise. Thus, for this first phase, a multi-resolution approach will be used, feeding the second phase with the different pre-classifications of the algorithm according to different resolution values.

4.4 Threshold choosing technique

The threshold choice involves automatically determining the boundary above which transformed measurements will be considered as unknown. Examples of this choice may be seen in the previous section (figure 5). According to our design criterion, we would like to obtain a TPR as high as possible keeping our FPR ideally at a zero value. Graphically over the examples in figure 5 (especially for the highest resolutions, where the non-uniform maneuver can be clearly identified), that implies getting the red line as low as possible, leaving only the central section over it (where the maneuver takes place, making its residue value high enough to get over our threshold).
As presented in (Guerrero et al., 2010), the residue value in (10) follows a Chi-squared probability distribution function (pdf) normalized by its degrees of freedom, n. The value of n is given by twice the number of 2D measurements contained in the interval minus the dimension of P (P=4 in the presented uniform model, as we are imposing 4 linear restrictions). For a valid segment residual, "res" behaves with distribution $\frac{1}{(kmax-kmin+1)}\chi^2_{2(kmax-kmin+1)-P}$, which has the following mean and variance:

$$\mu = 2 - \frac{P}{(kmax-kmin+1)} \qquad \sigma^2 = \frac{4}{(kmax-kmin+1)} - \frac{2P}{(kmax-kmin+1)^2} \tag{11}$$

The residue distribution allows us to establish our criterion based on the TPR value, but not the FPR (we have a distribution over the uniform measurements, not the unknown ones), which is the one constrained by the design criterion. We may use the Chevychev's inequality (Meyer, 1970) to determine a threshold which should leave the 99% of the measurements belonging to our model above it (TPR>=0.99), with $\mu + 3\sigma$ value. From the values exposed in (11) we get the following threshold value:

$$\text{thres}=2-\frac{4}{N}+3\sqrt{\frac{4}{N}-\frac{8}{N^2}} \quad N=(kmax-kmin+1) \tag{12}$$

This threshold depends on the resolution of the segment, N, which also influences the residue value in (10). It is interesting to notice that the highest threshold value is reached with the lowest resolution. This is a logical result, since to be able to maintain the TPR value (having fixed it with the inequality at 99%) with short segments, a high threshold value is required, in order to counteract the noise effects (while longer segments are more resistant to that noise and thus the threshold value may be lower).

We would like to determine how precisely our χ^2 distribution represents our normalized residue in non-uniform trajectories with estimated covariance matrix. In the following figures we compare the optimal result of the threshold choice (dotted lines), manually chosen, to the results obtained with equation (12). Figure 6 shows the used trajectories for this comparison, along with the proposed comparison between the optimal TPR and the one obtained with (12) for increasing threshold values.

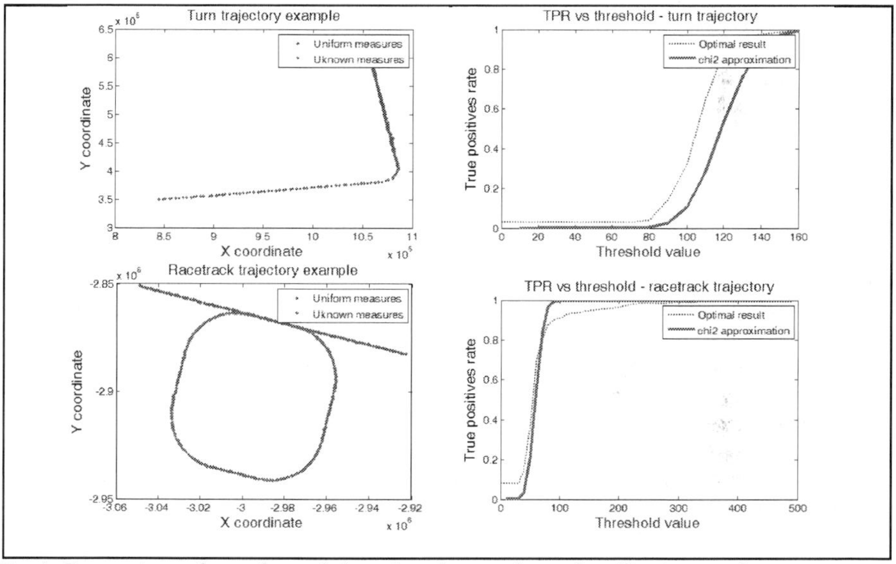

Fig. 6. Comparison of transformed domain values and pre-classification results

In the two trajectories in figure 6 we may appreciate two different distortion effects introduced by our approximation. The turn trajectory shows an underestimation of our TPR due to the inexactitude in the covariance matrix R_k . This inexactitude assumes a higher noise than the one which is present in the trajectory, and thus will make us choose a higher threshold than necessary in order to obtain the desired TPR margin.

In the racetrack trajectory we perceive the same underestimation at the lower values of the threshold, but then our approximation crosses the optimal results and reaches a value over it. This is caused by the second distortion effect, the maneuver's edge measurements. The measurements close to a maneuver beginning or end tend to have a higher residue value than the theoretical one for a uniform trajectory (due to their proximity to the non-uniform segments), making us increase the threshold value to classify them correctly (which causes the optimal result to show a lower TPR in the figure). These two effects show that a heuristic tuning may be required in our χ^2 distribution in order to adapt it to these distortion effects.

5. Machine learning techniques application

The algorithm's first phase, as has been detailed, ended with a set of pre-classification values based on the application of the domain transformation with different resolutions to every measurement in the trajectory. The objective of this second phase is to obtain a classification according to the analyzed model for each of these measurements, to be able to build the resulting segments from this data.

There are countless variants of machine learning techniques, so the choice of the ones presented here was not a trivial one. There was not a particular family of them more promising a-priori, so the decision tried to cover several objectives: they should be easy to replicate, general and, at the same time, cover different approaches in order to give the algorithm the chance to include the best alternative from a wide set of choices. This led to the choice of Weka®[1] as the integrated tool for these tests, trying to use the algorithms with their default parameters whenever possible (it will be indicated otherwise if necessary), even though the fine tuning of them gives us a very slight better performance, and the choice of representative well tested algorithms from different important families in machine learning: decision trees (C4.5) clustering (EM) neural networks (multilayer perceptron) and Bayesian networks, along with the simplified naive Bayes approach. We will describe each of these techniques briefly.

Decision trees are predictive models based on a set of "attribute-value" pairs and the entropy heuristic. The C 4.5 algorithm (Quinlan, 1993) allows continuous values for its variables.

Clustering techniques have the objective of grouping together examples with similar characteristics and obtain a series of models for them that, even though they may not cover all the characteristics of their represented members, can be representative enough of their sets as a whole (this definition adapts very well to the case in this chapter, since we want to obtain a representative set of common characteristics for measurements following our analyzed model). The EM algorithm (Dellaert, 2002) is based on a statistical model which represents the input data basing itself on the existence of k Gaussian probability distribution functions, each of them representing a different cluster. These functions are based on maximum likelihood hypothesis. It is important to realize that this is an unsupervised technique which does not classify our data, only groups it. In our problem, we will have to select the classification label afterwards for each cluster. In this algorithm, as well, we will introduce a non standard parameter for the number of clusters. The default configuration allows Weka to automatically determine this number, but, in our case, we only want two different clusters: one representing those measurements following the analyzed model and a different one for those unknown, so we will introduce this fact in the algorithm's configuration.

[1] Available online at http://www.cs.waikato.ac.nz/ml/weka/

Bayesian networks (Jensen & Graven-Nielsen, 2007) are directed acyclic graphs whose nodes represent variables, and whose missing edges encode conditional independencies between the variables. Nodes can represent any kind of variable, be it a measured parameter, a latent variable or a hypothesis. Special simplifications of these networks are Naive Bayes networks (Rish, 2001), where the variables are considered independent. This supposition, even though it may be considered a very strong one, usually introduces a faster learning when the number of training samples is low, and in practice achieves very good results.
Artificial neural networks are computational models based on biological neural networks, consisting of an interconnected group of artificial neurons, which process information using a connectionist approach to computation. Multilayer Perceptron (MP), (Gurney, 1997), are feed-forward neural networks having an input layer, an undetermined number of hidden layers and an output layer, with nonlinear activation functions. MP's are universal function approximators, and thus they are able to distinguish non-linearly separable data. One of the handicaps of their approach is the configuration difficulties which they exhibit (dealing mainly with the number of neurons and hidden layers required for the given problem). The Weka tool is able to determine these values automatically.

6. Classification refinement and segment construction

The algorithm's final phase must refine the results from the machine learning techniques and build the appropriate segments from the individual measurements classification. To perform this refinement, we will use the continuity in the movement of the aircrafts, meaning that no abrupt MM changes can be performed (every MM has to be sustained for a certain time-length). This means that situations where a certain measurement shows a classification value different to its surrounding values can be corrected assigning to it the one shared by its neighbours.
This correction will be performed systematically by means of a voting system, assigning the most repeated classification in its segment to the central measurement. This processing is similar to the one performed by median filters (Yin et al., 1996) widely used in image processing (Baxes, 1994).
The widow size for this voting system has to be determined. In the segment definition section the importance of the available information regarding the length of the possible non-uniform MM's was pointed out, in order to determine the resolution of the domain transformation, which is used as well for this window size definition. Choosing a too high value for our window size might cause the algorithm to incorrectly reclassify non-uniform measurements as uniform (if its value exceeds the length of the non-uniform segment they belong to) leading to an important increase in the FPR value (while the design criterion tries to avoid this fact during the three phases presented). Thus, the window size will have the value of the shortest possible non-uniform MM.
It also important to determine which measurements must be treated with this filtering process. Through the different previous phases the avoidance of FPR has been highlighted (by means of multi-resolution domain transformation and the proper election of the used machine learning technique), even at the cost of slightly decreasing the TPR value. Those considerations are followed in this final phase by the application of this filtering process only to measurements classified as non-uniform, due to their possible misclassification

caused by their surrounding noise. Figure 7 shows the results of this filtering process applied to an accelerated trajectory

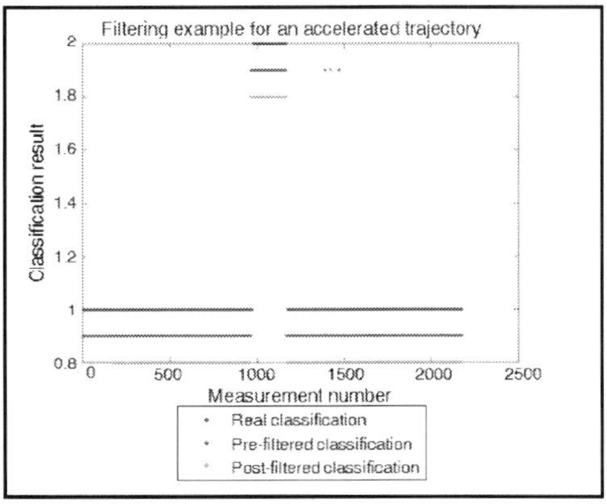

Fig. 7. Example filtering process applied to an accelerated trajectory

In figure 7, the lowest values (0.8 for post-filtered results, 0.9 for pre-filtered ones and 1 for the real classification) indicate that the measurement is classified as uniform, whereas their respective higher ones (1+ its lowest value) indicate that the measurement is classified as non-uniform. This figure shows that some measurements previously misclassified as non-uniform are corrected.

The importance of this filtering phase is not usually reflected in the TPR, bearing in mind that the number of measurements affected by it may be very small, but the number of output segments can vary its value significantly. In the example in figure 7, the pre-filtered classification would have output nine different segments, whereas the post-filtered classification outputs only three segments. This change highlights the importance of this filtering process.

The method to obtain the output segments is extremely simple after this median filter application: starting from the first detected measurement, one segment is built according to that measurement classification, until another measurement *i* with a different classification value is found. At that point, the first segment is defined with boundaries *[1, i-1]* and the process is restarted at measurement *i*, repeating this cycle until the end of the trajectory is reached.

7. Experimental validation

The division of the algorithm into different consecutive phases introduces validation difficulties, as the results are mutually dependant. In this whole work, we have tried to show those validations along with the techniques explanation when it was unavoidable (as occurred in the first phase, due to the influence of the choices in its different parameters) and postpone the rest of the cases for a final validation over a well defined test set (second and third phases, along with the overall algorithm performance).

This validation process is carried out by the generation of a set of test trajectories as representative as possible, implying not to use exact covariance matrixes, (but estimations of their value), and carefully choosing the shapes of the simulated trajectories. We have based our results on four kind of simulated trajectories, each having two different samples. Uniform, turn and accelerated trajectories are a direct validation of our three basic MM's identified, while the fourth trajectory type, racetrack, is a typical situation during landing procedures.

This validation will be divided into three different steps: the first one will use the whole data from these trajectories, obtain the transformed multi-resolution values for each measurement and apply the different presented machine learning techniques, analyzing the obtained results and choosing a particular technique to be included in the algorithm as a consequence of those results.

Having determined the used technique, the second step will apply the described refinement process to those classifications, obtaining the final classification results (along with their TPR and FPR values). Finally the segmentations obtained for each trajectory are shown along with the real classification of each trajectory, to allow the reader to perform a graphical validation of the final results.

7.1 Machine learning techniques validation

The validation method for the machine learning techniques still has to be determined. The chosen method is cross-validation (Picard and Cook, 1984) with 10 folds. This method ensures robustness in the percentages shown. The results output format for any of these techniques in Weka provides us with the number of correctly and incorrectly classified measurements, along with the confusion matrix, detailing the different class assignations. In order to use these values into our algorithm's framework, they have to be transformed into TPR and FPR values. They can be obtained from the confusion matrix, as shown in the following example:

Weka's raw output:

```
Correctly Classified Instances     10619          96.03  %
Incorrectly Classified Instances     439          3.97   %
=== Confusion Matrix ===
  a   b   <-- classified as
 345  37 |   a = uniform_model
   0 270 |   b = unknown_model
```

Algorithm parameters:

TPR = 345/37 = 0,903141361 FPR = 0/270 = 0

The selection criterion from these values must consider the design criterion of keeping a FPR value as low as possible, trying to obtain, at the same time, the highest possible TPR value. Also, we have introduced as their input only six transformed values for each measurement, corresponding to resolutions 11, 31, 51, 71, 91 and 111 (all of them expressed in number of measurements) The results presentation shown in table 1 provides the individual results for each trajectory, along with the results when the whole dataset is used as its input. The individual results do not include the completely uniform trajectories (due to their lack of FPR, having no non-uniform measurements). Figure 8 shows the graphical comparison of the different algorithms with the whole dataset according to their TPR and FPR values

Trajectory	C 4.5		EM Clustering		Bayesian networks		Naive Bayes		Multilayer perceptron	
	TPR	FPR	TPR	FPR	TPR	FPR	TPR	FPR	TPR	FPR
Racetr. 1	0,903	0	0,719	0	0,903	0	0,903	0	0,903	0
Racetr. 2	0,966	0,036	0,625	0	0,759	0	0,759	0	0,966	0,036
Turn 1	0,975	0	1	1	0,918	0	0,914	0	0,975	0
Turn 2	0,994	0,019	0,979	0	0,987	0	0,987	0	0,994	0,019
Accel. 1	0,993	0	0,993	0	0,993	0	0,993	0	0,993	0
Accel. 2	0,993	0,021	0,993	0,021	0,993	0,021	0,993	0,021	0,993	0,021
Whole dataset	0,965	0,078	0,941	0,003	0,956	0,096	0,956	0,096	0,973	0,155

Table 1. Results presentation over the introduced dataset for the different proposed machine learning techniques

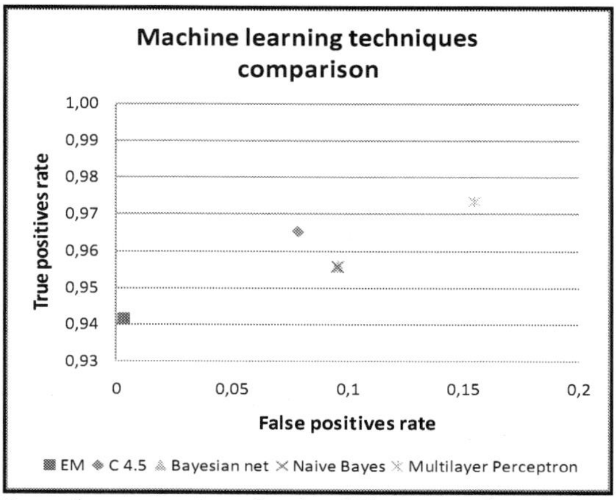

Fig. 8. TPR and FPR results comparison for the different machine learning techniques over the whole dataset.

From the results above we can determine that the previous phase has performed an accurate job, due to the fact that all the different techniques are able to obtain high TPR and low TPR results. When we compare them, the relationship between the TPR and the FPR does not allow a clear choice between the five techniques. If we recur to multi-objetive optimization terminology (Coello et al. 2007), (which is, in fact, what we are performing, trying to obtain a FPR as low as possible with a TPR as high as possible) we may discard the two Bayesian approaches, as they are dominated (in terms of Pareto dominance) by the C 4.5 solution. That leaves us the choice between EM (with the lowest FPR value), the C 4.5 (the most equilibrated between FPR and TPR values) and the multilayer perceptron (with the highest TPR). According to our design criterion, we will incorporate into the algorithm the technique with the lowest FPR: EM clustering.

7.2 Classification refinement validation

To obtain a more detailed performance analysis over the filtering results, we will detail the TPR and FPR values for each individual trajectory before and after this filtering phase. Also, to obtain a numerical validation over the segmentation quality we will detail the real and output number of segments for each of these trajectories. These results are shown in table 2.

Trajectory	Pre-filtered results		Post-filtered results		Number of segments	
	TPCP	TPFP	TPCP	TPFP	Real	Output
Racetr. 1	0,4686	0	0,4686	0	9	3
Racetr.2	0,5154	0	0,5154	0	9	3
Uniform 1	0,9906	0	1	0	1	1
Uniform 2	0,9864	0	0,9961	0	1	3
Turn 1	0,9909	0,0206	0,994	0,0206	3	3
Turn 2	0,9928	0	0,9942	0	3	3
Accel. 1	0,6805	0	0,6805	0	3	3
Accel. 2	0,9791	0	0,9799	0	3	3

Table 2. Comparison of TPR and FPR values for the dataset's trajectories, along with the final number of segments for this phase

In the previous results we can see that the filtering does improve the results in some trajectories, even though the numerical results over TPR and FPR are not greatly varied (the effect, as commented in the filtering section, is more noticeable in the number of segments, given that every measurement misclassified might have meant the creation of an additional output segment).

The overall segmentation output shows difficulties dealing with the racetrack trajectories. This is caused by the fact that their uniform segments inside the oval are close to two different non-uniform ones, thus increasing their transformed value to typical non-uniform measurements ones, being accordingly classified by the machine learning technique. However, these difficulties decrease the value of TPR, meaning that this misclassification can be corrected by the non-uniform models cycles which are applied after the described uniform one detailed through this work. The rest of the trajectories are segmented in a satisfactory way (all of them show the right number of output segments, apart from an additional non-uniform segment in one of the completely uniform ones, caused by the very high measuring noise in that area).

7.3 Overall graphical validation

Even though the previous section showed the different numerical results for every trajectory, the authors considered that a final visual validation is capital to enable the reader to perform the analysis of the segmentation quality, at least for one example of each kind of the different trajectories (focusing on the difficult cases detailed in the previous section).

Figure 9 shows the original trajectory with its correct classification along with the algorithm's results.

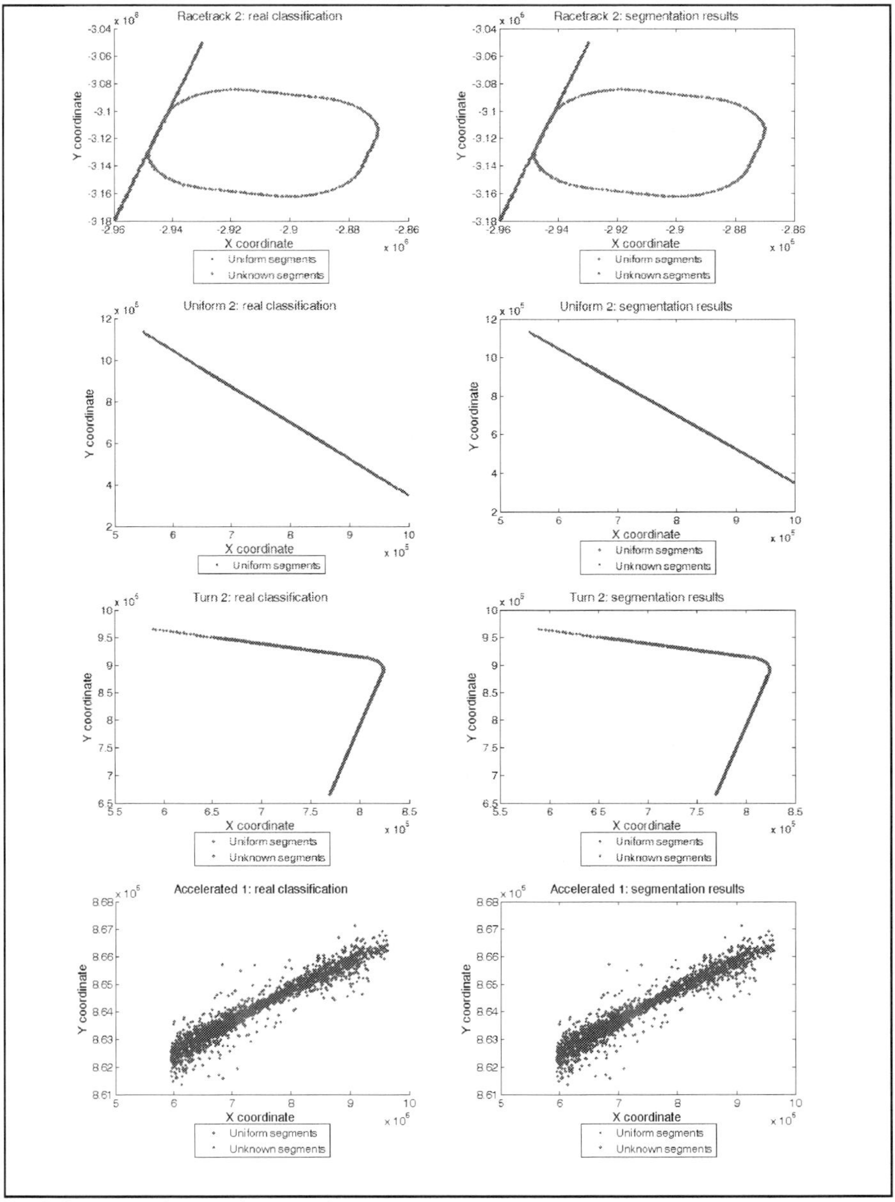

Fig. 9. Segmentation results overview

8. Conclusions

The automation of ATC systems is a complex issue which relies on the accuracy of its low level phases, determining the importance of their validation. That validation is faced in this work with an inherently offline processing, based on a domain transformation of the noisy measurements with three different motion models and the application of machine learning and filtering techniques, in order to obtain the final segmentation into these different models. This work has analyzed and defined in depth the uniform motion model and the algorithm's performance according to this model. The performance analysis is not trivial, since only one of the motion models in the algorithm is presented and the results obtained are, thus, only partial. Even so, these results are encouraging, having obtained good TPR and FPR values in most trajectory types, and a final number of segments which are reasonably similar to the real ones expected. Some issues have been pointed out, such as the behaviour of measurements belonging to uniform motion models when they are close to two different non-uniform segments (a typical situation during racetrack trajectories), but the final algorithm's results are required in order to deal with these issues properly. Future lines include the complete definition of the algorithm, including the non uniform motion models and the study of possible modifications in the domain transformation, in order to deal with the introduced difficulties, along with the validation with real trajectories.

9. References

Allchin, D.,(2001) "Error Types", *Perspectives on Science*, Vol.9, No.1, Pages 38-58. 2001.

Baxes, G.A. *(1994) "Digital Image Processing. Principles & Applications"*, Wiley and Sons

Coello, C. A., Lamont, G. B., Van Veldhuizen, D. A. (2007) *"Evolutionary Algorithms for Solving Multi-Objective Problems"* 2nd edition. Springer

Dellaert, F. (2002) *"The Expectation Maximization Algorithm"*. Technical Report number GIT-GVU-02-20. College of Computing, Georgia Institute of Technology

Drouilhet, P.R., Knittel, G.H., Vincent, A., Bedford, O. (1996) *"Automatic Dependent Surveillance Air Navigation System"*. U.S. Patent n. 5570095. October, 1996

Eibe, F. (2005) *"Data Mining: Practical Machine Learning Tools and Techniques"*. Second Edition. Morgan Kauffman

Famili, A., Sehn, W., Weber, R., Simoudis, E. (1997) "Data Preprocessing and Intelligent Data Analysis" *Intelligent Data Analysis Journal*. 1:1-28, March, 1997.

Fawcett, T. (2006) "An introduction to ROC analysis". *Pattern Recognition Letters*, 27. Pages: 861-874. International Association for Pattern Recognition

Garcia, J.; Perez, O.; Molina, J.M.; de Miguel, G.; (2006) *"Trajectory classification based on machine-learning techniques over tracking data"*. Proceedings of the 9th International Conference on Information Fusion. Italy. 2006.

Garcia, J., Molina, J.M., de Miguel, G., Besada, A. (2007) *"Model-Based Trajectory Reconstruction using IMM Smoothing and Motion Pattern Identification"*. Proceedings of the 10th International Conference on Information Fusion. Canada. July 2007.

Garcia, J., Besada, J.A., Soto, A. and de Miguel, G. (2009) "Opportunity trajectory reconstruction techniques for evaluation of ATC systems". *International Journal of Microwave and Wireless Technologies*. 1 : 231-238

Guerrero, J.L and Garcia J. (2008) *"Domain Transformation for Uniform Motion Identification in Air Traffic Trajectories"* Proceedings of the International Symposium on Distributed Computing and Artificial Intelligence (Advances in Soft Computing, Vol. 50), pp. 403-409, Spain, October 2008. Springer

Guerrero, J.L., Garcia, J., Molina, J.M. (2010) *"Air Traffic Control: A Local Approach to the Trajectory Segmentation Issue"*. Proceedings for the Twenty Third International Conference on Industrial, Engineering & Other Applications of Applied Intelligent Systems, part III, Lecture Notes in Artificial Intelligence, Vol. 6098, pp. 498-507. Springer

Gurney, K. (1997) *"An introduction to Neural Networks"*. CRC Press.

Jensen, F.B., Graven-Nielsen, T. (2007) *"Bayesian Networks and Decision Graphs"*. Second edition. Springer.

Kay, S.M. (1993) *"Fundamentals of Statistical Signal Processing, Volume I: Estimation Theory"*. Prentice Hall PTR.

Kennedy D., Gardner, A. B. (1998) "Tools for analysing the performance of ATC surveillance radars", *IEE Colloquium on Specifying and Measuring Performance of Modern Radar Systems*. March, 1998. 6/1-6/4.

Keogh, E, Chu, S., Hart, D., Pazzani, M. (2003) "Segmenting Time Series: A Survey and Novel Approach". In: *Data Mining in Time Series Databases*, second edition.. pp 1-21. World Scientific

Mann, R. Jepson, A.D. El-Maraghi, T. (2002) *"Trajectory segmentation using dynamic programming"*. Proceedings for the 16th International Conference on Pattern Recognition. 2002.

Meyer, P. (1970) *"Introductory Probability and Statistical Applications"* Second edition. Addison Wesley.

Pérez, O., García, J., Molina, J.M. (2006) *"Neuro-fuzzy Learning Applied to Improve the Trajectory Reconstruction Problem"*. Proceedings of the International Conference on Computational Intelligence for Modelling Control and Automation and International Conference on Intelligent Agents Web Technologies and International Commerce (CIMCA06). Australia, November 2006. IEEE Computer Society.

Picard, R.; Cook, D. (1984). "Cross-Validation of Regression Models". *Journal of the American Statistical Association* 79 (387). Pages 575–583.

Quinlan, J.R. (1993) *"C4.5: Programs for Machine Learning"*. Morgan Kaufmann

Rish, I. (2001) *"An empirical study of the naive Bayes classifier"*. IJCAI 2001 : Workshop on Empirical Methods in Artificial Intelligence.

Shipley, R. (1971) "Secondary Surveillance Radar in ATC Systems: A description of the advantages and implications to the controller of the introduction of SSR facilities". *Aircraft Engineering and Aerospace Technology*. 43: 20-21. MCB UP Ltd.

Wickens, C.D., Mavor, A.S., Parasuraman, R. and McGee, J. P. (1998) *"The Future of Air Traffic Control: Human Operators and Automation"*. The National Academies Press, Washington, D.C.

Yang, Y.E. Baldwin, J. Smith, A. Rannoch Corp., Alexandria, VA. (2002) *"Multilateration tracking and synchronization over wide areas"*. Proceedings of the IEEE Radar Conference. August 2002. IEEE Computer Society.

Yin, L., Yang, R., Gabbouj, M., Neuvo, Y. (1996) "Weighted Median Filters: A Tutorial", *IEEE Trans. on Circuits and Systems*, 43(3), pages. 157-192.

3

Distributed Compressed Sensing of Sensor Data

Vasanth Iyer
International Institute of Information Technology
Hyderabad A.P. India. 500 032

1. Introduction

Intelligent Information processing in distributed wireless sensor networks has many different optimizations by which redundancies in data can be eliminated, and at the same time the original source signal can be retrieved without loss. The data-centric nature of sensor network is modeled, which allows environmental applications to measure correlated data by periodic data aggregation. In the distributed framework, we explore how Compressed Sensing could be used to represent the measured signals in its sparse form, and model the framework to reproduce the individual signals from the ensembles in its sparse form expressed in equations(1,3). The processed signals are then represented with their common component; which is represented by its significant coefficients, and the variation components, which is also sparse are projected onto scaling and wavelet functions of the correlated component. The overall representation of the basis preserves the temporal (intra-signal) and spatial (inter-signal) characteristics. All of these scenarios correspond to measuring properties of physical processes that change smoothly in time, and in space, and thus are highly correlated. We show by simulation that the framework using cross-layer protocols can be extended using sensor fusion, and data-centric aggregation, to scale to a large number of nodes.

1.1 Cross Layer Sensor Nodes

Sensor network due to its constrained resources such as energy, memory, and range uses a cross layer model for efficient communications. The cross layer model uses *pre-processing*, *post-processing* and *routing*, to accomplish sensor measurements and communications with sensor nodes. Cross layer based routing protocols use different OSI layers to do multi-hop communications. Due to high deployment node densities and short bursts of wireless transmission, not all layers are connected, and can only be coordinated and scheduled by a higher level network function which keeps track of the node states. Due to this limited connectivity between layers, one needs to efficiently schedule the sensor nodes, and its states from the lower-level physical layers, to the higher routing and application layers. The energy spent at each layer needs to be carefully profiled so that any redundancy due to network scalability can further deteriorate the power-aware routing algorithm. One common motivation is to use the least number of bits to represent the data, as the transmission cost per bit increases non-linearly (Power Law) with distance (S. B. Lowen and M. C. Teich (1970)). The other relevant factors, which influence the accuracy of the measured sensor values, versus the total number of sensors deployed, can be divided into pre- and post processing of sensing application parameters. The lower-layer pre-processing involves, (a) the number of measurement needed so that the measured values can be represented without loss by using intra-sensor redundancy, (b) as the sensor measurements show temporal correlation with inter sensor data, the signal is further divided into many blocks which represent constant variance. In terms of the OSI layer, the pre-processing is done at the physical layer, in our case it is wireless channel with multi-sensor intervals. The network layer data aggregation is based on variable length pre-fix coding, which minimizes the number of bits before transmitting it to a sink. In terms of the OSI layers, data aggregation is done at the data-link layer periodically buffering, before the packets are routed through the upper network layer.

1.2 Computation Model

The sensor network model is based on network scalability the total number of sensors N, which can be very large upto many thousand nodes. Due to this fact an application needs to find the computation power in terms of the combined energy it has, and also the minimum accuracy of the data it can track and measure. The computation steps can be described in terms of the cross-layer protocol messages in the network model. The pre-processing needs to accomplish the minimal number of measurements needed, given by $x = \sum \vartheta(n)\Psi_n = \sum \vartheta(n_k)$, where Ψ_n^k is the best basis. The local coefficients can be represented by 2^j different levels, the search for best basis can be accomplished, using a binary search in $O(\lg m)$ steps. The post processing step involves efficient coding of the measured values, if there are m coefficients, the space required to store the computation can be accomplished in $O(\lg_2 m)$ bits. The routing of data using the sensor network needs to be power-aware, so these uses a distributed algorithm using cluster head rotation, which enhances the total lifetime of the sensor network. The computation complexity of routing in terms of the total number of nodes can be shown as $OC(\lg N)$, where C is the number of cluster heads and N total number of nodes. The computational bounds are derived for pre- and post processing algorithms for large data-sets, and is bounds are derived for a large node size in Section, Theoretical bounds.

1.3 Multi-sensor Data Fusion

Using the cross-layer protocol approach, we like to reduce the communication cost, and derive bounds for the number of measurements necessary for signal recovery under a given sparsity ensemble model, similar to Slepian-Wolf rate (Slepian (D. Wolf)) for correlated sources. At the same time, using the collaborative sensor node computation model, the number of measurements required for each sensor must account for the minimal features unique to that sensor, while at the same time features that appear among multiple sensors must be amortized over the group.

1.4 Chapter organization

Section 2 overviews the categorization of cross-layer pre-processing, CS theories and provides a new result on CS signal recovery. Section 3 introduces routing and data aggregation for our distributed framework and proposes two examples for routing. The performance analysis of cluster and MAC level results are discussed. We provide our detailed analysis for the DCS design criteria of the framework, and the need for pre-processing. In Section 4, we compare the results of the framework with a correlated data-set. The shortcomings of the upper layers which are primarily routing centric are contrasted with data centric routing using DHT, for the same family of protocols. In Section 5, we close the chapter with a discussion and conclusions. In appendices several proofs contain bounds for scalability of resources. For prerequisites and programming information using sensor applications you may refer to the book by (S. S. Iyengar and Nandan Parameshwaran (2010)) Fundamentals of Sensor Programming, Application and Technology.

2. Pre-Processing

As different sensors are connected to each node, the nodes have to periodically measure the values for the given parameters which are correlated. The inexpensive sensors may not be calibrated, and need processing of correlated data, according to intra and inter sensor variations. The pre-processing algorithms allow to accomplish two functions, one to use minimal number of measurement at each sensor, and the other to represent the signal in its loss-less sparse representation.

2.1 Compressive Sensing (CS)

The signal measured if it can be represented at a sparse Dror Baron (Marco F. Duarte) representation, then this technique is called the sparse basis as shown in equation (1), of the measured signal. The technique of finding a representation with a small number of significant coefficients is often referred to as Sparse Coding. When sensing locally many techniques have been implemented such as the Nyquist rate (Dror Baron (Marco F. Duarte)), which defines the minimum number of measurements needed to faithfully reproduce the original signal. Using CS it is further possible to reduce the number of measurement for a set of sensors with correlated measurements (Bhaskar Krishnamachari (Member)).

$$x = \sum \vartheta(n)\Psi_n = \sum \vartheta(n_k)\Psi_{n_k}, \tag{1}$$

Consider a real-valued signal $x \in R^N$ indexed as x(n), $n \in 1, 2, ..., N$. Suppose that the basis $\Psi = [\Psi_1, ..., \Psi_N]$ provides a K-sparse representation of x; that is, where x is a linear combination of K vectors chosen from, Ψ, n_k are the indices of those vectors, and $\vartheta(n)$ are the coefficients; the concept is extendable to tight frames (Dror Baron (Marco F. Duarte)). Alternatively, we can write in matrix notation $x = \Psi\vartheta$, where x is an $N \times 1$ column vector, the sparse basis matrix is $N \times N$ with the basis vectors Ψ_n as columns, and $\vartheta(n)$ is an $N \times 1$ column vector with K nonzero elements. Using $\| \cdot \|_p$Ato denote the ℓ_p norm, we can write that $\| \vartheta \|_p = K$; we can also write the set of nonzero indices $\Omega 1, ..., N$, with $|\Omega| = K$. Various expansions, including wavelets (Dror Baron (Marco F. Duarte)), Gabor bases (Dror Baron (Marco F. Duarte)), curvelets (Dror Baron (Marco F. Duarte)), are widely used for representation and compression of natural signals, images, and other data.

2.2 Sparse representation

A single measured signal of finite length, which can be represented in its sparse representation, by transforming into all its possible basis representations. The number of basis for the for each level j can be calculated from the equation as

$$A_{j+1} = A_j^2 + 1 \tag{2}$$

So staring at $j = 0$, $A_0 = 1$ and similarly, $A_1 = 1^2 + 1 = 2$, $A_2 = 2^2 + 1 = 5$ and $A_3 = 5^2 + 1 = 26$ different basis representations.

Let us define a framework to quantify the sparsity of ensembles of correlated signals $x_1, x2, ..., xj$ and to quantify the measurement requirements. These correlated signals can be represented by its basis from equation (2). The collection of all possible basis representation is called the sparsity model.

$$x = P\theta \tag{3}$$

Where P is the sparsity model of K vectors ($K << N$) and θ is the non zero coefficients of the sparse representation of the signal. The sparsity of a signal is defined by this model P, as there are many factored possibilities of $x = P\theta$. Among the factorization the unique representation of the smallest dimensionality of θ is the sparsity level of the signal x under this model, or ϵ which is the smallest interval among the sensor readings distinguished after cross-layer aggregation.

2.3 Distributed Compressive Sensing (DCS)

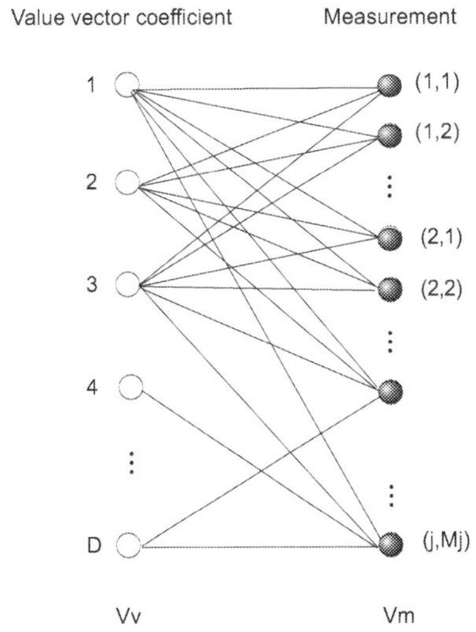

Fig. 1. Bipartite graphs for distributed compressed sensing.

DCS allows to enable distributed coding algorithms to exploit both intra-and inter-signal correlation structures. In a sensor network deployment, a number of sensors measure signals that are each individually sparse in the some basis and also correlated from sensor to sensor. If the separate sparse basis are projected onto the scaling and wavelet functions of the correlated sensors(common coefficients), then all the information is already stored to individually recover each of the signal at the joint decoder. This does not require any pre-initialization between sensor nodes.

2.3.1 Joint Sparsity representation

For a given ensemble X, we let $P_F(X) \subseteq P$ denote the set of feasible location matrices $P \in P$ for which a factorization $X = P\Theta$ exits. We define the joint sparsity levels of the signal ensemble as follows. The joint sparsity level D of the signal ensemble X is the number of columns of the smallest matrix $P \in P$. In these models each signal x_j is generated as a combination of two components: (i) a common component z_C, which is present in all signals, and (ii) an innovation component z_j, which is unique to each signal. These combine additively, giving

$$x_j = z_C + z_j, j \in \forall \tag{4}$$

$$X = P\Theta \tag{5}$$

We now introduce a bipartite graph $G = (V_V, V_M, E)$, as shown in Figure 1, that represents the relationships between the entries of the value vector and its measurements. The common and innovation components K_C and K_j, $(1 < j < J)$, as well as the joint sparsity $D = K_C + \sum K_J$. The set of edges E is defined as follows:

- The edge E is connected for all K_c if the coefficients are not in common with K_j.
- The edge E is connected for all K_j if the coefficients are in common with K_j.

A further optimization can be performed to reduce the number of measurement made by each sensor, the number of measurement is now proportional to the maximal overlap of the inter sensor ranges and not a constant as shown in equation (1). This is calculated by the common coefficients K_c and K_j, if there are common coefficients in K_j then one of the K_c coefficient is removed and the common Z_c is added, these change does not effecting the reconstruction of the original measurement signal x.

3. Post-Processing and Routing

The computation of this layer primarily deals with compression algorithms and distributed routing, which allows efficient packaging of data with minimal number of bits. Once the data are fused and compressed it uses a network protocol to periodically route the packets using multi-hoping. The routing in sensor network uses two categories of power-aware routing protocols, one uses distributed data aggregation at the network layer forming clusters, and the other uses MAC layer protocols to schedule the radio for best effort delivery of the multi-hop packets from source to destination. Once the data is snap-shotted, it is further aggregated into sinks by using Distributed Hash based routing (DHT) which keeps the number of hops for a query path length constant in a distributed manner using graph embedding James Newsome and Dawn Song (2003).

3.1 Cross-Layer Data Aggregation

Clustering algorithms periodically selects cluster heads (CH), which divides the network into k clusters which are in the CHs Radio range. As the resources at each node is limited the energy dissipation is evenly distributed by the distributed CH selection algorithm. The basic energy consumption for scalable sensor network is derived as below.
Sensor node energy dissipation due to transmission over a given range and density follows Power law, which states that energy consumes is proportional to the square of the distance in m^2 transmitted.

$$PowerLaw = 1^2 + 2^2 + 3^2 + 4^2 + ... + (d-1)^2 + d^2 \tag{6}$$

To sum up the total energy consumption we can write it in the form of Power Law equation [7]

$$PowerLaw = f(x) = ax^2 + o(x)^2 \tag{7}$$

Substituting d-distance for x and k number of bits transmitted, we equate as in equation (7).

$$PowerLaw = f(d) = kd^2 + o(d)^2 \tag{8}$$

Taking Log both sides of equation (8),

$$\log(f(d)) = 2\log d + \log k \tag{9}$$

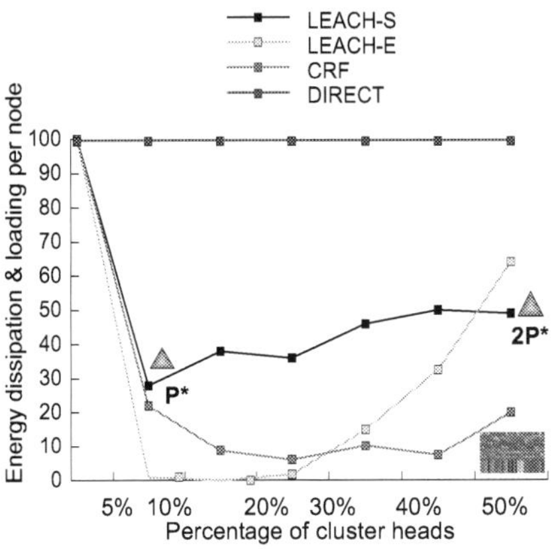

Fig. 2. Cost function for managing residual energy using LEACH routing.

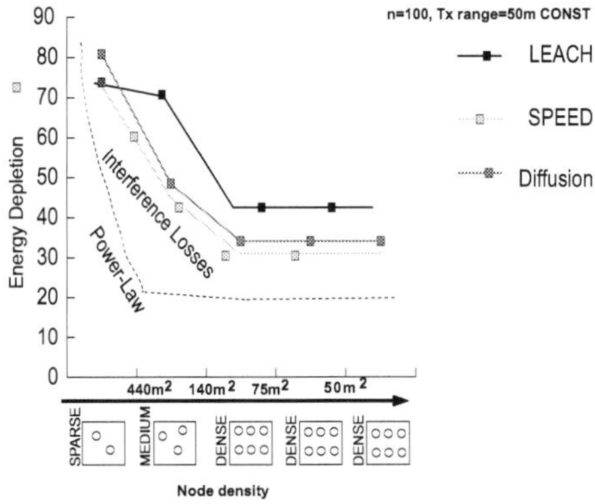

Fig. 3. Power-aware MAC using multi-hop routing.

Notice that the expression in equation (10) has the form of a linear relationship with slope k, and scaling the argument induces a linear shift of the function, and leaves both the form and slope k unchanged. Plotting to the log scale as shown in Figure 3, we get a long tail showing a few nodes dominate the transmission power compared to the majority, similar to the Power Law (S. B. Lowen and M. C. Teich (1970)).

Properties of power laws - Scale invariance: The main property of power laws that makes them interesting is their scale invariance. Given a relation $f(x) = ax^k$ or, any homogeneous polynomial, scaling the argument x by a constant factor causes only a proportionate scaling of the function itself. From the equation (10), we can infer that the property is scale invariant even with clustering c nodes in a given radius k.

$$f(cd) = k(cd^2) = c^k f(d) \alpha f(d) \tag{10}$$

This is validated from the simulation results (Vasanth Iyer (G. Rama Murthy)) obtained in Figure (2), which show optimal results, minimum loading per node (Vasanth Iyer (S.S. Iyengar)), when clustering is $\leq 20\%$ as expected from the above derivation.

3.2 MAC Layer Routing

The IEEE 802.15.4 (Joseph Polastre (Jason Hill)) is a standard for sensor network MAC interoperability, it defines a standard for the radios present at each node to reliably communicate with each other. As the radios consume lots of power the MAC protocol for best performance uses *Idle*, *Sleep* and *Listen* modes to conserve battery. The radios are scheduled to periodically listen to the channel for any activity and receive any packets, otherwise it goes to idle, or sleep mode. The MAC protocol also needs to take care of collision as the primary means of communication is using broadcast mode. The standard carrier sense multiple access (CSMA) protocol is used to share the channel for simultaneous communications. Sensor network variants of CSMA such as B-MAC and S-MAC Joseph Polastre (Jason Hill) have evolved, which allows to

Sensors	S_1	S_2	S_3	S_4	S_5	S_6	S_7	S_8
Value	4.7 ± 2.0	1.6 ± 1.6	3.0 ± 1.5	1.8 ± 1.0	4.7 ± 1.0	1.6 ± 0.8	3.0 ± 0.75	1.8 ± 0.5
Group	-	-	-	-	-	-	-	-

Table 1. A typical random measurements from sensors showing non-linearity in ranges

better handle passive listening, and used low-power listening(LPL). The performance characteristic of MAC based protocols for varying density (small, medium and high) deployed are shown in Figure 3. As it is seen it uses best effort routing (least cross-layer overhead), and maintains a constant throughput, the depletion curve for the MAC also follows the Power Law depletion curve, and has a higher bound when power-aware scheduling such LPL and Sleep states are further used for idle optimization.

3.2.1 DHT KEY Lookup

Topology of the overlay network uses an addressing which is generated by consistent hashing of the node-id, so that the addressing is evenly distributed across all nodes. The new data is stored with its $< KEY >$ which is also generated the same way as the node address range. If the specific node is not in the range the next node in the clockwise direction is assigned the data for that $< KEY >$. From theorem:4, we have that the average number of hops to retrieve the value for the $< KEY, VALUE >$ is only $O(\lg n)$ hops. The routing table can be tagged with application specific items, which are further used by upper layer during query retrieval.

4. Comparison of DCS and Data Aggregation

In Section 4 and 5, we have seen various data processing algorithms, in terms of communication cost they are comparable. In this Section, we will look into two design factors of the distributed framework:

1. Assumption1: How well the individual sensor signal sparsity can be represented.
2. Assumption2: What would be the minimum measurement possible by using joint sparsity model from equation (5).
3. Assumption3: The maximum possible basis representations for the joint ensemble coefficients.
4. Assumption4: A cost function search which allows to represent the best basis without overlapping coefficients.
5. Assumption5: Result validation using regression analysis, such package R (Owen Jones (Robert Maillardet)).

The design framework allows to pre-process individual sensor sparse measurement, and uses a computationally efficient algorithm to perform in-network data fusion.
To use an example data-set, we will use four random measurements obtained by multiple sensors, this is shown in Table 1. It has two groups of four sensors each, as shown the mean value are the same for both the groups and the variance due to random sensor measurements vary with time. The buffer is created according to the design criteria (1), which preserves the sparsity of the individual sensor readings, this takes three values for each sensor to be represented as shown in Figure (4).

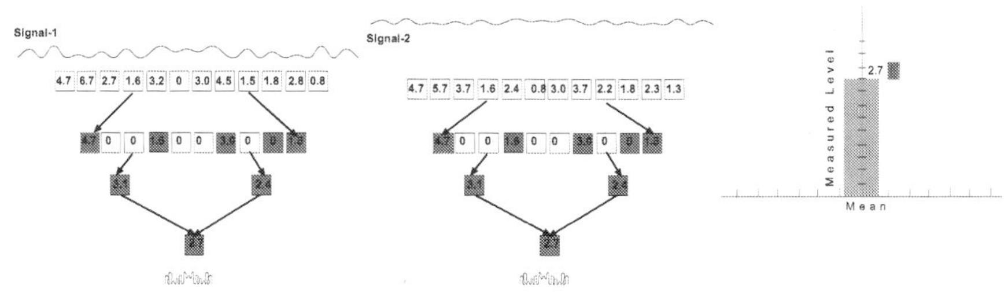

(a) Post-Processing and Data Aggregation

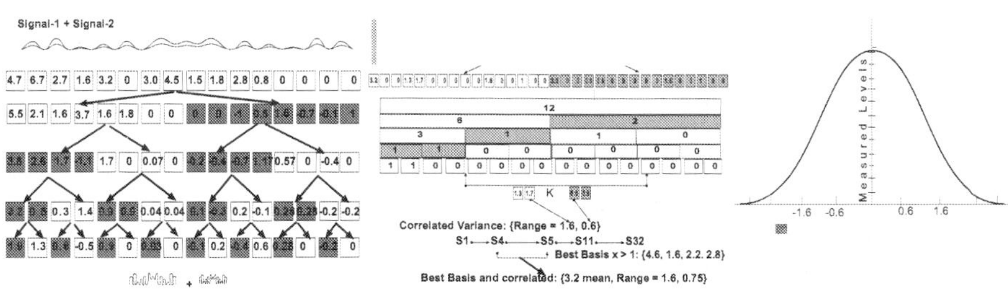

(b) Pre-Processing and Sensor Data Fusion

Fig. 4. Sensor Value Estimation with Aggregation and Sensor Fusion

In the case of post-processing algorithms, which optimizes on the space and the number of bits needed to represent multi-sensor readings, the fusing sensor calculates the average or the mean from the values to be aggregated into a single value. From our example data, we see that for both the data-sets gives the same end result, in this case $\mu = 2.7$ as shown in the output plot of Figure 4(a). Using the design criteria (1), which specifies the sparse representation is not used by post-processing algorithms. Due to this dynamic features are lost during data aggregation step.

The pre-processing step uses Discrete Wavelet Transform (DWT) (Arne Jensen and Anders la Cour-Harbo (2001)) on the signal, and may have to recursively apply the decomposition to arrive at a sparse representation, this pre-process is shown in Figure 4(b). This step uses the design criteria (1), which specifies the small number of significant coefficients needed to represent the given signal measured. As seen in Figure 4(b), each level of decomposition reduces the size of the coefficients. As memory is constrained, we use up to four levels of decomposition with a possible of 26 different representations, as computed by equation (2). These uses the design criteria (3) for lossless reconstruction of the original signal.

The next step of pre-processing is to find the best basis, we let a vector Basis of the same length as cost values representing the basis, this method uses Algorithm 1. The indexing of the two vector is the same and are enumerated in Figure of 4(b). In Figure 4(b), we have marked a basis with shaded boxes. This basis is then represented by the vector. The basis search, which is part of design criteria (4), allows to represent the best coefficients for inter and intra sensor features. It can be noticed that the values are not averages or means of the signal representation, it preserves the actual sensor outputs. As an important design criteria (2), which calibrates the minimum possible sensitivity of the sensor. The output in figure 4(b), shows the constant estimate of S_3, S_7 which is $Z_C = 2.7$ from equation (4).

Sensors	S_1	S_2	S_3	S_4	S_5	S_6	S_7	S_8
$i.i.d._1$	2.7	0	1.5	0.8	3.7	0.8	2.25	1.3
$i.i.d._2$	4.7	1.6	3	1.8	4.7	1.6	3	1.8
$i.i.d._3$	6.7	3.2	4.5	2.8	5.7	2.4	3.75	2.3

Table 2. Sparse representation of sensor values from Table:1

To represent the variance in four sensors, a basis search is performed which finds coefficients of sensors which matches the same columns. In this example, we find $Z_j = 1.6, 0.75$ from equation (4), which are the innovation component.

$$Basis = [0\,0\,1\,0\,1\,0\,0\,1\,1\,0\,0\,0\,0\,0\;\;0\,0\,0\,0\,0\,0\,0\,0\,0\,0\,0\,0\,0\,0\,0\,0\,0]$$

$$Correlated\ range = [0\,0\,0\,0\,1\,0\,0\,1\,0\,0\,0\,0\,0\,0\;\;0\,0\,0\,0\,0\,0\,0\,0\,0\,0\,0\,0\,0\,0\,0\,0\,0]$$

4.1 Lower Bound Validation using Covariance

The Figure 4(b) shows lower bound of the overlapped sensor i.i.d. of $S_1 - S_8$, as shown it is seen that the lower bound is unique to the temporal variations of S_2. In our analysis we will use a general model which allows to detect sensor faults. The binary model can result from placing a threshold on the real-valued readings of sensors. Let m_n be the mean normal reading and m_f the mean event reading for a sensor. A reasonable threshold for distinguishing between the two possibilities would be $0.5(\frac{m_n+m_f}{2})$. If the errors due to sensor faults and the fluctuations in the environment can be modeled by Gaussian distributions with mean 0 and a standard deviation σ, the fault probability p would indeed be symmetric. It can be evaluated using the tail probability of a Gaussian Bhaskar Krishnamachari (Member), the Q-function, as follows:

$$p = Q\frac{\left((0.5(\frac{m_n+m_f}{2}) - m_n)\right)}{\sigma} = Q\left(\frac{m_f - m_n}{2\sigma}\right) \tag{11}$$

From the measured i.i.d. value sets we need to determine if they have any faulty sensors. This can be shown from equation (11) that if the correlated sets can be distinguished from the mean values then it has a low probability of error due to sensor faults, as sensor faults are not correlated. Using the statistical analysis package R Owen Jones (Robert Maillardet), we determine the correlated matrix of the sparse sensor outputs as shown This can be written in a compact matrix form if we observe that for this case the covariance matrix is diagonal, this is,

$$\Sigma = \begin{pmatrix} \rho_1 & 0 & .. & 0 \\ 0 & \rho_2 & .. & 0 \\ \vdots & \vdots & \searrow & \vdots \\ 0 & 0 & .. & \rho_d \end{pmatrix} \tag{12}$$

The correlated co-efficient are shown matrix (13) the corresponding diagonal elements are highlighted. Due to overlapping reading we see the resulting matrix shows that S_1 and S_2 have higher index. The result sets is within the desired bounds of the previous analysis using DWT. Here we not only prove that the sensor are not faulty but also report a lower bound of the optimal correlated result sets, that is we use S_2 as it is the lower bound of the overlapping ranges.

$$\Sigma = \begin{pmatrix} \overrightarrow{4.0} & 3.20 & 3.00 & 2.00 & 2.00 & 1.60 & 1.5 & 1.0 \\ 3.2 & \overrightarrow{2.56} & 2.40 & 1.60 & 1.60 & 1.28 & 1.20 & 0.80 \\ 3.0 & 2.40 & \overrightarrow{2.250} & 1.50 & 1.50 & 1.20 & 1.125 & 0.75 \\ 2.0 & 1.60 & 1.50 & \overrightarrow{1.00} & 1.00 & 0.80 & 0.75 & 0.5 \\ 2.0 & 1.60 & 1.50 & 1.00 & \overrightarrow{1.00} & 0.80 & 0.75 & 0.5 \\ 1.6 & 1.28 & 1.20 & 0.80 & 0.80 & \overrightarrow{0.64} & 0.60 & 0.4 \\ 1.5 & 1.20 & 1.125 & 0.75 & 0.75 & 0.60 & \overrightarrow{0.5625} & 0.375 \\ 1.0 & 0.80 & 0.750 & 0.50 & 0.50 & 0.40 & 0.375 & \overrightarrow{0.250} \end{pmatrix} \tag{13}$$

5. Conclusion

In this topic, we have discussed a distributed framework for correlated multi-sensor measurements and data-centric routing. The framework, uses compressed sensing to reduce the number of required measurements. The joint sparsity model, further allows to define the system accuracy in terms of the lowest range, which can be measured by a group of sensors. The sensor fusion algorithms allows to estimate the physical parameter, which is being measured without any inter sensor communications. The reliability of the pre-processing and sensor faults are discussed by comparing DWT and Covariance methods.
The complexity model is developed which allows to describe the encoding and decoding of the data. The model tends to be easy for encoding, and builds more complexity at the joint decoding level, which are nodes with have more resources as being the decoders.
Post processing and data aggregation are discussed with cross-layer protocols at the network and the MAC layer, its implication to data-centric routing using DHT is discussed, and compared with the DCS model. Even though these routing algorithms are power-aware, the model does not scale in terms of accurately estimating the physical parameters at the sensor level, making sensor driven processing more reliable for such applications.

6. Theoretical Bounds

The computational complexities and its theoretical bounds are derived for categories of sensor pre-, post processing and routing algorithms.

6.1 Pre-Processing

Theorem 1. *The Slepian-Wolf rate as referenced in the region for two arbitrarily correlated sources x and y is bounded by the following inequalities, this theorem can be adapted using equation*

$$R_x \geq H\left(\frac{x}{y}\right), R_y \geq H\left(\frac{y}{x}\right) \text{ and } R_x + R_y \geq H(x,y) \tag{14}$$

Theorem 2. *minimal spanning tree (MST) computational and time complexity for correlated dendrogram. First considering the computational complexity let us assume n patterns in d-dimensional space. To make c clusters using $d_{min}(D_i, Dj)$ a distance measure of similarity. We need once for all, need to calculate $n(n-1)$ interpoint distance table. The space complexity is n^2, we reduce it to $\lg(n)$ entries. Finding the minimum distance pair (for the first merging) requires that we step through the complete list, keeping the index of the smallest distance. Thus, for the first step, the complexity is $O(n(n-1))(d^2+1) = O(n^2d^2)$. For clusters c the number of steps is $n(n-1) - c$ unused distances. The full-time complexity is $O(n(n-1) - c)$ or $O(cn^2d^2)$.*

Algorithm 1 DWT: Using a cost function for searching the best sparse representation of a signal.

1: Mark all the elements on the bottom level
2: Let $j = J$
3: Let $k = 0$
4: Compare the cost v_1 of the element k on level $(j-1)$ (counting from the left on that level) to the sum v_2 of the cost values of the element $2k$ and the $2k+1$ on the level j.
5: if $v_1 \leq v_2$, all marks below element k on level $j-1$ are deleted, and element k is marked.
6: if $v_1 > v_2$, the cost value v_1 of element k is replaced with v_2 $k = k+1$. If there are more elements on level j (if $k < 2^{j-1} - 1$)), go to step 4.
7: $j = j - 1$. If $j > 1$, go to step 3.
8: The marked sparse representation has the lowest possible cost value, having no overlaps.

6.2 Post-processing

Theorem 3. *Properties of Pre-fix coding: For any compression algorithm which assigns prefix codes and to uniquely be decodable. Let us define the* **kraft Number** *and is a measure of* **the size** *of L. We see that if L is 1, 2^{-L} is .5. We know that we cannot have more than two L's of .5. If there are more that two L's of .5, then $K > 1$. Similarly, we know L can be as large as we want. Thus, 2^{-L} can be as small as we want, so K can be as small as we want. Thus we can intuitively see that there must be a strict upper bound on K, and no lower bound. It turns out that a prefix-code only exists for the codes IF AND ONLY IF:*

$$K \leq 1 \tag{15}$$

The above equation is the Kraft inequality. The success of transmission can be further calculated by using the equation For a minimum pre-fix code $a = 0.5$ as $2^{-L} \leq 1$ for a unique decodability.
Iteration $a = 0.5$
In order to extend this scenario with distributed source coding, we consider the case of separate encoders for each source, x_n and y_n. Each encoder operates without access to the other source.
Iteration $a \geq 0.5 \leq 1.0$
As in the previous case it uses correlated values as a dependency and constructs the code-book. The compression rate or efficiency is further enhanced by increasing the correlated CDF higher than $a >$ 0.5. This produces very efficient code-book and the design is independent of any decoder reference information. Due to this a success threshold is also predictable, if $a = 0.5$ and the cost between $L = 1.0$ and 2.0 the success $= 50\%$ and for $a = 0.9$ and $L = 1.1$, the success $= 71\%$.

6.3 Distributed Routing

Theorem 4. *The Cayley Graph (S, E) of a group: Vertices corresponding to the underlying set S. Edges corresponding to the actions of the generators. (Complete) Chord is a Cayley graph for $(Zn, +)$. The routing nodes can be distributed using $S = Z \bmod n$ $(n = 2^m)$ very similar to our simulation results of LEACH (Vasanth Iyer (G. Rama Murthy)). Generators for one-way hashing can use these fixed length hash $1, 2, 4, , 2^m - 1$. Most complete Distributed Hash Table (DHTs) are Cayley graphs. Data-centric algorithm Complexity: where Z is the original ID and the key is its hash between $0 - 2^m$, ID + key are uniformly distributed in the chord (Vasanth Iyer (S. S. Iyengar)).*

7. References

S. Lowen and M. Teich. (1970). Power-Law Shot Noise, IEEE Trans Inform volume 36, pages 1302-1318, 1970.

Slepian, D. Wolf, J. (1973). Noiseless coding of correlated information sources. Information Theory, IEEE Transactions on In Information Theory, IEEE Transactions on, Vol. 19, No. 4. (06 January 2003), pp. 471-480.

Bhaskar Krishnamachari, S.S. Iyengar. (2004). Distributed Bayesian Algorithms for Fault-Tolerant Event Region Detection in Wireless Sensor Networks, In: *IEEE TRANSACTIONS ON COMPUTERS*,VOL. 53, NO. 3, MARCH 2004.

Dror Baron, Marco F. Duarte, Michael B. Wakin, Shriram Sarvotham, and Richard G. Baraniuk. (2005). Distributed Compressive Sensing. In Proc: *Pre-print*, Rice University, Texas, USA, 2005.

Vasanth Iyer, G. Rama Murthy, and M.B. Srinivas. (2008). Min Loading Max Reusability Fusion Classifiers for Sensor Data Model. In Proc: *Second international Conference on Sensor Technologies and Applications*, Volume 00 (August 25 - 31, SENSORCOMM 2008).

Vasanth Iyer, S.S. Iyengar, N. Balakrishnan, Vir. Phoha, M.B. Srinivas. (2009). FARMS: Fusionable Ambient Renewable MACS, In: *SAS-2009*,IEEE 9781-4244-2787, 17th-19th Feb, New Orleans, USA.

Vasanth Iyer, S. S. Iyengar, Rama Murthy, N. Balakrishnan, and V. Phoha. (2009). Distributed source coding for sensor data model and estimation of cluster head errors using bayesian and k-near neighborhood classifiers in deployment of dense wireless sensor networks, In Proc: *Third International Conference on Sensor Technologies and Applications SENSORCOMM*, 17-21 June. 2009.

Vasanth Iyer, S.S. Iyengar, G. Rama Murthy, Kannan Srinathan, Vir Phoha, and M.B. Srinivas. INSPIRE-DB: Intelligent Networks Sensor Processing of Information using Resilient Encoded-Hash DataBase. In Proc. Fourth International Conference on Sensor Technologies and Applications, IARIA-SENSORCOMM, July, 18th-25th, 2010, Venice, Italy (archived in the Computer Science Digital Library).

Vasanth Iyer, S.S. Iyengar, N. Balakrishnan, Vir. Phoha, M.B. Srinivas. (2009). FARMS: Fusionable Ambient Renewable MACS, In: *SAS-2009*,IEEE 9781-4244-2787, 17th-19th Feb, New Orleans, USA.

GEM: Graph EMbedding for Routing and DataCentric Storage in Sensor Networks Without Geographic Information. Proceedings of the First ACM Conference on Embedded Networked Sensor Systems (SenSys). November 5-7, Redwood, CA.

Owen Jones, Robert Maillardet, and Andrew Robinson. Introduction to Scientific Programming and Simulation Using R. Chapman & Hall/CRC, Boca Raton, FL, 2009. ISBN 978-1-4200-6872-6.

Arne Jensen and Anders la Cour-Harbo. Ripples in Mathematics, Springer Verlag 2001. 246 pp. Softcover ISBN 3-540-41662-5.

S. S. Iyengar, Nandan Parameshwaran, Vir V. Phoha, N. Balakrishnan, and Chuka D Okoye, Fundamentals of Sensor Network Programming: Applications and Technology. ISBN: 978-0-470-87614-5 Hardcover 350 pages December 2010, Wiley-IEEE Press.

4

Adaptive Kalman Filter for Navigation Sensor Fusion

Dah-Jing Jwo, Fong-Chi Chung
National Taiwan Ocean University, Keelung
Taiwan

Tsu-Pin Weng
EverMore Technology, Inc., Hsinchu
Taiwan

1. Introduction

As a form of optimal estimator characterized by recursive evaluation, the Kalman filter (KF) (Bar-Shalom, et al, 2001; Brown and Hwang, 1997, Gelb, 1974; Grewal & Andrews, 2001) has been shown to be the filter that minimizes the variance of the estimation mean square error (MSE) and has been widely applied to the navigation sensor fusion. Nevertheless, in Kalman filter designs, the divergence due to modeling errors is critical. Utilization of the KF requires that all the plant dynamics and noise processes are completely known, and the noise process is zero mean white noise. If the input data does not reflect the real model, the KF estimates may not be reliable. The case that theoretical behavior of a filter and its actual behavior do not agree may lead to divergence problems. For example, if the Kalman filter is provided with information that the process behaves a certain way, whereas, in fact, it behaves a different way, the filter will continually intend to fit an incorrect process signal. Furthermore, when the measurement situation does not provide sufficient information to estimate all the state variables of the system, in other words, the estimation error covariance matrix becomes unrealistically small and the filter disregards the measurement.

In various circumstances where there are uncertainties in the system model and noise description, and the assumptions on the statistics of disturbances are violated since in a number of practical situations, the availability of a precisely known model is unrealistic due to the fact that in the modelling step, some phenomena are disregarded and a way to take them into account is to consider a nominal model affected by uncertainty. The fact that KF highly depends on predefined system and measurement models forms a major drawback. If the theoretical behavior of the filter and its actual behavior do not agree, divergence problems tend to occur. The adaptive algorithm has been one of the approaches to prevent divergence problem of the Kalman filter when precise knowledge on the models are not available.

To fulfil the requirement of achieving the filter optimality or to preventing divergence problem of Kalman filter, the so-called adaptive Kalman filter (AKF) approach (Ding, et al,

2007; El-Mowafy & Mohamed, 2005; Mehra, 1970, 1971, 1972; Mohamed & Schwarz, 1999; Hide et al., 2003) has been one of the promising strategies for dynamically adjusting the parameters of the supposedly optimum filter based on the estimates of the unknown parameters for on-line estimation of motion as well as the signal and noise statistics available data. Two popular types of the adaptive Kalman filter algorithms include the innovation-based adaptive estimation (IAE) approach (El-Mowafy & Mohamed, 2005; Mehra, 1970, 1971, 1972; Mohamed & Schwarz, 1999; Hide et al., 2003) and the adaptive fading Kalman filter (AFKF) approach (Xia et al., 1994; Yang, et al, 1999, 2004;Yang & Xu, 2003; Zhou & Frank, 1996), which is a type of covariance scaling method, for which suboptimal fading factors are incorporated. The AFKF incorporates suboptimal fading factors as a multiplier to enhance the influence of innovation information for improving the tracking capability in high dynamic maneuvering.

The Global Positioning System (GPS) and inertial navigation systems (INS) (Farrell, 1998; Salychev, 1998) have complementary operational characteristics and the synergy of both systems has been widely explored. GPS is capable of providing accurate position information. Unfortunately, the data is prone to jamming or being lost due to the limitations of electromagnetic waves, which form the fundamental of their operation. The system is not able to work properly in the areas due to signal blockage and attenuation that may deteriorate the overall positioning accuracy. The INS is a self-contained system that integrates three acceleration components and three angular velocity components with respect to time and transforms them into the navigation frame to deliver position, velocity and attitude components. For short time intervals, the integration with respect to time of the linear acceleration and angular velocity monitored by the INS results in an accurate velocity, position and attitude. However, the error in position coordinates increase unboundedly as a function of time. The GPS/INS integration is the adequate solution to provide a navigation system that has superior performance in comparison with either a GPS or an INS stand-alone system. The GPS/INS integration is typically carried out through the Kalman filter. Therefore, the design of GPS/INS integrated navigation system heavily depends on the design of sensor fusion method. Navigation sensor fusion using the AKF will be discussed. A hybrid approach will be presented and performance will be evaluated on the loosely-coupled GPS/INS navigation applications.

This chapter is organized as follows. In Section 2, preliminary background on adaptive Kalman filters is reviewed. An IAE/AFKF hybrid adaptation approach is introduced in Section 3. In Section 4, illustrative examples on navigation sensor fusion are given. Conclusions are given in Section 5.

2. Adaptive Kalman Filters

The process model and measurement model are represented as

$$\mathbf{x}_{k+1} = \mathbf{\Phi}_k \mathbf{x}_k + \mathbf{w}_k \tag{1a}$$

$$\mathbf{z}_k = \mathbf{H}_k \mathbf{x}_k + \mathbf{v}_k \tag{1b}$$

where the state vector $\mathbf{x}_k \in \Re^n$, process noise vector $\mathbf{w}_k \in \Re^n$, measurement vector $\mathbf{z}_k \in \Re^m$, and measurement noise vector $\mathbf{v}_k \in \Re^m$. In Equation (1), both the vectors $\mathbf{w}_k$ and $\mathbf{v}_k$ are zero mean Gaussian white sequences having zero crosscorrelation with each other:

$$\mathrm{E}[\mathbf{w}_k\mathbf{w}_i^{\mathrm{T}}]=\begin{cases}\mathbf{Q}_k, & i=k\\ 0, & i\neq k\end{cases};\ \mathrm{E}[\mathbf{v}_k\mathbf{v}_i^{\mathrm{T}}]=\begin{cases}\mathbf{R}_k, & i=k\\ 0, & i\neq k\end{cases};\ \mathrm{E}[\mathbf{w}_k\mathbf{v}_i^{\mathrm{T}}]=\mathbf{0}\qquad \textit{for all } i \textit{ and } k \quad (2)$$

where $\mathbf{Q}_k$ is the process noise covariance matrix, $\mathbf{R}_k$ is the measurement noise covariance matrix, $\mathbf{\Phi}_k = e^{\mathbf{F}\Delta t}$ is the state transition matrix, and Δt is the sampling interval, $E[\cdot]$ represents expectation, and superscript "T" denotes matrix transpose.

The discrete-time Kalman filter algorithm is summarized as follow:

Prediction steps/time update equations:

$$\hat{\mathbf{x}}_{k+1}^{-} = \mathbf{\Phi}_k \hat{\mathbf{x}}_k \tag{3}$$

$$\mathbf{P}_{k+1}^{-} = \mathbf{\Phi}_k \mathbf{P}_k \mathbf{\Phi}_k^{\mathrm{T}} + \mathbf{Q}_k \tag{4}$$

Correction steps/measurement update equations:

$$\mathbf{K}_k = \mathbf{P}_k^{-}\mathbf{H}_k^{\mathrm{T}}[\mathbf{H}_k\mathbf{P}_k^{-}\mathbf{H}_k^{\mathrm{T}} + \mathbf{R}_k]^{-1} \tag{5}$$

$$\hat{\mathbf{x}}_k = \hat{\mathbf{x}}_k^{-} + \mathbf{K}_k[\mathbf{z}_k - \mathbf{H}_k\hat{\mathbf{x}}_k^{-}] \tag{6}$$

$$\mathbf{P}_k = [\mathbf{I} - \mathbf{K}_k\mathbf{H}_k]\mathbf{P}_k^{-} \tag{7}$$

A limitation in applying Kalman filter to real-world problems is that the *a priori* statistics of the stochastic errors in both dynamic process and measurement models are assumed to be available, which is difficult in practical application due to the fact that the noise statistics may change with time. As a result, the set of unknown time-varying statistical parameters of noise, $\{\mathbf{Q}_k, \mathbf{R}_k\}$, needs to be simultaneously estimated with the system state and the error covariance. Two popular types of the adaptive Kalman filter algorithms include the innovation-based adaptive estimation (IAE) approach (El-Mowafy and Mohamed, 2005; Mehra, 1970, 1971, 1972; Mohamed and Schwarz, 1999; Hide et al., 2003; Caliskan & Hajiyev, 2000) and the adaptive fading Kalman filter (AFKF) approach (Xia et al., 1994; Zhou & Frank, 1996), which is a type of covariance scaling method, for which suboptimal fading factors are incorporated.

2.1 The innovation-based adaptive estimation

The innovation sequences have been utilized by the correlation and covariance-matching techniques to estimate the noise covariances. The basic idea behind the covariance-matching approach is to make the actual value of the covariance of the residual consistent with its theoretical value. The implementation of IAE based AKF to navigation designs has been widely explored (Hide *et al*, 2003, Mohamed and Schwarz 1999). Equations (3)-(4) are the time update equations of the algorithm from k to step $k+1$, and Equations (5)-(7) are the measurement update equations. These equations incorporate a measurement value into *a priori* estimation to obtain an improved *a posteriori* estimation. In the above equations, $\mathbf{P}_k$ is the error covariance matrix defined by $E[(\mathbf{x}_k - \hat{\mathbf{x}}_k)(\mathbf{x}_k - \hat{\mathbf{x}}_k)^{\mathrm{T}}]$, in which $\hat{\mathbf{x}}_k$ is an estimation of the system state vector $\mathbf{x}_k$, and the weighting matrix $\mathbf{K}_k$ is generally referred to as the Kalman gain matrix. The Kalman filter algorithm starts with an initial condition value, $\hat{\mathbf{x}}_0^{-}$ and $\mathbf{P}_0^{-}$. When new measurement $\mathbf{z}_k$ becomes available with the progression of time, the estimation of states and the corresponding error covariance would follow recursively ad infinity. Mehra (1970, 1971, 1972) classified the adaptive approaches into four categories: Bayesian, maximum likelihood, correlation and covariance matching. The innovation sequences have been utilized by the correlation and covariance-matching techniques to estimate the noise covariances. The basic idea behind the covariance-matching approach is to make the actual value of the covariance of the residual consistent with its theoretical value.

From the incoming measurement $\mathbf{z}_k$ and the optimal prediction $\hat{\mathbf{x}}_k^-$ obtained in the previous step, the innovations sequence is defined as

$$\boldsymbol{\upsilon}_k = \mathbf{z}_k - \hat{\mathbf{z}}_k^- \tag{8}$$

The innovation reflects the discrepancy between the predicted measurement $\mathbf{H}_k\hat{\mathbf{x}}_k^-$ and the actual measurement $\mathbf{z}_k$. It represents the additional information available to the filter as a consequence of the new observation $\mathbf{z}_k$. The weighted innovation, $\mathbf{K}_k(\mathbf{z}_k - \mathbf{H}_k\hat{\mathbf{x}}_k^-)$, acts as a correction to the predicted estimate $\hat{\mathbf{x}}_k^-$ to form the estimation $\hat{\mathbf{x}}_k$. Substituting the measurement model Equation (1b) into Equation (8) gives

$$\boldsymbol{\upsilon}_k = \mathbf{H}_k(\mathbf{x}_k - \hat{\mathbf{x}}_k^-) + \mathbf{v}_k \tag{9}$$

which is a zero-mean Gaussian white noise sequence. An innovation of zero means that the two are in complete agreement. The mean of the corresponding error of an unbiased estimator is zero. By taking variances on both sides, we have the theoretical covariance, the covariance matrix of the innovation sequence is given by

$$\mathbf{C}_{\upsilon_k} = E[\boldsymbol{\upsilon}_k\boldsymbol{\upsilon}_k^{\mathrm{T}}] = \mathbf{H}_k\mathbf{P}_k^-\mathbf{H}_k^{\mathrm{T}} + \mathbf{R}_k \tag{10a}$$

which can be written as

$$\mathbf{C}_{\upsilon_k} = \mathbf{H}_k(\boldsymbol{\Phi}_k\mathbf{P}_k\boldsymbol{\Phi}_k^T + \boldsymbol{\Gamma}_k\mathbf{Q}_k\boldsymbol{\Gamma}_k^T)\mathbf{H}_k^{\mathrm{T}} + \mathbf{R}_k \tag{10b}$$

Defining $\hat{\mathbf{C}}_{\upsilon_k}$ as the statistical sample variance estimate of $\mathbf{C}_{\upsilon_k}$, matrix $\hat{\mathbf{C}}_{\upsilon_k}$ can be computed through averaging inside a moving estimation window of size N

$$\hat{\mathbf{C}}_{\upsilon_k} = \frac{1}{N}\sum_{j=j_0}^{k}\boldsymbol{\upsilon}_j\boldsymbol{\upsilon}_j^{\mathrm{T}} \tag{11}$$

where N is the number of samples (usually referred to the window size); $j_0 = k - N + 1$ is the first sample inside the estimation window. The window size N is chosen empirically (a good size for the moving window may vary from 10 to 30) to give some statistical smoothing. More detailed discussion can be referred to Gelb (1974), Brown & Hwang (1997), and Grewal & Andrews (2001).

The benefit of the adaptive algorithm is that it keeps the covariance consistent with the real performance. The innovation sequences have been utilized by the correlation and covariance-matching techniques to estimate the noise covariances. The basic idea behind the covariance-matching approach is to make the actual value of the covariance of the residual consistent with its theoretical value. This leads to an estimate of $\mathbf{R}_k$:

$$\hat{\mathbf{R}}_k = \hat{\mathbf{C}}_{\upsilon_k} - \mathbf{H}_k\mathbf{P}_k^-\mathbf{H}_k^{\mathrm{T}} \tag{12}$$

Based on the residual based estimate, the estimate of process noise $\mathbf{Q}_k$ is obtained:

$$\hat{\mathbf{Q}}_k = \frac{1}{N}\sum_{j=j_0}^{k}\Delta\mathbf{x}_j\Delta\mathbf{x}_j^{\mathrm{T}} + \mathbf{P}_k - \boldsymbol{\Phi}_k\mathbf{P}_{k-1}\boldsymbol{\Phi}_k^{\mathrm{T}} \tag{13}$$

where $\Delta\mathbf{x}_k = \mathbf{x}_k - \hat{\mathbf{x}}_k^-$. This equation can also be written in terms of the innovation sequence:

$$\hat{\mathbf{Q}}_k \approx \mathbf{K}_k \hat{\mathbf{C}}_{\upsilon_k} \mathbf{K}_k^T \tag{14}$$

For more detailed information derivation for these equations, see Mohamed & Schwarz (1999).

2.2 The adaptive fading Kalman filter

The idea of fading memory is to apply a factor to the predicted covariance matrix to deliberately increase the variance of the predicted state vector. The main difference between different fading memory algorithms is on the calculation of the scale factor.

A. Typical adaptive fading Kalman filter

One of the approaches for adaptive processing is on the incorporation of fading factors. Xia et al. (1994) proposed a concept of adaptive fading Kalman filter (AFKF) and solved the state estimation problem. In the AFKF, suboptimal fading factors are introduced into the nonlinear smoother algorithm. The idea of fading Kalman filtering is to apply a factor matrix to the predicted covariance matrix to deliberately increase the variance of the predicted state vector. In the so called AFKF algorithm, suboptimal fading factors are introduced into the algorithm.

The idea of fading Kalman filtering is to apply a factor matrix to the predicted covariance matrix to deliberately increase the variance of the predicted state vector:

$$\mathbf{P}_{k+1}^- = \boldsymbol{\lambda}_k \boldsymbol{\Phi}_k \mathbf{P}_k \boldsymbol{\Phi}_k^T + \mathbf{Q}_k \tag{15a}$$

or

$$\mathbf{P}_{k+1}^- = \boldsymbol{\lambda}_k (\boldsymbol{\Phi}_k \mathbf{P}_k \boldsymbol{\Phi}_k^T + \mathbf{Q}_k) \tag{15b}$$

where $\boldsymbol{\lambda}_k = diag(\lambda_1, \lambda_2 \ldots, \lambda_m)$. The main difference between various fading memory algorithms is on the calculation of scale factor $\boldsymbol{\lambda}_k$. One approach is to assign the scale factors as constants. When $\lambda_i \le 1$ ($i = 1,2,\ldots,m$), the filtering is in a steady state processing while $\lambda_i > 1$, the filtering may tend to be unstable. For the case $\lambda_i = 1$, it deteriorates to the standard Kalman filter. There are some drawbacks with constant factors, e.g., as the filtering proceeds, the precision of the filtering will decrease because the effects of old data tend to become less and less. The ideal way is to use time-varying factors that are determined according to the dynamic and observation model accuracy.

To increase the tracking capability, the time-varying suboptimal scaling factor is incorporated, for on-line tuning the covariance of the predicted state, which adjusts the filter gain, and accordingly the improved version of AFKF is developed. The optimum fading factor is:

$$\lambda_k = \max\left\{1, \frac{tr[\mathbf{N}_k]}{tr[\mathbf{M}_k]}\right\} \tag{16}$$

Some other choices of the factors are also used:

$$\lambda_k = \max\left\{1, \frac{1}{n} tr[\mathbf{N}_k \mathbf{M}_k^{-1}]\right\};\ \lambda_k = \max\left\{1, \frac{\alpha}{n} tr[\mathbf{N}_k \mathbf{M}_k^{-1}]\right\};\ \lambda_k = \max\left\{1, \alpha \frac{tr[\mathbf{N}_k]}{tr[\mathbf{M}_k]}\right\}$$

where $tr[\cdot]$ is the trace of matrix. The parameters are given by

$$\mathbf{M}_k = \mathbf{H}_k \mathbf{\Phi}_k \mathbf{P}_k \mathbf{\Phi}_k^T \mathbf{H}_k^T \tag{17}$$

$$\mathbf{N}_k = \mathbf{C}_0 - \mathbf{R}_k - \mathbf{H}_k \mathbf{Q}_k \mathbf{H}_k^T \tag{18a}$$

where

$$\mathbf{C}_0 = \begin{cases} \dfrac{\boldsymbol{\upsilon}_0 \boldsymbol{\upsilon}_0^T}{2}, k = 0 \\ \dfrac{[\lambda_k \boldsymbol{\upsilon}_k \boldsymbol{\upsilon}_k^T]}{1+\lambda_k}, k \geq 1 \end{cases} \tag{19}$$

Equation (18a) can be modified by multiplying an innovation enhancement weighting factor γ, and adding an additional term:

$$\mathbf{N}_k = \gamma \mathbf{C}_0 - \mathbf{R}_k - \mathbf{H}_k \mathbf{Q}_k \mathbf{H}_k^T \tag{18b}$$

In the AFKF, the key parameter is the fading factor matrix $\boldsymbol{\lambda}_k$. The factor γ is introduced for increasing the tracking capability through the increased weighting of covariance matrix of the innovation. The value of weighting factor γ is tuned to improve the smoothness of state estimation. A larger weighting factor γ provides stronger tracking capability, which is usually selected empirically. The fading memory approach tries to estimate a scale factor to increase the predicted variance components of the state vector. The variance estimation method directly calculates the variance factor for the dynamic model.

There are some drawbacks with a constant factor, e.g., as the filtering proceeds, the precision of the filtering will decrease because the effects of old data will become less and less. The ideal way is to use a variant scale factor that will be determined based on the dynamic and observation model accuracy.

B. The strong tracking Kalman filter

Zhou & Frank (1996) proposed a concept of strong tracking Kalman filter (STKF) (Zhou & Frank, 1996; Jwo & Wang, 2007) and solved the state estimation problem of a class of nonlinear systems with white noise. In the so called STKF algorithm, suboptimal fading factors are introduced into the nonlinear smoother algorithm. The STKF has several important merits, including (1) strong robustness against model uncertainties; (2) good real-time state tracking capability even when a state jump occurs, no matter whether the system has reached steady state or not. Zhou et al proved that a filter is called the STKF only if the filter satisfies the orthogonal principle stated as follows:

Orthogonal principle: The sufficient condition for a filter to be called the STKF only if the time-varying filter gain matrix be selected on-line such that the state estimation mean-square error is minimized and the innovations remain orthogonal (Zhou & Frank, 1996):

$$E[\mathbf{x}_k - \hat{\mathbf{x}}_k][\mathbf{x}_k - \hat{\mathbf{x}}_k]^T = \min$$

$$E[\boldsymbol{\upsilon}_{k+j} \boldsymbol{\upsilon}_k^T] = 0, \; k = 0,1,2..., \; j = 1,2... \tag{20}$$

Equation (20) is required for ensuring that the innovation sequence will be remained orthogonal.

The time-varying suboptimal scaling factor is incorporated, for on-line tuning the covariance of the predicted state, which adjusts the filter gain, and accordingly the STKF is developed. The suboptimal scaling factor in the time-varying filter gain matrix is given by:

$$\lambda_{i,k} = \begin{cases} \alpha_i c_k & ,\alpha_i c_k \geq 1 \\ 1 & ,\alpha_i c_k < 1 \end{cases} \tag{21}$$

where

$$c_k = \frac{tr[\mathbf{N}_k]}{tr[\boldsymbol{\alpha}\mathbf{M}_k]} \tag{22}$$

and

$$\mathbf{N}_k = \boldsymbol{\gamma}\mathbf{V}_k - \beta\mathbf{R}_k - \mathbf{H}_k\mathbf{Q}_k\mathbf{H}_k^T \tag{23}$$

$$\mathbf{M}_k = \mathbf{H}_k\boldsymbol{\Phi}_k\mathbf{P}_k\boldsymbol{\Phi}_k^T\mathbf{H}_k^T \tag{24}$$

$$\mathbf{V}_k = \begin{cases} \boldsymbol{\upsilon}_0\boldsymbol{\upsilon}_0^T, k = 0 \\ \dfrac{[\rho\mathbf{V}_{k-1} + \boldsymbol{\upsilon}_k\boldsymbol{\upsilon}_k^T]}{1+\rho}, k \geq 1 \end{cases} \tag{25}$$

The key parameter in the STKF is the fading factor matrix $\boldsymbol{\lambda}_k$, which is dependent on three parameters, including (1) α_i; (2) the forgetting factor (ρ); (3) and the softening factor (β). These parameters are usually selected empirically. $\alpha_i \geq 1, i = 1,2,\ldots,m$, which are *a priori* selected. If from *a priori* knowledge, we have the knowledge that $\mathbf{x}$ will have a large change, then a large α_i should be used so as to improve the tracking capability of the STKF. On the other hand, if no *a priori* knowledge about the plant dynamic, it is commonly select $\alpha_1 = \alpha_2 = \cdots = \alpha_m = 1$. In such case, the STKF based on multiple fading factors deteriorates to a STKF based on a single fading factor. The range of the forgetting factor is $0 < \rho \leq 1$, for which 0.95 is commonly used. The softening factor β is utilized to improve the smoothness of state estimation. A larger β (with value no less than 1) leads to better estimation accuracy; while a smaller β provides stronger tracking capability. The value is usually determined empirically through computer simulation and $\beta = 4.5$ is a commonly selected value.

C. The algorithm proposed by Yang, et al.

An adaptive factor depending on the discrepancy between predicted state from the dynamic model and the geometric estimated state by using measurements was proposed by Yang et al (1999, 2003, 2004), where they introduced an adaptive factor α incorporated into for regulating the error covariance

$$\mathbf{P}_{k+1}^- = (\boldsymbol{\Phi}_k\mathbf{P}_k\boldsymbol{\Phi}_k^T + \mathbf{Q}_k)/\alpha \tag{26}$$

where α is the single factor given by

$$\alpha = \begin{cases} 1 & |\tilde{\boldsymbol{\upsilon}}_k| \leq c_0 \\ \dfrac{c_0}{|\tilde{\boldsymbol{\upsilon}}_k|}\left(\dfrac{c_1 - |\tilde{\boldsymbol{\upsilon}}_k|}{c_1 - c_0}\right)^2 & c_0 < |\tilde{\boldsymbol{\upsilon}}_k| \leq c_1 \\ 0 & |\tilde{\boldsymbol{\upsilon}}_k| > c_1 \end{cases} \tag{27}$$

It is seen that Equation (15a) with $\lambda_k = 1/\alpha$ results in Equation (26). In Equation (27), $c_0 = 1$ and $c_1 = 3$ are commonly selected values, and

$$\tilde{\upsilon}_k = \frac{\|\upsilon_k\|}{\sqrt{\mathbf{C}_{\upsilon_k}}} \tag{28}$$

To avoid $\alpha = 0$, it is common to choose

$$\alpha = \begin{cases} 1 & |\tilde{\upsilon}_k| \le c \\ \dfrac{c}{|\tilde{\upsilon}_k|} & |\tilde{\upsilon}_k| > c \end{cases} \tag{29}$$

The *a priori* selected value α is usually selected empirically. If from *a priori* knowledge, we have the knowledge that $\mathbf{x}$ will have a large change, then a small α should be used so as to improve the tracking capability. The range of the factor is $0 < \alpha \le 1$. The factor is utilized to improve the smoothness of state estimation. A larger α (≤ 1) leads to better estimation accuracy; while a smaller α provides stronger tracking capability. The value is usually determined empirically through personal experience or computer simulation using a heuristic searching scheme. In the case that $\alpha = 1$, it deteriorates to a standard Kalman filter. In Equation (29), the threshold $c = 0.5$ is an average value commonly used. To increase the tracking capability, the time-varying suboptimal scaling factor need to be properly designed, for on-line tuning the covariance of the predicted state, which adjusts the filter gain, and accordingly the improved version of AFKF is able to provide better estimation accuracy.

2.3 The tuning logic for parameter adaptation

Another type of adaptation can be conducted by introducing a scaling factor directly to the $\mathbf{Q}_k$ and/or $\mathbf{R}_k$ matrices. To account for the greater uncertainty, the covariances need to be updated, through one of the following ways (Bakhache & Nikiforov, 2000; Jwo & Cho, 2007; Sasiadek, et al, 2000):

(1) $\mathbf{Q}_k \to \mathbf{Q}_{k-1} + \Delta\mathbf{Q}_k$; $\mathbf{R}_k \to \mathbf{R}_{k-1} + \Delta\mathbf{R}_k$

(2) $\mathbf{Q}_k \to \mathbf{Q}_k \alpha^{-(k+1)}$; $\mathbf{R}_k \to \mathbf{R}_k \beta^{-(k+1)}$, $\alpha \ge 1$; $\beta \ge 1$

(3) $\mathbf{Q}_k \to \alpha\mathbf{Q}_k$; $\mathbf{R}_k \to \beta\mathbf{R}_k$

For example, if (3) is utilized as an example, the filter equations can be augmented in the following way:

$$\mathbf{P}_{k+1}^- = \mathbf{\Phi}_k \mathbf{P}_k \mathbf{\Phi}_k^{\mathrm{T}} + \alpha\mathbf{Q}_k \tag{30}$$
$$\mathbf{K}_k = \mathbf{P}_k^- \mathbf{H}_k^{\mathrm{T}} [\mathbf{H}_k \mathbf{P}_k^- \mathbf{H}_k^{\mathrm{T}} + \beta\mathbf{R}_k]^{-1}$$

In case that $\alpha = \beta = 1$, it deteriorates to the standard Kalman filter.

To detect the discrepancy between $\hat{\mathbf{C}}_{\upsilon_k}$ and $\mathbf{C}_{\upsilon_k}$, we define the degree of mismatch (DOM)

$$\mathrm{DOM} = \mathbf{C}_{\upsilon_k} - \hat{\mathbf{C}}_{\upsilon_k} \tag{31}$$

Kalman filtering with motion detection is important in target tracking applications. The innovation information at the present epoch can be employed for timely reflect the change in vehicle dynamic. Selecting the degree of divergence (DOD) as the trace of innovation covariance matrix at present epoch (i.e., the window size is one), we have:

$$\xi = \upsilon_k^{\mathrm{T}} \upsilon_k = tr(\upsilon_k \upsilon_k^{\mathrm{T}}) \tag{32}$$

This parameter can be utilized for detection of divergence/outliers or adaptation for adaptive filtering. If the discrepancy for the trace of innovation covariance matrix between the present (actual) and theoretical value is used, the DOD parameter can be of the form:

$$\eta = \mathbf{\upsilon}_k^{\mathrm{T}} \mathbf{\upsilon}_k - tr(\mathbf{C}_{\upsilon_k}) \tag{33}$$

The other DOD parameter commonly use as a simple test statistic for an occurrence of failure detection is based on the normalized innovation squared, defined as the ratio given by:

$$\mu = \frac{\mathbf{\upsilon}_k^{\mathrm{T}} \mathbf{\upsilon}_k}{tr(\mathbf{C}_{\upsilon_k})} = \mathbf{\upsilon}_k^{\mathrm{T}} \mathbf{C}_{\upsilon_k}^{-1} \mathbf{\upsilon}_k \tag{34}$$

For each of the approaches, only one scalar value needs to be determined, and therefore the fuzzy rules can be simplified resulting in the decrease of computational efficiency.

The logic of adaptation algorithm using covariance-matching technique is described as follows. When the actual covariance value $\hat{\mathbf{C}}_{\upsilon_k}$ is observed, if its value is within the range predicted by theory $\mathbf{C}_{\upsilon_k}$ and the difference is very near to zero, this indicates that both covariances match almost perfectly. If the actual covariance is greater than its theoretical value, the value of the process noise should be decreased; if the actual covariance is less than its theoretical value, the value of the process noise should be increased. The fuzzy logic (Abdelnour,et al , 1993; Jwo & Chang, 2007; Loebis, et al, 2007; Mostov & Soloviev, 1996; Sasiadek, et al, 2000) is popular mainly due to its simplicity even though some other approaches such as neural network and genetic algorithm may also be applicable. When the fuzzy logic approach based on rules of the kind:

IF ⟨antecedent⟩ THEN ⟨consequent⟩

the following rules can be utilized to implement the idea of covariance matching:

A. $\hat{\mathbf{C}}_{\upsilon_k}$ is employed

(1) IF ⟨ $\hat{\mathbf{C}}_{\upsilon_k} \approx 0$ ⟩ THEN ⟨ $\mathbf{Q}_k$ is unchanged⟩ (This indicates that $\hat{\mathbf{C}}_{\upsilon_k}$ is near to zero, the process noise statistic should be remained.)

(2) IF ⟨ $\hat{\mathbf{C}}_{\upsilon_k} > 0$ ⟩ THEN ⟨ $\mathbf{Q}_k$ is increased⟩ (This indicates that $\hat{\mathbf{C}}_{\upsilon_k}$ is larger than zero, the process noise statistic is too small and should be increased.)

(3) IF ⟨ $\hat{\mathbf{C}}_{\upsilon_k} < 0$ ⟩ THEN ⟨ $\mathbf{Q}_k$ is decreased⟩ (This indicates that $\hat{\mathbf{C}}_{\upsilon_k}$ is less than zero, the process noise statistic is too large and should be decreased.)

B. DOM is employed

(1) IF ⟨ DOM ≈ 0 ⟩ THEN ⟨ $\mathbf{Q}_k$ is unchanged⟩ (This indicates that $\hat{\mathbf{C}}_{\upsilon_k}$ is about the same as $\mathbf{C}_{\upsilon_k}$, the process noise statistic should be remained.)

(2) IF ⟨ DOM > 0 ⟩ THEN ⟨ $\mathbf{Q}_k$ is decreased⟩ (This indicates that $\hat{\mathbf{C}}_{\upsilon_k}$ is less than $\mathbf{C}_{\upsilon_k}$, the process noise statistic should be decreased.)

(3) IF ⟨ DOM < 0 ⟩ THEN ⟨ $\mathbf{Q}_k$ is increased⟩ (This indicates that $\hat{\mathbf{C}}_{\upsilon_k}$ is larger than $\mathbf{C}_{\upsilon_k}$, the process noise statistic should be increased.)

C. DOD (μ) is employed

Suppose that μ is employed as the test statistic, and μ_T represents the chosen threshold. The following fuzzy rules can be utilized:

(1) IF $\langle \mu \geq \mu_T \rangle$ THEN $\langle \mathbf{Q}_k$ is increased$\rangle$ (There is a failure or maneuvering reported; the process noise statistic is too small and needs to be increased)

(2) IF $\langle \mu < \mu_T \rangle$ THEN $\langle \mathbf{Q}_k$ is decreased$\rangle$ (There is no failure or non maneuvering; the process noise statistic is too large and needs to be decreased)

3. An IAE/AFKF Hybrid Approach

In this section, a hybrid approach (Jwo & Weng, 2008) involving the concept of the two methods is presented. The proposed method is a hybrid version of the IAE and AFKF approaches. The ratio of the actual innovation covariance based on the sampled sequence to the theoretical innovation covariance will be employed for dynamically tuning two filter parameters - fading factors and measurement noise scaling factors. The method has the merits of good computational efficiency and numerical stability. The matrices in the KF loop are able to remain positive definitive.

The conventional KF approach is coupled with the adaptive tuning system (ATS) for providing two system parameters: fading factor and noise covariance scaling factor. In the ATS mechanism, both adaptations on process noise covariance (also referred to P-adaptation herein) and on measurement noise covariance (also referred to R-adaptation herein) are involved. The idea is based on the concept that when the filter achieves estimation optimality, the actual innovation covariance based on the sampled sequence and the theoretical innovation covariance should be equal. In other words, the ratio between the two should equal one.

(1) Adaptation on process noise covariance.

To account for the uncertainty, the covariance matrix needs to be updated, through the following way. The new $\overline{\mathbf{P}}_k^-$ can be obtained by multiplying $\mathbf{P}_k^-$ by the factor λ_P:

$$\overline{\mathbf{P}}_k^- = \lambda_P \mathbf{P}_k^- \tag{35}$$

and the corresponding Kalman gain is given by

$$\overline{\mathbf{K}}_k = \overline{\mathbf{P}}_k^- \mathbf{H}_k^T [\mathbf{H}_k \overline{\mathbf{P}}_k^- \mathbf{H}_k^T + \overline{\mathbf{R}}_k]^{-1} \tag{36a}$$

If representing the new variable $\overline{\mathbf{R}}_k = \lambda_R \mathbf{R}_k$, we have

$$\overline{\mathbf{K}}_k = \overline{\mathbf{P}}_k^- \mathbf{H}_k^T [\mathbf{H}_k \overline{\mathbf{P}}_k^- \mathbf{H}_k^T + \lambda_R \mathbf{R}_k]^{-1} \tag{36b}$$

From Equation (36b), it can be seen that the change of covariance is essentially governed by two of the parameters: $\overline{\mathbf{P}}_k^-$ and $\mathbf{R}_k$. In addition, the covariance matrix at the measurement update stage, from Equation (7), can be written as

$$\overline{\mathbf{P}}_k = [\mathbf{I} - \overline{\mathbf{K}}_k \mathbf{H}_k] \overline{\mathbf{P}}_k^- \tag{37a}$$

and

$$\overline{\mathbf{P}}_k = \lambda_P [\mathbf{I} - \overline{\mathbf{K}}_k \mathbf{H}_k] \mathbf{P}_k^- \tag{37b}$$

Furthermore, based on the relationship given by Equation (35), the covariance matrix at the prediction stage (i.e., Equation (4)) is given by

$$\overline{\mathbf{P}}_{k+1}^- = \mathbf{\Phi}_k \overline{\mathbf{P}}_k \mathbf{\Phi}_k^T + \mathbf{Q}_k \tag{38}$$

or, alternatively

$$\overline{\mathbf{P}}_{k+1}^{-} = \boldsymbol{\lambda}_P \boldsymbol{\Phi}_k \mathbf{P}_k \boldsymbol{\Phi}_k^{\mathrm{T}} + \mathbf{Q}_k \tag{39a}$$

On the other hand, the covariance matrix can also be approximated by

$$\overline{\mathbf{P}}_{k+1}^{-} = \boldsymbol{\lambda}_P \mathbf{P}_{k+1}^{-} = \boldsymbol{\lambda}_P (\boldsymbol{\Phi}_k \mathbf{P}_k \boldsymbol{\Phi}_k^{T} + \mathbf{Q}_k) \tag{39b}$$

where $\boldsymbol{\lambda}_P = diag(\lambda_1, \lambda_2 \ldots, \lambda_m)$. The main difference between different adaptive fading algorithms is on the calculation of scale factor $\boldsymbol{\lambda}_P$. One approach is to assign the scale factors as constants. When $\lambda_i \le 1$ ($i = 1,2,\ldots,m$), the filtering is in a steady state processing while $\lambda_i > 1$, the filtering may tend to be unstable. For the case $\lambda_i = 1$, it deteriorates to the standard Kalman filter. There are some drawbacks with constant factors, e.g., as the filtering proceeds, the precision of the filtering will decrease because the effects of old data tend to become less and less. The ideal way is to use time varying factors that are determined according to the dynamic and observation model accuracy.

When there is deviation due to the changes of covariance and measurement noise, the corresponding innovation covariance matrix can be rewritten as:

$$\overline{\mathbf{C}}_{\upsilon_k} = \mathbf{H}_k \overline{\mathbf{P}}_k^{-} \mathbf{H}_k^{\mathrm{T}} + \overline{\mathbf{R}}_k$$

and

$$\overline{\mathbf{C}}_{\upsilon_k} = \boldsymbol{\lambda}_P \mathbf{H}_k \mathbf{P}_k^{-} \mathbf{H}_k^{\mathrm{T}} + \boldsymbol{\lambda}_R \mathbf{R}_k \tag{40}$$

To enhance the tracking capability, the time-varying suboptimal scaling factor is incorporated, for on-line tuning the covariance of the predicted state, which adjusts the filter gain, and accordingly the improved version of AFKF is obtained. The optimum fading factors can be calculated through the single factor:

$$\lambda_i = (\boldsymbol{\lambda}_P)_{ii} = \max\left\{1, \frac{tr(\hat{\mathbf{C}}_{\upsilon_k})}{tr(\mathbf{C}_{\upsilon_k})}\right\}, \; i = 1,2\ldots,m \tag{41}$$

where $tr[\cdot]$ is the trace of matrix; $\lambda_i \ge 1$, is a scaling factor. Increasing λ_i will improve tracking performance.

(2) Adaptation on measurement noise covariance. As the strength of measurement noise changes with the environment, incorporation of the fading factor only is not able to restrain the expected estimation accuracy. For resolving these problems, the ATS needs a mechanism for R-adaptation in addition to P-adaptation, to adjust the noise strengths and improve the filter estimation performance.

A parameter which represents the ratio of the actual innovation covariance based on the sampled sequence to the theoretical innovation covariance matrices can be defined as one of the following methods:

(a) Single factor

$$\lambda_j = (\boldsymbol{\lambda}_R)_{jj} = \frac{tr(\hat{\mathbf{C}}_{\upsilon_k})}{tr(\mathbf{C}_{\upsilon_k})}, \; j = 1,2\ldots,n \tag{42a}$$

(b) Multiple factors

$$\lambda_j = \frac{(\hat{\mathbf{C}}_{\upsilon_k})_{jj}}{(\mathbf{C}_{\upsilon_k})_{jj}}, \; j = 1,2\ldots,n \tag{42b}$$

It should be noted that from Equation (40) that increasing $\mathbf{R}_k$ will lead to increasing $\mathbf{C}_{\upsilon_k}$, and vice versa. This means that time-varying $\mathbf{R}_k$ leads to time-varying $\mathbf{C}_{\upsilon_k}$. The value of $\boldsymbol{\lambda}_R$ is introduced in order to reduce the discrepancies between $\mathbf{C}_{\upsilon_k}$ and $\mathbf{R}_k$. The adaptation can be implemented through the simple relation:

$$\overline{\mathbf{R}}_k = \boldsymbol{\lambda}_R \mathbf{R}_k \tag{43}$$

Further detail regarding the adaptive tuning loop is illustrated by the flow charts shown in Figs. 1 and 2, where two architectures are presented. Fig. 1 shows the system architecture #1 and Fig. 2 shows the system architecture #2, respectively. In Fig. 1, the flow chart contains two portions, for which the block indicated by the dot lines is the adaptive tuning system (ATS) for tuning the values of both P and R parameters; in Fig. 2, the flow chart contains three portions, for which the two blocks indicated by the dot lines represent the R-adaptation loop and P-adaptation loop, respectively.

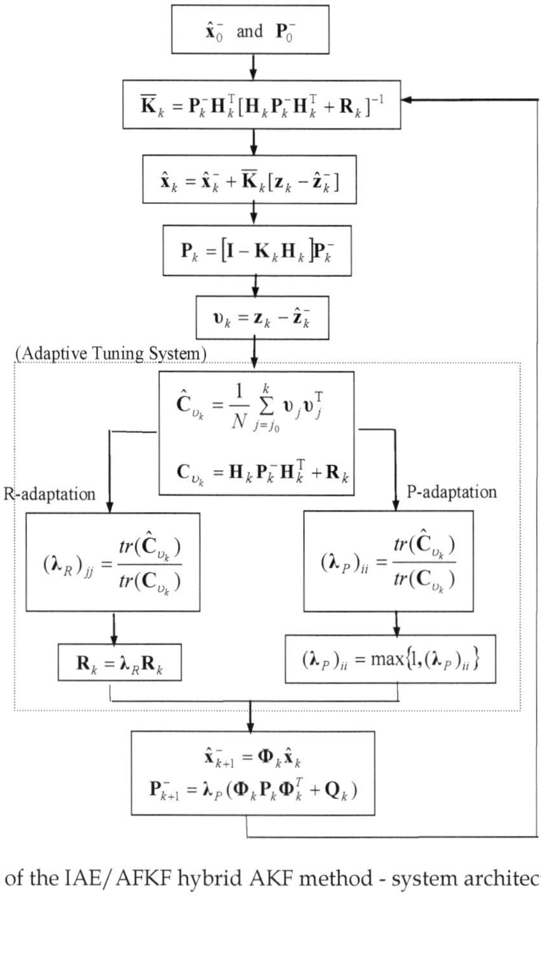

Fig. 1. Flow chart of the IAE/AFKF hybrid AKF method - system architecture #1

An important remark needs to be pointed out. When the system architecture #1 is employed, only one window size is needed. It can be seen that the measurement noise covariance of the innovation covariance matrix hasn't been updated when performing the fading factor calculation. In the system architecture #2, the latest information of the measurement noise strength has already been available when performing the fading factor calculation. However, one should notice that utilization of the 'old' (i.e., before R-adaptation) information is required. Otherwise, unreliable result may occur since the deviation of the innovation covariance matrix due to the measurement noise cannot be correctly detected. One strategy for avoiding this problem can be done by using two different window sizes, one for R-adaptation loop and the other for P-adaptation loop.

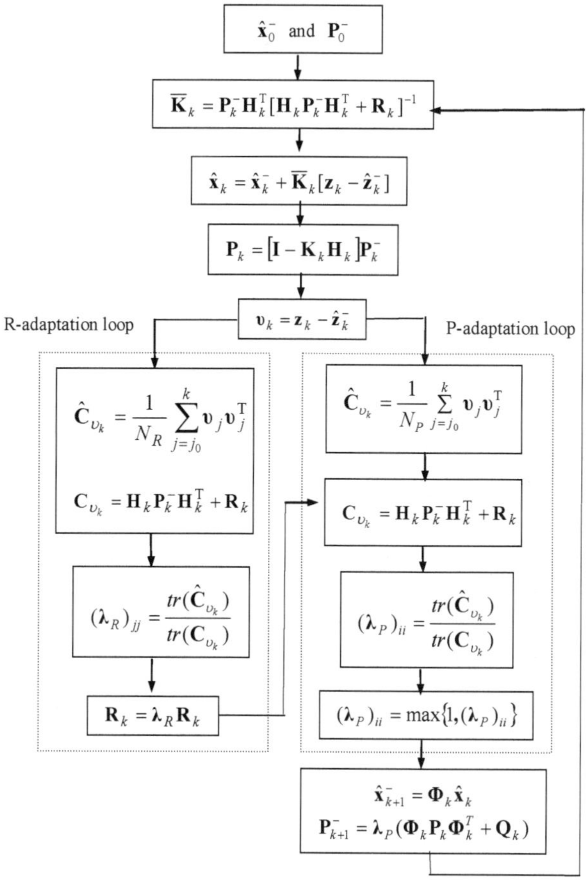

Fig. 2. Flow chart of the IAE/AFKF hybrid AKF method - system architecture #2

4. Navigation Sensor Fusion Example

In this section, two illustrative examples for GPS/INS navigation sensor fusion are provided. The loosely-coupled GPS/INS architecture is employed for demonstration. Simulation experiments were conducted using a personal computer. The computer codes were constructed using the Matlab® software. The commercial software Satellite Navigation (SATNAV) Toolbox by GPSoft LLC was used for generating the satellite positions and pseudoranges. The satellite constellation was simulated and the error sources corrupting GPS measurements include ionospheric delay, tropospheric delay, receiver noise and multipath. Assume that the differential GPS mode is used and most of the errors can be corrected, but the multipath and receiver thermal noise cannot be eliminated.

The differential equations describing the two-dimensional inertial navigation state are (Farrell, 1998):

$$\begin{bmatrix} \dot{n} \\ \dot{e} \\ \dot{v}_n \\ \dot{v}_e \\ \dot{\psi} \end{bmatrix} = \begin{bmatrix} v_n \\ v_e \\ a_n \\ a_e \\ \omega_r \end{bmatrix} = \begin{bmatrix} v_n \\ v_e \\ \cos(\psi)a_u - \sin(\psi)a_v \\ \sin(\psi)a_u + \cos(\psi)a_v \\ \omega_r \end{bmatrix} \quad (44)$$

where [a_u , a_v] are the measured accelerations in the body frame, ω_r is the measured yaw rate in the body frame, as shown in Fig. 3. The error model for INS is augmented by some sensor error states such as accelerometer biases and gyroscope drifts. Actually, there are several random errors associated with each inertial sensor. It is usually difficult to set a certain stochastic model for each inertial sensor that works efficiently at all environments and reflects the long-term behavior of sensor errors. The difficulty of modeling the errors of INS raised the need for a model-less GPS/INS integration technique. The linearized equations for the process model can be selected as

$$\frac{d}{dt}\begin{bmatrix} \delta n \\ \delta e \\ \delta v_n \\ \delta v_e \\ \delta\psi \\ \delta a_u \\ \delta a_v \\ \delta\omega_r \end{bmatrix} = \begin{bmatrix} 0 & 0 & 1 & 0 & 0 & 0 & 0 & 0 \\ 0 & 0 & 0 & 1 & 0 & 0 & 0 & 0 \\ 0 & 0 & 0 & 0 & -a_e & \cos(\psi) & -\sin(\psi) & 0 \\ 0 & 0 & 0 & 0 & -a_n & \sin(\psi) & \cos(\psi) & 0 \\ 0 & 0 & 0 & 0 & 0 & 0 & 0 & 1 \\ 0 & 0 & 0 & 0 & 0 & 0 & 0 & 0 \\ 0 & 0 & 0 & 0 & 0 & 0 & 0 & 0 \\ 0 & 0 & 0 & 0 & 0 & 0 & 0 & 0 \end{bmatrix} \begin{bmatrix} \delta n \\ \delta e \\ \delta v_n \\ \delta v_e \\ \delta\psi \\ \delta a_u \\ \delta a_v \\ \delta\omega_r \end{bmatrix} + \begin{bmatrix} 0 \\ 0 \\ u_{acc} \\ u_{acc} \\ u_{gyro} \\ u_{acc}^b \\ u_{acc}^b \\ u_{gyro}^b \end{bmatrix} \quad (45)$$

which can be utilized in the integration Kalman filter as the inertial error model. In Equation (45), δn and δe represent the east, and north position errors; δv_n and δv_e represent the east, and north velocity errors; $\delta\psi$ represents yaw angle; δa_u , δa_v , and $\delta\omega_r$ represent the accelerometer biases and gyroscope drift, respectively. The measurement model can be written as

$$\mathbf{z}_k = \begin{bmatrix} n_{INS} \\ e_{INS} \end{bmatrix} - \begin{bmatrix} n_{GPS} \\ e_{GPS} \end{bmatrix} = \begin{bmatrix} 1 & 0 & 0 & 0 & 0 & 0 & 0 & 0 \\ 0 & 1 & 0 & 0 & 0 & 0 & 0 & 0 \end{bmatrix} \begin{bmatrix} \delta n \\ \delta e \\ \delta v_n \\ \delta v_e \\ \delta \psi \\ \delta a_u \\ \delta a_v \\ \delta \omega_r \end{bmatrix} + \begin{bmatrix} v_n \\ v_e \end{bmatrix} \tag{46}$$

Further simplification of the above two models leads to

$$\frac{d}{dt}\begin{bmatrix} \delta n \\ \delta e \\ \delta v_n \\ \delta v_e \\ \delta \psi \end{bmatrix} = \begin{bmatrix} 0 & 0 & 1 & 0 & 0 \\ 0 & 0 & 0 & 1 & 0 \\ 0 & 0 & 0 & 0 & 0 \\ 0 & 0 & 0 & 0 & 0 \\ 0 & 0 & 0 & 0 & 0 \end{bmatrix} \begin{bmatrix} \delta n \\ \delta e \\ \delta v_n \\ \delta v_e \\ \delta \psi \end{bmatrix} + \begin{bmatrix} 0 \\ 0 \\ w_n \\ w_e \\ w_\psi \end{bmatrix} \tag{47}$$

and

$$\mathbf{z}_k = \begin{bmatrix} n_{INS} \\ e_{INS} \end{bmatrix} - \begin{bmatrix} n_{GPS} \\ e_{GPS} \end{bmatrix} = \begin{bmatrix} 1 & 0 & 0 & 0 & 0 \\ 0 & 1 & 0 & 0 & 0 \end{bmatrix} \begin{bmatrix} \delta n \\ \delta e \\ \delta v_n \\ \delta v_e \\ \delta \psi \end{bmatrix} + \begin{bmatrix} v_n \\ v_e \end{bmatrix} \tag{48}$$

respectively.

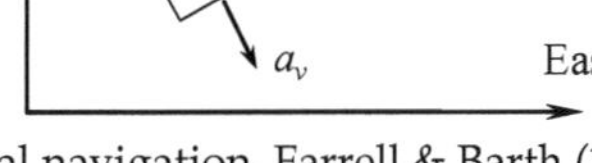

Fig. 3. Two-dimensional inertial navigation, Farrell & Barth (1999)

(A) Example 1: utilization of the fuzzy adaptive fading Kalman filter (FAFKF) approach

The first illustrative example is taken from Jwo & Huang (2009). Fig. 4 provides the strategy for the GPS/INS navigation processing based on the FAFKF mechanism. The GPS navigation solution based on the least-squares (LS) is solved at the first stage. The measurement is the residual between GPS LS and INS derived data, which is used as the measurement of the KF.

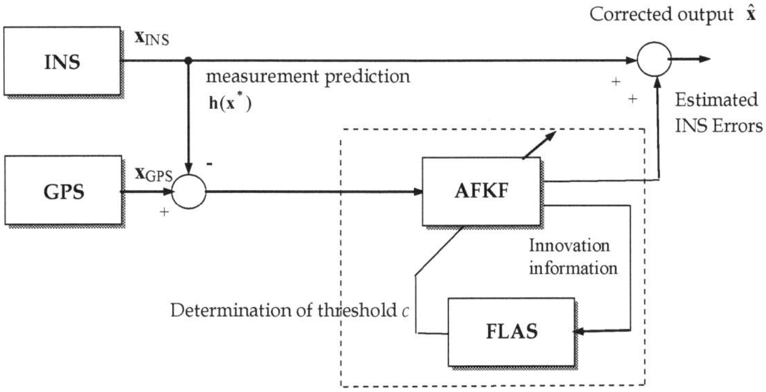

Fig. 4. GPS/INS navigation processing using the FAFKF for the illustrative example 1.

The experiment was conducted on a simulated vehicle trajectory originating from the (0, 0) m location. The simulated trajectory of the vehicle and the INS derived position are shown as in Fig. 5. The trajectory of the vehicle can be approximately divided into two categories according to the dynamic characteristics. The vehicle was simulated to conduct constant-velocity straight-line during the three time intervals, 0-200, 601-1000 and 1401-1600s, all at a speed of 10π m/s. Furthermore, it conducted counterclockwise circular motion with radius 2000 meters during 201-600 and 1001-1400s where high dynamic maneuvering is involved. The following parameters were used: window size N =10; the values of noise standard deviation are 2e-3 m/s^2 for accelerometers and 5e-4 m/s^2 for gyroscopes.
The presented FLAS is the *If-Then* form and consists of 3 rules. The $\bar{\boldsymbol{\upsilon}}$ and innovation covariance $\hat{\mathbf{C}}_{\upsilon_k}$ as the inputs. The fuzzy rules are designed as follows:

1. If $\bar{\boldsymbol{\upsilon}}$ is zero and $\hat{\mathbf{C}}_{\upsilon_k}$ is zero then c is large
2. If $\bar{\boldsymbol{\upsilon}}$ is zero and $\hat{\mathbf{C}}_{\upsilon_k}$ is small then c is large
3. If $\bar{\boldsymbol{\upsilon}}$ is zero and $\hat{\mathbf{C}}_{\upsilon_k}$ is large then c is small
4. If $\bar{\boldsymbol{\upsilon}}$ is small and $\hat{\mathbf{C}}_{\upsilon_k}$ is zero then c is small
5. If $\bar{\boldsymbol{\upsilon}}$ is small and $\hat{\mathbf{C}}_{\upsilon_k}$ is small then c is small
6. If $\bar{\boldsymbol{\upsilon}}$ is small and $\hat{\mathbf{C}}_{\upsilon_k}$ is large then c is zero
7. If $\bar{\boldsymbol{\upsilon}}$ is large and $\hat{\mathbf{C}}_{\upsilon_k}$ is zero then c is zero
8. If $\bar{\boldsymbol{\upsilon}}$ is large and $\hat{\mathbf{C}}_{\upsilon_k}$ is small then c is zero
9. If $\bar{\boldsymbol{\upsilon}}$ is large and $\hat{\mathbf{C}}_{\upsilon_k}$ is large then c is zero

The triangle membership functions for innovation mean value ($\bar{\boldsymbol{\upsilon}}$), innovation covariance ($\hat{\mathbf{C}}_{\upsilon_k}$) and threshold ($c$) are shown in Fig. 6. The center of area approach was used for the defuzzification. Fig. 7 shows the East and North components of navigation errors and the corresponding 1-σ bounds based on the AFKF method and FAFKF method, respectively. Fig. 8 provides the navigation accuracy comparison for AFKF and FAFKF. Fig. 9 gives the trajectories of the threshold c (the fuzzy logic output), and the corresponding fading factor λ_k, respectively.

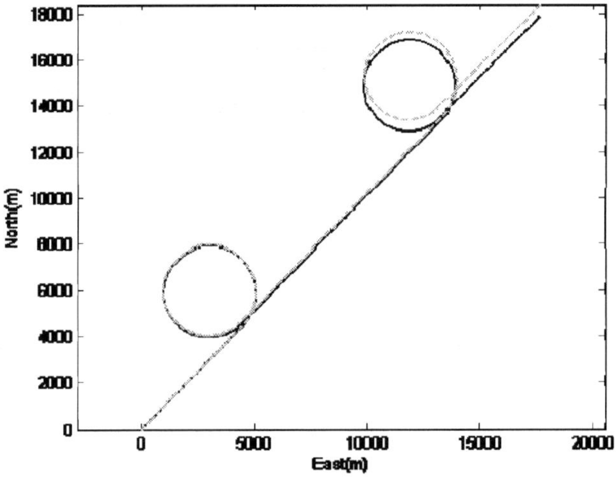

Fig. 5. Trajectory for the simulated vehicle (solid) and the INS derived position (dashed)

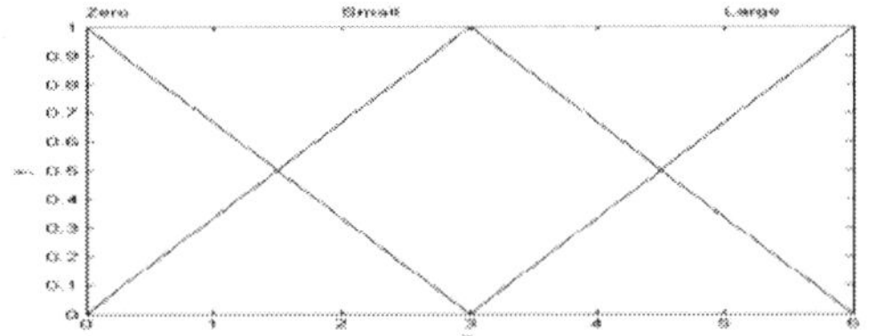

(a) Innovation mean value ($\overline{\mathbf{\upsilon}}$)

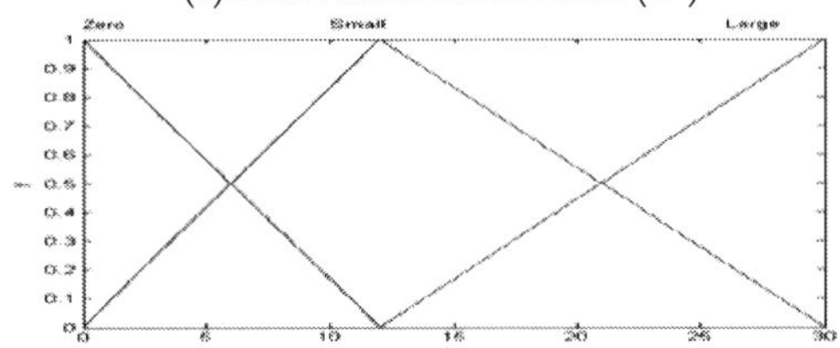

(b) Innovation covariance ($\hat{\mathbf{C}}_{\upsilon_k}$)

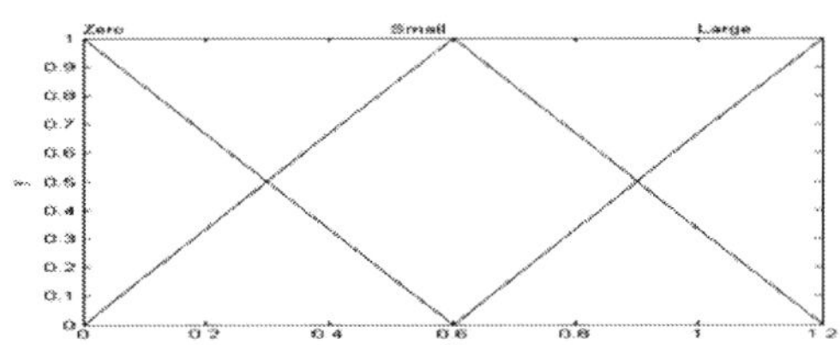

(c) Threshold c

Fig. 6. Membership functions for the inputs and output

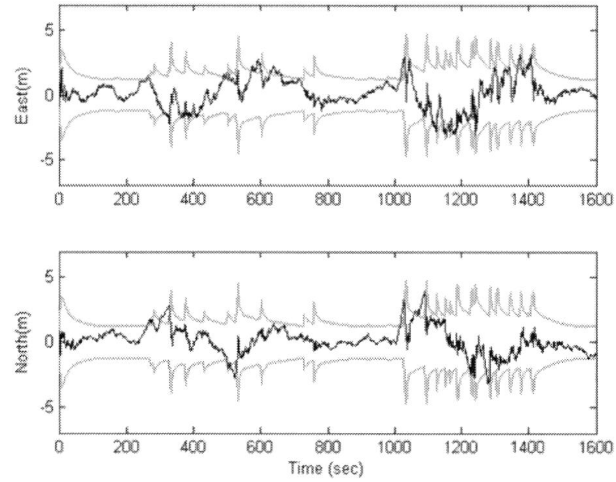

Fig. 7. East and north components of navigation errors and the 1-σ bound based on the FAFKF method

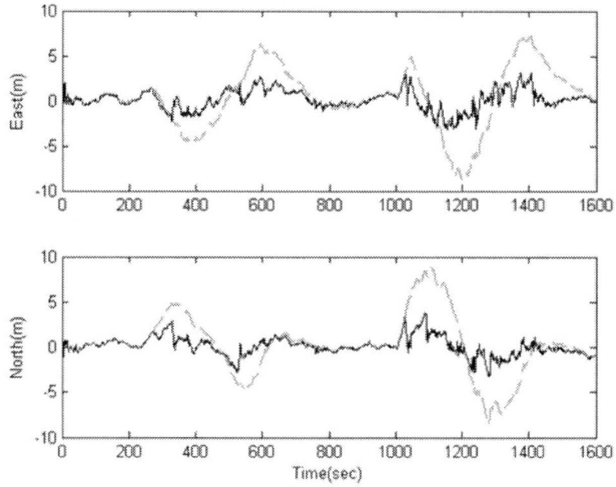

Fig. 8. Navigation accuracy comparison for AFKF and FAFKF

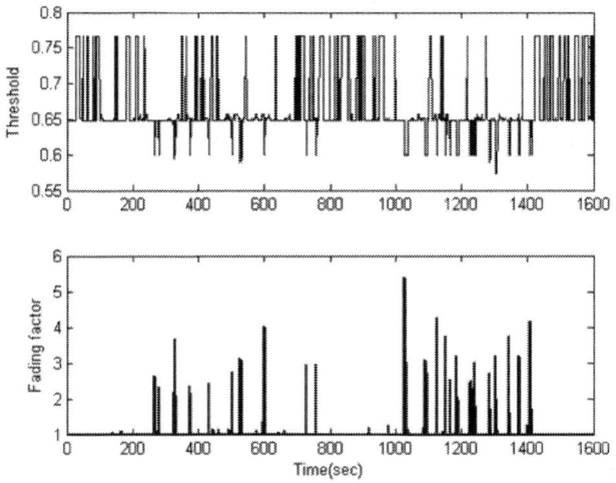

Fig. 9. Trajectories of the threshold c (top) from the fuzzy logic output, and the corresponding fading factor λ_k (bottom)

(B) Example 2: utilization of the IAE/AFKF Hybrid approach

The second example is taken from Jwo & Weng (2008). Fig. 10 shows the GPS/INS navigation processing using the IAE/AFKF Hybrid AKF. Trajectory for the simulated vehicle (solid) and the unaided INS derived position (dashed) is shown in Fig. 11. The trajectory of the vehicle can be approximately divided into two categories according to the dynamic characteristics. The vehicle was simulated to conduct constant-velocity straight-line during the three time intervals, 0-300, 901-1200 and 1501-1800s, all at a speed of 10π m/s. Furthermore, it conducted counterclockwise circular motion with radius 3000 meters during 301-900, and 1201-1500s where high dynamic maneuvering is involved. The following parameters were used: window size $N_p = 15$ $N_R = 20$; the values of noise standard deviation are 1e-3 m/s^2 for accelerometers and gyroscopes.

Fig. 12 provides the positioning solution from the integrated navigation system (without adaptation) as compared to the GPS navigation solutions by the LS approach, while Fig. 13 gives the positioning results for the integrated navigation system with and without adaptation. Substantial improvement in navigation accuracy can be obtained.

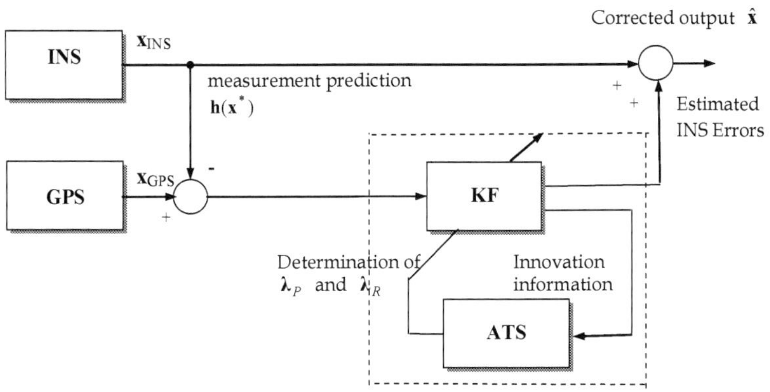

Fig. 10. GPS/INS navigation processing using the IAE/AFKF Hybrid AKF for the illustrative example 2

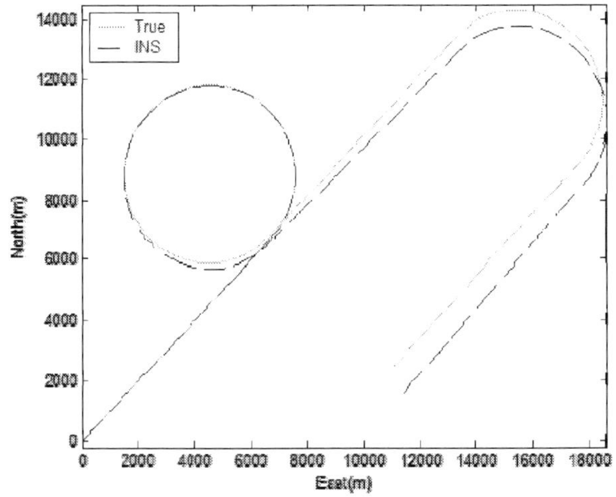

Fig. 11. Trajectory for the simulated vehicle (solid) and the INS derived position (dashed)

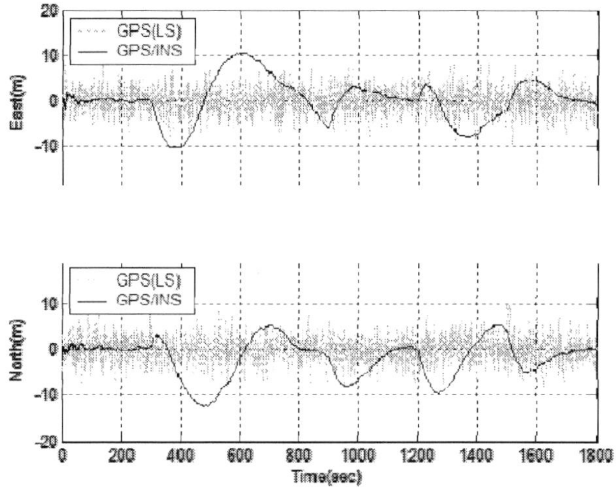

Fig. 12. The solution from the integrated navigation system without adaptation as compared to the GPS navigation solutions by the LS approach

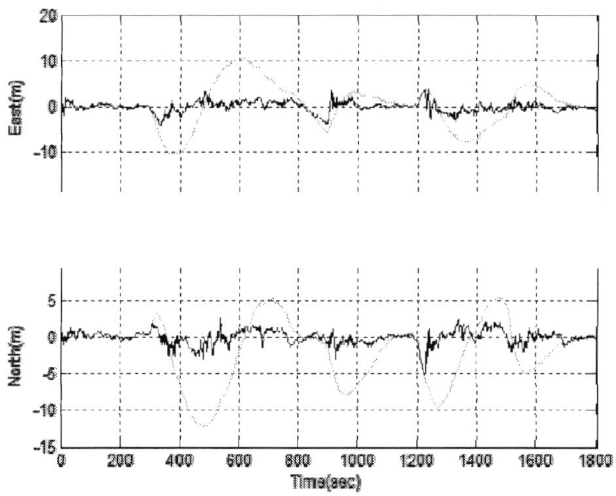

Fig. 13. The solutions for the integrated navigation system with and without adaptation

In the real world, the measurement will normally be changing in addition to the change of process noise or dynamic such as maneuvering. In such case, both P-adaptation and R-adaptation tasks need to be implemented. In the following discussion, results will be provided for the case when measurement noise strength is changing in addition to the change of process noise strength. The measurement noise strength is assumed to be changing with variances of the values $r = 4^2 \to 16^2 \to 8^2 \to 3^2$, where the 'arrows (→)' is employed for indicating the time-varying trajectory of measurement noise statistics. That is, it is assumed that the measure noise strength is changing during the four time intervals: 0-450s ($N(0,4^2)$), 451-900s ($N(0,16^2)$), 901-1350s ($N(0,8^2)$), and 1351-1800s ($N(0,3^2)$). However, the internal measurement noise covariance matrix $\mathbf{R}_k$ is set unchanged all the time in simulation, which uses $r_j \sim N(0,3^2)$, $j = 1,2\ldots,n$, at all the time intervals.

Fig. 14 shows the east and north components of navigation errors and the 1-σ bound based on the method without adaptation on measurement noise covariance matrix. It can be seen that the adaptation of P information without correct R information (referred to partial adaptation herein) seriously deteriorates the estimation result. Fig. 15 provides the east and north components of navigation errors and the 1-σ bound based on the proposed method (referred to full adaptation herein, i.e., adaptation on both estimation covariance and measurement noise covariance matrices are applied). It can be seen that the estimation accuracy has been substantially improved. The measurement noise strength has been accurately estimated, as shown in Fig. 16.

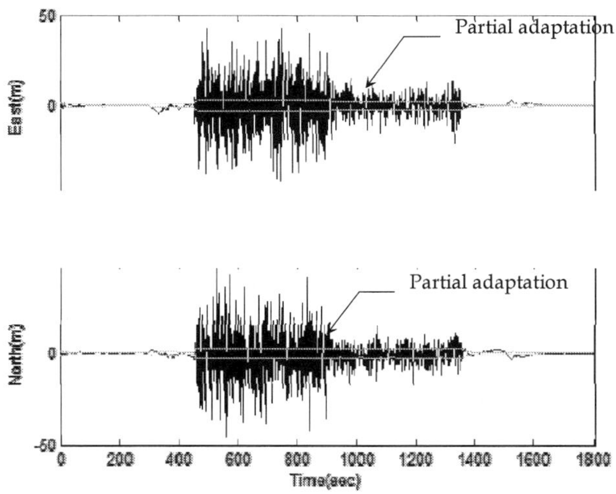

Fig. 14. East and north components of navigation errors and the 1-σ bound based on the method without measurement noise adaptation

It should also be mentioned that the requirement $(\lambda_P)_{ii} \geq 1$ is critical. An illustrative example is given in Figs. 17 and 18. Fig. 17 gives the navigation errors and the 1-σ bound when the threshold setting is not incorporated. The corresponding reference (true) and calculated standard deviations when the threshold setting is not incorporated is provided in Fig. 18. It is not surprising that the navigation accuracy has been seriously degraded due to the inaccurate estimation of measurement noise statistics.

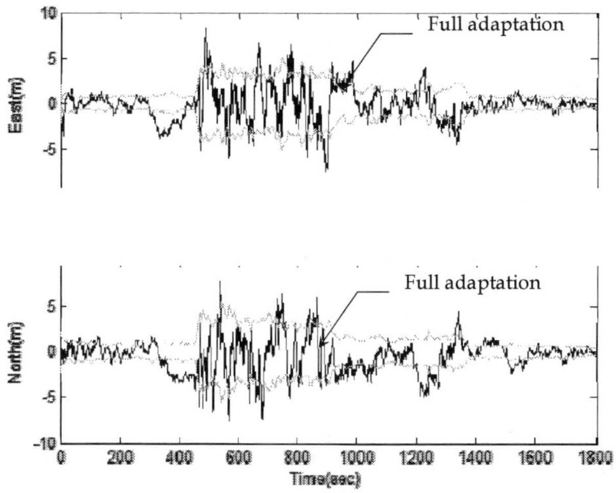

Fig. 15. East and north components of navigation errors and the 1-σ bound based on the proposed method (with adaptation on both estimation covariance and measurement noise covariance matrices)

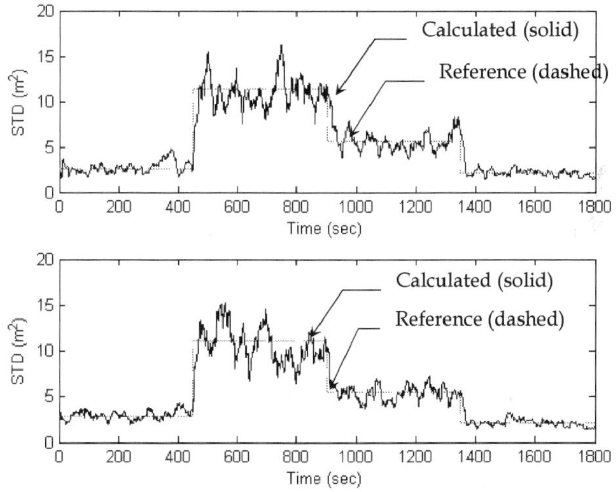

Fig. 16. Reference (true) and calculated standard deviations for the east (top) and north (bottom) components of the measurement noise variance values

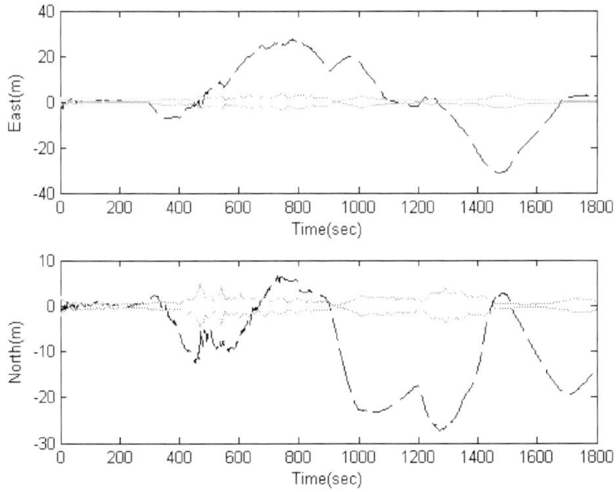

Fig. 17. East and north components of navigation errors and the 1-σ bound based on the proposed method when the threshold setting is not incorporated

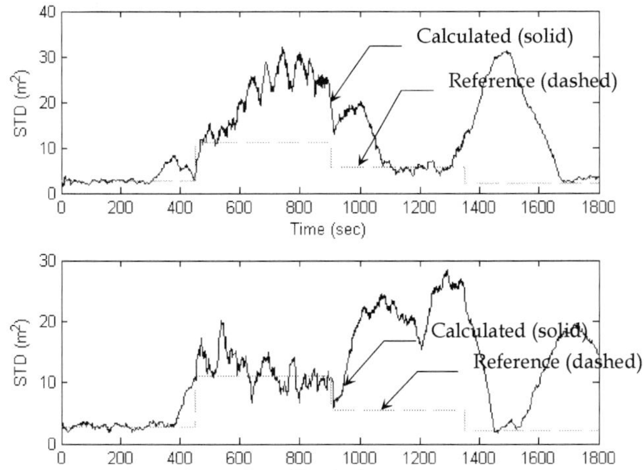

Fig. 18. Reference (true) and calculated standard deviations for the east and north components of the measurement noise variance values when the threshold setting is not incorporated

5. Conclusion

This chapter presents the adaptive Kalman filter for navigation sensor fusion. Several types of adaptive Kalman filters has been reviewed, including the innovation-based adaptive estimation (IAE) approach and the adaptive fading Kalman filter (AFKF) approach. Various types of designs for the fading factors are discussed. A new strategy through the hybridization of IAE and AFKF is presented with an illustrative example for integrated navigation application. In the first example, the fuzzy logic is employed for assisting the AFKF. Through the use of fuzzy logic, the designed fuzzy logic adaptive system (FLAS) has been employed as a mechanism for timely detecting the dynamical changes and implementing the on-line tuning of threshold c , and accordingly the fading factor, by monitoring the innovation information so as to maintain good tracking capability.

In the second example, the conventional KF approach is coupled by the adaptive tuning system (ATS), which gives two system parameters: the fading factor and measurement noise covariance scaling factor. The ATS has been employed as a mechanism for timely detecting the dynamical and environmental changes and implementing the on-line parameter tuning by monitoring the innovation information so as to maintain good tracking capability and estimation accuracy. Unlike some of the AKF methods, the proposed method has the merits of good computational efficiency and numerical stability. The matrices in the KF loop are able to remain positive definitive. Remarks to be noted for using the method is made, such as: (1) The window sizes can be set different, to avoid the filter degradation/divergence; (2) The fading factors $(\boldsymbol{\lambda}_P)_{ii}$ should be always larger than one while $(\boldsymbol{\lambda}_R)_{jj}$ does not have such limitation. Simulation experiments for navigation sensor fusion have been provided to illustrate the accessibility. The accuracy improvement based on the AKF method has demonstrated remarkable improvement in both navigational accuracy and tracking capability.

6. References

Abdelnour, G.; Chand, S. & Chiu, S. (1993). Applying fuzzy logic to the Kalman filter divergence problem. *IEEE Int. Conf. On Syst., Man and Cybernetics, Le Touquet, France,* pp. 630-634

Brown, R. G. & Hwang, P. Y. C. (1997). *Introduction to Random Signals and Applied Kalman Filtering,* John Wiley & Sons, New York, 3rd edn

Bar-Shalom, Y.; Li, X. R. & Kirubarajan, T. (2001). *Estimation with Applications to Tracking and Navigation,* John Wiley & Sons, Inc

Bakhache, B. & Nikiforov, I. (2000). Reliable detection of faults in measurement systems, *International Journal of adaptive control and signal processing,* 14, pp. 683-700

Caliskan, F. & Hajiyev, C. M. (2000). Innovation sequence application to aircraft sensor fault detection: comparison of checking covariance matrix algorithms, *ISA Transactions,* 39, pp. 47-56

Ding, W.; Wang, J. & Rizos, C. (2007). Improving Adaptive Kalman Estimation in GPS/INS Integration, *The Journal of Navigation,* 60, 517-529.

Farrell, I. & Barth, M. (1999) *The Global Positioning System and Inertial Navigation,* McCraw-Hill professional, New York

Gelb, A. (1974). *Applied Optimal Estimation.* M. I. T. Press, MA.

Grewal, M. S. & Andrews, A. P. (2001). *Kalman Filtering, Theory and Practice Using MATLAB*, 2nd Ed., John Wiley & Sons, Inc.

Hide, C, Moore, T., & Smith, M. (2003). Adaptive Kalman filtering for low cost INS/GPS, *The Journal of Navigation*, 56, 143-152

Jwo, D.-J. & Cho, T.-S. (2007). A practical note on evaluating Kalman filter performance Optimality and Degradation. *Applied Mathematics and Computation, 193,* pp. 482-505

Jwo, D.-J. & Wang, S.-H. (2007). Adaptive fuzzy strong tracking extended Kalman filtering for GPS navigation, *IEEE Sensors Journal*, 7(5), pp. 778-789

Jwo, D.-J. & Weng, T.-P. (2008). An adaptive sensor fusion method with applications in integrated navigation. *The Journal of Navigation*, 61, pp. 705-721

Jwo, D.-J. & Chang, F.-I., 2007, A Fuzzy Adaptive Fading Kalman Filter for GPS Navigation, *Lecture Notes in Computer Science,* LNCS 4681:820-831, Springer-Verlag Berlin Heidelberg.

Jwo, D.-J. & Huang, C. M. (2009). A Fuzzy Adaptive Sensor Fusion Method for Integrated Navigation Systems, *Advances in Systems Science and Applications*, 8(4), pp.590-604.

Loebis, D.; Naeem, W.; Sutton, R.; Chudley, J. & Tetlow S. (2007). Soft computing techniques in the design of a navigation, guidance and control system for an autonomous underwater vehicle, *International Journal of adaptive control and signal processing*, 21:205-236

Mehra, R. K. (1970). On the identification of variance and adaptive Kalman filtering. *IEEE Trans. Automat. Contr., AC-15,* pp. 175-184

Mehra, R. K. (1971). On-line identification of linear dynamic systems with applications to Kalman filtering. *IEEE Trans. Automat. Contr.,* AC-16, pp. 12-21

Mehra, R. K. (1972). Approaches to adaptive filtering. *IEEE Trans. Automat. Contr.*, Vol. AC-17, pp. 693-698

Mohamed, A. H. & Schwarz K. P. (1999). Adaptive Kalman filtering for INS/GPS. *Journal of Geodesy, 73 (4),* pp. 193-203

Mostov, K. & Soloviev, A. (1996). Fuzzy adaptive stabilization of higher order Kalman filters in application to precision kinematic GPS, *ION GPS-96,* Vol. 2, pp. 1451-1456, Kansas

Salychev, O. (1998). *Inertial Systems in Navigation and Geophysics,* Bauman MSTU Press, Moscow.

Sasiadek, J. Z.; Wang, Q. & Zeremba, M. B. (2000). Fuzzy adaptive Kalman filtering for INS/GPS data fusion. *15th IEEE int. Symp. on intelligent control, Rio Patras, Greece,* pp. 181-186

Xia, Q.; Rao, M.; Ying, Y. & Shen, X. (1994). Adaptive fading Kalman filter with an application, *Automatica*, 30, pp. 1333-1338

Yang, Y.; He H. & Xu, T. (1999). Adaptively robust filtering for kinematic geodetic positioning, *Journal of Geodesy*, 75, pp.109-116

Yang, Y. & Xu, T. (2003). An adaptive Kalman filter based on Sage windowing weights and variance components, *The Journal of Navigation*, 56(2), pp. 231-240

Yang, Y.; Cui, X., & Gao, W. (2004). Adaptive integrated navigation for multi-sensor adjustment outputs, *The Journal of Navigation*, 57(2), pp. 287-295

Zhou, D. H. & Frank, P. H. (1996). Strong tracking Kalman filtering of nonlinear time-varying stochastic systems with coloured noise: application to parameter estimation and empirical robustness analysis. *Int. J. control,* Vol. 65, No. 2, pp. 295-307

5

Fusion of Images Recorded with Variable Illumination

Luis Nachtigall and Fernando Puente León
Karlsruhe Institute of Technology
Germany

Ana Pérez Grassi
Technische Universität München
Germany

1. Introduction

The results of an automated visual inspection (AVI) system depend strongly on the image acquisition procedure. In particular, the illumination plays a key role for the success of the following image processing steps. The choice of an appropriate illumination is especially critical when imaging 3D textures. In this case, 3D or depth information about a surface can be recovered by combining 2D images generated under varying lighting conditions. For this kind of surfaces, diffuse illumination can lead to a destructive superposition of light and shadows resulting in an irreversible loss of topographic information. For this reason, directional illumination is better suited to inspect 3D textures. However, this kind of textures exhibits a different appearance under varying illumination directions. In consequence, the surface information captured in an image can drastically change when the position of the light source varies. The effect of the illumination direction on the image information has been analyzed in several works [Barsky & Petrou (2007); Chantler et al. (2002); Ho et al. (2006)]. The changing appearance of a texture under different illumination directions makes its inspection and classification difficult. However, these appearance changes can be used to improve the knowledge about the texture or, more precisely, about its topographic characteristics. Therefore, series of images generated by varying the direction of the incident light between successive captures can be used for inspecting 3D textured surfaces. The main challenge arising with the variable illumination imaging approach is the fusion of the recorded images needed to extract the relevant information for inspection purposes.

This chapter deals with the fusion of image series recorded using variable illumination direction. Next section presents a short overview of related work, which is particularly focused on the well-known technique photometric stereo. As detailed in Section 2, photometric stereo allows to recover the surface albedo and topography from a series of images. However, this method and its extensions present some restrictions, which make them inappropriate for some problems like those discussed later. Section 3 introduces the imaging strategy on which the proposed techniques rely, while Section 4 provides some general information fusion concepts and terminology. Three novel approaches addressing the stated information fusion problem are described in Section 5. These approaches have been selected to cover a wide spectrum of fusion strategies, which can be divided into model-based, statistical and filter-based methods. The performance of each approach are demonstrated with concrete automated visual inspection tasks. Finally, some concluding remarks are presented.

2. Overview of related work

The characterization of 3D textures typically involves the reconstruction of the surface topography or profile. A well-known technique to estimate a surface topography is photometric stereo. This method uses an image series recorded with variable illumination to reconstruct both the surface topography and the albedo [Woodham (1980)]. In its original formulation, under the restricting assumptions of Lambertian reflectance, uniform albedo and known position of distant point light sources, this method aims to determine the surface normal orientation and the albedo at each point of the surface. The minimal number of images necessary to recover the topography depends on the assumed surface reflection model. For instance, Lambertian surfaces require at least three images to be reconstructed. Photometric stereo has been extended to other situations, including non-uniform albedo, distributed light sources and non-Lambertian surfaces. Based on photometric stereo, many analysis and classification approaches for 3D textures have been presented [Drbohlav & Chantler (2005); McGunnigle (1998); McGunnigle & Chantler (2000); Penirschke et al. (2002)].

The main drawback of this technique is that the reflectance properties of the surface have to be known or assumed a priori and represented in a so-called reflectance map. Moreover, methods based on reflectance maps assume a surface with consistent reflection characteristics. This is, however, not the case for many surfaces. In fact, if location-dependent reflection properties are expected to be utilized for surface segmentation, methods based on reflectance maps fail [Lindner (2009)].

The reconstruction of an arbitrary surface profile may require demanding computational efforts. A dense sampling of the illumination space is also usually required, depending on the assumed reflectance model. In some cases, the estimation of the surface topography is not the goal, e.g., for surface segmentation or defect detection tasks. Thus, reconstructing the surface profile is often neither necessary nor efficient. In these cases, however, an analogous imaging strategy can be considered: the illumination direction is systematically varied with the aim of recording image series containing relevant surface information. The recorded images are then fused in order to extract useful features for a subsequent segmentation or classification step. The difference to photometric stereo and other similar techniques, which estimate the surface normal direction at each point, is that no surface topography reconstruction has to be explicitly performed. Instead, symbolic results, such as segmentation and classification results, are generated in a more direct way. In [Beyerer & Puente León (2005); Heizmann & Beyerer (2005); Lindner (2009); Pérez Grassi et al. (2008); Puente León (2001; 2002; 2006)] several image fusion approaches are described, which do not rely on an explicit estimation of the surface topography. It is worth mentioning that photometric stereo is a general technique, while some of the methods described in the cited works are problem-specific.

3. Variable illumination: extending the 2D image space

The choice of a suitable illumination configuration is one of the key aspects for the success of any subsequent image processing task. Directional illumination performed by a distant point light source generally yields a higher contrast than multidirectional illumination pat-

terns, more specifically, than diffuse lighting. In this sense, a variable directional illumination strategy presents an optimal framework for surface inspection purposes.
The imaging system presented in the following is characterized by a fixed camera position with its optical axis parallel to the z-axis of a global Cartesian coordinate system. The camera lens is assumed to perform an orthographic projection. The illumination space is defined as the space of all possible illumination directions, which are completely defined by two angles: the azimuth φ and the elevation angle θ; see Fig. 1.

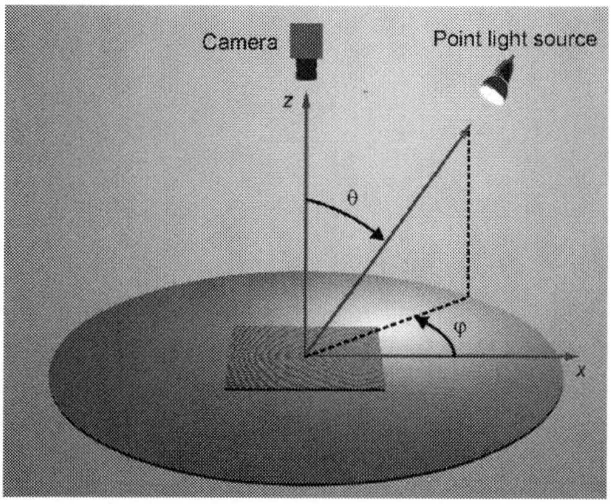

Fig. 1. Imaging system with variable illuminant direction.

An illumination series $\mathcal{S}$ is defined as a set of B images $g(\mathbf{x}, \mathbf{b}_b)$, where each image shows the same surface part, but under a different illumination direction given by the parameter vector $\mathbf{b}_b = (\varphi_b, \theta_b)^{\mathrm{T}}$:

$$\mathcal{S} = \{g(\mathbf{x}, \mathbf{b}_b), \quad b = 1, \ldots, B\}, \tag{1}$$

with $\mathbf{x} = (x, y)^{\mathrm{T}} \in \mathbb{R}^2$. The illuminant positions selected to generate a series $\{\mathbf{b}_b, \ b = 1, \ldots, B\}$ represent a discrete subset of the illumination space. In this sense, the acquisition of an image series can be viewed as the sampling of the illumination space.
Beside point light sources, illumination patterns can also be considered to generate illumination series. The term illumination pattern refers here to a superposition of point light sources. One approach described in Section 5 uses sector-shaped patterns to illuminate the surface simultaneously from all elevation angles in the interval $\theta \in [0°, 90°]$ given an arbitrary azimuth angle; see Fig. 2. In this case, we refer to a sector series $\mathcal{S}_s = \{g(\mathbf{x}, \varphi_b), \ b = 1, \ldots, B\}$ as an image series in which only the azimuthal position of the sector-shaped illumination pattern varies.

4. Classification of fusion approaches for image series

According to [Dasarathy (1997)] fusion approaches can be categorized in various different ways by taking into account different viewpoints like: application, sensor type and information hierarchy. From an application perspective we can consider both the application area and its final objective. The most commonly referenced areas are: defense, robotics, medicine and space. According to the final objective, the approaches can be divided into detection, recognition, classification and tracking, among others. From another perspective, the fusion

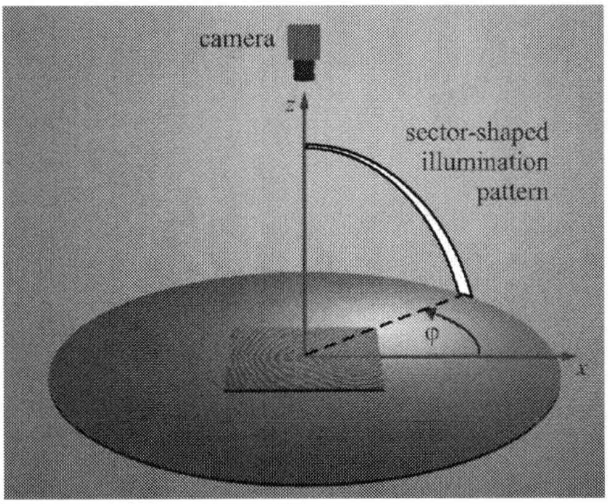

Fig. 2. Sector-shaped illumination pattern.

approaches can be classified according to the utilized sensor type into passive, active and a mix of both (passive/active). Additionally, the sensor configuration can be divided into parallel or serial. If the fusion approaches are analyzed by considering the nature of the sensors' information, they can be grouped into recurrent, complementary or cooperative. Finally, if the hierarchies of the input and output data classes (data, feature or decision) are considered, the fusion methods can be divided into different architectures: data input-data output (DAI-DAO), data input-feature output (DAI-FEO), feature input-feature output (FEI-FEO), feature input-decision output (FEI-DEO) and decision input-decision output (DEI-DEO). The described categorizations are the most frequently encountered in the literature. Table 1 shows the fusion categories according to the described viewpoints. The shaded boxes indicate those image fusion categories covered by the approaches presented in this chapter.

Application		Sensor		Data	
Application Domain	Fusion Objective	Sensor Type	Sensor Suite Configuration	Sensor Data	I/O Based Characterization
Defense	Detection	Active	Parallel	Recurrent	DAI-DAO
Robotics	Recognition	Passive	Serial	Complementary	DAI-FEO
Medical	Classification	Active/passive	-	Cooperative	FEI-FEO
Space	Tracking	-	-	-	FEI-DEO
-	-	-	-	-	DEI-DEO

Table 1. Common fusion classification scheme. The shaded boxes indicate the categories covered by the image fusion approaches treated in the chapter.

This chapter is dedicated to the fusion of images series in the field of automated visual inspection of 3D textured surfaces. Therefore, from the viewpoint of the application area, the approaches presented in the next section can be assigned to the field of robotics. The objectives of the machine vision tasks are the detection and classification of defects. Now, if we analyze the approaches considering the sensor type, we find that the specific sensor, i.e., the camera, is

a passive sensor. However, the whole measurement system presented in the previous section can be regarded as active, if we consider the targeted excitation of the object to be inspected by the directional lighting. Additionally, the acquisition system comprises only one camera, which captures the images of the series sequentially after systematically varying the illumination configuration. Therefore, we can speak here about serial virtual sensors.
More interesting conclusions can be found when analyzing the approaches from the point of view of the involved data. To reliably classify defects on 3D textures, it is necessary to consider all the information distributed along the image series simultaneously. Each image in the series contributes to the final decision with a necessary part of information. That is, we are fusing cooperative information. Now, if we consider the hierarchy of the input and output data classes, we can globally classify each of the fusion methods in this chapter as DAI-DEO approaches. Here, the input is always an image series and the output is always a symbolic result (segmentation or classification). However, a deeper analysis allows us to decompose each approach into a concatenation of DAI-FEO, FEI-FEO and FEI-DEO fusion architectures. Schemes showing these information processing flows will be discussed for each method in the corresponding sections.

5. Multi-image fusion methods

A 3D profile reconstruction of a surface can be computationally demanding. For specific cases, where the final goal is not to obtain the surface topography, application-oriented solutions can be more efficient. Additionally, as mentioned before, traditional photometric stereo techniques are not suitable to segment surfaces with location-dependent reflection properties. In this section, we discuss three approaches to segment, detect and classify defects by fusing illumination series. Each method relies on a different fusion strategy:

- Model-based method: In Section 5.1 a reflectance model-based method for surface segmentation is presented. This approach differs from related works in that reflection model parameters are applied as features [Lindner (2009)]. These features provide good results even with simple linear classifiers. The method performance is shown with an AVI example: the segmentation of a metallic surface. Moreover, the use of reflection properties and local surface normals as features is a general purpose approach, which can be applied, for instance, to defect detection tasks.
- Filter-based method: An interesting and challenging problem is the detection of topographic defects on textured surfaces like varnished wood. This problem is particularly difficult to solve due to the noisy background given by the texture. A way to tackle this issue is using filter-based methods [Xie (2008)], which rely on filter banks to extract features from the images. Different filter types are commonly used for this task, for example, wavelets [Lambert & Bock (1997)] and Gabor functions [Tsai & Wu (2000)]. The main drawback of the mentioned techniques is that appropriate filter parameters for optimal results have to be chosen manually. A way to overcome this problem is to use Independent Component Analysis (ICA) to construct or learn filters from the data [Tsai et al. (2006)]. In this case, the ICA filters are adapted to the characteristics of the inspected image and no manual selection of parameters are required. An extension of ICA for feature extraction from illumination series is presented in [Nachtigall & Puente León (2009)]. Section 5.2 describes an approach based on ICA filters and illumination series which allows a separation of texture and defects. The performance of this

method is demonstrated in Section 5.2.5 with an AVI application: the segmentation of varnish defects on a wood board.

- Statistical method: An alternative approach to detecting topographic defects on textured surfaces relies on statistical properties. Statistical texture analysis methods measure the spatial distribution of pixel values. These are well rooted in the computer vision world and have been extensively applied to various problems. A large number of statistical texture features have been proposed ranging from first order to higher order statistics. Among others, histogram statistics, co-occurrence matrices, and Local Binary Patterns (LBP) have been applied to AVI problems [Xie (2008)]. Section 5.3 presents a method to extract invariant features from illumination series. This approach goes beyond the defect detection task by also classifying the defect type. The detection and classification performance of the method is shown on varnished wood surfaces.

5.1 Model-based fusion for surface segmentation

The objective of a segmentation process is to separate or segment a surface into disjoint regions, each of which is characterized by specific features or properties. Such features can be, for instance, the local orientation, the color, or the local reflectance properties, as well as neighborhood relations in the spatial domain. Standard segmentation methods on single images assign each pixel to a certain segment according to a defined feature. In the simplest case, this feature is the gray value (or color value) of a single pixel. However, the information contained in a single pixel is limited. Therefore, more complex segmentation algorithms derive features from neighborhood relations like mean gray value or local variance.

This section presents a method to perform segmentation based on illumination series (like those described in Section 3). Such an illumination series contains information about the radiance of the surface as a function of the illumination direction [Haralick & Shapiro (1992); Lindner & Puente León (2006); Puente León (1997)]. Moreover, the image series provides an illumination-dependent signal for each location on the surface given by:

$$g_{\mathbf{x}}(\mathbf{b}) = g(\mathbf{x}, \mathbf{b}) \,, \tag{2}$$

where $g_{\mathbf{x}}(\mathbf{b})$ is the intensity signal at a fixed location $\mathbf{x}$ as a function of the illumination parameters $\mathbf{b}$. This signal allows us to derive a set of model-based features, which are extracted individually at each location on the surface and are independent of the surrounding locations. The features considered in the following method are related to the macrostructure (the local orientation) and to reflection properties associated with the microstructure of the surface.

5.1.1 Reflection model

The reflection properties of the surface are estimated using the Torrance and Sparrow model, which is suitable for a wide range of materials [Torrance & Sparrow (1967)]. Each measured intensity signal $g_{\mathbf{x}}(\mathbf{b})$ allows a pixel-wise data fit to the model. The reflected radiance L_{r} detected by the camera is assumed to be a superposition of a diffuse lobe L_{d} and a forescatter lobe L_{fs}:

$$L_{\mathrm{r}} = k_{\mathrm{d}} \cdot L_{\mathrm{d}} + k_{\mathrm{fs}} \cdot L_{\mathrm{fs}} . \tag{3}$$

The parameters k_{d} and k_{fs} denote the strength of both terms. The diffuse reflection is modeled by Lambert's cosine law and only depends on the angle of incident light on the surface:

$$L_{\mathrm{d}} = k_{\mathrm{d}} \cdot \cos(\theta - \theta_{\mathrm{n}}) . \tag{4}$$

The assignment of the variables θ (angle of the incident light) and θ_n (angle of the normal vector orientation) is explained in Fig. 3.

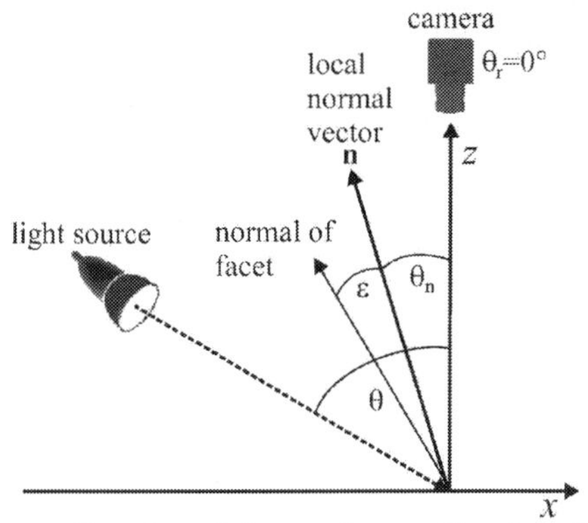

Fig. 3. Illumination direction, direction of observation, and local surface normal **n** are in-plane for the applied 1D case of the reflection model. The facet, which reflects the incident light into the camera, is tilted by ε with respect to the normal of the local surface spot.

The forescatter reflection is described by a geometric model according to [Torrance & Sparrow (1967)]. The surface is considered to be composed of many microscopic facets, whose normal vectors diverge from the local normal vector **n** by the angle ε; see Fig. 3. These facets are normally distributed and each one reflects the incident light like a perfect mirror. As the surface is assumed to be isotropic, the facets distribution function $p_\varepsilon(\varepsilon)$ results rotationally symmetric:

$$p_\varepsilon(\varepsilon) = c \cdot \exp\left(-\frac{\varepsilon^2}{2\sigma^2}\right) . \tag{5}$$

We define a surface spot as the surface area which is mapped onto a pixel of the sensor. The reflected radiance of such spots with the orientation θ_n can now be expressed as a function of the incident light angle θ:

$$L_{fs} = \frac{k_{fs}}{\cos(\theta_r - \theta_n)} \exp\left(-\frac{(\theta + \theta_r - 2\theta_n)^2}{8\sigma^2}\right) . \tag{6}$$

The parameter σ denotes the standard deviation of the facets' deflection, and it is used as a feature to describe the degree of specularity of the surface. The observation direction of the camera θ_r is constant for an image series and is typically set to $0°$. Further effects of the original facet model of Torrance and Sparrow, such as shadowing effects between the facets, are not considered or simplified in the constant factor k_{fs}.

The reflected radiance L_r leads to an irradiance reaching the image sensor. For constant small solid angles, it can be assumed that the radiance L_r is proportional to the intensities detected by the camera:

$$g_{\mathbf{x}}(\theta) \propto L_r(\theta). \tag{7}$$

Considering Eqs. (3)-(7), we can formulate our model for the intensity signals detected by the camera as follows:

$$g_{\mathbf{x}}(\theta) = k_{\mathrm{d}} \cdot \cos(\theta - \theta_{\mathrm{n}}) + \frac{k_{\mathrm{fs}}}{\cos(\theta_{\mathrm{r}} - \theta_{\mathrm{n}})} \exp\left(-\frac{(\theta + \theta_{\mathrm{r}} - 2\theta_{\mathrm{n}})^2}{8\sigma^2}\right). \tag{8}$$

This equation will be subsequently utilized to model the intensity of a small surface area (or spot) as a function of the illumination direction.

5.1.2 Feature extraction

The parameters related to the reflection model in Eq. (8) can be extracted as follows:

- First, we need to determine the azimuthal orientation $\phi(\mathbf{x})$ of each surface spot given by $\mathbf{x}$. With this purpose, a sector series $\mathcal{S}_{\mathrm{s}} = \{g(\mathbf{x}, \varphi_b), \ b = 1, \ldots, B\}$ as described in Section 3 is generated. The azimuthal orientation $\phi(\mathbf{x})$ for a position $\mathbf{x}$ coincides with the value of φ_b yielding the maximal intensity in $g_{\mathbf{x}}(\varphi_b)$.
- The next step consists in finding the orientation in the elevation direction $\vartheta(\mathbf{x})$ for each spot. This information can be extracted from a new illumination series, which is generated by fixing the azimuth angle φ_b of a point light source at the previously determined value $\phi(\mathbf{x})$ and then varying the elevation angle θ from 0° to 90°. This latter results in an intensity signal $g_{\mathbf{x}}(\theta)$, whose maximum describes the elevation of the surface normal direction $\vartheta(\mathbf{x})$. Finally, the reflection properties are determined for each location $\mathbf{x}$ through least squares fitting of the signal $g_{\mathbf{x}}(\theta)$ to the reflection model described in Eq. (8). Meaningful parameters that can be extracted from the model are, for example, the width $\sigma(\mathbf{x})$ of the forescatter lobe, the strengths $k_{\mathrm{fs}}(\mathbf{x})$ and $k_{\mathrm{d}}(\mathbf{x})$ of the lobes and the local surface normal given by:

$$\mathbf{n}(\mathbf{x}) = (\cos\phi(\mathbf{x})\sin\vartheta(\mathbf{x}), \sin\phi(\mathbf{x})\sin\vartheta(\mathbf{x}), \cos\vartheta(\mathbf{x}))^{\mathrm{T}}. \tag{9}$$

In what follows, we use these parameters as features for segmentation.

5.1.3 Segmentation

Segmentation methods are often categorized into region-oriented and edge-oriented approaches. Whereas the first ones are based on merging regions by evaluating some kind of homogeneity criterion, the latter rely on detecting the contours between homogeneous areas. In this section, we make use of region-oriented approaches. The performance is demonstrated by examining the surface of two different cutting inserts: a new part, and a worn one showing abrasion on the top of it; see Fig. 4.

5.1.3.1 Region-based segmentation

Based on the surface normal $\mathbf{n}(\mathbf{x})$ computed according to Eq. (9), the partial derivatives with respect to x and y, $p(\mathbf{x})$ and $q(\mathbf{x})$, are calculated. It is straightforward to use these image signals as features to perform the segmentation. To this end, a region-growing algorithm is applied to determine connected segments in the feature images [Gonzalez & Woods (2002)]. To suppress noise, a smoothing of the feature images is performed prior to the segmentation. Fig. 5 shows a pseudo-colored representation of the derivatives $p(\mathbf{x})$ and $q(\mathbf{x})$ for both the new and the worn cutting insert. The worn area can be clearly distinguished in the second feature image $q(\mathbf{x})$. Fig. 6 shows the segmentation results. The rightmost image shows two regions that correspond with the worn areas visible in the feature image $q(\mathbf{x})$. In this case, a subset of

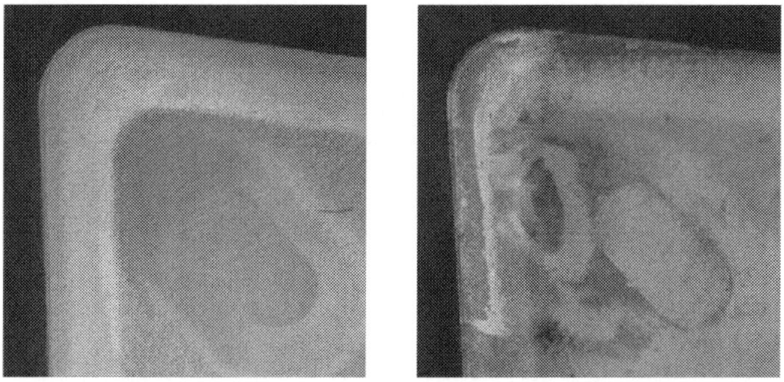

Fig. 4. Test surfaces: (left) new cutting insert; (right) worn cutting insert. The shown images were recorded with diffuse illumination (just for visualization purposes).

the parameters of the reflection model was sufficient to achieve a satisfactory segmentation. Further, other surface characteristics of interest could be detected by exploiting the remaining surface model parameters.

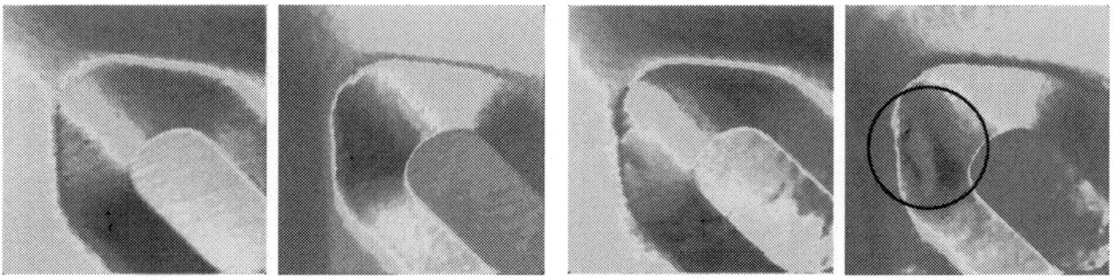

Fig. 5. Pseudo-colored representation of the derivatives $p(\mathbf{x})$ and $q(\mathbf{x})$ of the surface normal: (left) new cutting insert; (right) worn cutting insert. The worn area is clearly visible in area of the rightmost image as marked by a circle.

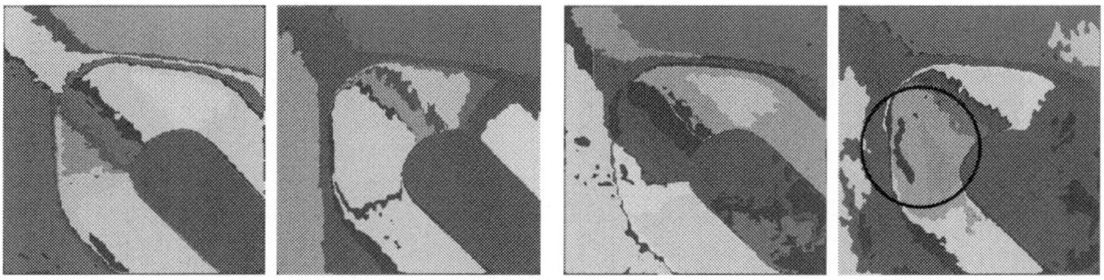

Fig. 6. Results of the region-based segmentation of the feature images $p(\mathbf{x})$ and $q(\mathbf{x})$: (left) new cutting insert; (right) worn cutting insert. In the rightmost image, the worn regions were correctly discerned from the intact background.

Fig. 7 shows a segmentation result based on the model parameters $k_{\mathrm{d}}(\mathbf{x})$, $k_{\mathrm{fs}}(\mathbf{x})$ and $\sigma(\mathbf{x})$. This result was obtained by thresholding the three parameter signals, and then combining them by a logical conjunction. The right image in Fig. 7 compares the segmentation result with a manual selection of the worn area.

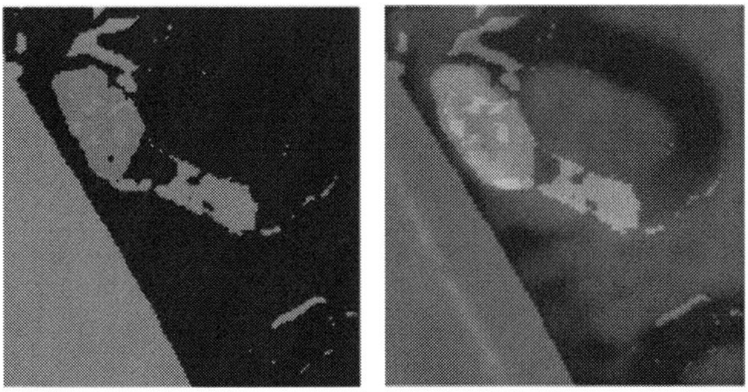

Fig. 7. Result of the region-based segmentation of the defective cutting insert based on the parameters of the reflection model: (left) segmentation result; (right) overlay of an original image, a selection of the defective area by an human expert (green), and the segmentation result (red). This result was achieved using a different raw dataset than for Figs. 5 and 6. For this reason, the cutting inserts are depicted with both a different rotation angle and a different magnification.

5.1.4 Discussion

The segmentation approach presented in this section utilizes significantly more information than conventional methods relying on the processing of a single image. Consequently, they are able to distinguish a larger number of surface characteristics. The region-based segmentation methodology allows exploiting multiple clearly interpretable surface features, thus enabling a discrimination of additional nuances. For this reason, a more reliable segmentation of surfaces with arbitrary characteristics can be achieved.
Fig. 8 illustrates the fusion process flow. Basically, the global DAI-DEO architecture can be

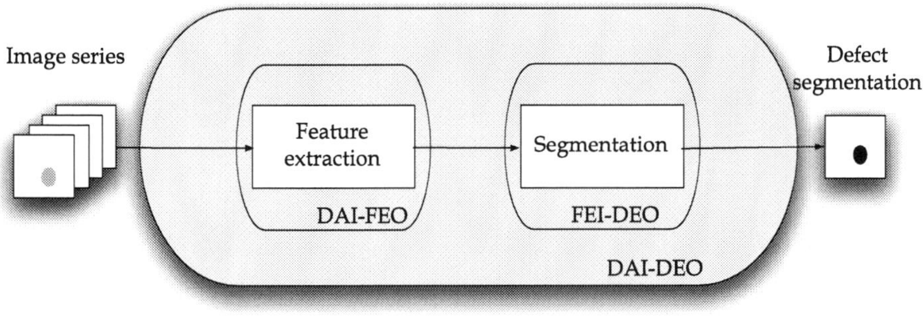

Fig. 8. Fusion architecture scheme for the model-based method.

seen as the concatenation of 2 fusion steps. First, features characterizing the 3D texture are extracted by fusing the irradiance information distributed along the images of the series. These features, e.g., surface normal and reflection parameters, are then combined in the segmentation step, which gives as output a symbolic (decision level) result.

5.2 Filter-based detection of topographic defects

Topographic irregularities on certain surfaces, e.g., metallic and varnished ones, can only be recognized reliably if the corresponding surface is inspected under different illumination directions. Therefore, a reliable automated inspection requires a series of images, in which each picture is taken under a different illumination direction. It is advantageous to analyze this series as a whole and not as a set of individual images, because the relevant information is contained in the relations among them.

In this section, a method for detection of topographical defects is presented. In particular for textured surfaces like wood boards, this problem can be difficult to solve due to the noisy background given by the texture. The following method relies on a stochastic generative model, which allows a separation of the texture from the defects. To this end, a filter bank is constructed from a training set of surfaces based on Independent Component Analysis (ICA) and then applied to the images of the surface to be inspected. The output of the algorithm consists of a segmented binary image, in which the defective areas are highlighted.

5.2.1 Image series

The image series used by this method are generated with a fixed elevation angle θ and a varying azimuth φ of a distant point light source. The number of images included in each series is $B = 4$, with $\varphi_b = 0°, 90°, 180°, 270°$. From a mathematical point of view, an image series can be considered as a vectorial signal $\mathbf{g}(\mathbf{x})$:

$$\mathbf{g}(\mathbf{x}) = \begin{pmatrix} g^{(1)}(\mathbf{x}) \\ \vdots \\ g^{(B)}(\mathbf{x}) \end{pmatrix}, \qquad (10)$$

where $g^{(1)}(\mathbf{x}), \ldots, g^{(B)}(\mathbf{x})$ denote the individual images of the defined series.

5.2.2 Overview of Independent Component Analysis

Generally speaking, Independent Component Analysis (ICA) is a method that allows the separation of one or many multivariate signals into statistically independent components. A stochastic generative model serves as a starting point for the further analysis. The following model states that a number m of observed random variables can be expressed as a linear combination of n statistically independent stochastic variables:

$$\mathbf{v} = \mathbf{A} \cdot \mathbf{s} = \sum_{i=1}^{n} \mathbf{a}_i \cdot s_i , \qquad (11)$$

where $\mathbf{v}$ denotes the observed vector $(m \times 1)$, $\mathbf{A}$ the mixing matrix $(m \times n)$, $\mathbf{s}$ the independent components vector $(n \times 1)$, $\mathbf{a}_i$ the basis vectors $(m \times 1)$ and s_i the independent components $(s_i \in \mathbb{R})$.

The goal of ICA is to find the independent components s_i of an observed vector:

$$\mathbf{s} = \mathbf{W} \cdot \mathbf{v} . \qquad (12)$$

In case that $m = n$, $\mathbf{W} = \mathbf{A}^{-1}$ holds. Note that the mixing matrix $\mathbf{A}$ is not known a priori. Thus, $\mathbf{A}$ (or $\mathbf{W}$) have to be estimated through ICA from the observed data, too. An overview

and description of different approaches and implementations of ICA algorithms can be found in [Hyvärinen & Oja (2000)].
The calculation of an independent component s_i is achieved by means of the inner product of a row vector $\mathbf{w}_i^{\mathrm{T}}$ of the ICA matrix $\mathbf{W}$ and an observed vector $\mathbf{v}$:

$$s_i = \langle \mathbf{w}_i, \mathbf{v} \rangle = \sum_{k=1}^{m} w_i^{(k)} \cdot v^{(k)}, \tag{13}$$

where $w_i^{(k)}$ and $v^{(k)}$ are the k-components of the vectors $\mathbf{w}_i$ and $\mathbf{v}$ respectively. This step is called feature extraction and the vectors $\mathbf{w}_i$, which can be understood as filters, are called feature detectors. In this sense, s_i can be seen as features of $\mathbf{v}$. However, in the literature, the concept of feature is not uniquely defined, and usually $\mathbf{a}_i$ is denoted as feature, while s_i corresponds to the amplitude of the feature in $\mathbf{v}$. In the following sections, the concept of feature will be used for s_i and $\mathbf{a}_i$ interchangeably.

5.2.3 Extending ICA for image series

The ICA generative model described in Eq. (11) can be extended and rewritten for image series as follows:

$$\mathbf{g}(\mathbf{x}) = \begin{pmatrix} g^{(1)}(\mathbf{x}) \\ \vdots \\ g^{(B)}(\mathbf{x}) \end{pmatrix} = \sum_{i=1}^{n} \begin{pmatrix} a_i^{(1)}(\mathbf{x}) \\ \vdots \\ a_i^{(B)}(\mathbf{x}) \end{pmatrix} s_i = \sum_{i=1}^{n} \mathbf{a}_i(\mathbf{x}) \cdot s_i \,. \tag{14}$$

The image series $\mathbf{a}_i(\mathbf{x})$, with $i = 1, \ldots, n$, form an image series basis. With this basis, an arbitrary $\mathbf{g}(\mathbf{x})$ can be generated using the appropriate weights s_i. The resulting feature detectors $\mathbf{w}_i(\mathbf{x})$ are in this case also image series. As shown in Eq. (13), the feature extraction is performed through the inner product of a feature detector and an observed vector, which, for the case of the image series, results in:

$$s_i = \langle \mathbf{w}_i(\mathbf{x}), \mathbf{g}(\mathbf{x}) \rangle = \sum_{b=1}^{B} \sum_{x=1}^{M} \sum_{y=1}^{N} w_i^{(b)}(\mathbf{x}) \cdot g^{(b)}(\mathbf{x}), \tag{15}$$

where $M \times N$ denotes the size of each image of the series.

5.2.4 Defect detection approach

In Fig. 9 a scheme of the proposed approach for defect detection in textured surfaces is shown. The primary idea behind this approach is to separate the texture or background from the defects. This is achieved through the generation of an image series using only the obtained ICA features that characterize the texture better than the defects. Subsequently, the generated image series is subtracted from the original one. Finally, thresholds are applied in order to generate an image with the segmented defects.

5.2.4.1 Learning of ICA features

The features (or basis vectors) are obtained from a set of selected image series that serves as training data. Image patches are extracted from these training surfaces and used as input data for an ICA algorithm, which gives as output the image series basis $\mathbf{a}_i(\mathbf{x})$ with $i = 1, \ldots, n$ and the corresponding feature detectors $\mathbf{w}_i(\mathbf{x})$. As input for the ICA algorithm, 50000 image patches (with size 8×8 pixels) taken from random positions of the training image set are used.

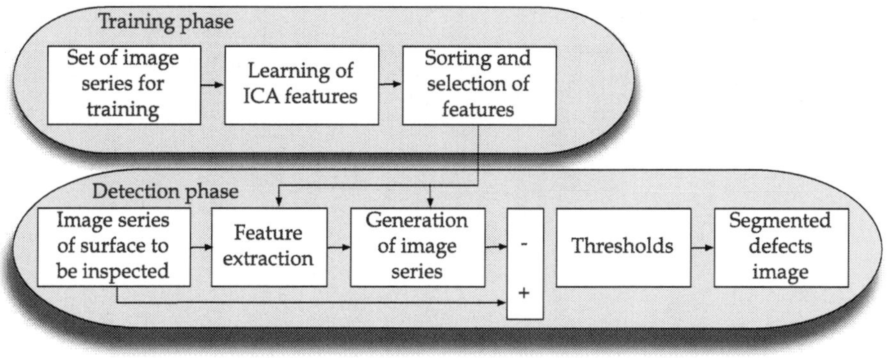

Fig. 9. Scheme of the proposed defect detection approach.

5.2.4.2 Sorting of features

Each feature learned by ICA remarks different aspects of the surface. In particular, some of them will characterize better the texture or background than the defects. In this sense, it is important to identify which of them are better suited to describe the background. The following proposed function $f(\mathbf{a}_i(\mathbf{x}))$ can be used as a measure for this purpose:

$$\begin{aligned} f(\mathbf{a}_i(\mathbf{x})) = \sum_{\mathbf{x}} & |a_i^{(1)}(\mathbf{x}) - a_i^{(2)}(\mathbf{x})| + |a_i^{(1)}(\mathbf{x}) - a_i^{(3)}(\mathbf{x})| + \\ & |a_i^{(1)}(\mathbf{x}) - a_i^{(4)}(\mathbf{x})| + |a_i^{(2)}(\mathbf{x}) - a_i^{(3)}(\mathbf{x})| + \\ & |a_i^{(2)}(\mathbf{x}) - a_i^{(4)}(\mathbf{x})| + |a_i^{(3)}(\mathbf{x}) - a_i^{(4)}(\mathbf{x})| . \end{aligned} \tag{16}$$

Basically, Eq. (16) gives a measure of the pixel intensity distribution similarity between the individual images $a_i^{(1,\ldots,4)}(\mathbf{x})$ of an image vector $\mathbf{a}_i(\mathbf{x})$. A low value of $f(\mathbf{a}_i(\mathbf{x}))$ denotes a high similarity. The image series of the basis $\mathbf{a}_i(\mathbf{x})$ are then sorted by this measure. As defects introduce local variations of the intensity distribution between the images of a series, the lower the value of $f(\mathbf{a}_i(\mathbf{x}))$, the better describes $\mathbf{a}_i(\mathbf{x})$ the background.

5.2.4.3 Defect segmentation

Once the features are sorted, the next step is to generate the background images of the surface to be inspected $\mathbf{g}_{\text{gen}}(\mathbf{x})$. This is achieved by using only the first k sorted features ($k < n$), which allows reproducing principally the background, while attenuating the defects' information. The parameter k is usually set to the half of the total number n of vectors that form the basis:

$$\mathbf{g}_{\text{gen}}(\mathbf{x}) = \begin{pmatrix} g_{\text{gen}}^{(1)}(\mathbf{x}) \\ \vdots \\ g_{\text{gen}}^{(4)}(\mathbf{x}) \end{pmatrix} = \sum_{i=1}^{k} \begin{pmatrix} a_i^{(1)}(\mathbf{x}) \\ \vdots \\ a_i^{(4)}(\mathbf{x}) \end{pmatrix} s_i = \sum_{i=1}^{k} \mathbf{a}_i(\mathbf{x}) \cdot s_i . \tag{17}$$

Whole images are simply obtained by generating contiguous image patches and then joining them together. The segmented defect image is obtained following the thresholding scheme shown in Fig. 10. This scheme can be explained as follows:

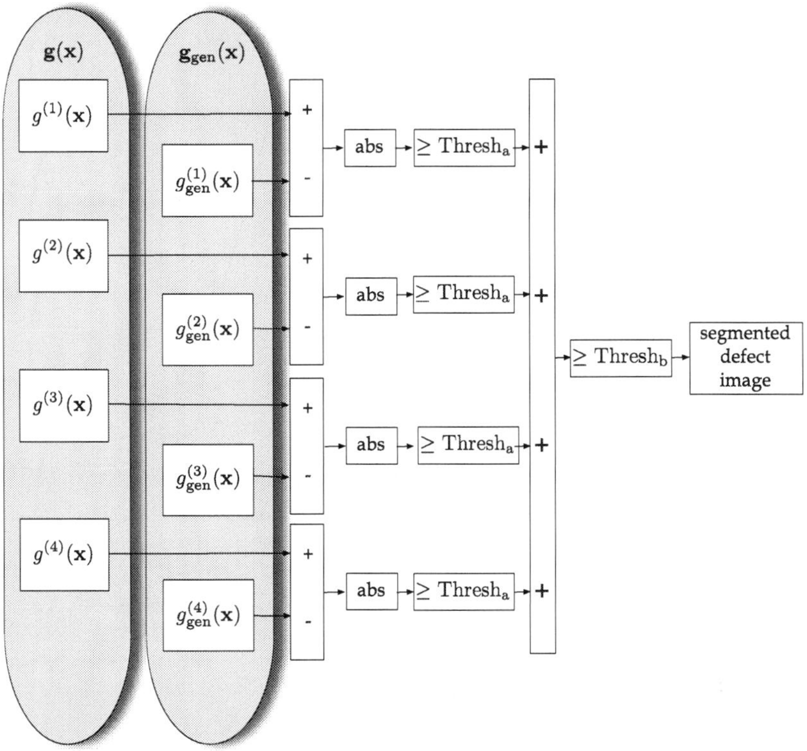

Fig. 10. Segmentation procedure of the filter-based method.

- When the absolute value of the difference between an original image $g^{(1,\ldots,4)}(\mathbf{x})$ and the generated one $g_{\text{gen}}^{(1,\ldots,4)}(\mathbf{x})$ exceeds a threshold Thresh_a, then these areas are considered as possible defects.
- When possible defective zones occur in the same position at least in Thresh_b different individual images of the series, then this area is considered as defective.

5.2.5 Experimental results

The proposed defect detection method was tested on varnished wood pieces. In Fig. 11, an example of an image series and the corresponding generated texture images is shown.

The tested surface contains two fissures, one in the upper and the other in the lower part of the images. The generated images reproduce well the original surface in the zones with no defects. On the contrary, the defective areas are attenuated and not clearly identifiable in these images.

The image indicating the possible defects and the final image of segmented defects, obtained following the thresholding scheme of Fig. 10, are shown in Fig. 12. The fissures have been clearly detected, as can be seen from the segmented image on the right side.

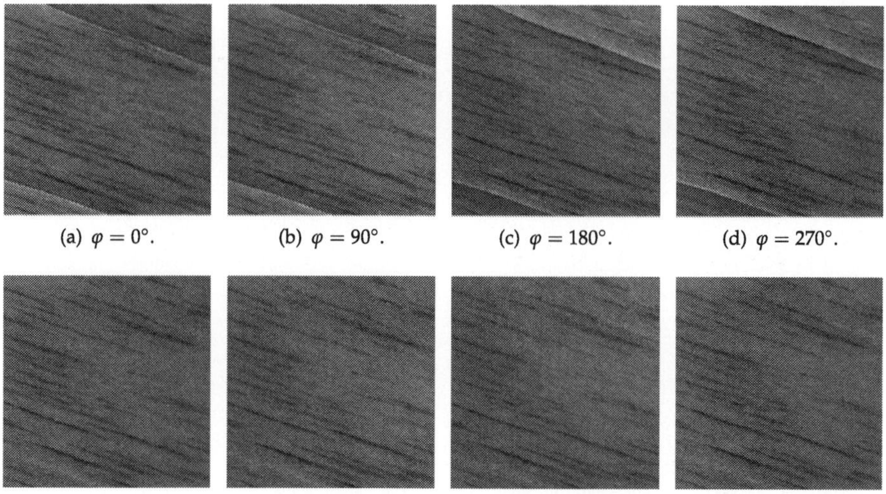

(a) $\varphi = 0°$. (b) $\varphi = 90°$. (c) $\varphi = 180°$. (d) $\varphi = 270°$.

(e) $\varphi = 0°$. (f) $\varphi = 90°$. (g) $\varphi = 180°$. (h) $\varphi = 270°$.

Fig. 11. Image series of a tested surface. (a)-(d): Original images. (e)-(h): Generated texture images.

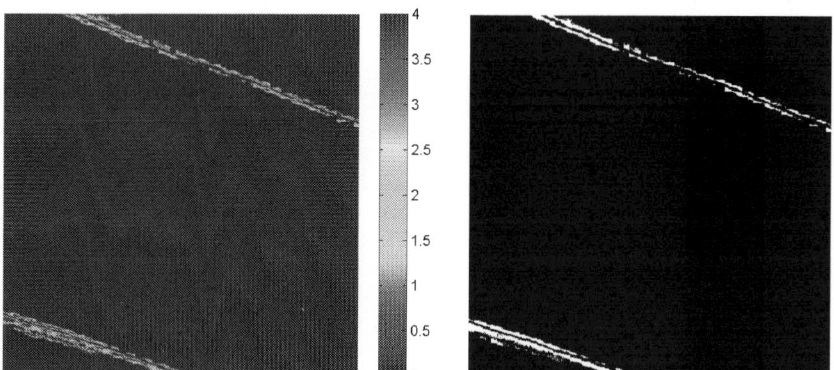

(a) Possible defects ($\text{Thresh}_a = 30$). (b) Segmented defect image ($\text{Thresh}_b = 2$).

Fig. 12. Possible defective areas and image of segmented defects of a varnished wood surface.

5.2.6 Discussion

A method for defect detection on textured surfaces was presented. The method relies on the fusion of an image series recorded with variable illumination, which provides a better visualization of topographical defects than a single image of a surface. The proposed method can be considered as filter-based: a filter bank (a set of feature detectors) is learned by applying ICA to a set of training surfaces. The learned filters allow a separation of the texture from the

defects. By application of a simple thresholding scheme, a segmented image of defects can be extracted. It is important to note that the defect detection in textured surfaces is a difficult task because of the noisy background introduced by the texture itself. The method was tested on defective varnished wood surfaces showing good results.
A scheme of the fusion architecture is shown in Fig. 13. The connected fusion blocks show the different processing steps. First, features are extracted from the image series through filtering with the learned ICA filters. A subset of these features is used to reconstruct filtered texture images. After subtracting the background from the original images, a thresholding scheme is applied in order to obtain a symbolic result showing the defect areas on the surface.

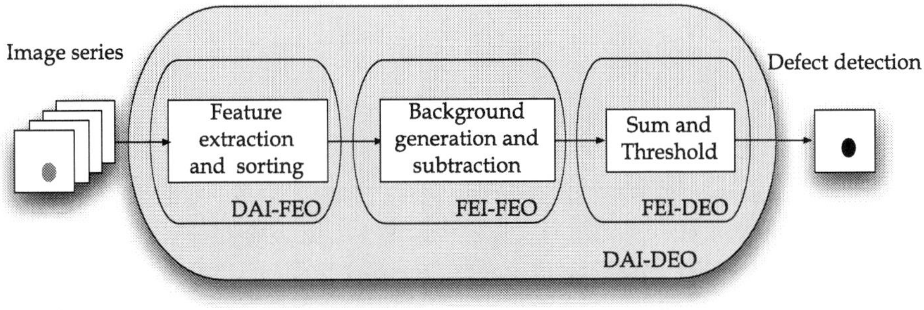

Fig. 13. Fusion architecture scheme of the ICA filter-based method.

5.3 Detection of surface defects based on invariant features

The following approach extracts and fuses statistical features from image series to detect and classify defects. The feature extraction step is based on an extended Local Binary Pattern (LBP), originally proposed by [Ojala et al. (2002)]. The resulting features are then processed to achieve invariance against two-dimensional rotation and translation. In order not to loose much discriminability during the invariance generation, two methods are combined: The invariance against rotation is reached by integration, while the invariance against translation is achieved by constructing histograms [Schael (2005); Siggelkow & Burkhardt (1998)]. Finally, a Support Vector Machine (SVM) classifies the invariant features according to a predefined set of classes. As in the previous case, the performance of this method is demonstrated with the inspection of varnished wood boards. In contrast to the previously described approach, the invariant-based method additionally provides information about the defect class.

5.3.1 Extraction of invariant features through integration

A pattern feature is called invariant against a certain transformation, if it remains constant when the pattern is affected by the transformation [Schulz-Mirbach (1995)]. Let $g(\mathbf{x})$ be a gray scale image, and let $\tilde{f}(g(\mathbf{x}))$ be a feature extracted from $g(\mathbf{x})$. This feature is invariant against a transformation $t(\mathbf{p})$, if and only if $\tilde{f}(g(\mathbf{x})) = \tilde{f}(t(\mathbf{p})\{g(\mathbf{x})\})$, where the $\mathbf{p}$ is the parameter vector describing the transformation.

A common approach to construct an invariant feature from $g(\mathbf{x})$ is integrating over the transformation space $\mathcal{P}$:

$$\tilde{f}(g(\mathbf{x})) = \int_{\mathcal{P}} f(t(\mathbf{p})\{g(\mathbf{x})\})\,\mathrm{d}\mathbf{p}\,. \tag{18}$$

Equation (18) is known as the Haar integral. The function $f := f(\mathbf{s})$, which is paremetrized by a vector $\mathbf{s}$, is an arbitrary, local kernel function, whose objective is to extract relevant information from the pattern. By varying the kernel function parameters defined in $\mathbf{s}$, different features can be obtained in order to achieve a better and more accurate description of the pattern.

In this approach, we aim at extracting invariant features with respect to the 2D Euclidean motion, which involves rotation and translation in $\mathbb{R}^2$. Therefore, the parameter vector of the transformation function is given as follows: $\mathbf{p} = (\tau_x, \tau_y, \omega)^{\mathrm{T}}$, where τ_x and τ_y denote the translation parameters in x and y direction, and ω the rotation parameter. In order to guarantee the convergence of the integral, the translation is considered cyclical [Schulz-Mirbach (1995)]. For this specific group, Eq. (18) can be rewritten as follows:

$$\tilde{f}^l(g(\mathbf{x})) = \int_{\mathcal{P}} f_l(t(\tau_x, \tau_y, \omega)\{g(\mathbf{x})\})\,\mathrm{d}\tau_x\,\mathrm{d}\tau_y\,\mathrm{d}\omega\,, \tag{19}$$

where $\tilde{f}^l(g(\mathbf{x}))$ denotes the invariant feature obtained with the specific kernel function $f_l := f(\mathbf{s}^l)$ and $l \in \{1, \ldots, L\}$. For the discrete case, the integration can be replaced by summations as:

$$\tilde{f}^l(g(\mathbf{x})) = \sum_{i=0}^{M-1}\sum_{j=0}^{N-1}\sum_{k=0}^{K-1} f_l(t_{ijk}\{g_{mn}\})\,. \tag{20}$$

Here, t_{ijk} and g_{mn} are the discrete versions of the transformation and the gray scale image respectively, $K = 360°/\Delta\omega$ and $M \times N$ denotes the image size.

5.3.2 Invariant features from series of images

In our approach, the pattern is not a single image g_{mn} but a series of images $\mathcal{S}$. The series is obtained by systematically varying the illumination azimuth angle $\varphi \in [0, 360°)$ with a fixed elevation angle θ. So, the number B of images in the series is given by $B = 360°/\Delta\varphi$, where $\Delta\varphi$ describes the displacement of the illuminant between two consecutive captures. As a consequence, each image of the series can be identified with the illumination azimuth used for its acquisition:

$$g_{mnb} = g(\mathbf{x}, \varphi_b) \quad \text{with} \quad \varphi_b = b\,\Delta\varphi \quad \text{and} \quad 0 \le b \le B-1\,. \tag{21}$$

Rewriting Eq. (20) to consider series of images, we obtain:

$$\tilde{f}^l(\mathcal{S}) = \sum_{i=0}^{M-1}\sum_{j=0}^{N-1}\sum_{k=0}^{K-1} f_l(t_{ijk}\{\mathcal{S}\})\,. \tag{22}$$

The transformed series of images $t_{ijk}\{\mathcal{S}\}$ can be defined as follows:

$$t_{ijk}\{\mathcal{S}\} =: \{\tilde{g}_{m'n'b'},\; b' = 1, \ldots, B\}\,, \tag{23}$$

where the vector $(m', n')^{\mathrm{T}}$ is the translated and rotated vector $(m, n)^{\mathrm{T}}$:

$$\begin{pmatrix} m' \\ n' \end{pmatrix} = \begin{pmatrix} \cos(k\Delta\omega) & \sin(k\Delta\omega) \\ -\sin(k\Delta\omega) & \cos(k\Delta\omega) \end{pmatrix} \begin{pmatrix} m \\ n \end{pmatrix} - \begin{pmatrix} i \\ j \end{pmatrix} . \tag{24}$$

The transformation of b in b' is a consequence of the rotation transformation and the use of directional light during the acquisition of the images. This transformation consists of a cyclical translation of the gray values along the third dimension of the series of images, which compensates the relative position changes of the rotated object with respect to the illumination source:

$$b' = (b + k) \bmod B . \tag{25}$$

From Eq. (25), it can be noticed that the resolution of the rotation transformation is limited by the resolution used during the image acquisition: $\Delta\omega = \Delta\varphi$.

5.3.2.1 Kernel function

As mentioned before, the kernel function has the aim of extracting relevant information used in the later classification step. As a consequence, its definition is closely related with the specific application (in our case the detection and classification of varnish defects on wood surfaces). In order to define an appropriate kernel function, two aspects related with the surface characteristics have to be considered:

- The information about the presence of topographic defects on the inspected surface and the type of these defects is partially contained in the intensity changes along the third dimension of the series of images. So, the kernel function should consider these changes.
- Intensity changes in the two dimensional neighborhood on each image of the series enclose also information about the presence and type of defects. The kernel function should be able to collect this information, too.

The kernel function applied to the transformed series of images can be written as follows:

$$f_l(t_{ijk}\{\mathcal{S}\}) = f_l\{\tilde{g}_{m'n'b'},\ b' = 1, \ldots, B\} =: f_{lijk}(\mathcal{S}) . \tag{26}$$

The kernel function f_{lijk} extracts the information of the image series, considering this latter as a whole. That is, the calculation of the kernel function for each value of i, j and k implies a first fusion process. Introducing $f_{lijk}(\mathcal{S})$ in Eq. (22), the invariant feature $\tilde{f}^l(\mathcal{S})$ can be expressed as:

$$\tilde{f}^l(\mathcal{S}) = \sum_{i=0}^{M-1} \sum_{j=0}^{N-1} \sum_{k=0}^{K-1} f_{lijk}(\mathcal{S}) . \tag{27}$$

The summations over i, j and k are necessary to achieve invariance against 2D rotation and translation. However, as a consequence of the summations, much information extracted by f_{lijk} gets lost. Therefore, the resulting feature $\tilde{f}^l(\mathcal{S})$ presents a low capability to discriminate between classes. For the application of interest, a high discriminability is especially important, because different kinds of varnish defects can be very similar. For this reason, the integration method to achieve invariance is used only for the rotation transformation, as explained in the following paragraphs.

5.3.2.2 Invariance against 2D rotation

We introduce an intermediate feature $\tilde{f}^{l}_{ij}(\mathcal{S})$, which is invariant against rotation. This feature is obtained by performing the summation over k in Eq. (27):

$$\tilde{f}^{l}_{ij}(\mathcal{S}) = \sum_{k=0}^{K-1} f_{lijk}(\mathcal{S}) . \tag{28}$$

5.3.2.3 Invariance against translation: fuzzy histogram

Next, it is necessary to achieve the invariance against translation. If this had to be done through integration, a summation over i and j in Eq. (27) should be performed:

$$\tilde{f}^{l}(\mathcal{S}) = \sum_{i=0}^{M-1} \sum_{j=0}^{N-1} \tilde{f}^{l}_{ij}(\mathcal{S}) . \tag{29}$$

An alternative to this summation is the utilization of histograms, which are inherently invariant to translation. This option has the advantage to avoid the loss of information resulting from the summation over i and j, so that the generated features have a better capability to represent different classes [Siggelkow & Burkhardt (1998)]. Then, considering all values of i and j, a fuzzy histogram $\mathcal{H}^{l}_{c}(\mathcal{S})$ is constructed from the rotation invariants $\tilde{f}^{l}_{ij}(\mathcal{S})$ [Schael (2005)], where $c = 1, \ldots, C$ denotes the histogram bins. Finally, the resulting histogram represents our feature against 2D Euclidean motion:

$$\tilde{f}^{l}(\mathcal{S}) = \mathcal{H}^{l}_{c}(\mathcal{S}). \tag{30}$$

5.3.3 Results

The presented method is used to detect and classify defects on varnished wood surfaces. Given the noisy background due to the substrate texture and the similarity between defect classes, the extracted feature should have good characteristics with regard to discriminability [Pérez Grassi et al. (2006)]. A first step in this direction was made by using histograms to achieve translation invariance instead of integration. Another key aspect is the proper selection of a kernel function f_{lijk}. For the results presented below, the kernel function is a vectorial function $\mathbf{f}_{lijk}(r_{1,l}, r_{2,l}, \alpha_l, \beta_l, a_l, \Delta\vartheta_l)$, whose q-th element is given by:

$$f^{q}_{lijk}(\mathcal{S}) = \frac{1}{B} \left| \tilde{g}_{\mathbf{u}^{q}_{l}} - \tilde{g}_{\mathbf{v}^{q}_{l}} \right| . \tag{31}$$

Here, the vectors $\mathbf{u}^{q}_{l}$ and $\mathbf{v}^{q}_{l}$ are defined as:

$$\mathbf{u}^{q}_{l} = \left(\begin{bmatrix} r_{1,l}\cos(\alpha_l + q\,\Delta\vartheta_l) \\ -r_{1,l}\sin(\alpha_l + q\,\Delta\vartheta_l) \end{bmatrix} ; 0 \right) , \quad \mathbf{v}^{q}_{l} = \left(\begin{bmatrix} r_{2,l}\cos(\beta_l + q\,\Delta\vartheta_l) \\ -r_{2,l}\sin(\beta_l + q\,\Delta\vartheta_l) \end{bmatrix} ; a_l \right) , \tag{32}$$

where $1 \le q \le Q_l$ and $Q_l = 360^\circ / \Delta\vartheta_l$. According to Eqs. (31) and (32), two circular neighborhoods with radii $r_{1,l}$ and $r_{2,l}$ are defined in the images $b = 0$ and $b = a_l$ respectively. Both circumferences are sampled with a frequency given by the angle $\Delta\vartheta_l$. This sampling results in Q_l points per neighborhood, which are addressed through the vectors $\mathbf{u}^{q}_{l}$ and $\mathbf{v}^{q}_{l}$ correspondingly. Each element $f^{q}_{lijk}(\mathcal{S})$ of the kernel function is obtained by taking the absolute value of the difference between the intensities in the positions $\mathbf{u}^{q}_{l}$ and $\mathbf{v}^{q}_{l}$ with the same q. In Fig. 14, the kernel function for a given group of parameters is illustrated. In this figure, the

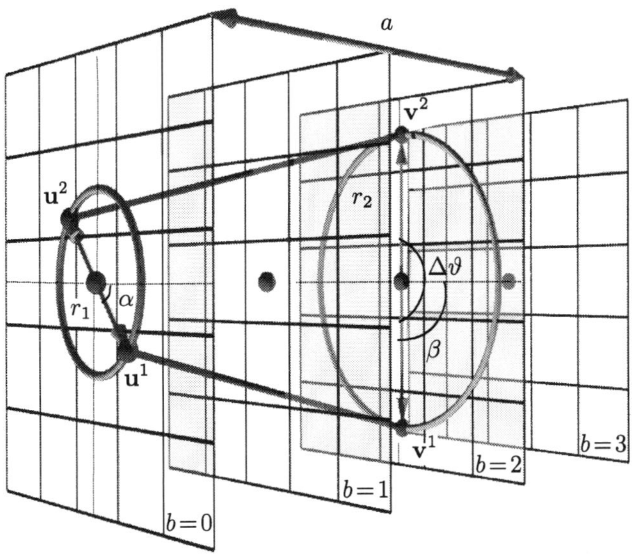

Fig. 14. Kernel function $\mathbf{f}_{lijk}$ for a image series with $B = 4\,(\Delta\varphi = 90^\circ)$. Function's parameters: $a_l = 2, r_{1,l} = 0.5\,r_{2,l}, \alpha_l = 45^\circ, \beta_l = 90^\circ$ and $\Delta\theta_l = 180^\circ\ (Q_l = 2)$. The lines between the points represent the absolut value of the difference (in the image, the subindex l has been suppressed from the function parameters to obtain a clearer graphic).

pairs of points $\mathbf{u}_l^q$ and $\mathbf{v}_l^q$ involved in the calculation of each element f_{lijk}^q of $\mathbf{f}_{lijk}$ are linked by segments.

Using the defined kernel function, a vectorial feature $\tilde{\mathbf{f}}_{ij}^l(\mathcal{S})$ invariant against rotation is obtained using Eq. (28), where $\tilde{\mathbf{f}}_{ij}^l(\mathcal{S}) = (f_{ij}^{l1}(\mathcal{S}), \ldots, f_{ij}^{lQ}(\mathcal{S}))$. Then, a fuzzy histogram $\mathcal{H}_c^l(\mathcal{S})$ is constructed from each element $\tilde{f}_{ij}^{lq}(\mathcal{S})$ of $\tilde{\mathbf{f}}_{ij}^l(\mathcal{S})$. This results in a sequence of Q histrograms $\mathcal{H}_c^{lq}$, which represents our final invariant feature:

$$\tilde{\mathbf{f}}^l(\mathcal{S}) = (\mathcal{H}_c^{l1}(\mathcal{S}), \ldots, \mathcal{H}_c^{lQ}(\mathcal{S})). \tag{33}$$

The performance of the resulting feature $\tilde{\mathbf{f}}^l(\mathcal{S})$ is tested in the classification of different varnish defects on diverse wood textures. The classification is performed by a Support Vector Machine (SVM) and the features $\tilde{\mathbf{f}}^l(\mathcal{S})$ are extracted locally from the image series by analyzing small image windows (32×32 pixels). Fig. 15 shows some classification results for five different classes: no defect, bubble, ampulla, fissure and crater. Theses results were generated using image series consisting of eight images ($B = 8$) and ten different parameter vectors of the kernel function ($L = 10$).

5.3.4 Discussion

The presented method extracts invariant features against rotation and translation from illumination series, which were generated varying the azimuth of an illumination source systematically. Taking the surface characteristics and the image acquisition process into account, a

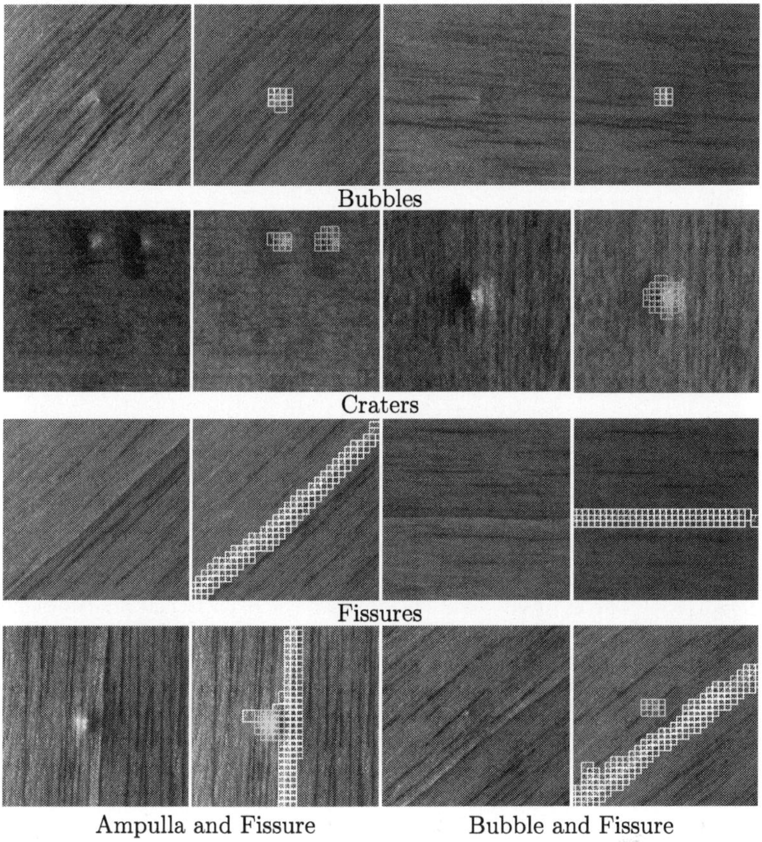

Fig. 15. Results: (left) single images of the image series; (right) classification result.

kernel function has been defined, which allows the extraction of relevant information. For the generation of the invariant features, two methods have been applied: The invariance against rotation has been achieved by integration over the transformation space, while the invariance against translation was obtained by building fuzzy histograms. The classification of the obtained features is performed by a SVM. The obtained features have been successfully used in the detection and classification of finishing defects on wood surfaces.

In Fig. 16 the fusion architecture is shown schematically. The information processing can be represented as a concatenation of different fusion blocks. The first and second processing steps perform the invariant feature extraction from the data. Finally, the SVM classifier generates a symbolic output (decision level data): the classes of the detected defects.

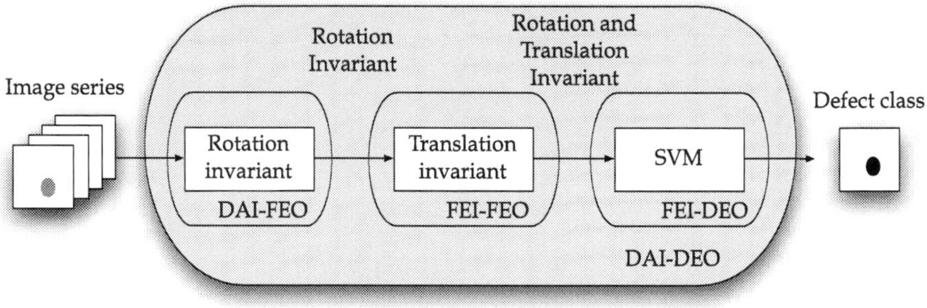

Fig. 16. Fusion architecture scheme for the method based on invariant features.

6. Conclusions

The illumination configuration chosen for any image acquisition stage plays a crucial role for the success of any machine vision task. The proposed multiple image strategy, based on the acquisition of images under a variable directional light source, results in a suitable framework for defect detection and surface assessment problems. This is mainly due to the enhanced local contrast achieved in the individual images. Another important fact is that the cooperative information distributed along the image series provides a better and more complete description of a surface topography. Three methods encompassing a wide field of signal processing and information fusion strategies have been presented. The potentials and benefits of using multi-image analysis methods and their versatility have been demonstrated with a variety of nontrivial and demanding machine vision tasks, including the inspection of varnished wood boards and machined metal pieces such as cutting inserts.

The fusion of images recorded with variable illumination direction has its roots in the well-known photometric stereo technique developed by [Woodham (1980)]. In its original formulation, the topography of Lambertian surfaces can be reconstructed. Since then, many authors have extended its applicability to surfaces with different reflection characteristics. In this chapter, a novel segmentation approach that estimates not only the surface normal direction but also reflectance properties was presented. As shown, these properties can be efficiently used as features for the segmentation step. This segmentation approach makes use of more information than conventional methods relying on single images, thus enabling a discrimination of additional surface properties. It was also shown, that, for some specific automated visual inspection problems, an explicit reconstruction of the surface profile is neither necessary nor efficient. In this sense, two novel problem-specific methods for detection of topographic defects were presented: one of them filter-based and the other relying on invariant statistical features.

Fusion of images recorded with variable illumination remains an open research area. Within this challenging field, some new contributions have been presented in this chapter. On the one hand, two application-oriented methods were proposed. On the other hand, a general segmentation method was presented, which can be seen as an extension of the well established photometric stereo technique.

7. References

Barsky, S. & Petrou, M. (2007). Surface texture using photometric stereo data: classification and direction of illumination detection, *Journal of Mathematical Imaging and Vision* **29**: 185–204.

Beyerer, J. & Puente León, F. (2005). Bildoptimierung durch kontrolliertes aktives Sehen und Bildfusion, *Automatisierungstechnik* **53**(10): 493–502.

Chantler, M. J., Schmidt, M., Petrou, M. & McGunnigle, G. (2002). The effect of illuminant rotation on texture filters: Lissajous's ellipses, Vol. 2352 of *Proceedings of the 7th European Conference on Computer Vision-Part III*, London, UK. Springer-Verlag, pp. 289–303.

Dasarathy, B. V. (1997). Sensor fusion potential exploitation-innovative architectures and illustrative applications, *Proceedings of the IEEE* **85**(1): 24–38.

Drbohlav, O. & Chantler, M. J. (2005). Illumination-invariant texture classification using single training images, Texture 2005: Proceedings of the 4th International Workshop on Texture Analysis and Synthesis, Beijing, China, pp. 31–36.

Gonzalez, R. C. & Woods, R. E. (2002). *Digital image processing*, Prentice Hall, Englewood Cliffs, NJ.

Haralick, R. M. & Shapiro, L. G. (1992). *Computer and Robot Vision*, Vol. II, Reading, MA: Addison-Wesley.

Heizmann, M. & Beyerer, J. (2005). Sampling the parameter domain of image series, Image Processing: Algorithms and Systems IV, San José, CA, USA, pp. 23–33.

Ho, Y.-X., Landy, M. & Maloney, L. (2006). How direction of illumination affects visually perceived surface roughness, *Journal of Vision* **6**: 634–348.

Hyvärinen, A. & Oja, E. (2000). Independent component analysis: algorithms and applications, *Neural Netw.* **13**(4-5): 411–430.

Lambert, G. & Bock, F. (1997). Wavelet methods for texture defect detection, *ICIP '97: Proceedings of the 1997 International Conference on Image Processing (ICIP '97) 3-Volume Set-Volume 3*, IEEE Computer Society, Washington, DC, USA, p. 201.

Lindner, C. (2009). *Segmentierung von Oberflächen mittels variabler Beleuchtung*, PhD thesis, Technische Universität München.

Lindner, C. & Puente León, F. (2006). Segmentierung strukturierter Oberflächen mittels variabler Beleuchtung, *Technisches Messen* **73**(4): 200–2007.

McGunnigle, G. (1998). *The classification of textured surfaces under varying illuminant direction*, PhD thesis, Heriot-Watt University.

McGunnigle, G. & Chantler, M. J. (2000). Rough surface classification using point statistics from photometric stereo, *Pattern Recognition Letters* **21**: 593–604.

Nachtigall, L. & Puente León, F. (2009). Merkmalsextraktion aus Bildserien mittels der Independent Component Analyse , *in* G. Goch (ed.), *XXIII. Messtechnisches Symposium des Arbeitskreises der Hochschullehrer für Messtechnik e.V. (AHMT)*, Shaker Verlag, Aachen, pp. 227–239.

Ojala, T., Pietikäinen, M. & Mäenpää, T. (2002). Multiresolution gray-scale and rotation invariant texture classification with local binary patterns, *IEEE Transactions on Pattern Analysis and Machine Intelligence* **24**(7): 971–987.

Penirschke, A., Chantler, M. J. & Petrou, M. (2002). Illuminant rotation invariant classification of 3D surface textures using Lissajous's ellipses, 2nd International Workshop on Texture Analysis and Synthesis, Copenhagen, pp. 103–107.

Pérez Grassi, A., Abián Pérez, M. A. & Puente León, F. (2008). Illumination and model-based detection of finishing defects, Reports on Distributed Measurement Systems, Shaker Verlag, Aachen, pp. 31–51.

Pérez Grassi, A., Abián Pérez, M. A., Puente León, F. & Pérez Campos, M. R. (2006). Detection of circular defects on varnished or painted surfaces by image fusion, *Proceedings of the IEEE International Conference on Multisensor Fusion and Integration for Intelligent Systems* .

Puente León, F. (1997). Enhanced imaging by fusion of illumination series, *in* O. Loffeld (ed.), *Sensors, Sensor Systems, and Sensor Data Processing*, Vol. 3100 of *Proceedings of SPIE*, SPIE, pp. 297–308.

Puente León, F. (2001). Model-based inspection of shot peened surfaces using fusion techniques, Vol. 4189 of *Proceedings of SPIE on Machine Vision and Three-Dimensional Imaging Systems for Inspection and Metrology*, SPIE, pp. 41–52.

Puente León, F. (2002). Komplementäre Bildfusion zur Inspektion technischer Oberflächen, *Technisches Messen* **69**(4): 161–168.

Puente León, F. (2006). Automated comparison of firearm bullets, *Forensic Science International* **156**(1): 40–50.

Schael, M. (2005). *Methoden zur Konstruktion invarianter Merkmale für die Texturanalyse*, PhD thesis, Albert-Ludwigs-Universität Freiburg.

Schulz-Mirbach, H. (1995). *Anwendung von Invarianzprinzipien zur Merkmalgewinnung in der Mustererkennung*, PhD thesis, Technische Universität Hamburg-Harburg.

Siggelkow, S. & Burkhardt, H. (1998). Invariant feature histograms for texture classification, *Proceedings of the 1998 Joint Conference on Information Sciences (JCIS'98)* .

Torrance, K. E. & Sparrow, E. M. (1967). Theory for off-specular reflection from roughened surfaces, *J. of the Optical Society of America* **57**(9): 1105–1114.

Tsai, D.-M., Tseng, Y.-H., Chao, S.-M. & Yen, C.-H. (2006). Independent component analysis based filter design for defect detection in low-contrast textured images, *ICPR '06: Proceedings of the 18th International Conference on Pattern Recognition*, IEEE Computer Society, Washington, DC, USA, pp. 231–234.

Tsai, D. M. & Wu, S. K. (2000). Automated surface inspection using Gabor filters, *The International Journal of Advanced Manufacturing Technology* **16**(7): 474–482.

Woodham, R. J. (1980). Photometric method for determining surface orientation from multiple images, *Optical Engineering* **19**(1): 139–144.

Xie, X. (2008). A review of recent advances in surface defect detection using texture analysis techniques, *Electronic Letters on Computer Vision and Image Analysis* **7**(3): 1–22.

Camera and laser robust integration in engineering and architecture applications

Pablo Rodriguez-Gonzalvez,
Diego Gonzalez-Aguilera and Javier Gomez-Lahoz
Department of Cartographic and Land Engineering
High Polytechnic School of Avila, Spain
University of Salamanca

1. Introduction

1.1 Motivation

The 3D modelling of objects and complex scenes constitutes a field of multi-disciplinary research full of challenges and difficulties, ranging from the accuracy and reliability of the geometry, the radiometric quality of the results up to the portability and cost of the products, without forgetting the aim of automatization of the whole procedure. To this end, a wide variety of passive and active sensors are available of which the digital cameras and the scanner laser play the main role. Even though these two types of sensors can work in a separate fashion, it is when are merged together when the best results are attained. The following table (Table 1) gives an overview of the advantages and limitations of each technology.

The comparison between the laser scanner and the digital camera (Table 1) stresses the incomplete character of the information derived from only one sensor. Therefore, we reach the conclusion that an integration of data sources and sensors must be achieved to improve the quality of procedures and results. Nevertheless, this sensor fusion poses a wide range of difficulties, derived not only from the different nature of the data (2D images and 3D scanner point clouds) but also from the different processing techniques related to the properties of each sensor. In this sense, an original sensor fusion approach is proposed and applied to the architecture and archaeology. This approach aims at achieving a high automatization level and provides high quality results all at once.

Scanner laser	Digital camera
↓ Not accurate extraction of lines	↑ High accuracy in the extraction of lines
↓ Not visible junctions	↑ Visible junctions
↓ Colour information available on low resolution.	↑ Colour information on high resolution
↑ Straightforward access to metric information	↓ Awkward and slow access to metric information
↑ High capacity and automatization in data capture	↓ Less capacity and automatization in data capture
↓ Data capture not immediate. Delays between scanning stations. Difficulties to move the equipment.	↑ Flexibility and swiftness while handling the equipment.
↑ Ability to render complex and irregular surfaces.	↓ Limitations in the renderization of complex and irregular surfaces
↓ High cost (60.000€-90.000€.)	↑ Low cost (From 100€)
↑ Not dependent on lighting conditions.	↓ Lighting conditions are demanding.
↓ 3D model is a "cloud" without structure and topology.	↑ The 3D model is accessed as a structured entity, including topology if desired.

Table 1. Comparison of advantages and drawbacks of laser scanner and digital camera.

1.2 State of the art

The sensor fusion, in particular concerning the laser scanner and the digital camera, appears as a promising possibility to improve the data acquisition and the geometric and radiometric processing of these data. According to Mitka (2009), the sensor fusion may be divided in two general approaches:

- *On-site integration*, that resides on a "physical" fusion of both sensors. This approach consists on a specific hardware structure that is previously calibrated. This solution provides a higher automatization and readiness in the data acquisition procedures but a higher dependency and a lack of flexibility in both the data acquisition and its processing. Examples of this kind of fusion are the commercial solutions of Trimble and Leica. Both are equipped with digital cameras that are housed in the inside of the device. These cameras exhibit a very poor resolution. (<1Mp). With the idea of accessing cameras with higher quality, other manufacturers present an exterior and calibrated frame to which a reflex camera can be attached. Faro Photon, Riegl LMS-Z620, Leica HDS6100 and Optech Ilris-3D are some of the laser systems that have incorporated this external sensor.

Even though these approaches may lead to the idea that the sensor fusion is a straightforward question, the actual praxis is rather different, since the photos shoot time must be simultaneous to the scanning time, thus the illumination conditions as well as other conditions regarding the position of the camera or the environment may be far from the desired ones.

- *Office integration,* that consists on achieving the sensor fusion on laboratory, as the result of a processing procedure. This approach permits more flexibility in the data acquisition since it will not require neither a previously fixed and rigid framework nor a predetermined time of exposure. Nevertheless, this gain in flexibility demands the challenge of developing an automatic or semi-automatic procedure that aims at "tunning" both different data sources with different constructive fundamentals. According to Kong et al., (2007), the sensor fusion can be divided in three categories: the sensorial level (low level), the feature level (intermediate level) and the decision level (high level). In the sensorial level raw data are acquired from diverse sensors. This procedure is already solved for the *onsite integration* case but it is really complicated to afford when sensors are not calibrated to each other. In this sense, the question is to compute the rigid transformation (rotation and translation) that renders the relationship between both sensors, besides the camera model (camera calibration). The feature level merges the extraction and matching of several feature types. The procedure of feature extraction includes issues such as corners, interest points, borders and lines. These are extracted, labeled, located and matched through different algorithms. The decision level implies to take advantage of hybrid products derived from the processed data itself combined with the expert decision taking.

Regarding the two first levels (sensorial and feature), several authors put forward the question of the fusion between the digital camera and the laser scanner through different approaches linked to different working environments. Levoy et al., (2000) in their project "Digital Michelangelo" carry on a camera pre-calibration facing integration with the laser scanner without any user interaction. In a similar context, Rocchini et al. (1999) obtain a fusion between the image and the laser model by means of an interactive selection of corresponding points. Nevertheless, both approaches are only applied to small objects such as sculptures and statues. With the idea of dealing with more complicated situations arising from complex scenes, Stamos and Allen, (2001) present an automatic fusion procedure between the laser model and the camera image. In this case, 3D lines are extracted by means of a segmentation procedure of the point clouds. After this, the 3D lines are matched with the borders extracted from the images. Some geometrical constraints, such as orthogonality and parallelism, that are common in urban scenes, are considered. In this way, this algorithm only works well in urban scenes where these conditions are met. In addition, the user must establish different kinds of thresholds in the segmentation process. All the above methodologies require the previous knowledge of the interior calibration parameters. With the aim of minimizing this drawback, Aguilera and Lahoz (2006) exploit a single view modelling to achieve an automatic fusion between a laser scanner and a not calibrated digital camera. Particularly, the question of the fusion between the two sensors is solved automatically through the search of 2D and 3D correspondences that are supported by the search of two spatial invariants: two distances and an angle. Nevertheless, some suppositions, such as the use of special targets and the presence of some geometric constraints on the image (vanishing points) are required to undertake the problem. More recently, Gonzalez-Aguilera et al. (2009) develop an automatic method to merge the digital image and the laser model by means of correspondences of the range image (laser) and the camera image. The main contribution of this approach resides on the use of a level hierarchy (pyramid) that takes advantage of the robust estimators, as well as of geometric constraints that ensure a higher accuracy and reliability. The data are processed and tested by means of software called USALign.

Although there are many methodologies that try to progress in the fusion of both sensors taking advantage of the sensorial and the feature level, the radiometric and spectral properties of the sensors has not received enough attention. This issue is critical when the matching concerns images from different parts of the electromagnetic spectrum: visible (digital camera), near infrared (laser scanner) and medium/far infrared (thermal camera) and when the aspiration is to achieve an automatization of the whole procedure. Due to the different ways through which the pixel is formed, some methodologies developed for the visible image processing context may work in an inappropriate way or do not work at all.

On this basis, this chapter on sensor fusion presents a method that has been developed and tested for the fusion of the laser scanner, the digital camera and the thermal camera. The structure of the chapter goes as follows: In the second part, we will tackle with the generalities related with the data acquisition and their pre-processing, concerning to the laser scanner, the digital camera and the thermal camera. In the third part, we will present the specific methodology based on a semi-automatic procedure supported by techniques of close range photogrammetry and computer vision. In the fourth part, a robust registration of sensors based on a spatial resection will be presented. In the fifth part, we will show the experimental results derived from the sensor fusion. A final part will devoted to the main conclusions and the expected future developments.

2. Pre-processing of data

In this section we will expose the treatment of the input data in order to prepare them for the established workflow.

2.1 Data Acquisition

The acquisition protocol has been established with the greatest flexibility as possible in such a way that the method can be applied both to favourable and unfavourable cases. In this sense, the factors that will condition the level of difficulty will be:

- Geometric complexity, directly related to the existence of complex forms as well as to the existence of occlusions.
- Radiometric complexity, directly related to the spectral properties of each sensor, as well as to different illumination conditions of the scene.
- Spatial and angular separation between sensors. The so called baseline will be a major factor when undertaking the correspondence between the sensors. This baseline will also condition the geometric and radiometric factors mentioned above. A short baseline will lead to images with a similar perspective view and consequently, to images easier to match and merge. On the contrary, a large baseline will produce images with big variations in perspective and so, with more difficulties for the correspondence. Nevertheless, rather than the length of the baseline, the critical factor will be the angle between the camera axis and the

average scanning direction. When this angle is large, the automatic fusion procedures will become difficult to undertake.

The following picture (Fig. 1) depicts the three questions mentioned above:

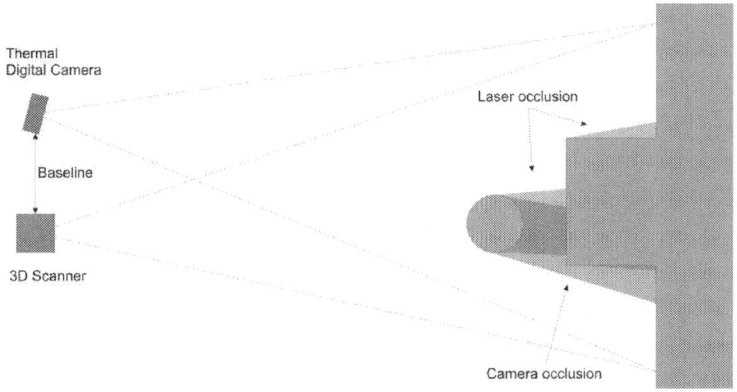

Fig. 1. Factors that influence the data acquisition with the laser scanner and the digital/thermal camera

Through a careful planning of the acquisition framework, taking into account the issues referred before, some rules and basic principles should be stated (Mancera-Taboada et al., 2009). These could be particularised for the case studies analyzed in section 5 focussing on objects related to the architectural and archaeological field. In all of them the input data are the following:

- The **point cloud** is the input data in the case of the laser scanner and exhibits a 3D character with specific metric and radiometric properties. Particularly, the cartesian coordinates *XYZ* associated to each of the points are accompanied by an intensity value associated to the energy of the return of each of the laser beams. The image that is formed from the point cloud, the range image, has radiometric properties derived from the wavelength of the electromagnetic spectrum, that is, the near or the medium infrared. This image depends on factors such as: the object material, the distance between the laser scanner and the object, the incidence angle between the scanner rays and the surface normal and the illumination of the scene. Also, in some cases, this value can be extended to a visible RGB colour value associated to each of the points.

- The **visible digital** image is the input data coming from the digital camera and presents a 2D character with specific metric and radiometric properties. Firstly, it is important that its geometric resolution must be in agreement with the object size and with the scanning resolution. The ideal would be that the number of elements in the point cloud would be the same that the number of pixels in the image. In this way, a perfect correspondence could be achieved between the image and the point cloud and we could obtain the maximum performance from both data sets. In addition, for a given field of view for each sensor, we should seek that the whole object could be covered by a single image. As far as this cannot be achieved we should rely on an image mosaic where each image (previously processed) should be registered in an individual fashion. On the other hand, from a radiometric point of view, the images obtained from the digital camera should present a homogeneous illumination, avoiding, as far as it is possible, the high contrasts and any backlighting.

- The **thermal digital** image is the input data coming from the thermal camera and presents a 2D character with specific metric and radiometric properties. From a geometric point of view they are low resolution images with the presence of high radial lens distortion. From a radiometric point of view the values distribution does not depend, as it does in the visible part of the electromagnetic spectrum, on the intensity gradient of the image that comes from part of the energy that is reflected by the object, but from the thermal gradient of the object itself as well as from the object emissivity. This represents a drawback in the fusion process.

2.2 Laser pre-processing

Aiming to extrapolate part of the approaches that had already been applied to images by the protogrammetric and the computer vision communities, one of the first stages of the laser pre-processing will concern to the transformation of the point cloud into the range image.

2.2.1 Generation of a range image

The range image generation process resides on the use of the collinearity equations (1) to project the points of the cloud over the image plane.

$$
\begin{aligned}
x_A &= -f \cdot \frac{r_{11}\cdot(X_A - X_S) + r_{12}\cdot(Y_A - Y_S) + r_{13}\cdot(Z_A - Z_S)}{r_{31}\cdot(X_A - X_S) + r_{32}\cdot(Y_A - Y_S) + r_{33}\cdot(Z_A - Z_S)} \\
y_A &= -f \cdot \frac{r_{21}\cdot(X_A - X_S) + r_{22}\cdot(Y_A - Y_S) + r_{23}\cdot(Z_A - Z_S)}{r_{31}\cdot(X_A - X_S) + r_{32}\cdot(Y_A - Y_S) + r_{33}\cdot(Z_A - Z_S)}
\end{aligned} \qquad (1)
$$

To obtain the photo coordinates (x_A, y_A) of a three-dimensional point (X_A, Y_A, Z_A) the value of the exterior orientation parameters $(X_S, Y_S, Z_S, \omega, \varphi, \kappa)$, must have been computed. These are the target unknowns we address when we undertake the sensors registration procedure. As this is a question that must be solved through an iterative process, it becomes necessary to provide the system of equations (1) with a set of initial solutions that will stand for the exterior orientation of the virtual camera. The registration procedure will lead to a set of corrections in such a way that the final result will be the desired position and attitude.

In this process it is necessary to define a focal length to perform the projection onto the range image. To achieve the best results and to preserve the initial configuration, the same focal length of the camera image will be chosen.

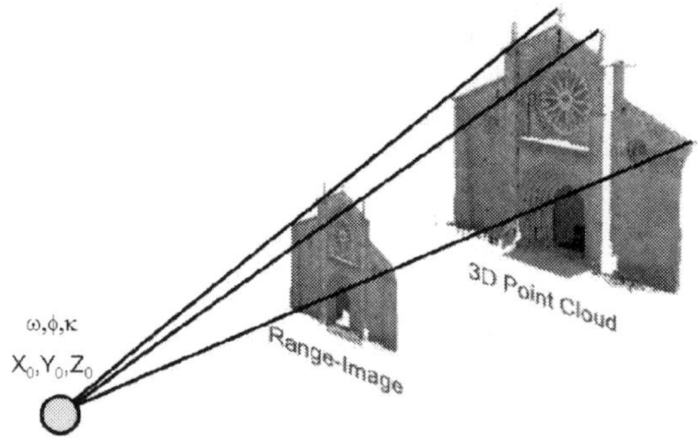

Fig. 2. Range-image generation from laser scanner point cloud

Likewise, in the procedure of generation of the *range-image* a simple algorithm of visibility (*depth correction*) should be applied since there is a high probability that two or more points of the point cloud can be projected on the same image pixel, so an incorrect discrimination of the visible and occluded parts would hinder the appropriate application of the matching procedures (section 3). This visibility algorithm consists on storing, for every pixel, the radiometric value, as well as the distance between the projected point and optic virtual camera centre (both in the laser coordinate system). In this way, every time that a point cloud receives a pair of photo-coordinates, the new pair will be received only if the former point happens to be closer to the point of view than the latter (Straßer, 1974).

2.2.2 Texture Regeneration

It is very common that the range image exhibits empty or white pixels because the object shape may lead to a non homogeneous distribution of the points in the cloud. Due to this, the perspective ray for a specific pixel may not intersect with a point in the cloud and consequently, it may happen that not all the points in the cloud have a correspondent point in the image. This lack of homogeneity in the range image texture drops the quality of the results in the matching processes because these are designed to work with the original conditions of real images. To overcome this drawback, the empty value of the pixel will be replaced by the value of some neighbouring pixels following an interpolation, based on distances (IDW - Inverse Distance Weighted) (Shepard, 1968). This method performs better than others because of its simplicity, efficiency and flexibility to adapt to swift changes in the data set. Its mathematical expression is

$$Z_k = \frac{\sum_{i=1}^{n} Z_i w_i}{\sum_{i=1}^{n} w_i} \tag{2}$$

where Z_k is the digital level of the empty pixel, Z_i are the digital values of the neighbouring pixels, w_i is the weighting factor and n is the number of points that are involved in the interpolation. Specifically this weighting factor is defined is the inverse of the square of distance between the pixel k and the i-th neighbouring pixel

$$w_i = \frac{1}{d_{k,i}^2} \tag{3}$$

The neighbouring area is defined as a standard mask of 3x3 pixels, although this size may change depending on the image conditions. In this way, we ensure a correct interpolation within the empty pixels of the image according to its specific circumstances.

Fig. 3. Before (Left) and after (Right) the texture regeneration

In (2) only one radiometric channel is addressed because the original point cloud data has only one channel (this is common for the intensity data) or because these data have been transformed from a RGB distribution in the original camera attached to the laser scanner to a single luminance value. At last, together with the creation of the range image, an equal size matrix is generated which stores the object coordinates corresponding to the point cloud. This matrix will be used in the sensor fusion procedure.

2.3 Pre-processing of the image

The target of the pre-processing of the image that comes from the digital camera and/or from the thermal camera is to provide high quality radiometric information for the point cloud. Nevertheless, before reaching this point, it is necessary to pre-process the original image in order to make it in tune with the range image in the further procedures. In the following lines we will present the steps in this pre-processing task.

2.3.1 Determination and correction of the radial distortion

One of the largest sources of error in the image is the existence of radial distortion. Particularly, in the context of the sensor fusion, the importance of the accurate determination and correction of the radial lens distortion resides in the fact that if this is not accurately corrected, we can expect that large displacements occur at the image edges, so this could lead to inadmissible errors in the matching process (Fig. 4).

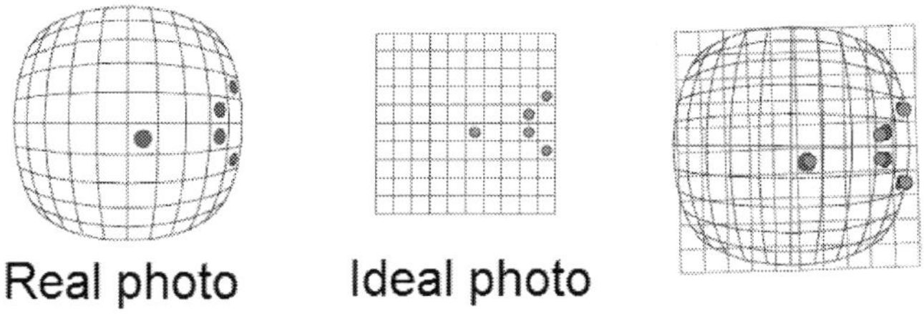

Fig. 4. Displacement due to the radial distortion (Right): Real photo (Left), Ideal Photo (Centre)

Please note in Fig. 4, how if the camera optical elements would be free from the radial distortion effects, the relationship between the image (2D) and the object (3D) would be linear, but such distortions are rather more complicated than this linear model and so, the transformation between image and object needs to account for this question.

On the other hand, in the determination of the radial distortion we find that its modelling is far from being simple because, first of all, there is little agreement at the scientific community on the standard model to render this phenomenon and this leads to difficulties in the comparison and interpretation of the different models and so, it is not easy to assess the accuracy of the methodology. As a result empirical approaches are rather used (Sánchez et al., 2004).

In our case, the radial distortion has been estimated by means of the so called Gaussian model as proposed by Brown (Brown, 1971). This model represents a "raw" determination of the radial distortion distribution and doses not account for any constraint to render the correlation between the focal length and such distribution(4).

$$dr = k_1 r'^3 + k_2 r'^5 \tag{4}$$

For the majority of the lenses and applications this polynomial can be reduced to the first term without a significant loss in accuracy.

Particularly, the parameters k_1 and k_2 in the Gaussian model have been estimated by means of the software sv3DVision Aguilera and Lahoz (2006), which enables to estimate these parameters from a single image. To achieve this, it takes advantage of the existence of diverse geometrical constraints such as straight lines and vanishing points. In those cases of study, such as archaeological cases, in which these elements are scarce, the radial distortion parameters have been computed with the aid of the open-source software Fauccal (Douskos et al., 2009).

Finally, it is important to state that the radial distortion parameters will require a constant updating, especially for consumer-grade compact cameras, since a lack of robustness and stability in their design will affect to the focal length stability. A detailed analysis of this question is developed by Sanz (2009) in its Ph.D thesis. Particularly, Sanz analysis as factors of unsteadiness of the radial lens distortion modelling the following: switching on and off, use of zooming and focus and setting of the diaphragm aperture.

Once the camera calibration parameters are known, they must be applied to correct the radial distortion effects. Nevertheless, the direct application of these parameters may produce some voids in the final image since the pixels are defined as entire numbers (Fig. 5), that is, neighbouring pixels in the original image may not maintain this condition after applying the distortion correction.

Fig. 5. Left: original image with radial distortion. Right: image without radial distortion, corrected by the direct method.

Trying to avoid this situation as well as applying an interpolation technique which would increase the computing time considerably, an indirect method based on Newton-Rapshon (Süli, 2003) has been adapted in order to correct images of radial lens distortion. Particularly, the corrected image matrix will be consider as the input data, so for every target position on such matrix (x_u,y_u), the corresponding position on the original image (x_d,y_d) will be computed.

2.3.2 Radiometric correction of the images

With the correction of the radial distortion, many of the problems of the image processing are solved but it is advisable to also correct radiometric problems such as:

Treatment of background of the visible image. Usually when we acquire an image, some additional information of the scene background that is not related with object of study is recorded. On the counterpart, the range image has as a main feature that there is any information at all corresponding to the background (by default, this information is white) because it has been defined from the distances to the object. This disagreement has an impact on the matching quality between the elements that are placed at the objects edges, since their neighbourhood and the radiometric parameters related with them become modified by scene background.

From all the elements that may appear at the background of an image shut at the outside (which is the case of the facades of architecture) the most common is the sky. This situation cannot be extrapolated to those elements in the inside or to those situations in which the illumination conditions are uniform (cloudy days), so this background correction would not be not necessary. Nevertheless, for the remaining cases in which the atmosphere appears clear, the background radiometry will be close to blue and, consequently it will turn necessary to proceed to its rejection. This is achieved thanks to its particular radiometric qualities. (Fig. 6).

Fig. 6. Before (Left) and after (Right) of rejecting the sky from camera image.

The easiest and automatic way is to compute the blue channel in the original image, that is, to obtain an image whose digital levels are the third coordinate in the RGB space and to filter it depending on this value. The sky radiometry exhibits the largest values of blue component within the image (close to a digital level of 1, ranging from 0 to 1), and far away from the blue channel values that may present the facades of buildings (whose digital level usually spans from 0.4 to 0.8). Thus, we just have to implement a conditional instruction by which all pixels whose blue channel value is higher than a certain threshold, (this threshold being controlled by the user), will be substituted by white.

Conversion of colour models: RGB->YUV. At this stage the RGB space radiometric information is transform into a scalar value of luminance. To achieve this, the YUV colour space is used because one of its main characteristics is that it is the model which renders more closely the human eye behaviour. This is done because the retina is more sensitive to the light intensity (luminance) than to the chromatic information. According to this, this space is defined by the three following components: Y (luminance component), U and V (chromatic components). The equation that relates the luminance of the YUV space with the coordinates of the RGB space is:

$$Y = 0,299 \cdot R + 0,587 \cdot G + 0,114 \cdot B \tag{5}$$

Texture extraction. With the target of accomplishing a radiometric uniformity that supports the efficient treatment of the images (range, visible and thermal) in its intensity values, a region based texture extraction has been applied. The texture information extraction for purposes of image fusion has been scarcely treated in the scientific literature but some experiments show that it could yield interesting results in those cases of low quality images (Rousseau et al., 2000; Jarc et al., 2007). The fusion procedure that has been developed will require, in particular, the texture extraction of thermal and range images. Usually, two filters are used for this type of task: Gabor (1946) or Laws (1980). In our case, we will use the Laws filter. Laws developed a set 2D convolution kernel filters which are composed by combinations of four one dimensional scalar filters. Each of these one dimensional filters will extract a particular feature from the image texture. These features are: level (L), edge (E), spot (S) and ripple (R). The one-dimensional kernels are as follows:

$$\begin{aligned} L5 &= \begin{bmatrix} 1 & 4 & 6 & 4 & 1 \end{bmatrix} \\ E5 &= \begin{bmatrix} -1 & -2 & 0 & 2 & 1 \end{bmatrix} \\ S5 &= \begin{bmatrix} -1 & 0 & 2 & 0 & -1 \end{bmatrix} \\ R5 &= \begin{bmatrix} 1 & -4 & 6 & -4 & 1 \end{bmatrix} \end{aligned} \tag{6}$$

By the convolution of these kernels we get a set of 5x5 convolution kernels:

$$\begin{matrix} L5L5 & E5L5 & S5L5 & R5L5 \\ L5E5 & E5E5 & S5E5 & R5E5 \\ L5S5 & E5S5 & S5S5 & R5S5 \\ L5R5 & E5R5 & S5R5 & R5R5 \end{matrix} \tag{7}$$

The combination of these kernels gives 16 different filters. From them, and according to (Jarc, 2007), the more useful are E5L5, S5E5, S5L5 and their transposed. Particularly, considering that our cases of study related with thermal camera correspond to architectural buildings, the filters E5L5 and L5E5 have been applied in order to extract horizontal and vertical textures, respectively.

Finally, each of the images filtered by the convolution kernels, were scaled for the range 0-255 and processed by histogram equalization and a contrast enhancement.

2.3.3 Image resizing

In the last pre-processing images step, it is necessary to bring the existing images (range, visible and thermal) to a common frame to make them agreeable. Particularly, the visible image that comes from the digital camera usually will have a large size (7-10Mp), while the range image and the thermal image will have smaller sizes. The size of the range image will depend on the points of the laser cloud while the size of the thermal image depends on the low resolution of this sensor. Consequently, it is necessary to resize images in order to have a similar size (width and height) because, on the contrary, the matching algorithms would not be successful.

An apparent solution would be to create a range and/or thermal image of the same size as the visible image. This solution presents an important drawback since in the case of the range image this would demand to increase the number of points in the laser cloud and, in the case of the thermal image, the number of thermal pixels. Both solutions would require new data acquisition procedures that would rely on the increasing of the scanning resolution in the case of the range image and, in the case of the thermal image, on the generation of a mosaic from the original images. Both approaches have been disregarded for this work because they are not flexible enough for our purposes. We have chosen to resize all the images after they have been acquired and pre-processed seeking to achieve a balance between the number of pixels of the image with highest resolution (visible), the image with lowest resolution (thermal) and the number of laser points. The equation to render this sizing transformation is the 2D affine transformation (8).

$$\mathbf{R}_{\mathrm{Img}} = \mathbf{C}_{\mathrm{Img}} \times \boldsymbol{A}_1$$
$$\mathbf{R}_{\mathrm{Img}} = \mathbf{T}_{\mathrm{Img}} \times \boldsymbol{A}_2 \quad (8)$$
$$\mathbf{A}_{1,2} = \begin{bmatrix} a & \mathrm{b} & \mathrm{c} \\ d & e & \mathrm{d} \\ 0 & 0 & 1 \end{bmatrix}$$

where $\mathbf{A_1}$ contains the affine transformation between range image and camera image, $\mathbf{A_2}$ contains the affine transformation between range image and thermal image , and $\mathbf{R_{Img}}$, $\mathbf{C_{Img}}$ y $\mathbf{T_{Img}}$ are the matrices of range image, the visible image and the thermal image, respectively.

After the resizing of the images we are prepared to start the sensor fusion.

3. Sensor fusion

One of the main targets of the fusion sensor strategy that we propose is the flexibility to use multiple sensors, so that the laser point cloud can be rendered with radiometric information and, vice versa, that the images can be enriched by the metric information provided by de laser scanner. Under this point of view, the sensor fusion processing that we will describe in the following pages will require extraction and matching approaches that can ensure: accuracy, reliability and unicity in the results.

3.1 Feature extraction

The feature extraction that will be applied over the visible, range and thermal images must yield high quality in the results with a high level of automatization, so a good approximation for the matching process can be established. More specifically, the approach must ensure the robustness of the procedure in the case of repetitive radiometric patterns, which is usually the case when dealing with buildings. Even more, we must aim at guarantying the efficient feature extraction from images from different parts of the electromagnetic spectrum. To achieve this, we will use an interest point detector that remains invariant to rotations and scale changes and an edge-line detector invariant to intensity variations on the images.

3.1.1 Extraction of interest points

In the case of range and visible images two different interest points detectors, Harris (Harris y Stephen, 1988) and Förstner (Förstner and Guelch, 1987), have been considered since there is not an universal algorithm that provide ideal results for each situation. Obviously, the user always will have the opportunity to choose the interest point detector that considers more adequate.

Harris operator provides stable and invariant spatial features that represent a good support for the matching process. This operator shows the following advantages when compared with other alternatives: high accuracy and reliability in the localization of interest points and invariance in the presence of noise. The threshold of the detector to assess the behaviour of the interest point is fixed as the relation between the eigenvector of the autocorrelation function of the kernel(9) and the standard deviation of the gaussian kernel. In addition, a non maximum elimination is applied to get the interest points:

$$R = \lambda_1\lambda_2 - k(\lambda_1 + \lambda_2) = |M| - k \cdot \mathrm{trace}(M)^2 \tag{9}$$

where R is the response parameter of the interest point, λ_1 y λ_2 are the eigenvectors of $\mathbf{M}$, k is an empiric value and $\mathbf{M}$ is the auto-correlation matrix. If R is negative, the point is labeled as edge, if R is small is labeled as a planar region and if it is positive, the point is labeled as interest point.

On the other hand, Förstner algorithm is one of the most widespread detectors in the field of terrestrial photogrammetry. Its performance (10) is based on analyzing the Hessian matrix and classifies the points as a point of interest based on the following parameters:

- The average precision of the point (w)
- The direction of the major axis of the ellipse (ϕ)
- The form of the confidence ellipse (q)

$$q = 1 - \left(\frac{\lambda_1 - \lambda_2}{\lambda_1 + \lambda_2}\right)^2 = \frac{4 \cdot |\mathbf{N}|}{\mathrm{tr}^2(\mathbf{N})} \qquad w = \frac{|\mathbf{N}|}{\frac{1}{2} \cdot \mathrm{tr}(\mathbf{N})} \tag{10}$$

where q is the ellipse circularity parameter, λ_1 and λ_2 are the eigenvalues of $\mathbf{N}$, w the point weight and $\mathbf{N}$ the Hessian matrix. The use of q-parameter allows us to avoid the edges which are not suitable for the purposes of the present approach

The recommended application of the selection criteria is as follows: firstly, remove those edges with a parameter (q) close to zero; next, check that the average precision of the point

(w) does not exceed the tolerance imposed by the user; finally, apply a non-maximum suppression to ensure that the confidence ellipse is the smallest in the neighbourhood.

3.1.2 Extraction of edges and lines

The extraction of edges and lines is oriented to the fusion of the thermal and range images which present a large variation in their radiometry due to their spectral nature: near infrared or visible (green) for the laser scanner and far infrared for the thermal camera. In this sense, the edge and lines procedure follows a multiphase and hierarchical flux based on the Canny algorithm (Canny, 1986) and the latter segmentation of such edges by means of the Burns algorithm (Burns et al., 1986).

Edge detection: Filter of Canny. The Canny edge detector is the most appropriate for the edge detection in images where there is a presence of regular elements because it meets three conditions that are determinant for our purposes:

- Accuracy in the location of edge ensuring the largest closeness between the extracted edges and actual edges.
- Reliability in the detection of the points in the edge, minimizing the probability of detecting false edges because of the presence of noise and, consequently, minimizing the loss of actual edges.
- Unicity in the obtaining of a unique edge, ensuring edges with a maximum width of one pixel.

Mainly, the Canny edge detector filter consists of a multi-phase procedure in which the user must choose three parameters: a standard deviation and two threshold levels. The result will be a binary image in which the black pixels will indicate the edges while the rest of the pixels will be white.

Line segmentation: Burns. The linear segments of an image represent one of the most important features of the digital processing since they support the interpretation in three dimensions of the scene. Nevertheless, the segmentation procedure is not straightforward because the noise and the radial distortion will complicate its accomplishment. Achieving a high quality segmentation will demand to extract as limit points of the segment those that best define the line that can be adjusted to the edge. To meet so, the segmentation procedure that has been developed is, once more, structured on a multi-phase fashion in which a series of stages are chained pursuing to obtain a set of segments (1D) defined by their limit points coordinates. The processing time of the segmentation phase will linearly depend on the number of pixels that have been labeled as edge pixels in the previous phase. From here, it becomes crucial the choice of the three Canny parameters, described above.

The segmentation phase starts with the scanning of the edge image (from up to down and from left to right) seeking for candidate pixels to be labeled as belonging to the same line. The basic idea is to group the edge pixels according to similar gradient values, being this step similar to the Burns method. In this way, every pixel will be compared with its eight neighbours for each of the gradient directions. The pixels that show a similar orientation will be labeled as belonging to the same edge: from here we will obtain a first clustering of the edges, according to their gradient.

Finally, aiming at depurating and adapting the segmentation to our purposes, the edges resulting from the labeling stage will be filtered by means of the edge least length parameter. In our case, we want to extract only those most relevant lines to describe the object in order to find the most favourable features to support the matching process. To do so, the length of the labeled edges is computed and compared with a threshold length set by the user. If this length is larger than the threshold value the edge will be turned into a segment which will receive as limit coordinates the coordinates of the centre of the first and last pixel in the edge. On the contrary, if the length is smaller than the threshold level, the edge will be rejected (Fig. 7).

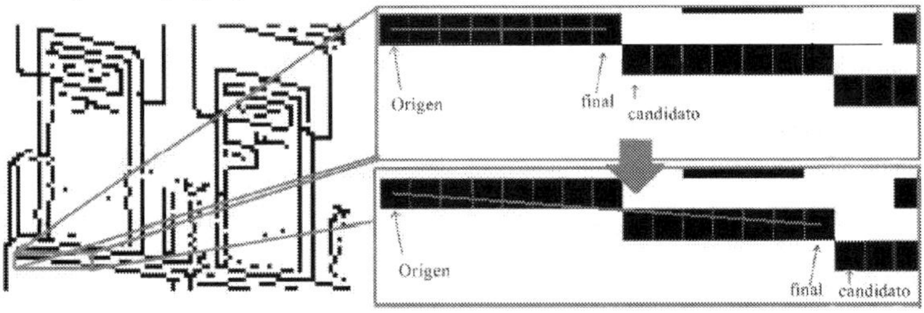

Fig. 7. Edge and line extraction with the Canny and Burns operators.

3.2 Matching

Taking into account that the images present in the fusion problem (range, visible and thermal) are very different in their radiometry, we must undertake a robust strategy to ensure a unique solution. To this end, we will deal with two feature based matching strategies: the interest point based matching strategy (Li and Zouh, 1995; Lowe, 2005) and the edge and lines based matching strategy (Dana and Anandan, 1993; Keller and Averbuch, 2006), both integrated on a hierarchical and pyramidal procedure.

3.2.1 Interest Points Based Matching

The interest point based matching will be used for the range and visible images fusion. To accomplish so, we have implemented a hierarchical matching strategy combining: correlation measures, matching, thresholding and geometrical constraints. Particularly, area-based and feature-based matching techniques have been used following the coarse-to-fine direction of the pyramid in such a way that the extracted interest points are matched among them according to their degree of similarity. At the lower levels of the pyramid, the matching task is developed through the closeness and grey level similarity within the neighbourhood. The area-based matching and cross-correlation coefficients are used as indicator (11).

$$\rho = \frac{\sigma_{HR}}{\sigma_H \sigma_R} \tag{11}$$

where p is the cross-correlation coefficient, σ_{HR} is the covariance between the windows of the visible image and the range image; σ_H is the standard deviation of the visible image and y σ_R is the standard deviation of the range image. The interest point based matching relays on closeness and similarity measures of the grey levels within the neighbourhood.

Later, at the last level of the pyramid, in which the image is processed at its real resolution the strategy will be based on the least squares matching (Grün, 1985). For this task, the initial approximations will be taken from the results of the area based matching applied on the previous levels. The localization and shape of the matching window is estimated from the initial values and recomputed until the differences between the grey levels comes to a minimum(12),

$$v = F(\bar{x}, \bar{y}) - G(ax_0 + by_0 + \Delta x + cx_0 + dy_0 + \Delta y)r_1 + r_0 \rightarrow \min \qquad (12)$$

where **F** and **G** represent the reference and the matching window respectively, $a,b,c,d,\Delta x$ y Δy are the geometric parameters of an affine transformation while r_1 and r_0 are the radiometric parameters of a linear transformation, more precisely, the gain and the offset, respectively.

Finally, even though the matching strategy has been applied in a hierarchical fashion, the particular radiometric properties of both images, especially the range image, may lead to many mismatches that would affect the results of the sensor fusion. Hence, the proposed approach has been reinforced including geometric constraints relying on the epipolar lines (Zhang et al., 1995; Han and Park, 2000). Particularly and taking into account the case of the laser scanner and the digital camera, given a 3D point in object space P, and being p_r and p_v its projections on the range and visible images, respectively and being O_l and O_c the origin of the laser scanner and the digital camera, respectively, we have that the plane defined by P, O_l and O_c is named the epipolar plane. The intersections of the epipolar plane with the range and visible image define the epipolar lines l_r and l_v. The location of an interest point on the range image p_r, that matches a point p_v on the visible image matching is constrained to lay at the epipolar line l_r of the range image (Fig. 8). To compute these epipolarity constraints, the Fundamental Matrix is used (Hartley, 1997) using eight homologous points as input (Longuet-Higgins, 1981). In this way, once we have computed the Fundamental Matrix we can build the epipolar geometry and limit the search space for the matching points to one dimension: the epipolar line. As long as this strategy is an iterative process, the threshold levels to be applied in the matching task will vary in an adaptative way until we have reduced the search as much as possible and reach the maximum accuracy and reliability.

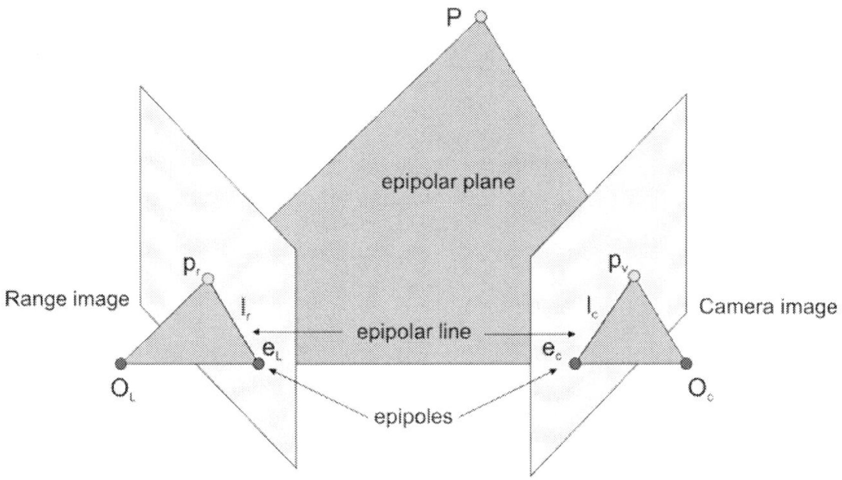

Fig. 8. Epipolar geometry used as geometric constraints in the matching process.

In order to ensure the accuracy of the Fundamental Matrix, the iterative strategy has been supported by RANSAC algorithm (RANdom SAmpling Consensus) (Fischler and Bolles, 1981). This technique computes the mathematical model for a randomly selected dataset and evaluates the number of points of the global dataset which satisfy this model by a given threshold. The final accepted model will be that one which incorporates the larger set of points and the minimum error.

3.2.2 Line based matching

The line based matching will be used for the range and thermal images fusion. Given the intrinsic properties of thermal image, it is not advisable to use the strategy outlined above since the radiometric response of thermal image is not related at all with the range image. This leads to a complication of the matching process when it is based on interest points and even to an ill-conditioned problem since a lot of interest points could not be matched.

The solution proposed takes advantage of line based matching (Hintz & Zhao, 1990; Schenk, 1986) that exploits the direction criterion, distance criterion and attribute similarity criterion in a combined way. Nevertheless, this matching process is seriously limited by the ill-conditioning of both images: the correspondence can be of several lines to one (due to discontinuities), several lines regarded as independent may be part of the same, some lines may be wrong or may not exist at all (Luhmman et al., 2006). This is the reason for the pre-processing of these images according to a texture filtering (Laws, 1980) as described in the section (2.3.2). This will yield four images with a larger radiometric similarity degree and with horizontal and vertical textures extracted on which we can support our line based matching.

On the following lines we describe the three criteria we have applied for the line based matching:

Direction criterion. We will take as an approach criterion to the line based matching the classification of these lines according to their direction. To this end, we take the edge orientation and the own gradient of the image as reference. The main goal in this first step is to classify the lines according to their horizontal and vertical direction, rejecting any other direction. In those cases in which we work with oblique images, a more sophisticated option could be applied to classify the linear segments according to the three main directions of the object (x,y,z) based on vanishing points (Gonzalez-Aguilera y Gomez-Lahoz, 2008).

Distance criterion. Once we have classified the lines according to their direction we will take their distance attribute as the second criterion to search for the homologous line. Obviously, considering the different radiometric properties of both images, an adaptative threshold should be established since the distance of a matched line could present variations.

Intersection criterion. In order to reinforce the matching of lines based on their distance, a specific strategy has been developed based on computing intersections between lines (corner points). Particularly, a buffer area (50x50 pixels) is defined where horizontal and vertical lines are enlarged to their intersection. In this sense, those lines that find a similar intersection points will be labelled as homologous lines.

As a result of the application of these three criterions, a preliminary line based matching based on the fundamental matrix will be performed (see section 3.2.1). More precisely, the best eight intersections of lines matched perform as input data in the fundamental matrix. Once we have computed the Fundamental Matrix we can build the epipolar geometry and limit the search space for the matching lines to one dimension: the epipolar line. As long as this strategy is an iterative process, the threshold levels to be applied in the matching task will vary in an adaptative way until we have reduced the search as much as possible and reach the maximum accuracy and reliability.

4. Spatial resection

Once we have solved the matching task, through which we have related the images to each other (range image, visible image and thermal image) we proceed to solve the spatial resection. The parameters to be determined are the exterior parameters of the cameras (digital and thermal) respect of the laser scanner.

The question of the spatial resection is well known on the classic aerial photogrammetry (Kraus, 1997). It is solved by the establishment of the relationship of the image points, the homologous object points and the point of view through a collinearity constraint (1).

We must have in mind that the precision of the data on both systems (image and object) is different since their lineage is different, so we must write an adequate weighting for the stochastic model. This will lead to the so called unified approach to least squares adjustment (Mikhail and Ackerman, 1976) in the form:

$$L + BV + AX = 0 \tag{13}$$

where **L** is the independent term vector, **B** is the jacobian matrix of the observations, **V** is the vector of the residuals, **A** is the jacobian matrix of the unknowns and **X** is the vector of unknowns. The normal equation system we get after applying the criterion of least squares is in the form:

$$A^T M^{-1} A\hat{x} + A^T M^{-1} L = 0 \qquad \text{where } M = \left[BW^{-1}B^T \right] \tag{14}$$

This equation is equivalent to the least squares solution we obtain when directly solving for the so called observation equation system. In this case we can say that the matrix **M** plays the role of weighting the equations (instead of the observations). Please note that this matrix is obtained from the weighting of the observations (through the matrix **W**) and from the functional relationship among them expressed the jacobian matrix (matrix **B**). In this way, this matrix operates in the equation system as a geometrical counterpart of the metrical relationship between the precision of the different observations (image and object).

From the equation (13) and its solution (14) we can obtain the adjusted residuals:

$$V = -W^{-1}B^T \left[BW^{-1}B^T \right]^{-1} \left[AX - L \right] \tag{15}$$

According to the covariance propagation law (Mikhail and Ackermann, 1976), the cofactor matrix of the estimated parameters is obtained from the equation:

$$\begin{aligned} Q_{\hat{x}} &= -\left(A^T M^{-1} A\right)^{-1} A^T M^{-1} Q_L \left(-M^{-1} A \left(A^T M^{-1} A\right)^{-1}\right) = \left(A^T M^{-1} A\right)^{-1} \\ Q_L &= BW^{-1}B^T = M \end{aligned} \tag{16}$$

and so, the covariance matrix of the spatial resection is given by:

$$C_{\hat{x}} = \sigma_0^2 Q_{\hat{x}} \tag{17}$$

The square root of the elements in the main diagonal of the matrix provides the standard deviation of the exterior orientation parameters.
Finally, the mean square error is obtained from:

$$\text{e.m.c.} = \sqrt{\frac{V^T W V}{2n - 6}} \tag{18}$$

On the other side, with the aim of comparing the results and analyzing its validity we have also solved the spatial resection by means of the so called Direct Linear Transformation

(DLT) (Abdel-Aziz, 1971). This method represented and innovation in phtogrammetry because allow us to relate the instrumental coordinates with the object coordinates without undertaking the intermediate steps (interior and exterior orientation). This approach allows us to solve without knowing camera parameters (focal length and principal point position) making the procedure especially interesting for non-metric cameras. Another advantage is that it could be solved as a linear model and thus, avoiding the iterative approach and the need of providing initial approximations for the unknowns

The DLT equations results from a re-parameterization of the collinearity equations (Kraus, 1997) in the following way,

$$\begin{bmatrix} x_A - x_p \\ y_A - y_p \\ -f \end{bmatrix} = \lambda \cdot R \cdot \begin{bmatrix} X_A - X_S \\ Y_A - Y_S \\ Z_A - Z_S \end{bmatrix} \tag{19}$$

in which (X_S, Y_S, Z_S) are the object coordinates of the point of view, (X_A, Y_A, Z_A) are the object coordinates of an object point and (x_A, y_A) are the image coordinates of an image point homologous of the first, f is the focal length, (x_p, y_p) are the image coordinates of the principal point, **R** is the 3x3 rotation matrix and λ is the scale factor.

If we expand the terms and divide the equations among them to eliminate the scale factor we have:

$$\begin{aligned} x_A &= \frac{(x_p r_{31} - f r_{11}) X_A + (x_p r_{32} - f r_{12}) Y_A + (x_p r_{33} - f r_{13}) Z_A - (x_p r_{31} - f r_{11}) X_S - (x_p r_{32} - f r_{12}) Y_S - (x_p r_{33} - f r_{13}) Z_S}{r_{31} X_A + r_{32} Y_A + r_{33} Z_A - (r_{31} X_S + r_{32} Y_S + r_{33} Z_S)} \\ y_A &= \frac{(y_p r_{31} - f r_{21}) X_A + (y_p r_{32} - f r_{22}) Y_A + (y_p r_{33} - f r_{23}) Z_A - (y_p r_{31} - f r_{21}) X_S - (y_p r_{32} - f r_{22}) Y_S - (y_p r_{33} - f r_{23}) Z_S}{r_{31} X_A + r_{32} Y_A + r_{33} Z_A - (r_{31} X_S + r_{32} Y_S + r_{33} Z_S)} \end{aligned} \tag{20}$$

Rearranging and renaming, we finally get the DLT expression:

$$x_A = \frac{L_1 X_A + L_2 Y_A + L_3 Z_A + L_4}{L_9 X_A + L_{10} Y_A + L_{11} Z_A + 1} \qquad y_A = \frac{L_5 X_A + L_6 Y_A + L_7 Z_A + L_8}{L_9 X_A + L_{10} Y_A + L_{11} Z_A + 1} \tag{21}$$

This expression relates image coordinates (x_A, y_A) with the object coordinates (X_A, Y_A, Z_A), and consequently, it is useful to reference the images to the laser model. The relationship between the mathematical parameters $(L_1, \ldots, L_{11})$ and the geometrical parameters is as follows:

$$
\begin{aligned}
&L_1 = \frac{x_p r_{31} - f r_{11}}{D} \quad L_2 = \frac{x_p r_{32} - f r_{12}}{D} \quad L_3 = \frac{x_p r_{33} - f r_{13}}{D} \\
&L_4 = \frac{\left(f r_{11} - x_p r_{31}\right) X_S + \left(f r_{12} - x_p r_{32}\right) Y_S + \left(f r_{13} - x_p r_{33}\right) Z_S}{D} \\
&L_5 = \frac{y_p r_{31} - f r_{21}}{D} \quad L_6 = \frac{y_p r_{32} - f r_{22}}{D} \quad L_7 = \frac{y_p r_{33} - f r_{23}}{D} \\
&L_8 = \frac{\left(f r_{21} - y_p r_{31}\right) X_S + \left(f r_{22} - y_p r_{32}\right) Y_S + \left(f r_{23} - y_p r_{33}\right) Z_S}{D} \\
&L_9 = \frac{r_{31}}{D} \quad L_{10} = \frac{r_{32}}{D} \quad L_{11} = \frac{r_{33}}{D} \\
&D = -\left(r_{31} X_S + r_{32} Y_S + r_{33} Z_S\right)
\end{aligned} \tag{22}
$$

The inverse relationship is:

$$
\begin{aligned}
&\begin{bmatrix} X_S \\ Y_S \\ Z_S \end{bmatrix} = \begin{bmatrix} L_1 & L_2 & L_3 \\ L_5 & L_6 & L_7 \\ L_9 & L_{10} & L_{11} \end{bmatrix}^{-1} \begin{bmatrix} -L_4 \\ -L_8 \\ -1 \end{bmatrix} \\
&x_p = \frac{L_1 L_9 + L_2 L_{10} + L_3 L_{11}}{L_9^2 + L_{10}^2 + L_{11}^2} \\
&y_p = \frac{L_5 L_9 + L_6 L_{10} + L_7 L_{11}}{L_9^2 + L_{10}^2 + L_{11}^2} \\
&R = \begin{bmatrix} r_{11} & r_{12} & r_{13} \\ r_{21} & r_{22} & r_{23} \\ r_{31} & r_{32} & r_{33} \end{bmatrix} = D \cdot \begin{bmatrix} \frac{x_p L_9 - L_1}{f} & \frac{x_p L_{10} - L_2}{f} & \frac{x_p L_{11} - L_3}{f} \\ \frac{y_p L_9 - L_5}{f} & \frac{y_p L_{10} - L_6}{f} & \frac{y_p L_{10} - L_7}{f} \\ L_9 & L_{10} & L_{11} \end{bmatrix} \\
&D^2 = \frac{1}{L_9^2 + L_{10}^2 + L_{11}^2}
\end{aligned} \tag{23}
$$

To solve the spatial resection both models are effective. Nevertheless, some differences must be remarked:

- DLT is a linear model and therefore it does not require neither an iterative process nor initial values for the first iteration (both derived from de Taylor series expansion).

- The number of parameters to be solved when using the DLT is 11 and so, we need at least to have measured 6 control points (2 equations for each point) whereas the number of parameters to be solved when using the collinearity equations is directly 6 (if we are only solving for the exterior orientation or 9 (if we are solving for the exterior orientation and for the three parameters of the interior orientation that the describe the camera without taking into account any systematic error such a as radial lens distortion). Therefore, we will need three control points in the first case, and five in the second case.

Concerning the reliability of the spatial resection, it is important to stress that in spite of robust computing methods that we have applied at the matching stage, there may still persist some mismatching on the candidates homologous points and so the final accuracy could be reduced. These blunders are not easy to detect because in the adjustment its influence is distributed over all the points. As is well known, the least squares approach allows to detect blunders when the geometry is robust, that is, when the conditioning of the design matrix **A** is good but when the geometry design is weak the high residual which should be related with the gross error is distributed over other residuals. Consequently, it becomes necessary to apply statistical tests such as the Test of Baarda (Baarda, 1968), and/or the Test of Pope (Pope, 1976), as well as robust estimators that can detect and eliminate such wrong observations.

Regarding the statistical tests, they are affected by some limitations, some of which are related with the workflow described up to here. These are:

- If the data set present a bias, that is, the errors do not follow a gaussian distribution the statistical tests will lose a large part of its performance
- Form the actual set of available statistical tests, only the test of Pope can work without knowing previously the variance of the observations. Unfortunately, this is usually the case in photogrammetry.
- As stated before, in the case of working under a weak geometry, the probability that these tests do not perform adequately greatly increases. In addition, these tests are only able of rejecting one observation at each iteration.

On the contrary, these statistical tests exhibit the advantage that they may be applied in a fully automated fashion, and thus avoiding the interaction with the user.

The test of **Baarda** (Baarda, 1968), assumes that the theoretical variance is not known and therefore will use the a priori variance (σ_0^2). It also works on the assumption that the standard deviation of the observations is known. The test is based on the fact that the residuals are normally (gaussian) distributed. The test indicator is the normalised residual (z_i), defined as:

$$z_i = \frac{(Pv)_i}{\sigma_0\sqrt{(PQ_{vv}P)_{ii}}} \tag{24}$$

where P is the matrix of weights, v_i is the i-th residual, and $\mathbf{Q_{vv}}$ is the cofactor matrix of the residuals. This indicator is compared with the critical value of the test to accept or reject the null hypothesis (H_0). It is defined by:

$$T_b \sim N_{\alpha/2} = \sqrt{F_{1,\infty,\alpha}} = \sqrt{\chi^2_{1,\infty,\alpha}} \tag{25}$$

Where α is the significance level, N represents the normal distribution, F is the distribution of Fischer-Snedecor and χ is the Square - Chi table.

The critical value of Baarda (T_b) takes into account the level of significance as well as the power of the test. Therefore, it is very common that certain combinations of α and β are used in the majority of cases. The most common is α=0,1 % and β=20%, which leads to a critical value of 3,291.

If the null hypothesis is rejected, we will assume that there is gross error among the observations. Therefore, the procedure will consist on eliminating from the adjustment the point with the largest typified residual and repeating the test of Baarda to check if there are more gross errors. The iterative application of this strategy is called *data snooping* (Kraus, 1997) and permits to detect multiple blunders and to reject them from the adjustment.

The test of **Pope** (Pope, 1976) is used when the a priori variance (σ_0^2) is not known or is not possible to be determined. In its place the a posteriori variance (26) is used.

$$\hat{\sigma}_0^2 = \frac{V^T P V}{r} \tag{26}$$

This statistic test is usually applied in Photogrammetry since it is very common that the a priori variance is not known. The null hypothesis (H_0) is that all the residuals (v_i) follow a normal (gaussian) distribution N(0,σ) such that its variance is the residual normalized variance.

$$\sigma \equiv \sigma_{\hat{V}_i} = \hat{\sigma}_0 \sqrt{q_{ii}} \tag{27}$$

where q_{vivi} is the i.th element of the main diagonal of the cofactor matrix of the residuals ($\mathbf{Q_{vv}}$). On the contrary, the alternative hypothesis (H_a) states that the in the set of observations there is a gross error that does not behave according to the normal distribution and, thus, must be eliminated. Thus, we establish as statistical indicator the standardised residuals (w_i) that is obtained as:

$$w_i = \frac{v_i}{\hat{\sigma}_0 \sigma_{Vi}} \tag{28}$$

Please note that in this test we use the standardised residuals (w_i), while in the test of Baarda we use the normalised residual (z_i). The only difference is the use of the a posteriori and a priori variance, respectively.

Since the residuals are computed using the a posteriori variance they will not be normally distributed (25)but rather will follow a Tau distribution. The critical value of the Tau distribution may be computed from the tables of the t-student distribution (Heck, 1981) according to:

$$\tau_{r,\alpha_0/2,} = \sqrt{\frac{r\cdot\left(t_{r-1,\alpha_0/2}\right)^2}{r-1+\left(t_{r-1,\alpha_0/2}\right)^2}} \tag{29}$$

where r are the degree of freedom of the adjustment and α_0 the significance level for a single observation that is computing from the total significance level (α) and the number of observations (n):

$$\alpha_0 = 1-\left(1-\alpha\right)^{\frac{1}{n}} \approx \frac{\alpha}{n} \tag{30}$$

If the alternative hypothesis is accepted, the standardised residual w_i will be regarded as a blunder and hence will be eliminated from the adjustment. The procedure is repeated until the null hypothesis is verified for all the remaining points in a similar way as has been done with the data snooping technique, described above.

In addition to the statistical tests described before it is possible (and recommended) to include in the parameter computation a robust estimator to complete the least squares technique. While the base for the statistical estimators is the progressive suppression of the gross errors, the robust estimators technique sets a low weighting of the bad observations and keeps them in the adjustment. These weights depend on the inverse of the magnitude of the residual itself and so error the bad observations are "punished" with low weights which leads in time to a worse residual and to lower weight. The main feature of the robust estimators is they minimize a function different than the sum of squares of the residuals and this is accomplished by modifying on each iteration the weight matrix.

There are many robust estimators (Domingo, 2000), because each of them modifies the weighting function in a particular way. The most common robust estimators are:

Sum Minimum $$p\left(v_i\right) = \frac{1}{\left|v_i\right|} \tag{31}$$

Huber

$$p(v) = \begin{cases} 1 & \text{para} \left|v\right|/\sigma \le a \\ \dfrac{a}{\left|v\right|/\sigma} & \text{para} \left|v\right|/\sigma > a \end{cases}$$

Modified Danish

$$p(v_i) = e^{-\left|v_i\right|^2}$$

In our case, the three robust estimators (31) have been implemented, adapted and combined with the statistical estimators in the spatial resection adjustment in order to detect the gross errors and to improve the accuracy and the reliability of the sensor fusion. Particularly, the robust estimators have been applied on the first iterations to filter the observations from the worst blunders and afterwards, the statistical tests have been applied to detect and eliminate the rest of the gross errors.

5. Experimental results

In order to assess the capabilities and limitations of the methodology of sensor fusion developed, some experiments have been undertaken by using the USALign software (González-Aguilera et al., 2009). In the following pages, tree case studies are outlined. The reasons for presenting these cases are based on the possibilities of integrating different sensors: laser scanner, digital camera and thermal camera.

5.1 Case of study: Hermitage of San Segundo

The church of San Segundo is a Romanesque church of the XI century (built between 1130 and 1160) placed at the banks of the river Adaja (Avila, Spain). Its south facade (studied for this case) is the only part that has been preserved from the original building.

5.1.1 Problem and goal

The principal facade of the hermitage of San Segundo presents a favourable shape for the sensor fusion since it is similar to a plane and exhibits a large number of singular elements. The sensors used for this work are: a phase shift laser scanner, Faro Photon 80, and a reflex digital camera, Nikon D80. The input data, acquired by these sensors are: a high density point cloud: 1.317.335 points with a spatial resolution of 6mm at a distance of 10 m with the cartesian coordinates (*xyz*) and an intensity value (*int*) from the near infrared part of the electromagnetic spectrum (specifically of 785nm); an image with a size of 3872 x 2592 pixels. This camera image is shut from a position close to the centre of the laser scanner.

The goal is to obtain a 3D textured mapping from the fusion of both sensors. In this way, we will be able to render with high accuracy the facade and consequently, to help on its documentation, dissemination and preservation.

5.1.2 Methodology and results

The laser point cloud is pre-processed to obtain the range image by means of the collinearity equation while the digital image is pre-processed in order to make both sources similar between them.

Particularly, in the generation of the range image a total of 6719 points have been processed. This step implies an improvement of the range image quality by correcting the empty pixels and by increasing the resolution which is usually lower than the digital camera resolution. The digital camera image is corrected of the effects of radial lens distortion. The three values of the RGB space are reduced to only the red channel because this is close enough to the wavelength of the laser Faro (Fig. 9)

Fig. 9. Input data. Left: Image acquired with the digital camera. Right: Range image acquired with the laser scanner.

The next step is to apply an interest point extraction procedure, by means of the Förstner operator working on criteria of precision and circularity. After it, a robust matching procedure based on a hierarchical approach is carried on with the following parameters: cross correlation coefficient: 0.70 and search kernel size: 15 pixels. As a result, we obtain 2677 interest points from which only 230 are identified as homologous points. This low percentage is due to the differences in textures of both images. In addition, the threshold chosen for the matching is high in order to provide good input data for the next step: the computation of the Fundamental Matrix. This Matrix is computed by means of the algorithm of Longuet-Higgins with a threshold of 2.5 pixels and represents the base for establishing the epipolar constraints. Once these are applied, the number of homologous points increased to 317 (Fig. 10)

Fig. 10. Point matching based on epipolar constraints. Left: Digital image. Right: range image.

The next step is to obtain the exterior parameters of the camera in the laser point cloud system. An iterative procedure based on the spatial resection adjustment is used in combination with robust estimators as well as the statistical test of Pope. 18 points are eliminated as a result of this process. The output is the position and attitude parameters of the camera related to the point cloud and some quality indices that give an idea of the accuracy of the fusion process of both sensors (Table 2).

Rotation (Grad)			Translation (mm)			Quality indices	
ω	φ	κ	X_0	Y_0	Z_0	σ_{XoYoZo} (mm)	$\sigma_{0,xy}$ (pixels)
107.6058	11.3030	2.5285	-252.0	1615.4	18.2	21.4	0.66

Table 2. Parameters and quality indices of the robust estimation of the spatial resection of the digital camera referenced to the laser scanner.

Finally, once the spatial resection parameters have been computed a texture map is obtained (Fig. 11). This allows us to integrate under the same product both the radiometric properties of the high resolution camera and the metric properties of the laser scanner.

Fig. 11. Left: Back projection error on pixels with a magnification factor of 10. Right: Texture mapping as the result of the fusion of both sensors

5.2 Case study 2: Rock paintings at the Cave of Llonín

The snaky shaped sign of the cave of Llonin, placed in Asturias (Spain) poses a special challenge for the sensor fusion of the laser scanner and the digital camera. This challenge is double: on one side, it is a geometrical challenge since we have to deal with an irregular surface composed by convex and concave elements and, on the other side, it is a radiometric challenge since the illumination conditions are poor as usual at underground places and besides this the preservation conditions of the paintings are deficient.

5.2.1 Problem and goal

The workspace is focused on the most important part of the rock paintings of the cave, the snaky shaped sign. The sensors used for this work are: a time of flight laser scanner, Trimble GX200, and a reflex digital camera, Nikon D80. The input data, acquired by these sensors are: a high density point cloud (153.889 points with a spatial resolution of 5 mm) with the cartesian coordinates (*xyz*) and an intensity value (*int*) from the visible part of the electromagnetic spectrum (specifically of 534nm, that is, green); an image with a size of 3872 x 2592 pixels.

The goal is to obtain a 3D textured mapping from the fusion of both sensors. In this way, we will be able to render with high accuracy the rocky paintings of the Cave of Llonín and, hence, we will contribute to its representation and preservation.

5.2.2 Methodology and results

The laser point cloud is pre-processed to obtain the range image by means of the collinearity equation while the digital image is pre-processed in order to make both sources similar between them.

Particularly, in the generation of the range image a total of 6480 points have been processed. This step yields an improvement in the image quality by enhancing the effects of the empty pixels and by increasing the resolution which is usually lower than the digital camera resolution. The digital image will be corrected of radial lens distortion effects and transformed from the RGB values to luminance values as described in the section (2.3.2) (Fig. 12).

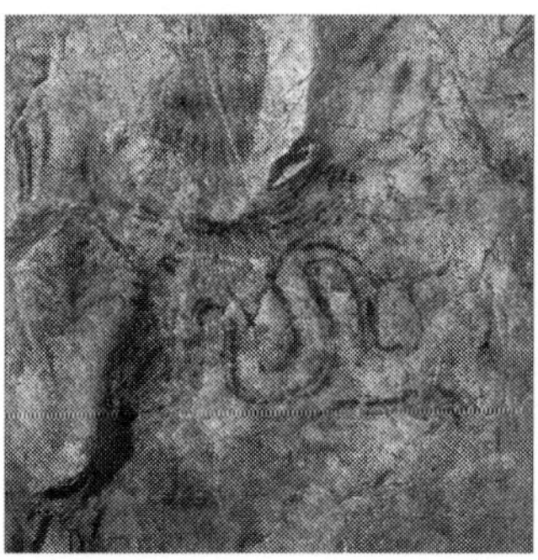

Fig. 12. Input data. Left: Image acquired with the camera. Right: Range image acquired with the laser scanner.

The next step is to apply an interest point extraction procedure, by means of the Harris operator and a robust matching procedure based on a hierarchical approach with the following parameters: cross correlation coefficient: 0.80 and search kernel size: 15 pixels. As a result, we obtain 1461 interest points from which only 14 are identified as homologous points. This low rate is due to the low uncertainty while trying to bridge the gap between the textures of both images. In addition, the threshold chosen for the matching is high to avoid bad results that could distort the computation of the Fundamental Matrix. This Matrix is computed by means of the algorithm of Longuet-Higgins with a threshold of 2.5 pixels and represents the base for establishing the epipolar constraints. This, in time, leads to an improvement of the procedure and thus the matching yields as much as 63 homologous points (Fig. 13).

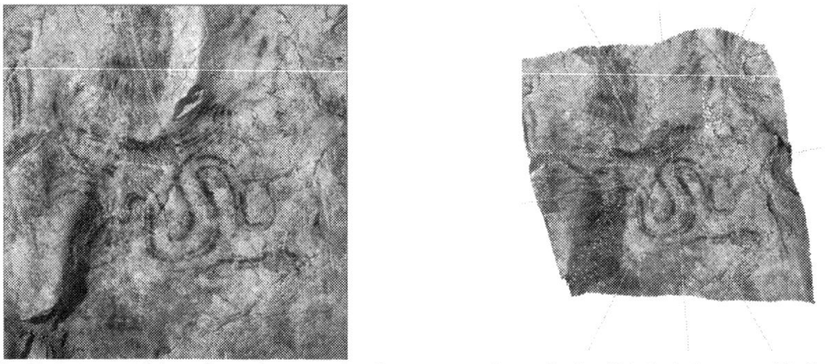

Fig. 13. Point matching based on epipolar constraints. Left: Digital image. Right: range image.

Afterwards, the exterior parameters of the camera are referenced to the laser point cloud in an iterative procedure based on the spatial resection adjustment in which robust estimators as well as the statistical test of Pope play a major role. As a result, we obtain the following parameters: position and attitude of the camera related to the point cloud and some quality indices that give an idea of the accuracy of the fusion process of both sensors (Table 3).

Rotation (Grad)			Translation (mm)			Quality indices	
ω	φ	κ	X_0	Y_0	Z_0	$\sigma_{X_0Y_0Z_0}$ (mm)	$\sigma_{0,xy}$ (píxeles)
122.3227	20.6434	16.9354	962.9	23665.1	-7921.1	124	2.5

Table 3. Parameters and quality indices of the robust estimation of the spatial resection of the digital camera referenced to the laser scanner.

Finally, once the spatial resection parameters are computed, a texture map is obtained (Fig. 14). This allows us to integrate under the same product both the radiometric properties of the high resolution camera and the metric properties of the laser scanner.

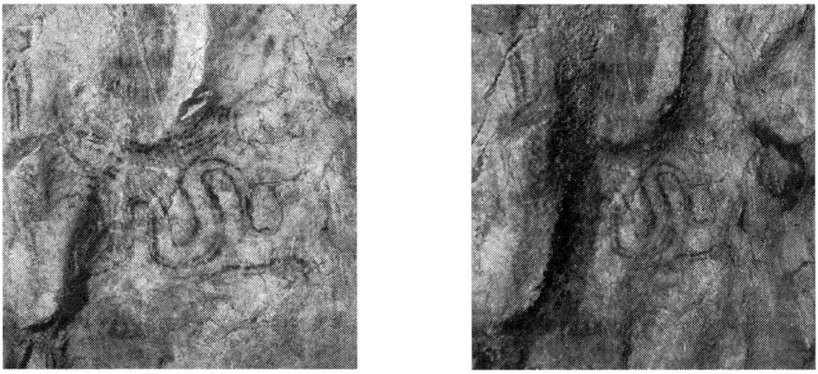

Fig. 14. Left: Back projection error on pixels with a magnification factor of 5. Right: Texture mapping as the result of the fusion of both sensors.

5.3 Case studio 3: architectural building

The next case study is related with a modern architectural building situated at the University of Vigo (Spain), and has a special interest in the context of the fusion of the laser scanner and the thermal image since the results could be exploited in the study of the energetic efficiency of the building.

5.3.1 Problem and goal

The basic problem is to overcome the radiometric problems due to the spectral differences of each sensor. The target is twofold: on one side, to solve the matching of two largely different images: the range image generated from the laser scanner and thermal image acquired with the thermal camera. On the other side, try to demonstrate the usefulness of the sensor fusion in order to attain hybrid products such as thermal 3D models and orthofotos. The following tables (Table 4), (Table 5) and figure (Fig. 15) show the technical specifications of the sensors.

	Principle	FOV	Range	Spot size	Speed	Accuracy	Wavelength	External Camera
Faro Photon 80	CW	H360° V320°	0.60-72m	3.3mm	120000 points/sec	2mm @25m	785 nm (Near Infrared)	Y

Table 4. Technical specifications: Faro Photon laser scanner

	Thermographic Measuring Range	Spatial Resolution	Spectral Range	FOV	Focusing Range	Image Resolution	Quantization
SC640 FLIRGX200	-40° at +1,500°	0.65 mrad (1cm at 30m)	7.5-13µm	24° (H) x 18° (V)	50 cm to infinity	640x480 pixels	14 bit

Table 5. Technical specifications: FLIR SC640 thermal camera

Fig. 15. Faro Photon (Left); FLIR SC640 thermal camera (Right).

5.3.2 Methodology and results

The workspace is the facade of a modern concrete building covered with panels and located at the University of Vigo (Spain). Particularly, the density of the laser scanner point cloud is high (above 2.8 million points with an object resolution of 10mm). This leads to a range image with enough resolution (1333x600 pixels) to ensure an adequate feature extraction.

Nevertheless, in the case of the thermal image, we find the opposite situation: the resolution is low (640x480 pixels) and the pixel size projected on the object taking into account the technical specifications and a shutting distance of 20 metres, is of 5 cm. The following image (Fig. 16) shows the input data of this case study.

Fig. 16. Input data: (Left) Range image (GSD 1 cm) obtained with the laser scanner Faro Photon. (Right) Thermal image (GSD 5 cm) acquired with the thermal camera SC640 FLIR.

In relation with the methodology we have developed, it can be divided in four parts: i) pre-processing of the range and thermal images ii) feature extraction and matching iii) registration of the images iv) generation of hybrid products.

The pre-processing automatic tasks to prepare the images for the matching process are diverse. Nevertheless, due to the specific properties of the images, the most important stage undertaken at this level is a texture extraction based on the Laws filters. In this way, we achieve to uniform the images. Particularly, the range and thermal images are convoluted with the filters E5L5 and L5E5 which are sensitive to horizontal and vertical edges respectively (Fig. 17). Both images of each case are added to obtain an output image free from any orientation bias.

(a) (b) (c) (d)

Fig. 17. Texture images derived from the range image (a)(b) and thermal image (c)(d).

Afterwards, we apply a feature extraction process and matching. Particularly, edges and lines are extracted by using the Canny and Burns operators, respectively. The working parameters for these operators are: deviation: (1), Gaussian kernel size: 5x5, superior threshold: 200, inferior threshold: 40 and minimum length of lines: 20 pixels. A total amount of 414 linear segments are extracted for the range image whereas the number of segments extracted for the thermal image is 487 (Fig. 18).

Fig. 18. Linear features extraction on the range image (Left) and on the thermal image (Right) after applying the Canny and Burns operators.

In the next step, and taking into account the extracted linear features and their attributes: direction, length and intersection, a feature based matching procedure is undertaken. Particularly, the intersection between the most favourable horizontal and vertical lines is computed and used as input data in the fundamental matrix. As a result, the epipolar constraints are applied iteratively to reinforce the lines matching and thus to compute the registration of thermal camera supported by robust estimators and the statistical test of Pope. The following table (Table 6) shows the results of this stage.

Rotation (Grad)			Translation (mm)			Quality indices	
ω	φ	κ	X_0	Y_0	Z_0	$\sigma_{X_0Y_0Z_0}$ (mm)	$\sigma_{0,xy}$ (pixels)
98.9243	184.2699	-1.3971	2087.3	-259.8	212.9	130	0.9

Table 6. Resulting parameters of the spatial resection supported by the test of Pope.

Finally, once both sensors are registered to each other the following products could be derived: a 3D thermal model and thermal orthofoto (Fig. 19). These hybrid products combine the qualitative properties of the thermal image with the quantitative properties of the laser point cloud. In fact, the orthophoto may be used as matrix where the rows and columns are related with the planimetric coordinates of the object while the pixel value represents the temperature.

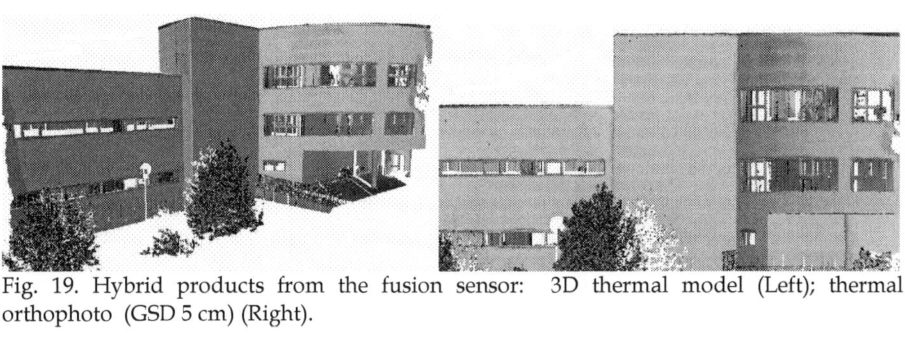

Fig. 19. Hybrid products from the fusion sensor: 3D thermal model (Left); thermal orthophoto (GSD 5 cm) (Right).

6. Conclusions and future perspectives

The presented chapter has presented and developed a semi-automatic fusion of three sensors: a terrestrial laser scanner, a reflex digital camera and a thermal camera. Through this new approach, a central issue for the integration of sensor technology has been solved efficiently using precise and reliable data processing schemes. It was demonstrated with different practical examples tested through the developed tool "USAlign".

With relation to the most relevant advantages of the proposed approach, we could remark on:

The integration of sensors, regarding the three sensors analyzed here (laser scanner, digital image and thermal image) is feasible and that an automatization of the process may be achieved. In this way, we can overcome the incomplete character of the information derived from only one sensor.

More specifically, we have seen that the initial difference between the sources: geometric differences, radiometric differences and spectral differences may be solved if we take advantage of the multiple procedures that the photogrammetric and the computer vision communities have been developing for the last two decades.

In this sense, it is also important to stress that these strategies must work: a) on a pre-processing and processing level; b) on a multi-disciplinary fashion where strategies are developed to take advantage of the strength of certain approaches while minimize the weaknesses of others; c) taking advantage of iterative and hierarchical approaches based on the idea that the first low accurate and simple solutions are the starting point of a better approximation that can only be undertaken if the previous one is good enough.

On the other hand, the main drawbacks that have been manifested from this work are:

The processing is still far away from acceptable computing times. At least on the unfavorable cases (case 2 and 3) we think that is still a long way to go on reducing the computing time. We think that seeking for a better integration of the diverse strategies that has been used or developing new ones may lead to an optimization in this sense.

Likewise the full automatization target is fairly improvable. The user interaction is required mainly to define threshold levels and there is a wide field of research to improve this. It is important to note that this improvement should not rely on a higher complexity of the procedures involved in the method since this would punish the previous question of the computation effort. So this is a sensitive problem that must be undertaken in holistic way.

The data and processing presented here deal with conventional image frames. It would be a great help if approaches to include line-scanning cameras or fish eye cameras would be proposed.

Finally regarding with future working lines, the advantages and drawbacks stated before point out the main lines to work on in the future. Some new strategies should be tested on the immediate future: to develop a line based computation of the spatial resection, to develop a self calibration process to render both the calibration parameters of each sensor and the relationship among them, to work on a better integration and automatization of the multiple procedures or to work on the generalization of this approaches to other fields like the panoramic images.

7. References

Abdel-Aziz, Y.I. & Karara, H.M. (1971). Direct linear transformation from comparator coordinates into space coordinates in close range photogrammetry. *Proceedings of the Symposium on close range photogrammetry*, pp. 1-18, The American Society of Photogrammetry: Falls Church.

Aguilera, D.G. & Lahoz, J. G. (2006). sv3DVision: didactical photogrammetric software for single image-based modeling", *Proceedings of International Archives of Photogrammetry, Remote Sensing and Spatial Information Sciences 36(6)*, pp. 171-179.

Baarda, W. (1968). A testing procedure for use in geodetic networks, *Netherlands Geodetic Commission Publications on Geodesy*. New Series, 2 (5), Delft.

Brown, D. C. (1971). Close Range Camera Calibration. *Photogrammetric Engineering*.

Burns, B. J., Hanson, A.R. & Riseman, E.M. (1986) Extracting Straight Lines, *IEEE Transactions on Pattern Analysis and Machine Intelligence*, pp. 425-455.

Canny, J. F. (1986). A computational approach to edge detection. *IEEE Trans. Pattern Analysis and Machine Intelligence*, pp. 679-698.

Dana, K. & Anandan, P. (1993). Registration of visible and infrared images, *Proceedings of the SPIE Conference on Architecture, Hardware and Forward-looking Infrared Issues in Automatic Target Recognition*, pp. 1-12, Orlando, May 1993.

Domingo, A. (2000). Investigación sobre los Métodos de Estimación Robusta aplicados a la resolución de los problemas fundamentales de la Fotogrametría. *PhD thesis*. Universidad de Cantabria.

Douskos V.; Grammatikopoulos L.; Kalisperakis I.; Karras G. & Petsa E. (2009). FAUCCAL: an open source toolbox for fully automatic camera calibration. *XXII CIPA Symposium on Digital Documentation, Interpretation & Presentation of Cultural Heritage*, Kyoto, 11-15October 2009.

Fischler, M. A., & R. C. Bolles, (1981). Random sample consensus: A paradigm for model fitting with application to image analysis and automated cartography. *Communications of the ACM, 24(6)*, pp- 381-395.

Förstner, W. & Guelch, E. (1987). A fast operator for detection and precise location of distinct points, corners and center of circular features. *ISPRS Conference on Fast Processing of Photogrammetric Data*, pp. 281-305, Interlaken, Switzerland.

Gabor, D. (1946) Theory of Communication, *Journal of Institute for Electrical Engineering*, Vol. 93, part III. n.° 26. pp. 429-457.

González-Aguilera, D. & Gómez-Lahoz, J. (2008). From 2D to 3D Through Modelling Based on a Single Image. *The Photogrammetric Record, vol. 23, n°. 122*, pp. 208-227.

González-Aguilera, D.; Rodríguez-Gonzálvez, P. & Gómez-Lahoz, J. (2009). An automatic procedure for co-registration of terrestrial laser scanners and digital cameras, *ISPRS Journal of Photogrammetry & Remote Sensing 64(3)*, pp. 308-316.

Grün, A. (1985). Adaptive least squares correlation: A powerful image matching technique. *South African Journal of Photogrammetry, Remote Sensing and Cartography 14 (3),* pp.175-187.

Han, J.H. & Park, J.S. (2000). Contour Matching Using Epipolar Geometry, *IEEE Trans. on Pattern Analysis and Machine Intelligence, 22(4),* pp.358-370.

Harris, C. & Stephens, M. J. (1988). A combined corner and edge detector. *Proceddings of Alvey Vision Conference.* pp. 147-151

Hartley, R. I. (1997). In defence of the 8-point algorithm. *IEEE Transactions on Pattern Analysis and Machine Intelligence, 19(6),* pp. 580-593.

Heck, (1981). The influence of individual observations on the result of a compensation and the search for outliers in the observations. *AVN, 88,* pp. 17-34.

Hintz, R.J. & Zhao, M. Z. (1990). Demonstration of Ideals in Fully Automatic line Matching of Overlapping Map Data, *Auto-Carto 9 Proceedings.* p.118.

Jarc, A.; Perˇs, J.; Rogelj, P.; Perˇse, M., & Kovaˇciˇc, S. (2007). Texture features for affine registration of thermal (FLIR) and visible images. *Proceedings of the 12th Computer Vision Winter Workshop,* Graz University of Technology, February 2007.

Keller, Y. & Averbuch, A. (2006) Multisensor Image Registration via Implicit Similarity. *IEEE Trans. Pattern Anal. Mach. Intell. 28(5),* pp. 794-801.

Kong, S. G.; Heo, J.; Boughorbel, F.; Zheng, Y.; Abidi, B. R.; Koschan, A.; Yi, M. & Abidi, M.A. (2007). Adaptive Fusion of Visual and Thermal IR Images for Illumination-Invariant Face Recognition, *International Journal of Computer Vision, Special Issue on Object Tracking and Classification Beyond the Visible Spectrum 71(2),* pp. 215-233.

Kraus, K. (1997). *Photogrammetry, Volume I, Fundamentals and Standard Processes.* Ed. Dümmler (4ª ed.) Bonn.

Laws, K. (1980). Rapid texture identification. *In SPIE Image Processing for Missile Guidance,* pp. 376–380.

Levoy, M.; Pulli, K.; Curless, B.; Rusinkiewicz, S.; Koller, D.; Pereira, L.; Ginzton, M.; Anderson, S.; Davis, J.; Ginsberg, J.; Shade, J. & Fulk, D. (2000). The Digital Michelangelo Project: 3-D Scanning of Large Statues. *Procedding of SIGGRAPH.*

Li, H. & Zhou, Y-T. (1995). Automatic EO/IR sensor image registration. *Proceedings of International Conference on Image Proccessing. Vol. 2,* pp.161-164.

Longuet-Higgins, H. C. (1981). A computer algorithm for reconstructing a scene from two projections. *Nature 293,* pp. 133-135.

Lowe, D. G. (2004). Distinctive image features from scale-invariant keypoints, *International Journal of Computer Vision, 60(2),* pp. 91-110.

Luhmann, T.; Robson, S.; Kyle, S. & Harley, I. (2006). *Close Range Photogrammetry: Principles, Methods and Applications.* Whittles, Scotland, 510 pages.

Mancera-Taboada, J., Rodríguez-Gonzálvez, P. & González-Aguilera, D. (2009). Turning point clouds into 3d models: The aqueduct of Segovia. *Workshop on Geographical Analysis, Urban Modeling, Spatial statistics,* pp. 520-532, Yongin (Korea)

Mikhail, E.M. & Ackerman, F. (1976) *Observations and least squares.* New York. University Press of America.

Mitka, B. & Rzonca, A. (2009). Integration of photogrammetric and 3D laser scanning data as a flexible and effective approach for heritage documentation. *Proceedings of 3D Virtual Reconstruction and Visualization of Complex Architectures,* Trento, Italy.

Pope, A. J. (1976). *The statistics of residuals and the detection of outliers*. NOAA Technical Report NOS 65 NGS 1, National Ocean Service, National Geodetic Survey, US Department of Commerce. Rockville, MD, Washington, 133pp.

Rocchini, C.; Cignoni, P. & Montani, C. (1999). Multiple textures stitching and blending on 3D objects. *10th Eurographics Rendering Workshop*, pp. 127-138.

Rousseau, F.; Fablet, R. & Barillot, C. (2000) Density based registration of 3d ultrasound images using texture information, *Electronic Letters on Computer Vision and Image Analysis*, pp. 1–7.

Sánchez, N.; Arias, B.; Aguilera, D. & Lahoz, J. (2004). Análisis aplicado de métodos de calibración de cámaras para usos fotogramétricos. *TopCart 2004*, ISBN 84-923511-2-8, pp. 113-114.

Sanz, E. (2009). Control de la deformación en sólidos mediante técnicas de fotogrametría de objeto cercano: aplicación a un problema de diseño estructural. *PhD thesis*. Universidad de Vigo.

Schenk T. (1986). A Robust Solution to the Line-Matching Problem in Photogrammetry and Cartography, *Photogrammetric Engineering and Remote Sensing 52(11)*, pp. 1779-1784.

Shepard, D. (1968). A two-dimensional interpolation function for irregularly-spaced data. *Proceedings of the ACM National Conference*, pp. 517–524.

Stamos, I., & Allen, P. K. (2001). Automatic registration of 3-D with 2-D imagery in urban environments. *IEEE International conference on computer vision* pp. 731-736.

Straßer, W. (1974) Schnelle Kurven-und Flaechendarstellung auf graphischen Sichtgeraeten, *PhD thesis*, TU Berlin.

Süli, E. & Mayers, D. (2003). *An Introduction to Numerical Analysis*, Cambridge University Press, ISBN 0-521-00794-1.

Zhang, Z.; Deriche, R.; Faugeras, O. & Luong, Q-T. (1995). A robust techniquc for matching two uncalibrated images through the recovery of the unknown epipolar geometry. *Artificial intelligence, 78(1-2)*, pp. 87-119.

7

Spatial Voting With Data Modeling

Holger Marcel Jaenisch, Ph.D., D.Sc.
Licht Strahl Engineering INC (LSEI)
United States of America
James Cook University
Australia

1. Introduction

Our detailed problem is one of having multiple orthogonal sensors that are each able to observe different objects, but none can see the whole assembly comprised of such objects. Further, our sensors are moving so we have positional uncertainties located with each observed object. The problem of associating multiple time based observations of a single object by fusing future estimate covariance updates with our best estimate to date and knowing which estimate to assign to which current location estimate becomes a problem in bias elimination or compensation. Once we have established which objects to fuse together, next we must determine which objects are close enough together to be related into a possible assembly. This requires a decision to determine which objects to group together. But if a group of nearby objects is found, how are their spatial locations best used? Simply doing a covariance update and combining their state estimates yields a biased answer, since the objects are "not" the same and "not" superimposed. Therefore, naive covariance updating yields estimates of assemblies within which we find no objects. Our proposed spatial correlation and voting algorithm solves this spatial object fusion problem.

The spatial voting (SV) concept for the object to assembly aggregation problem is based on the well-known principles of voting, geometry, and image processing using 2D convolution (Jaenisch et.al., 2008). Our concept is an adaptation of the subjects as covered in Hall and McCullen (2004) which are limited to multiple sensors, single assembly cases. Our concept is an extension to multiple orthogonal sensors and multiple assemblies (or aspects of the same assembly). Hall and McCullen describe general voting as a democratic process. Hard decisions from M sensors are counted as votes with a majority or plurality decision rule. For example, if M sensors observe a phenomena and make an identity declaration by ranking n different hypothesis, summing the number of sensors that declare each hypothesis to be true and taking the largest sum as the winner forms an overall declaration of identity. From this, it is easy to see that voting many times reduces to probabilities or confidences and their efficient mathematical combination. Typically, this is where either Bayes' rule or other covariance combining methods are used such as covariance updating and Klein's Boolean voting logic (Klein, 2004). However, all of these methods are still probabilistic.

SV reduces object location uncertainty using an analog method by stacking and tallying, which results in a vote. It is common with probabilistic methods to assume the assembly is at the center of the estimate with some uncertainty. In our spatial approach, we don't make that assumption. Rather, SV states that the object is located with confidence somewhere in the area. The larger the area, the higher the confidence that one or more objects will be contained within its boundary, which is the opposite approach taken in traditional covariance confidence updating.

2. Approach

In SV, the sensor report ellipses are stacked and the aggregation becomes a tally or vote. This results in a growing landscape of overlapping ellipses. By collecting assembly object estimates throughout one full epoch, a full landscape of all the best available assembly sensor reports and locations are obtained. By convolving this array with a 2-D spatial kernel, it is possible to achieve correlation based on a mission controlled setting for choosing a 2-D kernel of the necessary spatial extent. For our application, the grid exists as a 128 x 128 element array that is a total size of 128 x 128 meters. Each unit on the grid is 1 square meter, and we wish to fuse elements up to 5 meters apart using a suitable 5m x 5m kernel. Spatial averaging combines by blending high regions in the array that are approximately 5 meters apart or less into a continuous blob. The blob is then isolated by calculating an adaptive threshold from the frame and zeroing everything below the threshold. The resultant hills are projected down to the x and y-axis independently and the local sub pixel regions are extracted. The pixel regions are used to calculate spatial extent in the form of a covariance for the extracted region for the newly discerned assembly. Finally, each located assembly is evaluated to estimate total confidence of the assembly being significant or anomalous and the assembly labeled accordingly.

3. Algorithm Description

A flowchart for the SV algorithm is given in Fig. 1 on the top of the next page. SV has been implemented in MathCAD 14 and this implementation is included in Fig. 8 - 13 as a SV simulation shown later in this chapter. The SV simulation allows Monte Carlo cases to be generated (explained in Section 5). The example case described in this section is the first Monte Carlo case (FRAME=0) generated by the MathCAD simulation. To initialize the SV process, first define the dimensions of the detection space. For our example case, the size of the grid is 128 x 128 grid units. Each grid unit is 1 meter by 1 meter in size. Next, define the spatial extent over which objects are to be fused together as assemblies. This defines the size (or spatial extent) of the spatial convolution kernel (spatial correlator) that we apply to the detection space once the centroid and covariance defined ellipse representations (derived encompassing rectangles) are stacked. The kernel size is given by

$$Kernel\,Size = \frac{Spatial\,Extent}{Grid\,Resolution} \tag{1}$$

where kernel size is in number of grid units, and spatial extent and grid resolution are in meters.

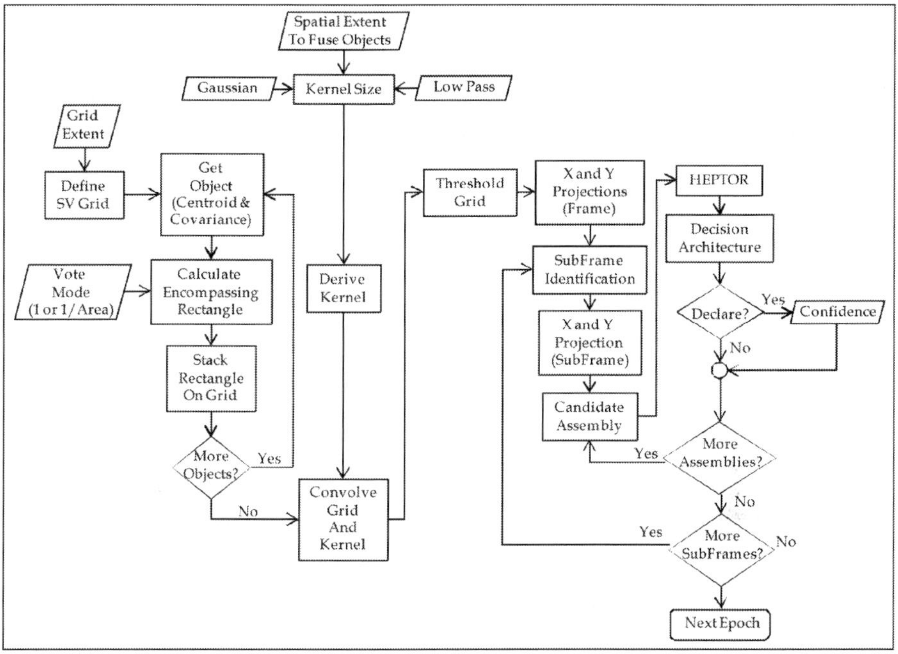

Fig. 1. Spatial Voting (SV) process flowchart.

The spatial convolution kernel (Jain, 1989) (NASA, 1962) is the equivalent kernel shown in Equation (2c), which is a 5m x 5m (with very little effect past 2m) matrix resulting from the convolution of the two low-pass or smoothing kernels used in image processing given in Equations (2a) and (2b).

$$Kernel_{LowPass} = \begin{bmatrix} 1 & 1 & 1 \\ 1 & 3 & 1 \\ 1 & 1 & 1 \end{bmatrix} \text{(a)} \quad Kernel_{Gaussian} = \begin{bmatrix} 1 & 2 & 1 \\ 2 & 4 & 2 \\ 1 & 2 & 1 \end{bmatrix} \text{(b)} \qquad (2)$$

(3m x 3m) (3m x 3m)

$$Kernel_{SpatialConvolutionKernel} = Kernel_{LowPass} ** Kernel_{Gaussian} = \begin{bmatrix} 1 & 3 & 4 & 3 & 1 \\ 3 & 11 & 16 & 11 & 3 \\ 4 & 16 & 24 & 16 & 4 \\ 3 & 11 & 16 & 11 & 3 \\ 1 & 3 & 4 & 3 & 1 \end{bmatrix} \text{(c) (5m x 5m)}$$

The spatial convolution kernel in Equation (2c) defines the shape of a Gaussian distribution, and by convolving the spatial convolution kernel with the detection space, it is converted into a correlation map describing how each pixel neighborhood in the detection space is correlated with the spatial convolution kernel.

To enlarge the kernel to match the spatial extent, the spatial convolution kernel in Equation (2c) is convolved with itself until the equivalent kernel size corresponds with the extent. The number of times that the kernel in Equation (2c) is convolved with itself is given in Equation (3), and the final equivalent kernel requiring convolving the original spatial convolution kernel n times with itself is given in Equation (4) as

$$N_{comb} = floor(\tfrac{1}{2}(Kernel\ Size - 3)) \tag{3}$$

$$Kernel_{SC} = Kernel_{SCK} ** Kernel_{n-1} \tag{4}$$

where $Kernel_{n-1}$ is the result of convolving the spatial convolution kernel with itself n-1 times.

The estimated object's position is described by the sensor report using position centroid and covariance (which defines the location and size of the uncertainty region). The centroid and covariance are given by

$$X = \begin{bmatrix} \mu_x \\ \mu_y \end{bmatrix} \qquad \Lambda = \begin{bmatrix} \sigma_{xx} & \sigma_{xy} \\ \sigma_{yx} & \sigma_{yy} \end{bmatrix} \qquad \mu_x = \frac{1}{N}\sum_i x_i \qquad \mu_y = \frac{1}{N}\sum_i y_i$$

$$\sigma_{xx} = \frac{1}{N}\sum_{i=1}^{N}(x_i - \mu_x)^2 \qquad \sigma_{xy} = \frac{1}{N}\sum_{i=1}^{N}(x_i - \mu_x)(y_i - \mu_y) \qquad \sigma_{yy} = \frac{1}{N}\sum_{i=1}^{N}(y_i - \mu_y)^2 \tag{5}$$

where x_i and y_i are the individual sensor reports of position estimates used to derive the centroid and covariance. We begin with the sensor report consisting of the position centroid X and the covariance Λ. From the covariance, the one sigma distance from the centroid along the semi-major (a) and semi-minor (b) axes of the ellipse are given by

$$a^2 = \frac{1}{2}\left[\sigma_{xx} + \sigma_{yy} + \sqrt{[\sigma_{yy} - \sigma_{xx}]^2 + 4\sigma_{xy}^{\ 2}}\right] \qquad b^2 = \frac{1}{2}\left[\sigma_{xx} + \sigma_{yy} - \sqrt{[\sigma_{yy} - \sigma_{xx}]^2 + 4\sigma_{xy}^{\ 2}}\right] \tag{6}$$

(along Semi-major axis) (along Semi-minor axis)

and the angle of rotation θ of the semi-major axis is given in Equation (7) and the lengths a and b and the rotation angle θ are used to define a rotated ellipse of the form given in Equation (7).

$$\theta = \frac{1}{2}\arctan\left(\frac{2\sigma_{xy}}{\sigma_{yy} - \sigma_{xx}}\right)$$

$$\frac{[(x-h)\cos(\theta) - (y-k)\sin(\theta)]^2}{a^2} + \frac{[(y-k)\sin(\theta) + (x-h)\sin(\theta)]^2}{b^2} = 1 \qquad \sigma_{xx} > \sigma_{yy}$$

$$\frac{[(x-h)\cos(\theta) - (y-k)\sin(\theta)]^2}{b^2} + \frac{[(y-k)\sin(\theta) + (x-h)\sin(\theta)]^2}{a^2} = 1 \qquad \sigma_{xx} < \sigma_{yy} \tag{7}$$

where h is the centroid x value, k is the centroid y value, and a and b are defined in Equation (6). The ellipse in Equation (7) defines the perimeter of the elliptical region, and to define the entire region encompassed by the ellipse, we simply change the equality (=) in Equation (7) to the less than or equal to (≤) inequality so that the function includes not only the boundary, but also the locations contained within the boundary.

Because the actual location of each object is unknown, the only information that is available is contained in the sensor report in the form of a centroid and covariance. It is an incorrect assumption that the object is located at the center of the ellipse; because if this were true then the covariance information would not be needed since the true position would be defined by the centroid alone.

The semi-major axis length, semi-minor axis length, and rotation angle are converted into covariance using

$$\sigma_{xx} = a\cdot\cos(\theta)^2 + b\cdot\sin(\theta)^2 \quad \sigma_{yy} = a\cdot\sin(\theta)^2 + b\cdot\cos(\theta)^2 \quad \sigma_{xy} = \sigma_{yx} = (b-a)\cdot\cos(\theta)\sin(\theta) \quad (8)$$

Fig. 2 shows 2 examples of starting with the rotation angle and semi-major and semi-minor axis lengths deriving the covariance matrix and corresponding ellipse.

$a = 234.0$, $b = 130.0$, $\theta = 148\,\mathrm{deg.}$ $\quad \Lambda = \begin{bmatrix} 207.803 & 42.109 \\ 42.109 & 166.323 \end{bmatrix}$

$a = 241.9$, $b = 97.1$, $\theta = 105.2\,\mathrm{deg.}$ $\quad \Lambda = \begin{bmatrix} 231.904 & -36.686 \\ -36.686 & 107.133 \end{bmatrix}$

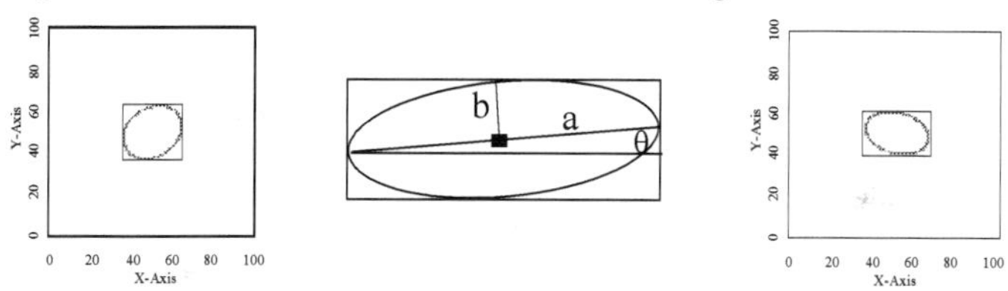

Fig. 2. Starting with the semi-major axis length, semi-minor axis length, and rotation angle, the covariance matrices and ellipses above are derived using Equation (8).

If the ellipses are placed into the detection grid directly, artifacts are introduced by aliasing and pixelization from the boundary of the ellipse. Also, as the size of an ellipse to place becomes small relative to the detection grid size, the overall shape approaches the rectangle. Therefore, to minimize scale dependent artifacts, encompassing rectangles with well-defined boundaries replace each ellipse (Press et.al., 2007). The semi-major axis of the ellipse is the hypotenuse of the triangle, and completing the rectangle yields the first approximation to an equivalent rectangle. Finally, the width of the rectangle is scaled to the semi-minor axis length to preserve the highest spatial confidence extent reported in the covariance. The length of the sides of the rectangle that are placed instead of the ellipse are given by

$$\left.\begin{aligned} x &= 2a\cos(\theta) \\ y &= Max(2a\sin(\theta), 2b\sin(\theta)) \end{aligned}\right\} if\ \sigma_{xx} > \sigma_{yy}$$
$$\left.\begin{aligned} x &= Max(2a\sin(\theta), 2b\sin(\theta)) \\ y &= 2a\cos(\theta) \end{aligned}\right\} if\ \sigma_{yy} > \sigma_{xx} \quad (9)$$

where θ again is the rotation angle of the semi-major axis given in Equation (7) above. The length of the semi-minor axis modifies the size of the rectangle subject to the conditions given in Equation (9), which preserves the axis with the greatest spatial location confidence. The value at each grid location inside of the rectangle is

$$Value = \frac{1}{N} = \frac{1}{x \cdot y} \quad (10)$$

where x and y are the sides of the rectangle, and if the analysis is done under the assumption that a smaller area increases the confidence that it contains an object. If on the other hand the converse is true, then N = 1, which implies that the confidence of an object being contained in a larger area is weighted higher than the confidence in a smaller area when the spatial vote or stacking occurs. Both forms may be used to determine how many pedigree covariance reports are associated with each respective assembly by using the sum of the values mapped into the assembly location as a checksum threshold.

Now that the rectangle extent and value is defined, the rectangles are stacked into the detection grid one at a time. This is accomplished by adding their value (1 or 1/Area depending on how scoring is done for testing sensor report overlap. If 1's are placed the number of overlaps is max value in subarray, if 1/Area is used sum>Area indicates overlap) in each rectangle to the current location in the grid where the rectangle is being stacked. Fig. 3 (left) shows as an example (obtained from the MathCAD 14 implementation in Fig. 8-13) 38 original sensor reports along a stretch of road, and (left center) is the detection grid after stacking the 38 rectangles that represent each of the sensor reports and applying the spatial convolution kernel.

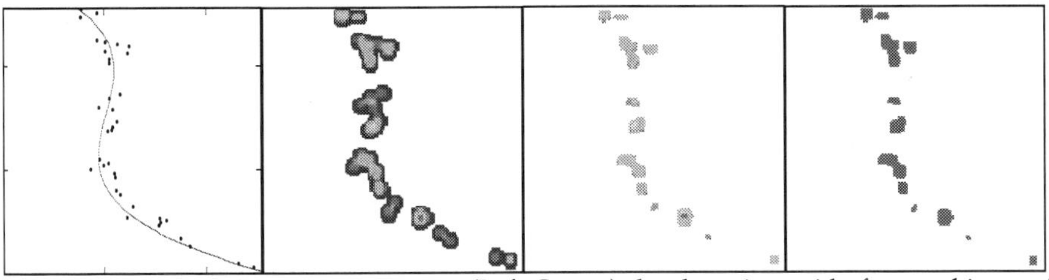

Fig. 3. (Left) Original 38 sensor reports, (Left Center) the detection grid after stacking and applying the spatial convolution kernel, (Right Center) After applying the threshold, and (Right) locations in the graph on the left converted into a 0/1 mask.

Next, automatically calculate a threshold to separate the background values in the detection grid from those that represent the assemblies (anomaly detection). This threshold is calculated as the minimum value of the non-zero grid locations plus a scale factor times the range of the values in the detection grid (set in the MathCAD implementation as 0.3 times the range (maximum minus minimum) of the non-zero values) in Fig. 3 (left center). Values that occur below this threshold are set to zero, while those that are above the threshold retain their values. Fig. 3 (right center) shows an example of applying the threshold to the detection grid in Fig. 3 (left center), resulting assembly blobs (fused objects) are shown. Also shown in Fig. 3 (right) is an example of the mask that is formed by setting all values above the threshold to one and all those below the threshold to zero.

In order to isolate the assemblies that now are simply blobs in the detection grid, we compute blob projections for both the x-axis and the y-axis of the grid by summing the mask in Fig. 3 (right) both across the rows (y-axis projection) and down the columns (x-axis projection). Fig. 4 shows examples of these assembly shadow projections, which are calculated using

$$DX_j = \sum_{k=0}^{ngrid-1} D_{k,j} \text{ and } DY_i = \sum_{k=0}^{ngrid-1} D_{i,k} \tag{11}$$

where D is the array shown in Fig. 3 (right), $ngrid$ is the grid size (128 for our example), DX_j is the x-axis projection for the jth column, and DY_i is the y-axis projection for the ith row.

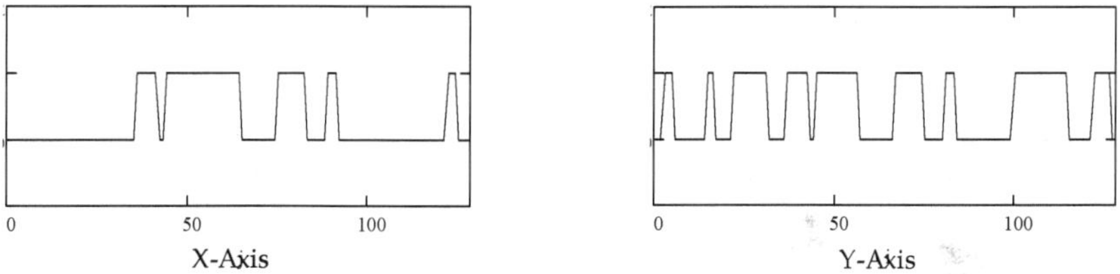

Fig. 4. Example assembly shadow projections for the x-axis (left) and y-axis (right) for the mask shown in Fig. 4 (right).

Once these assembly shadow projections are calculated, they are renormalized so that all non-zero locations have a value of one while zero locations remain zero. Using the assembly shadow projections, horizontal and vertical lines are placed across the detection grid corresponding to the transition points from zero to one and from one to zero in the graphs in Fig. 4. Regions on the grid that are formed by intersections of these lines are labeled 1 through 45 in Fig. 5, and are the candidate assemblies that are identified (including zero frames).

Each of the 45 candidate assembly subframes are processed to remove zero frames by determining if any non-zero locations exist within its boundary. This is done by extracting the assembly subframe into its own separate array and calculating the maximum value of the array. If the maximum value is non-zero, then at least one grid unit in the array is a part of an object assembly and is labeled kept.

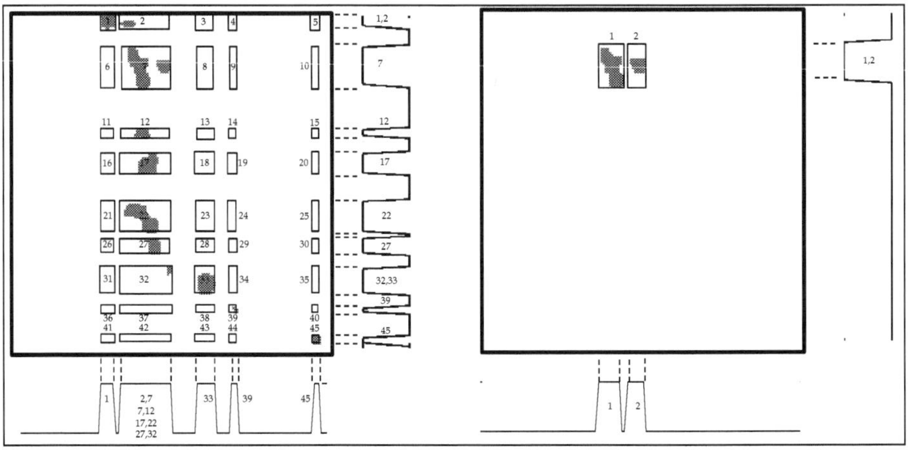

Fig. 5. (Left) Identification of candidate assembly subframes using the shadow projection in Equation (11) and Fig. 3, (Center) Applying the shadow projection algorithm a second time to Region 7 to further isolate assemblies. After processing the subframes a second time, a total of 12 candidate assemblies have been located.

This is repeated for each of the subframes that are identified. Once the subframes have been processed, we repeat this process on each subframe one at a time to further isolate regions within each subframe into its own candidate assembly. This results in subframes being broken up into smaller subframes, and for all subframes found, the centroid and covariance is calculated. This information is used by the object and assembly tracking routines to improve object and assembly position estimates as a function of motion and time. As a result of this processing, the number of candidate assembly subframes in Fig. 5 is reduced from 45 to 12 (the number of isolated red regions in the grid). The final results after applying the SV algorithm to the stacked rectangles in Fig. 6 (center) results in the graphic shown in Fig. 6 (right).

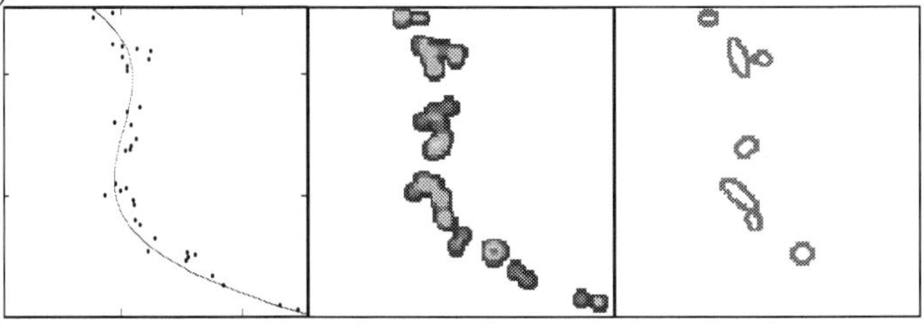

Fig. 6. (Left) Sensor reports, (Center) rectangles stacked in the detection grid with SV smoothing applied, (Right) final result after applying spatial voting.

4. Heptor

From an isolated SV target, we have available the geospatial distribution attributes (X and Y or latitude and longitude components characterized independently, including derivatives across cluster size transitions), and if physics based features exist, Brightness (including derivatives across cluster size transitions), Amplitude, Frequency, Damping, and Phase. Each of these attributes is characterized with a fixed template of descriptive parametric and non-parametric (fractal) features collectively termed a Heptor (vector of seven (7) features) and defined in Equations (12) - (18) as:

$$\sigma = \sqrt{\tfrac{1}{N-1}\sum_{j=1}^{N}(x_j-\bar{x})^2} \qquad (12) \qquad Skew = \tfrac{1}{N}\sum_{j=1}^{N}\left[\frac{x_j-\bar{x}}{\sigma}\right]^3 \qquad (13)$$

$$Kurt = \left\{\tfrac{1}{N}\sum_{j=1}^{N}\left[\frac{x_j-\bar{x}}{\sigma}\right]^4\right\}-3 \qquad (14) \qquad M6 = \left\{\tfrac{1}{N}\sum_{j=1}^{N}\left[\frac{x_j-\bar{x}}{\sigma}\right]^6\right\}-15 \qquad (15)$$

$$M8 = \left\{\tfrac{1}{N}\sum_{j=1}^{N}\left[\frac{x_j-\bar{x}}{\sigma}\right]^8\right\}-105 \qquad (16) \qquad \mathrm{Re}(J_{i+1}) = \min\left(\lim_{\Delta J\to 0}\left[\frac{\log\left(\frac{Range}{\sigma N J_i}\right)}{\log\left(\frac{1}{N}\right)}\right]\right) \qquad (17)$$

$$DH = 1+\log\left(\tfrac{1}{N}\sum_{j=1}^{N-1}\sqrt{1+\left(\tfrac{x_{j+1}-x_j}{Range}\right)^2}\right) \qquad (18)$$

The basic Heptor can be augmented by additional features that may exist, but in their absence, the Heptor represents an excellent starting point. Equations (19) to (23) lists some additional features that can be used to augment the Heptor.

$$\bar{x} = \tfrac{1}{N}\sum_{j=1}^{N}x_j \qquad (19) \qquad Min = \min(x) \qquad (20)$$

$$Max = \max(x) \qquad (21) \qquad Range = Max - Min \qquad (22)$$

$$ChiSq = N-(N-1)\sigma^2 \qquad (23)$$

The features are associated with a category variable (class) for 1=no target or nominal, and 2=target or off-nominal. The next step is to drive a classifier to associate the features with class in a practical fashion. Here we use the Data Model since very few examples are available, and not enough to discern statistical behavior. For this, we want to populate a knowledge base which encodes all examples encountered as observed and identified species. This mandates a scalable, bottom-up approach that is well suited to the Group Method of Data Handling (GMDH) approach to polynomial network representation.

5. SV Simulation in MathCAD 14

SV has been implemented in MathCAD 14, C, and Java. Included in this work (Figs. 8-13) is the MathCAD 14 implementation, which facilitates the ability to generate Monte Carlo ensemble cases used in deriving the Data Model decision architecture described in later sections of this chapter.

Spatial Voting Algorithm Demonstration

A. SV Initialization

$snglcmptgt \equiv 0$ Display Single Componet Targets? (0 = single components not recognized as targets)

$votemode := 0$ Vote mode = 0 for 1/N filling, and no single component targets. Vote mode = 1 for filling with 1's

$maxseparation := 5$ max obj separation $nsize := 128$ Grid Size $res := 1$ m

$isigma := 1$ For placing ellipses $ntgt := 3$ Number of targets per epoch $sx := 6$ Max number of components per target

B. Kernel Initialization

$i := 0..nsize-1$ $j := 0..nsize-1$ $t := nsize \cdot res$ $t = 128$ meters by $t = 128$ meters grid ($res = 1$ meter resolution)

$ksize1 := \frac{maxseparation}{res}$ $ksize1 = 5$ $ksize := floor\left(\frac{ksize1}{2}\right) \cdot 2 + 1$ $ksize = 5$ kernel size to detect the selected max separation

$ncomb := floor\left(\frac{ksize-3}{2}\right) - 1$ $ncomb = 0$ number of LP/G passes required to build ksize kernel starting with initial LP/G

Initial LowPass and Gaussian kernels $LP := \begin{pmatrix} 1 & 1 & 1 \\ 1 & 3 & 1 \\ 1 & 1 & 1 \end{pmatrix}$ $G := \begin{pmatrix} 1 & 2 & 1 \\ 2 & 4 & 2 \\ 1 & 2 & 1 \end{pmatrix}$

C. Calculate final correlator kernel $LPK_{nsize-1,nsize-1} := 0$ $GK_{nsize-1,nsize-1} := 0$ $ij := 0..2$ $ik := 0..2$

$LPK_{floor[(nsize+1) \cdot 0.5]-1+ij,\, floor[(nsize+1) \cdot 0.5]-1+ik} := \frac{LP_{ij,ik}}{11}$ $GK_{floor[(nsize+1) \cdot 0.5]-1+ij,\, floor[(nsize+1) \cdot 0.5]-1+ik} := \frac{G_{ij,ik}}{16}$

$KCOMB := FFTCONV(LPK, GK)$ $K1 := KCOMB$

$K2 := \left| \begin{array}{l} \text{if } ncomb \geq 1 \\ \quad \left| \begin{array}{l} \text{for } i \in 1..ncomb \\ \quad K1 \leftarrow FFTCONV(K1, KCOMB) \\ abc \leftarrow 0 \end{array} \right. \\ K1 \end{array} \right.$

$K2 := if(ksize1 \leq 2, LPK, K2)$

$K2 := if(ksize1 > 2 \wedge ksize1 \leq 4, GK, K2)$

$ij := 0..ksize-1$ $ik := 0..ksize-1$

$KF_{ij,ik} := K2_{ij+\frac{nsize}{2}-2,\, ik+\frac{nsize}{2}-2}$

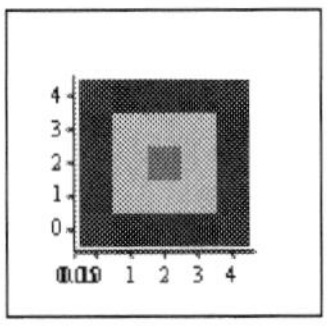

KF

D. Initialize detection grid and road

$A_{i,j} := 0$ $ir := 0..11$ $rx_{ir} := ir \cdot \frac{nsize-1}{11}$ $ry_{ir} := nsize \cdot RD(kkk1 + ir)$

$rdx^{\langle 0 \rangle} := rx$ $rdx^{\langle 1 \rangle} := rx^2$ $rdx^{\langle 2 \rangle} := rx^3$ $norder := 3$ $MM := FIT(12, 3, rdx, ry, 8)$

$irl := 0..nsize-1$ $rpoly_{irl} := \sum_{i=0}^{norder} \left(MM_i \cdot irl^i\right)$ $rpoly1_{ir} := \sum_{i=0}^{norder} \left[MM_i \cdot \left(rx_{ir}\right)^i\right]$

E. Initialize truth locations

$sy := \frac{nsize-1}{ntgt}$ $jtgt := 0..ntgt-1$ $k := 0..ntgt-1$ $ty_{jtgt} := floor[[(jtgt+1) \cdot sy + jtgt \cdot sy + 1] \cdot 0.5]$ $tx_{jtgt} := rpoly_{ty_{jtgt}}$

$tx1_{jtgt} := tx_{jtgt} + sx \cdot RD(kkk1 + jtgt)$ $ty1_{jtgt} := ty_{jtgt} + sx \cdot RD(kkk1 + jtgt \cdot 2)$ $rottheta := 180$

$\beta_k := RD[kkk1 + (k+1) \cdot 5] \cdot \frac{\pi}{180} \cdot rottheta$ $sval1_k := 9 \cdot RD[kkk1 + (k+1) \cdot 3]$

$sval2_k := 9 \cdot RD[kkk1 + (k+1) \cdot 4]$ $txx_k := sval1_k \cdot \cos(\beta_k)^2 + sval2_k \cdot \sin(\beta_k)^2$ $ncomp_k := 2 + 2 \cdot RD(kkk1 + 2 + k)$

$tyy_k := sval1_k \cdot \sin(\beta_k)^2 + sval2_k \cdot \cos(\beta_k)^2$ $txy_k := (sval2_k - sval1_k) \cdot \cos(\beta_k) \cdot \sin(\beta_k)$ $CT_k := \begin{pmatrix} txx_k & txy_k \\ txy_k & tyy_k \end{pmatrix}$

$jx_k := \left| \begin{array}{l} A \leftarrow 0 \\ \text{for } j \in 0..ncomp_k - 1 \\ \quad A_j \leftarrow tx1_k + txx_k \cdot [2 \cdot RD[kkk1 + (k+1+j) \cdot 6] - 1] \\ A \end{array} \right.$ $jy_k := \left| \begin{array}{l} A \leftarrow 0 \\ \text{for } j \in 0..ncomp_k - 1 \\ \quad A_j \leftarrow ty1_k + tyy_k \cdot [2 \cdot RD[kkk1 + (k+1+j) \cdot 7] - 1] \\ A \end{array} \right.$

$ix := MAPCOMP(jx, jy)_0$ $iy := MAPCOMP(jx, jy)_1$ $n := rows(ix)$ $RD(x) \equiv \frac{\sin\left[(x)^{\exp(1)}\right] + \cos\left[(x)^{\exp(1)}\right] + 2}{4}$

Fig. 8. Part 1 of MathCAD 14 implementation of SV.

A. Map in false alarm detections

```
FA := | m ← 0
      | for p ∈ 0..nsize − 1
      |   if RD[kkk1 + (p)·8] > 0.75
      |     | tmp ← [RD[kkk1 + (p)·8] − 0.8]·nsize
      |     | FA_{m,0} ← rpoly_p + tmp
      |     | FA_{m,1} ← p
      |     | m ← m + 1
      | FA

k := 0..rows(FA) − 1     ix_{n+k} := FA_{k,0}     iy_{n+k} := FA_{k,1}

n := rows(ix)     k := 0..n − 1          ix and iy are the detection centroids

roadx_{irl} := rpoly_{irl}     roady_{irl} := irl

min2(A, z) ≡ | a ← A
             | a ← z if z < a
             | a

max2(A, z) ≡ | a ← A
             | a ← z if z > a
             | a

MAPCOMP(jx, jy) ≡ | m ← 0
                  | for i ∈ 0..rows(jx) − 1
                  |   | n ← rows(jx_i)
                  |   | for j ∈ 0..n − 1
                  |   |   | ix_m ← (jx_i)_j
                  |   |   | iy_m ← (jy_i)_j
                  |   |   | m ← m + 1
                  | A_0 ← ix
                  | A_1 ← iy
                  | A
```

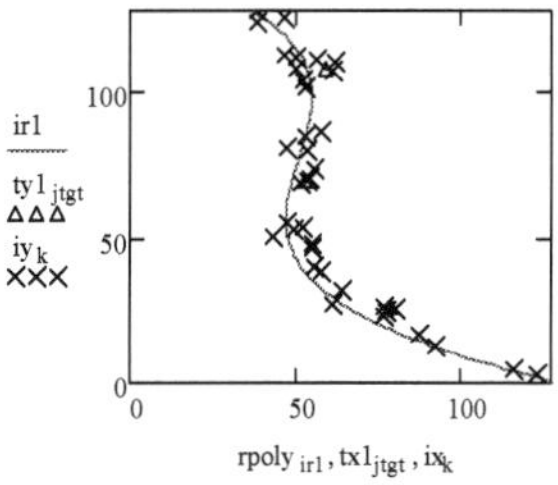

Triangles are truth targets, X's are detections

B. Assign detection covariances

```
β_k := RD[kkk1 + (k + 1)·9]·(π/180)·rottheta     svall1_k := 4·RD[kkk1 + (k + 1)·10]     sval2_k := 4·RD[kkk1 + (k + 1)·11]

txx_k := svall1_k·cos(β_k)^2 + sval2_k·sin(β_k)^2     tyy_k := svall1_k·sin(β_k)^2 + sval2_k·cos(β_k)^2     XA_k := (ix_k ; iy_k)     Centroids

txy_k := (sval2_k − svall1_k)·cos(β_k)·sin(β_k)     ix_k := floor(ix_k + 0.5)     iy_k := floor(iy_k + 0.5)

A1 := PLCC(A, ix, iy, C, 2, isigma, 0)     C_k := C_k·isigma^2     A1 is for display only     C_k := (txx_k txy_k ; txy_k tyy_k)     Covariances

I2_0 := A     I2_1 := ix     I2_2 := iy     I2_3 := C     I2_4 := votemode     I2_5 := maxseparation
```

C. Calculate Equivalent Rectangles and Place on SV Grid

```
AA := PLCR(I2)
```

D. Convolve SV Kernel and Grid

```
B := FFTCONV(AA_0, K2)
```

E. Auto calculate and apply threshold (D is now the 0/1 mask)

```
cmin := MIN(B)   cmax := MAX(B)   crng := cmax − cmin     fac := 0.3     D_{i,j} := if(B_{i,j} < cmin + fac·crng, 0, 1)     B1_{i,j} := B_{i,j}·D_{i,j}
```

F. Compute Shadowing For Isolation

$$DX_j := \sum_{k=0}^{nsize-1} D_{k,j} \quad DY_i := \sum_{k=0}^{nsize-1} D_{i,k} \quad DX_j := if(DX_j > 0, 1, 0) \quad DY_i := if(DY_i > 0, 1, 0)$$

G. Extract Candidate Assemblies

```
II_0 := AA_0   II_1 := DX   II_2 := DY   II_3 := B   II_4 := D   II_5 := snglcmptgt   II_6 := isigma   II_7 := votemode     IFRAMES := FRMS(II)

NTargets := rows(IFRAMES) − 1     D_{i,j} := 0     G_{i,j} := B_{i,j}·D_{i,j}     D := G     icolor := maxx(D)     isigma := 2
```

isigma here is for the target covariance

H. Draw Results (A1 and D)

```
Covar := CALCOV(IFRAMES^<8>)     icolor := if(icolor = 0, 1, icolor)     xcent := IFRAMES^<1>     ycent := IFRAMES^<2>

A1 := PLCC(A1, xcent, ycent, Covar, icolor, isigma, 1)     D := PLCC(D, xcent, ycent, Covar, icolor, isigma, 1)
```

I. Heptor Candidate Assemblies for Decision Architecture

```
AAA := HEPFRAME(IFRAMES, tx1, ty1)     kkk1 ≡ FRAME + 1
```

kkk1 is the Monte Carlo parameter to vary (increment by +1) FRAME increments using the Animation tool under Tools/Animation/Record

Fig. 9. Part 2 of MathCAD 14 implementation of SV.

Calculates Covariance Between 2 2-D arrays

```
COVAR(yc, nfiles, n) ≡ | for i ∈ 0..nfiles − 1
                       |   dm_i ← mean(yc^⟨i⟩)
                       | for i ∈ 0..nfiles − 1
                       |   for j ∈ 0..nfiles − 1
                       |     c_{j,i} ← 0
                       |     for k ∈ 0..n − 1
                       |       c_{j,i} ← c_{j,i} + (yc_{k,j} − dm_j)·(yc_{k,i} − dm_i)
                       | for i ∈ 0..nfiles − 1
                       |   for j ∈ 0..nfiles − 1
                       |     c_{j,i} ← c_{j,i} / (n − 1)  if n > 1
                       | c
```

Maps points around an ellipse (for plotting)

```
ADELL(A, x, y, C, ikul, sig) ≡ | nr ← rows(A)
                               | nc ← cols(A)
                               | sx ← √(C_{0,0})
                               | sy ← √(C_{1,1})
                               | ρ ← C_{0,1} / (sx · sy)
                               | cd11 ← sx
                               | cd12 ← 0.0
                               | cd21 ← ρ · sy
                               | cd22 ← 10^−10
                               | cd22 ← sy · √(1 − ρ²)  if 1 − ρ² > 0
                               | for i ∈ 0, 0.01..6.3
                               |   x1 ← cd11 · sig · cos(i) + cd12 · sig · sin(i)
                               |   x1 ← floor(x1 + 0.5) + x
                               |   y1 ← cd21 · sig · cos(i) + cd22 · sig · sin(i)
                               |   y1 ← floor(y1 + 0.5) + y
                               |   if y1 ≥ 0 ∧ y1 ≤ nr − 1 ∧ x1 ≥ 0 ∧ x1 ≤ nc − 1
                               |     A_{y1,x1} ← ikul
                               |     abc ← 0
                               | A
```

Loop to add multiple ellipses to a 2-D array (for plotting)

```
PLCC(D, xc, yc, C, ikul, isig, st) ≡ | n ← rows(xc)
                                     | if n − 1 ≥ st
                                     |   for i ∈ st..n − 1
                                     |     D ← ADELL(D, xc_i, yc_i, C_i, ikul, isig)
                                     |   abc ← 0
                                     | D
```

Calculates rectangle encompassing an ellipse

```
E2RC(I, i) ≡ | C ← (I_3)_i
             | θ ← 0
             | tmp ← C_{1,1} − C_{0,0}
             | θ ← 0.5 · atan[2 · (C_{0,1}) · (tmp)^−1]  if tmp ≠ 0
             | tmp ← √(tmp² + 4 · (C_{0,1})²)
             | a ← 0.5 · (C_{0,0} + C_{1,1} + tmp)
             | b ← 0.5 · (C_{0,0} + C_{1,1} − tmp)
             | xlen ← 2 · √a · sin(θ)
             | ylen ← 2 · √a · cos(θ)
             | xlen ← 2 · √b · cos(θ)  if 2 · √b · cos(θ) > xlen
             | if C_{0,0} > C_{1,1}
             |   xlen ← 2 · √a · cos(θ)
             |   ylen ← 2 · √a · sin(θ)
             |   ylen ← 2√b · cos(θ)  if 2√b · cos(θ) > ylen
             | xmn ← max2[floor[(I_1)_i − I_5 · 0.5 + 0.5], 2]
             | ymn ← max2[floor[(I_2)_i − I_5 · 0.5 + 0.5], 2]
             | xmx ← min2[floor[(I_1)_i + I_5 · 0.5 + 0.5], cols(I_0) − 3]
             | ymx ← min2[floor[(I_2)_i + I_5 · 0.5 + 0.5], rows(I_0) − 3]
             | for i ∈ ymn..ymx
             |   if ymx ≥ ymn ∧ xmx ≥ xmn
             |     for j ∈ xmn..xmx
             |       if I_4 = 0
             |         tmp ← (ymx − ymn + 1) · (xmx − xmn + 1)
             |         (I_0)_{i,j} ← (I_0)_{i,j} + 1/tmp
             |         imp ← 0
             |       (I_0)_{i,j} ← (I_0)_{i,j} + 1  otherwise
             |     imp ← 0
             | c_0 ← xmn
             | c_1 ← xmx
             | c_2 ← ymn
             | c_3 ← ymx
             | B_0 ← I_0
             | B_1 ← c
             | B
```

Rounds x to p decimal places

```
rflr(x, p) ≡ | x ← x · 10^p
             | x ← floor(x + 0.5)
             | x ← x · 10^−p
             | x
```

Builds output array from FRMS

```
OUT1(E, D, xmn, xmx, ymn, ymx, H, M, icol) ≡ | E_{icol,0} ← D
                                             | E_{icol,1} ← floor[(xmn + xmx) · 0.5]
                                             | E_{icol,2} ← floor[(ymn + ymx) · 0.5]
                                             | E_{icol,3} ← xmn
                                             | E_{icol,4} ← ymn
                                             | E_{icol,5} ← xmx
                                             | E_{icol,6} ← ymx
                                             | E_{icol,8} ← H
                                             | E_{icol,9} ← M
                                             | E
```

Calculate min of 1-D vector

```
min(A) ≡ | a ← A_0
         | for i ∈ 1..rows(A) − 1
         |   a ← A_i  if A_i < a
         | a
```

Calculate max of 1-D vector

```
max(A) ≡ | a ← A_0
         | for i ∈ 1..rows(A) − 1
         |   a ← A_i  if A_i > a
         | a
```

Calculates minimum of non-zero values in 2-D array A

```
MIN(A) ≡ | n ← 0
         | B_0 ← 0
         | for i ∈ 0..rows(A) − 1
         |   for j ∈ 0..cols(A) − 1
         |     if A_{i,j} ≠ 0
         |       B_n ← A_{i,j}
         |       n ← n + 1
         | minb ← B_0
         | for i ∈ 1..n − 1
         |   minb ← B_i  if B_i < minb
         | minb
```

Fig. 10. Part 3 of MathCAD 14 implementation of SV.

Single pass assembly isolation

```
SHAD(I) ≡ | F ← I_4
          | I_5 ← 1 if I_7 ≠ 0
          | tl ← (rows(I_0) · cols(I_0))^-1
          | E_0,9 ← 0
          | DDX ← PRCX(I_1)
          | DDY ← PRCX(I_2)
          | icol ← 1
          | for i ∈ 0..cols(DDX) − 1
          |   for j ∈ 0..cols(DDY) − 1
          |     | xL ← DDX_0,i
          |     | xH ← max(DDX^<i>)
          |     | yL ← DDY_0,j
          |     | yH ← max(DDY^<j>)
          |     | sum ← 0
          |     | sm1 ← 0
          |     | N ← 0
          |     | H ← 0
          |     | D ← 0
          |     | M ← 0
          |     | M_rows(I_0)−1,cols(I_0)−1 ← 0
          |     | for m ∈ xL..xH
          |     |   for L ∈ yL..yH
          |     |     | p ← L − yL
          |     |     | q ← m − xL
          |     |     | D_p,q ← (I_3)_L,m
          |     |     | M_L,m ← F_L,m
          |     |     | sm1 ← sm1 + (I_0)_L,m
          |     |     | H_p,q ← F_L,m · (I_3)_L,m
          |     |     | N ← N + 1 if (I_0)_L,m > 0
          |     |     | sum ← sum + (I_3)_L,m · F_L,m
          |     | for m ∈ xL..xH  if I_5 = 0 ∧ [sm1 ≤ (1 + tl) ∨ (I_6 = 0 ∧ N ≤ 1)]
          |     |   for L ∈ yL..yH
          |     |     F_L,m ← 0
          |     | if I_5 ≠ 0 ∨ [I_5 = 0 ∧ [sm1 > (1 + tl) ∨ (I_6 = 0 ∧ N > 1)]]  if sum > 0
          |     |   | E ← OUT1(E, D, xL, xH, yL, yH, H, M, icol)
          |     |   | icol ← icol + 1
          | E
```

Assembly isolation loop (recalculates shadow projection and calls SHAD for each candidate assembly)

```
FRMS(I) ≡ | G ← SHAD(I)
          | n ← rows(G) − 1
          | F_rows(I_0)−1,cols(I_0)−1 ← 0
          | n1 ← 1
          | if n ≥ 1
          |   | for i ∈ 1..n
          |   |   | D ← G_i,9
          |   |   | for j ∈ 0..cols(I_0) − 1
          |   |   |   | DX_j ← Σ_{k=0}^{rows(I_0)−1} D_k,j
          |   |   |   | DX_j ← 1 if DX_j > 1
          |   |   | for j ∈ 0..rows(I_0) − 1
          |   |   |   | DY_j ← Σ_{k=0}^{cols(I_0)−1} D_j,k
          |   |   |   | DY_j ← 1 if DY_j > 1
          |   |   | I_1 ← DX
          |   |   | I_2 ← DY
          |   |   | I_4 ← D
          |   |   | J ← SHAD(I)
          |   |   | if rows(J) > 1
          |   |   |   | for k ∈ 1..rows(J) − 1
          |   |   |   |   | for j ∈ 0..9
          |   |   |   |   |   E_n1,j ← J_k,j
          |   |   |   |   | n1 ← n1 + 1
          |   |   |   | ijk ← −1
          |   | G ← E
          | G
```

Calculates mean of 1-D array A

```
mean(A) ≡ | ym ← 0
          | for i ∈ 0..rows(A) − 1
          |   ym ← ym + A_i / rows(A)
          | ym
```

Identifies start and stop of each section of the shadow projection for use in SHAD

```
PRCX(D) ≡ | i ← 0
          | icol ← 0
          | istart ← 0
          | while i < rows(D) − 1
          |   | if D_i > 0
          |   |   | E_0,icol ← i
          |   |   | istart ← 1
          |   |   | i ← i + 1
          |   |   | while D_i > 0 ∧ i < (rows(D) − 1)
          |   |   |   | E_istart,icol ← i
          |   |   |   | i ← i + 1
          |   |   |   | istart ← istart + 1
          |   |   |   | break if i ≥ rows(D)
          |   |   | icol ← icol + 1
          |   | i ← i + 1 otherwise
          | E
```

Determines non-zero locations in each candidate assembly (A holds all candidate assemblies) and calls COVAR

```
CALCOV(A) ≡ | n ← rows(A)
            | covar_0 ← 0
            | if n − 1 ≥ 1
            |   | for i ∈ 1..n − 1
            |   |   | m ← 0
            |   |   | C ← A_i
            |   |   | B ← 0
            |   |   | for j ∈ 0..rows(C) − 1
            |   |   |   for k ∈ 0..cols(C) − 1
            |   |   |     if C_j,k ≠ 0
            |   |   |       | B_m,0 ← k
            |   |   |       | B_m,1 ← j
            |   |   |       | m ← m + 1
            |   |   | covar_i ← COVAR(B, 2, m)
            |   | abc ← 0
            | covar
```

Calculates max of 2-D array A

```
max(A) ≡ | mx ← A_0,0
         | for i ∈ 0..rows(A) − 1
         |   for j ∈ 0..rows(A) − 1
         |     mx ← A_i,j if A_i,j > mx
         | mx
```

Fig. 11. Part 4 of MathCAD 14 implementation of SV.

Heptor value J in Equation 17

```
J(A) ≡ | n ← rows(A)
       | ystat ← 1
       | yold ← 2
       | j ← 0
       | if (max(A) − min(A)) ≠ 0
       |   while |yold − Re(ystat)| > .0001
       |     yold ← Re(ystat)
       |     if Im(ystat) = 0
       |       lgr ← ln[|(Re(ystat))^−1|]
       |       lgi ← 1 − sign[(Re(ystat))^−1]
       |       lgi ← logi · π · 0.5
       |     otherwise
       |       xx ← Re(ystat) · (|ystat|)^−2
       |       yy ← −Im(ystat) · (|ystat|)^−2
       |       if xx · (|yy|)^−1 > 0
       |         acot ← atan(|yy| · xx^−1)
       |         abc ← 0
       |       if xx · (|yy|)^−1 = 0
       |         acot ← 0.5 · π
       |         abc ← 0
       |       if xx · (|yy|)^−1 < 0
       |         acot ← π + atan(|yy| · xx^−1)
       |         abc ← 0
       |       logr ← ln(xx^2 + yy^2) · 0.5
       |       logi ← sign(yy) · acot
       |     ystat ← max(A) − min(A)
       |     ystat ← ystat · n^−1 · Stdev(A)^−1
       |     ystat ← ln(ystat) · (ln(n^−1))^−1
       |     ystat ← ystat + lgr · (ln(n^−1))^−1
       |     ystat ← ystat + √−1 · lgi · (ln(n^−1))^−1
       |     j ← j + 1
       |   abc ← 0
       | h ← Re(ystat)
       | h ← 1 if h > 1
       | h ← 0 if h < 0
       | h ← h^−1 if h ≥ .5
       | h ← (1 − h)^−1 otherwise
       | h
```

Heptor (Equations 12 - 18) in this chapter

```
HEP(A) ≡ | ym ← (1 / rows(A)) · Σ_{i=0}^{rows(A)−1} A_i
         | h_0 ← sqrt( (1 / (rows(A) − 1)) · Σ_{i=0}^{rows(A)−1} (A_i − ym)^2 )
         | h_1 ← (1 / rows(A)) · Σ_{i=0}^{rows(A)−1} [(A_i − ym) · (h_0)^−1]^3
         | h_2 ← (1 / rows(A)) · Σ_{i=0}^{rows(A)−1} [(A_i − ym) · (h_0)^−1]^4 − 3
         | h_3 ← (1 / rows(A)) · Σ_{i=0}^{rows(A)−1} [(A_i − ym) · (h_0)^−1]^6 − 15
         | h_4 ← (1 / rows(A)) · Σ_{i=0}^{rows(A)−1} [(A_i − ym) · (h_0)^−1]^8 − 105
         | h_5 ← J(A)
         | A ← (A − min(A)) · (max(A) − min(A))^−1
         | M ← Σ_{i=0}^{rows(A)−2} sqrt( 1 + [A_{i+1} · (rows(A) − 1) − A_i · (rows(A) − 1)]^2 )
         | h_6 ← 1 + ln( M / (rows(A) − 1) ) · (ln(M))^−1
         | h
```

```
PLCR(I) ≡ | n ← rows(I_2)
          | if n − 1 ≥ 0
          |   for i ∈ 0..n − 1
          |     D1 ← E2RC(I,i)
          |     I_0 ← D1_0
          |     xm_i ← (D1_1)_0
          |     xx_i ← (D1_1)_1
          |     ym_i ← (D1_1)_2
          |     yx_i ← (D1_1)_3
          |   imp ← 0
          | E_0 ← I_0
          | E_1 ← xm
          | E_2 ← xx
          | E_3 ← ym
          | E_4 ← yx
          | E
```

PLCR places rectangles
Calls E2RC (ellipse to rectangle)
for multiple covariance ellipses
Returns array with rectangles
stacked along with min and max
x and y locations for each
rectangle extent

```
HEPFRAME(I,x,y) ≡ | for i ∈ 1..rows(I) − 1
                  |   A ← 0
                  |   m ← 0
                  |   for j ∈ 0..rows(I_{i,8}) − 1
                  |     for k ∈ 0..cols(I_{i,8}) − 1
                  |       A_m ← (I_{i,8})_{j,k}
                  |       m ← m + 1
                  |   H^⟨i−1⟩ ← HEP(A)
                  |   icls ← 2
                  |   for j ∈ 0..rows(x) − 1
                  |     if x_j ≥ I_{i,3} ∧ x_j ≤ I_{i,5} ∧ y_j ≥ I_{i,4} ∧ y_j ≤ I_{i,6}
                  |       icls ← 1
                  |       ijk ← −1
                  |   H_{7,i−1} ← icls
                  | H ← H^T
                  | w ← APPENDPRN("feats.out" ,H)
```

Calls Heptor for each
candidate assembly frame
and determines if a truth
location is within the assembly
(sets output variable for use
in Data Model K-G algorithm
used to derive the Decision
Architecture)

Fig. 12. Part 5 of MathCAD 14 implementation of SV.

2-D Convolution of A and B (Grid and kernel) using 1-D FFT

```
FFTCONV(A,B) ≡ | n ← rows(A)
               | twon ← 2·n
               | n1 ← floor(n/2)
               | A1[twon-1,twon-1] ← 0
               | B1[twon-1,twon-1] ← 0
               | for i ∈ 0..n-1
               |   for j ∈ 0..n-1
               |     | A1[i+n1,j+n1] ← A[i,j]
               |     | B1[i+n1,j+n1] ← B[i,j]
               | for i ∈ 0..twon-1
               |   | zA<i> ← FFT(A1<i>)
               |   | zB<i> ← FFT(B1<i>)
               | zA ← zA^T
               | zB ← zB^T
               | for i ∈ 0..twon-1
               |   | zA<i> ← FFT(zA<i>)
               |   | zB<i> ← FFT(zB<i>)
               | zA ← zA^T
               | zB ← zB^T
               | for i ∈ 0..twon-1
               |   for j ∈ 0..twon-1
               |     zC[i,j] ← zA[i,j]·zB[i,j]
               | for i ∈ 0..twon-1
               |   for j ∈ 0..twon-1
               |     zC[i,j] ← conj(zC[i,j])
               | for i ∈ 0..twon-1
               |   zC<i> ← FFT(zC<i>)
               | zC ← zC^T
               | for i ∈ 0..twon-1
               |   zC<i> ← FFT(zC<i>)
               | zC ← zC^T
               | C ← RC(zC)
               | for i ∈ 0..n-1
               |   for j ∈ 0..n-1
               |     D[i,j] ← Re(C[i+n1,j+n1])·twon
               | D
```

1-D Fast Fourier Transform (FFT)

```
FFT(Z) ≡ | n ← rows(Z)
         | x ← Re(Z)
         | y ← Im(Z)
         | j ← 0
         | n2 ← n/2
         | for i ∈ 1..n-2
         |   | n1 ← n2
         |   | while j ≥ n1
         |   |   | j ← j - n1
         |   |   | n1 ← n1·0.5
         |   | j ← j + n1
         |   | if i < j
         |   |   | t1 ← x[i]
         |   |   | x[i] ← x[j]
         |   |   | x[j] ← t1
         |   |   | t1 ← y[i]
         |   |   | y[i] ← y[j]
         |   |   | y[j] ← t1
         | n1 ← 0
         | n2 ← 1
         | m ← floor[ln(n)·(ln(2))^-1]
         | for i ∈ 0..m-1
         |   | n1 ← n2
         |   | n2 ← n2 + n2
         |   | a ← 0
         |   | for j ∈ 0..n1-1
         |   |   | c ← cos(-2·π·a·n^-1)
         |   |   | s ← sin(-2·π·a·n^-1)
         |   |   | a ← a + 2^(m-i-1)
         |   |   | for k ∈ j,j+n2..n-1
         |   |   |   | t1 ← c·x[k+n1] - s·y[k+n1]
         |   |   |   | t2 ← s·x[k+n1] + c·y[k+n1]
         |   |   |   | x[k+n1] ← x[k] - t1
         |   |   |   | y[k+n1] ← y[k] - t2
         |   |   |   | x[k] ← x[k] + t1
         |   |   |   | y[k] ← y[k] + t2
         | F ← (x + √-1·y)·(√n)^-1
         | F
```

Recenter for 2-D arrays (moves corners to the center and the center out to the 4 corners)

```
RC(A) ≡ | xlen ← cols(A)
        | ylen ← rows(A)
        | xsize ← floor(xlen/2)
        | ysize ← floor(ylen/2)
        | for i ∈ 0..ysize-1
        |   for j ∈ 0..xsize-1
        |     | B[i,j] ← A[i+ysize,j+xsize]
        |     | B[i+ysize,j+xsize] ← A[i,j]
        |     | B[i,j+xsize] ← A[i+ysize,j]
        |     | B[i+ysize,j] ← A[i,j+xsize]
        | B
```

```
MAX(A) ≡ | n ← 0
         | B[0] ← 0
         | for i ∈ 0..rows(A)-1
         |   for j ∈ 0..cols(A)-1
         |     if A[i,j] ≠ 0
         |       | B[n] ← A[i,j]
         |       | n ← n + 1
         | maxb ← B[0]
         | for i ∈ 1..n-1
         |   maxb ← B[i] if B[i] > maxb
         | maxb
```

Max non-zero values in 2-D array A

Fig. 13. Part 6 of MathCAD 14 implementation of SV.

The first 2 pages (Fig. 8 and 9) list the overall structure of the SV algorithm implementation (the main program body), and each of these 2 pages has been broken up into lettered sections with brief descriptions of each section. The remaining 4 pages (Fig. 10-13) are individual MathCAD programs that implement each of the specific functions used in SV, along with a general description of each function. When the MathCAD 14 document is loaded, a single case is generated. In order to vary the road and object placements, new individual cases can be generated by increasing the value of kkk1 (Fig. 9, Section I at the bottom of the figure) in integer steps. Alternatively, Monte Carlo cases can be generated using the Tool/Animation/Record pull down menu to load the movie recording capability in MathCAD 14. Place a fence around the kkk1 equation and set the FRAME variable to range from 0 to the number of Monte Carlos desired and set the time step to 1. The resultant HEPTOR features for each Monte Carlo are written into the file feats.out in the HEPFRAME function (note, delete this file from the directory containing the MathCAD 14 document before starting this process so that only the selected Monte Carlos are written into the file).

6. Classifier KG algorithm

To derive a general mathematical Data Model (Jaenisch and Handley, 2003), it is necessary to combine multiple input measurement variables to provide a classifier in the form of an analytical math model. Multivariate linear regression is used to derive an $O(3^n)$ Data Model fusing multiple input measurement sources or data sets and associated target label definitions. This is accomplished using a fast algorithm (flowchart in Fig. 14) that derives the coefficients of the approximation to the Kolmogorov-Gabor (KG) polynomial (which they proved to be a universal function or mathematical model for any dynamic process)

$$y(x_1, x_2, \ldots, x_L) = a_0 + \sum_i a_i x_i + \sum_i \sum_j a_{ij} x_i x_j + \sum_i \sum_j \sum_k a_{ijk} x_i x_j x_k + \cdots \quad (24)$$

which takes all available inputs in all possible combinations raised to all possible powers (orders).

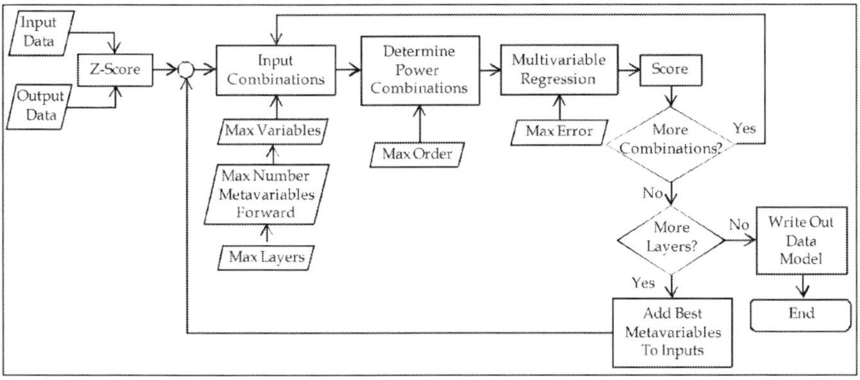

Fig. 14. Multivariable Data Model algorithm flowchart.

The full KG multinomial is impractical to derive directly. One method for approximating the KG polynomial is the Group Method of Data Handling (GMDH) algorithm (Madala and Ivakhnenko, 1994), which has been improved upon by the author into Data Modeling. Data Modeling uses multivariable linear regression to fit combinations of input variables (up to a user specified number at a time) to find the minimum error using either correlation or root sum square (RSS) differences between the regression output and the objective function. The best of these combinations (user specified number) are retained and used as metavariables (new inputs) and the process repeated at the next layer. Layering is terminated when overall desired RSS difference is minimized (Jaenisch and Handley, 2009). Figs. 16-20 on the following pages contain a MathCAD 14 implementation of Data Model K-G algorithm that was used to build the decision architecture in Section 7, and as before, Fig. 16 is broken up into sections for explanation.

7. Decision Architecture

It is possible to identify an optimal subset of the exemplars using available support vector finding machines; however, a good rule of thumb is to use 10% of the available exemplars. The SV algorithm in Figs. 8-13 was run for 50 epochs (FRAME ranging from 0 to 49), generating a total of 320 exemplars. The first 1/3 of these points (107 exemplars) was used as input into the MathCAD 14 document in Figs. 16-20. Fig. 16 shows the output results from this Data Model graphically at the bottom of the page. Two thresholds were set (lower threshold at 0.89 and an upper threshold at 1.92), and the exemplars cases which fell between the two thresholds were pulled out as the support vectors (87 of the 107 original cases were selected as support vectors) using the EXTR function provided.

Starting with these 87 exemplars, a new Data Model was generated using the decision architecture construction/execution flowchart in Fig. 15. Each node was constructed using the exemplars siphoned from the previous node (using EXTUP in the MathCAD document). The number of layers (nlay) was changed to 2 to make the Data Models shorter for publication in this work. A total of 3 nodes (bulk filter plus 2 resolvers) were required to learn these 87 support vector exemplars (with care taken to preserve each Data Model BASIC source code written out from the MathCAD 14 document at each siphon point along with the exemplar data).

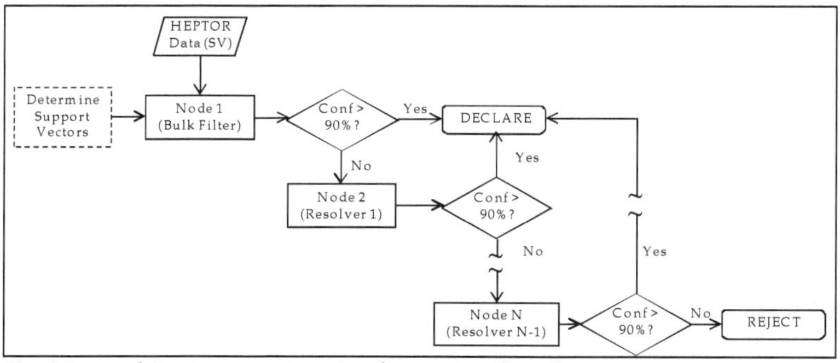

Fig. 15. Decision architecture construction/execution flowchart.

Derive Multi-Variable Data Model

A. Initialization

$prec := 2$ — **Calc Prec**
$exitc := 0.0001$ — **Exit Criteria**
$nfwd := 3$ — **# metvar forward**
$nlay := 4$ — **# Layers**
$maxvar := 3$ — **Max # ins per bldg blk**
$maxorder := 3$ — **Max bldg blk Order**
$X1 := READPRN("feats.out")$ — **Data file from SV**
$nins := 7$ — **# inputs**

$outcol := 7$ — **Output Data Col**
$nsamp := 107$ — **# samps to build DM**

B. Pull out samples and Sort into ascending order on output (for visualization)

$i := 0..nsamp - 1$ $j := 0..nins - 1$ $X2_{i,j} := X1_{i,j}$ $X2_{i,outcol} := X1_{i,outcol}$ $X2 := CSORT(X2, outcol)$ $X_{i,j} := X2_{i,j}$

$Y_i := X2_{i,outcol}$ $j := 0..cols(X) - 1$ $Xtmp := X2$ $npts := rows(X)$ $i := 0..npts - 1$

C. Supply names for inputs and output $InNam_j := concat("z", num2str(j + 1))$ **Input names (z1 to z7)** $OutName := "y"$

D. Z-score inputs and output

$xavg_j := rflr\left(mean\left(X^{\langle j\rangle}\right), prec\right)$ $xdev_j := rflr\left(ADEV\left(X^{\langle j\rangle}, npts\right), prec\right)$ $yavg := rflr(mean(Y), prec)$

$ydev := rflr(ADEV(Y, npts), prec)$ $X_{i,j} := \dfrac{X_{i,j} - xavg_j}{xdev_j}$ $Y_i := \dfrac{Y_i - yavg}{ydev}$

E. Perform Multivariable linear regression (K-G) algorithm process

$I_0 := X$ $I_1 := InNam$ $I_2 := Y$ $I_3 := nlay$ $I_4 := nfwd$ $I_5 := exitc$ $I_6 := maxvar$ $I_7 := maxorder$ $I_8 := prec$ $I_9 := nins$

$kgmodel := DM(I)$ Derive KG Data Model

F. Undo Z-scoring on output to score $kgmodel_i := kgmodel_i \cdot ydev + yavg$ $Y_i := Y_i \cdot ydev + yavg$

$rss := \sqrt{\sum_i \left(kgmodel_i - Y_i\right)^2}$ $rss = 2.99$

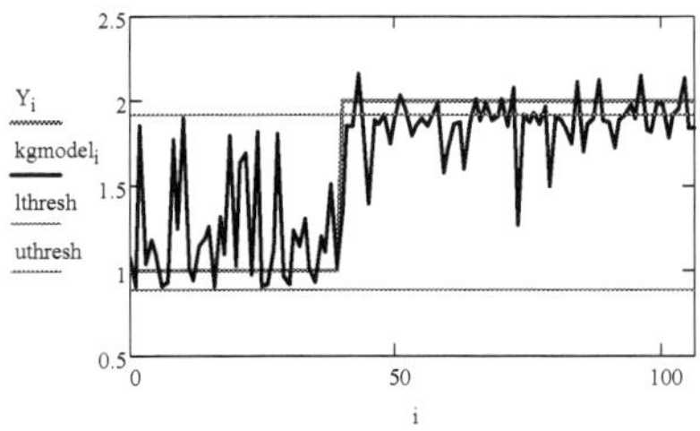

$lthresh \equiv 0.89$
$uthresh \equiv 1.92$

G. Tools for siphoning (used in decision architecture construction)

$B := EXTR(Xtmp, kgmodel, lthresh, uthresh)$ — Used to select support vectors (between thresholds)

$B := EXTUP(Xtmp, kgmodel, uthresh)$ — Enable for siphoning

H. Write out Data Model BASIC code

$f := "outbas.prn"$ $iscale_i := 1$ $jscale := 1$ KG output Data Model file $C1 := READPRN("fnldm.prn")$

$I1_0 := C1$ $I1_1 := OutName$ $I1_2 := yavg$ $I1_3 := ydev$ $I1_4 := f$ $I1_5 := prec$ $I1_6 := InNam$ $I1_7 := xavg$ $I1_8 := xdev$

$I1_9 := iscale$ $I1_{10} := jscale$ $COD := \left| \begin{array}{l} WHD(f, InNam) \\ WPG(I1) \end{array} \right.$

$$mean(A) \equiv \left| \begin{array}{l} ym \leftarrow 0 \\ \text{for } i \in 0..rows(A) - 1 \\ \quad ym \leftarrow ym + \dfrac{A_i}{rows(A)} \\ ym \end{array} \right.$$

Calculates the mean of 1-D vector A

$$rflr(x, p) \equiv \left| \begin{array}{l} x \leftarrow x \cdot 10^p \\ x \leftarrow floor(x + 0.5) \\ x \leftarrow x \cdot 10^{-p} \\ x \end{array} \right.$$

Rounds x to p decimal places precision

B — **Enable to write out siphoned data or support vectors**

COD — **Writes out the Data Model BASIC code**

Fig. 16. Part 1 of MathCAD 14 implementation to derive a multivariable Data Model.

Calculates the Average Deviation of x (n is the number of points in x)

```
ADEV(x,n) ≡ | avg ← 0
            | avgdev ← 0
            | for i ∈ 0..n − 1
            |     avg ← avg + x_i / n
            | for i ∈ 0..n − 1
            |   | x_i ← x_i − avg
            |   | avgdev ← avgdev + |x_i| / n
            | avgdev
```

Removes any duplications in output from COMBIN

```
REMDUP(A) ≡ | n ← rows(A)
            | ncols ← cols(A)
            | for i ∈ 0..n − 1
            |     A_{i,ncols} ← ∏_{j=0}^{ncols−1} A_{i,j}
            | A ← csort(A,ncols)
            | itot ← 1
            | for j ∈ 0..ncols − 1
            |     B_{0,j} ← A_{0,j}
            | if n > 1
            |   | for i ∈ 1..n − 1
            |   |   if A_{i,ncols} ≠ A_{i−1,ncols}
            |   |     | for j ∈ 0..ncols − 1
            |   |     |     B_{itot,j} ← A_{i,j}
            |   |     | itot ← itot + 1
            |   | abc ← 0
            | B
```

Embeds Z-score of input in BASIC code export

```
MV(I,z,j,k) ≡ | z ← concat["((" ,num2str[(I_9)_j],"*" ,z,"-"]
              | z ← concat[z,num2str[rflr[(I_7)_k,I_5]],")/("]
              | z ← concat[z,num2str[rflr[(I_8)_k,I_5]],"))"]
              | z
```

Makes temporary file names

```
NAM(i,j,k) ≡ vec2str( | tnam_0 ← 96 + i
                      | tnam_1 ← 96 + j − k )
```

Probability distribution

$$p(x,m,s) \equiv \exp\left[-0.5\cdot\left(\frac{x-m}{s}\right)^2\right]$$

Returns combinations
Each column of A is a variable
Each row of A is an example of that variable

```
COMBIN(A) ≡ | tot ← 0
            | icnt ← 0
            | iexit ← 0
            | mxc ← cols(A)
            | mxw ← rows(A)
            | maxcomb ← mxw^mxc
            | for i ∈ 0..mxc − 1
            |     ord_i ← 0
            | while iexit = 0
            |   | for i ∈ 0..mxw − 1
            |   |   | ord_{mxc−1} ← i
            |   |   | ifill ← 1
            |   |   | for k ∈ 0..mxc − 1
            |   |   |   | B_{tot,k} ← A_{ord_k,k}
            |   |   |   | if A_{ord_k,k} = ""
            |   |   |   |   | ifill ← 0
            |   |   |   |   | abc ← 0
            |   |   | tot ← tot + 1 if ifill = 1
            |   |   | icnt ← icnt + 1
            |   |   | if icnt ≥ maxcomb
            |   |   |   | iexit ← 1
            |   |   |   | break
            |   | break if iexit = 1
            |   | ic ← 1
            |   | iexit1 ← 0
            |   | while iexit1 = 0
            |   |   | s1 ← mxc − ic − 1
            |   |   | s2 ← mxc − ic − 2
            |   |   | for i ∈ s1,s2..0
            |   |   |   | if ord_i ≥ mxw − 1
            |   |   |   |   | ord_i ← 0
            |   |   |   |   | ic ← ic + 1
            |   |   |   |   | break
            |   |   |   | otherwise
            |   |   |   |   | ord_i ← ord_i + 1
            |   |   |   |   | iexit1 ← 1
            |   |   |   |   | break
            | for i ∈ 0..tot − 1
            |   for j ∈ 0..mxc − 1
            |     B1_{i,j} ← B_{i,j}
            | B1
```

Multivariable linear regression

```
FIT(n,v,din,dout,pc) ≡ | s_{n+1} ← 0
                       | a_{v+1,v+2} ← 0
                       | xl_1 ← 1
                       | for i ∈ 1..n
                       |   | for j ∈ 1..v
                       |   |     xl_{j+1} ← din_{i−1,j−1}
                       |   | xl_{v+2} ← dout_{i−1}
                       |   | for k ∈ 1..v + 1
                       |   |   for m ∈ 1..v + 2
                       |   |     | a_{k,m} ← a_{k,m} + xl_k·xl_m
                       |   |     | s_k ← a_{k,v+2}
                       |   | s_{v+2} ← s_{v+2} + xl_{v+2}·xl_{v+2}
                       | for i ∈ 2..v + 1
                       |     t_i ← a_{1,i}
                       | for i ∈ 1..v + 1
                       |   | j ← i
                       |   | while a_{j,i} = 0
                       |   |   | j ← j + 1
                       |   |   | break if j > v + 1
                       |   | break if j > v + 1
                       |   | for k ∈ 1..v + 2
                       |   |   | b ← a_{i,k}
                       |   |   | a_{i,k} ← a_{j,k}
                       |   |   | a_{j,k} ← b
                       |   | z1 ← (a_{i,i})^−1
                       |   | for k ∈ 1..v + 2
                       |   |     a_{i,k} ← z1·a_{i,k}
                       |   | for j ∈ 1..v + 1
                       |   |   if j ≠ i
                       |   |     | z1 ← −a_{j,i}
                       |   |     | for k ∈ 1..v + 2
                       |   |     |     a_{j,k} ← a_{j,k} + z1·a_{i,k}
                       | c_0 ← a_{1,v+2}
                       | for j ∈ 1..v
                       |   | c_j ← rflr(a_{j+1,v+2},pc)
                       |   | c_j ← str2num(num2str(c_j))
                       | c
```

Fig. 17. Part 2 of MathCAD 14 implementation to derive a multivariable Data Model.

```
WHD(f,Nam) ≡ | a_0 ← 39
             | tvar ← rows(Nam)
             | abc_0 ← "cls : on error resume next"
             | bb ← WRITEPRN(f,abc)
             | abc_0 ← "rem Holger Jaenisch, PhD, DSc"
             | abc_1 ← "rem Licht Strahl Engineering INC (LSEI)"
             | abc_2 ← "rem LSEI1@yahoo.com"
             | APPENDPRN(f,abc)
             | abc_0 ← concat("open " ,vec2str(a),"kggmdh.in" )
             | abc_0 ← concat(abc_0,vec2str(a)," for input as #1" )
             | abc_1 ← concat("open " ,vec2str(a),"kggmdh.out" )
             | abc_1 ← concat(abc_1,vec2str(a)," for output as #2" )
             | abc_2 ← "do until eof(1)"
             | abc_3 ← "input #1, "
             | for i ∈ 0..tvar − 2                          if tvar > 1
             |   abc_3 ← concat(abc_3,Nam_i,", " )
             | abc_3 ← concat(abc_3,Nam_(tvar−1))
             | APPENDPRN(f,abc)
```

Write Header of BASIC code for Data Model

```
RBLOCK(X,Y,a,flg,no,pc) ≡ | nvar ← cols(X)
                          | n ← rows(X)
                          | m ← 0
                          | for i ∈ 1..no
                          |   for j ∈ 0..nvar − 1
                          |     Z_(j,i−1) ← j + 1
                          |   B ← COMBIN(Z)
                          |   A ← REMDUP(B)
                          |   for p ∈ 0..rows(A) − 1
                          |     for j ∈ 0..n − 1
                          |       dj_(j,m) ← X_(j,A_(p,0)−1)
                          |       if i − 1 > 0
                          |         for k ∈ 1..i − 1
                          |           tmp ← A_(p,k) − 1
                          |           dj_(j,m) ← dj_(j,m)·X_(j,tmp)
                          |         jjj ← 1
                          |     m ← m + 1
                          | if flg = 0
                          |   a ← FIT(n,m,dj,Y,pc)
                          |   WRITEPRN("coeff.prn" ,a)
                          |   a ← READPRN("coeff.prn" )
                          | for i ∈ 0..n − 1
                          |   tot_i ← [a_0 + Σ_(j=0)^(m−1) (dj_(i,j)·a_(j+1))]
                          | tot
```

Uses Combinatorial Algorithm to determine power combinations and calls FIT

```
EXTUP(X,kg,ut) ≡ | m ← 0
                 | for i ∈ 0..rows(X) − 1
                 |   if kg_i ≥ ut
                 |     for j ∈ 0..7
                 |       A_(m,j) ← X_(i,j)
                 |     m ← m + 1
                 | A

EXTR(X,kg,lt,ut) ≡ | m ← 0
                   | for i ∈ 0..rows(X) − 1
                   |   if kg_i ≥ lt ∧ kg_i ≤ ut
                   |     for j ∈ 0..7
                   |       A_(m,j) ← X_(i,j)
                   |     m ← m + 1
                   | A
```

EXTR selects input exemplars between lt and ut, while EXTUP selects those above ut

```
SCR(z,n,cerr,rnk,nf,c) ≡ | ibreak ← 0
                         | if cerr < rnk_(nf−1,0)
                         |   for i ∈ 1..nf
                         |     if cerr < rnk_(i−1,0)
                         |       if i < nf
                         |         for k ∈ nf,nf − 1..i + 1
                         |           rnk_(k−1,0) ← rnk_(k−2,0)
                         |           for m ∈ 0..n − 1
                         |             rnk_(m,k) ← rnk_(m,k−1)
                         |           for m ∈ 0..n − 1
                         |             rnk_(m,nf+k) ← rnk_(m,nf+k−1)
                         |         jjj ← 1
                         |       for m ∈ 0..n − 1
                         |         rnk_(m,i) ← z_m
                         |         rnk_(m,i+nf) ← 0
                         |       for m ∈ 0..rows(c) − 1
                         |         rnk_(m,i+nf) ← c_m
                         |       rnk_(i−1,0) ← cerr
                         |       ibreak ← 1
                         |     break if ibreak ≠ 0
                         |   jjj ← 1
                         | rnk
```

Scores current layer object if current better than previous, stores

```
CHKEQN(I) ≡ | n ← rows(I_0)
            | ni ← cols(I_0)
            | for j ∈ 1..I_4
            |   cname ← NAM(I_2,j,0)
            |   cname ← concat(cname,".prn" )
            |   tmp ← READPRN(cname)
            |   nvar ← tmp_0
            |   norder ← tmp_1
            |   ncoef ← tmp_(nvar+2)
            |   for k ∈ 0..ncoef − 1
            |     a_k ← rflr(tmp_(nvar+3+k),I_6)
            |     a_k ← str2num(num2str(a_k))
            |   for k ∈ 0..nvar − 1
            |     imatch ← 0
            |     for m ∈ 0..ni − 1
            |       if tmp_(k+2) = (I_1)_m
            |         imatch ← 1
            |         x^<k> ← (I_0)^<m>
            |         break
            |     if imatch = 0
            |       fil ← concat("d" ,tmp_(k+2),".prn" )
            |       x^<k> ← READPRN(fil)
            |   z ← RBLOCK(x,x^<0>,a,1,norder,I_6)
            |   WRITEPRN(concat("d" ,cname),z)
            |   break if j = I_5
            | z
```

Reads Data Model coefficients from file and generates Data Model values

Fig. 18. Part 3 of MathCAD 14 implementation to derive a multivariable Data Model.

Main driver program for Data Model generation

```
DM(I) ≡ | errc ← I_5 + 1
        | Xi ← I_0
        | Nam ← I_1
        | ilay ← 0
        | while (errc > I_5) ∧ (ilay < I_3)
        |   | ilay ← ilay + 1
        |   | I1_0 ← Xi
        |   | I1_1 ← Nam
        |   | I1_2 ← I_2
        |   | I1_3 ← I_4
        |   | I1_4 ← I_6
        |   | I1_5 ← I_7
        |   | I1_6 ← I_8
        |   | r ← NEST(I1)
        |   | errc ← r_{0,0}
        |   | for i ∈ I_4 + 1..2·I_4
        |   |    WRITEPRN(NAM(ilay,i,I_4), r^⟨i⟩)
        |   | for i ∈ 0..I_4 − 1
        |   |   | I1_2 ← ilay
        |   |   | I1_4 ← I_4
        |   |   | I1_5 ← i + 1
        |   |   | I1_6 ← I_8
        |   |   | Xi^⟨i+I_9⟩ ← CHKEQN(I1)
        |   |   | Nam_{i+I_9} ← NAM(ilay, i + 1, 0)
        | A_{1,0} ← ilay
        | A_{2,0} ← I_4
        | for i ∈ 1..ilay
        |   for j ∈ 1..I_4
        |     | cn ← concat(NAM(i,j,0), ".prn")
        |     | tmp ← READPRN(cn)
        |     | A^⟨(i−1)·I_4+j⟩ ← tmp
        | WRITEPRN("fnldm.prn", A)
        | r^⟨1⟩
```

Input combinations used for Data Model, calls RBLOCK and SCR

```
NEST(I) ≡ | n ← rows(I_0)
          | nvar ← cols(I_0)
          | rank_{n−1,2·I_3} ← 0
          | for i ∈ 0..I_3 − 1
          |    rank_{i,0} ← 10^20
          | for i ∈ 0..n − 1
          |    a_i ← 1
          | for v1 ∈ 1..I_4
          |   | for j ∈ 0..nvar − 1
          |   |    Z_{j,v1−1} ← j + 1
          |   | B ← COMBIN(Z)
          |   | A ← REMDUP(B)
          |   | for v2 ∈ 1..I_5
          |   |   for j ∈ 0..rows(A) − 1
          |   |     | XA ← 0
          |   |     | for v3 ∈ 0..v1 − 1
          |   |     |    XA^⟨v3⟩ ← (I_0)^⟨(A_{j,v3}−1)⟩
          |   |     | z ← RBLOCK(XA, I_2, a, 0, v2, I_6)
          |   |     | coefA ← READPRN("coeff.prn")
          |   |     | c ← 0
          |   |     | c_0 ← v1
          |   |     | c_1 ← v2
          |   |     | for v3 ∈ 0..v1 − 1
          |   |     |    c_{v3+2} ← (I_1)_{A_{j,v3}−1}
          |   |     | c_{v1+2} ← rows(coefA)
          |   |     | for m ∈ 0..rows(coefA) − 1
          |   |     |   | iL ← m + v1 + 3
          |   |     |   | c_iL ← rflr(coefA_m, I_6)
          |   |     |   | c_iL ← str2num(num2str(c_iL))
          |   |     | err ← 0
          |   |     | for jj ∈ 0..n − 1
          |   |     |    err ← err + [(I_2)_jj − z_jj]^2
          |   |     | err ← √err
          |   |     | rank ← SCR(z, n, err, rank, I_3, c)
          | rank
```

BASIC Data Model export of K-G poly approximation (multilayer)

```
WOB(C,a,O,N) ≡ | m ← 1
               | e_0 ← concat(O, " = ", num2str(rflr(a_0, C_2)))
               | mm ← 1
               | for i ∈ 1..C_0
               |   | for j ∈ 0..C_1 − 1
               |   |    Z_{j,i−1} ← j + 1
               |   | B ← COMBIN(Z)
               |   | A ← REMDUP(B)
               |   | for j ∈ 0..rows(A) − 1
               |   |   | if rflr(a_mm, C_2) ≠ 0 ∧ |rflr(a_mm, C_2)| ≠ 1.0
               |   |   |   | e_m ← concat(O, " = ", O, " + ")
               |   |   |   | e_m ← concat(e_m, num2str(rflr(a_mm, C_2)))
               |   |   |   | for k ∈ 0..i − 1
               |   |   |   |    e_m ← concat[e_m, " * ", N_(A_{j,k}−1)]
               |   |   |   | m ← m + 1
               |   |   | otherwise
               |   |   |   | if rflr(a_mm, C_2) ≠ 0
               |   |   |   |   | if rflr(a_mm, C_2) = 1.0
               |   |   |   |   |   | e_m ← concat(O, " = ", O, " + ")
               |   |   |   |   |   | ijk ← −1
               |   |   |   |   | otherwise
               |   |   |   |   |   | e_m ← concat(O, " = ", O, " - ")
               |   |   |   |   |   | ijk ← −1
               |   |   |   |   | for k ∈ 0..i − 1
               |   |   |   |   |   | if k > 0
               |   |   |   |   |   |   | e_m ← concat(e_m, " * ")
               |   |   |   |   |   |   | ijk ← −1
               |   |   |   |   |   | e_m ← concat[e_m, N_(A_{j,k}−1)]
               |   |   |   |   | m ← m + 1
               |   |   |   | ijk ← −1
               |   |   | mm ← mm + 1
               | e
```

Fig. 19. Part 4 of MathCAD 14 implementation to derive a multivariable Data Model.

Switches value locations (Sorting)

```
SWT(I,x,y) ≡ | temp ← (I0)x
             | (I0)x ← (I0)y
             | (I0)y ← temp
             | temp ← (I1)x
             | (I1)x ← (I1)y
             | (I1)y ← temp
             | I
```

BASIC source code exportation (writes all except header)

```
WPG(I) ≡ | nl ← (I0)1,0
         | nf ← (I0)2,0
         | for i ∈ 1..nl
         |   for k ∈ 1..nf
         |     neqn ← k + (i − 1)·nf
         |     nvar ← (I0)0,neqn
         |     norder ← (I0)1,neqn
         |     for j ∈ 0..nvar − 1
         |       varj ← (I0)j+2,neqn
         |       for kk ∈ 0..rows(I6) − 1
         |         if (I6)kk = varj
         |           varj ← MV(I, varj, j, kk)
         |           ijk ← −1
         |     ncoeff ← (I0)nvar+2,neqn
         |     for j ∈ 0..ncoeff − 1
         |       bj ← (I0)nvar+3+j,neqn
         |     oname ← NAM(i,k,0)
         |     C0 ← norder
         |     C1 ← nvar
         |     C2 ← I5
         |     bline ← WOB(C,b,oname,var)
         |     APPENDPRN(I4,bline)
         |     break if i = nl
         |   break if i = nl
         | abc0 ← concat(I1," = ",oname,"*")
         | abc0 ← concat(abc0,num2str(rflr(I3,I5)))
         | abc0 ← concat(abc0," + ",num2str(rflr(I2,I5)))
         | abc1 ← concat(I1," = ",I1,"/",num2str(I10))
         | abc2 ← concat("print #2, ",I1)
         | abc3 ← "loop : close : end"
         | APPENDPRN(I4,abc)
```

```
CSORT(A,k) ≡ | n ← rows(A)
             | for i ∈ 1..n
             |   arri ← Ai−1,k
             |   brri ← i − 1
             | loc ← SORT2(n,arr,brr)1
             | for i ∈ 0..cols(A) − 1
             |   for j ∈ 1..n
             |     Bj−1,i ← Alocj,i
             | B
```

Converts sort2 into n column sort

Upper Sort routine branch

```
S2A(I) ≡ | if I2 + 1 ≤ I5
         |   for j ∈ I2 + 1..I5
         |     a ← (I0)j
         |     b ← (I1)j
         |     jf ← 0
         |     if j > 1
         |       for i ∈ j − 1, j − 2..1
         |         if (I0)i ≤ a
         |           jf ← 1
         |           break
         |         break if jf = 1
         |         (I0)i+1 ← (I0)i
         |         (I1)i+1 ← (I1)i
         |       abc ← 0
         |     i ← 0 if jf = 0
         |     (I0)i+1 ← a
         |     (I1)i+1 ← b
         |   abc ← 0
         | if I4 = 0
         |   I6 ← 1
         |   break
         | I5 ← (I3)(I4)
         | I2 ← (I3)I4−1
         | I4 ← I4 − 2
         | I
```

2 variable sort main program

```
SORT2(ir,arr,brr) ≡ | I0 ← arr
                    | I1 ← brr
                    | I2 ← 1
                    | istack0 ← 0
                    | I3 ← istack
                    | I4 ← 0
                    | I5 ← ir
                    | I6 ← 0
                    | while I6 = 0
                    |   I ← S2A(I) if I5 − I2 < 7
                    |   I ← S2B(I) otherwise
                    | A0 ← I0
                    | A1 ← I1
                    | A
```

Lower sort routine branch

```
S2B(I) ≡ | L ← I2
         | ir ← I5
         | k ← floor[(L + ir)·0.5]
         | I ← SWT(I,k,L + 1)
         | if (I0)L+1 > (I0)ir
         |   I ← SWT(I,L + 1,ir)
         |   abc ← 0
         | if (I0)L > (I0)ir
         |   I ← SWT(I,L,ir)
         |   abc ← 0
         | if (I0)L+1 > (I0)L
         |   I ← SWT(I,L + 1,L)
         |   abc ← 0
         | i ← L + 1
         | j ← ir
         | a ← (I0)L
         | b ← (I1)L
         | jf ← 0
         | while jf = 0
         |   while jf = 0
         |     i ← i + 1
         |     break if (I0)i ≥ a
         |   while jf = 0
         |     j ← j − 1
         |     break if (I0)j ≤ a
         |   break if j < i
         |   I ← SWT(I,i,j) otherwise
         | (I0)L ← (I0)j
         | (I0)j ← a
         | (I1)L ← (I1)j
         | (I1)j ← b
         | I4 ← I4 + 2
         | if I4 > 50
         |   kf ← 1
         |   break
         | if ir − i + 1 ≥ j − L
         |   (I3)(I4) ← ir
         |   (I3)I4−1 ← i
         |   ir ← j − 1
         | otherwise
         |   (I3)(I4) ← j − 1
         |   (I3)I4−1 ← L
         |   L ← i
         | I2 ← L
         | I5 ← ir
         | I
```

Fig. 20. Part 5 of MathCAD 14 implementation to derive a multivariable Data Model.

Fig. 21 shows the results of processing all of the 87 training exemplars thru the bulk filter and 2 resolver Data Models in this process (Jaenisch et.al., 2002)(2010). All examples for which the Data Model returns a value inside the lower and upper thresholds (labeled Declare on each graph) are declared targets, while those outside the upper and lower thresholds are deferred until the last resolver, where a reject decision is made. Rollup equations for each node in the decision architecture are also provided under each graph in Fig. 21. The coefficients in front of each variable are derived by first determining how many times the variable occurs in the actual multinomial, normalizing each by dividing by the number of occurrences of the least frequently occurring variable, summing the result, and dividing each result by the sum. By normalizing by the least frequently occurring variable first and then turning the number into a percentage by dividing by the result sum, the coefficients describe the key and critical feature contribution in the full Data Model.

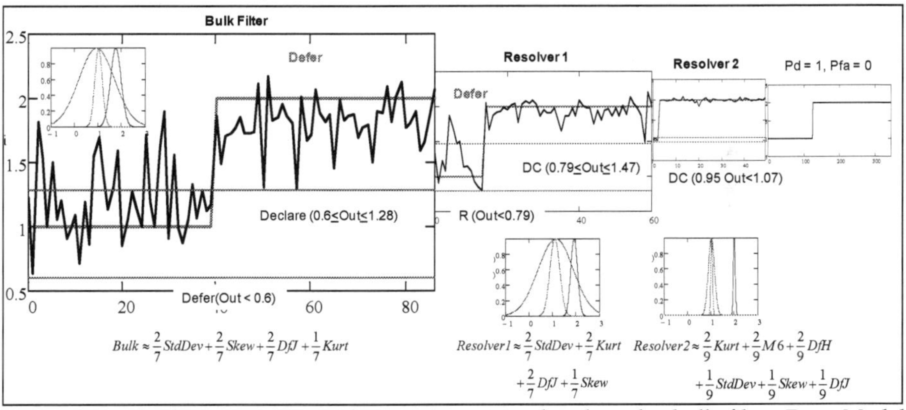

Fig. 21. Results from processing the training examples thru the bulk filter Data Model classifier and the ambiguity resolver. The entire decision architecture flows thru the bulk filter and, if required, as many of the ambiguity resolvers until either a reject or declare is determined.

The 3 BASIC files saved from deriving each of the nodes were combined together into the single decision architecture BASIC program given in Figs. 22 and 23. The value for each node in the decision architecture was converted into a confidence using the normal probability distribution defined by

$$Conf = \exp[-0.5(((Val - m)/s)^2)] \tag{25}$$

where Val is the value returned by the individual node in the decision architecture, m is the average between the upper and lower declare thresholds, and s (normally in the distribution the standard deviation) the value required so that Equation 25 returned a value of 0.9 (90% confidence) at the declaration thresholds. At the upper declaration threshold, no potential targets with a confidence of less than 90% are ever allowed to be declared, since they are labeled as defer by the decision architecture. All of the 320 examples were processed thru the decision architecture, yielding a probability of detection (Pd) of 0.65 and a probability of false alarm (Pfa) of 0.16.

```
CLS
ON ERROR RESUME NEXT
OPEN "feats.out" FOR INPUT AS #1
OPEN "dearch.out" FOR OUTPUT AS #2
DO UNTIL EOF(1)
INPUT #1, z1, z2, z3, z4, z5, z6, z7, trth
'z1 to z7 are heptor elements
'trth=truth class from SV file for comparison
GOSUB node1
IF p1 >= .9 THEN
 class=1
ELSE
 GOSUB node2
 IF p2 >= .9 THEN
  class=1
 ELSE
  GOSUB node3
  IF p3 >= .9 THEN
   class=1
  ELSE
   class=2
  END IF
 END IF
END IF
PRINT #2, class, trth
LOOP
CLOSE
END
node1:
aa=.35+.47*(z6-1.52)/(.14)
aa=aa-.52*(z1-370.42)/(73.83)
aa=aa+.4*(z2+.06)/(.56)
aa=aa-.07*(z6-1.52)/(.14)*(z6-1.52)/(.14)
aa=aa+.37*(z1-370.42)/(73.83)*(z6-1.52)/(.14)
aa=aa+.17*(z6-1.52)/(.14)*(z2+.06)/(.56)
aa=aa-.09*(z1-370.42)/(73.83)*(z1-370.42)/(73.83)
aa=aa+.33*(z1-370.42)/(73.83)*(z2+.06)/(.56)
aa=aa+.07*(z2+.06)/(.56)*(z2+.06)/(.56)
aa=aa-.04*(z6-1.52)/(.14)*(z6-1.52)/(.14)*(z6-1.52)/(.14)
aa=aa-.02*(z6-1.52)/(.14)*(z1-370.42)/(73.83)*(z6-1.52)/(.14)
aa=aa+.01*(z2+.06)/(.56)*(z6-1.52)/(.14)*(z6-1.52)/(.14)
aa=aa-.02*(z6-1.52)/(.14)*(z1-370.42)/(73.83)*(z1-370.42)/(73.83)
aa=aa-.05*(z6-1.52)/(.14)*(z1-370.42)/(73.83)*(z2+.06)/(.56)
aa=aa+.16*(z2+.06)/(.56)*(z2+.06)/(.56)*(z6-1.52)/(.14)
aa=aa-.02*(z1-370.42)/(73.83)*(z1-370.42)/(73.83)*(z2+.06)/(.56)
aa=aa+.09*(z2+.06)/(.56)*(z2+.06)/(.56)*(z1-370.42)/(73.83)
aa=aa-.02*(z2+.06)/(.56)*(z2+.06)/(.56)*(z2+.06)/(.56)
ab=.19-.14*(z3+.91)/(.53)
ab=ab-.39*(z1-370.42)/(73.83)
ab=ab+.41*(z6-1.52)/(.14)
ab=ab+.02*(z3+.91)/(.53)*(z3+.91)/(.53)
ab=ab-.05*(z1-370.42)/(73.83)*(z3+.91)/(.53)
ab=ab-.05*(z3+.91)/(.53)*(z6-1.52)/(.14)
ab=ab-.06*(z1-370.42)/(73.83)*(z1-370.42)/(73.83)
ab=ab-.01*(z1-370.42)/(73.83)*(z6-1.52)/(.14)
ab=ab-.1*(z6-1.52)/(.14)*(z6-1.52)/(.14)
ab=ab-.03*(z3+.91)/(.53)*(z3+.91)/(.53)*(z3+.91)/(.53)
ab=ab-.09*(z3+.91)/(.53)*(z1-370.42)/(73.83)*(z3+.91)/(.53)
ab=ab-.04*(z6-1.52)/(.14)*(z3+.91)/(.53)*(z3+.91)/(.53)
ab=ab+.08*(z3+.91)/(.53)*(z1-370.42)/(73.83)*(z1-370.42)/(73.83)
ab=ab-.16*(z3+.91)/(.53)*(z1-370.42)/(73.83)*(z6-1.52)/(.14)
ab=ab+.02*(z1-370.42)/(73.83)*(z1-370.42)/(73.83)*(z1-370.42)/(73.83)
ab=ab-.06*(z6-1.52)/(.14)*(z6-1.52)/(.14)*(z3+.91)/(.53)
ab=ab-.01*(z1-370.42)/(73.83)*(z1-370.42)/(73.83)*(z6-1.52)/(.14)
ab=ab+.08*(z6-1.52)/(.14)*(z6-1.52)/(.14)*(z1-370.42)/(73.83)
ab=ab-.01*(z6-1.52)/(.14)*(z6-1.52)/(.14)*(z6-1.52)/(.14)
ba=-.04+2*ab
ba=ba+.11*aa
ba=ba+.39*(z2+.06)/(.56)
ba=ba+1.3*ab*ab
ba=ba-2.28*aa*ab
ba=ba-.43*ab*(z2+.06)/(.56)
ba=ba+.24*aa*aa
ba=ba+.06*aa*(z2+.06)/(.56)
ba=ba-.03*(z2+.06)/(.56)*(z2+.06)/(.56)
ba=ba-.55*ab*ab*ab
ba=ba-.24*ab*aa*ab
ba=ba+.46*(z2+.06)/(.56)*ab*ab
ba=ba+.38*ab*aa*aa
ba=ba-2.29*ab*aa*(z2+.06)/(.56)
ba=ba-.67*aa*aa*aa
ba=ba-.79*(z2+.06)/(.56)*(z2+.06)/(.56)*ab
ba=ba+1.34*aa*aa*(z2+.06)/(.56)
ba=ba+.55*(z2+.06)/(.56)*(z2+.06)/(.56)*aa
ba=ba-.1*(z2+.06)/(.56)*(z2+.06)/(.56)*(z2+.06)/(.56)
da1=ba*.5+1.54
p1=EXP(-.5*((da1-.94)/.75) ^ 2)
RETURN
node2:
aa=-.58-.27*(z3+.98)/(.5)
aa=aa-.55*(z1-343.23)/(50.85)
aa=aa+1.12*(z6-1.54)/(.14)
aa=aa+1.16*(z3+.98)/(.5)*(z3+.98)/(.5)
aa=aa+.72*(z1-343.23)/(50.85)*(z3+.98)/(.5)
aa=aa-.53*(z3+.98)/(.5)*(z6-1.54)/(.14)
aa=aa+.32*(z1-343.23)/(50.85)*(z1-343.23)/(50.85)
aa=aa-.57*(z1-343.23)/(50.85)*(z6-1.54)/(.14)
aa=aa+.1*(z6-1.54)/(.14)*(z6-1.54)/(.14)
aa=aa+.19*(z3+.98)/(.5)*(z3+.98)/(.5)*(z3+.98)/(.5)
aa=aa+1.15*(z3+.98)/(.5)*(z1-343.23)/(50.85)*(z3+.98)/(.5)
aa=aa-.39*(z6-1.54)/(.14)*(z3+.98)/(.5)*(z3+.98)/(.5)
aa=aa+.48*(z3+.98)/(.5)*(z1-343.23)/(50.85)*(z1-343.23)/(50.85)
aa=aa-1.34*(z3+.98)/(.5)*(z1-343.23)/(50.85)*(z6-1.54)/(.14)
aa=aa-.02*(z1-343.23)/(50.85)*(z1-343.23)/(50.85)*(z1-343.23)/(50.85)
aa=aa+.21*(z6-1.54)/(.14)*(z6-1.54)/(.14)*(z3+.98)/(.5)
aa=aa-.34*(z1-343.23)/(50.85)*(z1-343.23)/(50.85)*(z6-1.54)/(.14)
aa=aa+.75*(z6-1.54)/(.14)*(z6-1.54)/(.14)*(z1-343.23)/(50.85)
aa=aa-.29*(z6-1.54)/(.14)*(z6-1.54)/(.14)*(z6-1.54)/(.14)
ab=.29+.3*(z6-1.54)/(.14)
ab=ab-.24*(z1-343.23)/(50.85)
ab=ab+.15*(z2+.23)/(.5)
ab=ab-.45*(z6-1.54)/(.14)*(z6-1.54)/(.14)
ab=ab+.69*(z1-343.23)/(50.85)*(z6-1.54)/(.14)
ab=ab-.85*(z6-1.54)/(.14)*(z2+.23)/(.5)
ab=ab-.31*(z1-343.23)/(50.85)*(z1-343.23)/(50.85)
ab=ab+1.02*(z1-343.23)/(50.85)*(z2+.23)/(.5)
ab=ab-.3*(z2+.23)/(.5)*(z2+.23)/(.5)
ab=ab-.3*(z6-1.54)/(.14)*(z6-1.54)/(.14)*(z6-1.54)/(.14)
ab=ab+.39*(z6-1.54)/(.14)*(z1-343.23)/(50.85)*(z6-1.54)/(.14)
ab=ab-.5*(z2+.23)/(.5)*(z6-1.54)/(.14)*(z6-1.54)/(.14)
ab=ab+.15*(z6-1.54)/(.14)*(z1-343.23)/(50.85)*(z1-343.23)/(50.85)
ab=ab-.04*(z6-1.54)/(.14)*(z1-343.23)/(50.85)*(z2+.23)/(.5)
ab=ab-.16*(z1-343.23)/(50.85)*(z1-343.23)/(50.85)*(z1-343.23)/(50.85)
ab=ab-.03*(z2+.23)/(.5)*(z2+.23)/(.5)*(z6-1.54)/(.14)
ab=ab+.46*(z1-343.23)/(50.85)*(z1-343.23)/(50.85)*(z2+.23)/(.5)
ab=ab-.13*(z2+.23)/(.5)*(z2+.23)/(.5)*(z1-343.23)/(50.85)
ab=ab-.05*(z2+.23)/(.5)*(z2+.23)/(.5)*(z2+.23)/(.5)
ba=.45-.88*ab
ba=ba+.46*aa
ba=ba+.11*(z3+.98)/(.5)
ba=ba+.74*ab*ab
ba=ba-.47*aa*ab
ba=ba-.47*ab*(z3+.98)/(.5)
ba=ba-.07*aa*aa
ba=ba-.99*aa*(z3+.98)/(.5)
ba=ba-.09*(z3+.98)/(.5)*(z3+.98)/(.5)
ba=ba+.86*ab*ab*ab
ba=ba-.14*ab*aa*ab
ba=ba-.64*(z3+.98)/(.5)*ab*ab
ba=ba+.19*ab*aa*aa
ba=ba-.3*ab*aa*(z3+.98)/(.5)
ba=ba-.13*aa*aa*aa
ba=ba+.49*(z3+.98)/(.5)*(z3+.98)/(.5)*ab
ba=ba+1.1*aa*aa*(z3+.98)/(.5)
ba=ba+.12*(z3+.98)/(.5)*(z3+.98)/(.5)*aa
ba=ba-.03*(z3+.98)/(.5)*(z3+.98)/(.5)*(z3+.98)/(.5)
da2=ba*.35+1.77
p2=EXP(-.5*((da2-1.13)/.75) ^ 2)
RETURN
node3:
aa=1.94+14.85*(z3+.96)/(.55)
aa=aa-12.06*(z4+8.56)/(4.29)
aa=aa+2.26*(z7-1.36)/(.02)
aa=aa-35.27*(z3+.96)/(.55)*(z3+.96)/(.55)
aa=aa+91.74*(z4+8.56)/(4.29)*(z3+.96)/(.55)
aa=aa-.31*(z3+.96)/(.55)*(z7-1.36)/(.02)
aa=aa-57.86*(z4+8.56)/(4.29)*(z4+8.56)/(4.29)
aa=aa+.8*(z4+8.56)/(4.29)*(z7-1.36)/(.02)
aa=aa-.09*(z7-1.36)/(.02)*(z7-1.36)/(.02)
aa=aa-9.12*(z3+.96)/(.55)*(z3+.96)/(.55)*(z3+.96)/(.55)
aa=aa+11.75*(z3+.96)/(.55)*(z4+8.56)/(4.29)*(z3+.96)/(.55)
aa=aa-6.98*(z7-1.36)/(.02)*(z3+.96)/(.55)*(z3+.96)/(.55)
aa=aa-2.62*(z3+.96)/(.55)*(z4+8.56)/(4.29)*(z4+8.56)/(4.29)
aa=aa+12.73*(z3+.96)/(.55)*(z4+8.56)/(4.29)*(z7-1.36)/(.02)
```

Fig. 22. BASIC source code for the decision architecture (Part 1 of 2).

```
aa=aa+.16*(z4+8.56)/(4.29)*(z4+8.56)/(4.29)*(z4+8.56)/(4.29)
aa=aa+.69*(z7-1.36)/(.02)*(z7-1.36)/(.02)*(z3+.96)/(.55)
aa=aa-6.08*(z4+8.56)/(4.29)*(z4+8.56)/(4.29)*(z7-1.36)/(.02)
aa=aa-1.16*(z7-1.36)/(.02)*(z7-1.36)/(.02)*(z4+8.56)/(4.29)
aa=aa-.14*(z7-1.36)/(.02)*(z7-1.36)/(.02)*(z7-1.36)/(.02)
ab=1.15+11.53*(z3+.96)/(.55)
ab=ab-11.27*(z4+8.56)/(4.29)
ab=ab+.72*(z6-1.55)/(.13)
ab=ab-28.13*(z3+.96)/(.55)*(z3+.96)/(.55)
ab=ab+73.45*(z4+8.56)/(4.29)*(z3+.96)/(.55)
ab=ab+.21*(z3+.96)/(.55)*(z6-1.55)/(.13)
ab=ab-47.14*(z4+8.56)/(4.29)*(z4+8.56)/(4.29)
ab=ab-1.2*(z4+8.56)/(4.29)*(z6-1.55)/(.13)
ab=ab+.6*(z6-1.55)/(.13)*(z6-1.55)/(.13)
ab=ab-.05*(z3+.96)/(.55)*(z3+.96)/(.55)*(z3+.96)/(.55)
ab=ab-7.74*(z3+.96)/(.55)*(z4+8.56)/(4.29)*(z3+.96)/(.55)
ab=ab+10.68*(z6-1.55)/(.13)*(z3+.96)/(.55)*(z3+.96)/(.55)
ab=ab+11.2*(z3+.96)/(.55)*(z4+8.56)/(4.29)*(z4+8.56)/(4.29)
ab=ab-23*(z3+.96)/(.55)*(z4+8.56)/(4.29)*(z6-1.55)/(.13)
ab=ab-2.98*(z4+8.56)/(4.29)*(z4+8.56)/(4.29)*(z4+8.56)/(4.29)
ab=ab-7.06*(z6-1.55)/(.13)*(z6-1.55)/(.13)*(z3+.96)/(.55)
ab=ab+12.47*(z4+8.56)/(4.29)*(z4+8.56)/(4.29)*(z6-1.55)/(.13)
ab=ab+7.43*(z6-1.55)/(.13)*(z6-1.55)/(.13)*(z4+8.56)/(4.29)
ab=ab+.15*(z6-1.55)/(.13)*(z6-1.55)/(.13)*(z6-1.55)/(.13)
ac=-2.24+2.01*(z7-1.36)/(.02)
ac=ac-1.26*(z1-341.35)/(48.93)
ac=ac-.55*(z2+.31)/(.48)
ac=ac+.68*(z7-1.36)/(.02)*(z7-1.36)/(.02)
ac=ac+.31*(z1-341.35)/(48.93)*(z7-1.36)/(.02)
ac=ac+.39*(z7-1.36)/(.02)*(z2+.31)/(.48)
ac=ac+.4*(z1-341.35)/(48.93)*(z1-341.35)/(48.93)
ac=ac-.77*(z1-341.35)/(48.93)*(z2+.31)/(.48)
ac=ac+.75*(z2+.31)/(.48)*(z2+.31)/(.48)
ac=ac-.4*(z7-1.36)/(.02)*(z7-1.36)/(.02)*(z7-1.36)/(.02)
ac=ac+.22*(z7-1.36)/(.02)*(z1-341.35)/(48.93)*(z7-1.36)/(.02)
ac=ac+.26*(z2+.31)/(.48)*(z7-1.36)/(.02)*(z7-1.36)/(.02)
ac=ac-.12*(z7-1.36)/(.02)*(z1-341.35)/(48.93)*(z1-341.35)/(48.93)
ac=ac+.75*(z7-1.36)/(.02)*(z1-341.35)/(48.93)*(z2+.31)/(.48)
ac=ac+.32*(z1-341.35)/(48.93)*(z1-341.35)/(48.93)*(z1-341.35)/(48.93)
ac=ac-.44*(z2+.31)/(.48)*(z2+.31)/(.48)*(z7-1.36)/(.02)
ac=ac-.24*(z1-341.35)/(48.93)*(z1-341.35)/(48.93)*(z2+.31)/(.48)
ac=ac+.01*(z2+.31)/(.48)*(z2+.31)/(.48)*(z1-341.35)/(48.93)
ac=ac+.14*(z2+.31)/(.48)*(z2+.31)/(.48)*(z2+.31)/(.48)
ba=.53-.33*ac
ba=ba+.01*ab
ba=ba-.24*aa
ba=ba+.04*ac*ac
ba=ba-.16*ab*ac
ba=ba-.17*ac*aa
ba=ba-.12*ab*ab
ba=ba-.1*ab*aa
ba=ba+.14*aa*aa
ba=ba-.06*ac*ac*ac
ba=ba+.13*ac*ab*ac
ba=ba+.53*aa*ac*ac
ba=ba+.31*ac*ab*ab
ba=ba+.15*ac*ab*aa
ba=ba-.02*ab*ab*ab
ba=ba-.06*aa*aa*ac
ba=ba-.15*ab*ab*aa
ba=ba-.08*aa*aa*ab
ba=ba+.01*aa*aa*aa
da3=ba*.11+1.94
p3=EXP(-.5*((da3-1.01)/.13) ^ 2)
RETURN
```

Fig. 23. BASIC source code for the decision architecture (Part 2 of 2).

8. Summary

We use the Spatial Voting (SV) process for fusing spatial positions in a 2-D grid. This process yields a centroid and covariance estimate as the basis of robust cluster identification. We calculate a series of geospatial features unique to the identified cluster and attempt to identify unique and consistent features to enable automated target recognition. We define the geospatial features and outline our process of deriving a decision architecture populated with Data Models. We attempt to identify the support vectors of the feature space and enable the smallest subsample of available exemplars to be used for extracting the analytical rule equations. We present details of the decision architecture derivation process. We construct ambiguity resolvers to further sieve and classify mislabeled sensor hits by deriving a new resolver Data Model that further processes the output from the previous layer. In this fashion through a cascade filter, we are able to demonstrate unique classification and full assignment of all available examples even in high dimensional spaces.

9. Acknowledgements

The author would like to thank James Handley (LSEI) for programming support and proofreading this document; and Dr. William "Bud" Albritton, Jr., Dr. Nat Albritton, Robert Caspers, and Randel Burnett (Amtec Corporation) for their assistance with applications development, as well as their sponsorship of and technical discussions with the author.

10. References

Hall, D.L., & McMullen, S.A.H. (2004), *Mathematical Techniques in Multisensor Data Fusion*, Artech House, ISBN 0890065586, Boston, MA, USA.

Jaenisch, H.M., Albritton, N.G., Handley, J.W., Burnett, R.B., Caspers, R.W., & Albritton Jr., W.P. (2008), "A Simple Algorithm For Sensor Fusion Using Spatial Voting (Unsupervised Object Grouping)", Proceedings of SPIE, Vol. 6968, pp. 696804-696804-12, ISBN 0819471593, 17-19 March 2008, Orlando, FL, USA.

Jaenisch, H.M., & Handley, J.W. (2009), "Analytical Formulation of Cellular Automata Rules Using Data Models", Proceeding of SPIE, Vol. 7347, pp. 734715-734715-13, ISBN 0819476137, 14-15 April 2009, Orlando, FL, USA.

Jaenisch, H.M., & Handley, J.W. (2003), "Data Modeling for Radar Applications", Proceedings of IEEE Radar Conference 2003, ISBN 0780379209, 18-19 May 2003, Huntsville, AL, USA.

Jaenisch, H.M., Handley, J.W., Albritton, N.G., Koegler, J., Murray, S., Maddox, W., Moren, S., Alexander, T., Fieselman, W., & Caspers, R.T., (2010), "Geospatial Feature Based Automatic Target Recognition (ATR) Using Data Models", Proceedings of SPIE, Vol. 7697, 5-9 April 2010, Orlando, FL, USA.

Jaenisch, H.M., Handley, J.W., Massey, S., Case, C.T., & Songy, C.G. (2002), "Network Centric Decision Architecture for Financial or 1/f Data Models", Proceedings of SPIE, Vol. 4787, pp. 86-97, ISBN 0819445541, 9-10 July 2002, Seattle, WA, USA.

Jain, A.K. (1989), *Fundamentals of Digital Image Processing*, Prentice-Hall, ISBN 0133361659, Englewood Cliffs, NJ.

Klein, L. (2004), *Sensor and Data Fusion*, SPIE Press, ISBN 0819454354, Bellingham, WA.

Madala, H, & Ivakhnenko, A. (1994), *Inductive Learning Algorithms for Complex Systems Modeling*, CRC Press, ISBN 0849344387, Boca Raton, FL.

National Aeronautics and Space Administration (NASA) (1962), *Celestial Mechanics and Space Flight Analysis*, Office of Scientific and Technical Information, Washington, DC.

Press, W.H., Teukolsky, S.A., Vetterling, W.T., & Flannery, B.P. (2007), *Numerical Recipes: The Art of Scientific Computing, 3rd Edition*, Cambridge University Press, ISBN 0521880688, Cambridge, UK.

8

Hidden Markov Model as a Framework for Situational Awareness

Thyagaraju Damarla
US Army Research Laboratory
2800 Powder Mill Road, Adelphi, MD
USA

Abstract
In this chapter we present a hidden Markov model (HMM) based framework for situational awareness that utilizes multi-sensor multiple modality data. Situational awareness is a process that comes to a conclusion based on the events that take place over a period of time across a wide area. We show that each state in the HMM is an event that leads to a situation and the transition from one state to another is determined based on the probability of detection of certain events using multiple sensors of multiple modalities - thereby using sensor fusion for situational awareness. We show the construction of HMM and apply it to the data collected using a suite of sensors on a Packbot.

1. Introduction

Situational awareness (SA) is a process of conscious effort to process the sensory data to extract actionable information to accomplish a mission over a period of time with or without interaction with the sensory systems. Most of the information is time dependent and they usually follow a sequence of states. This is where the Markov or hidden Markov models are useful in analyzing the data and to extract the actionable information from the sensors. To gain better understanding, the following section would elaborate on situation awareness.

1.1 Situation Awareness

Situational awareness means different things to different people. Experience plays a great role in the situational awareness. Based on one's experience, the interpretation of the situation will be different. For example, in the case of animal world, the situation assessment by the predator and prey will be different. The predator assesses the situation based on the past experience, circumstances, etc., and determines when to strike. Similarly, the prey assesses its situation based on its experience and determines the best route to take to escape from the imminent danger. The origins of SA are in the military (Smith, 2003) back in 1970's. Initial work is done in the area of analyzing and understanding what a pilot is observing and how he is making decisions based on the data provided to him in the cockpit and what he/she is able to observe outside through the windows. Some of it resulted in the design of modern cockpit and flight training facilities. The US Army defines the SA as[1]:

[1] `http://www.army.mil/armyBTKC/focus/sa/index.htm`

> *Situational Awareness is the ability to generate actionable knowledge through the use of timely and accurate information about the Army enterprise, its processes, and external factors.*

Endsley and Garland (Endsley & Mataric, 2000) defines SA as "SA is knowing what is going around you". There is usually a torrent of data coming through the sensors, situational awareness is sifting through all that data and extracting the information that is actionable and predicting the situation ahead. The awareness of the situation ahead lets one plan the data collection from the right set of sensors. SA allows selective attention to the information. Some other pertinent definitions are provided here (Beringer & Hancock, 1989):

> *SA requires an operator to "quickly detect, integrate and interpret data gathered from the environment. In many real-world conditions, situational awareness is hampered by two factors. First, the data may be spread throughout the visual field. Second, the data are frequently noisy"* (Green et al., 1995).

> *Situation awareness is based on the integration of knowledge resulting from recurrent situation awareness* (Sarter & Woods, 1991).

> *"Situation awareness is adaptive, externally-directed consciousness that has as its products knowledge about a dynamic task environment and directed action within that environment"*(Smith & Hancock, 1995).

In a sensor world, situation awareness is obtained by gathering data using multi-modal multiple sensors distributed over an area of interest. Each modality of sensor obtains the data within its operating range. For example video observes the data within its field of view. Acoustic sensors record the sound within its audible (sensitive) range. In this chapter, several sensor modalities will be considered and the data they present. Proper information from each sensor or from a combination of sensors will be extracted to understand the scene around. Extraction of the right information depends mostly on previous knowledge or previous situation awareness. Understanding of the contribution of each sensor modality to the SA is key to the development of algorithms pertinent to the SA. Clearly, the information one would like to obtain for SA depends on the mission. In order to help us better understand the functionality of each modality, three different missions are considered as exemplars here, namely, (a) urban terrain operations, (b) difficult terrain such as tunnels, caves, etc., and (c) battlefield.

1.1.1 Urban Terrain Operations

Since World War II, nation building after war has become a common practice, partly, to ensure the vanquished country does not become a pariah nation or some dictator does not take hold of the country. After World War II, Marshal plan was developed to help the countries. Recently, after Iraq war, coalition partners (US and UK) stayed back in Iraq to facilitate smooth functioning of the Iraqi government. However, the presence of foreign troops always incite mixed feelings among some people and may become the cause for friction resulting in urban war or operations. Moreover by year 2020, 85% of world's population live in the coastal cities (Maj. Houlgate, 2004) which cause friction among various ethnic groups that call for forces to quite the upraising necessitating the urban military operations. In general, the urban operations include (Press, 1998):

- Policing operations – to deter violence
- Raids

  - Evacuation of embassies
  - Seize ports and airfields
  - Counter weapons of mass destruction (WMD)
  - Seize enemy leaders
- Sustained urban combat

From the above list of operations that may take place in an urban area, clearing of buildings and protecting them is one of the major missions. Often, once a building is cleared, one may leave some sensors in the building to monitor the building for intruders. Another important operation is perimeter protection. In the case of perimeter protection, several sensors will be deployed around the perimeter of a building or a place. These sensors detect any person approaching the perimeter and report to the command center for further investigation and action. Next we consider operations in difficult terrain.

1.1.2 Operations in Difficult Terrain

In general, terrorists take advantage of the rugged terrain and often hide in the caves in the mountain range or bunkers in the ground. There are too many hiding places and one can not just walk in to these areas without risking their own lives. The operations required in these areas are quite different from those conducted in the urban areas. Often, one would send a robot equipped with sensors to monitor if there is any human activity in the caves/tunnels or to find any infrastructure, man made objects, etc.

Borders between warring nations and between rich and poor nations have become porous for illegal transportation of people, drugs, weapons, etc. Operations in these areas include: (a) detection of tunnels using various sensing modalities and (b) making sure that the tunnels remain cleared once they are cleared. Detection of tunnels require different kind of sensors.

1.1.3 Operations in open battlefield

This is the traditional cold war scenario where the war is fought in an open area. Here the situation awareness requires knowing where the enemy is, how big is the enemy, where the firing is coming from, and the type of weapons used, etc. Furthermore, one would like to know, not only the firing location but also the impact point of the mortars and rockets. The launch location helps in taking action to mitigate the enemy and its firing weaponry, etc., and the knowledge of impact location helps in assessing the damage to provide the necessary medical and other support to control and confine the damage.

Clearly, the requirements for different operations are different. To be successful in the operations, one need to have a clear understanding of the situation. Situation awareness comes from the sensors deployed on the ground and in the air, and human intelligence. The sensor data is processed for right information to get the correct situation awareness. The next section presents various sensors that could be used to monitor the situation.

1.2 Sensor Suite for Situational Awareness

Traditionally, when the subject of sensors comes up, immediately, Radar, and video sensors come to one's mind. With the advent of very large scale integrated (VLSI) circuits, other sensor modalities have been developed and used extensively in modern times. Main reasons for development of new sensor modalities are: (a) limited capability of existing sensors, (b) high power consumption by traditional sensors, (c) wide area of operation requiring many sensors, (d) limited field of view by Radar and video and (e) new modalities offer better insight in to the situation. Most of the sensors for situation awareness are deployed in an area of interest and left there for days, weeks, and months before attending to them. This necessitated the need for low power, low cost and large quantities of sensors that could be deployed in the field.

Now, we will present some of the sensors that may be deployed in the field and discuss their utility.

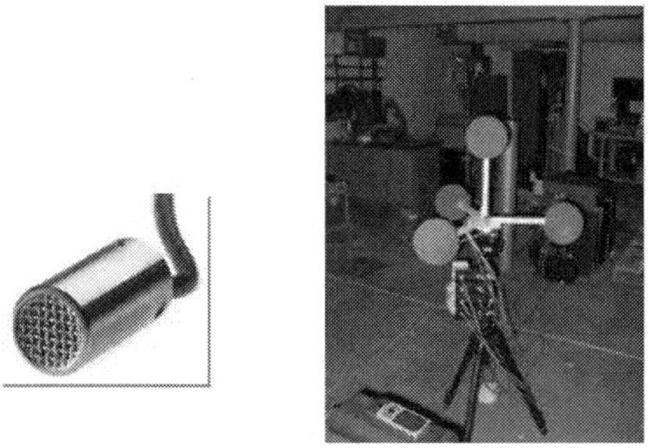

(a) (b)

Fig. 1. (a) Single microphone and (b) an array (tetrahedral) of microphones

Acoustic Sensors: While the imaging sensors (for example: camera, video) act as the eyes, the acoustic sensors fulfill the role of ears in the sensing world. These microphones capture the sounds generated by various events taking place in their vicinity, such as, a vehicle traveling on a nearby road, mortar/rocket launch and detonations, sound of bullets whizzing by and of course sounds made by people, animals, etc., to name few. These are passive sensors, that is, they do not transmit any signals unlike the Radar, hence they can be used for stealth operations. There are several types of microphones, namely, condenser, piezoelectric, dynamic, carbon, magnetic and micro-electro mechanical systems (MEMS) microphones. Each microphone has its own characteristic response in terms of sensitivity to the sound pressure and the frequency of operation. Each application demands a different type of microphone to be used depending on the signals that are being captured by the microphone. For example, detection of motor vehicles require the microphones that have the frequency response equal or greater than the highest engine harmonic frequency. On the other hand to capture a transient event such as a shock wave generated by a super sonic bullet require a microphone with frequency response of 100 kHz or more. When the microphones are used in an array configuration, such as, linear, circular or tetrahedral array, the signals from all the microphones can be processed for estimating the angle of arrival (AoA) of the target. Figure 1 shows a single microphone and a tetrahedral array. The microphones in the tetrahedral array Figure 1b are covered by foam balls to reduce the wind noise.

Seismic Sensors: These are also called geophones. These sensors are used to detect the vibrations in the ground caused by the events taking place in the sensing range of the sensors. Just as in the case of acoustic sensors, the seismic sensors are passive sensors. Typical applications for these sensors include (a) detection of vehicles (both civilian and military vehicles) by capturing the signals generated by a moving vehicles, (b) perimeter protection – by capturing the vibrations caused by footsteps of a person walking, (c) explosion, etc. The Indonesian tsunami in December 2004 was devastating to the people. However, several animals sensed the vibrations in the ground caused by the giant waves coming to the shore and ran to the hills or elevated areas and survived the tsunami. Figure 2 shows different seismic sensors. The spikes are used to couple the the sensor to the ground by burying the spikes in the ground.

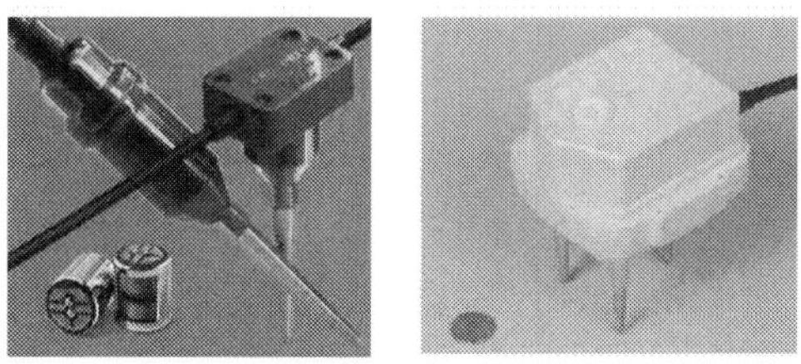

Fig. 2. Different seismic sensors

Magnetic Sensors: Magnetic (B-field) sensors can be used to detect ferromagnetic materials carried by people, e.g., keys, firearms, and knives. These sensors may also detect the usage of computer monitors. There are several types of magnetic sensors, namely, (a) flux gate magnetometer and (b) coil type magnetic sensor. The coil type magnetic sensor has high frequency response compared to the flux gate magnetometer. One can use multiple sensors in order to detect the flux change in all three X, Y and Z directions. The sensitivity of the magnetic sensor depends on the type and as well as the construction of the sensor. Figure 3 shows two types of magnetic sensors.

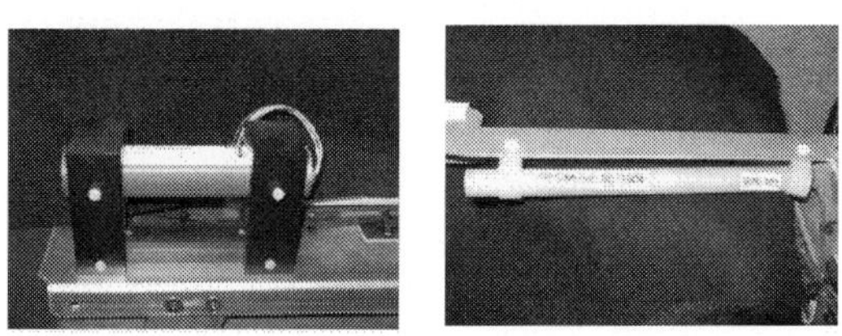

(a) (b)

Fig. 3. (a) Flux gate magnetometer, (b) Coil type magnetic sensor

Electrostatic or E-field Sensors: These are passive sensors that detect static electric charge built-up on the targets or any electric field in the vicinity of the sensor. Some of the sources of the static electric charge are (a) clothes rubbing against the body, (b) combing hair, and (c) bullet or projectile traveling in the air builds up charge on the bullet, etc. All the electric transmission lines have electric field surrounding the lines – this field gets perturbed by a target in the vicinity – and can be detected by E-field sensors. Figure 4 shows some of the E-field sensors that are commercially available.

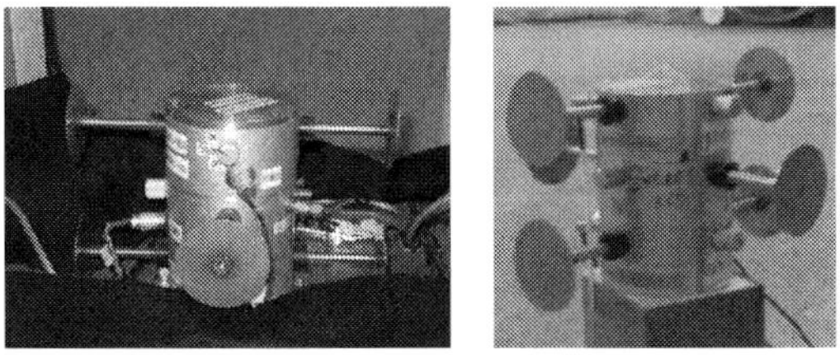

Fig. 4. E-field sensors

Passive Infrared (PIR) Sensor: These are passive sensors that detect infrared radiation by the targets. These are motion detectors. If a person walks in front of them, the sensor generates an output proportional to the temperature of the body and inversely proportional to the distance between the person and the sensor. Figure 5 shows a picture of PIR sensor.

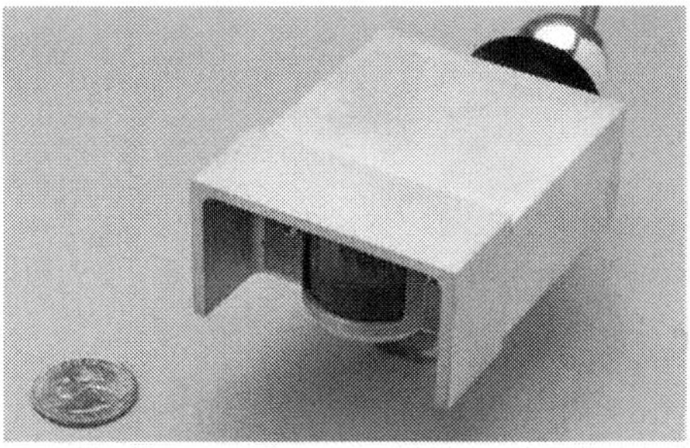

Fig. 5. Passive Infra Red sensor

Chemical Sensor: These sensors are similar to the carbon monoxide detectors used in buildings. Some of the sensors can detect multiple chemicals. Usually, these sensors employ several wafers. Each wafer reacts to a particular chemical in the air changing the resistivity of the wafer. The change in the resistivity in turn changes the output voltage indicating the presence of that chemical.

Infra Red Imagers: There are several IR imagers depending on the frequency band they operate at, namely, long wave IR, medium wave IR, and forward looking infrared (FLIR). These sensors take the thermal image of the target in their field of view. A typical IR imager's picture is shown in Figure 6.

Fig. 6. Visible and IR cameras

Visible Imagers: These are regular video cameras. They take the pictures in visible spectra and have different resolution and different field of view depending on the lens used. Figure 6 shows a picture of a typical video camera.
In the next section, we present the description of the unattended ground sensors.

1.2.1 Unattended Ground Sensors

A typical unattended ground sensor (UGS) is a suite of multi-modal sensor package with a processor facilitating the collection of data from all the sensors and having a capability to process the data and extracting the information relevant to the mission. A typical UGS sensor consists of acoustic, seismic, magnetic and both IR and visible cameras. The non-imaging sensors are often called activity detection sensors. As the name implies, these sensors are utilized to detect any activity within the receptive field of the sensors, such as a person walking/running, vehicle moving, etc. Once the activity sensors detect a target, they cue the imaging sensors to capture a picture of the target which will be sent to the command control center. Target/activity detection algorithms run on the processor in the UGS system. There are algorithms running when to cue the imagers and which one of the pictures to transmit to the command and control center in order to reduce the bandwidth of the communication channel. In general activity detection sensors consume low power, hence reduce the power consumption by the UGS prolonging the battery life.

UGS are in general placed in the area of interest conspicuously and left to operate for several days or months. In general these are low power sensors that meant to last for several days or months before replacing the batteries. There are several manufacturers that make the UGS systems.

1.3 Techniques for Situational Awareness

In order to assess the situation, sensor information is needed. Based on the history of sensor information/output when a particular event took place, one can infer same event has taken place if similar information/output is observed. Such inference can be made using Bayesian nets or hidden Markov model. If several events are observed in sequence, then such a sequence of events can be modeled using Markov or Hidden Markov chain. In the following subsection, both Bayesian nets and Hidden Markov models will be described.

1.3.1 Bayesian Belief Networks

Bayesian belief networks (BBN) are directed acyclic graphical networks with nodes representing variables and arcs (links between nodes) representing the dependency relationship between the corresponding variables. Quite often, the relationship between the variables is known but can not quantify it in absolute terms. Hence, the relationship is described in probabilistic terms. For example, if there are clouds then there is a chance of rain. Of course, there need not be rain every time a cloud is formed. Similarly, if a person walks in front of a seismic sensor, the sensor detects periodic vibrations caused by footfalls, however, if periodic vibrations are observed it does not mean there is a person walking. One of the uses of BBN is in situations that require statistical inference.

Bayesian methods provide a way for reasoning about partial beliefs under conditions of uncertainty using a probabilistic model, encoding probabilistic information that permits us to compute the probability of an event. The main principle of Bayesian techniques lies in the inversion formula:

$$p(H|e) = \frac{p(e|H)p(H)}{p(e)}$$

where H is the hypothesis, $p(e|H)$ is the likelihood, $p(H)$ is called the prior probability, $p(H|e)$ is the posterior probability, and $p(e)$ is the probability of evidence. Belief associated with the hypothesis H is updated based on this formula when new evidence arrives. This approach forms the basis for reasoning with Bayesian belief networks. Figure 7 show how the evidence is collected using hard and soft methods.

Nodes in Bayesian networks (Pearl, 1986; 1988) represent hypotheses, and information is transmitted from each node (at which evidence is available or belief has been updated) to adjacent nodes in a directed graph. Use of Bayesian rule for large number of variables require estimation of joint probability distributions and computing the conditional probabilities. For example, if no assumption on the dependencies is made, that is, all variables are dependent on each other, then

$$p(A,B,C,D,E) = p(A|B,C,D,E)\ p(B|C,D,E)\ p(C|D,E)\ p(D|E)\ p(E) \tag{1}$$

If the dependencies are modeled as shown in Figure 8, then the joint probability distribution is much simpler and is given by

$$p(A,B,C,D,E) = p(A|B)\ p(B|C,E)\ p(C|D)\ p(D)\ p(E) \tag{2}$$

Let $G(V,E)$ is a directed acyclic graph with a set of vertices $V = \{v_1, v_2, \cdots, v_n\}$ and a set of edges $E = \left\{e_{1,2}, e_{1,3}, \cdots, e_{i,j}\right\}$, with $i \neq j \in \{1,2,\cdots,n\}$. Note that the directed edge $e_{i,j}$

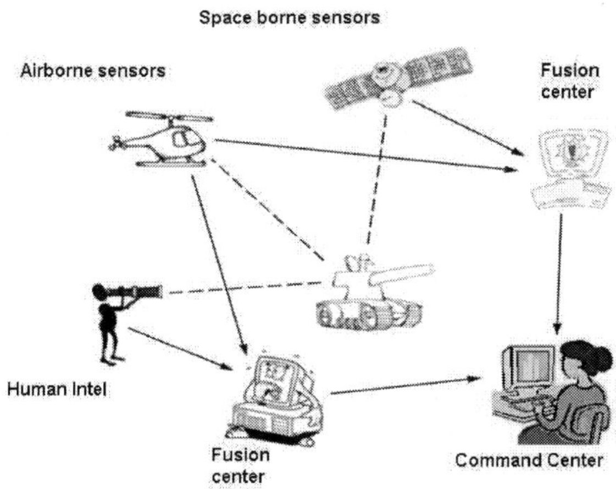

Fig. 7. Evidence Collection for Situational Awareness

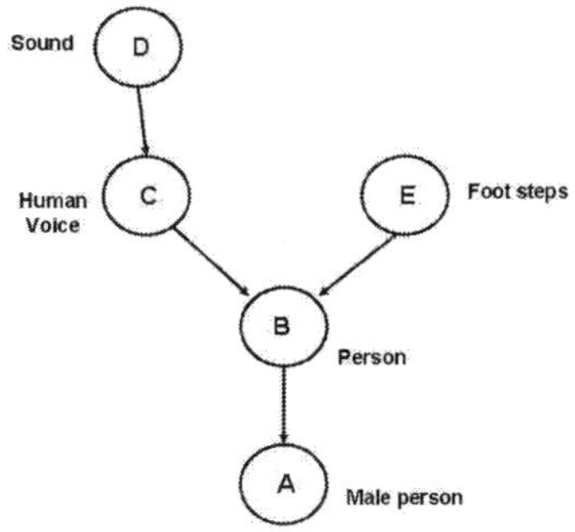

Fig. 8. Node dependency in a BBN

connects the vertex v_i to vertex v_j and it exists if and only if there is a relationship between nodes v_i and v_j. Node v_i is the parent of node v_j and v_j is the descendant of node v_i. Let us denote the random variable associated with the node v_i by X_{v_i}. For simplicity, let us denote $X_i = X_{v_i}$. Let $pa(v_i)$ denote the parent nodes of the node v_i. For a Bayesian belief network the following properties must be satisfied:

- Each variable is *conditionally independent* of its non-descendants
- Each variable is dependent on its parents

This property is called the *local Markov property*. Then the joint probability distribution is given by

$$p\left(X_1, X_2, \cdots, X_n\right) = \prod_{i=1}^{n} p\left(X_i \middle| \, pa(X_i)\right) \tag{3}$$

Now it is possible to associate meaning to the links in the Bayesian belief network and hence what we need to specify to turn the graphical dependence structure of a BBN into a probability distribution. In Figure 8 the nodes labeled 'sound' and 'human voice' are related. The node 'sound' is the parent node of 'human voice' node since without sound there is no human voice. The link shows that relation. Similarly nodes in Figure 8 are related to others with certain probability. Each node in the BBN represents a state and provides the situation awareness.

A closely related process to BBN is a Markov process. Both Markov and Hidden Markov process are presented in the next section.

1.3.2 Markov & Hidden Markov Models (HMM)

In probability theory, people studied how the past experiments effect the future experiments. In general, the outcome of the next experiment is dependent on the outcome of the past experiments. For example, a student's grades in the previous tests may affect the grades in the final test. In the case of student grades, a teacher might have specified a particular formula or weightage given to each test for assessing the final grade. However, if the experiments are chance experiments, prediction of the next experiment's outcome may be difficult. Markov introduced a new chance process where the outcome of the given experiment only influences the outcome of the next experiment. This is called the Markov process and is characterized by:

$$p(X_n| \, X_{n-1}, X_{n-2}, \cdots, X_1) = p(X_n| \, X_{n-1}) \tag{4}$$

In real world situations, the Markov process occurs quite frequently, for example, rain falls after clouds are formed.

One of the important application of Markov model is in speech recognition where the states are hidden but the measured parameters depend on the state the model is in. This important model is called the hidden Markov model (HMM). A more detailed description of the model is presented in the next section.

2. Hidden Markov Model

Consider a scenario, where there are several sensors deployed along a road as shown in Figure 9. These sensors could be acoustic, seismic, or video sensors. For the sake of discussion, let us assume they are acoustic sensors. In the case of a tracked vehicle, for example, a tank, the track makes slap noise as each segment (shoe) of the track slaps the road as it moves. The engine of a vehicle has a fundamental frequency associated with the engine cylinder's firing rate and its harmonics will be propagated through the atmosphere. The tires make noise due to friction between the road and the tire. These sounds will be captured by the sensors. The sound level decreases inversely proportional to the distance R between the vehicle and the sensor. Moreover, there is wind noise that gets added to the the vehicle sound. As a result each sensor records the vehicle sound plus the noise as voltage; generated by the microphone associated with the sensor. Let us assume that each sensor is capable of recording 'M' discrete levels of voltage $V = \{v_1, v_2, \cdots, v_M\}$ where V is called the alphabet. In this experiment, let us assume only one vehicle is allowed to pass at a time. After the first vehicle completes its run, the second vehicle is allowed to pass, and so on till all the vehicles complete their runs. Let the experiment consist of using some random process for selecting initial sensor. An observation is made by measuring the voltage level at the sensor. A new sensor is selected according to some random process associated with the current sensor. Again another

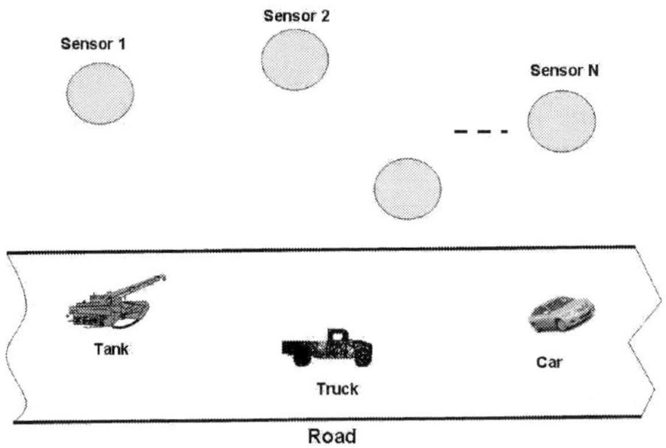

Fig. 9. Vehicle Identification

observation is made. The process is repeated with other sensors. The entire process generates a sequence of observations $O = O_1, O_2, \cdots, O_M$, where $O_i \in V$. This is similar to the urn and ball problem presented in (Rabiner, 1989). One of the problems could be; given the observation sequence, what is the probability that it is for car, truck or tank?
An HMM in Figure 10 is characterized by (Rabiner, 1989):

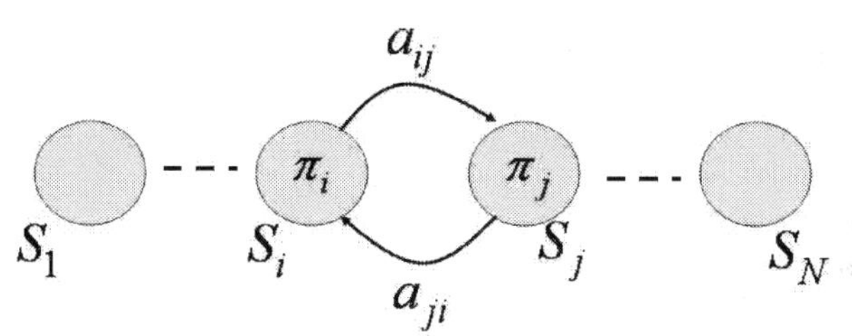

Fig. 10. An hidden Markov model

1. The number of states N. Let S denote the set of states, given by, $S = \{S_1, S_2, \cdots, S_N\}$ and we denote the state at time t as $q_t \in S$.
2. Size of the alphabet M, that is, the number of distinct observable symbols $V = \{v_1, v_2, \cdots, v_M\}$.
3. The state transition probability distribution $A = \left\{a_{ij}\right\}$ where

$$a_{ij} = P\left[q_{t+1} = S_j \mid q_t = S_i\right], \ 1 \leq i, j \leq N. \quad (5)$$

4. The probability distribution of each alphabet v_k in state j, $B = \left\{b_j(v_k)\right\}$, where

$$b_j(v_k) = P\left[v_k \; at \; t \mid q_t = S_j\right], \quad 1 \le j \le N; \; 1 \le k \le M. \tag{6}$$

5. The initial state distribution $\pi = \{\pi_i\}$ where

$$\pi_i = P\left[q_1 = S_i\right], \quad 1 \le i \le N. \tag{7}$$

Clearly, the HMM is completely specified if N, M, A, B, π are specified and it can be used to generate an observation sequence $O = O_1, O_2, \cdots, O_T$ (Rabiner, 1989). Three questions arise with HMMs, namely,

- Question 1: Given the observation sequence $O = O_1, O_2, \cdots, O_T$, and the model $\lambda = \{A, B, \pi\}$, how does one compute the $P(O \mid \lambda)$, that is, the probability of the observation sequence,
- Question 2: Given the observation sequence $O = O_1, O_2, \cdots, O_T$, and the model λ, how does one compute the optimal state sequence $Q = q_1 q_2 \cdots q_T$ that best explains the observed sequence, and
- Question 3: How does one optimizes the model parameters $\lambda = \{A, B, \pi\}$ that maximizes $P(O \mid \lambda)$.

Getting back to the problem posed in Figure 9, we will design a separate N-state HMM for each vehicle passage. It is assumed that the vehicles travel at near constant velocity and the experiment starts when the vehicle approaches a known position on the road. For training purposes the experiment is repeated with each vehicle traveling at different positions on the road, for example, left, right, middle or some other position. Now, for each HMM a model has to be built. In section 3.4 we show how to build an HMM. This is same as finding the solution to the question 3. Answer to question 2 provides the meaning to the states. Recognition of the observations is given by the solution to the question 1.

2.1 Solutions to the questions

In this section we will provide the answer to question 1 as it is the most important one that most of the practical situations demand. The answers to the other questions can be found in reference(Rabiner, 1989) or books on HMM.

Solution to Question 1: Given the observation sequence O and the model λ, estimate $P(O \mid \lambda)$. Let the observed sequence is

$$O = O_1, O_2, \cdots, O_T$$

and one specific state sequence that produced the observation O is

$$Q = q_1, q_2, \cdots, q_T$$

where q_1 is the initial state. Then

$$P(O \mid Q, \lambda) = \prod_{t=1}^{T} P(O_t \mid q_t, \lambda) \tag{8}$$

Invoking (6) we get

$$P(O \mid Q, \lambda) = b_{q_1}(O_1) \cdot b_{q_2}(O_2) \cdots b_{q_T}(O_T). \tag{9}$$

The probability of the state sequence Q can be computed using (5) and (7) and is given by

$$P(Q \mid \lambda) = \pi_{q_1} a_{q_1 q_2} a_{q_2 q_3} \cdots a_{q_{T-1} q_T}. \tag{10}$$

Finally, the probability of the observation sequence O is obtained by summing over all possible Q and is given by

$$P(O \mid \lambda) = \sum_{all\ Q} P(O \mid Q, \lambda)\ P(Q \mid \lambda) \tag{11}$$

There are efficient ways to compute the probability of the observation sequence given by (11) which will not be discussed here. Interested people should consult (Rabiner, 1989).

3. HMM framework for Situational Awareness

One of the advantages of using multiple sensors with multiple modalities is to detect various events with high confidence. Situational awareness is achieved based on the sequence of events observed over a period of time. These events may take place in a closed area or on a wide area. In the case of wide area, one would require multiple sensors distributed over the entire region of interest. Situational awareness leads to better response in a timely manner either to mitigate the situation or to take appropriate action proactively rather than reactively. Since the situational awareness is achieved based on the sequence of events observed - hidden Markov model (HMM) (Rabiner, 1989) is ideally suited. Researchers used HMM for situational awareness for traffic monitoring (Bruckner et al., 2007) and learning hand grasping movements for robots (Bernardin et al., 2003).

Sensor fusion is supposed to lead to a better situational awareness. However fusion of multimodal data is a difficult thing to do as there are few joint probability density functions exist for mixed modalities. Fusion mostly depends on the application at hand. The problem is further complicated if one has to fuse the events that take place over a period of time and over a wide area. If they are time dependent, relevance of the data observed at different times become an issue. We opted to do fusion of information, that is, probability of detection of an event. In a majority of the cases Bayesian networks (Singhal & Brown, 1997; 2000) are used for fusion. In this chapter we use Dempster-Shafer fusion (Hall & Llinas, 2001; Klein, 2004) for fusion of multi-modal multi-sensor data.

3.1 Example scenario for Situational Awareness in an urban terrain

Some of the situational awareness problems that may be of interest are discussed here. In a situation where we are monitoring a building (Damarla, 2008), we would like to know if there is any activity taking place. In particular, we placed a robot inside an office room (in stealth mode, various sensors will be placed and camouflaged to avoid detection) as shown in Figure 11.

Figure 12 shows the robot with 4 microphones, 3-axis seismic sensor, PIR, chemical sensor, 3 coil type magnetometer (one coil for each axis X, Y and Z), three flux gate magneto meter, 3-axis E-field sensor, visible video and IR imaging sensors. The goal is to assess the situation based on the observations of various sensor modalities over a period of time in the area covered by the sensor range. We enacted the data collection scenario with several features built-in to observe the happenings inside the office room and assess the situation.

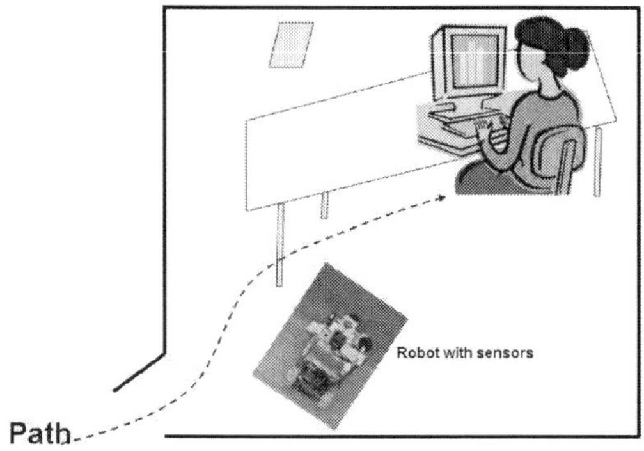

Fig. 11. Robot full of sensors monitoring activities in an office room

Fig. 12. Robot with different sensors

Data Collection Scenario:

- A person walks into the office room - this triggers PIR, B & E-field and seismic sensors.
- She occasionally talks - the acoustic sensor picks up the voice.
- She sits in front of a computer.
- She turns on the computer.

- B & E-field sensors observe the power surge caused by turning on the computer.
- Acoustic sensors observe the characteristic chime of Windows turning on.
- The person's movements are picked up by the PIR sensor.
- Visible video shows a pattern on the computer screen showing activity on the computer.
- The IR imager picks up the reflected thermal profile of the person in front of the monitor.

- She types on the keyboard - sound is detected by the acoustic sensor.
- She turns off the computer.
  - Windows turning off sound is observed by the acoustic sensor.
  - The power surge after shutdown is observed by the B-field sensor.

In the next section we present the data from various sensors and show the events detected by each sensor and also present some of the signal processing done to identify the events.

3.2 Processing of sensor data for information

We process the data from sensors in order to extract the features corresponding to various events - depending on the situation and application these extracted features will be different even for the same sensor, e.g., voice versus chime.

Acoustic sensor data analysis: In the case of acoustic sensors, we try to look for any human or machine activity - this is done by observing the energy levels in 4 bands, that is, 20 - 250Hz, 251 - 500Hz, 501 - 750Hz and 751 - 1000Hz corresponding to voice indicative of human presence. These four energy levels become the feature set and a classifier (Damarla et al., 2007; 2004; Damarla & Ufford, 2007) is trained with this feature set collected with a person talking and not talking. The algorithm used to detect a person is presented in the references (Damarla et al., 2007; 2004; Damarla & Ufford, 2007) and the algorithm is provided here.

Classifier: Let $X = [X_1, X_2, \cdots, X_N]^T$ is a vector of N features, where T denotes the transpose. Assuming they obey the normal distribution, then the multi-variate normal probability distribution of the pattern X is given by

$$p(X) = \frac{1}{(2\pi)^{N/2} |\Sigma|^{1/2}} exp\left\{-1/2 (X - M)^T \Sigma^{-1} (X - M)\right\},$$

where the mean, M and the covariance matrix Σ are defined as

$$M = E\{X\} = [m_1, m_2, \cdots, m_N]^T$$

$$\Sigma = E\left\{(X - M)(X - M)^T\right\} = \begin{bmatrix} \sigma_{11} & \sigma_{12} & \cdots & \sigma_{1N} \\ \sigma_{21} & \sigma_{22} & \cdots & \sigma_{2N} \\ \cdots & \cdots & \cdots & \cdots \\ \sigma_{N1} & \sigma_{N2} & \cdots & \sigma_{NN} \end{bmatrix},$$

and $\sigma_{pq} = E\left\{(x_p - m_p)(x_q - m_q)^T\right\}$, $p, q = 1, 2, \cdots, N$. We assume that for each category i, where $i \in \{1, \cdots, R\}$, R denotes the number of classes (in our case $R = 2$, person present and person not present), we know the a priori probability and the particular N-variate normal probability function $P\{X \mid i)$. That is, we know R normal density functions. Let us denote the mean vectors M_i and the covariance matrices Σ_i for $i = 1, 2, \cdots, R$, then we can write

$$p(X \mid i) = \frac{1}{(2\pi)^{N/2} |\Sigma_i|^{1/2}} exp\left\{ -\frac{1}{2}(X - M_i)^T \Sigma_i^{-1} (X - M_i) \right\} \tag{12}$$

where $M_i = (m_{i1}, m_{i2}, \cdots, m_{iN})$. Let us define H_0 and H_1 as the null and human present hypotheses. The likelihood of each hypothesis is defined as the probability of the observation, i.e., feature, conditioned on the hypothesis,

$$l_{H_j}(X_s) = p\left(X_s \mid H_j\right) \tag{13}$$

for $j = 1, 2$ and $s \in S$, where S ={acoustic, PIR, seismic}. The conditional probability is modeled as a Gaussian distribution given by (12),

$$p\left(X_s \mid H_j\right) = \aleph\left(X_s; \mu_{s,j}, \sigma_{s,j}^2\right). \tag{14}$$

Now, (13)-(14) can be used to determine the posterior probability of human presence given a single sensor observation. Namely,

$$p(H_i \mid X_s) = \frac{l_{H_1}(X_s)\, p(H_1)}{l_{H_0}(X_s)\, p(H_0) + l_{H_1}(X_s)\, p(H_1)} \tag{15}$$

where $p(H_0)$ and $p(H_1)$ represent the prior probabilities for the absence and presence of a human, respectively. We assumes an uninformative prior, i.e., $p(H_0) = p(H_1) = 0.5$.

In the office room scenario, we are looking for any activity on the computer - the Windows operating system produces a distinct sound whenever a computer is turned on or off. This distinct sound has a 75-78Hz tone and the data analysis looks for this tone. The acoustic data process is depicted in the flow chart sown in Figure 13 and Figure 14 shows the spectrum of the acoustic data when a person is talking and when Windows operating system comes on. The output of the acoustic sensor is P_i, $i = 1, 2, 3$, corresponding to three situations, namely, (i) a person talking, (ii) computer chime and (iii) no acoustic activity.

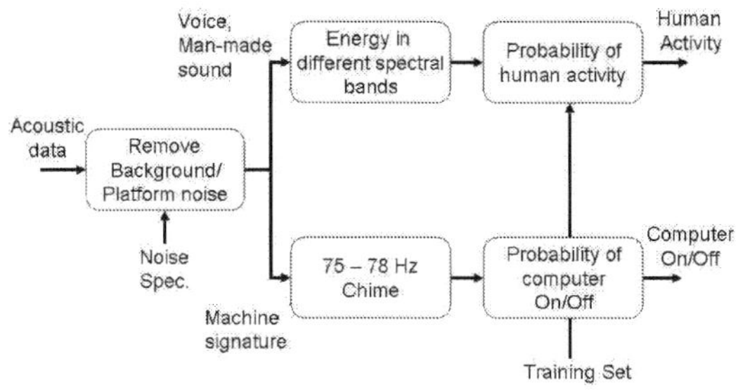

Fig. 13. Flow chart for acoustic sensor data analysis

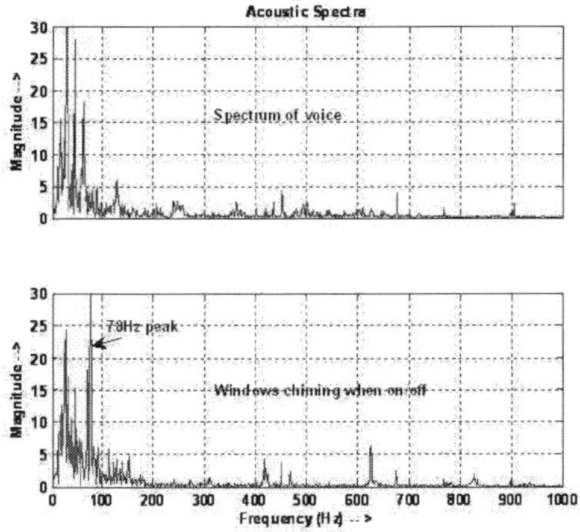

Fig. 14. Spectrum of voice and computer chime

Seismic Sensor Data Analysis: We analyze the seismic data for footfalls of a person walking. The gait frequency of normal walk is around 1-2Hz. We use the envelope of the signal instead of the signal itself to extract the gait frequency (Damarla et al., 2007; Houston & McGaffigan, 2003). We also look for the harmonics associated with the gait frequency. Figure 15 shows the flow chart for seismic data analysis. We use the 2-15Hz band to determine the probability of person walking in the vicinity. The seismic sensor provides two probabilities, (i) probability of a person walking and (ii) probability of nobody present.

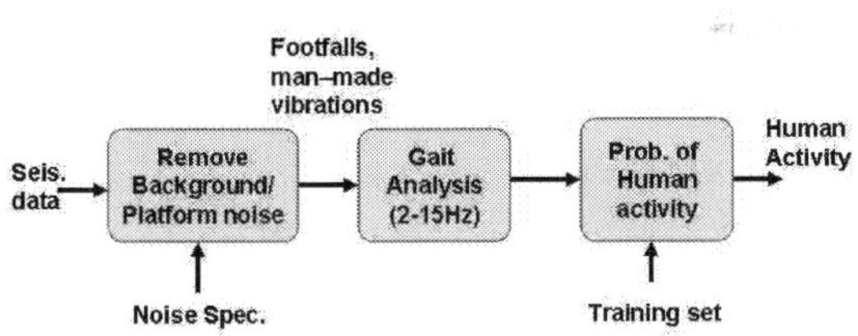

Fig. 15. Flow chart for seismic sensor data analysis

PIR sensor data analysis: These are motion detectors, if a person walks in front of them, they will give an output proportional to the temperature of the body and inversely proportional to the distance of the person from the sensor. Figure 16 shows the PIR sensor data collected in the office room. Clearly, one can see a large amplitude when a person walked by the sensor. The smaller amplitudes correspond to the person seated in the chair in front of the computer and moving slightly (note that the chair is obstructing the full view of the person) and only part of the body is seen by the PIR sensor. In order to assess the situation, both seismic and PIR sensor data can be used to determine whether a person entered the office room. The seismic sensor does not require line of sight unlike the PIR sensor - they complement each other.

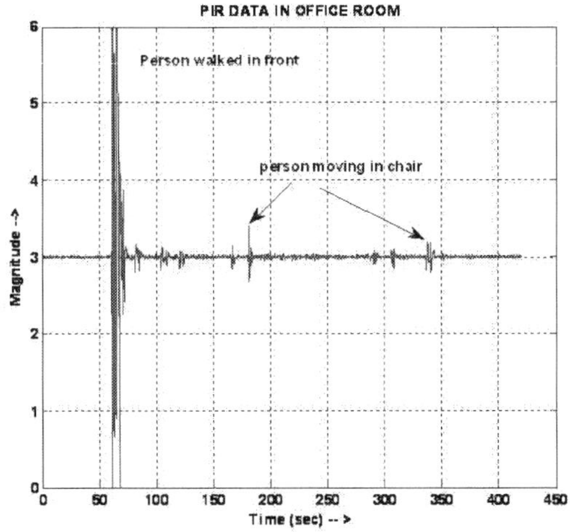

Fig. 16. PIR sensor output

Magnetic sensor (B-field sensor) Data Analysis: We used both Flux gate and coil magnetometers. The former has low frequency response while the coil magnetometer provides high frequency response. A total of six sensors: three flux gate magnetometers, one for each direction X, Y, and Z and three coil magnetometers were used. The coil magneto-meters are placed in X, Y, and Z axes to measure the magnetic flux in respective direction. Figure 17 shows clearly the change in magnetic flux when a computer is turned on and off. Similar signals are observed in Y and Z axes.

E-Field Sensor data analysis: We used three E-field sensors - one in each axis. The output of X-axis E-field sensor data is shown in Figure 18. A spike appears when the computer is turned on in the E-field sensor output, however, we did not observe any spike or change in amplitude when the computer is turned off.

Visible and IR imaging sensors: Several frames of visible and IR images of the office room and its contents are taken over a period of time. In this experiment, the images are used to determine if the computers are on or off and if anybody is sitting in front of the computer to assess the situation. Due to limited field of view of these sensors, only a partial view of the room is visible – often it is difficult to observe a person in the room. Figure 19 shows a frame of visible image showing only the shoulder of a person sitting in front of a computer. Figure 20 shows an IR frame showing a thermal image of the person in front of the computer due to reflection. Most of the thermal energy radiated by the person in front of the computer monitor is reflected by the monitor and this reflected thermal energy is detected by the IR imager. The IR imager algorithm processes the silhouette reflected from the monitor – first Hough transform (Hough, 1962) is used to determine the line patterns of an object and then using elliptical and rectangular models to detect a person (Belongie et al., 2002; Dalal & Triggs, 2005; Wang et al., 2007) in front of the monitor and provide the probability of a person being present in the room. The visible imager algorithm determines the brightness of the monitor

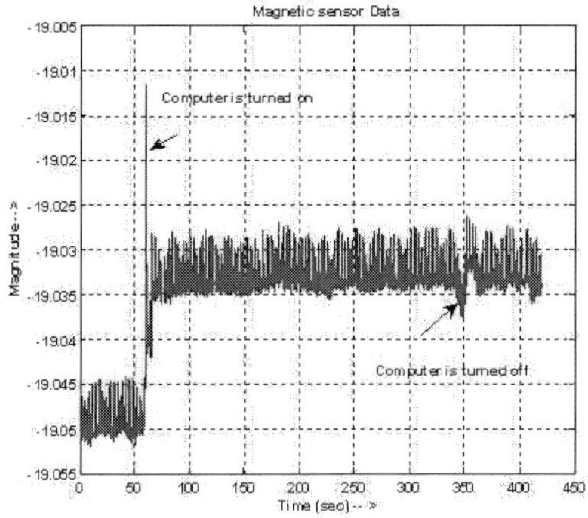

Fig. 17. Flux gate magnetometer output in X-axis

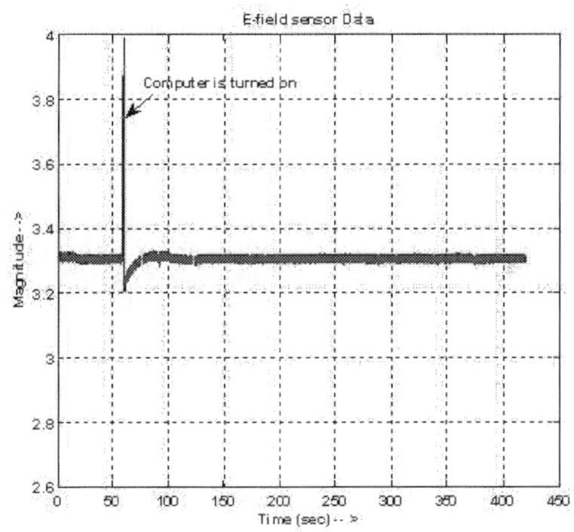

Fig. 18. E-field sensor output in X-axis

and varying patterns and provides the probability that the computer is on. In the next section we present the framework for HMM.

In the next section 3.3, we present an HMM with hypothetical states and how they can be reached based on the information observed. Although we present that these states are determined based on the output of some process, hence making them deterministic rather than the

Fig. 19. Visible image showing a person in front of computer before it is turned on

Fig. 20. IR image frame showing thermal reflection of person in front of the computer

hidden states, it is shown like this for conceptual purposes only. In section 3.4 we present the HMM where the states are hidden and can be reached only by particular observations.

3.3 Relation between HMM states and various states of Situational Awareness

Based on the situation we are interested in assessing, the HMM is designed with four states as shown in Figure 21. The states are as follows:

- S_0 denotes the state when there is no person in the office room,
- S_1 denotes the state when a person is present in the office room,
- S_2 denotes the state when a person is sitting in front of a computer and
- S_3 denotes the state when a computer is in use.

The above mentioned states are just a sample and can be extended to any number based on the situation one is trying to assess on the basis of observations using multi-modal sensors. We now discuss how each state is reached, what sensor data is used and how they are used. This also illustrates that the HMM also achieves the sensor fusion as each state transition is made on the observations of all or a subset of sensors.

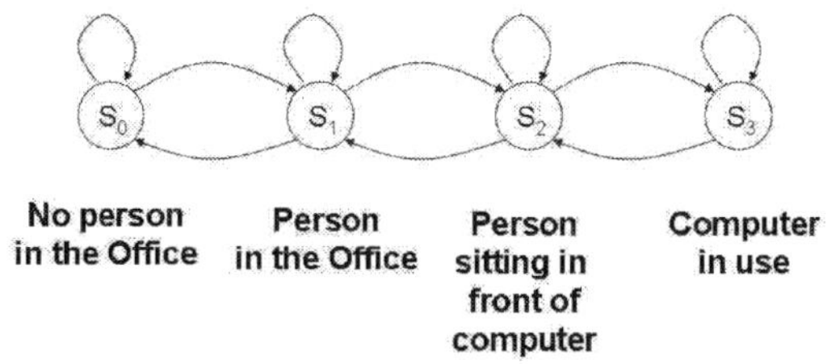

Fig. 21. Various states of HMM

State S_0: This is the initial state of the HMM. We use acoustic, seismic, PIR and visible video data to determine the presence of a person. Each sensor gives probability of detection, probability of no detection and confidence level denoted by (Pd, Pnd, Pc) as shown in Figure 22. These probabilities are fused using the Dempster-Shafer (Hall & Llinas, 2001; Klein, 2004) fusion paradigm to determine the overall probability. There will be transition from state S_0 to S_1 if this probability exceeds a predetermined threshold otherwise it will remain in state S_0. The Dempster-Shafer fusion paradigm used is presented here.

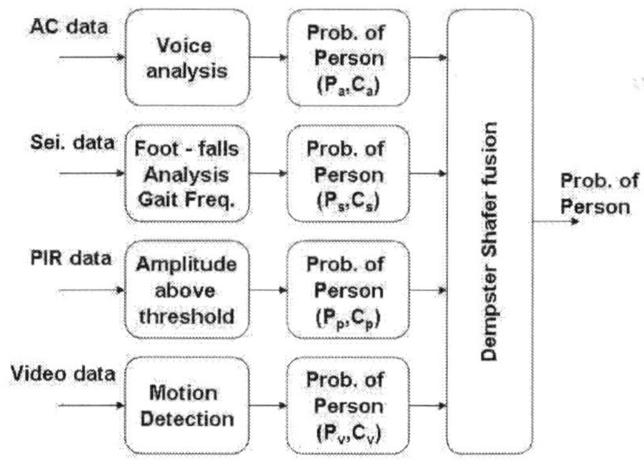

Fig. 22. Data processing in state S_0

Dempster-Shafer fusion rule: To combine the results from two sensors (s_1 and s_2), the fusion algorithm uses the Dempster-Shafer Rule of combination (Hall & Llinas, 2001; Klein, 2004): The total probability mass committed to an event Z defined by the combination of evidence represented by $s_1(X)$ and $s_2(Y)$ is given by

$$s_{1,2}(Z) = s_1(Z) \oplus s_2(Z) = K \sum_{X \cap Y = Z} s_1(x) s_2(Y) \tag{16}$$

where $\oplus$ denotes the orthogonal sum and K the normalization factor is:

$$K^{-1} = 1 - \sum_{X \cap Y = \phi} s_1(X) s_2(Y) \tag{17}$$

This is basically the sum of elements from the set of Sensor 1 who intersect with Sensor 2 to make Z, divided by 1 minus the sum of elements from s_1 that have no intersection with s_2. The rule is used to combine all three probabilities (Pd, Pnd, Pc) of sensors s_1 and s_2. The resultant probabilities are combined with the probabilities of the next sensor.

State S_1: This is the state when there is a person in the room. There are three transitions that can take place while in this state, namely, (1) transition to state S_2, (2) transitions back to state S_0 and (3) stays in the same state.

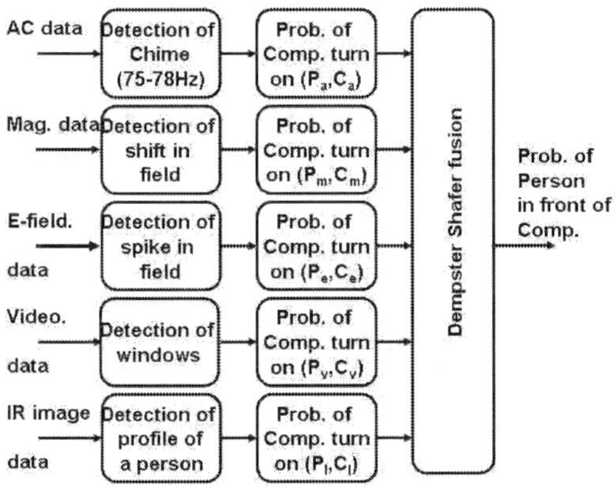

Fig. 23. Data processing in state S_1

Transition to S_2 happens if any one of the following takes place: (a) if the computer turn on chime is heard, (b) if magnetic and E-field sensors detect flux change and E-field by the respective sensors, (c) if the IR imager detects an image on the monitor and (d) if the visible imager detects changing images that appear during the windows turning on process.

Transition to S_0 takes place if there is no activity on any of the sensors.

The HMM remain in state S_1 if there is activity in the PIR, acoustic or seismic but not any of the events described for the case of transition to S_2. Figure 23 shows the data processing in each sensor modality.

State S_2**:** This is the state where a person is in front of the computer. The transition from this state either to S_3 or to S_1 depends on the following: (a) there is keyboard activity or the IR imager detects a hand on the keyboard and the PIR detects slight motion. S_2 to S_1 takes place when the computer is turned off - as detected by acoustic and magnetic sensors.

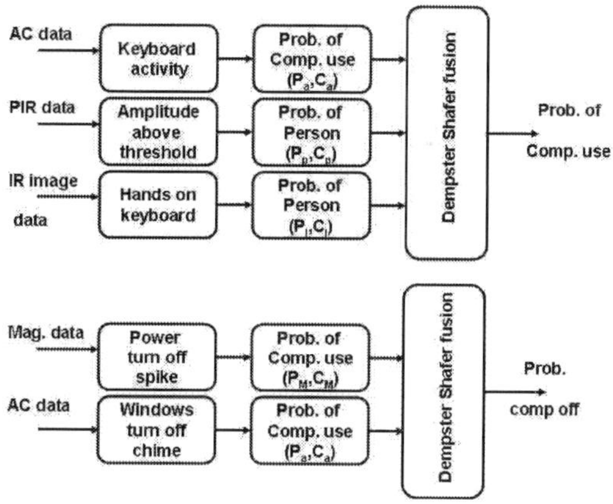

Fig. 24. Data processing in state S_2

State S_3**:** This is the state where the computer is in use. As long as keyboard activity is detected using acoustic and IR imagers the state remains in state S_3, if no keyboard activity is detected, it will transition to S_2.

Data processing in state S_2 is shown in Figure 24. Data processing in S_3 is straight forward.

We discussed what processing is done at each state and how the probabilities are estimated. The transition probabilities of HMM are generated based on several observations with people entering into the computer room, sitting in front of the computer, turning it on, using it for a period of time, turning it off and leaving the office room.

Data processing of various sensors depends on the state of the machine and the confidence levels of various sensor modalities are also changed based on the state of the HMM. For example, in state S_2 the PIR sensor output monitoring a person in a chair produces small amplitude changes as shown in Figure 16 - in normal processing those outputs will not result in high probability – however in this case they will be given high probability. In state S_3 the acoustic sensor determines the tapping on the keyboard, this sound is often very light and the sensor is given high confidence levels than normal. In order to accommodate such varying confidence levels based on the state – it is necessary the state information should be part of the processing in a deterministic system. In a HMM where the states are automatically transition based on the outputs of sensor observations. In the next section 3.4 an HMM is built for the above problem.

3.4 Generation of HMM for the Example Scenario

In the previous section, we showed how the states could be set up based on the outputs of various sensor processes. The processes used are:

Process	**Output random variable**
Acoustic data analysis for human voice	X_1
Acoustic data analysis for computer chime	X_2
Seismic data analysis for footstep detection	X_3
PIR data analysis	X_4
Magnetic sensor data analysis	X_5
E-field sensor data analysis	X_6
Motion detection in imagers	X_7
Detection of image in IR data	X_8

Clearly some processes can be combined to reduce the number of variables. For example, acoustic and seismic data can be processed together for detection of human presence. Less number of variables simplify the code table needed to train the HMM. Or one can use the output of process in Figure 22 as one variable, output of process in Figure 23 as another variable and so on. Let us assume that each variable gives a binary output, that is, in the case of acoustic data analysis $X_1 = 0$ implies no human voice, $X_1 = 1$ implying the presence of human voice. At each instant of time we observe $X = \{X_1, X_2, \cdots, X_8\}$ which can take $2^8 = 256$ different values. Each distinct vector X is an alphabet and there are 256 alphabets.

The data collection scenario in section 3.1 is enacted several times and each enactment is made with some variation. While enacting the scenario, for each time step t, we make an observation $O^t = \{O_1^t, O_2^t, \cdots, O_8^t\}$, where $O_i = X_i$. Each observation O^t is associated with a state S_i, for $i \in \{0,1,2,3,4\}$ based on the ground truth. For example, let the observation at time step t is $O^t = \{0,0,1,0,0,0,0,0\}$ is associated with state S_0 if there is no person present or it is associated with state S_1 if there is person in the room. This is the training phase. This association generates a table of 9 columns, first 8 columns corresponding to the observations and the 9th column corresponding to the states.

This table should be as large as possible. Next, the HMM model $\lambda = \{A, B, \pi\}$ will be developed.

3.5 Computation of transition probabilities for HMM

In this section we estimate the model parameters π, A, and B. The number of states $N = 4$ by design. The number of alphabet, the different possible observations, $M = 256$.

Estimation of π: $\pi = \{\pi_i\}, \forall i \in \{1, 2, \cdots, N\}$, where π_i is the initial state probability distribution (7) for the state S_i, that is, $\pi_i = p[q_1 = S_i]$. This can be computed by counting how many times S_i has appeared as an initial state. Let this number is denoted by n_i^1 and dividing it by the total number of experiments n_e. Then

$$\pi_i = \frac{n_i^1}{n_e} \tag{18}$$

O_1	O_2	O_3	O_4	O_5	O_6	O_7	O_8	State
0	0	1	0	0	0	0	0	0
0	0	1	0	0	0	0	0	0
0	0	1	0	0	0	0	0	0
1	0	1	0	0	0	0	0	1
1	0	1	1	0	0	0	0	1
⋮	⋮	⋮	⋮	⋮	⋮	⋮	⋮	⋮
0	0	0	0	0	0	1	1	2
0	0	0	1	0	0	1	1	3
0	0	1	0	0	0	0	0	0

Table 1. Exemplar observations and the state assignment

Estimation of A: A is the state transition probability distribution $A = \left\{a_{ij}\right\}$ where

$$a_{ij} = p\left[q_{t+1} = S_j \mid q_t = S_i\right], \quad 1 \le i,j \le N$$

In order to compute a_{ij}, we need to estimate how many times the state S_i to S_j in the Table 1, let this number is denoted by n_{ij}. Note that n_{ij} need not be equal to n_{ji}. Then

$$a_{ij} = \frac{n_{ij}}{n_T} \tag{19}$$

where n_T denotes the total number of rows in the Table 1.

Estimation of B: B is the probability distribution of each alphabet v_k in state j, $B = \left\{b_j(v_k)\right\}$, where

$$b_j(v_k) = p\left[v_k \; at \; t \mid q_t = S_j\right], \quad 1 \le j \le N; \; 1 \le k \le M.$$

In order to compute $b_j(v_k)$, first we count the number of times n_j the state S_j has occurred in Table 1. Out of these count the number of times the pattern $v_k = \{O_1, O_2, \cdots, O_8\}$ has occurred and denote this number by n_{v_k}. Then

$$b_j(v_k) = \frac{n_{v_k}}{n_j} \tag{20}$$

Now we have showed how to compute the model $\lambda = \{A, B, \pi\}$ and it can be used to determine the state and hence the situation when a new pattern is observed. It is worth noting several educational institutes have developed HMM packages for the MATLAB programming language and are available on the Internet *HMM Toolbox*.

In this chapter we showed how the HMM can be used to provide the situational awareness based on its states. We also showed how to build a HMM. We showed that fusion happens in HMM.

4. References

Belongie, S., Malik, J. & Puzicha, J. (2002). Shape matching and object recognition using shape contexts, *IEEE Trans. Pattern Anal. Mach. Intell.* **Vol. 24**(No. 4): 509–522.

Beringer, D. & Hancock, P. (1989). Summary of the various definitions of situation awareness, *Proc. of Fifth Intl. Symp. on Aviation Psychology* **Vol. 2**(No.6): 646 – 651.

Bernardin, K., Ogawara, K., Ikeuchi, K. & Dillmann, R. (2003). A hidden markov model based sensor fusion approach for recognizing continuous human grasping sequences, *Proc. 3rd IEEE International Conference on Humanoid Robots* pp. 1 – 13.

Bruckner, D., Sallans, B. & Russ, G. (2007). Hidden markov models for traffic observation, *Proc. 5th IEEE Intl. Conference on Industrial Informatics* pp. 23 – 27.

Dalal, N. & Triggs, B. (2005). Histograms of oriented gradients for human detection, *IEEE Computer Society Conference on Computer Vision and Pattern Recognition (CVPR'05)* **Vol. 1**: 886 – 893.

Damarla, T. (2008). Hidden markov model as a framework for situational awareness, *Proc. of Intl. Conference on Information Fusion, Cologne, Germany* .

Damarla, T., Kaplan, L. & Chan, A. (2007). Human infrastructure & human activity detection, *Proc. of Intl. Conference on Information Fusion, Quebec City, Canada* .

Damarla, T., Pham, T. & Lake, D. (2004). An algorithm for classifying multiple targets using acoustic signatures, *Proc. of SPIE* **Vol. 5429**(No.): 421 – 427.

Damarla, T. & Ufford, D. (2007). Personnel detection using ground sensors, *Proc. of SPIE* **Vol. 6562**: 1 – 10.

Endsley, M. R. & Mataric, M. (2000). *Situation Awareness Analysis and Measurement*, Lawrence Earlbaum Associates, Inc., Mahwah, New Jersey.

Green, M., Odom, J. & Yates, J. (1995). Measuring situational awareness with the ideal observer, *Proc. of the Intl. Conference on Experimental Analysis and Measurement of Situation Awareness*.

Hall, D. & Llinas, J. (2001). *Handbook of Multisensor Data Fusion*, CRC Press: Boca Raton.

HMM Toolbox (n.d.).
URL: `www.cs.ubc.ca/~murphyk/Software/HMM/hmm.html`

Hough, P. V. C. (1962). Method and means for recognizing complex patterns, *U.S. Patent 3069654* .

Houston, K. M. & McGaffigan, D. P. (2003). Spectrum analysis techniques for personnel detection using seismic sensors, *Proc. of SPIE* **Vol. 5090**: 162 – 173.

Klein, L. A. (2004). *Sensor and Data Fusion - A Tool for Information Assessment and Decision Making*, SPIE Press, Bellingham, Washington, USA.

Maj. Houlgate, K. P. (2004). Urban warfare transforms the corps, *Proc. of the Naval Institute* .

Pearl, J. (1986). Fusion, propagation, and structuring in belief networks, *Artificial Intelligence* **Vol. 29**: 241 – 288.

Pearl, J. (1988). *Probabilistic Reasoning in Intelligent Systems: Networks of Plausible Inference*, Morgan Kaufmann Publishers, Inc.

Press, D. G. (1998). Urban warfare: Options, problems and the future, *Summary of a conference sponsored by MIT Security Studies Program* .

Rabiner, L. R. (1989). A tutorial on hidden markov models and selected applications in speech recognition, *Proc. of the IEEE* **Vol. 77**(2): 257 – 285.

Sarter, N. B. & Woods, D. (1991). Situation awareness: A critical but ill-defined phenomenon, *Intl. Journal of Aviation Psychology* **Vol. 1**: 45–57.

Singhal, A. & Brown, C. (1997). Dynamic bayes net approach to multimodal sensor fusion, *Proc. of SPIE* **Vol. 3209**: 2 – 10.

Singhal, A. & Brown, C. (2000). A multilevel bayesian network approach to image sensor fusion, *Proc. ISIF, WeB3* pp. 9 – 16.

Smith, D. J. (2003). Situation(al) awareness (sa) in effective command and control, *Wales* .

Smith, K. & Hancock, P. A. (1995). The risk space representation of commercial airspace, *Proc. of the* 8th *Intl. Symposium on Aviation Psychology* pp. 9 – 16.

Wang, L., Shi, J., Song, G. & Shen, I. (2007). Object detection combining recognition and segmentation, *Eighth Asian Conference on Computer Vision (ACCV)* .

Multi-sensorial Active Perception for Indoor Environment Modeling

Luz Abril Torres-Méndez
Research Centre for Advanced Studies - Campus Saltillo
Mexico

1. Introduction

For many applications, the information provided by individual sensors is often incomplete, inconsistent, or imprecise. For problems involving detection, recognition and reconstruction tasks in complex environments, it is well known that no single source of information can provide the absolute solution, besides the computational complexity. The merging of multisource data can create a more consistent interpretation of the system of interest, in which the associated uncertainty is decreased.
Multi-sensor data fusion also known simply as sensor data fusion is a process of combining evidence from different information sources in order to make a better judgment (Llinas & Waltz, 1990; Hall, 1992; Klein, 1993). Although, the notion of data fusion has always been around, most multisensory data fusion applications have been developed very recently, converting it in an area of intense research in which new applications are being explored constantly. On the surface, the concept of fusion may look to be straightforward but the design and implementation of fusion systems is an extremely complex task. Modeling, processing, and integrating of different sensor data for knowledge interpretation and inference are challenging problems. These problems become even more difficult when the available data is incomplete, inconsistent or imprecise.

In robotics and computer vision, the rapid advance of science and technology combined with the reduction in the costs of sensor devices, has caused that these areas together, and before considered as independent, strength the diverse needs of each. A central topic of investigation in both areas is the recovery of the tridimensional structure of large-scale environments. In a large-scale environment the complete scene cannot be captured from a single referential frame or given position, thus an active way of capturing the information is needed. In particular, having a mobile robot able to build a 3D map of the environment is very appealing since it can be applied to many important applications. For example, virtual exploration of remote places, either for security or efficiency reasons. These applications depend not only on the correct transmission of visual and geometric information but also on the quality of the information captured. The latter is closely related to the notion of active perception as well as the uncertainty associated to each sensor. In particular, the behavior any artificial or biological system should follow to accomplish certain tasks (e.g., extraction, simplification and filtering), is strongly influenced by the data supplied by its sensors. This data is in turn dependent on the perception criteria associated with each sensorial input (Conde & Thalmann, 2004).

A vast body of research on 3D modeling and virtual reality applications has been focused on the fusion of intensity and range data with promising results (Pulli et al., 1997; Stamos & Allen, 2000) and recently (Guidi et al., 2009). Most of these works consider the complete acquisition of 3D points from the object or scene to be modeled, focusing mainly on the registration and integration problems.

In the area of computer vision, the idea of extracting the shape or structure from an image has been studied since the end of the 70's. Scientists in computer vision were mainly interested in methods that reflect the way the human eye works. These methods, known as "shape-from-X", extract depth information by using visual patterns of the images, such as shading, texture, binocular vision, motion, among others. Because of the type of sensors used in these methods, they are categorized as passive sensing techniques, i.e., data is obtained without emitting energy and involve typically mathematical models of the image formation and how to invert them. Traditionally, these models are based on physical principles of the light interaction. However, due to the difficulties to invert them, is necessary to assume several aspects about the physical properties of the objects in the scene, such as the type of surface (Lambertian, matte) and *albedo*, which cannot be suitable to real complex scenes.

In the robotics community, it is common to combine information from different sensors, even using the same sensors repeatedly over time, with the goal of building a model of the environment. Depth inference is frequently achieved by using sophisticated, but costly, hardware solutions. Range sensors, in particular laser rangefinders, are commonly used in several applications due to its simplicity and reliability (but not its elegance, cost and physical robustness). Besides of capturing 3D points in a direct and precise manner, range measurements are independent of external lighting conditions. These techniques are known as active sensing techniques. Although these techniques are particularly needed in non-structured environments (e.g., natural outdoors, aquatic environments), they are not suitable for capturing complete 2.5D maps with a resolution similar to that of a camera. The reason for this is that these sensors are extremely expensive or, in other way, impractical, since the data acquisition process may be slow and normally the spatial resolution of the data is limited. On the other hand, intensity images have a high resolution which allows precise results in well-defined objectives. These images are easy to acquire and give texture maps in real color images.

However, although many elegant algorithms based on traditional approaches for depth recovery have been developed, the fundamental problem of obtaining precise data is still a difficult task. In particular, achieving geometric correctness and realism may require data collection from different sensors as well as the correct fusion of all these observations.
Good examples are the stereo cameras that can produce volumetric scans that are economical. However, these cameras require calibration or produce range maps that are incomplete or of limited resolution. In general, using only 2D intensity images will provide

sparse measurements of the geometry which are non-reliable unless some simple geometry about the scene to model is assumed. By fusing 2D intensity images with range finding sensors, as first demonstrated in (Jarvis, 1992), a solution to 3D vision is realized - circumventing the problem of inferring 3D from 2D.

One aspect of great importance in the 3D modeling reconstruction is to have a fast, efficient and simple data acquisition process from the sensors and yet, have a good and robust reconstruction. This is crucial when dealing with dynamic environments (e.g., people walking around, illumination variation, etc.) and systems with limited battery-life. We can simplify the way the data is acquired by capturing only partial but reliable range information of regions of interest. In previous research work, the problem of tridimensional scene recovery using incomplete sensorial data was tackled for the first time, specifically, by using intensity images and a limited number of range data (Torres-Méndez & Dudek, 2003; Torres-Méndez & Dudek, 2008). The main idea is based on the fact that the underlying geometry of a scene can be characterized by the visual information and its interaction with the environment together with its inter-relationships with the available range data. Figure 1 shows an example of how a complete and dense range map is estimated from an intensity image and the associated partial depth map. These statistical relationships between the visual and range data were analyzed in terms of small patches or neighborhoods of pixels, showing that the contextual information of these relationships can provide information to infer complete and dense range maps. The dense depth maps with their corresponding intensity images are then used to build 3D models of large-scale man-made indoor environments (offices, museums, houses, etc.)

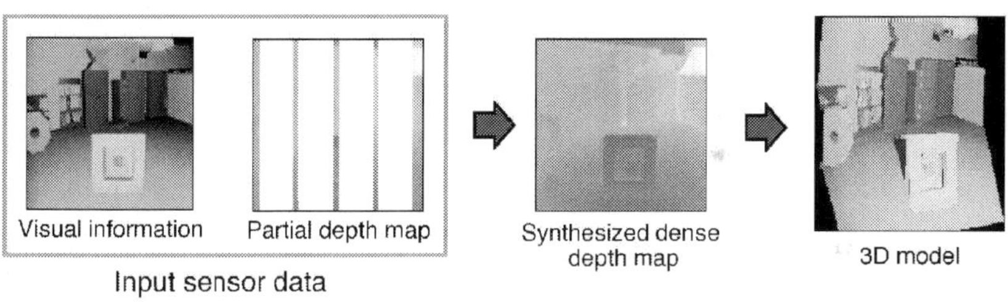

Fig. 1. An example of the range synthesis process. The data fusion of intensity and incomplete range is carried on to reconstruct a 3D model of the indoor scene. Image taken from (Torres-Méndez, 2008).

In that research work, the sampling strategies for measuring the range data was determined beforehand and remain fixed (vertical and horizontal lines through the scene) during the data acquisition process. These sampling strategies sometimes carried on critical limitations to get an ideal reconstruction as the quality of the input range data, in terms of the geometric characteristics it represent, did not capture the underlying geometry of the scene to be modeled. As a result, the synthesis process of the missing range data was very poor.

In the work presented in this chapter, we solve the above mentioned problem by selecting in an optimal way the regions where the initial (minimal) range data must be captured. Here, the term *optimal* refers in particular, to the fact that the range data to be measured must truly represent relevant information about the geometric structure. Thus, the input range data, in this case, must be good enough to estimate, together with the visual information, the rest of the missing range data.

Both sensors (camera and laser) must be fused (i.e., registered and then integrated) in a common reference frame. The fusion of visual and range data involves a number of aspects to be considered as the data is not of the same nature with respect to their resolution, type and scale. The images of real scene, i.e., those that represent a meaningful concept in their content, depend on the regularities of the environment in which they are captured (Van Der Schaaf, 1998). These regularities can be, for example, the natural geometry of objects and their distribution in space; the natural distributions of light; and the regularities that depend on the viewer's position. This is particularly difficult considering the fact that at each given position the mobile robot must capture a number of images and then analyze the optimal regions where the range data should be measured. This means that the laser should be directed to those regions with accuracy and then the incomplete range data must be registered with the intensity images before applying the statistical learning method to estimate complete and dense depth maps.
The statistical studies of these images can help to understand these regularities, which are not easily acquired from physical or mathematical models. Recently, there has been some success when using statistical methods to computer vision problems (Freeman & Torralba, 2002; Srivastava et al., 2003; Torralba & Oliva, 2002). However, more studies are needed in the analysis of the statistical relationships between intensity and range data. Having meaningful statistical tendencies could be of great utility in the design of new algorithms to infer the geometric structure of objects in a scene.

The outline of the chapter is as follows. In Section 2 we present related work to the problem of 3D environment modeling focusing on approaches that fuse intensity and range images. Section 3 presents our multi-sensorial active perception framework which statistically analyzes natural and indoor images to capture the initial range data. This range data together with the available intensity will be used to efficiently estimate dense range maps. Experimental results under different scenarios are shown in Section 4 together with an evaluation of the performance of the method.

2. Related Work

For the fundamental problem in computer vision of recovering the geometric structure of objects from 2D images, different monocular visual cues have been used, such as shading, defocus, texture, edges, etc. With respect to binocular visual cues, the most common are the obtained from stereo cameras, from which we can compute a depth map in a fast and economical way. For example, the method proposed in (Wan & Zhou, 2009), uses stereo vision as a basis to estimate dense depth maps of large-scale scenes. They generate depth map mosaics, with different angles and resolutions which are combined later in a single large depth map. The method presented in (Malik and Choi, 2008) is based in the shape from focus approach and use a defocus measure based in an optic transfer function implemented in the Fourier domain. In (Miled & Pesquet, 2009), the authors present a novel method based on stereo that help to estimate depth maps of scene that are subject to changes in illumination. Other works propose to combine different methods to obtain the range maps. For example, in (Scharstein & Szeliski, 2003) a stereo vision algorithm and structured light are used to reconstruct scenes in 3D. However, the main disadvantage of above techniques is that the obtained range maps are usually incomplete or of limited resolution and in most of the cases a calibration is required.

Another way of obtaining a dense depth map is by using range sensors (e.g., laser scanners), which obtain geometric information in a direct and reliable way. A large number of possible 3D scanners are available on the market. However, cost is still the major concern and the more economical tend to be slow. An overview of different systems available to 3D shape of objects is presented in (Blais, 2004), highlighting some of the advantages and disadvantages of the different methods. Laser Range Finders directly map the acquired data into a 3D volumetric model thus having the ability to partly avoid the correspondence problem associated with visual passive techniques. Indeed, scenes with no textural details can be easily modeled. Moreover, laser range measurements do not depend on scene illumination.

More recently, techniques based on learning statistics have been used to recover the geometric structure from 2D images. For humans, to interpret the geometric information of a scene by looking to one image is not a difficult task. However, for a computational algorithm this is difficult as some *a priori* knowledge about the scene is needed.
For example, in (Torres-Méndez & Dudek, 2003) it was presented for the first time a method to estimate dense range map based on the statistical correlation between intensity and available range as well as edge information. Other studies developed more recently as in (Saxena & Chung, 2008), show that it is possible to recover the missing range data in the sparse depth maps using statistical learning approaches together with the appropriate characteristics of objects in the scene (e.g., edges or cues indicating changes in depth). Other works combine different types of visual cues to facilitate the recovery of depth information or the geometry of objects of interest.
In general, no matter what approach is used, the quality of the results will strongly depend on the type of visual cues used and the preprocessing algorithms applied to the input data.

3. The Multi-sensorial Active Perception Framework

This research work focuses on recovering the geometric (depth) information of a man-made indoor scene (e.g., an office, a room) by fusing photometric and partial geometric information in order to build a 3D model of the environment.
Our data fusion framework is based on an active perception technique that captures the limited range data in regions statistically detected from the intensity images of the same scene. In order to do that, a perfect registration between the intensity and range data is required. The registration process we use is briefly described in Section 3.2. After registering the partial range with the intensity data we apply a statistical learning method to estimate the unknown range and obtain a dense range map. As the mobile robot moves at different locations to capture information from the scene, the final step is to integrate all the dense range maps (together with intensity) and build a 3D map of the environment.

The key role of our active perception process concentrates on capturing range data from places where the visual cues of the images show depth discontinuities. Man-made indoor environments have inherent geometric and photometric characteristics that can be exploited to help in the detection of this type of visual cues.

First, we apply a statistical analysis on an image database to detect regions of interest on which range data should be acquired. With the internal representation, we can assign confidence values according to the ternary values obtained. These values will indicate the filling order of the missing range values. And finally, we use a non-parametric range synthesis method in (Torres-Méndez & Dudek, 2003) to estimate the missing range values and obtain a dense depth map. In the following sections, all these stages are explained in more detail.

3.1 Detecting regions of interest from intensity images

We wish to capture limited range data in order to simplify the data acquisition process. However, in order to have a good estimation of the unknown range, the quality of this initial range data is crucial. That is, it should represent the depth discontinuities existing in the scene. Since we have only information from images, we can apply a statistical analysis on the images and extract changes in depth.

Given that our method is based on a statistical analysis, the type of images to analyze in the database must contain characteristics and properties similar to the scenes of interest, as we focus on man-made scenes, we should have images containing those types of images. However, we start our experiments using a public available image database, the van Hateren database, which contains scenes of natural images. As this database contains important changes in depth in their scenes, this turns out to be the main characteristic to be considered so that our method can be functional.

The statistical analysis of small patches implemented is based in part on the Feldman and Yunes algorithm (Feldman & Yunes, 2006). This algorithm extracts characteristics of interest from an image through the observation of an image database and obtains an internal representation that concentrates the relevant information in a form of a ternary variable. To generate the internal representation we follow three steps. First, we reduce (in scale) the images in the database (see Figure 2). Then, each image is divided in patches of same size (e.g. *13 x13* pixels), with these patches we make a new database which is decomposed in its principal components by applying PCA to extract the most representative information, which is usually contained, in the first five eigenvectors. In Figure 3, the eigenvectors are depicted. These eigenvectors are the filters that are used to highlight certain characteristics on the intensity images, specifically the regions with relevant geometric information.
The last step consists on applying a threshold in order to map the images onto a ternary variable where we assign *-1* value to very low values, *1* to high values and *0* otherwise. This way, we can obtain an internal representation

$$\xi_i : G \to \{-1,0,1\}^k , \qquad (1)$$

where k represents the number of filters (eigenvectors). G is the set of pixels of the scaled image.

Fig. 2. Some of the images taken from the van Hateren database. These images are reduced by a scaled factor of 2.

Fig. 3. The first 5 eigenvectors (zoomed out). These eigenvectors are used as filters to highlight relevant geometric information.

The internal representation gives information about the changes in depth as it is shown in Figure 4. It can be observed that, depending on the filter used, the representation gives a different orientation on the depth discontinuities in the scene. For example, if we use the first filter, the highlighted changes are the horizontal ones. If we applied the second filter, the discontinuities obtained are the vertical ones.

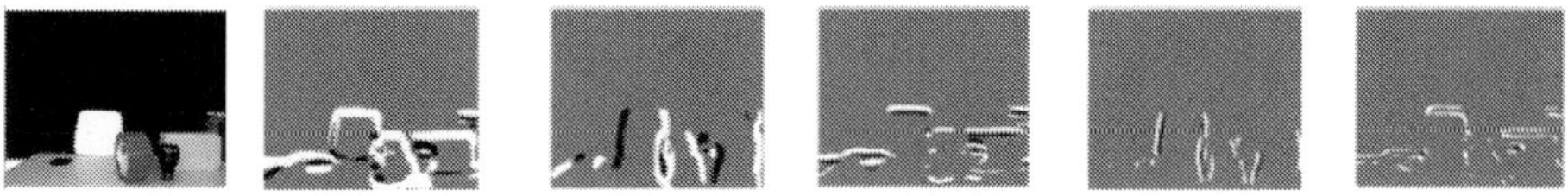

Fig. 4. The internal representation after the input image is filtered.

This internal representation is the basis to capture the initial range data from which we can obtain a dense range map.

3.2 Obtaining the registered sparse depth map

In order to obtain the initial range data we need to register the camera and laser sensors, i.e., the corresponding reference frame of the intensity image taken from the camera with the reference frame of the laser rangefinder. Our data acquisition system consists of a high resolution digital camera and a 2D laser rangefinder (laser scanner), both mounted on a pan unit and on top of a mobile robot. Registering different types of sensor data, which have different projections, resolutions and scaling properties is a difficult task. The simplest and easiest way to facilitate this sensor-to-sensor registration is to vertically align their center of projections (optical center for the camera and mirror center for the laser) are aligned to the center of projection of the pan unit. Thus, both sensors can be registered with respect to a common reference frame. The laser scanner and camera sensors work with different coordinate systems and they must be adjusted one to another. The laser scanner delivers spherical coordinates whereas the camera puts out data in a typical image projection. Once the initial the range data is collected we apply a post-registration algorithm which uses their projection types in order to do an image mapping.

The image-based registration algorithm is similar to that presented in (Torres-Méndez & Dudek, 2008) and assumes that the optical center of the camera and the mirror center of the laser scanner are vertically aligned and the orientation of both rotation axes coincide (see Figure 5). Thus, we only need to transform the panoramic camera data into the laser coordinate system. Details of the algorithm we use are given in (Torres-Méndez & Dudek, 2008).

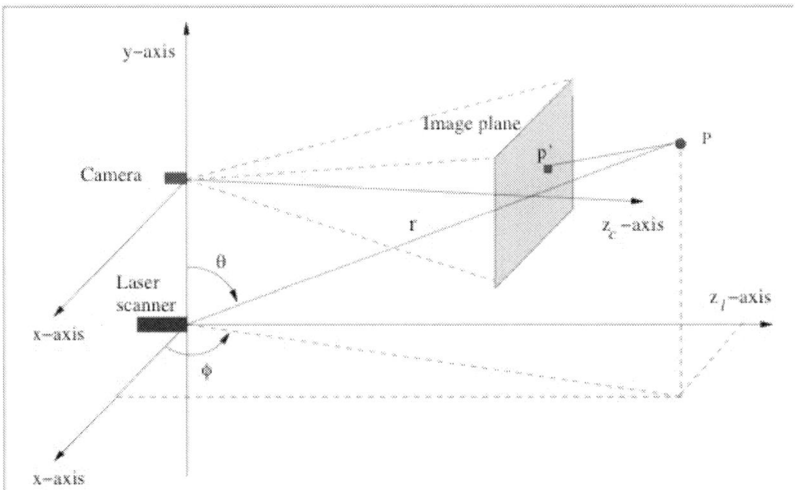

Fig. 5. Camera and laser scanner orientation and world coordinate system. Image taken from (Torres-Méndez & Dudek, 2008).

3.3 The range synthesis method

After obtaining the internal representation and a registered sparse depth map, we can apply the range synthesis method in (Torres-Méndez & Dudek, 2008). In general, the method estimates dense depth maps using intensity and partial range information. The Markov Random Field (MRF) model is trained using the (local) relationships between the observed range data and the variations in the intensity images and then used to compute the unknown range values. The Markovianity condition describes the local characteristics of the pixel values (in intensity and range, called voxels). The range value at a voxel depends only on neighboring voxels which have direct interactions on each other. We describe the non-parametric method in general and skip the details of the basis of MRF; the reader is referred to (Torres-Méndez & Dudek, 2008) for further details.

In order to compute the maximum *a posteriori* (MAP) for a depth value R_i of a voxel V_i, we need first to build an approximate distribution of the conditional probability $P(f_i \mid f_{N_i})$ and sample from it. For each new depth value $R_i \in R$ to estimate, the samples that correspond to

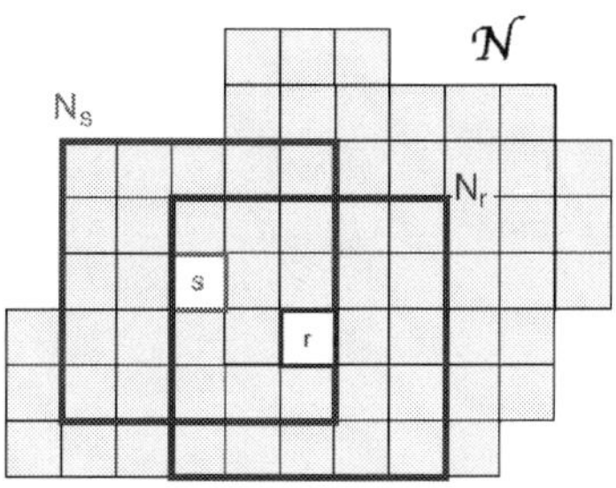

Fig. 6. A sketch of the neighborhood system definition.

the neighborhood system of voxel i, i.e., N_i, are taken and the distribution of R_i is built as a histogram of all possible values that occur in the sample. The neighborhood system N_i (see Figure 6) is an infinite real subset of voxels, denoted by $\mathcal{N}_{\text{real}}$. Taking the MRF model as a basis, it is assumed that the depth value R_i depends only on the intensity and range values of its immediate neighbors defined in N_i. If we define a set

$$\Gamma(R_i) = \{N^* \subset \mathcal{N}_{real} : \left\| N_i - N^* \right\| = 0\}, \tag{2}$$

that contains all occurrences of N_i in $\mathcal{N}_{\text{real}}$, then the conditional probability distribution of R_i can be estimated through a histogram based on the depth values of voxels representing each N_i in $\Gamma(R_i)$. Unfortunately, the sample is finite and there exists the possibility that no neighbor has exactly the same characteristics in intensity and range, for that reason we use the heuristic of finding the most similar value in the available finite sample $\Gamma'(R_i)$, where $\Gamma'(R_i) \subseteq \Gamma(R_i)$. Now, let A_p be a local neighborhood system for voxel p, which is composed for neighbors that are located within radius r and is defined as:

$$A_p = \{A_q \in N \,|\, \text{dist}(p,q) \le r\}. \tag{3}$$

In the non-parametric approximation, the depth value R_p of voxel V_p with neighborhood N_p, is synthesized by selecting the most similar neighborhood N_{best} to N_p.

$$N_{best} = \arg\min \left\| N_p - A_q \right\|, \ A_q \in A_p. \tag{4}$$

All neighborhoods A_q in A_p that are similar to N_{best} are included in $\Gamma'(R_p)$ as follows:

$$\left\| N_p - A_q \right\| < (1-\varepsilon) \left\| N_p - N_{best} \right\|. \tag{5}$$

The similarity measure between two neighborhoods N_a and N_b is described over the partial data of the two neighborhoods and is calculated as follows:

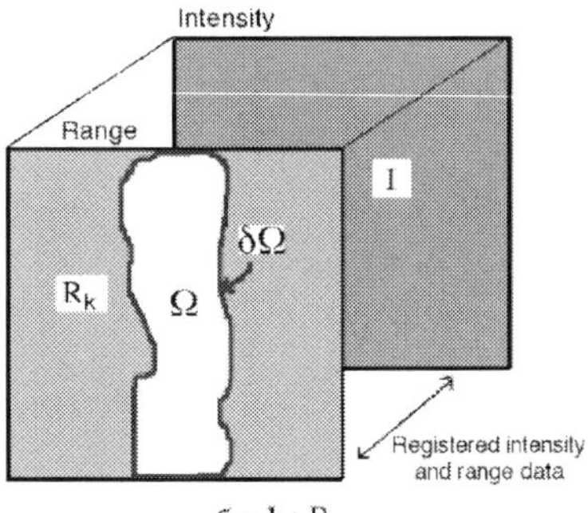

Fig. 7. The notation diagram. Taken from (Torres-Méndez, 2008).

$$\|N_a - N_b\| = \sum_{\vec{v} \in N_a, N_b} G(\sigma, \vec{v} - \vec{v}_0) \cdot D \tag{6}$$

$$D = \sqrt{\left(I_{\vec{v}}^{a} - I_{\vec{v}}^{b}\right)^2 + \left(R_{\vec{v}}^{a} - R_{\vec{v}}^{b}\right)^2}, \tag{7}$$

where $\vec{v}_0$ represents the voxel located in the center of the neighborhood N_a and N_b, $\vec{v}$ is the neighboring pixel of $\vec{v}_0$. I_a and R_a are the intensity and range values to be compared. G is a Gaussian kernel that is applied to each neighborhood so that voxels located near the center have more weight that those located far from it. In this way we can build a histogram of depth values R_p in the center of each neighborhood in $\Gamma'(R_i)$.

3.3.1 Computing the priority values to establish the filling order

To achieve a good estimation for the unknown depth values, it is critical to establish an order to select the next voxel to synthesize. We base this order on the amount of available information at each voxel's neighborhood, so that the voxel with more neighboring voxels with already assigned intensity and range is synthesized first. We have observed that the reconstruction in areas with discontinuities is very problematic and a probabilistic inference is needed in these regions. Fortunately, such regions are identified by our internal representation (described in Section 3.1) and can be used to assign priority values. For example, we assign a high priority to voxels which ternary value is *1*, so these voxels are synthesized first; and a lower priority to voxels with ternary value *0* and -1, so they are synthesized at the end.

The region to be synthesized is indicated by $\Omega=\{w_i | i \in A\}$, where $w_i = R(x_i,y_i)$ is the unknown depth value located at pixel coordinates (x_i,y_i). The input intensity and the known range value together conform the source region and is indicated by ς (see Figure 6). This region is used to calculate the statistics between the input intensity and range for the reconstruction. If V_p is the voxel with an unknown range value, inside Ω and N_p is its neighborhood, which is an *nxn* window centered at V_p, then for each voxel $V_p \in \Omega$, we calculate its priority value as follows

$$P(V_p) = \frac{\sum_{i \in N_p} C(V_i)F(V_i)}{|N_p| - 1}, \tag{8}$$

where $|\cdot|$ indicates the total number of voxels in N_p. Initially, the priority value of $C(V_i)$ for each voxel $V_p \in \Omega$ is assigned a value of *1* if the associated ternary value is *1*, *0.8* if its ternary value is *0* and 0.2 if -1. $F(V_i)$ is a flag function, which takes value *1* if the intensity and range values of V_i are known, and *0* if its range value is unknown. In this way, voxels with greater priority are synthesized first.

3.4 Integration of dense range maps

We have mentioned that at each position the mobile robot takes an image, computes its internal representation to direct the laser range finder on the regions detected and capture range data. In order to produce a complete 3D model or representation of a large environment, we need to integrate *dense* panoramas with depth from multiple viewpoints. The approach taken is based on a hybrid method similar to that in (Torres-Méndez & Dudek, 2008) (the reader is advised to refer to the article for further details).

In general, the integration algorithm combines a geometric technique, which is a variant of the ICP algorithm (Besl & McKay, 1992) that matches 3D range scans, and an image-based technique, the SIFT algorithm (Lowe, 1999), that matches intensity features on the images. Since dense range maps with its corresponding intensity images are given as an input, their integration to a common reference frame is easier than having only intensity or range data separately.

4. Experimental Results

In order to evaluate the performance of the method, we use three databases, two of which are available on the web. One is the Middlebury database (Hiebert-Treuer, 2008) which contains intensity and dense range maps of 12 different indoor scenes containing objects with a great variety of texture. The other is the USF database from the CESAR lab at Oak Ridge National Laboratory. This database has intensity and dense range maps of indoor scenes containing regular geometric objects with uniform textures. The third database was created by capturing images using a stereo vision system in our laboratory. The scenes contain regular geometric objects with different textures. As we have ground truth range data from the public databases, we first simulate sparse range maps by eliminating some of the range information using different sampling strategies that follows different patterns (squares, vertical and horizontal lines, etc.) The sparse depth maps are then given as an input to our algorithm to estimate dense range maps. In this way, we can compare the ground-truth dense range maps with those synthesized by our method and obtain a quality measure for the reconstruction.

To evaluate our results we compute a well-know metric, called mean absolute residual (MAR) error. The MAR error of two matrices R_1 and R_2 is defined as

$$\mathrm{MAR} = \frac{\sum_{i,j} \left| R_1(i,j) - R_2(i,j) \right|}{\#\,\text{unknown range voxels}} \tag{9}$$

In general, just computing the MAR error is not a good mechanism to evaluate the success of the method. For example, when there are few results with a high MAR error, the average of the MAR error elevates. For this reason, we also compute the absolute difference at each pixel and show the result as an image, so we can visually evaluate our performance.
In all the experiments, the size of the neighborhood N is *3x3* pixels for one experimental set and *5x5* pixels for other. The search window varies between *5* and *10* pixels. The missing range data in the sparse depth maps varies between *30%* and *50%* of the total information.

4.1 Range synthesis on sparse depth maps with different sampling strategies

In the following experiments, we have used the two first databases described above. For each of the input range maps in the databases, we first simulate a sparse depth map by eliminating a given amount of range data from these dense maps. The areas with missing depth values follow an arbitrary pattern (vertical, horizontal lines, squares). The size of these areas depends on the amount of information that is eliminated for the experiment (from *30%* up to *50%*). After obtaining a simulated sparse depth map, we apply the proposed algorithm. The result is a synthesized dense range map. We compare our results with the ground truth range map computing the MAR error and also an image of the absolute difference at each pixel.

Figure 8 shows the experimental setup of one of the scenes in the Middlebury database. In 8b the ground truth range map is depicted. Figure 9 shows the synthesized results for different sampling strategies for the baby scene.

(a) Intensity image. (b) Ground truth dense range map. (c) Ternary variable image.

Fig. 8. An example of the experimental setup to evaluate the method (Middlebury database).

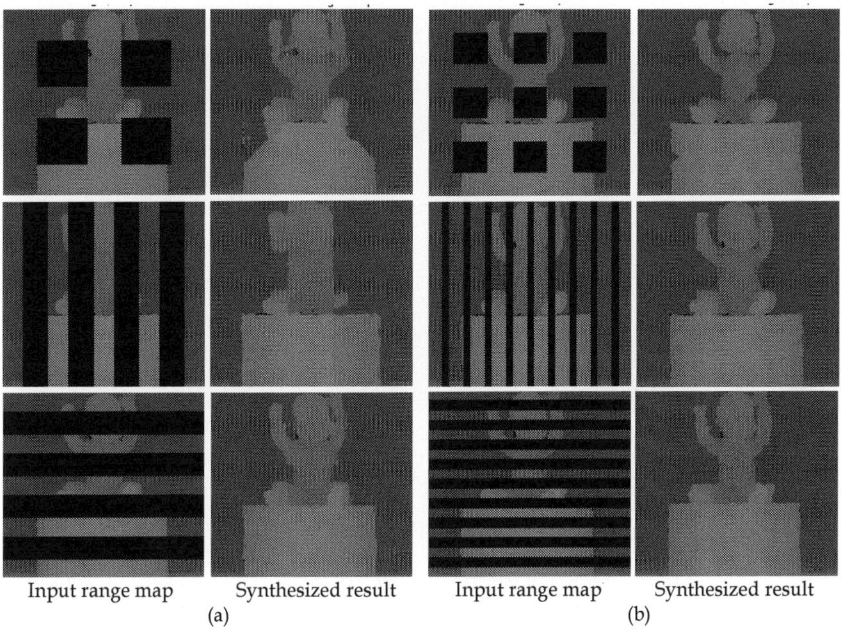

Fig. 9. Experimental results after running our range synthesis method on the baby scene.

The first column shows the incomplete depth maps and the second column the synthesized dense range maps. In the results shown in Figure 9a, most of the missing information is concentrated in a bigger area compared to 9b. It can be observed that for some cases, it is not possible to have a good reconstruction as there is little information about the inherent statistics in the intensity and its relationship with the available range data. In the synthesized map corresponding to the set in Figure 9a following a sampling strategy of vertical lines, we can observe that there is no information of the object to be reconstructed and for that reason it does not appear in the result. However, in the set of images of Figure 9b the same sampling strategies were used and the same amount of range information as of 9a is missing, but in these incomplete depth maps the unknown information is distributed in four different regions. For this reason, there is much more information about the scene and the quality of the reconstruction improves considerably as it can be seen. In the set of Figure 8c, the same amount of unknown depth values is shown but with a greater distribution over the range map. In this set, the variation between the reconstructions is small due to the amount of available information. A factor that affects the quality of the reconstruction is the existence of textures in the intensity images as it affects the ternary variable computation. For the case of the Middlebury database, the images have a great variety of textures, which affects directly the values in the ternary variable as it can be seen in Figure 8c.

(a) Intensity image.

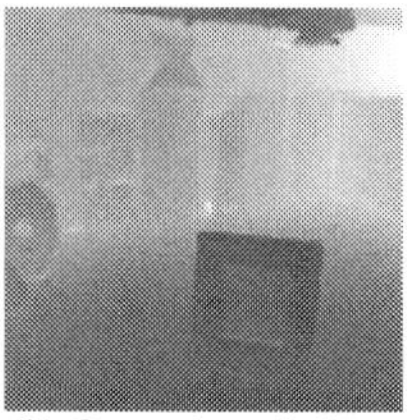

(b) Ground truth dense range map.

(c) Ternary variable image.

Fig. 10. An example of the experimental setup to evaluate the proposed method (USF database).

4.2 Range synthesis on sparse depth maps obtained from the internal representation

We conducted experiments where the sparse depth maps contain range data only on regions indicated by the internal representation. Therefore, apart from greatly reducing the acquisition time, the initial range would represent all the relevant variations related to depth discontinuities in the scene. Thus, it is expected that the dense range map will be estimated more efficiently.

In Figure 10 an image from the USF database is shown with its corresponding ground truth range map and ternary variable image. In the USF database, contrary to the Middlebury database, the scenes are bigger and objects are located at different depths and the texture is uniform. Figure 10c depicts the ternary variable, which represents the initial range given as an input together with the intensity image to the range synthesis process. It can be seen that the discontinuities can be better appreciated in objects as they have a uniform texture. Figure 11 shows the synthesized dense range map. As before, the quality of the reconstruction depends on the available information. Good results are obtained as the known range is distributed around the missing range. It is important to determine which values inside the available information have greater influence on the reconstruction so we can give to them a high priority.
In general, the experimental results show that the ternary variable influences in the quality of the synthesis, especially in areas with depth discontinuities.

Fig. 11. The synthesized dense range map of the initial range values indicated in figure 10c.

4.3 Range synthesis on sparse depth maps obtained from stereo

We also test our method by using real sparse depth maps by acquiring pair of images directly from the stereo vision system, obtaining the sparse depth map, the internal representation and finally synthesizing the missing depth values in the map using the non-parametric MRF model. In Figure 12, we show the input data to our algorithm for three different scenes acquired in our laboratory. The left images of the stereo pair for each scene are shown in the first column. The sparse range maps depicted on Figure 12b are obtained from the Shirai's stereo algorithm (Klette & Schlns, 1998) using the epipolar geometry and the Harris corner detector (Harris & Stephens, 1988) as constraints. Figure 12c shows the ternary variable images used to compute the priority values to establish the synthesis order. In Figure 13, we show the synthesized results for each of the scenes shown in Figure 12. From top to bottom we show the synthesized results for iterations at different intervals. It can be seen that the algorithm first synthesizes the voxels with high priority, that is, the contours where depth discontinuities exists. This gives a better result as the synthesis process progresses. The results vary depending on the size of the neighborhood *N* and the size of the searching window *d*. On one hand, if *N* is more than *5x5* pixels, it can be difficult to find a neighborhood with similar statistics. On the other hand, if *d* is big, for example, it considers the neighborhoods in the whole image, then the computing time increases accordingly.

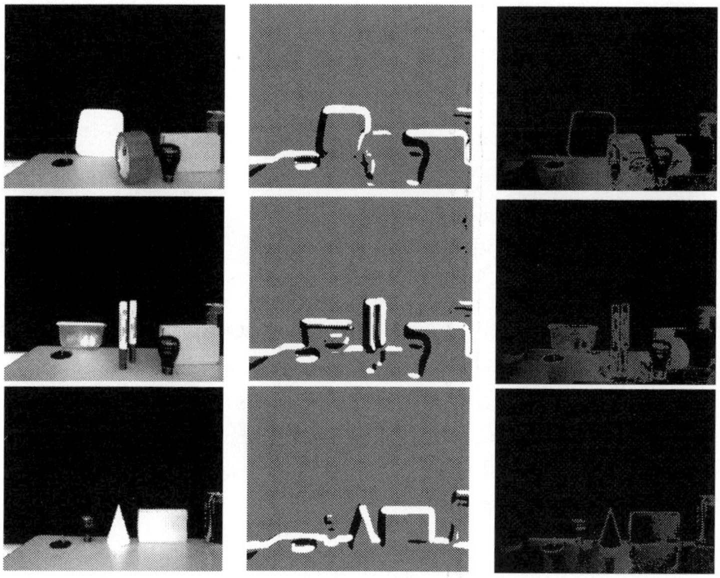

(a) Left (stereo) image. (b) Ternary variable images. (c) Sparse depth maps.

Fig. 12. Input data for three scenes captured in our laboratory.

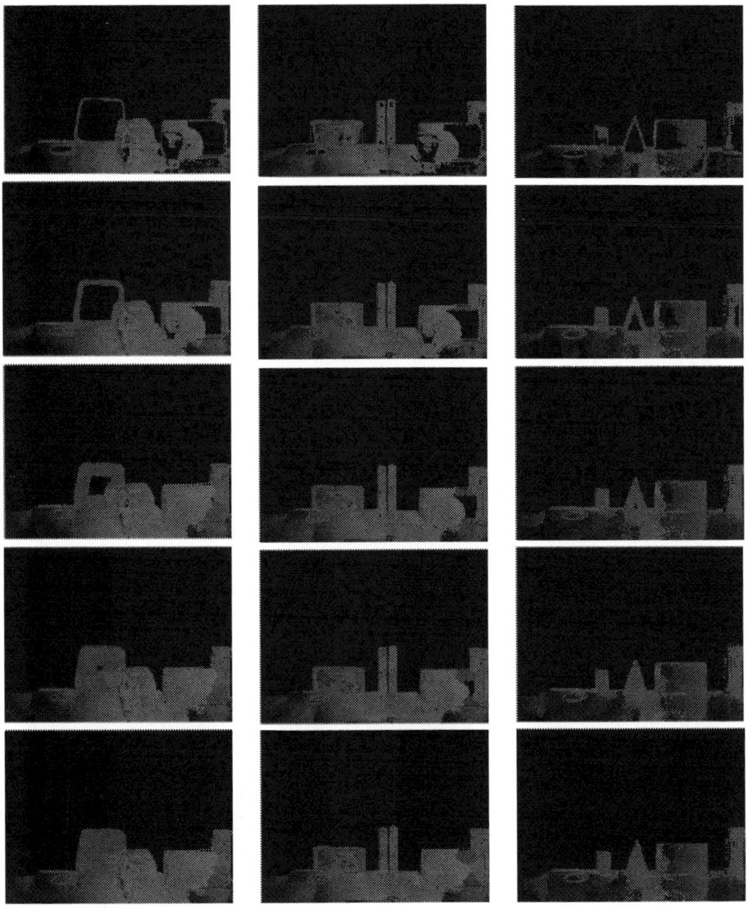

(a) Scene 1 (b) Scene 2 (c) Scene 3

Fig. 13. Experimental results of the three different scenes shown in Figure 11. Each row shows the results at different steps of the range synthesis algorithm.

5. Conclusion

We have presented an approach to recover dense depth maps based on the statistical analysis of visual cues. The visual cues extracted represent regions indicating depth discontinuities in the intensity images. These are the regions where range data should be captured and represent the range data given as an input together with the intensity map to the range estimation process. Additionally, the internal representation of the intensity map is used to assign priority values to the initial range data. The range synthesis is improved as the orders in which the voxels are synthesized are established from these priority values.

The quality of the results depends on the amount and type of the initial range information, in terms of the variations captured on it. In other words, if the correlation between the intensity and range data available represents (although partially) the correlation of the intensity near regions with missing range data, we can establish the statistics to be looked for in such available input data.
Also, as in many non-deterministic methods, we have seen that the results depend on the suitable selection of some parameters. One is the neighborhood size (N) and the other the radius of search (r). With the method here proposed the synthesis near the edges (indicated by areas that present depth discontinuities) is improved compared to prior work in the literature.

While a broad variety of problems have been covered with respect to the automatic 3D reconstruction of unknown environments, there remain several open problems and unanswered questions. With respect to the data collection, a key issue in our method is the quality of the observable range data. In particular, with the type of the geometric characteristics that can be extracted in relation to the objects or scene that the range data represent. If the range data do not capture the inherent geometry of the scene to be modeled, then the range synthesis process on the missing range values will be poor. The experiments presented in this chapter were based on acquiring the initial range data in a more directed way such that the regions captured reflect important changes in the geometry.

6. Acknowledgements

The author gratefully acknowledges financial support from CONACyT (CB-2006/55203).

7. References

Besl, P.J. & McKay, N.D. (1992). A method for registration of 3D shapes. *IEEE Transactions on Pattern Analysis and Machine Intelligence*, Vol. 4, No. 2, 239-256, 1992.

Blais, F. (2004). A review of 20 years of range sensor development. *Journal of Electronic Imaging*, Vol. 13, No. 1, 231–240, 2004.

Conde, T. & Thalmann, D. (2004). An artificial life environment for autonomous virtual agents with multi-sensorial and multi-perceptive features. Computer Animation and Virtual Worlds, Vol. 15, 311-318, ISSN: 1546-4261.

Feldman, T. & Younes, L. (2006). Homeostatic image perception: An artificial system. *Computer Vision and Image Understanding*, Vol. 102, No. 1, 70–80, ISSN:1077-3142.

Freeman, W.T. & Torralba, A. (2002). Shape recipes: scene representations that refer to the image. *Adv. In Neural Information Processing Systems* 15 (NIPS).

Guidi, G. & Remondino, F. & Russo, M. & Menna, F. & Rizzi, A. & Ercoli, S. (2009). A Multi-Resolution Methodology for the 3D Modeling of Large and Complex Archeological Areas. *Internation Journal of Architectural Computing*, Vol. 7, No. 1, 39-55, Multi Science Publishing.

Hall, D. (1992). *Mathematical Techniques in Multisensor Data Fusion*. Boston, MA: Artech House.

Harris, C. & Stephens, M. (1988). A combined corner and edge detector. In *Fourth Alvey Vision Conference*, Vol. 4, pp. 147–151, 1988, Manchester, UK.

Hiebert-Treuer, B. (2008). Stereo datasets with ground truth.

http://vision.middlebury.edu/stereo/data/scenes2006/.
Jarvis, R.A. (1992). 3D shape and surface colour sensor fusion for robot vision. *Robotica,* Vol. 10, 389–396.
Klein, L.A. (1993). *Sensor and Data Fusion Concepts and Applications.* SPIE Opt. Engineering Press, Tutorial Texts, Vol. 14.
Klette, R. & Schlns, K. (1998). *Computer vision: three-dimensional data from images.* Springer-Singapore. ISBN: 9813083719, 1998.
Llinas, J. & Waltz, E. (1990). *Multisensor Data Fusion.* Boston, MA: Artech House.
Lowe, D.G. (1999). Object recognition from local scale-invariant features. In *Proceedings of the International Conference on Computer Vision* ICCV, 1150–1157.
Malik, A.S. & Choi, T.-S. (2007). Application of passive techniques for three dimensional cameras. *IEEE Transactions on Consumer Electronics,* Vol. 53, No. 2, 258–264, 2007.
Malik, A. S. & Choi, T.-S. (2008). A novel algorithm for estimation of depth map using image focus for 3D shape recovery in the presence of noise. *Pattern Recognition,* Vol. 41, No. 7, July 2008, 2200-2225.
Miled, W. & Pesquet, J.-C. (2009). A convex optimization approach for depth estimation under illumination variation. *IEEE Transactions on image processing,* Vol. 18, No. 4, 2009, 813-830.
Pulli, K. & Cohen, M. & Duchamp, M. & Hoppe, H. & McDonald, J. & Shapiro, L. & Stuetzle, W. (1997). Surface modeling and display from range and color data. *Lectures Notes in Computer Science* 1310: 385-397, ISBN: 978-3-540-63507-9, Springer Berlin.
Saxena, A. & Chung, S. H. (2008). 3D depth reconstruction from a single still image. *International journal of computer vision,* Vol. 76, No. 1, 2008, 53-69.
Scharstein, D. & Szeliski, R. (2003). High-accuracy stereo depth maps using structured light. *IEEE Computer Society Conference on Computer Vision and Pattern Recognition,* Vol. 1, pp. 195–202.
Stamos, I. & Allen, P.K. (2000). 3D model construction using range and image data. In *Proceedings of the International Conference on Vision and Pattern Recognition,* 2000.
Srivastava, A., Lee, A.B., Simoncelli, E.P. & Zhu, S.C. (2003). On advances in statistical modeling of natural images. *Journal of the Optical Society of America,* Vol. 53, No. 3, 375–385, 2003.
Torralba, A. & Oliva, A. (2002). Depth estimation from image structure. *IEEE Trans. Pattern Analysis and Machine Intelligence,* Vol. 24, No. 9, 1226–1238, 2002.
Torres-Méndez, L. A. & Dudek, G. (2003). Statistical inference and synthesis in the image domain for mobile robot environment modeling. In *Proc. of the IEEE/RSJ Conference on Intelligent Robots and Systems,* Vol. 3, pp. 2699–2706, October, Las Vegas, USA.
Torres-Méndez, L. A. & Dudek, G. (2008). Inter-Image Statistics for 3D Environment Modeling. *International Journal of Computer Vision,* Vol. 79, No. 2, 137-158, 2008. ISSN: 0920-5691.
Torres-Méndez, L. A. (2008). *Inter-Image Statistics for Mobile Robot Environment Modeling.* VDM Verlag Dr. Muller, 2008, ISBN: 3639068157.
Van Der Schaaf, A. (1998). Natural Image Statistics and Visual Processing. PhD thesis, Rijksuniversiteit Groningen, 1998.
Wan, D. & Zhou, J. (2009). Multiresolution and wide-scope depth estimation using a dual-PTZ-camera system. *IEEE Transactions on Image Processing,* Vol. 18, No. 3, 677–682.

10

Mathematical Basis of Sensor Fusion in Intrusion Detection Systems

Ciza Thomas
Assistant Professor, College of Engineering, Trivandrum
India

Balakrishnan Narayanaswamy
Associate Director, Indian Institute of Science, Bangalore
India

1. Introduction

Intrusion Detection Systems (IDS) gather information from a computer or a network, and analyze this information to identify possible security breaches against the system or the network. The network traffic (with embedded attacks) is often complex because of multiple communication modes with deformable nature of user traits, evasion of attack detection and network monitoring tools, changes in users' and attackers' behavior with time, and sophistication of the attacker's attempts in order to avoid detection. This affects the accuracy and the reliability of any IDS. An observation of various IDSs available in the literature shows distinct preferences for detecting a certain class of attack with improved accuracy, while performing moderately on other classes. The availability of enormous computing power has made it possible for developing and implementing IDSs of different types on the same network. With the advances in sensor fusion, it has become possible to obtain a more reliable and accurate decision for a wider class of attacks, by combining the decisions of multiple IDSs.

Clearly, sensor fusion for performance enhancement of IDSs requires very complex observations, combinations of decisions and inferences via scenarios and models. Although, fusion in the context of enhancing the intrusion detection performance has been discussed earlier in literature, there is still a lack of theoretical analysis and understanding, particularly with respect to correlation of detector decisions. The theoretical study to justify why and how the sensor fusion algorithms work, when one combines the decisions from multiple detectors has been undertaken in this chapter. With a precise understanding as to why, when, and how particular sensor fusion methods can be applied successfully, progress can be made towards a powerful new tool for intrusion detection: the ability to automatically exploit the strengths and weaknesses of different IDSs. The issue of performance enhancement using sensor fusion is therefore a topic of great draw and depth, offering wide-ranging implications and a fascinating community of researchers to work within.

The mathematical basis for sensor fusion that provides enough support for the acceptability of sensor fusion in performance enhancement of IDSs is introduced in this chapter. This chapter justifies the novelties and the supporting proof for the Data-dependent Decision (DD) fusion architecture using sensor fusion. The neural network learner unit of the Data-dependent Decision fusion architecture aids in improved intrusion detection sensitivity and false alarm reduction. The theoretical model is undertaken, initially without any knowledge of the available detectors or the monitoring data. The empirical evaluation to augment the mathematical analysis is illustrated using the DARPA data set as well as the real-world network taffic. The experimental results confirm the analytical findings in this chapter.

2. Related Work

Krogh & Vedelsby (1995) prove that at a single data point the quadratic error of the ensemble estimator is guaranteed to be less than or equal to the average quadratic error of the component estimators. Hall & McMullen (2000) state that if the tactical rules of detection require that a particular certainty threshold must be exceeded for attack detection, then the fused decision result provides an added detection up to 25% greater than the detection at which any individual IDS alone exceeds the threshold. This added detection equates to increased tactical options and to an improved probability of true negatives Hall & McMullen (2000). Another attempt to illustrate the quantitative benefit of sensor fusion is provided by Nahin & Pokoski (1980). Their work demonstrates the benefits of multisensor fusion and their results also provide some conceptual rules of thumb.

Chair & Varshney (1986) present an optimal data fusion structure for distributed sensor network, which minimizes the cumulative average risk. The structure weights the individual decision depending on the reliability of the sensor. The weights are functions of probability of false alarm and the probability of detection. The maximum *a posteriori* (MAP) test or the Likelihood Ratio (L-R) test requires either exact knowledge of the *a priori* probabilities of the tested hypotheses or the assumption that all the hypotheses are equally likely. This limitation is overcome in the work of Thomopoulos et al. (1987). Thomopoulos et al. (1987) use the Neyman-Pearson test to derive an optimal decision fusion. Baek & Bommareddy (1995) present optimal decision rules for problems involving n distributed sensors and m target classes.

Aalo & Viswanathan (1995) perform numerical simulations of the correlation problems to study the effect of error correlation on the performance of a distributed detection systems. The system performance is shown to deteriorate when the correlation between the sensor errors is positive and increasing, while the performance improves considerably when the correlation is negative and increasing. Drakopoulos & Lee (1995) derive an optimum fusion rule for the Neyman-Pearson criterion, and uses simulation to study its performance for a specific type of correlation matrix. Kam et al. (1995) considers the case in which the class-conditioned sensor-to-sensor correlation coefficient are known, and expresses the result in compact form. Their approach is a generalization of the method adopted by Chair & Varshney (1986) for solving the data fusion problem for fixed binary local detectors with statistically independent decisions. Kam et al. (1995) uses Bahadur-Lazarsfeld expansion of the probability density functions. Blum et al. (1995) study the problem of locally most powerful detection for correlated local decisions.

The next section attempts a theoretical modeling of sensor fusion applied to intrusion detection, with little or no knowledge regarding the detectors or the network traffic.

3. Theoretical Analysis

The choice of when to perform the fusion depends on the types of sensor data available and the types of preprocessing performed by the sensors. The fusion can occur at the various levels like, 1) input data level prior to feature extraction, 2) feature vector level prior to identity declaration, and 3) decision level after each sensor has made an independent declaration of identity.

Sensor fusion is expected to result in both qualitative and quantitative benefits for the intrusion detection application. The primary aim of sensor fusion is to detect the intrusion and to make reliable inferences, which may not be possible from a single sensor alone. The particular quantitative improvement in estimation that results from using multiple IDSs depends on the performance of the specific IDSs involved, namely the observational accuracy. Thus the fused estimate takes advantage of the relative strengths of each IDS, resulting in an improved estimate of the intrusion detection. The error analysis techniques also provide a means for determining the specific quantitative benefits of sensor fusion in the case of intrusion detection. The quantitative benefits discover the phenomena that are likely rather than merely chance of occurrences.

3.1 Mathematical Model

A system of n sensors $IDS_1, IDS_2, ..., IDS_n$ is considered; corresponding to an observation with parameter x; $x \in \Re^m$. Consider the sensor IDS_i to yield an output s^i; $s^i \in \Re^m$ according to an unknown probability distribution p_i. The decision of the individual IDSs that take part in fusion is expected to be dependent on the input and hence the output of IDS_i in response to the input x_j can be written more specifically as s^i_j. A successful operation of a multiple sensor system critically depends on the methods that combine the outputs of the sensors, where the errors introduced by various individual sensors are unknown and not controllable. With such a fusion system available, the fusion rule for the system has to be obtained. The problem is to estimate a fusion rule $f : \Re^{nm} \rightarrow \Re^m$, independent of the sample or the individual detectors that take part in fusion, such that the expected square error is minimized over a family of fusion rules.

To perform the theoretical analysis, it is necessary to model the process under consideration. Consider a simple fusion architecture as given in Fig. 1 with n individual IDSs combined by means of a fusion unit. To start with, consider a two dimensional problem with the detectors responding in a binary manner. Each of the local detector collects an observation $x_j \in \Re^m$ and transforms it to a local decision $s^i_j \in \{0, 1\}, i = 1, 2, ..., n$, where the decision is 0 when the traffic is detected normal or else 1. Thus s^i_j is the response of the ith detector to the network connection belonging to class $j = \{0, 1\}$, where the classes correspond to normal traffic and the attack traffic respectively. These local decisions s^i_j are fed to the fusion unit to produce an unanimous decision $y = s_j$, which is supposed to minimize the overall cost of misclassification and improve the overall detection rate.

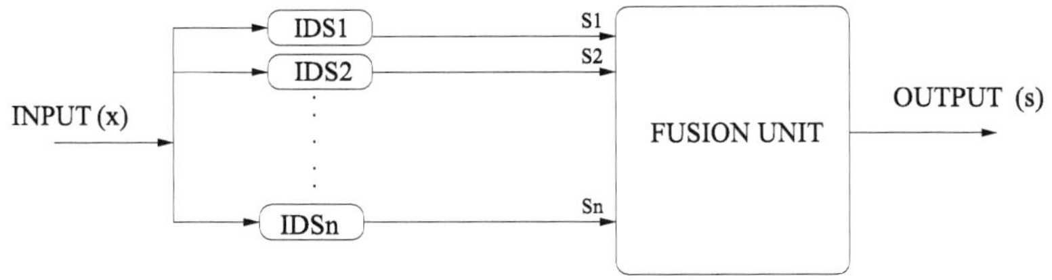

Fig. 1. Fusion architecture with decisions from n IDSs

The fundamental problem of network intrusion detection can be viewed as a detection task to decide whether network connection x is a normal one or an attack. Assume a set of unknown features $e = \{e_1, e_2, ..., e_m\}$ that are used to characterize the network traffic. The feature extractor is given by $e_e(x) \subset e$. It is assumed that this observed variable has a deterministic component and a random component and that their relation is additive. The deterministic component is due to the fact that the class is discrete in nature, i.e., during detection, it is known that the connection in either normal or an attack. The imprecise component is due to some random processes which in turn affects the quality of extracted features. Indeed, it has a distribution governed by the extracted feature set often in a nonlinear way. By ignoring the source of distortion in extracted network features $e_e(x)$, it is assumed that the noise component is random (while in fact it may not be the case when all possible variations can be systematically incorporated into the base-expert model).

In a statistical framework, the probability that x is identified as normal or as attack after a detector s_θ observes the network connection can be written as:

$$s^i = s_{\theta_i}(e_e(x)) \tag{1}$$

where x is the sniffed network traffic, e_e is a feature extractor, and θ_i is a set of parameters associated to the detector indexed i. There exists several types of intrusion detectors, all of which can be represented by the above equation.

Sensor fusion results in the combination of data from sensors competent on partially overlapping frames. The output of a fusion system is characterized by a variable s, which is a function of uncertain variables $s^1, ..., s^n$, being the output of the individual IDSs and given as:

$$s = f(s^1, ..., s^n) \tag{2}$$

where $f(.)$ corresponds to the fusion function. The independent variables (i.e., information about any group of variables does not change the belief about the others) $s^1, ..., s^n$, are imprecise and dependent on the class of observation and hence given as:

$$s_j = f(s_j^1, ..., s_j^n) \tag{3}$$

where j refers to the class of the observation.

Variance of the IDSs determines how good their average quality is when each IDS acts individually. Lower variance corresponds to a better performance. Covariance among detectors measures the dependence of the detectors. The more the dependence, the lesser the gain benefited out of fusion.

Let us consider two cases here. In the first case, n responses are available for each access and these n responses are used independent of each other. The average of variance of s_j over all $i = 1, 2, ..., n$, denoted as $(\sigma_{av}^j)^2$ is given as:

$$(\sigma_{av}^j)^2 = \frac{1}{n}\sum_{i=1}^{n}(\sigma_i^j)^2 \tag{4}$$

In the second case, all n responses are combined using the mean operator. The variance over many accesses is denoted by $(\sigma_{fusion}^j)^2$ and is called the variance of average given by:

$$(\sigma_{fusion}^j)^2 = \frac{1}{n^2}\sum_{i=1}^{n}(\sigma_i^j)^2 + \frac{1}{n^2}\sum_{i=1,i\neq k}^{n}\sum_{k=1,i\neq k}^{n}\rho_{i,k}^j\sigma_i^j\sigma_k^j \tag{5}$$

where $\rho_{i,k}^j$ is the correlation coefficient between the ith and kth detectors and for j taking the different class values. The first term is the average variance of the base-experts while the second term is the covariance between ith and kth detectors for $i \neq k$. This is because the term $\rho_{i,k}^j\sigma_i^j\sigma_k^j$ is by definition equivalent to correlation. On analysis, it is seen that:

$$(\sigma_{fusion}^j)^2 \leq (\sigma_{av}^j)^2 \tag{6}$$

When two detector scores are merged by a simple mean operator, the resultant variance of the final score will be reduced with respect to the average variance of the two original scores. Since $0 \leq \rho_{m,n}^j \leq 1$,

$$\frac{1}{n}(\sigma_{av}^j)^2 \leq (\sigma_{fusion}^j)^2 \tag{7}$$

Equation 6 and equation 7 give the lower and upper bound of $(\sigma_{fusion}^j)^2$, attained with correlation and uncorrelation respectively. Any positive correlation results in a variance between these bounds. Hence, by combining responses using the mean operator, the resultant variance is assured to be smaller than the average (not the minimum) variance.

Fusion of the scores reduces variance, which in turn results in reduction of error (with respect to the case where scores are used separately). To measure explicitly the factor of reduction in variance,

$$\frac{1}{n}(\sigma_{av}^j)^2 \leq (\sigma_{fusion}^j)^2 \leq (\sigma_{av}^j)^2 \tag{8}$$

Factor of reduction in variance, $(v_r) = \frac{(\sigma_{av}^j)^2}{(\sigma_{fusion}^k)^2}$

$1 \leq v_r \leq n$

This clearly indicates that the reduction in variance is more when more detectors are used, i.e., increasing n, the better will be the combined system, even if the hypotheses of underlying IDSs are correlated. This comes at a cost of increased computation, proportional to the value of n. The reduction in variance of the individual classes results in lesser overlap between the class distributions. Thus the chances of error reduces, which in turn results in an improved detection. This forms the argument in this chapter for why fusion using multiple detectors works for intrusion detection application.

Following common possibilities encountered on combining two detectors are analyzed:

1. combining two uncorrelated experts with very different performances;
2. combining two highly correlated experts with very different performances;
3. combining two uncorrelated experts with very similar performances;
4. combining two highly correlated experts with very similar performances.

Fusing IDSs of similar and different performances are encountered in almost all practical fusion problems. Considering the first case, without loss of generality it can be assumed that system 1 is better than system 2, i.e., $\sigma_1 < \sigma_2$ and $\rho = 0$. Hence, for the combination to be better than the best system, i.e., system 1, it is required that

$$(\sigma^j_{fusion})^2 < (\sigma^j_1)^2; \quad \frac{(\sigma^j_1)^2 + (\sigma^j_2)^2 + 2\rho\sigma^j_1\sigma^j_2}{4} < (\sigma^j_1)^2; \quad (\sigma^j_2)^2 < 3(\sigma^j_1)^2 - 2\rho\sigma^j_1\sigma^j_2 \tag{9}$$

The covariance is zero in general for cases 1 and 3. Hence, the combined system will benefit from the fusion when the variance of one $((\sigma^j_2)^2)$ is at most less than 3 times of the variance of the other $(\sigma^j_1)^2$ since $\rho = 0$. Furthermore, correlation [or equivalently covariance; one is proportional to the other] between the two systems penalizes this margin of $3(\sigma^j_1)^2$. This is particularly true for the second case since $\rho > 0$. Also, it should be noted that $\rho < 0$ (which implies negative correlation) could allow for larger $(\sigma^j_2)^2$. As a result, adding another system that is negatively correlated, but with large variance (hence large error) will improve fusion $((\sigma^j_{fusion})^2 < \frac{1}{n}(\sigma^j_{av})^2)$. Unfortunately, with IDSs, two systems are either positively correlated or not correlated, unless these systems are jointly trained together by algorithms such as negative correlation learning Brown (2004). For a given detector i, s_i for $i = 1, ..., n$, will tend to agree with each other (hence positively correlated) most often than to disagree with each other (hence negatively correlated). By fusing scores obtained from IDSs that are trained independently, one can almost be certain that $0 \leq \rho_{m,n} \leq 1$.

For the third and fourth cases, we have $(\sigma^j_1)^2 \approx (\sigma^j_2)^2$. Hence, $\rho(\sigma^j_2)^2 < (\sigma^j_1)^2$. Note that for the third case with $\rho \approx 0$, the above constraint gets satisfied. Hence, fusion will definitely lead to better performance. On the other hand, for the fourth case where $\rho \approx 1$, fusion may not necessarily lead to better performance.

From the above analysis using a mean operator for fusion, the conclusion drawn are the following:

The analysis explains and shows that fusing two systems of different performances is not always beneficial. The theoretical analysis shows that if the weaker IDS has (class-dependent) variance three times larger that of the best IDS, the gain due to fusion breaks down. This is even more true for correlated base-experts as correlation penalizes this limit further. It is also seen that fusing two uncorrelated IDSs of similar performance always result in improved performance. Finally, fusing two correlated IDSs of similar performance will be beneficial only when the covariance of the two IDSs are less than the variance of the IDSs.

It is necessary to show that a lower bound of accuracy results in the case of sensor fusion. This can be proved as follows:

Given the fused output as $s = \sum_i w_i s_i$, the quadratic error of a sensor indexed i, (e_i), and also the fused sensor, (e_{fusion}) are given by:

$$e_i = (s_i - c)^2 \tag{10}$$

and

$$e_{fusion} = (s_{fusion} - c)^2 \tag{11}$$

respectively, where w_i is the weighting on the ith detector, and c is the target. The ambiguity of the sensor is defined as:

$$a_i = (s_i - s)^2 \tag{12}$$

The squared error of the fused sensor is seen to be equal to the weighted average squared error of the individuals, minus a term which measures average correlation. This allows for non-uniform weights (with the constraint $\sum_i w_i = 1$). Hence, the general form of the ensemble output is $s = \sum_i w_i s_i$.

The ambiguity of the fused sensor is given by:

$$a_{fusion} = \sum_i w_i a_i = \sum_i w_i (s_i - s)^2 \tag{13}$$

On solving equation 13, the error due to the combination of several detectors is obtained as the difference between the weighted average error of individual detectors and the ambiguity among the fusion member decisions.

$$e_{fusion} = \sum_i w_i (s_i - c)^2 - \sum_i w_i (s_i - s)^2 \tag{14}$$

The ambiguity among the fusion member decisions is always positive and hence the combination of several detectors is expected to be better than the average over several detectors. This result turns out to be very important for the focus of this chapter.

4. Solution Approaches

In the case of fusion problem, the solution approaches depend on whether there is any knowledge regarding the traffic and the intrusion detectors. This section initially considers no knowledge of the IDSs and the intrusion detection data and later with a knowledge of available IDSs and evaluation dataset. There is an arsenal of different theories of uncertainty and methods based on these theories for making decisions under uncertainty. There is no consensus as to which method is most suitable for problems with epistemic uncertainty, when information is scarce and imprecise. The choice of heterogeneous detectors is expected to result in decisions that conflict or be in consensus, completely or partially. The detectors can be categorized by their output s_i, i.e., probability (within the range [0, 1]), Basic Probability Assignment (BPA) m (within the range [0, 1]), membership function (within the range [0, 1]), distance metric (more than or equal to zero), or log-likelihood ratio (a real number).

Consider a body of evidence $(F; m)$, where F represents the set of all focal elements and m their corresponding basic probability assignments. This analysis without any knowledge of the system or the data, attempts to prove the acceptance of sensor fusion in improving the intrusion detection performance and hence is unlimited in scope. In this analysis the Dempster-Shafer fusion operator is used since it is more acceptable for intrusion detection application as explained below.

Dempster-Shafer theory considers two types of uncertainty; 1) due to the imprecision in the evidence, and 2) due to the conflict. Non specificity and strife measure the uncertainty due to imprecision and conflict, respectively. The larger the focal elements of a body of evidence, the more imprecise is the evidence and, consequently, the higher is non specificity. When the evidence is precise (all the focal elements consist of a single member), non specificity is zero. The importance of Dempster-Shafer theory in intrusion detection is that in order to track statistics, it is necessary to model the distribution of decisions. If these decisions are probabilistic assignments over the set of labels, then the distribution function will be too complicated to retain precisely. The Dempster-Shafer theory of evidence solves this problem by simplifying the opinions to Boolean decisions, so that each detector decision lies in a space having 2^{Θ} elements, where Θ defines the working space. In this way, the full set of statistics can be specified using 2^{Θ} values.

4.1 Dempster-Shafer Combination Method

Dempster-Shafer (DS) theory is required to model the situation in which a classification algorithm cannot classify a target or cannot exhaustively list all of the classes to which it could belong. This is most acceptable in the case of unknown attacks or novel attacks or the case of zero *a priori* knowledge of data distribution. DS theory does not attempt to formalize the emergence of novelties, but it is a suitable framework for reconstructing the formation of beliefs when novelties appear. An application of decision making in the field of intrusion detection illustrates the potentialities of DS theory, as well as its shortcomings.

The DS rule corresponds to conjunction operator since it builds the belief induced by accepting two pieces of evidence, i.e., by accepting their conjunction. Shafer developed the DS theory of evidence based on the model that all the hypotheses in the FoD are exclusive and the frame is exhaustive. The purpose is to combine/aggregate several independent and equi-reliable sources of evidence expressing their belief on the set. The aim of using the DS theory of fusion is that with any set of decisions from heterogeneous detectors, sensor fusion can be modeled as utility maximization. DS theory of combination conceives novel categories that classify empirical evidence in a novel way and, possibly, are better able to discriminate the relevant aspects of emergent phenomena. Novel categories detect novel empirical evidence, that may be fragmentary, irrelevant, contradictory or supportive of particular hypotheses. The DS theory approach for quantifying the uncertainty in the performance of a detector and assessing the improvement in system performance, consists of three steps:

1. Model uncertainty by considering each variable separately. Then a model that considers all variables together is derived.
2. Propagate uncertainty through the system, which results in a model of uncertainty in the performance of the system.
3. Assess the system performance enhancement.

In the case of Dempster-Shafer theory, Θ is the Frame of Discernment (FoD), which defines the working space for the desired application. FoD is expected to contain all propositions of which the information sources (IDSs) can provide evidence. When a proposition corresponds to a subset of a frame of discernment, it is said that the frame discerns that proposition. It is expected that the elements of the frame of discernment, Θ are assumed to be exclusive propositions. This is a constraint, which always gets satisfied in intrusion detection application because of the discrete nature of the detector decision. The belief of likelihood of the traffic to be in an anomalous state is detected by various IDSs by means of a mass to the subsets of the FoD.

The DS theory is a generalization of the classical probability theory with its additivity axiom excluded or modified. The probability mass function (p) is a mapping which indicates how the probability mass is assigned to the elements. The Basic Probability Assignment (BPA) function (m) on the other hand is the set mapping, and the two can be related $\forall\ A \subseteq \Theta$ as $m(A) = \sum_{B \epsilon A} p(B)$ and hence obviously $m(A)$ relates to a belief structure. The mass m is very near to the probabilistic mass p, except that it is shared not only by the single hypothesis but also to the union of the hypotheses.

In DS theory, rather than knowing exactly how the probability is distributed to each element $B \in \Theta$, we just know by the BPA function m that a certain quantity of a probability mass is somehow divided among the focal elements. Because of this less specific knowledge about the allocation of the probability mass, it is difficult to assign exactly the probability associated with the subsets of the FoD, but instead we assign two measures: the (1) belief (*Bel*) and (2) plausibility (*Pl*), which correspond to the lower and upper bounds on the probability,

i.e., $Bel(A) \leq p(A) \leq Pl(A)$

where the belief function, $Bel(A)$, measures the minimum uncertainty value about proposition A, and the Plausibility, $Pl(A)$, reflects the maximum uncertainty value about proposition A.

The following are the key assumptions made with the fusion of intrusion detectors:

- If some of the detectors are imprecise, the uncertainty can be quantified about an event by the maximum and minimum probabilities of that event. Maximum (minimum) probability of an event is the maximum (minimum) of all probabilities that are consistent with the available evidence.
- The process of asking an IDS about an uncertain variable is a random experiment whose outcome can be precise or imprecise. There is randomness because every time a different IDS observes the variable, a different decision can be expected. The IDS can be precise and provide a single value or imprecise and provide an interval. Therefore, if the information about uncertainty consists of intervals from multiple IDSs, then there is uncertainty due to both imprecision and randomness.

If all IDSs are precise, then the pieces of evidence from these IDSs point precisely to specific values. In this case, a probability distribution of the variable can be build. However, if the IDSs provide intervals, such a probability distribution cannot be build because it is not known as to what specific values of the random variables each piece of evidence supports.

Also the additivity axiom of probability theory $p(A) + p(\bar{A}) = 1$ is modified as $m(A) + m(\bar{A}) + m(\Theta) = 1$, in the case of evidence theory, with uncertainty introduced by the term $m(\Theta)$. $m(A)$ is the mass assigned to A, $m(\bar{A})$ is the mass assigned to all other propositions that are not A in FoD and $m(\Theta)$ is the mass assigned to the union of all hypotheses when the detector is ignorant. This clearly explains the advantages of evidence theory in handling an uncertainty where the detector's joint probability distribution is not required.

The equation $Bel(A) + Bel(\bar{A}) = 1$, which is equivalent to $Bel(A) = Pl(A)$, holds for all subsets A of the FoD if and only if $Bel's$ focal points are all singletons. In this case, Bel is an additive probability distribution. Whether normalized or not, the DS method satisfies the two axioms of combination: $0 \leq m(A) \leq 1$ and $\sum_{A \subseteq \Theta} m(A) = 1$. The third axiom $\sum m(\phi) = 0$ is not satisfied by the unnormalized DS method. Also, independence of evidence is yet another requirement for the DS combination method.

The problem is formalized as follows: Considering the network traffic, assume a traffic space Θ, which is the union of the different classes, namely, the attack and the normal. The attack class have different types of attacks and the classes are assumed to be mutually exclusive. Each IDS assigns to the traffic, the detection of any of the traffic sample $x \in \Theta$, that denotes the traffic sample to come from a class which is an element of the FoD, Θ. With n IDSs used for the combination, the decision of each one of the IDSs is considered for the final decision of the fusion IDS.

This chapter presents a method to detect the unknown traffic attacks with an increased degree of confidence by making use of a fusion system composed of detectors. Each detector observes the same traffic on the network and detects the attack traffic with an uncertainty index. The frame of discernment consists of singletons that are exclusive ($A_i \cap A_j = \phi, \forall i \neq j$) and are exhaustive since the FoD consists of all the expected attacks which the individual IDS detects or else the detector fails to detect by recognizing it as a normal traffic. All the constituent IDSs that take part in fusion is assumed to have a global point of view about the system rather than separate detectors being introduced to give specialized opinion about a single hypothesis.

The DS combination rule gives the combined mass of the two evidence m_1 and m_2 on any subset A of the FoD as $m(A)$ given by:

$$m(A) = \frac{\sum_{X \cap Y = A} m_1(X) m_2(Y)}{1 - \sum_{X \cap Y = \phi} m_1(X) m_2(Y)} \tag{15}$$

The numerator of Dempster-Shafer combination equation 15 represents the influence of aspects of the second evidence that confirm the first one. The denominator represents the influence of aspects of the second evidence that contradict the first one. The denominator of equation 15 is $1 - k$, where k is the conflict between the two evidence. This denominator is for normalization, which spreads the resultant uncertainty of any evidence with a weight factor, over all focal elements and results in an intuitive decision. i.e., the effect of normalization consists of eliminating the conflicting pieces of information between the two sources to combine, consistently with the intersection operator. Dempster-Shafer rule does not apply if the two evidence are completely contradictory. It only makes sense if $k < 1$. If the two evidence are completely contradictory, they can be handled as one single evidence over alternative possibilities whose BPA must be re-scaled in order to comply with equation 15. The meaning of Dempster-Shafer rule 15 can be illustrated in the simple case of two evidence on an observation A. Suppose that one evidence is $m_1(A) = p$, $m_1(\Theta) = 1 - p$ and that another evidence is $m_2(A) = q$, $m(\Theta) = 1 - q$. The total evidence in favor of A = The denominator of equation 15 = $1 - (1 - p)(1 - q)$. The fraction supported by both the bodies of evidence = $\frac{pq}{(1-p)(1-q)}$

Specifically, if a particular detector indexed i taking part in fusion has probability of detection $m_i(A)$ for a particular class A, it is expected that fusion results in the probability of that class as $m(A)$, which is expected to be more that $m_i(A)$ $\forall$ i and A. Thus the confidence in detecting a particular class is improved, which is the key aim of sensor fusion. The above analysis is simple since it considers only one class at a time. The variance of the two classes can be merged and the resultant variance is the sum of the normalized variances of the individual classes. Hence, the class label can be dropped.

4.2 Analysis of Detection Error Assuming Traffic Distribution

The previous sections analyzed the system without any knowledge about the underlying traffic or detectors. The Gaussian distribution is assumed for both the normal and the attack traffic in this section due to its acceptability in practice. Often, the data available in databases is only an approximation of the true data. When the information about the goodness of the approximation is recorded, the results obtained from the database can be interpreted more reliably. Any database is associated with a degree of accuracy, which is denoted with a probability density function, whose mean is the value itself. Formally, each database value is indeed a random variable; the mean of this variable becomes the stored value, and is interpreted as an approximation of the true value; the standard deviation of this variable is a measure of the level of accuracy of the stored value.

Assuming the attack connection and normal connection scores to have the mean values $y^i_{j=I} = \mu_I$ and $y^i_{j=NI} = \mu_{NI}$ respectively, $\mu_I > \mu_{NI}$ without loss of generality. Let σ_I and σ_{NI} be the standard deviation of the attack connection and normal connection scores. The two types of errors committed by IDSs are often measured by False Positive Rate (FP_{rate}) and False Negative Rate (FN_{rate}). FP_{rate} is calculated by integrating the attack score distribution from a given threshold T in the score space to ∞, while FN_{rate} is calculated by integrating the normal distribution from $-\infty$ to the given threshold T. The threshold T is a unique point where the error is minimized, i.e., the difference between FP_{rate} and FN_{rate} is minimized by the following criterion:

$$T = argmin(|FP_{rate_T} - FN_{rate_T}|) \tag{16}$$

At this threshold value, the resultant error due to FP_{rate} and FN_{rate} is a minimum. This is because the FN_{rate} is an increasing function (a cumulative density function, cdf) and FP_{rate} is a decreasing function $(1 - cdf)$. T is the point where these two functions intersect. Decreasing the error introduced by the FP_{rate} and the FN_{rate} implies an improvement in the performance of the system.

$$FP_{rate} = \int_T^{\infty} (p^{k=NI})dy \tag{17}$$

$$FN_{rate} = \int_{-\infty}^{T} (p^{k=I})dy \tag{18}$$

The fusion algorithm accepts decisions from many IDSs, where a minority of the decisions are false positives or false negatives. A good sensor fusion system is expected to give a result that accurately represents the decision from the correctly performing individual sensors, while minimizing the decisions from erroneous IDSs. Approximate agreement emphasizes precision, even when this conflicts with system accuracy. However, sensor fusion is concerned solely with the accuracy of the readings, which is appropriate for sensor applications. This is true despite the fact that increased precision within known accuracy bounds would be beneficial in most of the cases. Hence the following strategy is being adopted:

- The false alarm rate FP_{rate} can be fixed at an acceptable value α_0 and then the detection rate can be maximized. Based on the above criteria a lower bound on accuracy can be derived.
- The detection rate is always higher than the false alarm rate for every IDS, an assumption that is trivially satisfied by any reasonably functional sensor.
- Determine whether the accuracy of the IDS after fusion is indeed better than the accuracy of the individual IDSs in order to support the performance enhancement of fusion IDS.
- To discover the weights on the individual IDSs that gives the best fusion.

Given the desired false alarm rate which is acceptable, $FP_{rate} = \alpha_0$, the threshold (T) that maximizes the TP_{rate} and thus minimizes the FN_{rate};

$$TP_{rate} = Pr[\sum_{i=1}^{n} w_i s_i \geq T \, |attack] \tag{19}$$

$$FP_{rate} = Pr[\sum_{i=1}^{n} w_i s_i \geq T|normal] = \alpha_0 \tag{20}$$

The fusion of IDSs becomes meaningful only when $FP \leq FP_i \quad \forall i$ and $TP \geq TP_i \quad \forall i$. In order to satisfy these conditions, an adaptive or dynamic weighting of IDSs is the only possible alternative. Model of the fusion output is given as:

$$s = \sum_{i=1}^{n} w_i s_i \quad and \quad TP_i = Pr[s_i = 1|attack], \quad FP_i = Pr[s_i = 1|normal] \tag{21}$$

where TP_i is the detection rate and FP_i is the false positive rate of any individual IDS indexed i. It is required to provide a low value of weight to any individual IDS that is unreliable, hence meeting the constraint on false alarm as given in equation 20. Similarly, the fusion improves the TP_{rate}, since the detectors get appropriately weighted according to their performance.

Fusion of the decisions from various IDSs is expected to produce a single decision that is more informative and accurate than any of the decisions from the individual IDSs. Then the question arises as to whether it is optimal. Towards that end, a lower bound on variance for the fusion problem of independent sensors, or an upper bound on the false positive rate or a lower bound on the detection rate for the fusion problem of dependent sensors is presented in this chapter.

4.2.1 Fusion of Independent Sensors

The decisions from various IDSs are assumed to be statistically independent for the sake of simplicity so that the combination of IDSs will not diffuse the detection. In sensor fusion, improvements in performances are related to the degree of error diversity among the individual IDSs.

Variance and Mean Square Error of the estimate of fused output

The successful operation of a multiple sensor system critically depends on the methods that combine the outputs of the sensors. A suitable rule can be inferred using the training examples, where the errors introduced by various individual sensors are unknown and not controllable. The choice of the sensors has been made and the system is available, and the fusion rule for the system has to be obtained. A system of n sensors $IDS_1, IDS_2, ..., IDS_n$ is considered; corresponding to an observation with parameter x, $x \in \Re^m$, sensor IDS_i yields output s^i, $s^i \in \Re^m$ according to an unknown probability distribution p_i. A training $l-$sample (x_1, y_1), (x_2, y_2), ..., (x_l, y_l) is given where $y_i = (s_i^1, s_i^2, ..., s_i^n)$ and s_j^i is the output of IDS_i in response to the input x_j. The problem is to estimate a fusion rule $f : \Re^{nm} \rightarrow \Re^m$, based on the sample, such that the expected square error is minimized over a family of fusion rules based on the given $l-$sample.

Consider n independent IDSs with the decisions of each being a random variable with Gaussian distribution of zero mean vector and covariance matrix diagonal $(\sigma_1^2, \sigma_2^2, \ldots, \sigma_n^2)$. Assume s to be the expected fusion output, which is the unknown deterministic scalar quantity to be estimated and $\hat{s}$ to be the estimate of the fusion output. In most cases the estimate is a deterministic function of the data. Then the mean square error (MSE) associated with the estimate $\hat{s}$ for a particular test data set is given as $E[(s-\hat{s})^2]$. For a given value of s, there are two basic kinds of errors:

- Random error, which is also called precision or estimation variance.
- Systematic error, which is also called accuracy or estimation bias.

Both kinds of errors can be quantified by the conditional distribution of the estimates $pr(\hat{s}-s)$. The MSE of a detector is the expected value of the error and is due to the randomness or due to the estimator not taking into account the information that could produce a more accurate result.

$$MSE = E[(s-\hat{s})^2] = Var(\hat{s}) + (Bias(\hat{s},s))^2 \tag{22}$$

The MSE is the absolute error used to assess the quality of the sensor in terms of its variation and unbiasedness. For an unbiased sensor, the MSE is the variance of the estimator, or the root mean squared error ($RMSE$) is the standard deviation. The standard deviation measures the accuracy of a set of probability assessments. The lower the value of $RMSE$, the better it is as an estimator in terms of both the precision as well as the accuracy. Thus, reduced variance can be considered as an index of improved accuracy and precision of any detector. Hence, the reduction in variance of the fusion IDS to show its improved performance is proved in this chapter. The Cramer-Rao inequality can be used for deriving the lower bound on the variance of an estimator.

Cramer-Rao Bound (CRB) for fused output

The Cramer-Rao lower bound is used to get the best achievable estimation performance. Any sensor fusion approach which achieves this performance is optimum in this regard. CR inequality states that the reciprocal of the Fisher information is an asymptotic lower bound on the variance of any unbiased estimator $\hat{s}$. Fisher information is a method for summarizing the influence of the parameters of a generative model on a collection of samples from that model. In this case, the parameters we consider are the means of the Gaussians. Fisher information is the variance, (σ^2) of the score (partial derivative of the logarithm of the likelihood function of the network traffic with respect to σ^2).

$$score = \frac{\partial}{\partial\sigma^2} ln(L(\sigma^2;s)) \tag{23}$$

Basically, the score tells us how sensitive the log-likelihood is to changes in parameters. This is a function of variance, σ^2 and the detection s and this score is a sufficient statistic for variance. The expected value of this score is zero, and hence the Fisher information is given by:

$$E\left\{[\frac{\partial}{\partial\sigma^2} ln(L(\sigma^2;s))]^2|\sigma^2\right\} \tag{24}$$

Fisher information is thus the expectation of the squared score. A random variable carrying high Fisher information implies that the absolute value of the score is often high.

Cramer-Rao inequality expresses a lower bound on the variance of an unbiased statistical estimator, based on the Fisher information.

$$\sigma^2 \geq \frac{1}{Fisher\ information} = \frac{1}{E\left\{[\frac{\partial}{\partial\sigma^2} ln(L(\sigma^2; X))]^2|\sigma^2\right\}} \tag{25}$$

If the prior probability of detection of the various IDSs are known, the weights $w_{i|i=1,---n}$ can be assigned to the individual IDSs. The idea is to estimate the local accuracy of the IDSs. The decision of the IDS with the highest local accuracy estimate will have the highest weighting on aggregation. The best fusion algorithm is supposed to choose the correct class if any of the individual IDS did so. This is a theoretical upper bound for all fusion algorithms. Of course, the best individual IDS is a lower bound for any meaningful fusion algorithm. Depending on the data, the fusion may sometimes be no better than Bayes. In such cases, the upper and lower performance bounds are identical and there is no point in using a fusion algorithm. A further insight into CRB can be gained by understanding how each IDS affects it. With the architecture shown in Fig. 1, the model is given by $\hat{s} = \sum_{i=1}^{n} w_i s_i$. The bound is calculated from the effective variance of each one of the IDSs as $\hat{\sigma_i^2} = \frac{\sigma_i^2}{w_i^2}$ and then combining them to have the CRB as $\frac{1}{\sum_{i=1}^{n} \frac{1}{\hat{\sigma_i^2}}}$.

The weight assigned to the IDSs is inversely proportional to the variance. This is due to the fact that, if the variance is small, the IDS is expected to be more dependable. The bound on the smallest variance of an estimation $\hat{s}$ is given as:

$$\hat{\sigma^2} = E[(\hat{s} - s)^2] \geq \frac{1}{\sum_{i=1}^{n} \frac{w_i^2}{\sigma_i^2}} \tag{26}$$

It can be observed from equation 26 that any IDS decision that is not reliable will have a very limited impact on the bound. This is because the non-reliable IDS will have a much larger variance than other IDSs in the group; $\hat{\sigma_n^2} \gg \hat{\sigma_1^2}, ---, \hat{\sigma_{n-1}^2}$ and hence $\frac{1}{\hat{\sigma_n^2}} \ll \frac{1}{\hat{\sigma_1^2}}, ---, \frac{1}{\hat{\sigma_{n-1}^2}}$. The bound can then be approximated as $\frac{1}{\sum_{i=1}^{n-1} \frac{1}{\hat{\sigma_i^2}}}$.

Also, it can be observed from equation 26 that the bound shows asymptotically optimum behavior of minimum variance. Then, $\hat{\sigma_i^2} > 0$ and $\hat{\sigma_{min}^2} = min[\hat{\sigma_i^2}, ---, \hat{\sigma_n^2}]$, then

$$CRB = \frac{1}{\sum_{i=1}^{n} \frac{1}{\hat{\sigma_i^2}}} < \hat{\sigma_{min}^2} \leq \hat{\sigma_i^2} \tag{27}$$

From equation 27 it can also be shown that perfect performance is apparently possible with enough IDSs. The bound tends to zero as more and more individual IDSs are added to the fusion unit.

$$CRB_{n\to\infty} = Lt_{n\to\infty} \frac{1}{\frac{1}{\hat{\sigma_1^2}} + --- + \frac{1}{\hat{\sigma_n^2}}} \tag{28}$$

For simplicity assume homogeneous IDSs with variance $\hat{\sigma^2}$;

$$CRB_{n\to\infty} = Lt_{n\to\infty}\frac{1}{\frac{n}{\hat{\sigma^2}}} = Lt_{n\to\infty}\frac{\hat{\sigma^2}}{n} = 0 \tag{29}$$

From equation 28 and equation 29 it can be easily interpreted that increasing the number of IDSs to a sufficiently large number will lead to the performance bounds towards perfect estimates. Also, due to monotone decreasing nature of the bound, the IDSs can be chosen to make the performance as close to perfect.

4.2.2 Fusion of Dependent Sensors

In most of the sensor fusion problems, individual sensor errors are assumed to be uncorrelated so that the sensor decisions are independent. While independence of sensors is a good assumption, it is often unrealistic in the normal case.

Setting bounds on false positives and true positives

As an illustration, let us consider a system with three individual IDSs, with a joint density at the IDSs having a covariance matrix of the form:

$$\bigwedge = \begin{bmatrix} 1 & \rho_{12} & \rho_{13} \\ \rho_{21} & 1 & \rho_{23} \\ \rho_{31} & \rho_{32} & 1 \end{bmatrix} \tag{30}$$

The false alarm rate (α) at the fusion center, where the individual decisions are aggregated can be written as:

$$\alpha_{max} = 1 - Pr(s_1 = 0, s_2 = 0, s_3 = 0|normal) = 1 - \int_{-\infty}^{t}\int_{-\infty}^{t}\int_{-\infty}^{t} P_s(s|normal)ds \tag{31}$$

where $P_s(s|normal)$ is the density of the sensor observations under the hypothesis *normal* and is a function of the correlation coefficient, ρ. Assuming a single threshold, T, for all the sensors, and with the same correlation coefficient, ρ between different sensors, a function $F_n(T|\rho) = Pr(s_1 = 0, s_2 = 0, s_3 = 0)$ can be defined.

$$F_n(T|\rho) = \int_{-\infty}^{-\infty} F^n(\frac{T - \sqrt{\rho}y}{\sqrt{1-\rho}})f(y)dy \tag{32}$$

where $f(y)$ and $F(X)$ are the standard normal density and cumulative distribution function respectively.

$F^n(X) = [F(X)]^n$

Equation 31 can be written depending on whether $\rho > \frac{-1}{n-1}$ or not, as:

$$\alpha_{max} = 1 - \int_{-\infty}^{\infty} F^3(\frac{T - \sqrt{\rho}y}{\sqrt{1-\rho}})f(y)dy \quad for \quad 0 \le \rho < 1 \tag{33}$$

and

$$\alpha_{max} = 1 - F^3(T\,|\rho) \quad for \quad -0.5 \leq \rho < 1 \tag{34}$$

With this threshold T, the probability of detection at the fusion unit can be computed as:

$$TP_{min} = 1 - \int_{-\infty}^{\infty} F^3(\frac{T - S - \sqrt{\rho}y}{\sqrt{1-\rho}})f(y)dy \quad for \quad 0 \leq \rho < 1 \tag{35}$$

and

$$TP_{min} = 1 - F^3(T - S\,|\rho) \quad for \quad -0.5 \leq \rho < 1 \tag{36}$$

The above equations 33, 34, 35, and 36, clearly showed the performance improvement of sensor fusion where the upper bound on false positive rate and lower bound on detection rate were fixed. The system performance was shown to deteriorate when the correlation between the sensor errors was positive and increasing, while the performance improved considerably when the correlation was negative and increasing.

The above analysis were made with the assumption that the prior detection probability of the individual IDSs were known and hence the case of bounded variance. However, in case the IDS performance was not known *a priori*, it was a case of unbounded variance and hence given the trivial model it was difficult to accuracy estimate the underlying decision. This clearly emphasized the difficulty of sensor fusion problem, where it becomes a necessity to understand the individual IDS behavior. Hence the architecture was modified as proposed in the work of Thomas & Balakrishnan (2008) and shown in Fig. 2 with the model remaining the same. With this improved architecture using a neural network learner, a clear understanding of each one of the individual IDSs was obtained. Most other approaches treat the training data as a monolithic whole when determining the sensor accuracy. However, the accuracy was expected to vary with data. This architecture attempts to predict the IDSs that are reliable for a given sample data. This architecture is demonstrated to be practically successful and is also the true situation where the weights are neither completely known nor totally unknown.

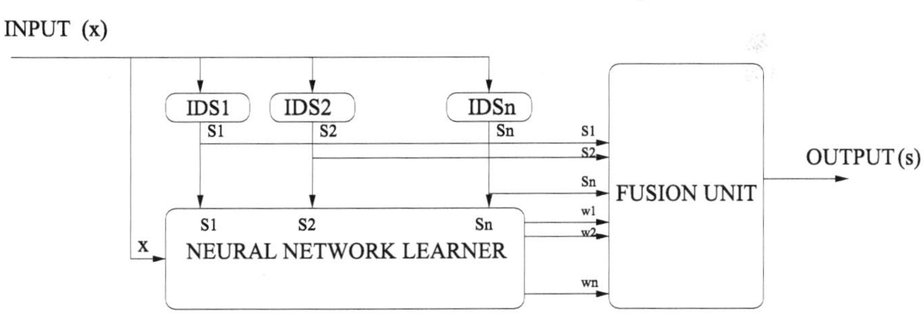

Fig. 2. Data-Dependent Decision Fusion architecture

4.3 Data-Dependent Decision Fusion Scheme

It is necessary to incorporate an architecture that considers a method for improving the detection rate by gathering an in-depth understanding on the input traffic and also on the behavior of the individual IDSs. This helps in automatically learning the individual weights for the combination when the IDSs are heterogeneous and shows difference in performance. The architecture should be independent of the dataset and the structures employed, and has to be used with any real valued data set.

A new data-dependent architecture underpinning sensor fusion to significantly enhance the IDS performance is attempted in the work of Thomas & Balakrishnan (2008; 2009). A better architecture by explicitly introducing the data-dependence in the fusion technique is the key idea behind this architecture. The disadvantage of the commonly used fusion techniques which are either implicitly data-dependent or data-independent, is due to the unrealistic confidence of certain IDSs. The idea in this architecture is to properly analyze the data and understand when the individual IDSs fail. The fusion unit should incorporate this learning from input as well as from the output of detectors to make an appropriate decision. The fusion should thus be data-dependent and hence the rule set has to be developed dynamically. This architecture is different from conventional fusion architectures and guarantees improved performance in terms of detection rate and the false alarm rate. It works well even for large datasets and is capable of identifying novel attacks since the rules are dynamically updated. It also has the advantage of improved scalability.

The Data-dependent Decision fusion architecture has three-stages; the IDSs that produce the alerts as the first stage, the neural network supervised learner determining the weights to the IDSs' decisions depending on the input as the second stage, and then the fusion unit doing the weighted aggregation as the final stage. The neural network learner can be considered as a pre-processing stage to the fusion unit. The neural network is most appropriate for weight determination, since it becomes difficult to define the rules clearly, mainly as more number of IDSs are added to the fusion unit. When a record is correctly classified by one or more detectors, the neural network will accumulate this knowledge as a weight and with more number of iterations, the weight gets stabilized. The architecture is independent of the dataset and the structures employed, and can be used with any real valued dataset. Thus it is reasonable to make use of a neural network learner unit to understand the performance and assign weights to various individual IDSs in the case of a large dataset.

The weight assigned to any IDS not only depends on the output of that IDS as in the case of the probability theory or the Dempster-Shafer theory, but also on the input traffic which causes this output. A neural network unit is fed with the output of the IDSs along with the respective input for an in-depth understanding of the reliability estimation of the IDSs. The alarms produced by the different IDSs when they are presented with a certain attack clearly tell which sensor generated more precise result and what attacks are actually occurring on the network traffic. The output of the neural network unit corresponds to the weights which are assigned to each one of the individual IDSs. The IDSs can be fused with the weight factor to produce an improved resultant output.

This architecture refers to a collection of diverse IDSs that respond to an input traffic and the weighted combination of their predictions. The weights are learned by looking at the response of the individual sensors for every input traffic connection. The fusion output is represented as:

$$s = F_j(w_j^i(x_j, s_j^i), s_j^i), \tag{37}$$

where the weights w_j^i are dependent on both the input x_j as well as individual IDS's output s_j^i, where the suffix j refers to the class label and the prefix i refers to the IDS index. The fusion unit used gives a value of one or zero depending on the set threshold being higher or lower than the weighted aggregation of the IDS's decisions.

The training of the neural network unit by back propagation involves three stages: 1) the feed forward of the output of all the IDSs along with the input training pattern, which collectively form the training pattern for the neural network learner unit, 2) the calculation and the back propagation of the associated error, and 3) the adjustments of the weights. After the training, the neural network is used for the computations of the feedforward phase. A multilayer network with a single hidden layer is sufficient in our application to learn the reliability of the IDSs to an arbitrary accuracy according to the proof available in Fausett (2007).

Consider the problem formulation where the weights $w_1, ..., w_n$, take on constrained values to satisfy the condition $\sum_{i=1}^{n} w_i = 1$. Even without any knowledge about the IDS selectivity factors, the constraint on the weights assures the possibility to accuracy estimate the underlying decision. With the weights learnt for any data, it becomes a useful generalization of the trivial model which was initially discussed. The improved efficient model with good learning algorithm can be used to find the optimum fusion algorithms for any performance measure.

5. Results and Discussion

This section includes the empirical evaluation to support the theoretical analysis on the acceptability of sensor fusion in intrusion detection.

5.1 Data Set

The proposed fusion IDS was evaluated on two data, one being the real-world network traffic embedded with attacks and the second being the DARPA-1999 (1999). The real traffic within a protected University campus network was collected during the working hours of a day. This traffic of around two million packets was divided into two halves, one for training the anomaly IDSs, and the other for testing. The test data was injected with 45 HTTP attack packets using the HTTP attack traffic generator tool called libwhisker Libwhisker (n.d.). The test data set was introduced with a base rate of 0.0000225, which is relatively realistic. The MIT Lincoln Laboratory under DARPA and AFRL sponsorship, has collected and distributed the first standard corpora for evaluation of computer network IDSs. This MIT- DARPA-1999 (1999) was used to train and test the performance of IDSs. The data for the weeks one and three were used for the training of the anomaly detectors and the weeks four and five were used as the test data. The training of the neural network learner was performed on the training data for weeks one, two and three, after the individual IDSs were trained. Each of the IDS was trained on distinct portions of the training data (ALAD on week one and PHAD on week three), which is expected to provide independence among the IDSs and also to develop diversity while being trained.

The classification of the various attacks found in the network traffic is explained in detail in the thesis work of Kendall (1999) with respect to DARPA intrusion detection evaluation dataset and is explained here in brief. The attacks fall into four main classes namely, Probe, Denial of Service(DoS), Remote to Local(R2L) and the User to Root (U2R). The Probe or Scan attacks automatically scan a network of computers or a DNS server to find valid IP addresses, active ports, host operating system types and known vulnerabilities. The DoS attacks are designed to disrupt a host or network service. In R2L attacks, an attacker who does not have an account on a victim machine gains local access to the machine, exfiltrates files from the machine or modifies data in transit to the machine. In U2R attacks, a local user on a machine is able to obtain privileges normally reserved for the unix super user or the windows administrator.

Even with the criticisms by McHugh (2000) and Mahoney & Chan (2003) against the DARPA dataset, the dataset was extremely useful in the IDS evaluation undertaken in this work. Since none of the IDSs perform exceptionally well on the DARPA dataset, the aim is to show that the performance improves with the proposed method. If a system is evaluated on the DARPA dataset, then it cannot claim anything more in terms of its performance on the real network traffic. Hence this dataset can be considered as the base line of any research Thomas & Balakrishnan (2007). Also, even after ten years of its generation, even now there are lot of attacks in the dataset for which signatures are not available in database of even the frequently updated signature based IDSs like Snort (1999). The real data traffic is difficult to work with; the main reason being the lack of the information regarding the status of the traffic. Even with intense analysis, the prediction can never be 100 percent accurate because of the stealthiness and sophistication of the attacks and the unpredictability of the non-malicious user as well as the intricacies of the users in general.

5.2 Test Setup

The test set up for experimental evaluation consisted of three Pentium machines with Linux Operating System. The experiments were conducted with IDSs, PHAD (2001), ALAD (2002), and Snort (1999), distributed across the single subnet observing the same domain. PHAD, is based on attack detection by extracting the packet header information, whereas ALAD is application payload-based, and Snort detects by collecting information from both the header and the payload part of every packet on time-based as well as on connection-based manner. This choice of heterogeneous sensors in terms of their functionality was to exploit the advantages of fusion IDS Bass (1999). The PHAD being packet-header based and detecting one packet at a time, was totally unable to detect the slow scans. However, PHAD detected the stealthy scans much more effectively. The ALAD being content-based has complemented the PHAD by detecting the Remote to Local (R2L) and the User to Root (U2R) with appreciable efficiency. Snort was efficient in detecting the Probes as well as the DoS attacks.

The weight analysis of the IDS data coming from PHAD, ALAD, and Snort was carried out by the Neural Network supervised learner before it was fed to the fusion element. The detectors PHAD and ALAD produces the IP address along with the anomaly score whereas the Snort produces the IP address along with severity score of the alert. The alerts produced by these IDSs are converted to a standard binary form. The Neural Network learner inputs these decisions along with the particular traffic input which was monitored by the IDSs.

The neural network learner was designed as a feed forward back propagation algorithm with a single hidden layer and 25 sigmoidal hidden units in the hidden layer. Experimental proof is available for the best performance of the Neural Network with the number of hidden units being $log(T)$, where T is the number of training samples in the dataset Lippmann (1987). The values chosen for the initial weights lie in the range of -0.5 to 0.5 and the final weights after training may also be of either sign. The learning rate is chosen to be 0.02. In order to train the neural network, it is necessary to expose them to both normal and anomalous data. Hence, during the training, the network was exposed to weeks 1, 2, and 3 of the training data and the weights were adjusted using the back propagation algorithm. An epoch of training consisted of one pass over the training data. The training proceeded until the total error made during each epoch stopped decreasing or 1000 epochs had been reached. If the neural network stops learning before reaching an acceptable solution, a change in the number of hidden nodes or in the learning parameters will often fix the problem. The other possibility is to start over again with a different set of initial weights.

The fusion unit performed the weighted aggregation of the IDS outputs for the purpose of identifying the attacks in the test dataset. It used binary fusion by giving an output value of one or zero depending the value of the weighted aggregation of the various IDS decisions. The packets were identified by their timestamp on aggregation. A value of one at the output of the fusion unit indicated the record to be under attack and a zero indicated the absence of an attack.

5.3 Metrics for Performance Evaluation

The detection accuracy is calculated as the proportion of correct detections. This traditional evaluation metric of detection accuracy was not adequate while dealing with classes like U2R and R2L which are very rare. The cost matrix published in KDD'99 Elkan (2000) to measure the damage of misclassification, highlights the importance of these two rare classes. Majority of the existing IDSs have ignored these rare classes, since it will not affect the detection accuracy appreciably. The importance of these rare classes is overlooked by most of the IDSs with the metrics commonly used for evaluation namely the false positive rate and the detection rate.

5.3.1 ROC and AUC

ROC curves are used to evaluate IDS performance over a range of trade-offs between detection rate and the false positive rate. The Area Under ROC Curve (AUC) is a convenient way of comparing IDSs. AUC is the performance metric for the ROC curve.

5.3.2 Precision, Recall and F-score

Precision (P) is a measure of what fraction of the test data detected as attack are actually from the attack class. Recall (R) on the other hand is a measure of what fraction of attack class is correctly detected. There is a natural trade-off between the metrics precision and recall. It is required to evaluate any IDS based on how it performs on both recall and precision. The metric used for this purpose is F-score, which ranges from [0,1]. The F-score can be considered as the harmonic mean of recall and precision, given by:

$$F\text{-}score = \frac{2 * P * R}{P + R} \tag{38}$$

Higher value of F-score indicates that the IDS is performing better on recall as well as precision.

Attack type	Total attacks	Attacks detected	% detection
Probe	37	22	59%
DoS	63	24	38%
R2L	53	6	11%
U2R/Data	37	2	5%
Total	190	54	28%

Table 1. Attacks of each type detected by PHAD at a false positive of 0.002%

Attack type	Total attacks	Attacks detected	% detection
Probe	37	6	16%
DoS	63	19	30%
R2L	53	25	47%
U2R/Data	37	10	27%
Total	190	60	32%

Table 2. Attacks of each type detected by ALAD at a false positive of 0.002%

5.4 Experimental Evaluation

All the IDSs that form part of the fusion IDS were separately evaluated with the same two data sets; 1) real-world traffic and 2) the DARPA 1999 data set. Then the empirical evaluation of the data-dependent decision fusion method was also observed. The results support the validity of the data-dependent approach compared to the various existing fusion methods of IDS. It can be observed from tables 1, 2 and 3 that the attacks detected by different IDS were not necessarily the same and also that no individual IDS was able to provide acceptable values of all performance measures. It may be noted that the false alarm rates differ in the case of snort as it was extremely difficult to try for a fair comparison with equal false alarm rates for all the IDSs because of the unacceptable ranges for the detection rate under such circumstances.

Table 4 and Fig. 3 show the improvement in performance of the Data-dependent Decision fusion method over each of the three individual IDSs. The detection rate is acceptably high for all types of attacks without affecting the false alarm rate.

The real traffic within a protected University campus network was collected during the working hours of a day. This traffic of around two million packets was divided into two halves, one for training the anomaly IDSs, and the other for testing. The test data was injected with 45 HTTP attack packets using the HTTP attack traffic generator tool called libwhisker Libwhisker (n.d.). The test data set was introduced with a base rate of 0.0000225, which is relatively realistic. The comparison of the evaluated IDS with various other fusion techniques is illustrated in table 5 with the real-world network traffic.

The results evaluated in Table 6 show that the accuracy (Acc.) and AUC are not good metrics with the imbalanced data where the attack class is rare compared to the normal class. Accuracy was heavily biased to favor majority class. Accuracy when used as a performance measure assumed target class distribution to be known and unchanging, and the costs of FP and FN to be equal. These assumptions are unrealistic. If metrics like accuracy and AUC are to be used, then the data has to be more balanced in terms of the various classes. If AUC was to be used as an evaluation metric a possible solution was to consider only the area under

Attack type	Total attacks	Attacks detected	% detection
Probe	37	10	27%
DoS	63	30	48%
R2L	53	26	49%
U2R/Data	37	30	81%
Total	190	96	51%

Table 3. Attacks of each type detected by Snort at a false positive of 0.02%

Attack type	Total attacks	Attacks detected	% detection
Probe	37	28	76%
DoS	63	40	64%
R2L	53	29	55%
U2R/Data	37	32	87%
Total	190	129	68%

Table 4. Attacks of each type detected by Data-dependent Decision Fusion architecture at a false positive of 0.002%

the ROC curve until the FP-rate reaches the prior probability. The results presented in Table 5 indicate that the Data-dependent Decision fusion method performs significantly better for attack class with high recall as well as high precision as against achieving the high accuracy alone.

The ROC Semilog curves of the individual IDSs and the DD fusion IDS are given in Fig. 4, which clearly show the better performance of the DD fusion method in comparison to the three individual IDSs, PHAD, ALAD and Snort. The log-scale was used for the x-axis to identify the points which would otherwise be crowded on the x-axis.

Detector/ Fusion Type	Total Attacks	TP	FP	Precision	Recall	F-score
PHAD	45	10	45	0.18	0.22	0.20
ALAD	45	18	45	0.29	0.4	0.34
Snort	45	11	400	0.03	0.24	0.05
OR	45	28	470	0.06	0.62	0.11
AND	45	8	29	0.22	0.18	0.20
SVM	45	23	94	0.2	0.51	0.29
ANN	45	25	131	0.16	0.56	0.25
Data-dependent Decision Fusion	45	27	42	0.39	0.6	0.47

Table 5. Comparison of the evaluated IDSs with various evaluation metrics using the real-world data set

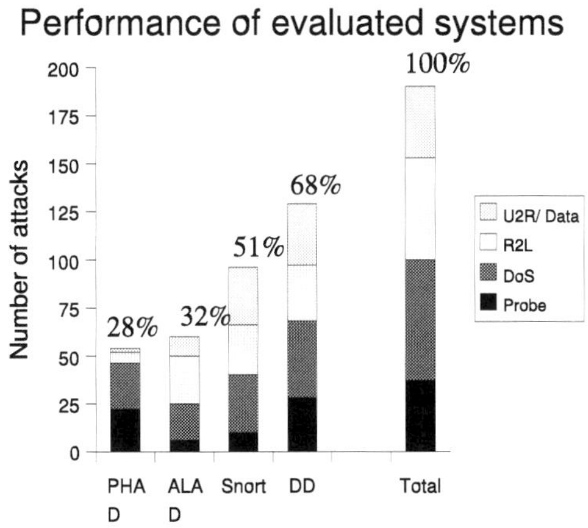

Fig. 3. Performance of Evaluated Systems

Detection/ Fusion	P	R	Acc.	AUC	F-Score
PHAD	0.35	0.28	0.99	0.64	0.31
ALAD	0.38	0.32	0.99	0.66	0.35
Snort	0.09	0.51	0.99	0.75	0.15
Data-Dependent fusion	0.39	0.68	0.99	0.84	0.50

Table 6. Performance Comparison of individual IDSs and the Data-Dependent Fusion method

6. Conclusion

A discussion on the mathematical basis for sensor fusion in IDS is included in this chapter. This study contributes to fusion field in several aspects. Firstly, considering zero knowledge about the detection systems and the traffic data, an attempt is made to show the improved performance of sensor fusion for intrusion detection application. The later half of the chapter takes into account the analysis of the sensor fusion system with a knowledge of data and sensors that are seen in practice. Independent as well as dependent detectors were considered and the study clarifies the intuition that independence of detectors is crucial in determining the success of fusion operation. If the individual sensors were complementary and looked at different regions of the attack domain, then the data-dependent decision fusion enriches the analysis on the incoming traffic to detect attack with appreciably low false alarms. The approach is tested with the standard DARPA IDS traces, and offers better performance than any of the individual IDSs. The individual IDSs that are components of this architecture in this particular work were PHAD, ALAD and Snort with detection rates 0.28, 0.32 and 0.51 respectively. Although the research discussed in this chapter has thus far focused on the three

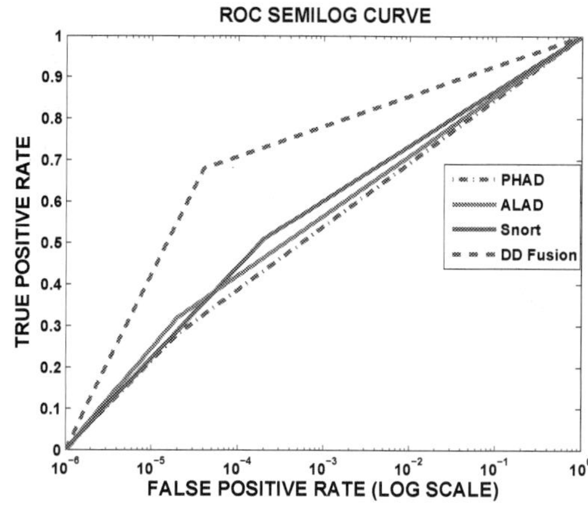

Fig. 4. ROC Semilog curve of individual and combined IDSs

IDSs, namely, PHAD, ALAD and Snort, the algorithm works well with any IDS. The result of the Data-dependent Decision fusion method is better than what has been predicted by the Lincoln Laboratory after the DARPA IDS evaluation. An intrusion detection of 68% with a false positive of as low as 0.002% is achieved using the DARPA data set and detection of 60% with a false positive of as low as 0.002% is achieved using the real-world network traffic. The figure of merit, F-score of the data-dependent decision fusion method has improved to 0.50 for the DARPA data set and to 0.47 for the real-world network traffic.

7. References

Aalo, V. & Viswanathan, R. (1995). On distributed detection with correlated sensors: Two examples, *IEEE Transactions on Aerospace and Electronic Systems* **Vol. 25**(No. 3): 414–421.

ALAD (2002). Learning non stationary models of normal network traffic for detecting novel attacks, *SIGKDD*.

Baek, W. & Bommareddy, S. (1995). Optimal m-ary data fusion with distributed sensors, *IEEE Transactions on Aerospace and Electronic Systems* **Vol. 31**(No. 3): 1150–1152.

Bass, T. (1999). Multisensor data fusion for next generation distributed intrusion detection systems, *IRIS National Symposium*.

Blum, R., Kassam, S. & Poor, H. (1995). Distributed detection with multiple sensors - part ii: Advanced topics, *Proceedings of IEEE* pp. 64–79.

Brown, G. (2004). Diversity in neural network ensembles, *PhD thesis* .

Chair, Z. & Varshney, P. (1986). Optimal data fusion in multiple sensor detection systems, *IEEE Transactions on Aerospace and Electronic Systems* **Vol. 22**(No. 1): 98–101.

DARPA-1999 (1999). `http://www.ll.mit.edu/IST/ideval/data/data_index.html`.

Drakopoulos, E. & Lee, C. (1995). Optimum multisensor fusion of correlated local, *IEEE Transactions on Aerospace and Electronic Systems* **Vol. 27**: 593–606.

Elkan, C. (2000). Results of the kdd'99 classifier learning, *SIGKDD Explorations*, pp. 63–64.

Fausett, L. (2007). *My Life*, Pearson Education.

Hall, D. H. & McMullen, S. A. H. (2000). *Mathematical Techniques in Multi-Sensor Data Fusion*, Artech House.

Kam, M., Zhu, Q. & Gray, W. (1995). Optimal data fusion of correlated local decisions in multiple sensor detection systems, *IEEE Transactions on Aerospace and Electronic Systems* **Vol. 28**: 916–920.

Kendall, K. (1999). *A database of computer attacks for the evaluation of intrusion detection sytsems*, Thesis.

Krogh, A. & Vedelsby, J. (1995). Neural network ensembles, cross validation, and active learning, *NIPS* (No.7): 231–238.

Libwhisker (n.d.). rfp@wiretrip.net/libwhisker.

Lippmann, R. (1987). An introduction to computing with neural nets, *IEEE ASSP Magazine*, pp. 4–22.

Mahoney, M. & Chan, P. (2003). An analysis of the 1999 darpa /lincoln laboratory evaluation data for network anomaly detection, *Technical Report CS-2003-02*, Publisher.

McHugh, J. (2000). Improvement in intrusion detection with advances in sensor fusion, *ACM Transactions on Information and System Security* **Vol. 3**(4): 543–552.

Nahin, P. & Pokoski, J. (1980). Nctr plus sensor fusion equals iffn or can two plus two equal five?, *IEEE Transactions on Aerospace and Electronic Systems* **Vol. AES-16**(No. 3): 320–337.

PHAD (2001). Detecting novel attacks by identifying anomalous network packet headers, *Technical Report CS-2001-2*.

Snort (1999). www.snort.org/docs/snort_htmanuals/htmanual_260.

Thomas, C. & Balakrishnan, N. (2007). Usefulness of darpa data set in intrusion detection system evaluation, *Proceedings of SPIE International Defense and Security Symposium*.

Thomas, C. & Balakrishnan, N. (2008). Advanced sensor fusion technique for enhanced intrusion detection, *Proceedings of IEEE International Conference on Intelligence and Security Informatics*, IEEE, Taiwan.

Thomas, C. & Balakrishnan, N. (2009). Improvement in intrusion detection with advances in sensor fusion, *IEEE Transactions on Information Forensics and Security* **Vol. 4**(3): 543–552.

Thomopoulos, S., Vishwanathan, R. & Bougoulias, D. (1987). Optimal decision fusion in multiple sensor systems, *IEEE Transactions on Aerospace and Electronic Systems* **Vol. 23**(No. 5): 644–651.

11

Sensor Fusion for Position Estimation in Networked Systems

Giuseppe C. Calafiore, Luca Carlone and Mingzhu Wei
Politecnico di Torino
Italy

1. Introduction

Recent advances in wireless communication have enabled the diffusion of networked systems whose capability of acquiring information and acting on wide areas, in a decentralized and autonomous way, represents an attractive peculiarity for many military and civil applications. Sensor networks are probably the best known example of such systems: cost reduction in producing smart sensors has allowed the deployment of constellations of low-cost low-power interconnected nodes, able to sense the environment, perform simple computation and communicate within a given range (Akyildiz et al., 2002). Another example is mobile robotics, whose development has further stressed the importance of distributed control and cooperative task management in formations of agents (Siciliano & Khatib, 2008). A non-exhaustive list of emerging applications of networked systems encompasses target tracking, environmental monitoring, smart buildings surveillance and supervision, water quality and bush fire surveying (Martinez & Bullo, 2006).

The intrinsically distributed nature of measurements acquired by the nodes requires the system to perform a fusion of sensor perceptions in order to obtain relevant information from the environment in which the system is deployed. This is the case of environmental monitoring, in which the nodes may measure the trend of variables of interest over a geographic region, in order to give a coherent overview on the scenario of observation. As in this last example, most of the mentioned fields of application require that each node has precise knowledge of its geometric position for correctly performing information fusion, since actions and observations are location-dependent. Other cases in which it is necessary to associate a position to each node are formation control, which is based on the knowledge of agent positions, and location aware routing, which benefits from the position information for optimizing the flow of data through the network, to mention but a few.

In this chapter we discuss the problem of *network localization*, that is the estimation of node positions from internodal measurements, focusing on the case of pairwise distance measurements. In Section 2 the estimation problem is first introduced, reporting the related literature on the topic. In Section 2.1 we consider the case of localization from range-only measurements, whereas in Section 3 we formalize the estimation problem at hand. Five approaches for solving network localization are extensively discussed in Section 4, where we report the theoretical basis of each technique, the corresponding convergence properties and numerical experiments in realistic simulation setups. The first three localization methods, namely a *gradient-based method*, a *Gauss-Newton* approach and a *trust region* method are local, since they require a reasonable initial guess on node position to successfully estimate the actual network configuration. We then present two global techniques, respectively a *global continuation* approach and a technique based on *semidefinite programming* (SDP), which are demonstrated, under suitable conditions, to retrieve the actual configuration, regardless the available prior knowledge on node positions. Several comparative results are presented in Sections 5 and 6. A brief discussion on distributed localization techniques is reported in Section 7 and conclusions are draws in Section 8.

2. Network Localization

When dealing with a network with a large number of nodes a manual configuration of node positions during system set up, when possible, is an expensive and time consuming task. Moreover, in many applications, such as mobile robotics, nodes can move autonomously, thus positions need be tracked as time evolves. A possible solution consists in equipping each node with a GPS sensor, hence allowing the nodes to directly measure their location. Such an approach is often infeasible in terms of cost, weight burden, power consumption, or when the network is deployed in GPS-denied areas. As the above mentioned factors could be technological barriers, a wide variety of solutions for computing node locations through effective and efficient procedures was proposed in the last decade. The so-called *indirects methods* are finalized at determining absolute node positions (with respect to a local or global reference frame) from partial relative measurements between nodes, that is, each node may measure the relative position (angle and distance, angle only or distance only) from a set of *neighbor* nodes, and the global absolute positions of all nodes need be retrieved. This problem is generically known as *network localization*.

If all relative measurements are gathered to some "central elaboration unit" which performs estimation over the whole network, the corresponding localization technique is said to be *centralized*. This is the approach that one implicitly assumes when writing and solving a problem: all the data that is relevant for the problem description is available to the problem solver. In a *distributed* setup, however, each node communicates only with its *neighbors*, and performs local computations in order to obtain an estimate of its own position. As a consequence, the communication burden is equally spread among the network, the computation is decentralized and entrusted to each agent, improving both efficiency and robustness of the estimation process.

In the most usual situation of planar networks, i.e., networks with nodes displaced in two-dimensional space, three main variations of the localization problem are typically considered in the literature, depending on the type of relative measurements available to the nodes. A first case is when nodes may take noisy measurements of the full relative position (coordinates or, equivalently, range and angle) of neighbors; this setup has been recently surveyed in (Barooah & Hespanha, 2007). The localization problem with full position measurements is a linear estimation problem that can be solved efficiently via a standard least-squares approach, and the networked nature of the problem can also be exploited to devise distributed algorithms (such as the Jacobi algorithm proposed in (Barooah & Hespanha, 2007)).

A second case arises, instead, when only angle measurements between nodes are available. This case, which is often referred to as *bearing localization*, can be attacked via maximum likelihood estimation as described in (Mao et al., 2007). This localization setup was pioneered by Stanfield (Stanfield, 1947), and further studied in (Foy, 1976).

In the last case, which is probably the most common situation in practice, each node can measure only distances from a subset of other nodes in the formation. This setup that we shall name *range localization*, has quite a long history, dating at least back to the eighties, and it is closely related to the so-called molecule problem studied in molecular biology, see (Hendrickson, 1995). However, it still attracts the attention of the scientific community for its relevance in several applications; moreover, recent works propose innovative and efficient approaches for solving the problem, making the topic an open area of research.

2.1 Range localization

The literature on range-based network localization is heterogeneous and includes different approaches with many recent contributions. Most authors formulated the problem in the form of a minimization over a non-linear and non-convex cost function. A survey on both technological and algorithmic aspects can be found in (Mao et al., 2007). In (Howard et al., 2001) the distance constraints are treated using mass-spring models, hence the authors formulate the network localization problem as a minimization of the energy of the overall mass-spring system. The localization problem has also been solved using suitable non linear optimization techniques, like simulated annealing, see (Kannan et al., 2006). First attempts to reduce the computational effort of optimization by breaking the problem into smaller subproblems traces back to (Hendrickson, 1995), in which a divide-and-conquer algorithm is proposed. Similar considerations are drawn in (Moore et al., 2004), where clustering is applied to the network in order to properly reconstruct network configuration. In (More, 1983) the issue of local minima is alleviated using objective function smoothing. In (Biswas & Ye, 2004) the optimization problem is solved using semidefinite programming (SDP), whereas in (Tseng, 2007) network localization is expressed in the form of second-order cone programming (SOCP); sum of squares (SOS) relaxation is applied in (Nie, 2009). Other approaches are based on coarse distance or mere connectivity measurements, see (Niculescu & Nath, 2001) or (Savarese et al., 2002).
Range localization naturally leads to a strongly NP-hard non-linear and non-convex optimization problem (see (Saxe, 1979)), in which convergence to a global solution cannot in general be guaranteed. Moreover the actual reconstruction of a unique network configuration from range measurements is possible only under particular hypotheses on the topology of the networked formation (graph rigidity, see (Eren et al., 2004)). It is worth noticing that localization in an absolute reference frame requires that a subset of the nodes (*anchor nodes* or *beacons*) already knows its exact location in the external reference frame. Otherwise, localization is possible only up to an arbitrary roto-translation. This latter setup is referred to as *anchor-free* localization; see, e.g., (Priyantha et al., 2003).

Notation

I_n denotes the $n \times n$ identity matrix, $\mathbf{1}_n$ denotes a (column) vector of all ones of dimension n, $\mathbf{0}_n$ denotes a vector of all zeros of dimension n, $e_i \in \mathbb{R}^n$ denotes a vector with all zero entries, except for the i-th position, which is equal to one. We denote with $\lfloor x \rfloor$ the largest integer smaller than or equal to x. Subscripts with dimensions may be omitted when they can be easily inferred from context.

For a matrix X, X_{ij} denotes the element of X in row i and column j, and $X^\top$ denotes the transpose of X. $X > 0$ (resp. $X \geq 0$) denotes a positive (resp. non-negative) matrix, that is a matrix with all positive (resp. non-negative) entries. $\|X\|$ denotes the spectral (maximum singular value) norm of X, or the standard Euclidean norm, in case of vectors. For a square matrix $X \in \mathbb{R}^{n,n}$, we denote with $\sigma(X) = \{\lambda_1(X), \ldots, \lambda_n(X)\}$ the set of eigenvalues, or *spectrum*, of X, and with $\rho(X)$ the spectral radius: $\rho(X) \doteq \max_{i=1,\ldots,n} |\lambda_i(X)|$, where $\lambda_i(X)$, $i = 1, \ldots, n$, are the eigenvalues of X ordered with decreasing modulus, i.e. $\rho(X) = |\lambda_1(X)| \geq |\lambda_2(X)| \geq \cdots | \geq |\lambda_n(X)|$.

3. Problem Statement

We now introduce a formalization of the range-based localization problem. Such model is the basis for the application of the optimization techniques that are presented in the following sections and allows to estimate network configuration from distance measurement.
Let $\mathcal{V} = \{v_1, \ldots, v_n\}$ be a set of n nodes (agents, sensors, robots, vehicles, etc.), and let $\mathcal{P} = \{p_1, \ldots, p_n\}$ denote a corresponding set of positions on the Cartesian plane, where $p_i = [x_i \ y_i]^\top \in \mathbb{R}^2$ are the coordinates of the i-th node. We shall call $\mathcal{P}$ a *configuration* of nodes. Consider a set $\mathcal{E}$ of m distinct unordered pairs $e_1, \ldots, e_m$, where $e_k = (i, j)$, and suppose that we are given a corresponding set of nonnegative scalars $d_1, \ldots, d_m$ having the meaning of distances between node i and j.
We want to determine (if one exists) a node configuration $\{p_1, \ldots, p_n\}$ that matches the given set of internodal distances, i.e. such that

$$\|p_i - p_j\|^2 = d_{ij}^2, \quad \forall \ (i,j) \in \mathcal{E},$$

or, if exact matching is not possible, that minimizes the sum of squared mismatch errors, i.e. such that the cost

$$f = \frac{1}{2} \sum_{(i,j)\in\mathcal{E}} \left(\|p_i - p_j\|^2 - d_{ij}^2 \right)^2 \tag{1}$$

is minimized. When the global minimum of f is zero we say that exact matching is achieved, otherwise no geometric node configuration can exactly match the given range data, and we say that approximate matching is achieved by the optimal configuration.
The structure of the problem can be naturally described using graph formalism: nodes $\{v_1, \ldots, v_n\}$ represent the vertices of a graph $\mathcal{G}$, and pairs of nodes $(i, j) \in \mathcal{E}$ between which the internodal distance is given represent graph edges. The cost function f has thus the meaning of accumulated quadratic distance mismatch error over the graph edges. We observe that in practical applications the distance values d_{ij} come from noisy measurements of actual distances between node pairs in a real and existing configuration of nodes in a network. The purpose of network localization is in this case to estimate the actual node positions from the distance measurements. However, recovery of the true node position from distance measurements is only possible if the underlying graph is *generically globally rigid* (ggr), (Eren et al., 2004). A network is said to be globally rigid if is congruent with any network which shares the same underlying graph and equal corresponding information on distances. Generically global rigidity is a stronger concept that requires the formation to remain globally rigid also up to non trivial flexes. Rigidity properties of a network strongly depends on the so called *Rigidity matrix* $R \in \mathbb{R}^{m \times 2n}$, in which each row is associated to an edge e_{ij}, and the four nonzero entries of the row can be computed as $x_i - x_j, y_i - y_j, x_j - x_i, y_j - y_i$ (with $p_i = [x_i, y_i]^\top$), and are located respectively in column $2i - 1, 2i, 2j - 1, 2j$. In particular a network is globally rigid if R has rank $2n - 3$.
If a planar network is generically globally rigid the objective function in (1) has a unique global minimum, if the positions of at least three non-collinear nodes is known and fixed in advance (anchor nodes), or it has several equivalent global minima corresponding to congruence transformations (roto-translation) of the configuration, if no anchors are specified. If the graph is not ggr, instead, there exist many different geometric configurations (also called *flexes*) that match exactly or approximately the distance data and that correspond to equivalent global minima of the cost f. In this work we are not specifically interested in rigidity conditions that

render the global minimum of f unique. Instead, we focus of numerical techniques to compute *a* global minimum of f, that is one possible configuration that exactly or approximately matches the distance data. Clearly, if the problem data fed to the algorithm correspond to a ggr graph with anchors, then the resulting solution will indeed identify univocally a geometric configuration. Therefore, we here treat the problem in full generality, under no rigidity assumptions. Also, in our approach we treat under the same framework both anchor-based and anchor-free localization problems. In particular, when anchor nodes are specified at fixed positions, we just set the respective node position variables to the given values, and eliminate these variables from the optimization. Therefore, the presence of anchors simply reduces the number of free variables in the optimization.

4. Approaches to Network Localization

In this section we review several techniques for solving network localization from range measurements. The first technique is a simple *gradient algorithm* in which the optimization is performed by iterative steps in the direction of the gradient. This approach is able to find a local minimizer of the objective function and requires only first-order information, making the implementation easy and fast. A critical part of the gradient algorithm is the computation of a suitable stepsize. Exact line search prescribes to compute the stepsize by solving a unidimensional optimization problem, hence involving further computational effort in solving the localization. In this context we recall a simple and effective alternative for computing the stepsize, called Barzilai-Borwein stepsize from the name of the authors that proposed it in (Barzilai & Borwein, 1988).

The second technique is a Gauss-Newton (or *iterative least-squares*) approach which is successfully employed in several examples of range localization. We will show how iterative least-squares method converges to the global optimum only in case the initial guess for optimization is reasonably close to the actual configuration. Otherwise the algorithm is only able to retrieve a configuration that corresponds to a local optimum of the objective function. It is worth noticing that, apart from the previous consideration, the algorithm can provide a fast method for obtaining a local solution of the problem.

The third technique is a *trust-region* method which is based on the iterative minimization of a convex approximation of the cost function. The underlying idea is similar to the iterative least-squares: at each step the optimization is performed over a quadratic function which locally resemble the behavior of the objective function. The minimizer of the quadratic approximation is searched over a trust region (a suitable neighborhood of the current point), hence if the approximated solution can assure an appropriate decrease of the objective function the trust region is expanded, otherwise it is contracted. The higher order approximation of the objective function allows trust region to enhance convergence properties, expanding the domain of application of the technique. The improved convergence comes at the price of numerical efficiency, although the trust region method provides a good trade-off between numerical efficiency and global convergence.

In the chapter we further present another solution to the range localization, which is named *global continuation*. This technique was firstly introduced for determining protein structure and for the interpretation of the NMR (Nuclear Magnetic Resonance) data. Global continuation method is based on the idea of iterative smoothing the original cost function into a function that has fewer local minima. Applying a mathematical tool known as *Gaussian transform* the objective function is converted into a convex function and a *smoothing parameter* controls

how much the initial function changes in the transformation. For large values of the smoothing parameter the transformed function is convex, whereas smaller values correspond to less smoothed functions. When the parameter is zero the original cost function is recovered. The result is that the initial smoothing succeeds in moving the initial guess closer to the global optimum of the objective function, then a decreasing sequence of smoothing parameters assures the method to reach the global minimum of the original function. According to the previous considerations the method guarantees the convergence to the global optimum with high probability regardless the initial guess of the optimization. In the chapter it is shown how the robustness of the approach implies a further computation effort which may be unsustainable for nodes with limited computational resources.
Finally we describe a technique which has recently attracted the attention of the research community. The approach, whose first contributions can be found in (Doherty et al., 2001) and (Biswas & Ye, 2004), is based on a relaxation of the original optimization problem and solved using *semidefinite programming* (SDP). This technique is the most computational demanding with respect to the previous approaches, although distributed techniques can be implemented to spread the computational burden on several nodes.
These centralized approaches for minimizing the cost (1) work iteratively from a starting initial guess. As mentioned above the gradient method, the Gauss-Newton approach, the trust region method are local, hence the initial guess plays a fundamental role in the solution of the problem: such techniques may fail to converge to the global optimum, if the initial guess is not close enough to the global solution. In Figure 1 we report an example of node configuration and a possible initial guess for optimization. The Global Continuation method employs iteratively a local approach on a smoothed objective function and this allows the solution to be resilient on perturbations of the initial guess. Finally the Semi-definite Programming approach is proved to retrieve the correct network configuration in the case of exact distance measurements, although it can be inaccurate in the practical case of noisy measurements. The

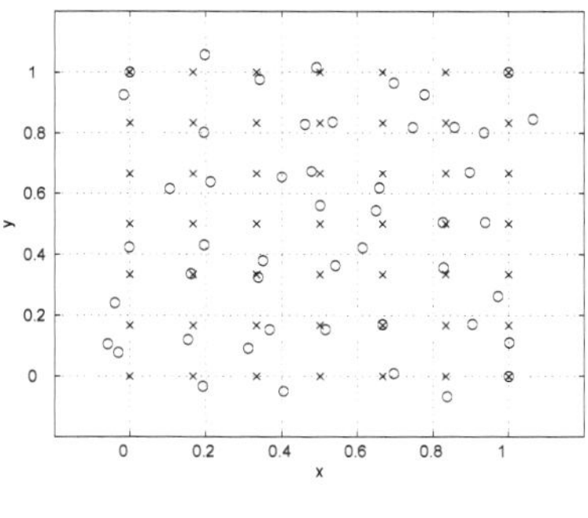

Fig. 1. Actual node configuration (circles) and initial position guess (asterisks).

minimization objective (1) can be rewritten as

$$f(p) = \frac{1}{2} \sum_{(i,j) \in \mathcal{E}} g_{ij}^2(p), \quad g_{ij}(p) \doteq \|p_i - p_j\|^2 - d_{ij}^2, \tag{2}$$

and we let $p^{(0)}$ denote the vector of initial position estimates. We next describe the five centralized methods to determine a minimum of the cost function, starting from $p^{(0)}$.

4.1 A gradient-based method

The most basic iterative algorithm for finding a local minimizer of $f(p)$ is the so called *gradient method* (GM). Let $p^{(\tau)}$ be the configuration computed by the algorithm at iteration τ, being $p^{(0)}$ the given initial configuration: at each iteration the solution is updated according to the rule

$$p^{(\tau+1)} = p^{(\tau)} - \alpha_\tau \nabla f(p^{(\tau)}), \tag{3}$$

where α_τ is the step length, which may be computed at each iteration via exact or approximate line search, and where

$$\nabla f(p) \quad = \quad \sum_{(i,j)\in\mathcal{E}} g_{ij}(p)\nabla g_{ij}(p) \tag{4}$$

where gradient ∇g_{ij} is a row vector of n blocks, with each block composed of two entries, thus $2n$ entries in total, and with the only non-zero terms corresponding to the blocks in position i and j:

$$\nabla g_{ij}(p) \quad = \quad 2[\mathbf{0}_2^\top \ \cdots \ \mathbf{0}_2^\top \ (p_i - p_j)^\top \ \mathbf{0}_2^\top \ \cdots \ \mathbf{0}_2^\top \ (p_j - p_i)^\top \ \mathbf{0}_2^\top \ \cdots \ \mathbf{0}_2^\top].$$

The gradient method is guaranteed to converge to a local minimizer whenever $\{p : f(p) \leq f(p^{(0)})\}$ is bounded and the step lengths satisfy the Wolfe conditions, see, e.g., (Nocedal & Wright, 2006). Although the rate of convergence of the method can be poor, we are interested in this method here since it requires first-order only information (no Hessian needs be computed) and it is, in the specific case at hand, directly amenable to distributed implementation, as discussed in Section 7.

4.1.1 The Barzilai and Borwein scheme

A critical part of the gradient algorithm is the computation of suitable stepsizes α_τ. Exact line search prescribes to compute the stepsize by solving the unidimensional optimization problem

$$\min_\alpha f(p^{(\tau)} - \alpha \nabla f(p^{(\tau)})).$$

Determining the optimal α can however be costly in terms of evaluations of objective and gradient. Moreover, an approach based on exact or approximate line search is not suitable for the decentralized implementation. Barzilai and Borwein (BB) in (Barzilai & Borwein, 1988) proposed an alternative simple and effective technique for selection of the step size, which requires few storage and inexpensive computations. The BB approach prescribes to compute the step size according to the formula

$$\alpha_\tau = \frac{\|p^{(\tau)} - p^{(\tau-1)}\|^2}{(p^{(\tau)} - p^{(\tau-1)})^\top (\nabla f(p^{(\tau)}) - \nabla f(p^{(\tau-1)}))}, \tag{5}$$

hence no line searches or matrix computations are required to determine α_τ. In the rest of the chapter the BB stepsize will be employed for solving the network localization with the gradient method.

4.1.2 Numerical experiments and convergence results

In this section we discuss some numerical experiments that show interesting properties of the gradient-based localization approach.

We first focus on convergence results in the case of exact distance measurements. In the following tests we use generically globally rigid (**ggr**) graphs with n nodes. Hence, by choosing at least three non colinear anchor nodes, the global solution of the localization problem is unique and defines the corresponding geometric configuration of the nodes. One approach to build a **ggr** realization of the networked system is reported in (Eren et al., 2004), and summarized in the following procedure: consider at least 3 non collinear anchor nodes on the plane, then sequentially add new nodes, each one connected with at least 3 anchors or previously inserted nodes. The obtained network is called a *trilateration graph* and it is guaranteed to be **ggr**, see Theorem 8 of (Eren et al., 2004). An example of trilateration graph is reported in Figure 2(a). This technique is fast and easy to implement, however it does not consider that, in

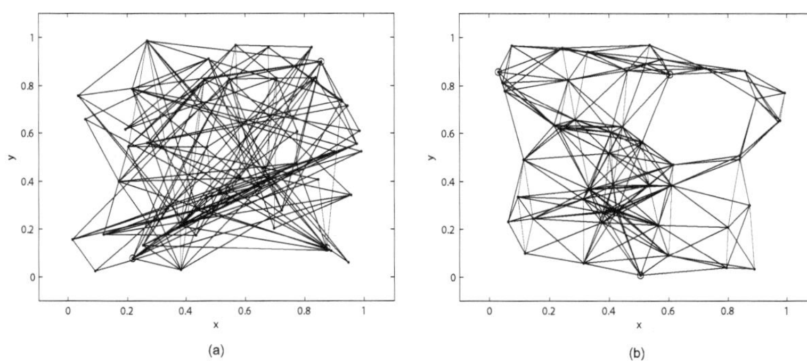

Fig. 2. (a) Example of trilateration graph with nodes in the unit square, $[0,1]^2$; (b) Example of geometric random graph with nodes in the unit square.

practical setups, the *sensing radius* of each node is limited, i.e. edges in the graph may appear only between nodes whose distance is less than the sensing range R. In order to work on more realistic graphs in the numerical tests, we hence use *random geometric graphs*, that are graphs in which nodes are deployed at random in the unit square $[0,1]^2$, and an edge exists between a pair of nodes if and only if their geometrical distance is smaller than R. It has been proved in (Eren et al., 2004) that if $R > 2\sqrt{2}\sqrt{\frac{\log(n)}{n}}$, the graphs produced by the previous technique are **ggr** with high probability. An example of geometric graph with $R = 0.3$ and $n = 50$ is shown in Figure 2(b).

We consider the configuration generated as previously described as the "true" configuration (which is of course unknown in practice), and then, we use the distance measurements from this configuration as the data for the numerical tests. Hence the global optimum of the objective function is expected to correspond to the value zero of the objective function. Convergence properties of the gradient method are evaluated under the settings mentioned above. According to (Moré & Wu, 1997), we consider p_i^*, $i = 1, 2, ..., n$ a solution to the network localization problem, i.e., the gradient algorithm successfully attained the global optimum of the objective function, if it satisfies:

$$| \|p_i - p_j\| - d_{ij} | \leq \varepsilon, \quad (i,j) \in \mathcal{E} \tag{6}$$

where ε is a given tolerance. The technique is local hence it is expected to be influenced

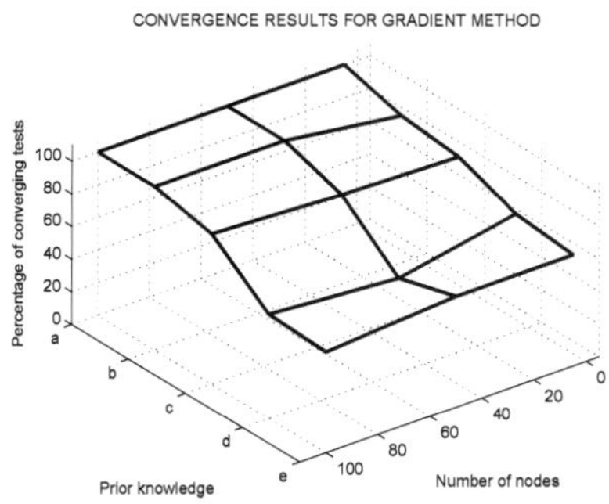

Fig. 3. Percentage of convergence test depending on network size and goodness of initial guess for the GM approach.

by the initial guess for the optimization. In particular, we considered five levels of a-priori knowledge on the configuration:

a) Good prior knowledge: initial guess for the algorithms is drawn from a multivariate Normal distribution centered at the true node positions, with standard deviation $\sigma_p = 0.1$;

b) Initial guess is drawn from a multivariate Normal distribution with $\sigma_p = 0.5$;

c) Bad prior knowledge: Initial guess is drawn from a multivariate Normal distribution with $\sigma_p = 1$;

d) Only the area where nodes are deployed is known: initial guess is drawn uniformly over the unit square;

e) No prior information is available: initial guess is drawn randomly around the origin of the reference frame.

In Figure 3 we report the percentage of test in which convergence is observed for different network sizes and different initial guess on non-anchors position (for each setting we performed 100 simulation runs). The gradient method shows high percentage of convergence when good prior knowledge is available.
The second test is instead related to the localization performance in function of the number of anchors in the network. We consider a realistic setup in which there are 50 non-anchor nodes and the number of anchors ranges from 3 to 10, displaced in the unit square. Two nodes are connected by an edge if their distance is smaller than 0.3 and distance measurement are affected by noise in the form:

$$d_{ij} = \tilde{d}_{ij} + \epsilon_d \ \forall \ (i,j) \in \mathcal{E} \tag{7}$$

where $\tilde{d}_{ij}$ is the true distance among node i and node j, d_{ij} is the corresponding measured quantity and ϵ_d is a zero mean white noise with standard deviation σ_d. In the following test we consider $\sigma_d = 5 \cdot 10^{-3}$. In order to measure the localization effectiveness, we define the *node positioning error* ϕ_i^* at node i as the Euclidean distance between the estimated position p_i^*

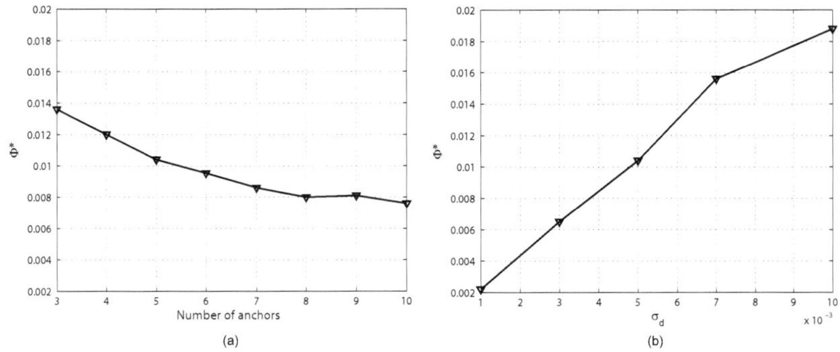

Fig. 4. (a) Localization error for different numbers of anchor nodes, using gradient method; (b) Localization error for different standard deviation of distance measurement noise.

and the true position p_i of the node. The *localization error* Φ^* is further defined as the mean value of the local positioning errors of all the nodes in the network:

$$\Phi^* = \frac{1}{n}\sum_{i=1}^{n} \|p_i - p_i^*\|.$$

It can be seen from Figure 4(a) that the localization error shows low sensitivity on the tested number of anchors, and the downward slope of the curve is not remarked (see tests on SDP, Section 4.5.3, for comparison).

The third test is aimed at studying the localization error for different standard deviations of the distance noise σ_d. The results, considering 3 anchor nodes, are reported in Figure 4(b). It is worth noting that the statistics about the localization error are performed assuming convergence to the global optimum of the technique, hence a good initial guess was used for optimization in the second and third test. In this way we can disambiguate the effects of convergence (Figure 3), from the effect of distance noise propagation (Figures 4(a) and 4(b)).

4.2 Gauss-Newton method

We next discuss a *Gauss-Newton* (GN) approach based on successive linearization of the component costs and *least-squares* iterates.

At each iteration τ of this method, we linearize $g_{ij}(p)$ around the current solution $p^{(\tau)}$, obtaining

$$g_{ij}(p) \simeq g_{ij}(p^{(\tau)}) + \nabla g_{ij}(p^{(\tau)})(p - p^{(\tau)}). \tag{8}$$

Stacking all g_{ij} elements in vector g, in lexicographical order, we have that

$$g(p) \simeq g(p^{(\tau)}) + R(p^{(\tau)})\delta_p(\tau),$$

where $\delta_p(\tau) \doteq p - p^{(\tau)}$, and

$$R(p) \doteq \begin{bmatrix} \nabla g_{i_1 j_1}(p) \\ \vdots \\ \nabla g_{i_m j_m}(p) \end{bmatrix} \in \mathbb{R}^{m,2n}, \tag{9}$$

where m is the number of node pairs among which a relative distance measurement exists. Matrix R is usually known as the *rigidity matrix* of the configuration, see (Eren et al., 2004). Using the approximation in (8), we thus have that

$$\begin{aligned} f(p) &\simeq \frac{1}{2} \sum_{(i,j)\in\mathcal{E}} \left(g_{ij}(p^{(\tau)}) + \nabla g_{ij}(p^{(\tau)})\delta_p(\tau) \right)^2 \\ &= \frac{1}{2} \| g(p^{(\tau)}) + R(p^{(\tau)})\delta_p(\tau) \|^2. \end{aligned}$$

The update step is then computed by determining a minimizing solution for the approximated f, which corresponds to the least-squares solution

$$\delta_p^*(\tau) = -R^+(p^{(\tau)})g(p^{(\tau)}),$$

where R^+ denotes the Moore-Penrose pseudo-inverse of R. Thus, the updated configuration is given by

$$p^{(\tau+1)} = p^{(\tau)} - R^+(p^{(\tau)})g(p^{(\tau)}), \tag{10}$$

and the process is repeated until no further decrease is observed in f, that is until the relative decrease $(f^{(\tau)} - f^{(\tau+1)})/f^{(\tau)}$ goes below a given threshold.
Notice that in the case when anchor nodes are present the very same approach can be used, with the only prescription that the columns of R corresponding to anchors need be eliminated. Specifically, if there are $b > 0$ anchor nodes, we define the reduced rigidity matrix $R_r(p^{(\tau)}) \in \mathbb{R}^{m,2(n-b)}$ as the sub-matrix obtained from $R(p^{(\tau)})$ by removing the pairs of columns corresponding to the anchor nodes, and we define the vector of free variables $\tilde{p}$ as the sub-vector of p containing the coordinates of non-anchor nodes (positions of anchors are fixed, and need not be updated). The iteration then becomes

$$\tilde{p}^{(\tau+1)} = \tilde{p}^{(\tau)} - R_r^+(p^{(\tau)})g(p^{(\tau)}).$$

The described iterative technique is a version of the classical Gauss-Newton method, for which convergence to a local minimizer is guaranteed whenever the initial level set $\{p : f(p) \le f(p^{(0)})\}$ is bounded, and R_r has full rank at all steps; see, e.g., (Nocedal & Wright, 2006).

4.2.1 Numerical experiments and convergence results

We now present the convergence results for the Gauss-Newton approach, according to the simulation setup presented in 4.1.2. As in the previous example, when no prior information is available we build the initial guess for optimization randomly drawing non-anchor nodes around the origin of the reference frame. It is worth noticing that the initial guess cannot be fixed exactly in the origin otherwise the rank loss in the *rigidity matrix* prevents the application of least squares approach. We denote this first setup as (e) in Figure 5. In the cases prior knowledge on the area in which the network is deployed is available, node positions are initialized randomly in the unit square, $[0,1]^2$. This situation is denoted with (d) in Figure 5. Finally the cases labeled with (a), (b), (c) in Fig. 5 correspond to the case the nodes have some prior information on their geometric location, although this information can be accurate (a), not very accurate (b) or inaccurate (c), see Section 4.1.2. The local nature of the approach is remarked by the 3D plot but is this case the region of attraction of the global minimum is

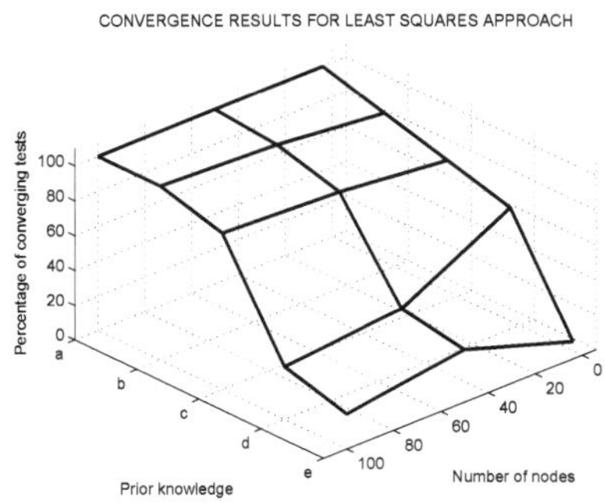

Fig. 5. Percentage of convergence test depending on network size and goodness of initial guess for the GN approach.

smaller and the technique is prone to incur in local minima when starting from poor initial guess. This issue becomes more critical as the number of nodes increases.

We repeated the localization error tests for different measurement noise and number of anchors nodes obtaining exactly the same results as in the gradient-based case. This is however an intuitive result when the initial guess of local techniques is sufficiently close to the global optimum of the objective function: all the techniques simply reaches the same minimum and the localization errors simply depend on the error propagation from distance measurement noise.

4.3 Trust Region approach

The third technique that we examine for application to the problem at hand is a *trust region* (TR) method based on quadratic approximation of the cost function f. At each iteration of this method, the minimizer of the approximated cost function is searched over a suitable neighborhood Δ of the current point (the so-called *trust region*, usually spherical or ellipsoidal). When an adequate decrease of the objective is found in the trust region, the trust region is expanded, otherwise it is contracted, and the process is repeated until no further progress is possible.

The quadratic approximation of f around a current configuration $p^{(\tau)}$ is given by

$$\begin{aligned} f(p) &\simeq q_\tau(p) \\ &\doteq f(p^{(\tau)}) + \nabla f(p^{(\tau)})\delta_p(\tau) + \frac{1}{2}\delta_p^\top(\tau)\nabla^2 f(p^{(\tau)})\delta_p(\tau), \end{aligned}$$

where, using the notation introduced in the previous section,

$$\begin{aligned} \nabla f(p) &= \sum_{(i,j)\in\mathcal{E}} 2g_{ij}(p)\nabla g_{ij}(p) \\ &= 2g^\top(p)R(p), \end{aligned} \tag{11}$$

and the Hessian matrix $\nabla^2 f \in \mathbb{R}^{2n,2n}$ is given by

$$\nabla^2 f(p) = 2\sum_{(i,j)\in\mathcal{E}} \left(\nabla g_{ij}^\top(p)\nabla g_{ij}(p) + g_v(p)\nabla^2 g_{ij}(p)\right), \tag{12}$$

where the Hessian matrix $\nabla^2 g_{ij}(p) \in \mathbb{R}^{2n,2n}$ is composed of $n \times n$ blocks of size 2×2: all blocks are zero, except for the four blocks in position $(i,i),(i,j),(j,i),(j,j)$, which are given by

$$\begin{aligned} [\nabla^2 g_{ij}(p)]_{i,i} &= 2I_2, \quad & [\nabla^2 g_{ij}(p)]_{i,j} &= -2I_2, \\ [\nabla^2 g_{ij}(p)]_{j,i} &= -2I_2, \quad & [\nabla^2 g_{ij}(p)]_{j,j} &= 2I_2, \end{aligned}$$

where I_2 denotes the 2×2 identity matrix.

Given a current configuration $p^{(\tau)}$ and trust region Δ_τ, we solve the trust-region subproblem:

$$\min_{\delta_p(\tau) \in \Delta_\tau} q_\tau(p).$$

Let $\delta_p^*(\tau)$ be the resulting optimal solution, and let $p^* = p^{(\tau)} + \delta_p^*(\tau)$. Then, we compute the ratio between actual and approximated function decrease:

$$\rho_\tau = \frac{f(p^{(\tau)}) - f(p^*)}{q_\tau(p^{(\tau)}) - q_\tau(p^*)},$$

and update the solution and trust region according to the following rules:

$$p^{(\tau+1)} = \begin{cases} p^{(\tau)} + \delta_p^*(\tau), & \text{if } \rho_\tau > \eta_0 \\ p^{(\tau)}, & \text{if } \rho_\tau \leq \eta_0 \end{cases}$$

$$\xi_{\tau+1} = \begin{cases} \sigma_1 \min\{\|\delta_p^*(\tau)\|, \xi_\tau\}, & \text{if } \rho_\tau < \eta_1 \\ \sigma_2 \xi_\tau, & \text{if } \rho_\tau \in [\eta_1, \eta_2) \\ \sigma_3 \xi_\tau, & \text{if } \rho_\tau \geq \eta_2 \end{cases} \tag{13}$$

where $\xi_{\tau+1}$ is the radius of the trust region $\Delta_{\tau+1}$, and $\eta_0 > 0, 0 < \eta_1 < \eta_2 < 1; 0 < \sigma_1 < \sigma_2 < 1 < \sigma_3$ are parameters that have typical values set by experience to $\eta_0 = 10^{-4}, \eta_1 = 0.25, \eta_2 = 0.75; \sigma_1 = 0.25, \sigma_2 = 0.5, \sigma_3 = 4$. The conjugate gradient method is usually employed to solve the trust-region subproblem, see (More, 1983) for further implementation details.

4.3.1 Numerical experiments and convergence results

In this section we report the results on the application of the Trust Region approach to the network localization problem. We now focus on the convergence properties of the approach whereas further comparative experiments are presented in Section 5. The simulation are performed according to the setup described in Section 4.1.2 and 4.2.1. Figure 6 shows the percentage of convergence for different initial guesses of the optimization and for different network sizes. The statistics are performed over 100 simulation runs. The trust region approach provides better convergence properties with respect to Gauss-Newton approach, although also showing degrading performance under scarce prior knowledge. Regarding the sensitivity to the number of anchors and to the measurement noise, the results reported in Section 4.1.2 hold (see also the final remarks of Section 4.2.1).

4.4 Global Continuation approach

The *global continuation* (GC) method is based on the idea of gradually transforming the original objective function into smoother functions having fewer local minima. Following the

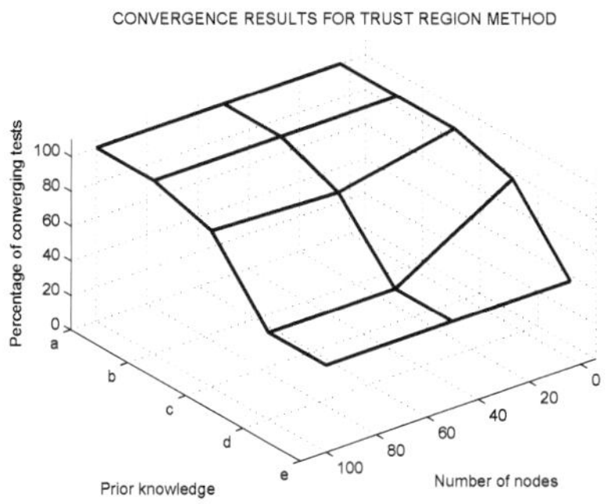

Fig. 6. Percentage of convergence test depending on network size and goodness of initial guess for TR approach.

approach of (More, 1983), the smoothed version of the cost function is obtained by means of the Gaussian transform: For a function $f : \mathbb{R}^n \to \mathbb{R}$ the Gaussian transform is defined as

$$\varphi(x) \doteq \langle f \rangle_\lambda(x) = \frac{1}{\pi^{n/2}} \int_{R^n} f(x + \lambda u) \exp(-\|u\|^2) du. \tag{14}$$

Intuitively, $\varphi(x)$ is the average value of $f(z)$ in the neighborhood of x, computed with respect to a Gaussian probability density. The parameter λ controls the degree of smoothing: large λ implies a high degree of smoothing, whereas for $\lambda \to 0$ the original function f is recovered. The Gaussian transform of the cost function in (1) can be computed explicitly, see Theorem 4.3 on (More, 1983).

Proposition 1 (Gaussian transform of localization cost). *Let f be given by (1). Then, the Gaussian transform of f is given by*

$$\varphi_\lambda(p) = f(p) + \gamma + 8\lambda^2 \sum_{(i,j)\in\mathcal{E}} \|p_i - p_j\|^2, \tag{15}$$

where

$$\gamma = 8m\lambda^4 - 4\lambda^2 \sum_{(i,j)\in\mathcal{E}} d_{ij}^2.$$

It is interesting to observe that, for suitably large value of λ, the transformed function $\varphi_\lambda(p)$ is *convex*. This fact is stated in the following proposition.

Proposition 2 (Convexification of localization cost). *Let $f(p)$ be given by (1), and let $\varphi_\lambda(p)$ be the Gaussian transform of $f(p)$. If*

$$\lambda > \frac{1}{2} \max_{(i,j)\in\mathcal{E}} d_{ij} \tag{16}$$

then $\varphi_\lambda(p)$ is convex.

Proof. From (1) and (15) we have that

$$\varphi_\lambda(p) = \gamma + \sum_{(i,j)\in\mathcal{E}} 8\lambda^2 r_{ij}^2(p) + (r_{ij}^2(p) - d_{ij}^2)^2,$$

where we defined $r_{ij}(p) \doteq \|p_i - p_j\|$. Let

$$h_{ij}(r_{ij}) = 8\lambda^2 r_{ij}^2 + (r_{ij}^2 - d_{ij}^2)^2.$$

Then

$$\begin{aligned} h'_{ij} \doteq \frac{\mathrm{d}h_{ij}}{\mathrm{d}r_{ij}} &= 4r_{ij}(r_{ij}^2 - d_{ij}^2 + 4\lambda^2) \\ h''_{ij} \doteq \frac{\mathrm{d}^2 h_{ij}}{\mathrm{d}r_{ij}^2} &= 4(3r_{ij}^2 - d_v^2 + 4\lambda^2). \end{aligned}$$

Note that $h'_{ij} > 0$ if $4\lambda^2 > d_{ij}^2 - r_{ij}^2$, and $h''_{ij} > 0$ if $4\lambda^2 > d_{ij}^2 - 3r_{ij}^2$. Since $r_{ij} \geq 0$ it follows that, for $4\lambda^2 > d_{ij}^2$, both h'_{ij} and h''_{ij} are positive. Therefore, if

$$\lambda > \frac{1}{2} \max_{(i,j)\in\mathcal{E}} d_{ij} \tag{17}$$

then functions h_{ij} are increasing and convex, for all (i,j). Observe next that function $r_{ij}(p)$ is convex in p (it is the norm of an affine function of p), therefore by applying the composition rules to $h_{ij}(r_{ij}(p))$ (see Section 3.2.4 of (Boyd, 2004)), we conclude that this latter function is convex. Convexity of $\varphi_\lambda(p)$ then immediately follows since the sum of convex functions is convex. □

The key idea in the global continuation approach is to define a sequence $\{\lambda_k\}$ decreasing to zero as k increases, and to compute a corresponding sequence of points $\{p^*(\lambda_k)\}$ which are the global minimizers of functions $\varphi_{\lambda_k}(p)$. The following strong result holds.

Proposition 3 (Theorem 5.2 of (More, 1983)). *Let $\{\lambda_k\}$ be a sequence converging to zero, and let $\{p^*(\lambda_k)\}$ be the corresponding sequence of global minimizers of $\varphi_{\lambda_k}(p)$. If $\{p^*(\lambda_k)\} \to p^*$ then p^* is a global minimizer of $f(p)$.*

In practice, we initialize λ to a value λ_1 that guarantees convexity of φ_λ, so that the initial computed point is guaranteed to be the global minimizer of φ_λ. Then, λ is slightly decreased and a new minimizer is computed using the previous point as the starting guess. The process is iterated until $\lambda = 0$, that is until the original cost function f is minimized. Each iteration in this procedure requires the solution of an unconstrained minimization problem, which can be suitably performed using a trust-region method. The various steps of the global continuation method are summarized in the next section.

4.4.1 Global Continuation algorithm

Set the total number M of major iterations. Given an initial guess p_0 for the configuration:

1. Let $k = 1$. Compute a convexifying parameter

$$\lambda_k = \frac{1}{2} \max_{(i,j)\in\mathcal{E}} d_{ij};$$

2. Compute a (hopefully global) minimizer p_k^* of $\varphi_{\lambda_k}(p)$ using a trust-region method with initial guess p_{k-1};
3. If $\lambda_k = 0$, exit and return $p^* = p_k^*$;

4. Let $k = k + 1$. Update λ:
$$\lambda_k = \frac{M-k}{M-1}\lambda_1;$$

5. Go to step 2).

In step 2) of the algorithm, a quadratic approximation of $\varphi_{\lambda_k}(p)$ is needed for the inner iterations of the trust-region method. More precisely, the trust-region algorithm shall work with the following approximation of φ_λ around a current point $\bar{p}$:

$$\begin{aligned}\varphi_\lambda(p) &\simeq q_\lambda(p)\\ &\doteq \varphi_\lambda(\bar{p}) + \nabla\varphi_\lambda(\bar{p})\delta_p + \frac{1}{2}\delta_p^\top \nabla^2\varphi_\lambda(\bar{p})\delta_p,\end{aligned}$$

where $\delta_p = p - \bar{p}$. Due to the additive structure of (15), the gradient and Hessian of φ_λ are computed as follows:

$$\begin{aligned}\nabla\varphi_\lambda(p) &= \nabla f(p) + 8\lambda^2 \sum_{(i,j)\in\mathcal{E}} \nabla g_{ij}(p)\\ \nabla^2\varphi_\lambda(p) &= \nabla^2 f(p) + 8\lambda^2 \sum_{(i,j)\in\mathcal{E}} \nabla^2 g_{ij}(p).\end{aligned}$$

4.4.2 Numerical experiments and convergence results

Repeating the localization test performed for the techniques presented so far, we report the percentage of convergence for the Global Continuation approach in Figure 7. The different levels of prior knowledge are the same as in Sections 4.1.2 and 4.2.1. We choose a number of major (or outer) iterations $M = 11$. The global continuation method, although computationally

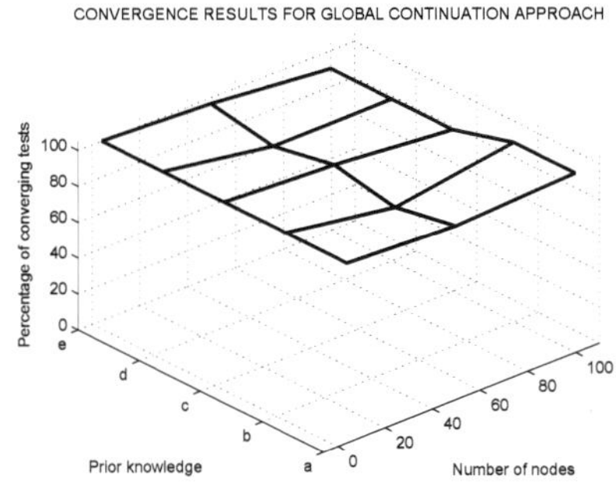

Fig. 7. Percentage of convergence test depending on network size and goodness of initial guess for GC approach.

more intensive than the previous two methods (see Section 5), shows instead a remarkable insensitivity to the initial guess, and therefore it is suitable for applications in which little or no prior knowledge is available. In few cases the number of converging experiments is less than 100%, but this issue can be alleviated by increasing the number of major iterations, hence making a more gradual smoothing. Further results on computational effort required by the technique in reported in the Section 5.

4.5 Semidefinite Programming-based localization

In this section we describe an approach to network localization, which is based on *semidefinite programming* (SDP). First attempts to solve the range localization problem using convex optimization trace back to (Doherty et al., 2001); the authors model some upper bounds on distance measurement as convex constraints, in the form:

$$\|p_i - p_j\| \leq d_{ij}, \quad (i,j) \in \mathcal{E}. \tag{18}$$

The previous convex constraints can only impose internodal distances to be less than a given sensing range or less or equal to a measured distance d_{ij}. However, as stated in Section 3, we want to impose equality constraints in the form:

$$\|p_i - p_j\|^2 = d_{ij}^2, \quad (i,j) \in \mathcal{E}, \tag{19}$$

Such constraints are non convex, and the SDP network localization approach is based on a relaxation of the original problem. If only inequality conditions like (18) are used it is possible to assure good localization accuracy only when non-anchor nodes are in the convex hull of the anchors, whereas these localization approaches tend to perform poorly when anchors are placed in the interior of the network (Biswas et al., 2006).
The rest of this section is structured as follows. The SDP relaxation is presented in Section 4.5.1. Then in Section 4.5.2 some relevant properties of the SDP approach are discussed. In Section 4.5.3 some numerical examples are reported. Finally, a gradient refinement phase is presented in Section 4.5.4, for the purpose of enhancing localization performance when the distance measurements are affected by noise.

4.5.1 Problem relaxation

In the previous sections, we found it convenient to stack the information on node positions, $p_i = [x_i \; y_i]^\top$, $i = 1, \ldots, n$, in the column vector $p \doteq [p_1^\top \; p_2^\top \; \cdots \; p_n^\top]^\top \in \mathbb{R}^{2n}$. Here, we modify the notation and pack the variables p_i as follows

$$p \;=\; \begin{bmatrix} x_1 & x_2 & \ldots & x_n \\ y_1 & y_2 & \ldots & y_n \end{bmatrix} = [p_1 \; p_2 \; \ldots \; p_n] \in \mathbb{R}^{2\times n},$$

As mentioned in Section 3 if an anchor-based setup is considered the columns of p are simply deleted and the corresponding Cartesian positions are substituted in the problem formulation, with known vectors $a_k \in \mathbb{R}^2$. In the following we recall the relaxation approach of (Biswas et al., 2006) and (Biswas & Ye, 2004).
Starting from equation (19) we can distinguish constraints which are due to measurements between two non-anchor nodes and measurements in which an anchor node is involved. For this purpose we partition the set $\mathcal{E}$ into two sets, respectively called $\mathcal{E}_p$ (including all edges between non-anchor nodes) and $\mathcal{E}_a$ (including all edges incident on one anchor node). We further define $m_p = |\mathcal{E}_p|$ and $m_a = |\mathcal{E}_a|$, where $|S|$ denotes the cardinality of the set S. Therefore the localization problem can be rewritten as:

$$\begin{aligned} \|p_i - p_j\|^2 &= d_{ij}^2, \quad \forall (i,j) \in \mathcal{E}_p \\ \|a_k - p_j\|^2 &= d_{kj}^2, \quad \forall (k,j) \in \mathcal{E}_a \end{aligned}$$

where d_{ij} is the distance measurement between non-anchor nodes i and j and d_{kj} is the distance measurement between non-anchor node j and anchor node k.

If we define the standard unit vector e_i as a column vector of all zeros, except a unit entry in the i-th position, it is possible to write the following equalities:

$$\begin{aligned} \|p_i - p_j\|^2 &= (e_i - e_j)^\top p^\top p(e_i - e_j), \ \forall (i,j) \ \in \mathcal{E}_p \\ \|a_k - p_j\|^2 &= \begin{pmatrix} a_k \\ -e_j \end{pmatrix}^\top \begin{pmatrix} I_2 & p \\ p^\top & Y \end{pmatrix} \begin{pmatrix} a_k \\ -e_j \end{pmatrix}, \ \forall \ (k,j) \in \mathcal{E}_a, \quad Y = p^\top p, \end{aligned}$$

Then the matrix form of the localization problem can be rewritten as:

$$\begin{array}{ll} \textbf{find} & p \in \mathbb{R}^{(2\times n)}, Y \in \mathbb{R}^{(n\times n)} \\ \text{s.t.} & (e_i - e_j)^\top Y (e_i - e_j) = d_{ij}^2, \ \forall \ (i,j) \in \mathcal{E}_p \\ & \begin{pmatrix} a_k \\ -e_j \end{pmatrix}^\top \begin{pmatrix} I_2 & p \\ p^T & Y \end{pmatrix} \begin{pmatrix} a_k \\ -e_j \end{pmatrix} = d_{kj}^2, \ \forall \ (k,j) \in \mathcal{E}_a; \\ & Y = p^\top p. \end{array} \tag{20}$$

Equation (20) can be relaxed to a semidefinite program by simply substituting the constraint $Y = p^\top p$ with $Y \succeq p^\top p$. According to (Boyd, 2004) the previous inequality is equivalent to:

$$Z = \begin{pmatrix} I_2 & p \\ p^\top & Y \end{pmatrix} \succeq 0.$$

Then the relaxed problem (20) can be stated in standard SDP form:

$$\begin{array}{ll} \textbf{min} & 0 \\ \text{s.t.} & (1;0;\mathbf{0})^\top Z(1;0;\mathbf{0}) = 1 \\ & (0;1;\mathbf{0})^\top Z(0;1;\mathbf{0}) = 1 \\ & (1;1;\mathbf{0})^\top Z(1;1;\mathbf{0}) = 2 \\ & (0;e_i - e_j)^\top Z(0;e_i - e_j) = d_{ij}^2, \ \forall \ (i,j) \in \mathcal{E}_p, \\ & \begin{pmatrix} a_k \\ -e_j \end{pmatrix}^\top Z \begin{pmatrix} a_k \\ -e_j \end{pmatrix} = d_{kj}^2, \ \forall \ (k,j) \in \mathcal{E}_a, \\ & Z \succeq 0. \end{array} \tag{21}$$

Problem (21) is a feasibility convex program whose solution can be efficiently retrieved using interior-point algorithms, see (Boyd, 2004). As specified in Section 4.5.2 the approach is proved to attain the actual node position, regardless the initial guess chosen for optimization. It is clear that constraints in (21) are satisfied only if all distance measurements exactly match internodal distances in network configuration. For example, in the ideal case of perfect distance measurements, the optimal solution satisfies all the constraints and corresponds to the actual node configuration. In practical applications, however, the distance measurements are noisy, and, in general, no configuration does exist that satisfies all the imposed constraints. In such a case it is convenient to model the problem so to minimize the error on constraint satisfaction, instead of the stricter feasibility form (21). Hence the objective function can be rewritten as the sum of the error between the measured ranges and the distances between the nodes in the estimated configuration:

$$f_{SDP}(p) = \sum_{(i,j)\in\mathcal{E}_p} \left| \|p_i - p_j\|^2 - d_{ij}^2 \right| + \sum_{(k,j)\in\mathcal{E}_a} \left| \|a_k - p_j\|^2 - d_{kj}^2 \right| \tag{22}$$

It is worth noticing that, if the square of the errors is considered instead of the absolute value, the problem formulation exactly matches the one presented in Section 3. By introducing slack variables u_s and l_s, the corresponding optimization problem can be stated as follows:

$$\begin{array}{ll} \min & \sum_{(i,j)\in\mathcal{E}_p}(u_{ij}+l_{ij})+\sum_{(k,j)\in\mathcal{E}_a}(u_{kj}+l_{kj}) \\ \text{s.t.} & (1;0;\mathbf{0})^\top Z(1;0;\mathbf{0})=1 \\ & (0;1;\mathbf{0})^\top Z(0;1;\mathbf{0})=1 \\ & (1;1;\mathbf{0})^\top Z(1;1;\mathbf{0})=2 \\ & (0;e_i-e_j)^\top Z(0;e_i-e_j)-u_{ij}+l_{ij}=d_{ij}^2,\ \forall\ (i,j)\in\mathcal{E}_p, \\ & \begin{pmatrix} a_k \\ -e_j \end{pmatrix}^\top Z \begin{pmatrix} a_k \\ -e_j \end{pmatrix} - u_{kj}+l_{kj}=d_{kj}^2,\ \forall\ (i,j)\in\mathcal{E}_a, \\ & u_{ij},u_{kj},l_{ij},l_{kj}\geq 0, \\ & Z\succeq 0. \end{array} \tag{23}$$

The previous semidefinite convex program allows to efficiently solve the range localization; moreover it has global convergence properties as we describe in the following section.

4.5.2 Analysis of SDP-based network localization

In the ideal situation of agents that can take noiseless measurements of internodal distances, and when the network reconstruction is unique, the SDP approach allows to estimate the exact network configuration, (Biswas et al., 2006), (Biswas & Ye, 2004). The solution of the feasibility problem (21) is then:

$$Z^*=\begin{pmatrix} I_2 & p^* \\ p^{*\top} & Y^* \end{pmatrix},\quad Y^*=p^{*\top}p^*. \tag{24}$$

Hence the problem with the relaxed condition $Y\succeq p^\top p$ allows to retrieve the solution that satisfies the original problem with the constraint $Y=p^\top p$. Further discussion on conditions that make a network uniquely localizable and their connection with rigidity theory are reported in (So & Ye, 2007).
When dealing with noisy distance measurements, the SDP solution is no longer guaranteed to attain the global minimum of the objective function. In such a case the approach with relaxed constraints may provide inaccurate position estimation. In particular the matrix Y^* may have rank higher than 2, i.e., the estimated solution lies in a higher dimensional space than the planar dimension of the original problem. In (Biswas & Ye, 2004) the higher dimensional solution is simply projected in $\mathbb{R}^2$, but this comes at a price of rounding errors which may influence localization performance. For the purpose of improving position estimation accuracy in Section 4.5.4 we further describe a gradient refinement phase that may be added to the SDP localization.
We further observe that the SDP network localization, as expressed in (21), is able to retrieve the actual network configuration in case we consider a **ggr** graph, i.e., the global optimum of the objective function is unique. If the solution is not unique, the SDP approach returns a central solution that is the mean value of the global optima positions (So & Ye, 2007). We conclude this section with a remark on the complexity of the SDP network localization approach.

Remark 1. *Let $c=m_p+m_a+3$ be the number of constraints in the SDP formulation of the range localization problem (23) and ε be a positive number. Assume that a ε-solution of (23) is required, that is we are looking for an optimal configuration of the network that corresponds to a value of the objective function that is at most ε above the global minimum. Then the total number of interior-point* *algorithm iterations is smaller than* $\sqrt{n+c}\log\frac{1}{\varepsilon}$, *and the worst-case complexity of the SDP approach is* $O(\sqrt{n+c}(n^3+n^2c+c^3\log\frac{1}{\varepsilon}))$.

4.5.3 Numerical experiments

For numerical experiments we consider a geometric random graph with nodes in the unit square and sensing radius $R = 0.3$. We focus on the noisy case in which distance measurement are affected by noise with standard deviation $\sigma_d = 5 \cdot 10^{-3}$, according to the model (7). The gradient method, Gauss-Newton technique, the trust region approach and the global continuation were verified to be quite insensitive to the number of anchors. The SDP solution in presence of noise, however, is influenced by the number of anchors and on their placement. In order to show the effect of anchors on localization performance we consider a network with 50 non-anchor nodes and we varied the number of anchors from 3 to 10. Results are reported in Figure 8(a). We further tested the effects of anchor placement on localization performance: we

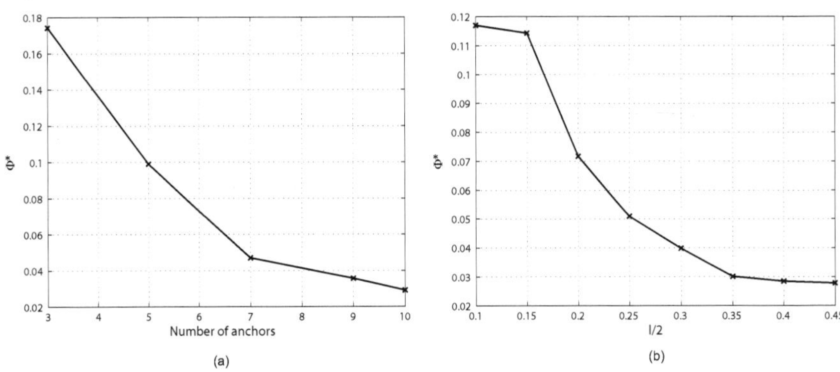

Fig. 8. (a) Localization error for different number of anchor nodes, using SDP approach; (b) Localization error for different anchor placements, using SDP approach. Four anchor nodes are displaced on the vertices of a square centered in [0.5, 0.5] and side l.

consider a network in the unit square, with four anchors disposed on the vertices of a smaller square with side l, centered in $[0.5, 0.5]$. For a small value of l the anchors are in the interior of the network, whereas as l increases the anchors tends to be placed on the boundary of the formation. It is possible to observe that the latter case, i.e., when the non-anchor nodes are in the convex hull of the anchors, the localization error is remarkably reduced, see Figure 8(b).

4.5.4 SDP with local refinement

As mentioned in Section 4.5.1, when distance measurements are affected by some measurement noise, the SDP can be inaccurate. On the other hand the reader can easily realize from the numerical experiments presented so far, that the local approaches assures better accuracy when an accurate initial guess is available. Therefore in a situation in which no a-priori information on node position is available to the problem solver and distance measures are supposed to be noisy, one may take the best of both local and global approaches by subdividing the localization problem into two phases (Biswas et al., 2006): (i) apply the SDP relaxation in order to have a rough estimate of node position; (ii) refine the imprecise estimated configuration with a local approach. For example one can use the gradient method described in Section 4.1, which is simple and has good convergence properties at a time. Moreover the gradient approach can be easily implemented in a distributed fashion, as discussed in Section 7. Numerical results on the SDP with local refinement are presented in Section 6.

5. Performance Evaluation of Local Approaches

We now compare the local techniques presented so far, i.e., the gradient method, the Gauss-Newton approach and the trust region approach. Global continuation is also reported for comparison, although it has global convergence capability. We consider a first setup that exemplifies the case of a network of sensors in which few nodes are equipped with GPS (anchors), whereas others use indirect estimation approaches (like the ones presented so far) for localization. For a numerical example, we considered the case of n nodes located on terrain according to the configuration shown Figure 9(b). This actual configuration should be estimated autonomously by the agents using as prior knowledge a given initial guess configuration, as the one shown in Figure 9(a). Four anchor nodes are selected at the external vertices of the network. Simulations were performed with $n = 49$ nodes. We test the convergence of the tech-

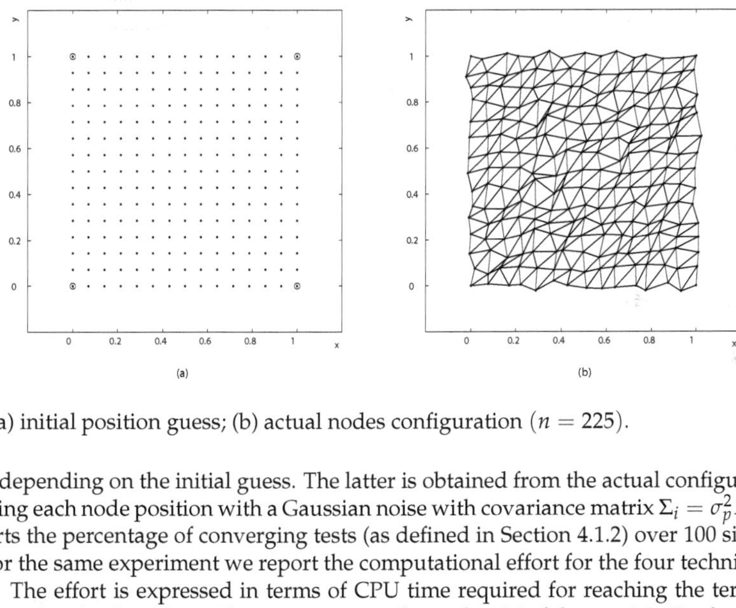

Fig. 9. (a) initial position guess; (b) actual nodes configuration ($n = 225$).

niques, depending on the initial guess. The latter is obtained from the actual configuration by perturbing each node position with a Gaussian noise with covariance matrix $\Sigma_i = \sigma_p^2 I_2$. Figure 10 reports the percentage of converging tests (as defined in Section 4.1.2) over 100 simulation runs. For the same experiment we report the computational effort for the four techniques, see Table 1. The effort is expressed in terms of CPU time required for reaching the termination condition of each algorithm. The tests were performed in Matlab on a MacBook, with 2.26 GHz clock frequency and 4 GB RAM.

It is possible to observe that the Gauss-Newton is the less resilient when the initial guess is not accurate, although it is fast and converges in few iterations. The Gradient method and the trust region approach have similar convergence properties and they require a comparable computational effort: the trust region approach is able to converge in few iterations, since it

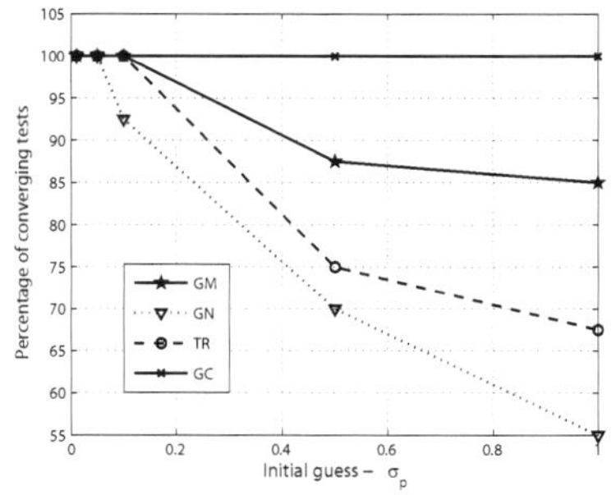

Fig. 10. Percentage of convergence vs. goodness of initial guess.

Table 1. CPU time for gradient method (GM), Gauss-Newton (GN), trust region (TR) and global continuation (GC) approach for different values of σ_p. Time is expressed in seconds.

σ_p	GM	GN	TR	GC
0.01	0.2955	0.0264	0.0751	2.2362
0.05	0.3292	0.0393	0.0635	2.2280
0.1	0.3657	0.0869	0.0930	2.2437
0.5	0.4449	0.7493	0.2316	2.3654
1	0.5217	1.4703	0.3443	2.5524

uses also second order information on the objective function (i.e., the Hessian). The gradient method, however, requires simpler update steps, but this comes at the price at a bigger number of iteration required for the technique to converge. Finally the global continuation converged in all the test performed, whereas the computational effort required is remarkably higher than the other approaches. Table 1 also enlightens how global continuation takes no advantage from good prior knowledge, since the initial smoothing moves the initial guess to the minimizer of the convexified function, regardless the starting guess of the optimization.

6. Localization Performance of Global Approaches

In this section we analyze the localization performance of the global approaches introduced so far, i.e., the global continuation approach and the SDP relaxation. We further compare the SDP with a local refinement, in which a gradient method is added in cascade to the SDP approach, as described in Section 4.5.4. We consider the rigid lattice shown in Figure 9, with $n = 49$ and we report the localization error for different standard deviations of the noise on distance measures σ_d. The reader can observe that the GC approach and the SDP with gradient refinement show exactly the same localization errors. This is, however, quite intuitive, since they reach the same optimum of the objective function. On the other hand, Table 2 reports the mean CPU time observed in the experiments. The SDP approach requires, in terms of CPU time, an order of magnitude more computational effort than the global continuation approach. This issue becomes critical as the network size increases, making the techniques practically unusable, for networks with more that 200 nodes. We remark that this problem

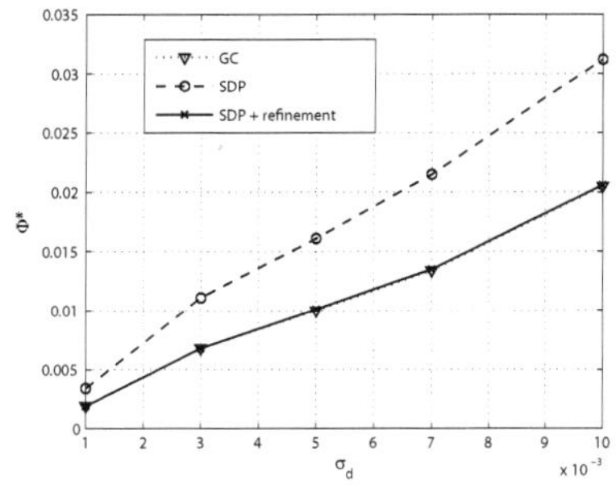

Fig. 11. Localization error of the configuration estimated with global continuation (dotted line with triangle), SDP (dashed line with circle) and SDP with gradient refinement (dotted line with cross).

Table 2. CPU time for global continuation (GC) approach, semidefinite programming and SDP with gradient refinement. Time is expressed in seconds.

σ_d	GC	SDP	SDP + GM
0.001	2.2942	20.1295	20.3490
0.003	2.3484	18.5254	18.9188
0.005	1.7184	16.5945	16.8349
0.007	1.7191	15.8923	16.1929
0.01	1.7360	15.8138	16.1093

has been addressed with some forms of distributed implementation of the SDP approach, see in (Biswas et al., 2006). Some discussion on distributed network localization is reported in the following section.

7. A Note on Distributed Range Localization

The techniques mentioned above are centralized since they require all the data needed for problem solution (i.e. distance measurements and anchor positions) to be available to a central units which perform network localization and then communicates to each node the estimated position. This may of course be highly undesirable due to intensive communication load over the central units and the agents. Moreover, since all the computation is performed by a single unit, for large networks the computational effort can be just too intensive. Also, the system is fragile, since failure in the central elaboration unit or in communication would compromise the functioning of the whole network. According to these considerations, *distributed* approaches are desirable for solving network localization. In a distributed setup each node communicates only with its *neighbors*, and performs local computations in order to obtain an estimate of its own position. As a consequence, the communication burden is equally spread among the network, the computation is decentralized and entrusted to each agent, improving both efficiency and robustness of the estimation process. Literature on decentralized network localization includes the application of distributed weighted-multidimensional scaling (Costa et al., 2006), and the use of barycentric coordinates for localizing the nodes under the hypothesis that non-anchor nodes lie in the convex hull of anchors (Khan et al., 2009). An extension of the SDP framework to distributed network localization can be found in (Biswas et al., 2006), whereas contributions in the anchor-free setup include (Xunxue et al., 2008). We conclude the chapter with a brief outline of a distributed extension of the gradient method presented in Section 4.1. We first notice that the gradient information which is needed by the node for an update step requires local-only information. Each node, in fact, can compute the local gradient as:

$$\nabla_i f(p) = \sum_{j \in \mathcal{N}_i} (p_i - p_j)^\top g_{ij}(p), \tag{25}$$

where $\nabla_i f(p)$ denote the i-th 1×2 block in the gradient $\nabla f(p)$ in (11) and $\mathcal{N}_i$ are the neighbors of the node i. It follows that the portion of gradient $\nabla_i f(p)$ can be computed individually by node i by simply querying the neighbors for their current estimated positions. For iterating the gradient method each node also needs the stepsize α_τ, which depends on some global information. The expression of the stepsize (5), however, is particularly suitable for decentralized computation, as we can notice by rewriting (5) in the following form:

$$\alpha_\tau = \frac{\sum_{i=1}^{n} \|p_i^{(\tau)} - p_i^{(\tau-1)}\|^2}{\sum_{i=1}^{n} (p_i^{(\tau)} - p_i^{(\tau-1)})^\top (\nabla_i f(p^{(\tau)}) - \nabla_i f(p^{(\tau-1)}))}, \tag{26}$$

It is easy to observe that each summand that composes the sum at the denominator and the numerator of α_τ is a local quantity available at node i. Hence a distributed averaging method, like the one proposed in (Xiao et al., 2006), allows each node to retrieve the quantities $\frac{1}{n}\sum_{i=1}^{n} \|p_i^{(\tau)} - p_i^{(\tau-1)}\|^2$ and $\frac{1}{n}\sum_{i=1}^{n} (p_i^{(\tau)} - p_i^{(\tau-1)})^\top (\nabla_i f(p^{(\tau)}) - \nabla_i f(p^{(\tau-1)}))$. By simply dividing these quantities each node can obtain the stepsize α_τ and can locally update its estimated position according to the distributed gradient rule:

$$p_i^{(\tau+1)} = p_i^{(\tau)} - \alpha_\tau \nabla_i f(p^{(\tau)}). \tag{27}$$

Similar considerations can be drawn about the Gauss-Newton approach. On the other hand it can be difficult to derive a distributed implementation of the global continuation and trust region approaches, limiting their effectiveness in solving the network localization problem.

8. Conclusion

In this chapter we review several centralized techniques for solving the network localization problem from range measurements. We first introduce the problem of information fusion aimed at the estimation of node position in a networked system, and we focus on the case in which nodes can take pairwise distance measurements. The problem setup is naturally modeled using graph formalism and network localization is expressed as an optimization problem. Suitable optimization methods are then applied for finding a minimum of the cost function which, under suitable conditions, corresponds to the actual network configuration. In the chapter we analyze five numerical techniques for solving the network localization problem under range-only measurements, namely a gradient method, an Gauss-Newton algorithm, a Trust-Region method, a Global Continuation approach and a technique based on semidefinite programming. The methods are described in details and compared, in terms of computational efficiency and convergence properties. Several tests and examples further define possible applications of the presented models, allowing the reader to approach the problem of position estimation in networked system paying attention to both theoretical and practical aspects. The

first three techniques (GM, GN and TR) are local in the sense that the optimization techniques are able to attain the global optimum of the objective function only when some initial guess on node configuration is available and this guess is sufficiently close to actual node positions. The convergence properties of these techniques are tested through extensive simulations. The gradient method can be implemented easily and requires only first order information. In this context we recall a simple and effective procedure for computing the stepsize, called Barzilai-Borwein stepsize. The Gauss-Newton approach, although being the fastest and most efficient method, is prone to convergence to local minima and it is therefore useful only when good a-priori knowledge of the node position is available. The trust-region method has better convergence properties with respect to the previous techniques, providing a good compromise between numerical efficiency and convergence. We also present two global approaches, a global continuation approach and a localization technique based on semidefinite programming (SDP). Global continuation, although computationally intensive, shows convergence to the global optimum regardless the initial guess on node configuration. Moreover it allows to compute accurate position estimates also in presence of noise. Finally the SDP approach is able to retrieve the exact node position in the case of noiseless distance measurements, by relaxing the original problem formulation. In the practical case of noisy measure, the approach tends to be inaccurate, and the localization error heavily depends on the number of anchor nodes and on their placement. In order to improve the localization accuracy we also discuss the possibility of adding a local refinement to the SDP estimate, evaluating this solution in terms of precision and computational effort.
We conclude the chapter by discussing how decentralized implementations of the network localization algorithms can be derived, and reviewing the state-of-the-art on distributed range-based position estimation.

9. References

Akyildiz, I., Su, W., Sankarasubramniam, Y. & Cayirci, E. (2002). A survey on sensor networks, *IEEE Communication Magazine* **40**(8): 102–114.

Barooah, P. & Hespanha, J. (2007). Estimation on graphs from relative measurements, *IEEE Control Systems Magazine* **27**(4): 57–74.

Barzilai, J. & Borwein, J. (1988). Two-point step size gradient methods, *IMA J. Numer. Anal.* **8**: 141–148.

Biswas, P., Lian, T., Wang, T. & Ye, Y. (2006). Semidefinite programming based algorithms for sensor network localization, *ACM Transactions on Sensor Networks (TOSN)* **2**(2): 220.

Biswas, P. & Ye, Y. (2004). Semidefinite programming for ad hoc wireless sensor network localization, *Proceedings of the Third International Symposium on Information Processing in Sensor Networks (IPSN)*, pp. 2673–2684.

Boyd, S., V. L. (2004). *Convex optimization*, Cambridge University Press.

Costa, J., Patwari, N. & Hero, A. (2006). Distributed weighted-multidimensional scaling for node localization in sensor networks, *ACM Transactions on Sensor Networks* **2**(1): 39–64.

Doherty, L., Pister, K. & El Ghaoui, L. (2001). Convex position estimation in wireless sensor networks, *IEEE INFOCOM*, Vol. 3, pp. 1655–1663.

Eren, T., Goldenberg, D., Whiteley, W., Yang, Y., Morse, A., Anderson, B. & Belhumeur, P. (2004). Rigidity, computation, and randomization in network localization, *IEEE INFOCOM*, Vol. 4, pp. 2673–2684.

Foy, W. (1976). Position-location solutions by Taylor-series estimation, *IEEE Transaction on Aerospace and Electronic Systems AES-12 (2)*, pp. 187–194.

Hendrickson, B. (1995). The molecule problem: Exploiting structure in global optimization, *SIAM Journal on Optimization* **5**(4): 835–857.

Howard, A., Mataric, M. & Sukhatme, G. (2001). Relaxation on a mesh: a formalism for generalized localization, *EEE/RSJ Int. Conf. on Intelligent Robots and Systems (IROS'01)*.

Kannan, A., Mao, G. & Vucetic, B. (2006). Simulated annealing based wireless sensor network localization, *Journal of Computers* **1**(2): 15–22.

Khan, U., Kar, S. & Moura, J. (2009). Distributed sensor localization in random environments using minimal number of anchor nodes, *IEEE Transactions on Signal Processing* **57**: 2000–2016.

Mao, G., Fidan, B. & Anderson, B. (2007). Wireless sensor network localization techniques, *Computer Networks* **51**(10): 2529–2553.

Martinez, S. & Bullo, F. (2006). Optimal sensor placement and motion coordination for target tracking, *Automatica* **42**(4): 661–668.

Moore, D., Leonard, J., Rus, D. & Teller, S. (2004). Robust distributed network localization with noisy range measurements, *Proceedings of the Second ACM Conference on Embedded Networked Sensor Systems (SenSys '04)*, pp. 50–61.

Moré, J. & Wu, Z. (1997). Global continuation for distance geometry problems, *SIAM Journal on Optimization* **7**(3): 814–836.

More, J.J., S. D. (1983). Computing a trust region step, *SIAM Journal on Scientific and Statistical Computing* **4**: 553–57.

Niculescu, D. & Nath, B. (2001). Ad hoc positioning system (aps), *in Proceedings of IEEE GLOBECOM '01*, pp. 2926–2931.

Nie, J. (2009). Sum of squares method for sensor network localization, *Computational Optimization and Applications* **43**(2): 151–179.

Nocedal, J. & Wright, S. (2006). *Numerical Optimization*, Springer.

Priyantha, N., Balakrishnan, H., Demaine, E. & Teller, S. (2003). Anchor-free distributed localization in sensor networks, *Proceedings of the 1st international conference on Embedded networked sensor systems*, pp. 340–341.

Savarese, C., Rabaey, J. & Langendoen, K. (2002). Robust positioning algorithms for distributed ad-hoc wireless sensor networks, *USENIX Annual Technical Conference*, pp. 317–327.

Saxe, J. (1979). Embeddability of weighted graphs in k-space is strongly NP-hard, *Proceedings of the 17th Allerton Conference in Communications, Control and Computing*, pp. 480–489.

Siciliano, B. & Khatib, O. (2008). *Springer Handbook of Robotics*, Springer-Verlag.

So, A. & Ye, Y. (2007). Theory of semidefinite programming for sensor network localization, *Mathematical Programming* **109**(2): 367–384.

Stanfield, R. (1947). Statistical theory of DF finding, *Journal of IEE* **94**(5): 762–770.

Tseng, P. (2007). Second-order cone programming relaxation of sensor network localization, *SIAM Journal on Optimization* **18**(1): 156–185.

Xiao, L., Boyd, S. & Lall, S. (2006). Distributed average consensus with time-varying Metropolis weights, *Unpublished manuscript* . `http://www.stanford.edu/~boyd/papers/avg_metropolis.html`.

Xunxue, C., Zhiguan, S. & Jianjun, L. (2008). Distributed localization for anchor-free sensor networks, *Journal of Systems Engineering and Electronics* **19**(3): 405–418.

M2SIR: A Multi Modal Sequential Importance Resampling Algorithm for Particle Filters

Thierry Chateau and Yann Goyat
University of Clermont-Ferrand (Lasmea) and LCPC
France

1. Introduction

Multi-sensor based state estimation is still challenging because sensors deliver correct measures only for nominal conditions (for example the observation of a camera can be identified for a bright and non smoggy day and illumination conditions may change during the tracking process). It results that the fusion process must handle with different probability density functions (pdf) provided by several sensors. This fusion step is a key operation into the estimation process and several operators (addition, multiplication, mean, median,...) can be used, which advantages and drawbacks.

In a general framework, the state is given by a hidden variable $\mathbf{X}$ that define "what we are looking for" and that generates the observation, provided by several sensors. Figure 1 is an illustration of this general framework. Let $\mathbf{Z}$ be a random vector that denotes the observations (provided by several sensors). State estimation methods can be divided in two main categories. The first family is based on optimisation theory and the state estimation problem is reformulated as the optimisation of an error criteria into the observation space. The second family proposes a probabilistic framework in which the distribution of the state given the observation has to be estimated ($p(\mathbf{X}|\mathbf{Z})$). Bayes rule is widely used to do that:

$$p(\mathbf{X}|\mathbf{Z}) = \frac{p(\mathbf{Z}|\mathbf{X})p(\mathbf{X})}{p(\mathbf{Z})} \quad (1)$$

When the state is composed by a random continuous variable, the associated distribution are represented by two principal methods: the first one, consists in the définition of an analytic representation of the distribution by a parametric function. A popular solution is given by Gaussian or mixture of Gaussian models. The main drawback of this approach is that it assumes that the general shape of the distribution if known (for example a Gaussian representing an unimodal shape). The second category of methods consists in approximate the distribution by samples, generated in a stochastic way from Monte-Carlo techniques. The resulting model is able to handle with non linear model and unknown distributions.

This chapter presents the probabilistic framework of state estimation from several sensors and more specifically, stochastic approaches that approximate the state distribution as a set of samples. Finally, several simple fusion operators are presented and compared with an original algorithm called *M2SIR*, on both synthetic and real data.

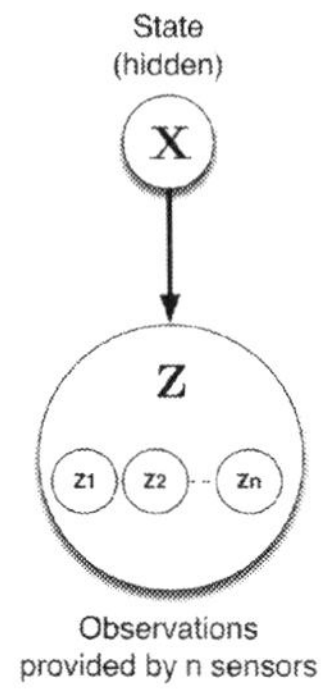

Fig. 1. State estimation synoptic: multi sensors observations are generated by the hidden state to be estimated.

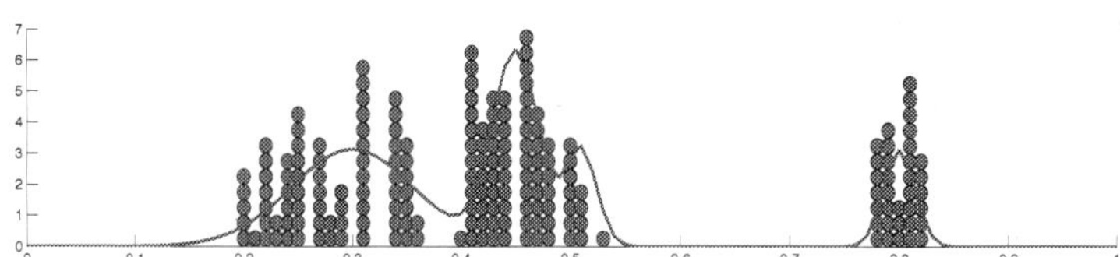

Fig. 2. Probability distribution approximation of the blue curve with unweighted samples (red balls). (best viewed in color)

2. Monte-Carlo Algorithm for Probability Distribution Function Approximation

This sections presents current methods used in state estimation to approximate probability distributions using Monte-Carlo algorithms.

2.1 Sampling Distributions

Two main approaches can be used to approximate a distribution. The first one is based on a parametric model of the law and the resulting challenge is how to estimated the model parameters, from measures. The main drawback of this method is that a parametric form has to be chosen for the law (for example a gaussian model). The second approach is based on an approximation of the law with a set of samples, using Monte-Carlo methods. The model developed hereafter is based on this approach. Figure 2, shows the approximation of a probability function from state $\mathbf{X}$ with N unweighted samples:

$$p(\mathbf{X}) \approx \frac{1}{N} \sum_{n=1}^{N} \delta(\mathbf{X} - \mathbf{X}^n), \text{ is equivalent to } p(\mathbf{X}) \approx \{\mathbf{X}^n\}_{n=1}^{N} \tag{2}$$

with δ the Kronecker function. Figure 3 shows that the same distribution may be also approximate by a sum of N samples with associated weights π^n, $n \in 1...N$, such as $\sum_{n=1}^{N} \pi^n = 1$:

$$p(\mathbf{X}) \approx \sum_{n=1}^{N} \pi^n \delta(\mathbf{X} - \mathbf{X}^n), \text{ is equivalent to } p(\mathbf{X}) \approx \{\mathbf{X}^n, \pi^n\}_{n=1}^{N} \tag{3}$$

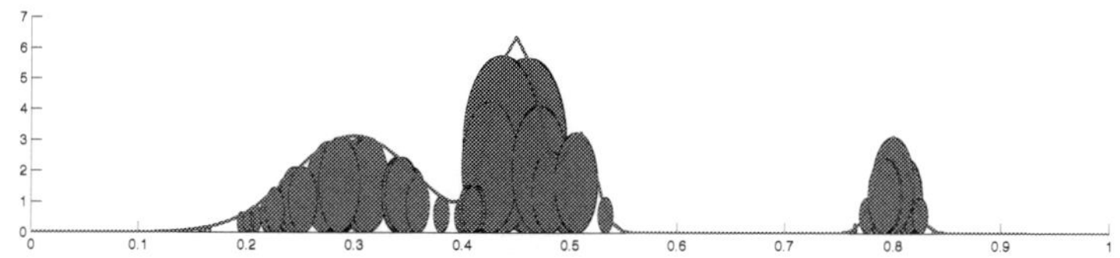

Fig. 3. Probability distribution approximation of the blue curve with weighted samples (red ellipsoids, from which the area is proportional to the weight). (best viewed in color)

2.2 Dynamic Law Sampling: Particle Filters

Filtering is a general research topic that consists in estimating the dynamic configuration (state) of a process from a sequence of observation. The state is a random vector, indexed by a discrete time, from which the associated probability distribution has to be estimated.
Let $\mathbf{X}_t$, be the state of the process to be tracked at time t. We define $\mathcal{X} \doteq \{\mathbf{X}_t\}_{t=1,...,T}$ as the state sequence for a temporal analysis windows. In a same way, let $\mathbf{Z}_t$ be the observation at time t and $\mathcal{Z} \doteq \{\mathbf{z}_t\}_{t=1,...,T}$ the observation sequence for a temporal analysis window. The system state $\mathbf{X}_t$ provides an observation $\mathbf{Z}_t$. By definition, the state sequence to be estimated is composed by hidden variables that are linked with the observation sequence by an observation function. Considering a probabilistic framework in which both state and observation are random variables, a solution of the tracking problem is given by the estimation of the posterior distribution $P(\mathbf{X}_t|\mathbf{Z}_t)$, from the prior distribution $P(\mathbf{X}_{t-1|}\mathbf{Z}_{t-1})$, the transition distribution $P(\mathbf{X}_{t|}\mathbf{X}_{t-1})$ and the likelihood function $P(\mathbf{X}_{t|}\mathbf{Z}_t)$.

2.2.1 Probabilistic Sequential Tracking

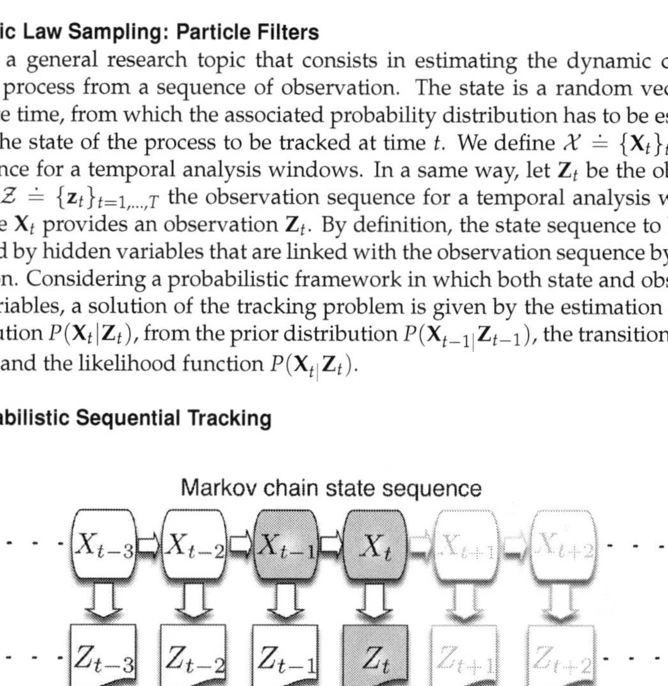

Fig. 4. Online tracking. The current state depends only on the current observation and the previous state.

Temporal filtering of a state sequence can be formalised with a first order Markov process (the current state depends only on the current observation and the previous state) as illustrated on fig. 4). In this recursive Markov process framework, sequential probabilistic tracking, the estimation of the posterior state distribution $p(\mathbf{X}_t|\mathbf{Z}_{1:t})$ at time t, is made according to the previous sequence of observation $\mathbf{Z}_{1:t}$. The Bayes rule is used update the current state:

$$p(\mathbf{X}_t|\mathbf{Z}_{1:t}) = \frac{p(\mathbf{Z}_t|\mathbf{X}_t)p(\mathbf{X}_t|\mathbf{Z}_{1:t-1})}{p(\mathbf{Z}_t|\mathbf{Z}_{1:t-1})}, \tag{4}$$

where the prior $p(\mathbf{X}_t|\mathbf{Z}_{1:t-1})$ is given by Chapman-Kolmogorov equation:

$$p(\mathbf{X}_t|\mathbf{Z}_{1:t-1}) = \int_{\mathbf{X}_{t-1}} p(\mathbf{X}_t|\mathbf{X}_{t-1})p(\mathbf{X}_{t-1}|\mathbf{Z}_{1:t-1})d\mathbf{X}_{t-1}. \tag{5}$$

In equation (5), $p(\mathbf{X}_t|\mathbf{X}_{t-1})$ is the temporal transition law, that gives prediction for time t, and $p(\mathbf{X}_{t-1}|\mathbf{Z}_{1:t-1})$ is a the posterior at time $t-1$. When equation (5) is substituted into equation (4), the following general expression of the sequential Bayesian filter is obtained:

$$p(\mathbf{X}_t|\mathbf{Z}_{1:t}) = C^{-1}p(\mathbf{Z}_t|\mathbf{X}_t)\int_{\mathbf{X}_{t-1}} p(\mathbf{X}_t|\mathbf{X}_{t-1})p(\mathbf{X}_{t-1}|\mathbf{Z}_{1:t-1})d\mathbf{X}_{t-1}, \tag{6}$$

where $C = p(\mathbf{Z}_t|\mathbf{Z}_{1:t-1})$ is a normalisation term.
This equation (6) defines the probability law for a dynamic state system, at current time t, from the dynamic state law at previous time and the current observation. However, in practice the resolution of this equation in the general case, is untrackable. A solution can be proposed using an approximation of the law to be estimated with samples generated by stochastic methods like Monte-Carlo algorithms. Particle filters is a popular and widely used algorithm that provides an efficient solution.

2.2.2 Particle Filters

Particle filters can be produced by several algorithms. The most popular is based in the algorithm *SIR* (Sequential Importance Resampling) M. Isard & A. Blake (1998): independent particles are generated from the previous posterior distribution (approximated by a set of particles) and evaluated in a parallel way in order to generate a set of particles at time t. The advantage of this algorithm is that it can be easily distributed on a parallel architechture. A second family of algorithm uses a sequential exploration with a Markov Chain Monte-Carlo *MCMC* MacKay (2003)Khan et al. (2004), in order to generate a Markov chain of particles, transition between two particles is related to the observation function. The advantage of MCMC particle filters is that several exploration strategies can be defined, and more specially marginalised strategies. This chapter focus on *SIR* based particle filters

2.3 *SIR* Based Particle Filters

Particle filters are based on an exploration strategy of the state space, driven by the previous state distribution and the transition distribution. *SIR* (*Sequential Importance Resampling*) algorithm uses an Importance Sampling step to efficiently generate samples.
We assume that an approximation of the $t-1$ posterior probability distribution $p(\mathbf{X}_{t-1}|\mathbf{Z}_{1:t-1})$, is given by N weighted samples $\{\mathbf{X}_{t-1}^n, \pi_{t-1}^n\}_{n=1}^N$:

$$p(\mathbf{X}_{t-1}|\mathbf{Z}_{1:t-1}) \approx \sum_{n=1}^{N} \pi_{t-1}^n \delta(\mathbf{X}_{t-1} - \mathbf{X}_{t-1}^n), \tag{7}$$

where π_{t-1}^n is the weight associated to the nth sample, $n \in 1...N$, such as $\sum_{n=1}^N \pi_{t-1}^n = 1$. A discrete approximation of the Chapman Kolmogorov equation (5) is given by:

$$p(\mathbf{X}_t|\mathbf{Z}_{1:t-1}) \approx \sum_{n=1}^{N} \pi_{t-1}^n p(\mathbf{X}_t|\mathbf{X}_{t-1}^n), \tag{8}$$

where $p(\mathbf{X}_t|\mathbf{X}_{t-1})$ is the transition distribution of the system. The law, defined by equation (8) is a mixture of N components $p(\mathbf{X}_t|\mathbf{X}^n_{t-1})$, weighted with π^n_{t-1}. A discrete form of the recursive Bayesian filter (6) is approximated by:

$$p(\mathbf{X}_t|\mathbf{Z}_{1:t}) \approx C^{-1}p(\mathbf{Z}_t|\mathbf{X}_t)\sum_{n=1}^{N}\pi^n_{t-1}p(\mathbf{X}_t|\mathbf{X}^n_{t-1}). \tag{9}$$

Since no analytical expression of the likelihood $p(\mathbf{Z}_t|\mathbf{X}_t)$, is available, a sampling strategy is also proposed. An importance sampling algorithm is applied to generate a new set of particles from the previous set $\{\mathbf{X}^n_{t-1}, \pi^n_{t-1}\}^N_{n=1}$, using the prediction distribution for each sample. The result is a set of N samples $\mathbf{X}^n_t$ generated by :

$$\mathbf{X}^n_t \sim q(\mathbf{X}_t) = \sum_{n=1}^{N}\pi^n_{t-1}p(\mathbf{X}_t|\mathbf{X}^n_{t-1}) \tag{10}$$

For each sample $\mathbf{X}^n_t$ the likelihhod is estimated with: $\pi^n_t = P(\mathbf{Z}_t|\mathbf{X}^n_t)$. The filter provides a set of N weighted samples $\{\mathbf{X}^n_t, \pi^n_t\}^N_{n=1}$, which is an approximation $p(\mathbf{X}_t|\mathbf{Z}_{1:t})$of the posterior at time t. Figure 5 illustrates the *SIR* algorithm for a simple state of dimension one. The algorithm is divided in three steps:

- (a) Importance sampling: draw particles according to their weight from the set of particles at time $t-1$. This process duplicates particles with a strong weight and removes particles with a light weight. The resulting set of particle approximates the same distribution than the weighted set from which they are drawn.
- (b) Prediction step: move each particle according to a proposal function $p(\mathbf{X}^*|\mathbf{X})$. When no information on the evolution process is available, a random step strategy can be used $p(\mathbf{X}^*|\mathbf{X}) = \mathcal{N}(0, \sigma)$.
- (c) Estimation step: the weight of each particle is computed according to the likelihood function of the observation $\mathbf{Z}_t$, given a sample $\mathbf{X}^n_t : \pi^n_t = P(\mathbf{Z}_t|\mathbf{X}^n_t)$

Diffusion of particles from $t-1$ to t provides filtering properties to the algorithm *SIR*. The particles are attracted toward high probability areas of the state space, from their previous position. The main drawback of this algorithm is that it requires a number of particles which grows in an exponential way related to the size of the state vectorIsard & MacCormick (2001); Smith & Gatica-Perez (2004). For high dimensional problems, MCMC methods with marginalized sampling strategies are preferred (see MacKay (2003) for further information).

2.4 Data Fusion for *SIR* Particle Filters

Classical data fusion algorithms are based on data association Bar-Shalom & Fortmann (1988); Gorji et al. (2007); Karlsson & Gustafsson (2001); Oh et al. (2004); Read (1979); Sarkka et al. (2004); Vermaak et al. (2005). Particle filtering in a visual tracking context has been introduced in M. Isard & A. Blake (1998). Then, extention to tracking with data fusion has been developed in P. Pérez & A. Blake (2004) (a wide bibliography is proposed) in an audiovisual context: different cues are modeled by data likelihood function and intermittent cues are handled. Particle filtering is now very popular for data fusion within a tracking context. Klein J. Klein et al. (2008) propose to introduce belief functions and different combination rules to access particles weight for road obstacle tracking. In D. Marimon et al. (2007), the fusion process allows the selection of available cue. In a multiple cameras tracking context, Wang Y.D. Wang & A.

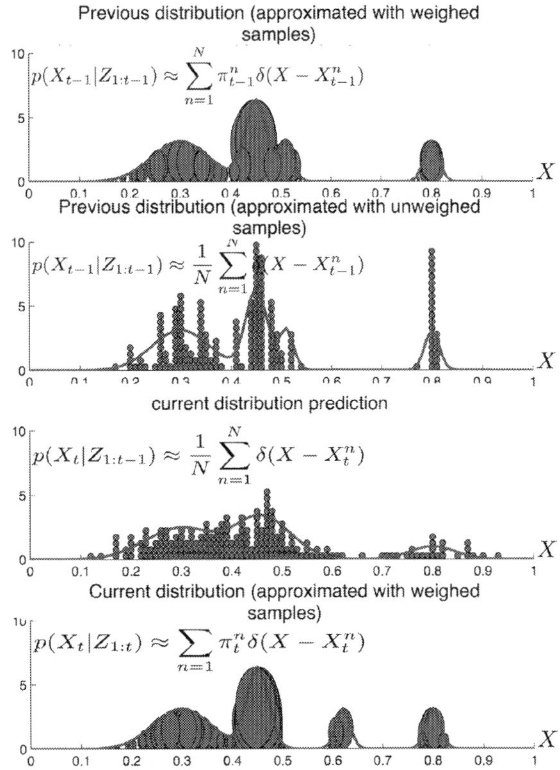

Fig. 5. Illustration of the diffusion of a set of particles with the *SIR* algorithm, with a proposal function $\mathcal{N}(0, \sigma = 0.06)$. (0) : posterior distribution at $t-1$ (blue curve) and it approximation with weighted particles (red ellipsoids with an area proportional to the weight). (a) : the same posterior distribution at $t-1$ (blue curve) and its approximation with unweighted particles, after the importance resampling algorithm. (b) : posterior distribution at t (blue curve) and it approximation with unweighted particles, generated using the proposal function $\mathcal{N}(0, \sigma = 0.06)$. (c) :probability distribution at t (blue curve) and it approximation by weighted particles according to the likelihhod function at time t.

Kassim (2007) propose to adapt the importance sampling method to the data quality. For a similar application, Du W. Du et al. (2007) propose to combine an independent transition ker-

Algorithm 1 (*SIR*) particle filter

Input:
- a set of particles and associated weights that approximates the state posterior distribution X at time $t-1$ **:** $\{X_{t-1}^n, \pi_{t-1}^n\}_{n=1}^N$
- the proposal law $p(X_t|X_{t-1})$
- the observation Z_t **at time** t.
1. importance sampling :
for $n = 1$ to N **do**
(a) sampling: draw a particle $X_{t-1}^i, i \in \{1, ..., N\}$, according to the weight π_{t-1}^i
(b) prediction: draw a proposal X_t^n according to $p(\mathbf{X_t}|\mathbf{X_{t-1}})$
(c) associate to X_t^n the weight $\mathbf{ß_t^n} = P(Z_t|X_t^n)$, likelihood of the observation Z_t given the state X_t^n.
end for
2. weight normalisation step: $\pi_t^n = \frac{\pi_t^n}{\sum \pi_t^n}$
output: a set of particles that approximates the posterior distribution at time t **:** $\{X_t^n, \pi_t^n\}_{n=1}^N$

nel with a booster function to get a mixture function. We propose a new importance sampling algorithm allowing to handle with several sources.

3. M2SIR Algorithm

When the observation is provided by several sources, the likelihood associated to each particle results to the fusion of several weights. This fusion is then a challenging operation because several operators can be used, with advantages and drawbacks. We are proposing to merge observations intrinsically during the re-sampling step of the particle filter .The resulting algorithm (see Algorithm 2) is a variant of the CONDENSATION algorithm M. Isard & A. Blake (1998). The difference between this algorithm and CONDENSATION is that the weight associated to each particle is a weight vector (composed of weights generated from observations of each source) and that the sampling step is provided by the M2SIR algorithm developed in the following section.

Algorithm 2 M2SIR particle filter

Init : particles $\{(\mathbf{X}_0^{\prime n}, \mathbf{1}/N)\}_{n=1}^N$ according to the initial distribution $\mathbf{X}_0$
for $t = 1, ..., T_{end}$ **do**
Prediction : generation of $\{(\mathbf{X}_t^n, \mathbf{1}/N)\}_{n=1}^N$ from $p(\mathbf{X}_t|\mathbf{X}_{t-1} = \mathbf{X}_{t-1}^{\prime n})$
Observation : estimation of the weight vector according to the various sources $\{(\mathbf{X}_t^n, \mathbf{ß}_t^n)\}_{n=1}^N$ with $\mathbf{ß}_t^n \propto \mathbf{p}(\mathbf{Z}_t|\mathbf{X}_t = \mathbf{X}_t^n)$
Sampling : build $\{(\mathbf{X}_{t-1}^{\prime n}, \mathbf{1}/N)\}_{n=1}^N$ from $\{(\mathbf{X}_0^n, \boldsymbol{\pi}_0^n)\}_{n=1}^N$ using M2SIR)
Estimation : $\hat{\mathbf{X}}_t \doteq \frac{1}{N}\sum_{n=1}^N \mathbf{X}_t^n$
end for
Output : The set of estimated states during the video sequence $\{\hat{\mathbf{X}}_t\}_{t=1,...,T_{end}}$

We consider the estimation of the posterior $p(\mathbf{X}_t|\mathbf{Z}_{0:t})$ at time t, by a set of N particles $\{(\mathbf{X}_t^n, \boldsymbol{\pi}_t^n)\}_{n=1}^N$ with N associated weight vector $\boldsymbol{\pi}_t^n$. The weight vector, of size M given by the number of observations (sources), is composed by the weights related to the sources. For readability, we omit the temporal index t in the following equations. The aim of the proposed multi modal sequential importance resampling algorithm (M2SIR) is to generate a new particle with a three step approach, illustrated in Fig. 6 in the case of three sources

1. M samples (one for each source) are drawn using an Importance Sampling strategy. The resulting output of the step is a set of M candidate samples and their associated weight vector: $\{\mathbf{X}^{(i)}, \boldsymbol{\pi}^{(i)}\}_{i=1,...,M}$
2. A likelihood ratio vector $\mathbf{r}$ of size M is then built from likelihood ratios estimated for each candidate sample. (see below for more details).
3. The selected candidate sample is finally given by an importance sampling strategy operated on a normalized likelihood ratio vector.

The M likelihood ratios used in step two, called r_i ($i = 1, .., M$) are computed by:

$$r_i \doteq \prod_{j=1}^{M} \prod_{k=1}^{M} \left(\frac{\pi_j^i}{\pi_j^k} \right) \tag{11}$$

where π_j^i denotes the weight associated to particle i, from the sensor j Equation 11 can be written in a simplest way using log ratio:

$$lr_i = \sum_{j=1}^{M} \sum_{k=1}^{M} \left[\log(\pi_j^i) - \log(\pi_j^k) \right] \tag{12}$$

where lr_i denotes the log of r_i. Finally, lr_i is given by:

$$lr_i = M \sum_{j=1}^{M} \left[\log(\pi_j^i) - \frac{1}{M} \sum_{k=1}^{M} \log(\pi_j^k) \right] \tag{13}$$

If $\mathbf{l}r \doteq (lr_1, ..., Lr_M)^T$ denotes the vector composed by the log ratios lr_i and $\boldsymbol{\pi}^k \doteq (\log \pi_1^k, ..., \log \pi_M^k)^T$ denotes the vector composed by the log of π_j^k, $\mathbf{l}r$ can be written:

$$\mathbf{l}r \doteq M \begin{pmatrix} \mathbf{1}_{(1\times M)} \left(\mathbf{l}\text{ß}^{1} - \frac{1}{M} \Sigma_{k=1}^{M} \mathbf{l}\text{ß}^{\mathbf{k}} \right) \\ \mathbf{1}_{(1\times M)} \left(\mathbf{l}\text{ß}^{2} - \frac{1}{M} \Sigma_{k=1}^{M} \mathbf{l}\text{ß}^{\mathbf{k}} \right) \\ \cdots \\ \mathbf{1}_{(1\times M)} \left(\mathbf{l}\boldsymbol{\pi}^{M} - \frac{1}{M} \Sigma_{k=1}^{M} \mathbf{l}\boldsymbol{\pi}^{k} \right) \end{pmatrix} \tag{14}$$

with $\mathbf{1}_{(1\times M)}$ a matrix of size one line and M columns filled by ones. if $\mathbf{C}_\pi \doteq \frac{1}{M} \Sigma_{k=1}^{M} \mathbf{l}\boldsymbol{\pi}^k$, $\mathbf{l}r$ can be written:

$$\mathbf{l}r = M \begin{pmatrix} \mathbf{1}_{(1\times M)} \left(\mathbf{l}_{\boldsymbol{\pi}^1} - \mathbf{C}_\pi \right) \\ \mathbf{1}_{(1\times M)} \left(\mathbf{l}_{\boldsymbol{\pi}^2} - \mathbf{C}_\pi \right) \\ \cdots \\ \mathbf{1}_{(1\times M)} \left(\mathbf{l}_{\boldsymbol{\pi}^M} - \mathbf{C}_\pi \right) \end{pmatrix} \tag{15}$$

$\mathbf{l}r$ represents an unnormalized log. weight vector and the final normalized weight vector is given by:

$$\mathbf{c} \doteq C_c.\exp(\mathbf{l}r) \quad (16)$$

$$C_c \doteq \mathbf{1}_{(1\times M)}\mathbf{l}r \quad (17)$$

$\mathbf{r}$ is then used in step three to select a sample for the M candidates with a importance sampling strategy.

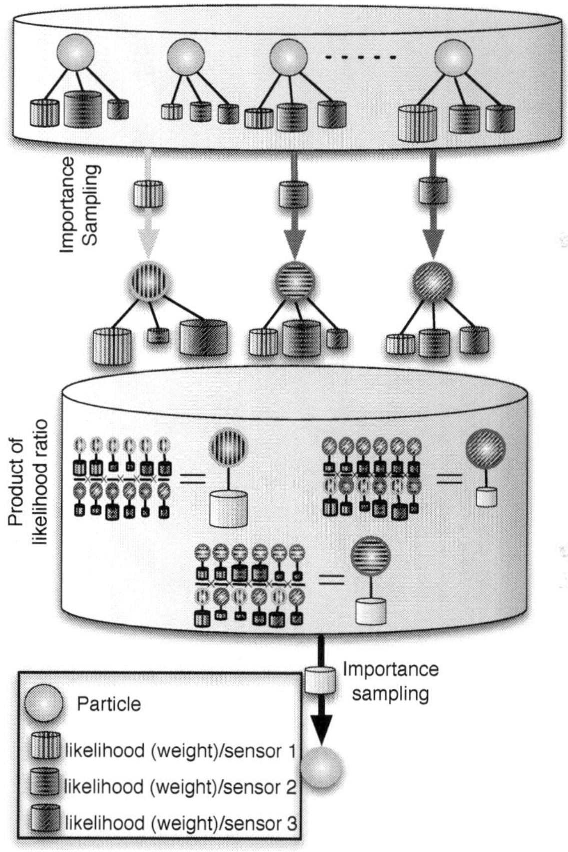

Fig. 6. synoptic of the M2SIR algorithm in the case of three sources: 1)Three particles are drawn using importance sampling (one for each sensor weight distribution). 2) Likelihood ratio are then computed for the three particles. 3) The final particle is drawn with importance sampling from the three ratios.

Algorithm 3 M2SIR Multi Modal Sampling

Input : Particle set and associated weight vector $\{\mathbf{X}^{(i)}, \boldsymbol{\pi}^{i}\}_{i=1,...,N}$, M sources
for $n = 1$ to N **do**
- Choose M candidate particles on the basis of $\{\mathbf{X}^{(i)}, \boldsymbol{\pi}^{(i)}\}_{i=1,...,N}$ and build $\{\mathbf{X}^{*(j)}, \boldsymbol{\pi}^{*(j)}\}_{j=1,...,M}$ where $\mathbf{X}^{*(j)}$ is derived from an *importance sampling* drawn on source j weights;
- Calculate vector $\mathbf{l}_r$ based on Equation 15, and then calculate confidence vector $\mathbf{c} \doteq C_c.\exp(\mathbf{l}_r)$
- Select the designated particle $\mathbf{X}^{e(n)}$ from among the candidate particles by proceeding with an *importance sampling* drawing.

end for
Output : Particle set $\{\mathbf{X}^{e(i)}\}_{i=1,...,N}$ composed of the selected particles.

4. Experiments on Synthetic Data

To validate the method, experiments have been achieved on synthetic data. In this section, we show the behavior of the sampling process for several toy examples.The aim of this experiment is to compare three fusion strategies for importance sampling:

1. Importance sampling using a sum operator, called SSIR. For each particle, a global weight is computed by the sum of the weight provided by each sensor :

$$\pi^i = \sum_{j=1}^{M} \pi_j^i \tag{18}$$

2. Importance sampling using a product operator, called PSIR. For each particle, a global weight is computed by the product of the weight provided by each sensor :

$$\pi^i = \prod_{j=1}^{M} \pi_j^i \tag{19}$$

3. Importance sampling using the M2SIR algorithm presented in the previous section.

Two synthetic set of 3 input distributions have been generated:

1. The first sequence illustrates two dissonant sensors (cf. figure 7)). Sensors two and three provide two different Gaussian distributions while sensor one is blind (it distribution follows a uniform random law).
2. The second sequence is an example of two sensors providing the same information (cf. figure8)). Distributions of sensors two and three follow the same Gaussian law while sensor one is blind.

Figure 7 shows, for the first sequence, the resulting distributions computed by SSIR, PSIR and M2SIR algorithms. In this example, both the SSIR and M2SIR methods give a resulting pdf reporting the two modes present in the original distributions of sensors two and three. The PSIR method provides a third ghost mode between modes of sensors 2 and 3. The second example (cf. fig 8) shows that the SSIR method generates a noisy distribution, resulting to the blind sensor. PSIR and M2SIR gives close distributions, decreasing the variance of sensors 2 and 3.

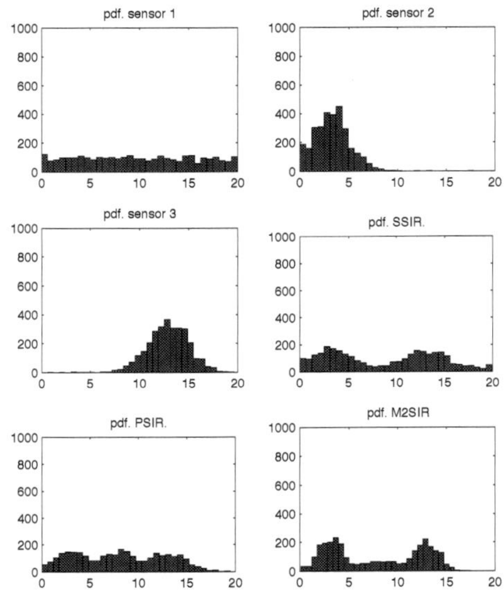

Fig. 7. Illustration of multi-source sampling algorithm for a three sensor fusion step. The distribution provided from sensor one is blind (follows a uniform law) while the distribution provided by sensors two and three are dissonant (the maximum of the two distribution is different).

5. Application to Visual Tracking of Vehicles From a Camera and a Laser Sensor

The M2SIR algorithm has been used in a vehicle tracking application using a sensor composed by a camera and a laser range finder. The objective of this system is to accurately estimate the trajectory of a vehicle travelling through a curve. The sensor, installed in a curve, is composed of three cameras placed on a tower approximately five meters high to cover the beginning, middle, and end of the curve, in addition to a laser range finder laid out parallel to the ground. Since the cameras offer only limited coverage, their observations do not overlap and we will be considering in the following discussion that the system can be divided into three subsystems, each composed of a camera-rangefinder pair, with a recalibration between each pair performed by means of rigid transformations. The object tracking procedure is intended to estimate the state of an object at each moment within a given scene, based on a scene observation sequence. Figure 9 shows the synoptic of the tracking process. A particle filter is used with three associated models:

- The state model is composed by the location of the vehicle (position and orientation given into a global reference frame), the velocity and the steering angle.

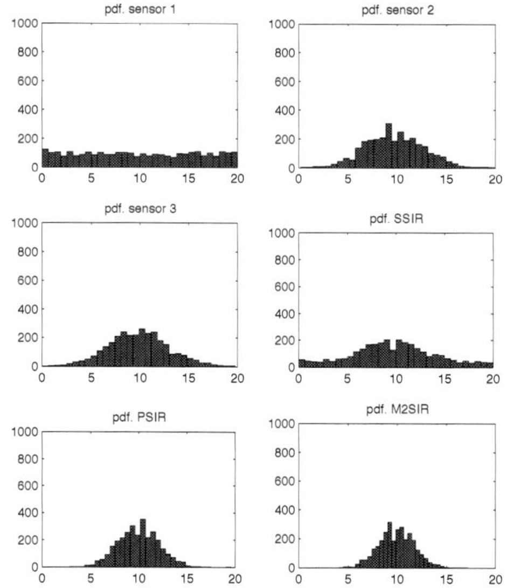

Fig. 8. Illustration of multi-source sampling algorithm for a three sensor fusion step. Distribution provided from sensor one is blind (follows a uniform law) while distribution provided by sensors two and three are the same (Gaussian law).

- The likelihood model (or observation function) is divided in two parts. The first observation is provided by a foreground/background algorithm developed in Goyat et al. (2006). The second observation is achieved by a laser sensor.
- The prediction model assume that the state prediction can be driven by a bicycle model.

Details of this application can be find here Goyat et al. (2009).

5.1 Experiments

Experiments have been achieved in order to compare several fusion algorithms on real data. In order to estimate the precision of the algorithms, ground truth has been acquired using a RTKGPS[1]. A set of twenty sequences at different velocities and under different illumination conditions has been acquired with the associated RTKGPS trajectories. A calibration step gives the homography between the image plane and and GPS ground plane such as an average error can be computed in centimeters into the GPS reference frame. Table 1 shows the estimated precision provided by each sensor without fusion and by the three fusion strategies: PSIR, SSIR and M2SIR. The fusion strategy increases the accuracy of the estimation. Moreover results provided by the M2SIR are slighty better than SSIR and PSIR. An other set of twenty sequences has been acquired with a unplugged sensor with provides constant measures. Table

[1] Real Time Kinematics GPS with a precision up to 1cm

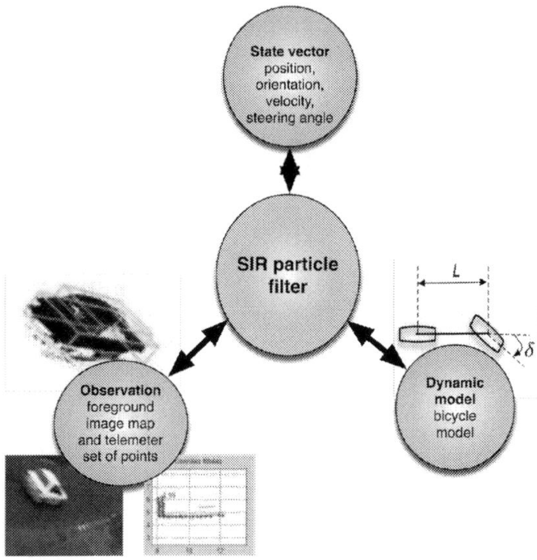

Fig. 9. Synoptic of the fusion based tracking application. A particle filter (SIR) is proposed with a five dimensional state vector, a bicycle evolution model and observations provided by a camera and a laser scanner.

2 shows the estimated precision provided by three fusion strategies. The SSIR fusion strategy provides a poor precision comparing to PSIR and M2SIR.

	Vision only	Laser only	SSIR	PSIR	M2SIR
mean/cm	0.20	0.55	0.16	0.16	0.15
std.	0.16	0.50	0.10	0.11	0.10

Table 1. Trajectories error for three fusion strategies.

	SSIR	PSIR	M2SIR
mean/cm	0.22	0.12	0.12
std.	0.12	0.07	0.07

Table 2. Trajectories error for three fusion strategies (one sensor has been unplugged to provide wrong data (constant).

6. Conclusion

Particle filters are widely used algorithms to approximate, in a sequential way, probability distributions of dynamic systems. However, when observations are provided by several sensors, a data fusion step is necessary to update the system. We have presented several fusion operators and compare them on both synthetic and real data. The M2SIR algorithm is a multi

Fig. 10. Illustration of the observations provided by the two sensors. The reference frame is defined by a GPS antenna on the top of the vehicle. The estimated position is represented by a virtual GPS antenna associated to each sensor (green dash for vision and red dash for laser). The green cube represents the projection of the 3D vehicle model for the estimated state (vision). Red dashes are the projection of laser measures into the image.

modal sequential importance resampling algorithm. This method, based on likelihood ratios, can be used easily within a particle filter algorithm. Experiments show that the method deals efficiently with both blind and dissonant sensors.
Fusion operators have been used for a vehicle tracking application, and experiments have shown that the sensor fusion increases the precision of the estimation.

7. References

Bar-Shalom, Y. & Fortmann, T. (1988). *Alignement and Data Association*, New-York: Academic.

D. Marimon, Y. Maret, Y. Abdeljaoued & T. Ebrahimi (2007). Particle filter-based camera tracker fusing marker and feature point cues, *IS&T/SPIE Conf. on visual Communications and image Processing*, Vol. 6508, pp. 1–9.

Gorji, A., Shiry, S. & Menhaj, B. (2007). Multiple Target Tracking For Mobile Robots using the JPDAF Algorithm, *IEEE International Conference on Tools with Artificial Intelligence (ICTAI)*, Greece.

Goyat, Y., Chateau, T., Malaterre, L. & Trassoudaine, L. (2006). Vehicle trajectories evaluation by static video sensors, *9th International IEEE Conference on Intelligent Transportation Systems Conference (ITSC 2006)*, Toronto, Canada.

Goyat, Y., Chateau, T. & Trassoudaine, L. (2009). Tracking of vehicle trajectory by combining a camera and a laser rangefinder, *Springer MVA : Machine Vision and Application* **online**.

Isard, M. & MacCormick, J. (2001). Bramble: A bayesian multiple-blob tracker, *Proc. Int. Conf. Computer Vision, vol. 2 34-41*, Vancouver, Canada.

J. Klein, C. Lecomte & P. Miche (2008). Preceding car tracking using belief functions and a particle filter, *ICPR08*, pp. 1–4.

Karlsson, R. & Gustafsson, F. (2001). Monte carlo data association for multiple target tracking, *In IEEE Target tracking: Algorithms and applications*.

Khan, Z., Balch, T. & Dellaert, F. (2004). An MCMC-based particle filter for tracking multiple interacting targets, *European Conference on Computer Vision (ECCV)*, Prague, Czech Republic, pp. 279–290.

M. Isard & A. Blake (1998). Condensation – conditional density propagation for visual tracking, *IJCV : International Journal of Computer Vision* **29**(1): 5–28.

MacKay, D. (2003). *Information Theory, Inference and Learning Algorithms.*, Cambridge University Press.

Oh, S., Russell, S. & Sastry, S. (2004). Markov chain monte carlo data association for multiple-target tracking, *IEEE Conference on Decision and Control*, Island.

P. Pérez, J. & A. Blake (2004). Data fusion for visual tracking with particles, *Proceedings of the IEEE* **92**(2): 495–513.

Read, D. (1979). An algorithm for tracking multiple targets, *IEEE Transactions on Automation and Control* **24**: 84–90.

Sarkka, S., Vehtari, A. & Lampinen, J. (2004). Rao-blackwellized particle filter for multiple target tracking, *7th International Conference on Information Fusion*, Italy.

Smith, K. & Gatica-Perez, D. (2004). Order matters: A distributed sampling method for multi-object tracking, *British Machine Vision Conference (BMVC)*, London, UK.

Vermaak, J., Godsill, J. & Pérez, P. (2005). Monte carlo filtering for multi-target tracking and data association, *IEEE Transactions on Aerospace and Electronic Systems* **41**: 309–332.

W. Du, Y. Maret & J. Piater (2007). Multi-camera people tracking by collaborative particle filters and principal axis-based integration, *ACCV*, pp. 365–374.

Y.D. Wang, J. & A. Kassim (2007). Adaptive particle filter for data fusion of multiple cameras, *The Journal of VLSI Signal Processing* **49**(3): 363–376.

13

On passive emitter tracking in sensor networks

Regina Kaune
Fraunhofer FKIE
Germany

Darko Mušicki
Hanyang University
Korea

Wolfgang Koch
Fraunhofer FKIE
Germany

1. Introduction

Many applications require fast and accurate localization and tracking of non-cooperative emitters. In many cases, it is advantageous not to conceal the observation process by using active sensors, but to work covertly with passive sensors. The estimation of the emitter state is based on various types of passive measurements by exploiting signals emitted by the targets. In other applications there is no choice but to exploit received signals only. Typical examples include search and rescue type operations.

Some passive measurements can be taken by single sensors: e.g. bearing measurements (AOA: Angle of Arrival) and frequency measurements (FOA: Frequency of Arrival). The emitter state can be estimated based on a set of measurements of a single passive observer. This problem is called the Target Motion Analysis (TMA) problem which means the process of estimating the state of a radiating target from noisy incomplete measurements collected by one or more passive observer(s). The TMA problem includes localization of stationary as well as tracking of moving emitters. The TMA problem based on a combination of AOA and FOA measurements is considered by Becker in (Becker, 2001). Becker investigates and discusses the TMA problem with many characteristic features such as observability conditions, combination of various types of measurements, etc., (Becker, 1999; 2005) .

Alternatively, measurements can be obtained from a network of several spatially dislocated sensors. Here, a minimum of two sensors is often needed. Measurements of Time Difference of Arrival (TDOA) and Frequency Difference of Arrival (FDOA) belong to this group.

TDOA measurements are obtained in the following way: several distributed, time-synchronized sensors measure the Time of Arrival (TOA) of signals transmitted from the emitter. The difference between two TOA measurements of the same signal gives one TDOA measurement. Alternatively, TDOA measurements can be obtained by correlating signals received by the sensors. A time standard can be used for time synchronization.

In the absence of noise and interference, a single TDOA measurement localizes the emitter on a hyperboloid with the two sensors as foci. By taking additional independent TDOA measurements from at least four sensors, the three-dimensional emitter location is estimated from the intersections of three or more hyperboloids. If sensors and emitter lie in the same plane, one TDOA measurement defines a hyperbola describing possible emitter locations. Therefore, the localization using TDOA measurements is called hyperbolic positioning. The sign of the measurement defines the branch of the hyperbola on which the emitter is located. The two-dimensional emitter location is found at the intersection of two or more hyperbolae from at least three sensors. This intersection point can be calculated by analytical solution, see e.g. (K. C. Ho, 2008; So et al., 2008). Alternatively, a pair of two sensors moving along arbitrary but known trajectories can be used for localizing an emitter using TDOA measurements. In this case, the emitter location can be estimated by filtering and tracking methods based on further measurements over time. This chapter is focused on the localization of unknown, non-cooperative emitters using TDOA measurements from a sensor pair. Some results have already been published in (Kaune, 2009).
The localization and tracking a non-cooperative emitter can be improved by combining different kinds of passive measurements, particularly in the case of a moving emitter.
One possibility is based on bearing measurements. A pair of one azimuth and one TDOA measurement is processed at each time step. The additional AOA measurement can solve the ambiguities appearing in processing TDOA measurements only. Another possibility considers two sensors measuring the FDOA between two frequencies of arrival (Mušicki et al., 2010; Mušicki & Koch, 2008). These measurements can be taken by the same sensors as the TDOA measurements. The TDOA/FDOA measurement pairs can be obtained by using the Complex Ambiguity function (CAF). The combination of TDOA and FDOA measurements improves the estimation performance strongly.

This chapter gives an overview of the topic of passive emitter tracking. Section 2 describes the situation of a single passive observer. Important steps of solving the passive emitter tracking problems are presented. When assessing an estimation task, it is important to know the best estimation accuracy that can be obtained with the measurements. The Cramér Rao Lower Bound (CRLB) provides a lower bound on the estimation accuracy for any unbiased estimator and reveals characteristic features of the estimation problem.
Powerful estimation algorithms must be applied to obtain useful estimates of the emitter state. For passive emitter tracking, measurements and states are not linearly related. Therefore, only nonlinear estimation methods are appropriate. Passive emitter tracking is a complex problem. Depending on the types of measurements, various estimation methods can be applied showing different localization performance in various scenarios. The goal of this chapter is to provide a review of the state of the art. The discussion is not restricted to one chosen method but presents an overview of different methods. The algorithms are not shown in detail; therefore, a look at the references is necessary to implement them. In the appendix, a toolbox of methods makes several estimation methods available which are applied in this chapter. Firstly, the maximum likelihood estimator (MLE) as a direct search method, which evaluates at each estimate the complete measurement dataset. Secondly, Kalman filter based solutions which recursively update the emitter state estimates. The tracking problem is nonlinear; thus the Extended Kalman Filter (EKF) provides an analytic approximation, while the Unscented Kalman Filter (UKF) deterministically selects a small number of points and transforms these points nonlinearly. Thirdly, Gaussian Mixture (GM) filters will be discussed, which approxi-

mate the posterior density by a GM (a weighted sum of Gaussian density functions). Additionally, some basics on the CRLB and the Normalized Estimation Error Squared (NEES) are presented.
In sections 3, 4, 5 passive emitter tracking using TDOA, a combination of TDOA and AOA and a combination of TDOA and FDOA is investigated, respectively. Finally, conclusions are drawn.

2. Review of TMA techniques

Passive emitter tracking using a single passive observer is part of the TMA problem which addresses the process of estimating the state of an emitter from noisy, incomplete measurements collected by a passive observer (Becker, 1999; 2001; 2005, and references cited therein). Typical applications can be found in passive sonar, infrared (IR), or passive radar tracking systems.

2.1 Solution of the TMA problem

The TMA problem is solved in three consecutive steps:

- The first step is the calculation and analysis of the CRLB. It is a lower bound for the achievable estimation accuracy and reveals characteristic features of the TMA problem under consideration.
- The main step is the development of an algorithm that effectively estimates the target state from the noisy measurements collected by the observer.
- A final third step is necessary in the TMA solution process. It increases the estimation accuracy by observer motions.

These three steps can be applied to passive emitter tracking in sensor networks as well, while the third step is not as important as in the single observer case.
In the following, the solution of the TMA problem is analyzed in detail:
In evaluating an estimation problem, it is important to know the optimal estimation accuracy achievable from the measurements. It is well known that the CRLB provides a lower bound on the achievable estimation accuracy; for explicit formulas see A.1. The investigation of the CRLB provides insight into the parametric dependencies of the TMA problem under consideration. It reveals characteristic features of the localization and tracking process. For the two-dimensional TMA problem based on AOA and FOA measurements, it has been discussed in detail, (Becker, 1992). It proved that the orientation of the error ellipses of bearings and frequency measurements significantly differ. One bearing measurement provides a strip of infinite length in the position space and two frequency measurements give a strip of infinite length in the position space, too. The error ellipses of the bearing and the frequency measurements are rotated with respect to each other. Therefore, there is a gain in accuracy by combining angle and frequency measurements in the TMA situation.
The main step of the TMA problem is the development of an algorithm that effectively estimates the emitter state from noisy measurements collected by the observer. These algorithms require the modeling of the emitter dynamics and the measurement process. The system or dynamics model describes the evolution of the emitter state with time. Let $\mathbf{e}_k \in \mathbb{R}^{n_e}$ be the emitter state at time t_k, where n_e is the dimension of the state vector, involving position and velocity. Using the evolution function f, the emitter state can be modeled from the previous time step t_{k-1} by adding white Gaussian noise; we obtain the dynamic model:

$$\mathbf{e}_k = f(\mathbf{e}_{k-1}) + \mathbf{v}_k, \quad \mathbf{v}_k \sim \mathcal{N}(\mathbf{0}, \mathbf{Q}), \tag{1}$$

where $\mathbf{v}_k \sim \mathcal{N}(\mathbf{0}, \mathbf{Q})$ means that $\mathbf{v}_k$ is zero-mean normal distributed with covariance $\mathbf{Q}$. The measurement model relates the noisy measurements $\mathbf{z}_k \in \mathbb{R}^{n_z}$ to the state, where n_z is the dimension of the measurement vector. The measurement function $h(\mathbf{e})$ is a function of the emitter state, nonlinear or linear, and reflects the relations between the emitter state and the measurements. Thus, the measurement process is modeled by adding white Gaussian noise $\mathbf{u}_k$:

$$\mathbf{z}_k = h(\mathbf{e}_k) + \mathbf{u}_k, \quad \mathbf{u}_k \sim \mathcal{N}(\mathbf{0}, \mathbf{R}), \tag{2}$$

where $\mathbf{R}$ is the covariance of the measurement noise.
An estimation algorithm must be found to solve the emitter tracking problem. Based on all available measurements $Z_k = \{\mathbf{z}_1, \mathbf{z}_2, \ldots, \mathbf{z}_k\}$ up to time t_k we seek to estimate the emitter state $\mathbf{e}_k$. Therefore, it is required to compute the posterior probability density function $p(\mathbf{e}_k|Z_k)$. A short review of available estimation algorithms is given in A.3 and include:

- As a direct method, maximum likelihood estimation (MLE) evaluates at each time step the complete measurement dataset. In many cases, a numerical iterative search algorithm is needed to implement MLE.
- Recursive Kalman-type filter algorithms can be used as well. They are Bayesian estimators and construct the posterior density using the Bayes rule. Since the measurement equation in passive emitter tracking is often nonlinear, nonlinear versions of it must be used: the Extended Kalman filter (EKF) provides an analytic approximation, while the Unscented Kalman filter (UKF) deterministically selects a small number of points and transforms these points according to the nonlinearity.
- Gaussian Mixture (GM) filters approximate the required densities by Gaussian Mixtures, weighted sums of Gaussians. The approximation can be made as accurate as desirable by adapting the number of mixture components appropriately, see (Ristic et al., 2004).

In passive tracking, the emitter may not be observable from available measurements in some situations. If the observer is moving directly in direction of the stationary emitter, for example, the emitter is not observable from bearing measurements only. In the literature, necessary and sufficient observability criteria using angle measurements and using a combination of angle and frequency measurements have been derived (Becker, 1993; 1996). In general, ambiguities can be resolved by suitable observer maneuvers, which depend on the type of measurements and the emitter model as well. A measurement set consisting of different measurement types often results in less restrictive observability conditions.
In an application, the user should always strive to get the maximum of attainable estimation accuracy. Estimation accuracy can firstly be influenced by the choice of the estimation algorithm and, secondly, by the choice of the emitter-observer geometry over time, via observer motion. The estimation accuracy highly depends on the emitter-observer geometry. The emitter-observer geometry may be changed by observer maneuvers. Thus, the final step in solving the TMA problem is to find an optimal observer maneuver creating a geometry that maximizes the estimation accuracy. In the literature, several criteria have been used, one of them is maximizing the determinant of the Fisher Information Matrix (FIM) $\mathbf{J}$.

2.2 TMA based on bearing and frequency measurements

The standard TMA method is based on bearing measurements taken at different points along the sensor trajectory, see Figure 1. It has been the topic of much research in the literature.

Already a single bearing measurement provides information on the emitter position. In addition, or instead of bearing measurements, measurements of the Doppler-shifted frequency can be taken, (Becker, 1992). Frequency measurements depend on the emitter-sensor-motion, more precisely on the radial component of the relative velocity vector. Frequency drift and frequency hopping have an impact on the quality of frequency measurements and have to be taken into account. The location methods based on bearing or frequency measurements differ significantly. The substantial differences between both methods lead to a significant integration gain when the combined set of bearing and frequency measurements is processed.

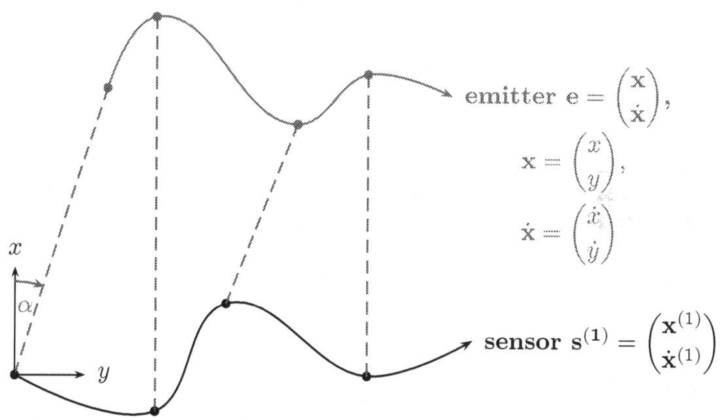

Fig. 1. TMA problem based on azimuth measurements (dashed lines)

3. Exploitation of TDOA measurements

The problem of passive emitter tracking can be considered in a network of senors as well. Various types of measurements can be obtained only with a network of sensors. TDOA measurements belong to this group. Several displaced, time-synchronized sensors measure the TOA of a signal transmitted from the emitter. The difference between two TOA measurements gives one TDOA measurement. In this chapter a network of two sensors building a sensor pair is regarded. They take measurements from an unknown emitter over time.

3.1 Problem statement

For a demonstration of the special features, the three-dimensional localization problem is not more enlightening than the two-dimensional one. Therefore, for easy understanding and presenting, the further text is restricted to the special case, where the trajectories of the sensors and the emitter lie in a plane.
Let $\mathbf{e}_k$ be the emitter state at time t_k:

$$\mathbf{e}_k = (\mathbf{x}_k^T, \dot{\mathbf{x}}_k^T)^T, \tag{3}$$

where $\mathbf{x}_k = (x_k, \ y_k)^T \in \mathbb{R}^2$ denotes the position and $\dot{\mathbf{x}}_k = (\dot{x}_k, \ \dot{y}_k)^T \in \mathbb{R}^2$ the velocity. Two sensors with the state vectors

$$\mathbf{s}_k^{(i)} = \left(\mathbf{x}_k^{(i)^T}, \dot{\mathbf{x}}_k^{(i)^T}\right)^T, \qquad i = 1, 2, \tag{4}$$

observe the emitter and receive the emitted signal. The sensors have a navigation system to know their own position and speed. Therefore their state vectors are known at every time.
To simplify, the emitter is assumed to be stationary, i.e. $\dot{\mathbf{x}}_k = 0$, while the sensors move along their trajectories with a constant speed.
The speed of propagation is the speed of light c, the TOA measurement can be expressed by:

$$t_0 + \frac{1}{c}||\mathbf{x}_k - \mathbf{x}_k^{(i)}||,$$

where $|| \cdot ||$ denotes the vector norm. t_0 is the emission time of the signal and $||\mathbf{r}_k^{(i)}|| = ||\mathbf{x}_k - \mathbf{x}_k^{(i)}||$ is the range between emitter and sensor i, $i = 1, 2$, at time t_k, where $\mathbf{r}_k^{(i)}$ denotes the emitter position relative to sensor i.
The TOA measurement consists of the unknown time of emission t_0 and the time the signal needs for propagating the relative vector between the emitter and sensor i. Calculating the difference between the TOA measurements eliminates the unknown time t_0 and yields the TDOA measurement at time t_k:

$$h_k^t = \frac{1}{c}\left(||\mathbf{x}_k - \mathbf{x}_k^{(1)}|| - ||\mathbf{x}_k - \mathbf{x}_k^{(2)}||\right).$$

The measurement in the range domain is obtained by multiplication with the speed of the light c:

$$h_k^{\mathrm{r}} = ||\mathbf{x}_k - \mathbf{x}_k^{(1)}|| - ||\mathbf{x}_k - \mathbf{x}_k^{(2)}||.$$

The measurement equation is a function of the unknown emitter position $\mathbf{x}_k$, the emitter speed is not important. Furthermore, the positions of the sensors which are changing over time are parameters of the measurement equation, the sensor speed is irrelevant. The two-dimensional vector of position $\mathbf{x}_k$ of the emitter is to be estimated. The emitter is stationary, its position is independent of the time and it holds for all time step t_k:

$$\mathbf{x}_k = \mathbf{x}_0.$$

A typical TDOA situation is illustrated in Figure 2. The two sensors move at the edge of the observation area in an easterly direction indicated by the arrows. They observe a stationary emitter. A single accurate, i.e. noise-free, TDOA measurement defines a hyperbola as possible emitter location. In Figure 2, the red curve shows the branch of the hyperbolae on which the emitter must be placed.
The combination of two measurements of the stationary emitter taken over time leads to an ambiguity of the emitter position. The two detection results are the true position of the emitter and the position mirrored along the connecting line between the sensors. This ambiguity can be resolved in various ways, e.g. by a maneuver of the sensors, the addition of a third sensor, or an additional bearing measurement. Alternatively, sensors which are sensitive only in the hemisphere can be used, and thus able to observe only this half-space. Here the sensors are positioned at the edge of the observation area, e.g. on a coast for the observation of a ground emitter or on the edge of a hostile territory.

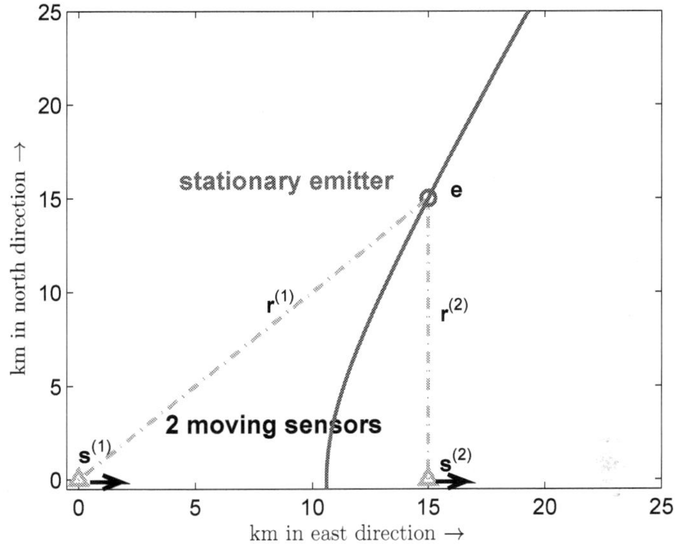

Fig. 2. TDOA scenario

The measurement process is modeled by adding white Gaussian noise to the measurement function. We get the measurement equation in the range domain at time t_k:

$$z_k^r = h_k^r + u_k^r, \quad u_k^r \sim \mathcal{N}(0, \sigma_r^2) \tag{5}$$

where σ_r denotes the standard deviation of the measurement error in the range domain. The measurement noise u_k^r is i.i.d., the measurement error is independent from time to time, i.e. mutually independent, and identically distributed.

3.2 Quantitative analysis

Two different emitter tracking scenarios are considered to compare the performance of four different estimation algorithms which solve the nonlinear emitter localization problem, the results have already been published in (Kaune, 2009). The results presented here are based on 100 measurements averaged over 1000 independent Monte Carlo simulations with a measurement interval of two seconds. The measurement standard deviation in the range domain σ_r is assumed to be 200 m. This corresponds to a measurement standard deviation in the time domain σ_t of about 0.67 μs.

In the first scenario, sensors, separated by a distance of 20 km, fly one after the other in east direction at a constant speed of 100 m/s. The second scenario analyzes a parallel flight of the sensors. Sensors at $(1,1)$ km and $(16,1)$ km fly side by side in parallel at a constant speed of 100 m/s in north direction.

3.2.1 CRLB investigation

The CRLB for the TDOA scenario at time t_k with the measurements z_i and the time-dependent measurement functions $h(\mathbf{x}_i), i = 1, \ldots, k$, can be computed as:

$$\mathrm{J}_k = \frac{1}{\sigma_r^2} \sum_{i=1}^{k} \left(\frac{\partial h(\mathbf{x}_i)}{\partial \mathbf{x}_k} \right)^T \frac{\partial h(\mathbf{x}_i)}{\partial \mathbf{x}_k}, \tag{6}$$

with entries of the Jacobian at time t_i:

$$\frac{\partial h(\mathbf{x}_i)}{\partial x_i} = \frac{x_i - x_i^{(1)}}{||\mathbf{r}_i^{(1)}||} - \frac{x_i - x_i^{(2)}}{||\mathbf{r}_i^{(2)}||} \quad \text{and} \quad \frac{\partial h(\mathbf{x}_i)}{\partial y_i} = \frac{y_i - y_i^{(1)}}{||\mathbf{r}_i^{(1)}||} - \frac{y_i - y_i^{(2)}}{||\mathbf{r}_i^{(2)}||}. \tag{7}$$

This shows that the CRLB depends only on the relative position of the sensors and the emitter, the measurement accuracy and the number of measurements.
The FIM J_1 at time t_1 will usually be singular since we cannot estimate the full position vector $\mathbf{x}$ from a single TDOA measurement without additional assumptions, see (Van Trees, 1968). In the present case these assumptions concern the area in which the emitter is supposed to be. These assumptions about the prior distribution on $\mathbf{x}$ are added to the FIM at time t_1.
For visualization, the estimation accuracy is given as the square root of the trace of the 2×2 CRLB matrix.
Figure 3 shows a plot of the CRLB in the plane for the two investigated scenarios without taking into account of prior information. The initial sensor positions are marked with green triangles, and the red circle designates the position of the emitter. For a grid of possible emitter

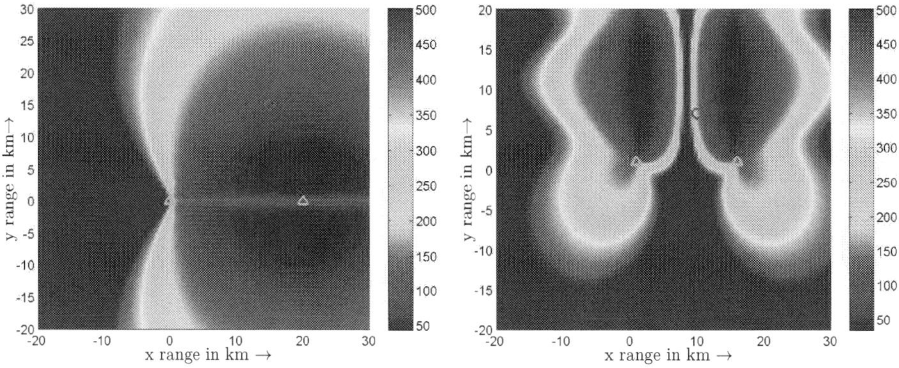

Fig. 3. CRLB in the plane, values cut off at 500 m: (a) scenario 1 (b) scenario 2, colorbar in m.

positions in the plane the Fisher information J_{100} after 100 measurements is computed by Equation (6). The associated CRLB J_{100}^{-1} is calculated and the square root of the trace is shown. Values larger than 500 m have been cut off for better visualization. The color bar shows the localization accuracy in m. The localization accuracy can be read from the figure for any emitter location in the plane.
In the first scenario, the emitter lies exactly in the area of optimal approach to the target.

In the second scenario, it is near the region of divergence which indicates poor localization performance.

3.2.2 Results

For comparison of the estimation methods, the Root Mean Square Error (RMSE), the squared distance of the estimate to the true target location $\mathbf{x}_k$ is used in Monte Carlo simulations. They are averaged over N, the number of Monte Carlo runs. Let $\hat{\mathbf{x}}_k^{(i)}$ be the estimate of the ith run at time t_k. Than, the RMSE at time t_k is computed as:

$$\mathrm{RMSE}_k = \sqrt{\frac{1}{N}\sum_{i=1}^{N}(\mathbf{x}_k - \hat{\mathbf{x}}_k^{(i)})^T(\mathbf{x}_k - \hat{\mathbf{x}}_k^{(i)})}. \tag{8}$$

Four estimation algorithms which solve the nonlinear emitter localization problem are investigated and compared.

- The **Maximum Likelihood Estimate (MLE)** is that value of $\mathbf{x}_k$ which maximizes the likelihood function (30). Since there is no closed-form ML solution for $\mathbf{x}_k$, a numerical iterative search algorithm is needed to find the minimum of the quadratic form, see equation (42). In our case, the simplex method due to Nelder and Mead is used. It is initialized with a central point from the observation area in scenario 1, in the second scenario the initialization point is chosen at a distance of up to about 5 km from the true target position. Being a batch algorithm, the MLE evaluates, at each update, the complete measurement dataset. It attains the CRLB when properly initialized. One disadvantage of the ML estimator is the higher computational effort in comparison to the Kalman filters, as can be seen in Table 1. Table 1 shows the computational efforts of the different estimation algorithms for a Monte Carlo simulation with 1000 runs for the first scenario. One advantage of the MLE is the superior performance in comparison to the Kalman filters.
- The **Extended Kalman filter (EKF)** approximates the nonlinear measurement equation by its first-order Taylor series expansion:

$$\widehat{\mathbf{H}}_k = \frac{(\mathbf{x}_k - \mathbf{x}_k^{(1)})^T}{||\mathbf{x}_k - \mathbf{x}_k^{(1)}||} - \frac{(\mathbf{x}_k - \mathbf{x}_k^{(2)})^T}{||\mathbf{x}_k - \mathbf{x}_k^{(2)}||}. \tag{9}$$

  Then, the Kalman filter equations are applied. The EKF is highly sensitive to the initialization and works only if the initial value is near the true target position. The EKF may not reach the CRLB even in the case of a good initialization. Initial values are chosen from a parametric approach similar to the approach described in (Mušicki & Koch, 2008): the first measurement is used for initialization. It defines a hyperbola as possible emitter locations from which several points are taken. These points initialize a ML estimate which evaluates a sequence of first measurements. The best result is the initial value of the EKF and the UKF. The computational efforts shown in Table 1 include this phase of initialization.

- The **Unscented Kalman filter (UKF)** (see (Julier & Uhlmann, 2004)) uses the Gaussian representation of the posterior density via a set of deterministically chosen sample points. These sample points are propagated through the Unscented Transform (UT).

Since the nonlinearity is in the measurement equation, the UT is applied in the update step. Then the KF equations are carried out.
The initialization is the same as in the EKF. Poor initialization values result in divergent tracks like in the EKF case.

Time in sec			
EKF	UKF	MLE	GS
49	80	939	90

Table 1. Comparison of computational effort

- The static **Gaussian Mixture** (GM) filter overcomes the initialization difficulties of the Kalman filter like EKF and UKF. It approximates the posterior density by a Gaussian Mixture (GM)((Tam et al., 1999)), a weighted sum of Gaussian density functions. The computational effort of finding a good initialization point is omitted here. The first measurement is converted into a Gaussian sum. The algorithmic procedure for computation of weights w_g, means $\mathbf{x}_g$ and covariances $\mathbf{P}_g$ is the same as in (Mušicki & Koch, 2008). The mapping of the TDOA measurement into the Cartesian state space consists of several steps:
  - present the $\pm\sigma_r$ hyperbolae in the state space,
  - choose the same number of points on each hyperbolae,
  - inscribe an ellipse in the quadrangle of two points on the $+\sigma_r$ and two points on the $-\sigma_r$ hyperbola,
  - the center of the ellipse is the mean, the ellipse the covariance and the square root of the determinant the weight of the Gaussian summand.

  An EKF is started for each mean and covariance, the weights are updated with the posterior probability. The final mean is computed as weighted sum of the individual EKF means: $\bar{\mathbf{x}} = \sum_{g=1}^{n} w_g \mathbf{x}_g$, where n is the number of Gaussian terms.

The performance of these four estimation algorithms is investigated in two different tracking scenarios. In the first scenario, the emitter at $(15, 15)$ km lies in a well-locatable region. MLE shows good performance. The results of EKF and UKF are shown in Figure 4. They perform well and the NEES, see appendix A.2, lies in the 95% interval $[1.878, 2.126]$ for both filters, as can be seen from Figure 4 (b). For this scenario the static GM filter shows no improvement compared to a single EKF or UKF.
Scenario 2 analyzes a parallel flight of the sensors. The CRLB for the emitter position in $(10, 7)$ km indicates poor estimation accuracy. EKF and UKF have heavy initialization problems, both have a high number of diverging tracks. Also the MLE suffers from difficulties of divergence. The initialization with a GM results in 9 simultaneously updated EKFs. The sampling from the GM approximation of the first measurement is presented in Figure 5 (a). The black solid lines are the $\pm\sigma_r$ hyperbolae. The sampling points are displayed in blue. They give an intelligent approximation of the first measurement. In Figure 5 (b) the RMSE of the GM filter and the MLE are plotted in comparison to the CRLB. In this scenario the GM filter, the bank of 9 EKFs, shows good performance. After an initial phase, it nears asymptotically the CRLB. The results of a single KF are unusable, they are higher than 10^5 m and for better visibility

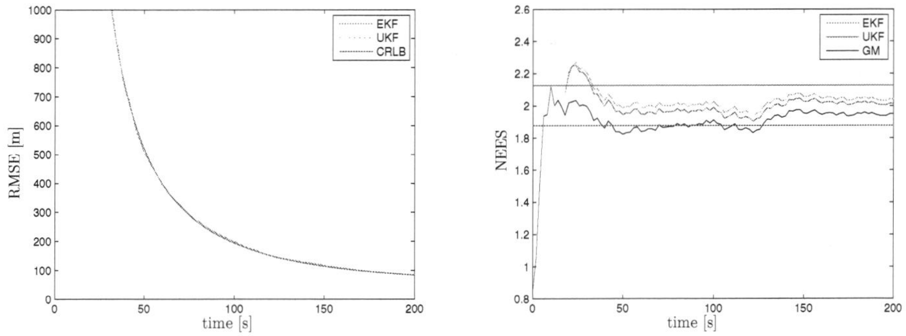

Fig. 4. (a) RMSE for EKF and UKF and (b) NEES for scenario 1

not presented. The MLE is initialized as described above and produces good results near the CRLB. Its performance is better than the performance of the GM filter. The CRLB are shown with initial assumptions.

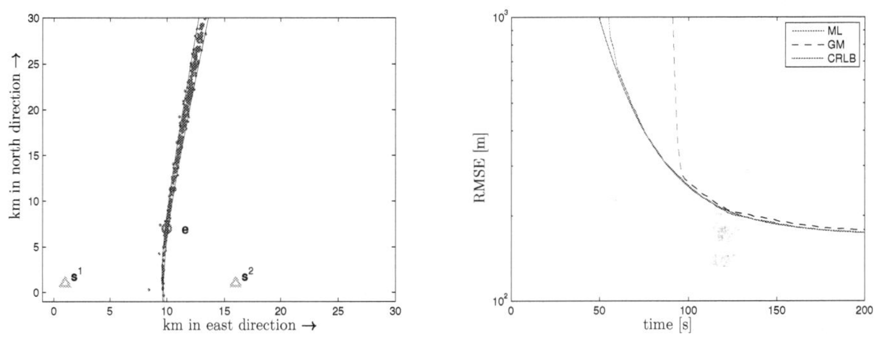

Fig. 5. (a) Sampling from the GM approximation and (b) RMSE for scenario 2

4. Combination of TDOA and AOA measurements

The combination of various types of measurements may lead to a gain in estimation accuracy. Particularly in the case of a moving emitter, it is advantageous to fuse different kinds of measurements. One possibility is that one sensor of the sensor pair is additionally able to take the bearing measurements.

4.1 Problem statement

Let $\mathbf{s}^{(1)}$ be the location of the sensor, which takes the bearing measurements. The additional azimuth measurement function at time t_k is:

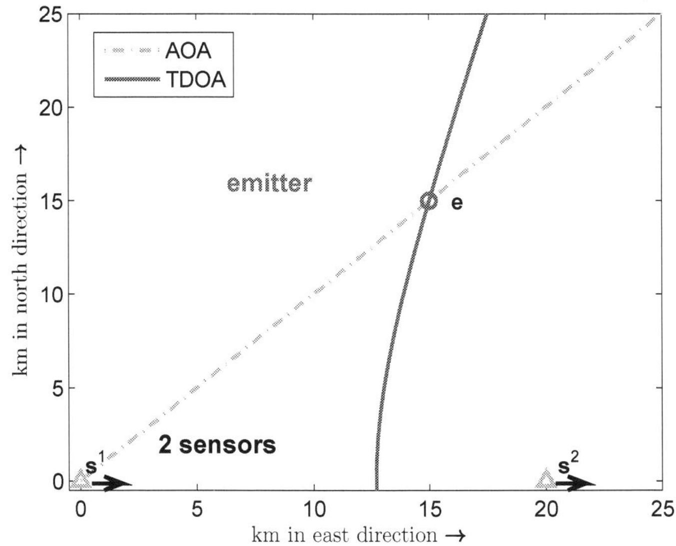

Fig. 6. Combination of one TDOA and one azimuth measurement

$$h_k^{\alpha} = \arctan\left(\frac{x_k - x_k^{(1)}}{y_k - y_k^{(1)}}\right) \tag{10}$$

Addition of white noise yields:

$$z_k^{\alpha} = h_k^{\alpha} + u_k^{\alpha}, \quad u_k^{\alpha} \sim \mathcal{N}(0, \sigma_{\alpha}^2), \tag{11}$$

where σ_{α} is the standard deviation of the AOA measurement.

Figure 6 shows the measurement situation after taking a pair of one azimuth and one TDOA measurement. At each time step, two nonlinear measurements are taken, which must be processed with nonlinear estimation algorithms.

4.2 Quantitative analysis

A moving emitter with one maneuver is considered to compare the performance of an estimator using single azimuth measurements and an estimator using the fused measurement set of azimuth and TDOA measurements. At the maneuvering time the emitter changes the flight direction and its velocity. The observer which takes the azimuth measurements flies at a constant speed of 50 m/s on a circular trajectory for observability reasons, see Figure 7. This sensor takes every 2nd second azimuth measurements from the maneuvering emitter. TDOA measurements are gained from the network of the moving sensor and a stationary observer which lies in the observation space. TDOA measurements are also taken every 2nd second.

Thus, at each time step a pair of one azimuth and one TDOA measurement can be processed. The azimuth measurement standard deviation is assumed to be 1 degree and the TDOA measurement standard deviation is assumed to be 200 m in the range domain.

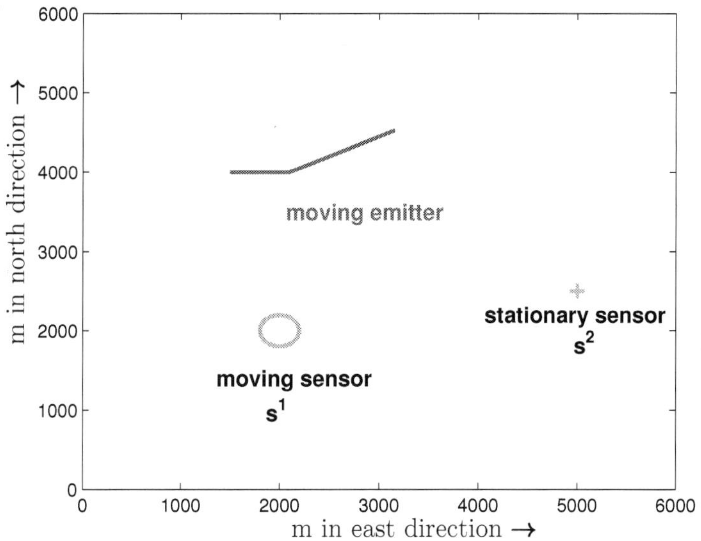

Fig. 7. Measurement situation

4.2.1 CRLB investigation

The CRLB of the combination of TDOA and AOA measurements is calculated over the fused Fisher information of the single Fisher informations. The Fisher information at time t_k is the sum of the FIMs based on the TDOA and the AOA measurements:

$$\mathrm{J}_k = \frac{1}{\sigma_r^2} \sum_{i=1}^{k} \left(\frac{\partial h^r(\mathbf{e}_i)}{\partial \mathbf{e}_k} \right)^T \frac{\partial h^r(\mathbf{e}_i)}{\partial \mathbf{e}_k} + \frac{1}{\sigma_\alpha^2} \sum_{i=1}^{k} \left(\frac{\partial h^\alpha(\mathbf{e}_i)}{\partial \mathbf{e}_k} \right)^T \frac{\partial h^\alpha(\mathbf{e}_i)}{\partial \mathbf{e}_k}, \tag{12}$$

with entries of the Jacobian of the AOA measurement equation:

$$\frac{\partial h^\alpha(\mathbf{e}_i)}{\partial x_i} = \frac{y_i - y_i^{(1)}}{||\mathbf{r}_i^{(1)}||^2} \tag{13}$$

$$\frac{\partial h^\alpha(\mathbf{e}_i)}{\partial y_i} = -\frac{x_i - x_i^{(1)}}{||\mathbf{r}_i^{(1)}||^2} \tag{14}$$

$$\frac{\partial h^\alpha(\mathbf{e}_i)}{\partial \dot{x}_i} = \frac{\partial h^\alpha(\mathbf{e}_i)}{\partial \dot{y}_i} = 0. \tag{15}$$

Therefore, the localization accuracy depends on the sensor-emitter geometry, the standard deviation of the TDOA and the azimuth measurements and the number of measurements.

4.2.2 Results

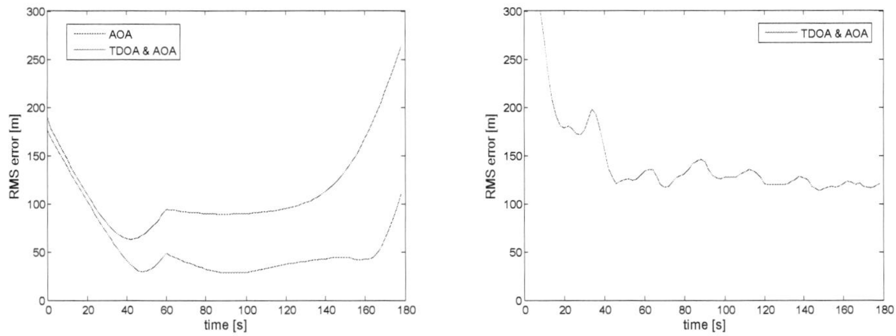

(a) MLE (b) UT

Fig. 8. Comparison of AOA and a combination of AOA and TDOA

Three estimation algorithms are compared:

- MLE based on azimuth-only measurements: It works with knowledge of the emitter dynamic: the state of the target is modeled using the dynamic with one maneuver and of a constant velocity before and after the maneuvering time. The 7-dimensional emitter state is to be estimated, including the maneuvering time and the two speed vectors of the two segments of the emitter trajectory. The modeling of the emitter dynamic and the algorithms for the MLE are implemented like in (Oispuu & Hörst, 2010), where piece-wise curvilinearly moving targets are considered. The processing of the measurements is done after taking the complete measurement dataset in retrospect. The 7-dimensional emitter state can be computed for every time step or alternatively for a single reference time step.
- MLE based on the combination of azimuth and TDOA measurements. The algorithm is the same algorithm as for the AOA only case. The TDOA measurements are basis of the optimization, too.
- A filter which uses the combined measurement set of azimuth and TDOA measurements: it transforms at each time step the measurement pair of azimuth and TDOA measurement $\{z^{\alpha}, z^{t}\}$ into the Cartesian state space. At each time step, using the UT an estimation of the emitter state in the Cartesian state space and an associated covariance are obtained. Emitter tracking is started with the first measurement pair and performed in parallel to gaining the measurements.
  The UT consists of two steps:

- Computation of the distance from sensor $\mathbf{s}^{(1)}$ to the emitter:

$$||\mathbf{r}^{(1)}|| = \frac{||\mathbf{x}^{(1)} - \mathbf{x}^{(2)}||^2 - z^{t2}}{2\left[\left(\mathbf{x}^{(2)} - \mathbf{x}^{(1)}\right)^T \begin{pmatrix}\sin(z^\alpha)\\ \cos(z^\alpha)\end{pmatrix} - z^t\right]} \tag{16}$$

- Calculation of the emitter location:

$$\hat{\mathbf{x}} = \mathbf{x}^{(1)} + ||\mathbf{r}^{(1)}|| \begin{pmatrix}\cos(z^\alpha)\\ \sin(z^\alpha)\end{pmatrix}; \tag{17}$$

The measurement pair and its associated measurement covariance $\mathbf{R} = \text{diag}[\sigma_\alpha^2, \sigma_r^2]$, where diag[] means the diagonal matrix, is processed using the UT. I.e., several sigma points in the two-dimensional measurement space are selected and transformed. We obtain an estimation of the emitter state in the Cartesian state space and an associated covariance. A linear Kalman filter is started with the position estimate and the associated covariance. The update is performed in the Cartesian state space by transforming the incoming measurement pair using the unscented transform. This filter uses as model for the emitter dynamic the model for a inertially moving target. This model does not describe correctly the emitter dynamic but addition of white Gaussian process noise can correct the error of the model.

In Figure 8 the results based on 1000 Monte Carlo runs are presented. Figure 8 (a) shows the comparison between the MLE only based on azimuth measurements and based on a combination of azimuth and TDOA measurements. The MLE delivers for each Monte Carlo run one 7-dimensional estimate of the emitter state from which the resulting emitter trajectory is computed. The RMS error to the true emitter trajectory is shown. Using the combined measurement set, the performance is significant better than the AOA only results. Figure 8 (b) visualizes the results of the linear KF using the UT. At each time step, an estimate of the emitter state is computed. In spite of an insufficient dynamic model, the emitter state is estimated quite fair in the beginning. But due to the incorrect dynamic model, the localization accuracy in the end is about 120 m. The MLE based on the combined measurement set shows better performance than the filter using the UT.

5. Combination of TDOA and FDOA measurements

A combination of TDOA and FDOA measurements increases the performance compared to single TDOA measurements (see (Mušicki et al., 2010)). A minimum of two sensors is needed to gain FDOA measurements at one time step. The omnidirectional antennas which measure the TOA can measure the frequency of the received signal as well. Frequency measurements depend on the relative motion between the emitter and the sensors. The radial component of the relative speed vector determines the frequency shift which is necessary to obtain nonzero FDOA values.

5.1 Problem statement

The FDOA measurement function depends not only on the emitter position but also on its speed and course, for easy understanding the subscript k for the time step is omitted in this

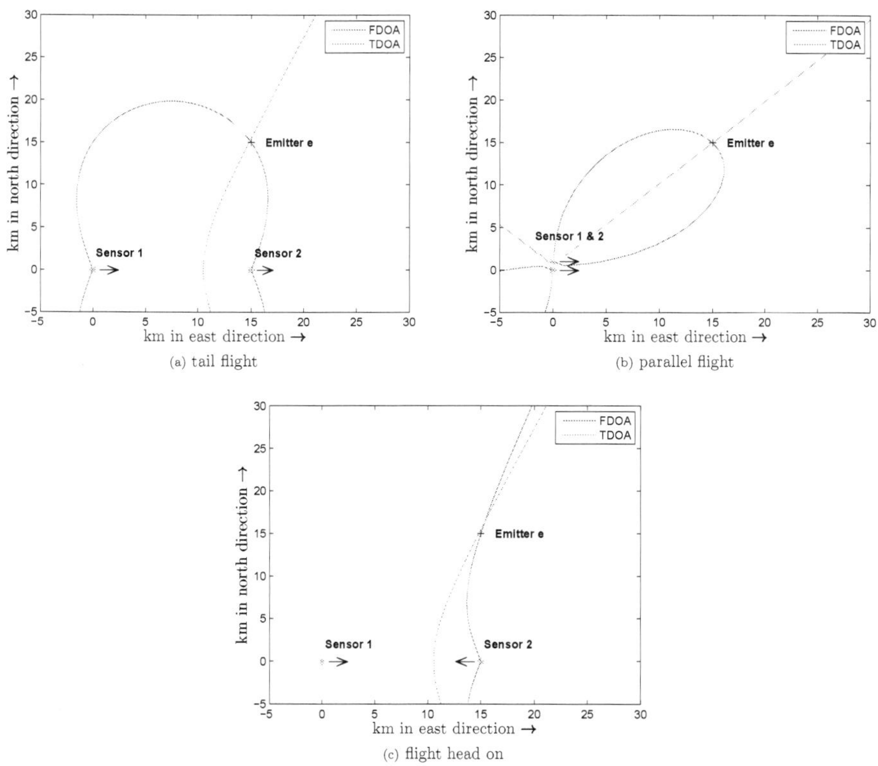

Fig. 9. Combination of TDOA and FDOA measurements in three different scenarios

section if it is clear from the context:

$$h^{ff} = \frac{f_0}{c}\left((\dot{\mathbf{x}}^{(1)} - \dot{\mathbf{x}})^T \frac{\mathbf{r}^{(1)}}{||\mathbf{r}^{(1)}||} - (\dot{\mathbf{x}}^{(2)} - \dot{\mathbf{x}})^T \frac{\mathbf{r}^{(2)}}{||\mathbf{r}^{(2)}||}\right), \tag{18}$$

where f_0 is carrier frequency of the signal. Multiplication with $\frac{c}{f_0}$ yields the measurement equation in the velocity domain:

$$h^f = (\dot{\mathbf{x}}^{(1)} - \dot{\mathbf{x}})^T \frac{\mathbf{r}^{(1)}}{||\mathbf{r}^{(1)}||} - (\dot{\mathbf{x}}^{(2)} - \dot{\mathbf{x}})^T \frac{\mathbf{r}^{(2)}}{||\mathbf{r}^{(2)}||}. \tag{19}$$

Under the assumption of uncorrelated measurement noise from time step to time step and from the TDOA measurements, we obtain the FDOA measurement equation in the velocity domain:

$$z^f = h^f + u_f, \quad u_f \sim \mathcal{N}(0, \sigma_f^2), \tag{20}$$

where σ_f is the standard deviation of the FDOA measurement. The associated TDOA/ FDOA measurement pairs may be obtained by using the CAF ((Stein, 1981)). For each TDOA value the associated FDOA value can be calculated. Nonlinear estimation algorithms are needed to process the pair of TDOA and FDOA measurements and to estimate the emitter state.
Figure 9 shows the situation for different sensor headings after taking one pair of TDOA and FDOA measurements. The green curve, i.e. the branch of hyperbola, indicates the ambiguity after the TDOA measurement. The ambiguity after the FDOA measurement is plotted in magenta. The intersection of both curves presents a gain in information for the emitter location. This gain is very high if sensors move behind each other.

5.2 Quantitative analysis

In the following, a scenario with a moving emitter is investigated to compare the performance of two filters which exploit a combination of TDOA and FDOA and one filter based on single TDOA measurements. The presented filters are GM filters which approximate the required densities by a weighted sum of Gaussian densities.

5.2.1 CRLB investigation

The Fisher information at time t_k is the sum of the Fisher information based on the TDOA and the FDOA measurements:

$$\mathrm{J}_k = \frac{1}{\sigma_r^2}\sum_{i=1}^{k}\left(\frac{\partial h^r(\mathbf{e}_i)}{\partial \mathbf{e}_k}\right)^T \frac{\partial h^r(\mathbf{e}_i)}{\partial \mathbf{e}_k} + \frac{1}{\sigma_f^2}\sum_{i=1}^{k}\left(\frac{\partial h^f(\mathbf{e}_i)}{\partial \mathbf{e}_k}\right)^T \frac{\partial h^f(\mathbf{e}_i)}{\partial \mathbf{e}_k}, \tag{21}$$

with entries of the Jacobian of the FDOA measurement equation:

$$\frac{\partial h^f(\mathbf{e})}{\partial x} = D_x^{(1)} - D_x^{(2)} \tag{22}$$

$$\frac{\partial h^f(\mathbf{e})}{\partial y} = D_y^{(1)} - D_y^{(2)} \tag{23}$$

$$\frac{\partial h^f(\mathbf{e})}{\partial \dot{x}} = \frac{x - x^{(2)}}{||\mathbf{r}^{(2)}||} - \frac{x - x^{(1)}}{||\mathbf{r}^{(1)}||} \tag{24}$$

$$\frac{\partial h^f(\mathbf{e})}{\partial \dot{y}} = \frac{y - y^{(2)}}{||\mathbf{r}^{(2)}||} - \frac{y - y^{(1)}}{||\mathbf{r}^{(1)}||}, \tag{25}$$

with

$$D_x^{(i)} = \frac{(\dot{x}^{(i)} - \dot{x}) - \frac{1}{||\mathbf{r}^{(i)}||^2}\left[(\dot{\mathbf{x}}^{(i)} - \dot{\mathbf{x}})^T\mathbf{r}^{(i)}\right](x - x^{(i)})}{||\mathbf{r}^{(i)}||}, \quad i = 1,2 \tag{26}$$

$$D_y^{(i)} = \frac{(\dot{y}^{(i)} - \dot{y}) - \frac{1}{||\mathbf{r}^{(i)}||^2}\left[(\dot{\mathbf{x}}^{(i)} - \dot{\mathbf{x}})^T\mathbf{r}^{(i)}\right](y - y^{(i)})}{||\mathbf{r}^{(i)}||}, \quad i = 1,2. \tag{27}$$

The CRLB depends not only on the sensors-emitter geometry and the measurement standard deviations but also on the velocity. A nonzero radial component of the relative velocity vector is needed to obtain nonzero FDOA values.

The CRLB for one time scan, a pair of one TDOA and one FDOA measurement, is plotted in Figure 10. Assumed is a standard deviation of TDOA of 200 m ($0.67 \mu s$) and a standard deviation of FDOA of 4 m/s, this corresponds to a standard deviation in the frequency domain of 40 Hz, assuming a carrier frequency of about 3 GHz. The color bar shows the values for the localization accuracy in m. In these situations, the maximal gain in localization accuracy is obtained when the sensors fly one after the other. The results for the parallel flight can be improved if the distance of the sensors is increased.

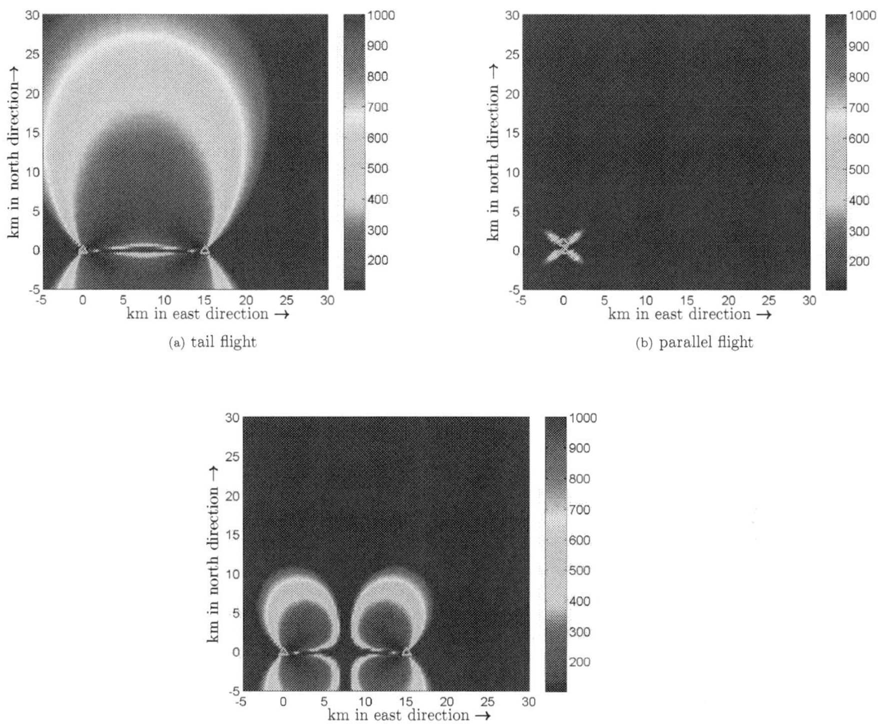

(a) tail flight (b) parallel flight (c) flight head on

Fig. 10. CRLB for the combination of TDOA and FDOA for one time scan

5.2.2 Results

Both TDOA and FDOA measurement equations are nonlinear. Therefore nonlinear estimation algorithms are needed to process the combined measurement set. The performance of three different estimation algorithms is investigated in a scenario with a moving emitter.
The investigated scenario and the results are described in (Mušicki et al., 2010). The emitter is assumed to move at a constant speed in x-direction of -10 m/s. Due to observability reasons, sensors perform maneuvers, they move with a constant speed, but not velocity, of 100 m/s. The results shown here are the product of a Monte Carlo simulation with 1000 runs with a

sampling interval of two seconds. A total of 80 s is regarded, the maneuver is performed at 40 s. The maximum emitter speed constraint is set to $V_{\max} = 15$ m/s. Measurement standard deviation σ_r for TDOA is assumed to be 100 m in the range domain, and the standard deviation σ_f for FDOA is assumed to be 10 mm/s in the velocity domain.
The three investigated algorithms are:

- The GMM-ITS (Gaussian Mixture Measurement presentation-Integrated Track Splitting) filter using TDOA and FDOA measurements is a dynamic GM filter with integrated track management, see (Mušicki et al., 2010) (TFDOA in Figure 11). In (Mušicki et al., 2010) is demonstrated that the simultaneous processing of the measurement pair is equivalent to processing first the TDOA measurement and than the FDOA measurement. The filter is initialized with the GM approximation of the first TDOA measurement. One cycle of the filter consists of several steps:
  - prior GM approximation of the updated density in the state space computed using previous measurements
  - prediction in the state space for each component of the GM
  - filtering with the incoming TDOA measurement:
    (a) GM representation of the TDOA measurement,
    (b) new components of the estimated state is obtained by updating each component of the predicted state space by each component of the TDOA GM,
    (c) control of the number of new estimated state components (pruning and merging)
  - filtering with the incoming FDOA measurement: each component of the state presentation is filtered with an EKF: updated density
- The GMM-ITS filter using single TDOA is a dynamic GM filter using only TDOA measurements. The processing is the same as in the GMM ITS filter, where the update process is only done with the TDOA measurements (TDOA in Figure 11)
- The static GM filter (fixed number of components) based on the combination of TDOA and FDOA measurements (static GM in Figure 11). The filter is initialized with the presentation of the TDOA measurement as a GM. The update is performed as EKF for the TDOA measurement as well as for the FDOA measurement, the filter based only on TDOA measurements is presented in 3.2.2.

Figure 11 presents the RMSE of the three described filters in comparison to the CRLB. The period after the sensor maneuvers, when the RMSE decreases, is zoomed in. In this scenario of a moving emitter, the filter based only on TDOA measurements shows poor performance. The combination of the various measurement types of TDOA and FDOA increases the estimation accuracy significantly. The static GM filter shows good performance with estimation errors of about 30 m. The dynamic GM filter is nearly on the CRLB in the final phase with estimation errors of about 10 m. This shows the significant gain in estimation accuracy combing different types of measurements.

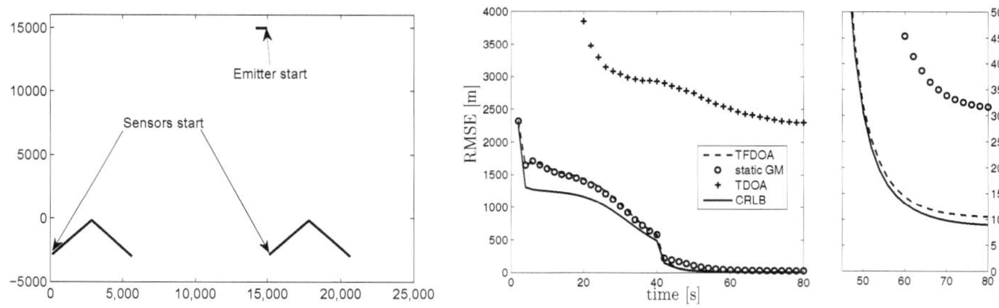

Fig. 11. (a) Scenario, (b) RMSE of the mobile emitter tracking (©[2010] IEEE)[1]

6. Conclusions

Passive emitter tracking in sensor networks is in general superior to emitter tracking using single sensors. Even a pair of sensors improves the performance strongly. The techniques of solving the underlying tracking problem are the same as in the single sensor case. The first step should be the investigation of the CRLB to know the optimal achievable estimation accuracy using the available measurement set. It reveals characteristic features of localization and gives an insight into the parametric dependencies of the passive emitter tracking problem under consideration. It shows that the estimation accuracy is often strongly dependent on the geometry. Secondly, a powerful estimation algorithm is needed to solve the localization problem. In passive emitter tracking, states and measurements are not linearly related. Therefore, only methods that appropriately deal with nonlinearities can be used. This chapter provides a review of different nonlinear estimation methods. Depending on the type of measurement and on different requirements in various scenarios, different estimation algorithms can be the methods of choice. E.g., to obtain good results near the CRLB the MLE is an appropriate method. Here, the computational effort is higher compared to alternatives such as Kalman filters. Tracking from the first measurement is possible using the UT in the TDOA/AOA case or using the GM filter or the GMM-ITS filter. They overcome the initialization difficulties of single Kalman Filters. The UT transform the measurement into the Cartesian state space and the GM filter and GMM-ITS filter approximate the first measurement by a Gaussian Mixture, a weighted sum of Gaussian densities. The first measurement is transformed into the Cartesian space and converted into a Gaussian sum. The tracking with the GM filter and GMM-ITS filter shows good performance and results near the CRLB.
For passive emitter tracking in sensor networks different measurement types can be gained by exploiting the signal coming from the target. Some of them can be taken by single sensors: e. g. bearing measurements. Others are only gained in the sensor network, a minimum of two sensors is needed. The combination of different measurements leads to a significant gain in estimation accuracy.

7. References

Bar-Shalom, Y., Li, X. R. & Kirubarajan, T. (2001). *Estimation with Applications to Tracking and Navigation: Theory Algorithms and Software*, Wiley & Sons.

[1] both figures have reprinted from (Mušicki et al., 2010)

Becker, K. (1992). An Efficient Method of Passive Emitter Location, *IEEE Trans. Aerosp. Electron. Syst.* **28**(4): 1091–1104.

Becker, K. (1993). Simple Linear Theory Approach to TMA Observability, *IEEE Trans. Aerosp. Electron. Syst.* **29, No. 2**: 575–578.

Becker, K. (1996). A General Approach to TMA Observability from Angle and Frequency Measurements, *IEEE Trans. Aerosp. Electron. Syst.* **32, No. 1**: 487–494.

Becker, K. (1999). Passive Localization of Frequency-Agile Radars from Angle and Frequency Measurements, *IEEE Trans. Aerosp. Electron. Syst.* **53, No. 4**: 1129 – 1144.

Becker, K. (2001). *Advanced Signal Processing Handbook*, chapter 9: Target Motion Analysis (TMA), pp. 1–21.

Becker, K. (2005). Three-Dimensional Target Motion Analysis using Angle and Frequency Measurements, *IEEE Trans. Aerosp. Electron. Syst.* **41**(1): 284–301.

Julier, S. J. & Uhlmann, J. K. (2004). Unscented Filtering and Nonlinear Estimation, *Proc. IEEE* **92**(3): 401–422.

K. C. Ho, L. Y. (2008). On the Use of a Calibration Emitter for Source Localization in the Presence of Sensor Position Uncertainty, *IEEE Trans. on Signal Processing* **56, No. 12**: 5758 – 5772.

Kaune, R. (2009). Gaussian Mixture (GM) Passive Localization using Time Difference of Arrival (TDOA), *Informatik 2009 — Workshop Sensor Data Fusion: Trends, Solutions, Applications*.

Mušicki, D., Kaune, R. & Koch, W. (2010). Mobile Emitter Geolocation and Tracking Using TDOA and FDOA Measurements, *IEEE Trans. on Signal Processing* **58, Issue 3, Part 2**: 1863 – 1874.

Mušicki, D. & Koch, W. (2008). Geolocation using TDOA and FDOA measurements, *Proc. 11th International Conference on Information Fusion*, pp. 1–8.

Oispuu, M. & Hörst, J. (2010). Azimuth-only Localization and Accuracy Study for Piecewise Curvilinearly Moving Targets, *International Conference on Information Fusion*.

Ristic, B., Arulampalam, S. & Gordon, N. (2004). *Beyond the Kalman Filter, Particle Filters for Tracking Applications*, Artech House.

So, H. C., Chan, Y. T. & Chan, F. K. W. (2008). Closed-Form Formulae for Time-Difference-of-Arrival Estimation, *IEEE Trans. on Signal Processing* **56, No. 6**: 2614 – 2620.

Stein, S. (1981). Algorithms for Ambiguity Function Processing, *IEEE Trans. Acoustic, Speech and Signal Processing* **29**(3): 588–599.

Tam, W. I., Plataniotis, K. N. & Hatzinakos, D. (1999). An adaptive Gaussian sum algorithm for radar tracking, *Elsevier Signal Processing* **77**: 85 – 104.

Van Trees, H. L. (1968). *Detection, Estimation and Modulation Theory, Part I*, New York: Wiley & Sons.

A. Appendix: Toolbox of methods

A.1 Cramér Rao investigation

It is important to know the optimum achievable localization accuracy that can be attained with the measurements. This optimum estimation accuracy is given by the Cramér Rao lower bound (CRLB); it is a lower bound for an unbiased estimator and can be asymptotically achieved by unbiased estimators (Bar-Shalom et al., 2001; Van Trees, 1968). The investigation of the CRLB reveals characteristic features of the estimation problem under consideration. The CRLB can be used as a benchmark to asses the performance of the investigated estimation methods. The CRLB is calculated from the inverse of the Fisher Information Matrix (FIM) $\mathbf{J}$. The CR inequality reads:

$$\mathbb{E}\left[(\hat{\mathbf{e}}_k - \mathbf{e}_k)(\hat{\mathbf{e}}_k - \mathbf{e}_k)^T\right] \geq \mathbf{J}_k^{-1}, \tag{28}$$

$$\mathbf{J}_k = \mathbb{E}\left[\nabla_{\mathbf{e}_k} \ln p(Z_k|\mathbf{e}_k)(\nabla_{\mathbf{e}_k} \ln p(Z_k|\mathbf{e}_k))^T\right], \tag{29}$$

where $\hat{\mathbf{e}}$ determines the estimate and $\mathbb{E}[\cdot]$ determines the expectation value.
The Fisher information $\mathbf{J}$ uses the Likelihood function, the conditional probability $p(Z_k|\mathbf{e}_k)$, for calculation:

$$p(Z_k|\mathbf{e}_k) = \left(\frac{1}{\sqrt{\det(2\pi\mathbf{R})}}\right) \exp\left(-\frac{1}{2}\sum_{i=1}^{k}(z_i - h(\mathbf{e}_i))^T\mathbf{R}^{-1}(z_i - h(\mathbf{e}_i))\right), \tag{30}$$

where $Z_k = \{z_1, z_2, \ldots, z_k\}$ is the set of measurements up to time t_k. Under the assumption of non-correlation of the measurement noise from time to time the calculation of the CRLB is performed for the reference time t_k with the measurement set $Z_k = \{z_1, \ldots, z_k\}$ and the time dependent measurement functions $\{h(\mathbf{e}_1), \ldots, h(\mathbf{e}_k)\}$. The computation results from the inverse of the Fisher information $\mathbf{J}_k$ at reference time t_k:

$$\mathbf{J}_k = \sum_{i=1}^{k}\left(\frac{\partial h(\mathbf{e}_i)}{\partial \mathbf{e}_k}\right)^T \mathbf{R}^{-1}\frac{\partial h(\mathbf{e}_i)}{\partial \mathbf{e}_k}, \tag{31}$$

where

$$\frac{\partial h(\mathbf{e}_i)}{\partial \mathbf{e}_k} = \frac{\partial h(\mathbf{e}_i)}{\partial \mathbf{e}_i}\frac{\partial \mathbf{e}_i}{\partial \mathbf{e}_k}. \tag{32}$$

For the stationary scenario the state vector $\mathbf{e}$ of the emitter is the same at each time step. That means,

$$\frac{\partial h(\mathbf{e}_i)}{\partial \mathbf{e}_i} = \frac{\partial h(\mathbf{e}_i)}{\partial \mathbf{e}_k} \quad \forall i. \tag{33}$$

For the mobile emitter case, we obtain, using the dynamic equation of the inertially target motion,

$$\mathbf{e}_k = \mathbf{F}_{k|k-1}\mathbf{e}_{k-1}, \tag{34}$$

where $\mathbf{F}_{k|k-1}$ is the evolution matrix which relates the target state from time t_k to time t_{k-1}, the FIM at reference time t_k

$$\mathbf{J}_k = \sum_{i=1}^{k}\mathbf{F}_{k|i}^{-1\,T}\left(\frac{\partial h(\mathbf{e}_i)}{\partial \mathbf{e}_i}\right)^T \mathbf{R}^{-1}\left(\frac{\partial h(\mathbf{e}_i)}{\partial \mathbf{e}_i}\right)\mathbf{F}_{k|i}^{-1}. \tag{35}$$

At time t_1 the FIM $\mathbf{J}_1$ is usually singular and not invertible, because the state vector $\mathbf{e}_k$ cannot be estimated based on a single measurement without additional assumptions. Thus, we incorporate additional assumptions. These assumptions may concern the area in which the emitter is attended to be. This prior information about a prior distribution of $\mathbf{e}$ can be added to the FIM at time t_1 as artificial measurement:

$$\mathbf{J}_1^{pr} = \mathbf{J}_1 + \mathbf{J}_{pr}, \tag{36}$$

where $\mathbf{J}_{pr}$ is the prior Fisher information. Under the Gaussian assumption of $\mathbf{e}$ follows:

$$\mathbf{J}_{pr} = \mathbf{P}_{pr}^{-1}, \tag{37}$$

where $\mathbf{P}_{pr}$ is the covariance of the prior distribution.
The prior information reduces the bound in the initial phase, but has little impact on later time steps.

A.2 NEES

Consistency is necessary for filter functionality, thus the normalized estimation error squared, the NEES is investigated, see (Bar-Shalom et al., 2001). A consistent estimator describes the size of the estimation error by its associated covariance matrix adequately. Filter consistency is necessary for the practical applicability of a filter.
The computation of the NEES requires the state estimate $\mathbf{e}_{k|k}$ at time t_k, its associated covariance matrix $\mathbf{P}_{k|k}$ and the true state $\mathbf{e}_k$.
Let $\tilde{\mathbf{e}}_{k|k}$ be the error of $\mathbf{e}_{k|k}$: $\tilde{\mathbf{e}}_{k|k} := \mathbf{e}_k - \mathbf{e}_{k|k}$. The NEES is defined by this term:

$$\epsilon_k = \tilde{\mathbf{e}}_{k|k}^T \mathbf{P}_{k|k}^{-1} \tilde{\mathbf{e}}_{k|k}. \tag{38}$$

thus, ϵ_k is the squared estimation error $\tilde{\mathbf{e}}_{k|k}$ which is normalized with its associated covariance $\mathbf{P}_{k|k}^{-1}$. Under the assumption that the estimation error is approximately Gaussian distributed and the filter is consistent, ϵ_k is χ^2 distributed with n_e degrees of freedom, where n_e is the dimension of $\mathbf{e}$: $\epsilon_k \sim \chi^2_{n_e}$. Then:

$$\mathbb{E}\left[\epsilon_k\right] = n_e. \tag{39}$$

The test will be based on the results of N Monte Carlo Simulations that provide N independent samples ϵ_k^i, $i = 1, \ldots, N$, of the random variable ϵ_k. The sample average of these N samples is

$$\bar{\epsilon}_k = \frac{1}{N} \sum_{i=1}^{N} \epsilon_k^i. \tag{40}$$

If the filter is consistent, $N\bar{\epsilon}_k$ will have a χ^2 density with Nn_e degrees of freedom.
Hypothesis H_0, that the state estimation errors are consistent with the filter calculated covariances is accepted if $\bar{\epsilon}_k \in [a_1, a_2]$, where the acceptance interval is determined such that:

$$P\left\{\bar{\epsilon}_k \in [a_1, a_2] \,|H_0\right\} = 1 - \alpha. \tag{41}$$

In this chapter, we apply the 95% probability concentration region for $\bar{\epsilon}_k$, i.e. α is $0,05$.
In the TDOA scenario of a stationary emitter, the dimension n_e of the emitter is 2, so the number of degrees of freedom for the NEES is equal to 2. Basis of the test are the results of $N = 1000$ Monte Carlo simulations, we get a total of 2000 degrees of freedom. The interval $[1.878, 2.126]$ is obtained for 2000 degrees of freedom with the values of the χ^2 table as two-sided acceptance interval.

A.3 Estimation algorithms overview

Powerful estimation algortihms must be found that effectively estimates the emitter state from the noisy measurements. Due to the fact that for passive emitter tracking, measurements and states are not linearly related, only nonlinear methods can be applied. We concentrate on some representatives of the number on nonlinear estimation methods with a focus on the Gaussian Mixture filter which shows good performance in nonlinear measurement situations, (Mušicki et al., 2010).

A.3.1 MLE

The MLE is a direct search method and computes at each time step the optimal emitter state based on the complete measurement dataset. It stores the complete measurement dataset and belongs to the batch algorithms. The MLE provides that value of $\mathbf{e}_k$ which maximizes the Likelihood function, the conditional probability density function, (30). This means that the MLE minimizes the quadratic form:

$$g(\mathbf{e}_k) = \sum_{i=1}^{k}(z_i - h(\mathbf{e}_i))^T\mathbf{R}^{-1}(z_i - h(\mathbf{e}_i)) \tag{42}$$

with respect to $\mathbf{e}_k$. Since there is no closed-form MLE solution for $\mathbf{e}_k$ in passive emitter tracking using TDOA, FDOA and AOA, a numerical iterative search algorithm is needed to find the minimum of the quadratic form. Therefore, application of MLE suffers from the same problems as the numerical algorithms. The ML method attains asymptotically the CRLB when properly initialized. One disadvantage of the MLE is the high computational effort in comparison to the Kalman filters.

A.3.2 EKF

The Extended Kalman filter (EKF) is a recursive Bayesian estimator which approximates the nonlinearities by linearization. The Bayes theorem which expresses the posterior probability density function of the state based on all available measurement information is used to obtain an optimal estimate of the state:

$$p(\mathbf{e}_k|Z_k) = \frac{p(z_k|\mathbf{e}_k)p(\mathbf{e}_k|Z_{k-1})}{p(z_k|Z_{k-1})}, \tag{43}$$

with $p(z_k|Z_{k-1}) = \int p(z_k|\mathbf{e}_k)p(\mathbf{e}_k|Z_{k-1})d\mathbf{e}_k$.
The filter consists of two steps, prediction using the dynamic equation and update, using the Bayes theorem to process the incoming measurement. Processing a combination of two measurements is the same as filtering first with one measurement and then processing the result with the other measurement, as shown in (Mušicki et al., 2010).
In passive target tracking using TDOA, angle and FDOA measurements, the nonlinearity is in the measurement equations. Thus, the EKF approximates the measurement equations by its first-order Taylor series expansions. Here, the TDOA and AOA measurement functions are differentiated with respect to the position coordinates and the FDOA measurement function is differentiated with respect to the position and velocity coordinates:

$$\widehat{\mathbf{H}}_k^t = \frac{(\mathbf{r}_k^{(1)})^T}{||\mathbf{r}_k^{(1)}||} - \frac{(\mathbf{r}_k^{(2)})^T}{||\mathbf{r}_k^{(2)}||} \tag{44}$$

$$\widehat{\mathbf{H}}_k^\alpha = \frac{\begin{pmatrix} y_k - y_k^{(1)} \\ x_k^{(1)} - x_k \end{pmatrix}^T}{||\mathbf{r}_k^{(1)}||^2} \tag{45}$$

$$\widehat{\mathbf{H}}_k^f = \begin{bmatrix} \mathbf{D}_k^{(1)} - \mathbf{D}_k^{(2)} \\ \frac{\mathbf{r}_k^{(2)}}{||\mathbf{r}_k^{(2)}||} - \frac{\mathbf{r}_k^{(1)}}{||\mathbf{r}_k^{(1)}||} \end{bmatrix}^T, \tag{46}$$

where

$$\mathbf{D}_k^{(i)} = \frac{(\dot{\mathbf{x}}_k^{(i)} - \dot{\mathbf{x}}_k) - \frac{1}{||\mathbf{r}_k^{(i)}||^2}\left[(\dot{\mathbf{x}}_k^{(i)} - \dot{\mathbf{x}}_k)^T \mathbf{r}_k^{(i)}\right]\mathbf{r}_k^{(i)}}{||\mathbf{r}_k^{(i)}||}, \quad i = 1,2. \tag{47}$$

Then the Kalman filter equations are applied. The EKF is highly sensitive to the initialization and works satisfactorily only if the initial value is near the true target position.

A.3.3 UKF

The Unscented Kalman Filter (UKF) (see (Julier & Uhlmann, 2004)) deterministically selects a small number of sigma points. These sigma points are propagated through a nonlinear transformation. Since the nonlinearities in passive target tracking are in the measurement equations, the Unscented Transform (UT) is applied in the update step. In the state space, sample points and their weights are deterministically chosen. They represent mean and covariance of the density. The sample points are propagated through the UT. This produces the sampling points in the measurement space. Furthermore a covariance and a cross covariance is computed. Than the Filter Equations are passed.
Alternatively, the UT can be used to transform measurements in the state space. In this chapter, measurements of the two-dimensional measurement space of TDOA and azimuth measurements and their associated measurement covariances are converted into the Cartesian state space. A position estimate and the associate position coavariance in the Cartesian state space is obtained.
The UT algorithm is very simple and easy to apply, no complex Jacobians must be calculated. The initialization is very important. A proper initialization is substantial for good results.

A.3.4 Gaussian Mixture Filter

The Gaussian Mixture (GM) Filter overcomes the initialization difficulties and divergence problems of the Kalman filter like EKF and UKF. It is a recursive Bayesian estimator like the Kalman filters which uses the Chapman-Kolmogoroff equation for the prediction step and the Bayes equation for the estimation update. The key idea is to approximate the posterior density $p(\mathbf{e}_k|Z_k)$ by a weighted sum of Gaussian density functions. Applying Bayes rule, the posterior density can be expressed using the likelihood function $p(z_k|\mathbf{e}_k)$. Therefore, the main step is to approximate the likelihood function by a GM:

$$p(z_k|\mathbf{e}_k) \approx p_A(z_k|\mathbf{e}_k) = \sum_{i=1}^{c_k} w_k^i \mathcal{N}\left(z_k^i; \hat{z}_{k|k}^i, \mathbf{R}_{k|k}^i\right), \tag{48}$$

where w_k^i are the weights such that $\sum_{i=1}^{c_k} w_k^i = 1$ and p_A is the density of approximation which must not be a probability density i. e. does not necessarily integrate to one.
The posterior density is:

$$p(\mathbf{e}_k|Z_k) = \frac{p(z_k|\mathbf{e}_k)p(\mathbf{e}_k|Z_{k-1})}{\int p(z_k|\mathbf{e}_k)p(\mathbf{e}_k|Z_{k-1})d\mathbf{e}_k}, \tag{49}$$

from which one can see, that multiplying $p(z_k|\mathbf{e}_k)$ by any constant will not change the posterior density.
The approximation of the likelihood is performed in the state space and can be made as accurate as desirable through the choice of the number of mixture components. The problem is to

formulate an algorithmic procedure for computation of weights, means and covariances. The number of components can increase exponentially over time.
We describe two types of GM filters, a dynamic GM filter and a static GM filter.

Dynamic GM filter

The dynamic GM filter represents both the measurement likelihood $p(z_k|\mathbf{e}_k)$ and the state estimate $p(\mathbf{e}_k|Z_k)$ in the form of Gaussian mixtures in the state space. The algorithm is initialized by approximating the likelihood function after the first measurement in the state space. This Gaussian Mixture yields a modelling of the state estimate too. New incoming TDOA measurements are converted into a Gaussian mixture in the state space. Each component of the state estimate is updated by each measurement component to produce one component of the updated emitter state estimate pdf $p(\mathbf{e}_k|Z_k)$. This update process is linear and performed by a standard Kalman filter. The number of emitter state estimate components increases exponentially in time. Therefore, their number must be controlled by techniques of pruning and merging.
For each time step the state estimate is obtained by the mean and the covariance:

$$\hat{\mathbf{e}}_k = \sum_{g=1}^{S_k M_k} \xi(g)\hat{\mathbf{e}}_{k|k}(g) \tag{50}$$

$$\mathbf{P}_{k|k} = \sum_{g=1}^{S_k M_k} \xi(g) \left(\mathbf{P}_{k|k} + \hat{\mathbf{e}}_{k|k}(g)\hat{\mathbf{e}}_{k|k}^T(g)\right) - \hat{\mathbf{e}}_{k|k}\hat{\mathbf{e}}_{k|k}^T. \tag{51}$$

The GM filter equations can be applied to all passive emitter tracking situations in this chapter. The measurement likelihoods must be presented by their GM.

Static GM filter

The static GM filter represents the likelihood function $p(z_1|\mathbf{e}_1)$ after taking the first measurement. The representation in the state space is used. Using the Bayesian equation this likelihood can be used to present the posterior density $p(\mathbf{e}_1|z_1)$. The component of the Gaussian Mixture are restricted to the number of the components of this Gaussian Sum representation. For each new incoming measurement an EKF is performed to update the posterior density.
The algorithmic procedure for computation of weights w_g, means $\mathbf{e}_g$ and covariances $\mathbf{P}_g$ of the GM is the same as in the dynamic case. The first measurement is converted into a Gaussian sum. The computational effort of finding a good initialization point for a single KF is omitted here. An EKF is started for each mean and covariance, the weights are updated with the probabilities $p(z|\mathbf{e})$. The filter output is the weighted sum of the individual estimates and covariances:

$$\hat{\mathbf{e}}_k = \sum_{g=1}^{n} w(g)\hat{\mathbf{e}}_{k|k}(g) \tag{52}$$

$$\mathbf{P}_{k|k} = \sum_{g=1}^{n} w(g) \left(\mathbf{P}_{k|k} + \hat{\mathbf{e}}_{k|k}(g)\hat{\mathbf{e}}_{k|k}^T(g)\right) - \hat{\mathbf{e}}_{k|k}\hat{\mathbf{e}}_{k|k}^T, \tag{53}$$

where n is the number of Gaussian terms.

14

Fuzzy-Pattern-Classifier Based Sensor Fusion for Machine Conditioning

Volker Lohweg and Uwe Mönks
Ostwestfalen-Lippe University of Applied Sciences, inIT - Institute Industrial IT, Lemgo Germany

1. Introduction

Sensor and Information fusion is recently a major topic not only in traffic management, military, avionics, robotics, image processing, and e.g. medical applications, but becomes more and more important in machine diagnosis and conditioning for complex production machines and process engineering. Several approaches for multi-sensor systems exist in the literature (e.g. Hall, 2001; Bossé, 2007).

In this chapter an approach for a Fuzzy-Pattern-Classifier Sensor Fusion Model based on a general framework (e.g. Bocklisch, 1986; Eichhorn, 2000; Schlegel, 2004; Lohweg, 2004; Lohweg, 2006; Hempel, 2008; Herbst 2008; Mönks, 2009; Hempel 2010) is described. An application of the fusion method is shown for printing machines. An application on quality inspection and machine conditioning in the area of banknote production is highlighted.

The inspection of banknotes is a high labour intensive process, where traditionally every note on every sheet is inspected manually. Machines for the automatic inspection and authentication of banknotes have been on the market for the past 10 to 12 years, but recent developments in technology have enabled a new generation of detectors and machines to be developed. However, as more and more print techniques and new security features are established, total quality, security in banknote printing as well as proper machine conditions must be assured (Brown, 2004). Therefore, this factor necessitates amplification of a sensorial concept in general. Such systems can be used to enhance the stability of inspection and condition results for user convenience while improving machine reliability.

During printed product manufacturing, measures are typically taken to ensure a certain level of printing quality. This is particularly true in the field of security printing, where the quality standards, which must be reached by the end-products, i.e. banknotes, security documents and the like, are very high. Quality inspection of printed products is conventionally limited to the optical inspection of the printed product. Such optical inspection can be performed as an off-line process, i.e. after the printed product has been processed in the printing press, or, more frequently, as an in-line process, i.e. on the printing press, where the printing operation is carried out. Usually only the existence or appearance of colours and their textures are checked by an optical inspection system.

In general, those uni-modal systems have difficulties in detection of low degradation errors over time (Ross 2006; Lohweg, 2006). Experienced printing press operators may be capable of identifying degradation or deviation in the printing press behaviour, which could lead to the occurrence of printing errors, for instance characteristic noise produced by the printing press. This ability is however highly dependent on the actual experience, know-how and attentiveness of the technical personnel operating the printing press. Furthermore, the ability to detect such changes in the printing press behaviour is intrinsically dependent on personnel fluctuations, such as staff reorganisation, departure or retirement of key personnel, etc. Moreover, as this technical expertise is human-based, there is a high risk that this knowledge is lost over time. The only available remedy is to organize secure storage of the relevant technical knowledge in one form or another and appropriate training of the technical personnel.

Obviously, there is need for an improved inspection system which is not merely restricted to the optical inspection of the printed end-product, but which can take other factors into account than optical quality criteria. A general aim is to improve the known inspection techniques and propose an inspection methodology that can ensure a comprehensive quality control of the printed substrates processed by printing presses, especially printing presses which are designed to process substrates used in the course of the production of banknotes, security documents and such like.

Additionally, a second aim is to propose a method, which is suited to be implemented as an expert system designed to facilitate operation of the printing press. In this context, it is particularly desired to propose a methodology, which is implemented in an expert system adapted to predict the occurrence of printing errors and machine condition and provide an explanation of the likely cause of errors, should these occur. An adaptive learning model, for both, conditioning and inspection methods based on sensor fusion and fuzzy interpretation of data measures is presented here.

2. Data Analysis and Knowledge Generation

In this section some general ideas for sensor and information fusion are presented for clarity. The basic concept of fused information relies on the fact that the lack of information which is supplied by sensors should be completed by a fusion process. It is assumed that, for example, two sensory information sources S_1 and S_2 with different active physical principles (e.g. pressure and temperature) are connected in a certain way. Then symbolically the union of information is described as follows (Luo, 1989):

$$Perf(S_1 \cup S_2) > Perf(S_1) + Perf(S_2) . \tag{1}$$

The performance *Perf* of a system should be higher than the performance of the two mono-sensory systems, or at least, it should be ensured that:

$$Perf(S_1 \cup S_2) > \max\left(Perf(S_1), Perf(S_2)\right) . \tag{2}$$

The fusion process incorporates performance, effectiveness and benefit. With fusion of different sources the perceptual capacity and plausibility of a combined result should be increased. It should be pointed out the above mentioned terms are not strictly defined as such. Moreover, they depend on a specific application as pointed out by Wald (Wald, 1999):

"Information fusion expresses the means and the tools for the alliance of data origination from different sources; it aims to obtain information of greater quality, the exact definition of greater quality will depend on the application."

The World Model (Luo, 1989) describes the fusion process in terms of a changing environment (cf. Fig. 1). The environment reacts on the system which controls (weighting factors A_i) a local fusion process based on different sensors S_i. On the basis of sensor models and the behaviour state of the sensors it is possible to predicate the statistical characteristics of the environment. Based on the World Model the environment stands for a general (printing) production machine. The fusion process generates in a best-case-scenario plausible and confident information which is necessary and sufficient for a stable decision.

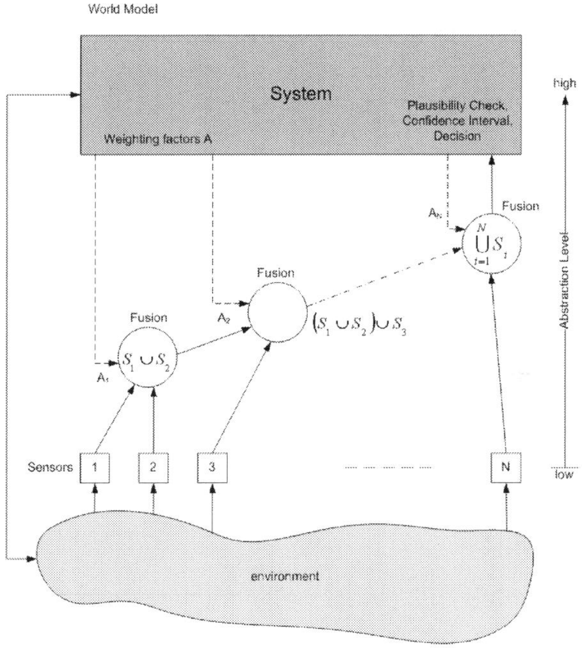

Fig. 1. World Model flow chart for multi-sensor information fusion (Luo, 1989)

2.1 Pitfalls in Sensor Fusion

In today's production world we are able to generate a huge amount of data from analogue or digital sensors, PLCs, middleware components, control PCs and if necessary from ERP systems. However, creating reliable knowledge about a machine process is a challenge because it is a known fact that Data $\neq$ Information $\neq$ Knowledge .

Insofar, a fusion process must create a low amount of data which creates reliable knowledge. Usually the main problems in sensor fusion can be described as follows: Too much data, poor models, bad features or too many features, and applications are not analysed properly. One major misbelieve is that machine diagnosis can be handled only based on the generated data - knowledge about the technical, physical, chemical, or other processes are indispensable for modeling a multi-sensor system.

Over the last decade many researchers and practitioners worked on effective multi-sensor fusion systems in many different areas. However, it has to be emphasized that some "Golden Rules" were formed which should be considered when a multi-sensor fusion system is researched and developed. One of the first who suggested rules (dirty secrets) in military applications were Hall and Steinberg (Hall, 2001a). According to their "Dirty Secrets" list, ten rules for automation systems should be mentioned here as general statements.

1. The system designers have to understand the production machine, automation system, etc. regarding its specific behaviour. Furthermore, the physical, chemical, biological and other effects must be conceived in detail.
2. Before designing a fusion system, the technical data in a machine must be measured to clarify which kind of sensor must be applied.
3. A human expert who can interpret measurement results is a must.
4. There is no substitute for an excellent or at least a good sensor. No amount of data from a not understood or not reliable data source can substitute a single accurate sensor that measures the effect that is to be observed.
5. Upstream sins still cannot be absolved by downstream processing. Data fusion processing cannot correct for errors in the pre-processing (or a wrong applied sensor) of individual data. "Soft" sensors are only useful if the data is known as reliable.
6. Not only may the fused result be worse than the best sensor - but failure to address pedigree, information overload, and uncertainty may show a worst result.
7. There is no such thing as a magic fusion algorithm. Despite claims of the contrary, no algorithm is optimal under all conditions. Even with the use of agent systems, ontologies, Dempster-Shafer and neuro-fuzzy approaches - just to name a few - the perfect algorithm is not invented yet. At the very end the application decides which algorithms are necessary.
8. The data are never perfectly de-correlated. Sources are in most cases statistically dependent.
9. There will never be enough training data available in a production machine. Therefore, hybrid methods based on models and training data should be used to apply Machine Learning and Pattern Recognition.
10. Data fusion is not a static process. Fusion algorithms must be designed so that the time aspect has to be considered.

2.2 Single-sensor vs. Multi-sensor Systems

Many detection systems are based on one main sensory apparatus. They rely on the evidence of a single source of information (e.g. photo-diode scanners in vending machines, greyscale-cameras in inspection systems, etc.). These systems, called unimodal systems, have to contend with a variety of general difficulties and have usually high false error rates in classification. The problems can be listed as follows; we refer to (Ross, 2006):

1. *Raw data noise*: Noisy data results from not sufficiently mounted or improperly maintained sensors. Also illumination units which are not properly maintained can cause trouble. Also, in general, machine drives and motors can couple different kinds of noise into the system.
2. *Intraclass variations*: These variations are typically caused by changing the sensory units in a maintenance process or by ageing of illuminations and sensors over a period of time.
3. *Interclass variations*: In a system which has to handle a variety of different production states over a period of time, there may be interclass similarities in the feature space of multiple flaws.
4. *Nonuniversality*: A system may not be able to create expedient and stable data or features from a subset of produced material.

Some of the above mentioned limitations can be overcome by including multiple information sources. Such systems, known as multimodal systems, are expected to be more reliable, due to the presence of multiple, partly signal-decorrelated, sensors. They address the problems of nonuniversality, and in combination with meaningful interconnection of signals (fusion), the problem of interclass variations. At least, they can inform the user about problems with intraclass variations and noise.

A generic multi-sensor system consists of four important units: a) the sensor unit which captures raw data from different measurement modules resp. sensors; b) the feature extraction unit which extracts an appropriate feature set as a representation for the machine to be checked; c) the classification unit which compares the actual data with their corresponding machine data stored in a database; d) the decision unit which uses the classification results to determine whether the obtained results represent e.g. a good printed or valid banknote. In multimodal systems information fusion can occur in any of the units. Generally three fusion types, depending on the abstraction level, are possible. The higher the abstraction level, the more efficient is the fusion. However, the high abstraction level fusion is not necessarily more effective due to the fact that data reduction methods are used. Therefore, information loss will occur (Beyerer, 2006).

1. *Signal level fusion – Sensor Association Principle*. At signal level all sensor signals are combined. It is necessary that the signals are comparable in a sense of data amount resp. sampling rate (adaption), registration, and time synchronisation.
2. *Feature level fusion – Feature Association Principle*. At feature level all signal descriptors (features) are combined. This is necessary if the signals are not comparable or complementary in a sense of data amount resp. sampling rate (adaption), registration, and time synchronisation. Usually this is the case if images and 1D-sensors are in use. There is no spatio-temporal coherence between the sensor signals.
3. *Symbol level fusion – Symbol Association Principle*. At symbol level all classification results are combined. In this case the reasoning (the decision) is based e.g. on probability or fuzzy membership functions (possibility functions). This is necessary if the signals are not comparable or complementary in a sense of data amount resp. sampling rate (adaption), registration, synchronisation and expert's know-how has to be considered.

Table 1 summarises the above mentioned fusion association principles.

It is stated (Ross, 2006) that generic multimodal sensor systems which integrate information by fusion at an early processing stage are usually more efficient than those systems which perform fusion at a later stage. Since input signals or features contain more information about the physical data than score values at the output of classifiers, fusion at signal or feature level is expected to provide better results. In general, fusion at feature level is critical under practical considerations, because the dimensionality of different feature sets may not be compatible. Therefore, the classifiers have the task to adapt the different dimensionalities onto a common feature space. Fusion in the decision unit is considered to be rigid, due to the availability of limited information and dimensionality.

Fusion Level	*Signal Level*	*Feature Level*	*Symbol Level*
Type of Fusion	Signals, Measurement Data	Signal Descriptors, Numerical Features	Symbols, Objects, Classes, Decisions
Objectives	Signal and Parameter Estimation	Feature Estimation, Descriptor Estimation	Classification, Pattern Recognition
Abstraction Level	low	middle	high
Applicable Data Models	Random Variables, Random Processes	Feature Vectors, Random Variable Vectors	Probability Distributions, Membership Functions
Fusion Conditions (spatio-temporal)	Registration / Synchronisation (*Alignment*)	Feature Allocation (*Association*)	Symbol Allocation (*Association*)
Complexity	high	middle	low

Table 1. Fusion levels and their allocation methods (Beyerer, 2006)

3. General Approach for Security Printing Machines

Under practical considerations, many situations in real applications can occur where information is not precise enough. This behaviour can be divided into two parts. The first part describes the fact that the information itself is uncertain. In general, the rules and the patterns describe a system in a vague way. This is because the system behaviour is too complex to construct an exact model, e.g. of a dynamic banknote model. The second part describes the fact that in real systems and applications many problems can occur, such as signal distortions and optical distortions. The practice shows that decisions are taken even on vague information and model imperfectness. Therefore, fuzzy methods are valuable for system analysis.

3.1 Detection Principles for Securities

In the general approach, different methods of machine conditioning and print flaw detection are combined, which can be used for vending or sorting machines as well as for printing machines.

3.1.1 Visible Light-based Optical Inspection

Analysis of the behaviour of the printing press is preferably performed by modelling characteristic behaviours of the printing press using appropriately located sensors to sense operational parameters of the functional components of the printing press which are exploited as representative parameters of the characteristic behaviours. These characteristic behaviours comprise of:

1. faulty or abnormal behaviour of the printing press, which leads to or is likely to lead to the occurrence of printing errors; and/or
2. defined behaviours (or normal behaviours) of the printing press, which leads to or is likely to lead to good printing quality.

Further, characteristic behaviours of the printing press can be modelled with a view to reduce false errors or pseudo-errors, i.e. errors that are falsely detected by the optical inspection system as mentioned above, and optimise the so-called alpha and beta errors. Alpha error is understood to be the probability to find bad sheets in a pile of good sheets, while beta error is understood to be the probability to find good printed sheets in a pile of bad printed sheets. According to (Lohweg, 2006), the use of a multi-sensor arrangement (i.e. a sensing system with multiple measurement channels) efficiently allows reducing the alpha and beta errors.

3.1.2 Detector-based Inspection

We have not exclusively used optical printing inspection methods, but also acoustical and other measurements like temperature and pressure of printing machines. For the latter cepstrum methods are implemented (Bogert, 1963). According to (Lohweg, 2006), the inherent defects of optical inspection are overcome by performing an in-line analysis of the behaviour of the printing press during the processing of the printed sheets. The monitored machine is provided with multiple sensors which are mounted on functional components of the printing press. As these sensors are intended to monitor the behaviour of the printing press during processing of the printed substrates, the sensors must be selected appropriately and be mounted on adequate functional machine components. The actual selection of sensors and location thereof depend on the configuration of the printing press, for which the behaviour is to be monitored. These will not be the same, for instance, for an intaglio printing press, an offset printing press, a vending machine or a sorting machine as the behaviours of these machines are not identical. It is not, strictly speaking, necessary to provide sensors on each and every functional component of the machine. But also the sensors must be chosen and located in such a way that sensing of operational parameters of selected functional machine components is possible. This permits a sufficient, precise and representative description of the various behaviours of the machine. Preferably, the sensors should be selected and positioned in such a way as to sense and monitor operational parameters which are virtually de-correlated. For instance, monitoring the respective rotational speeds of two cylinders which are driven by a common motor is not being very useful as the two parameters are directly linked to one another. In contrast, monitoring the current, drawn by an electric motor used as a drive and the contact pressure between two cylinders of the machine provides a better description of the behaviour of the printing press. Furthermore, the selection and location of the sensors should be made in view of the actual set of behaviour patterns one desires to monitor and of the classes of printing errors one wishes to detect. As a general rule, it is appreciated that sensors might be provided on the printing press in order to sense any combination of the following operational parameters:

1. processing speed of the printing press, i.e. the speed at which the printing press processes the printed substrates;
2. rotational speed of a cylinder or roller of the printing press;
3. current drawn by an electric motor driving cylinders of the printing unit of the printing press;

4. temperature of a cylinder or roller of the printing press;
5. pressure between two cylinders or rollers of the printing press;
6. constraints on bearings of a cylinder or roller of the printing press;
7. consumption of inks or fluids in the printing press; and/or
8. position or presence of the processed substrates in the printing press (this latter information is particularly useful in the context of printing presses comprising of several printing plates and/or printing blankets as the printing behaviour changes from one printing plate or blanket to the next).

Depending on the particular configuration of the printing press, it might be useful to monitor other operational parameters. For example, in the case of an intaglio printing press, monitoring key components of the so called wiping unit (Lohweg, 2006) has shown to be particularly useful in order to derive a representative model of the behaviour of the printing press, as many printing problems in intaglio printing presses are due to a faulty or abnormal behaviour of the wiping unit.

In general, multiple sensors are combined and mounted on a production machine. One assumption which is made in such applications is that the sensor signals should be de-correlated at least in a weak sense. Although this strategy is conclusive, the main drawback is based on the fact that even experts have only vague information about sensory cross correlation effects in machines or production systems. Furthermore, many measurements which are taken traditionally result in ineffective data simply because the measurement methods are suboptimal.

Therefore, our concept is based on a prefixed data analysis before classifying data. The classifier's learning is controlled by the data analysis results. The general concept is based on the fact that multi-sensory information can be fused with the help of a Fuzzy-Pattern-Classifier chain, which is described in section 5.

4. Fuzzy Multi-sensor Fusion

It can hardly be said that information fusion is a brand new concept. As a matter of fact, it has already been used by humans and animals intuitively. Techniques required for information fusion include various subjects, including artificial intelligence (AI), control theory, fuzzy logic, and numerical methods and so on. More areas are expected to join in along with consecutive successful applications invented both in defensive and civilian fields.

Multi-sensor fusion is the combination of sensory data or data derived from sensory data and from disparate sources such that the resulting information is in some sense better than for the case that the sources are used individually, assuming the sensors are combined in a good way. The term 'better' in that case can mean more accurate, more complete, or more reliable. The fusion procedure can be obtained from direct or indirect fusion. *Direct fusion* is the fusion of sensor data from some homogeneous sensors, such as acoustical sensors; *indirect fusion* means the fused knowledge from prior information, which could come from human inputs. As pointed out above, multi-sensor fusion serves as a very good tool to obtain better and more reliable outputs, which can facilitate industrial applications and compensate specialised industrial sub-systems to a large extent.

The primary objective of multivariate data analysis in fusion is to summarise large amounts of data by means of relatively few parameters. The underlying theme behind many multivariate techniques is reduction of features. One of these techniques is the Principal Components Analysis (PCA), which is also known as the Karhunen-Loéve transform (KLT) (Jolliffe, 2002).

Fuzzy-Pattern-Classification in particular is an effective way to describe and classify the printing press behaviours into a limited number of classes. It typically partitions the input space (in the present instance the variables - or operational parameters - sensed by the multiple sensors provided on functional components of the printing press) into categories or pattern classes and assigns a given pattern to one of those categories. If a pattern does not fit directly within a given category, a so-called "goodness of fit" is reported. By employing fuzzy sets as pattern classes, it is possible to describe the degree to which a pattern belongs to one class or to another. By viewing each category as a fuzzy set and identifying a set of fuzzy "if-then" rules as assignment operators, a direct relationship between the fuzzy set and pattern classification is realized. Figure 2 is a schematic sketch of the architecture of a fuzzy fusion and classification system for implementing the machine behaviour analysis. The operational parameters P_1 to P_n sensed by the multi-sensor arrangement are optionally preprocessed prior to feeding into the pattern classifier. Such preprocessing may in particular include a spectral transformation of some of the signals output by the sensors. Such spectral transformation will in particular be envisaged for processing the signal's representative of vibrations or noise produced by the printing press, such as the characteristic noise or vibration patterns of intaglio printing presses.

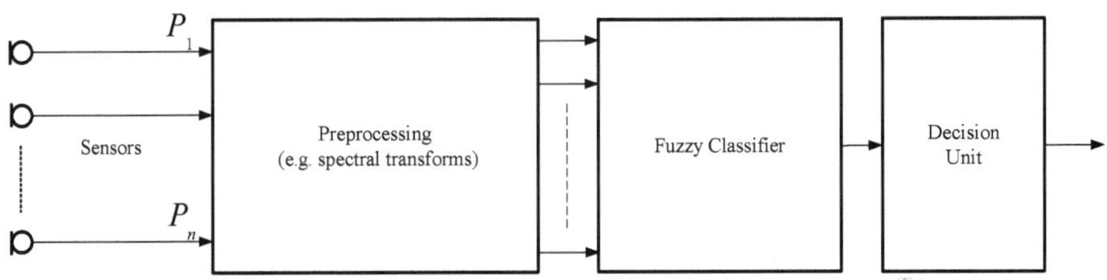

Fig. 2. Multi-sensor fusion approach based on Fuzzy-Pattern-Classifier modelling

5. Modelling by Fuzzy-Pattern-Classification

Fuzzy set theory, introduced first by Zadeh (Zadeh, 1965), is a framework which adds uncertainty as an additional feature to aggregation and classification of data. Accepting vagueness as a key idea in signal measurement and human information processing, fuzzy membership functions are a suitable basis for modelling information fusion and classification. An advantage in a fuzzy set approach is that class memberships can be trained by measured information while simultaneously expert's know-how can be taken into account (Bocklisch, 1986).

Fuzzy-Pattern-Classification techniques are used in order to implement the machine behaviour analysis. In other words, sets of fuzzy-logic rules are applied to characterize the behaviours of the printing press and model the various classes of printing errors which are likely to appear on the printing press. Once these fuzzy-logic rules have been defined, they can be applied to monitor the behaviour of the printing press and identify a possible correspondence with any machine behaviour which leads or is likely to lead to the occurrence of printing errors. Broadly speaking, Fuzzy-Pattern-Classification is a known technique that concerns the description or classification of measurements. The idea behind Fuzzy-Pattern-Classification is to define the common features or properties among a set of patterns (in this case the various behaviours a printing press can exhibit) and classify them into different predetermined classes according to a determined classification model. Classic modelling techniques usually try to avoid vague, imprecise or uncertain descriptive rules. Fuzzy systems deliberately make use of such descriptive rules. Rather than following a binary approach wherein patterns are defined by "right" or "wrong" rules, fuzzy systems use relative "if-then" rules of the type "if *parameter alpha* is equal to (greater than, ...less than) *value beta*, then *event A* always (often, sometimes, never) happens". Descriptors "always", "often", "sometimes", "never" in the above exemplary rule are typically designated as "linguistic modifiers" and are used to model the desired pattern in a sense of gradual truth (Zadeh, 1965; Bezdek, 2005). This leads to simpler, more suitable models which are easier to handle and more familiar to human thinking. In the next sections we will highlight some Fuzzy-Pattern-Classification approaches which are suitable for sensor fusion applications.

5.1 Modified-Fuzzy-Pattern-Classification

The Modified-Fuzzy-Pattern-Classifier (MFPC) is a hardware optimized derivate of Bocklisch's Fuzzy-Pattern-Classifier (FPC) (Bocklisch, 1986). It should be worth mentioning here that Hempel and Bocklisch (Hempel, 2010) showed that even non-convex classes can be modelled within the framework of Fuzzy-Pattern-Classification. The ongoing research on FPC for non-convex classes make the framework attractive for Support Vector Machine (SVM) advocates.

Inspired from Eichhorn (Eichhorn, 2000), Lohweg et al. examined both, the FPC and the MFPC, in detail (Lohweg, 2004). MFPC's general concept of simultaneously calculating a number of membership values and aggregating these can be valuably utilised in many approaches. The author's intention, which yields to the MFPC in the form of an optimized structure, was to create a pattern recognition system on a Field Programmable Gate Array (FPGA) which can be applied in high-speed industrial environments (Lohweg, 2009). As MFPC is well-suited for industrial implementations, it was already applied in many applications (Lohweg, 2006; Lohweg, 2006a; Lohweg, 2009; Mönks, 2009; Niederhöfer, 2009). Based on membership functions $\mu(m,\mathbf{p})$, MFPC is employed as a useful approach to modelling complex systems and classifying noisy data. The originally proposed unimodal MFPC fuzzy membership function $\mu(m,\mathbf{p})$ can be described in a graph as:

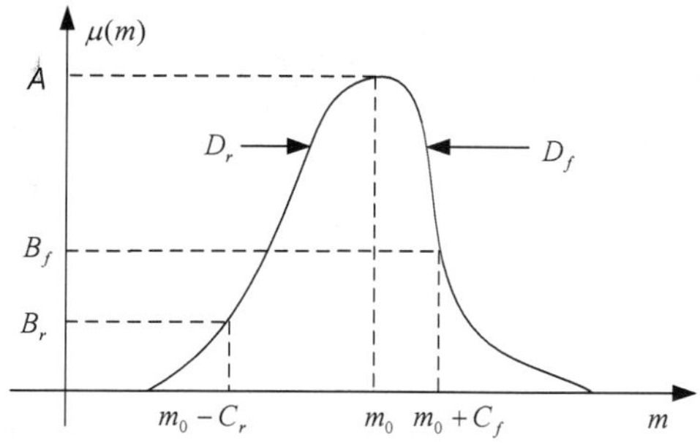

Fig. 3. Prototype of a unimodal membership function

The prototype of a one-dimensional potential function $\mu(m,\mathbf{p})$ can be expressed as follows (Eichhorn, 2000; Lohweg, 2004):

$$\mu(m,\mathbf{p}) = A \cdot 2^{-d(m,\mathbf{p})}, \tag{3}$$

with the difference measure

$$d(m,\mathbf{p}) = \begin{cases} \left(\dfrac{1}{B_r} - 1\right) \cdot \left(\dfrac{|m - m_0|}{C_r}\right)^{D_r} &, \forall m < m_0 \\ \left(\dfrac{1}{B_f} - 1\right) \cdot \left(\dfrac{|m - m_0|}{C_f}\right)^{D_f} &, \forall m \geq m_0 \end{cases}. \tag{4}$$

As for Fig. 3, the potential function $\mu(m,\mathbf{p})$ is a function concerning parameters A and the parameter vector $\mathbf{p}$ containing coefficients m_0, B_r, B_f, C_r, C_f, D_r, and D_f. A is denoted as the amplitude of this function, and in hardware design usually set $A = 1$. The coefficient m_0 is featured as center of gravity. The parameters B_r and B_f determine the value of the membership function on the boundaries $m_0 - C_r$ and $m_0 + C_f$ correspondingly. In addition, rising and falling edges of this function are described by $\mu(m_0 - C_r, \mathbf{p}) = B_r$ and $\mu(m_0 + C_f, \mathbf{p}) = B_f$. The distance from the center of gravity is interpreted by C_r and C_f. The parameters D_r and D_f depict the decrease in membership with the increase of the distance from the center of gravity m_0. Suppose there are M features considered, then Eq. 3 can be reformulated as:

$$\mu(\mathbf{m},\mathbf{p}) = 2^{-\frac{1}{M}\sum_{i=0}^{M-1} d_i(m_i, \mathbf{p}_i)}. \tag{5}$$

With a special definition ($A = 1$, $B_r = B_f = 0.5$, $C_r = C_f$, $D_r = D_f$) Modified-Fuzzy-Pattern Classification (Lohweg, 2004; Lohweg 2006; Lohweg 2006a) can be derived as:

$$\mu_{MFPC}(\mathbf{m},\mathbf{p}) = 2^{-\frac{1}{M}\sum_{i=0}^{M-1} d_i(m_i,\mathbf{p}_i)}, \tag{6}$$

where

$$d_i(m_i,\mathbf{p}_i) = \left(\frac{|m_i - m_{0,i}|}{C_i}\right)^D, \quad m_{0,i} = \frac{1}{2}(m_{\max_i} + m_{\min_i}), \quad C_i = (1 + 2\cdot P_{CE})\cdot(\frac{m_{\max_i} - m_{\min_i}}{2}). \tag{7}$$

The parameters $m_{\max}$ and $m_{\min}$ are the maximum and minimum values of a feature in the training set. The parameter m_i is the input feature which is supposed to be classified. Admittedly, the same objects should have similar feature values that are close to each other. In such a sense, the resulting value of $m_i - m_{0,i}$ ought to fall into a small interval, representing their similarity. The value P_{CE} is called elementary fuzziness ranging from zero to one and can be tuned by experts' know-how. The same implies to $D = (2, 4, 8, \ldots)$. The aggregation is performed by a fuzzy averaging operation with a subsequent normalization procedure.

As an instance of FPC, MFPC was addressed and successfully hardware-implemented on banknote sheet inspection machines. MFPC utilizes the concept of membership functions in fuzzy set theory and is capable of classifying different objects (data) according to their features, and the outputs of the membership functions behave as evidence for decision makers to make judgments. In industrial applications, much attention is paid on the costs and some other practical issues, thus MFPC is of great importance, particularly because of its capability to model complex systems and hardware implementability on FPGAs.

5.2 Adaptive Learning Model for Modified-Fuzzy-Pattern-Classification

In this section we present an adaptive learning model for fuzzy classification and sensor fusion, which on one hand adapts itself to varying data and on the other hand fuses sensory information to one score value. The approach is based on the following facts:

1. The sensory data are in general correlated or
2. Tend to correlate due to material changes in a machine.
3. The measurement data are *time-variant*, e.g., in a production process many parameters are varying imperceptively.
4. The definition of "good" production is always human-centric. Therefore, a committed quality standard is defined at the beginning of a production run.
5. Even if the machine parameters change in a certain range the quality could be in order.

The underlying scheme is based on membership functions (local classifiers) $\mu_i(m_i,\mathbf{p}_i)$, which are tuned by a learning (training) process. Furthermore, each membership function is weighted with an attractor value A_i, which is proportional to the eigenvalue of the corresponding feature m_i. This strategy leads to the fact that the local classifiers are trained based on committed quality and weighted by their attraction specified by a Principal Component Analysis' (PCA) (Jolliffe, 2002) eigenvalues. The aggregation is again performed by a fuzzy averaging operation with a subsequent normalization procedure.

5.2.1 Review on PCA

The Principal Components Analysis (PCA) is effective, if the amount of data is high while the feature quantity is small (< 30 features). PCA is a way of identifying patterns in data, and expressing the data in such a way as to highlight their similarities and differences. Since patterns in data are hard to find in data of high dimensions, where the graphical representation is not available, PCA is a powerful tool for analysing data. The other main advantage of PCA is that once patterns in the data are found, it is possible to compress the data by reducing the number of dimensions without much loss of information. The main task of the PCA is to project input data into a new (sub-)space, wherein the different input signals are de-correlated. The PCA is used to find weightings of signal importance in the measurement's data set.

PCA involves a mathematical procedure which transforms a set of correlated response variables into a smaller set of uncorrelated variables called principal components. More formally it is a linear transformation which chooses a new coordinate system for the data set such that the greatest variance by any projection of the set is on the first axis, which is also called the first principal component. The second greatest variance is on the second axis, and so on. Those created principal component variables are useful for a variety of things including data screening, assumption checking and cluster verification. There are two possibilities to perform PCA: first applying PCA to a covariance matrix and second applying PCA to a correlation matrix. When variables are not normalised, it is necessary to choose the second approach: Applying PCA to raw data will lead to a false estimation, because variables with the largest variance will dominate the first principal component. Therefore in this work the second method in applying PCA to standardized data (correlation matrix) is presented (Jolliffe, 2002).

In the following the function steps of applying PCA to a correlation matrix is reviewed concisely. If there are M data vectors $\mathbf{x}_{1N}^T \dots \mathbf{x}_{MN}^T$ each of length N, the projection of the data into a subspace is executed by using the Karhunen-Loéve transform (KLT) and their inverse, defined as:

$$\mathbf{Y} = \mathbf{W}^T \cdot \mathbf{X} \text{ and } \mathbf{X} = \mathbf{W} \cdot \mathbf{Y}, \tag{8}$$

where $\mathbf{Y}$ is the output matrix, $\mathbf{W}$ is the KLT transform matrix followed by the data (input) matrix:

$$\mathbf{X} = \begin{pmatrix} x_{11} & x_{12} & \cdots & x_{1N} \\ x_{21} & x_{22} & \cdots & x_{2N} \\ \vdots & \vdots & \cdots & \vdots \\ x_{M1} & x_{M2} & \cdots & x_{MN} \end{pmatrix}. \tag{9}$$

Furthermore, the expectation value $E(\bullet)$ (average $\overline{x}$) of the data vectors is necessary:

$$\overline{\mathbf{x}} = E(X) = \begin{pmatrix} E(x_1) \\ E(x_2) \\ \vdots \\ E(x_M) \end{pmatrix} = \begin{pmatrix} \overline{x}_1 \\ \overline{x}_2 \\ \vdots \\ \overline{x}_M \end{pmatrix}, \text{ where } \overline{x}_i = \frac{1}{N}\sum_{i=1}^{N} x_i . \tag{10}$$

With the help of the data covariance matrix

$$\mathbf{C} = E\left[(\mathbf{x}-\overline{\mathbf{x}})(\mathbf{x}-\overline{\mathbf{x}})^T\right] = \begin{pmatrix} c_{11} & c_{12} & \cdots & c_{1M} \\ c_{21} & c_{22} & \cdots & c_{2M} \\ \vdots & \vdots & \cdots & \vdots \\ c_{M1} & {}_{M2} & \cdots & c_{MM} \end{pmatrix}, \tag{11}$$

the correlation matrix $\boldsymbol{R}$ is calculated by:

$$\mathbf{R} = \begin{pmatrix} 1 & \rho_{12} & \cdots & \rho_{1N} \\ \rho_{21} & 1 & \cdots & \rho_{2N} \\ \vdots & \vdots & \cdots & \vdots \\ \rho_{N1} & \rho_{N2} & \cdots & 1 \end{pmatrix}, \text{ where } \rho_{ij} = \frac{c_{ij}}{\sqrt{c_{ii}c_{jj}}}. \tag{12}$$

The variables c_{ii} are called variances; the variables c_{ij} are called covariances of a data set. The correlation coefficients are described as ρ_{ij}. Correlation is a measure of the relation between two or more variables. Correlation coefficients can range from -1 to +1. The value of -1 represents a perfect negative correlation while a value of +1 represents a perfect positive correlation. A value of 0 represents no correlation. In the next step the eigenvalues λ_i and the eigenvectors $\mathbf{V}$ of the correlation matrix are computed by Eq. 13, where $\text{diag}(\lambda)$ is the diagonal matrix of eigenvalues of **C**:

$$\text{diag}(\lambda) = \mathbf{V}^{-1} \cdot \mathbf{R} \cdot \mathbf{V}. \tag{13}$$

The eigenvectors generate the KLT matrix and the eigenvalues represent the distribution of the source data's energy among each of the eigenvectors. The cumulative energy content for the *p*th eigenvector is the sum of the energy content across all of the eigenvectors from 1 through *p*. The eigenvalues have to be sorted in decreasing order:

$$\begin{pmatrix} \lambda_1 & \cdots & 0 \\ \vdots & \ddots & \vdots \\ 0 & \cdots & \lambda_M \end{pmatrix}, \text{ where } \lambda_1 \geq \lambda_2 \geq \cdots \geq \lambda_M. \tag{14}$$

The corresponding vectors $\mathbf{v}_i$ of the matrix $\mathbf{V}$ have also to be sorted in decreasing order like the eigenvalues, where $\mathbf{v}_1$ is the first column of matrix $\mathbf{V}$, $\mathbf{v}_2$ the second and $\mathbf{v}_M$ is the last column of matrix $\mathbf{V}$. The eigenvector $\mathbf{v}_1$ corresponds to eigenvalue λ_1, eigenvector $\mathbf{v}_2$ to eigenvalue λ_2 and so forth. The matrix **W** represents a subset of the column eigenvectors as basis vectors. The subset is preferably as small as possible (two eigenvectors). The energy distribution is a good indicator for choosing the number of eigenvectors. The cumulated energy should map approx. 90 % on a low number of eigenvectors. The matrix $\mathbf{Y}$ (cf. Eq. 8) then represents the Karhunen-Loéve transformed data (KLT) of matrix $\mathbf{X}$ (Lohweg, 2006a).

5.2.2 Modified Adaptive-Fuzzy-Pattern-Classifier

The adaptive Fuzzy-Pattern-Classifier core based on the world model (Luo, 1989) consists of M local classifiers (MFPC), one for each feature. It can be defined as

$$AFPC = diag(\mu_i) = \begin{bmatrix} \mu_1(m_1,\mathbf{p}_1) & 0 & 0 & 0 \\ 0 & \mu_2(m_2,\mathbf{p}_2) & 0 & 0 \\ 0 & 0 & \ddots & 0 \\ 0 & 0 & 0 & \mu_M(m_M,\mathbf{p}_M) \end{bmatrix}. \tag{15}$$

The adaptive fuzzy inference system (AFIS), is then described with a length M unit vector $\mathbf{u} = (1,\ldots,1)^T$ and the attractor vector $\mathbf{A} = (A_1, A_2, \ldots, A_M)^T$ as

$$\mu_{AFIS} = \frac{1}{\mathbf{A}^T \cdot \mathbf{u}} \mathbf{A}^T \cdot diag(\mu_i) \cdot \mathbf{u}, \tag{16}$$

which can be written as

$$\mu_{AFIS} = \frac{1}{\sum_{i=1}^{M} A_i} \cdot \sum_{i=1}^{M} A_i \cdot 2^{-d_i}. \tag{17}$$

The adaptive Fuzzy-Pattern-Classifier model output μ_{AFIS} can be interpreted as a score value in the range of $\{0\ldots1\}$. If $\mu_{AFIS} = 1$, a perfect match is reached, which can be assumed as a measure for a "good" system state, based on an amount of sensor signals. The score value $\mu_{AFIS} = 0$ represents the overall "bad" measure decision for a certain trained model. As it will be explained in section 6 the weight values of each parameter are taken as the weighted components of eigenvector one (PC1) times the square roots of the corresponding eigenvalues:

$$A_i = \left| v_{1i} \cdot \sqrt{\lambda_1} \right|. \tag{18}$$

With Eq. 17 the Modified-Adaptive-Fuzzy-Pattern-Classifier (MAFPC) results then in

$$\mu_{MAFPC} = \frac{1}{\sum_{i=1}^{M} \left| v_{1i} \cdot \sqrt{\lambda_1} \right|} \cdot \sum_{i=1}^{M} \left| v_{1i} \cdot \sqrt{\lambda_1} \right| \cdot 2^{-d_i}. \tag{19}$$

In section 6.1 an application with MAFPC will be highlighted.

5.3 Probabilistic Modified-Fuzzy-Pattern-Classifier

In many knowledge-based industrial applications there is a necessity to train using a small data set. It is typical that there are less than ten up to some tens of training examples. Having only such a small data set, the description of the underlying universal set, from which these examples are taken, is very vague and connected to a high degree of uncertainty. The heuristic parameterisation methods for the MFPC presented in section 5.1 leave a high degree of freedom to the user which makes it hard to find optimal parameter values. In this section we suggest an automatic method of learning the fuzzy membership

functions by estimating the data set's probability distribution and deriving the function's parameters automatically from it. The resulting *Probabilistic MFPC (PMFPC)* membership function is based on the MFPC approach, but leaves only one degree of freedom leading to a shorter learning time for obtaining stable and robust classification results (Mönks, 2010).
Before obtaining the different PMFPC formulation, it is reminded that the membership functions are aggregated using a fuzzy averaging operator in the MFPC approach. Consequently, on the one hand the PMFPC membership functions can substitute the MFPC membership function. On the other hand the fuzzy averaging operator used in the MFPC can be substituted by any other operator. Actually, it is also possible to substitute both parts of the MFPC at the same time (Mönks, 2010), and in all cases the application around the classifier remains unchanged. To achieve the possibility of exchanging the MFPC's core parts, its formulation of Eq. 6 is rewritten to

$$\mu_{MFPC}(\mathbf{m},\mathbf{p}) = 2^{-\frac{1}{M}\sum_{i=0}^{M-1} d_i(m_i,\mathbf{p}_i)} = \left(\prod_{i=1}^{M} 2^{-d_i(m_i,\mathbf{p}_i)}\right)^{\frac{1}{M}}, \tag{20}$$

revealing that the MFPC incorporates the geometric mean as its fuzzy averaging operator. Also, the unimodal membership function, as introduced in Eq. 3 with $A=1$, is isolated clearly, which shall be replaced by the PMFPC membership function described in the following section.

5.3.1 Probabilistic MFPC Membership Function

The PMFPC approach is based on a slightly modified MFPC membership function

$$\mu(m,\mathbf{p}) = 2^{-ld\left(\frac{1}{B}\right)d(m,\mathbf{p})} \in [0,1]. \tag{21}$$

D and B are automatically parameterised in the PMFPC approach. P_{CE} is yet not automated to preserve the possibility of adjusting the membership function slightly without needing to learn the membership functions from scratch. The algorithms presented here for automatically parameterising parameters D and B are inspired by former approaches: Bocklisch as well as Eichhorn developed algorithms which allow obtaining a value for the (MFPC) potential function's parameter D automatically, based on the used training data set. Bocklisch also proposed an algorithm for the determination of B. For details we refer to (Bocklisch, 1987) and (Eichhorn, 2000). However, these algorithms yield parameters that do not fulfil the constraints connected with them in all practical cases (cf. (Mönks, 2010)). Hence, we propose a probability theory-based alternative described in the following.
Bocklisch's and Eichhorn's algorithms adjust D after comparing the actual distribution of objects to a perfect uniform distribution. However, the algorithms tend to change D for every (small) difference between the actual distribution and a perfect uniform distribution. This explains why both algorithms do not fulfil the constraints when applied to random uniform distributions.
We actually stick to the idea of adjusting D with respect to the similarity of the actual distribution compared to an artificial, ideal uniform distribution, but we use probability theoretical concepts. Our algorithm basically works as follows: At first, the empirical

cumulative distribution function (ECDF) of the data set under investigation is determined. Then, the ECDF of an artificial perfect uniform distribution in the range of the actual distribution is determined, too. The similarity between both ECDFs is expressed by its correlation factor which is subsequently mapped to D by a parameterisable function.

5.3.1.1 Determining the Distributions' Similarity

Consider a sorted vector of n feature values $\mathbf{m}=(m_1,m_2,\dots,m_n)$ with $m_1 \le m_2 \le \dots \le m_n$, thus $m_{\min}=m_1$ and $m_{\max}=m_n$. The corresponding empirical cumulative distribution function $P_m(x)$ is determined by $P_m(x)=\frac{|\tilde{\mathbf{m}}|}{n}$ with $\tilde{\mathbf{m}}=(m_i | m_i \le x \; \forall i \in \mathbb{N}_n)$, where $|\mathbf{x}|$ denotes the number of elements in vector $\mathbf{x}$ and $\mathbb{N}_n=[1,2,\dots,n]$. The artificial uniform distribution is created by equidistantly distributing n values u_i, hence $\mathbf{u}=(u_1,u_2,\dots,u_n)$, with $u_i=m_1+(i-1)\cdot\frac{m_n-m_1}{n-1}$. Its ECDF $P_u(x)$ is determined analogously by substituting $\mathbf{m}$ with $\mathbf{u}$. In the next step, the similarity between both distribution functions is computed by calculating the *correlation factor* (Polyanin, 2007)

$$c=\frac{\sum_{i=1}^{k}\left(P_m[x_i]-\bar{P}_m\right)\left(P_u[x_i]-\bar{P}_u\right)}{\sqrt{\sum_{i=1}^{k}\left(P_m[x_i]-\bar{P}_m\right)^2\sum_{i=1}^{k}\left(P_u[x_i]-\bar{P}_u\right)^2}}, \tag{22}$$

where $\bar{P}_a$ is the mean value of $P_a(x)$, computed as $\bar{P}_a=\frac{1}{k}\sum_{i=1}^{k}P_a[x_i]$. The correlation factor must now be mapped to D while fulfilling Bocklisch's constraints on D (Bocklisch, 1987). Therefore, the average influence $\bar{\alpha}(D)$ of the parameter D on the MFPC membership function, which is the base for PMFPC membership function, is investigated to derive a mapping based on it. First $\alpha_D(x)$ is determined by taking $\frac{\partial}{\partial D}\mu(x,D)$ with $x=\frac{m-m_0}{C}$, $x>0$:

$$\alpha_D(x)=\frac{\partial}{\partial D}\mu(x,D)=\frac{\partial}{\partial D}2^{-x^D}=\ln(2)\left(-2^{-x^D}\right)x^D\ln(x). \tag{23}$$

The locations x represent the distance to the membership function's mean value m_0, hence $x=0$ is the mean value itself, $x=1$ is the class boundary m_0+C, $x=2$ twice the class boundary and so on. The average influence of D on the membership function $\bar{\alpha}(D)=\frac{1}{x_r-x_l}\int_{x_l}^{x_r}\alpha_D(x)\,dx$ is evaluated for $-1\le x\le 1$: This interval bears the most valuable information since all feature values of the objects in the training data set are included in this interval, and additionally those of the class members are expected here during the classification process, except from only a typically neglectable number of outliers. The mapping of $D: c\to[2,20]$, which is derived in the following, must take D's average influence into consideration, which turns out to be exponentially decreasing (Mönks, 2010).

5.3.1.2 Mapping the Distributions' Similarity to the Edge's Steepness

In the general case, the correlation factor c can take values from the interval $[-1,1]$, but when evaluating distribution functions, the range of values is restricted to $c \in [0,1]$, which is because probability distribution functions are monotonically increasing. This holds for both distributions, $P_m(x)$ as well as $P_u(x)$. It follows $c \geq 0$. The interpretation of the correlation factor is straight forward. A high value of c means that the distribution $P_m(x)$ is close to a uniform distribution. If $P_m(x)$ actually was a uniform distribution, $c = 1$ since $P_m(x) = P_u(x)$. According to Bocklisch, D should take a high value here. The more $P_m(x)$ differs from a uniform distribution, the more $c \to 0$, the more $D \to 2$. Hence, the mapping function $D(c)$ must necessarily be an increasing function with taking the exponentially decreasing average influence of D on the membership function $\bar{\alpha}(D)$ into consideration (cf. (Mönks, 2010)). An appropriate mapping $D: c \to [2,20]$ is an exponentially increasing function which compensates the changes of the MFPC membership function with respect to changes of c. We suggest the following heuristically determined exponential function, which achieved promising results during experiments:

$$D(c) = 19^{c^{2q}} + 1 \Rightarrow D(c) \in [2,20], \tag{24}$$

where q is an adjustment parameter. This formulation guarantees that $D \in [2,20] \; \forall c$ since $c \in [0,1]$. Using the adjustment parameter q, D is adjusted with respect to the aggregation operator used to fuse all n membership functions representing each of the n features. Each fuzzy aggregation operator behaves differently. For a fuzzy averaging operator $h(\mathbf{a})$, Dujmović introduced the objective measure of global andness ρ_g (for details cf. (Dujmović, 2007), (Mönks, 2009)). Assuming $q = 1$ in the following cases, it can be observed that, when using aggregation operators with a global andness $\rho_g^{h(\mathbf{a})} \to 0$, the aggregated single, n-dimensional membership function is more fuzzy than that one obtained when using an aggregation operator with $\rho_g^{h(\mathbf{a})} \to 1$, where the resulting function is sharp. This behaviour should be compensated by adjusting D in such a way, that the aggregated membership functions have comparable shapes: at some given correlation factor c, D must be increased if ρ_g is high and vice versa. This is achieved by mapping the aggregation operator's global andness to q, hence $q: \rho_g \to \mathbb{R}$. Our suggested solution is a direct mapping of the global andness to the adjustment parameter q, hence $q(\rho_g) = \rho_g \Rightarrow q \in [0,1]$. The mapping in Eq. 24 is now completely defined and consistent with Bocklisch's constraints and the observations regarding the aggregation operator's andness.

5.3.1.3 Determining the Class Boundary Membership Parameter

In addition to the determination of D, we present an algorithm to automatically parameterise the class boundary membership B. This parameter is a measure for the membership $\mu(m,\mathbf{p})$ at the locations $m \in \{m_0 + C, m_0 - C\}$. The algorithm for determining B is based on the algorithm Bocklisch developed, but was not adopted as it stands since it has

some disadvantages if this algorithm is applied to distributions with a high density especially on the class boundaries. For details cf. (Bocklisch, 1987).
When looking at the MFPC membership functions, the following two constraints on B can be derived: (i) The probability of occurrence is the same for every object in uniform distributions, also on the class boundary. Here, B should have a high value. (ii) For distributions where the density of objects decreases when going towards the class boundaries B should be assigned a small value, since the probability that an object occurs at the boundary is smaller than in the centre.
Hence, for sharp membership functions ($D \to 20$) a high value for B should be assigned, while for fuzzy membership functions ($D \to 2$) the value of B should be low. $B = f(D)$ must have similar properties like $\bar{\alpha}(D)$, meaning B changes quickly where $\bar{\alpha}(D)$ changes quickly and vice versa. We adopted Bocklisch's suitable equation for computing the class boundary membership (Bocklisch, 1987):

$$B = \frac{1}{1 + \left(\dfrac{1}{B_{\max}} - 1\right) \cdot \left(\dfrac{D_{\max}}{D}\right)^{1+\frac{1}{q}}}, \tag{25}$$

where $B_{\max} \in (0,1)$ stands for the maximum possible value of B with a proposed value of 0.9, $D_{\max} = 20$ is the maximum possible value of D and q is identical in its meaning and value to q as used in Eq. 24.

5.3.1.4 An Asymmetric PMFPC Membership Function Formulation

A data set may be represented better if the membership function was formulated asymmetrically instead of symmetrically as is the case with Eq. 21. This means

$$\mu(m, \mathbf{p}) = \begin{cases} 2^{-ld\left(\frac{1}{B_r}\right)\left(\frac{|m-m_0|}{C_r}\right)^{D_r}}, & m \le m_0 \\ 2^{-ld\left(\frac{1}{B_f}\right)\left(\frac{|m-m_0|}{C_f}\right)^{D_f}}, & m > m_0 \end{cases}, \tag{26}$$

where $m_0 = \frac{1}{M}\sum_{i=1}^{M} m_i$, $m_i \in \mathbf{m}$ is the arithmetic mean of all feature values. If m_0 was computed as introduced in Eq. 7, the resulting membership function would not describe the underlying feature vector $\mathbf{m}$ appropriately for asymmetrical feature distributions. A new computation method must therefore also be applied to $C_r = m_0 - m_{\min} + P_{CE} \cdot (m_{\max} - m_{\min})$ and $C_f = m_{\max} - m_0 + P_{CE} \cdot (m_{\max} - m_{\min})$ due to the change to the asymmetrical formulation. To compute the remaining parameters, the feature vector must be split into the left side feature vector $\mathbf{m}_r = (m_i | m_i \le m_0)$ and the one for the right side $\mathbf{m}_f = (m_i | m_i \ge m_0)$ for all $m_i \in \mathbf{m}$. They are determined following the algorithms presented in the preceding sections 5.3.1.2 and 5.3.1.3, but using only the feature vector for one side to compute this side's respective parameter.
Using Eq. 26 as membership function, the Probabilistic Modified-Fuzzy-Pattern-Classifier is defined as

$$\mu_{PMFPC}(\mathbf{m},\mathbf{p}) == \begin{cases} \left(\prod_{i=1}^{M} 2^{-ld\left(\frac{1}{B_r}\right)\left(\frac{|m-m_0|}{C_r}\right)^{D_r}} \right)^{\frac{1}{M}} &, m \leq m_0 \\ \left(\prod_{i=1}^{M} 2^{-ld\left(\frac{1}{B_f}\right)\left(\frac{|m-m_0|}{C_f}\right)^{D_f}} \right)^{\frac{1}{M}} &, m > m_0 \end{cases}, \quad (27)$$

having in mind, that the geometric mean operator can be substituted by any other fuzzy averaging operator. An application is presented in section 6.2.

6. Applications

6.1 Machine Condition Monitoring

The approach presented in section 4 and 5.1 was tested in particular with an intaglio printing machine in a production process. As an interesting fact print flaws were detected at an early stage by using multi-sensory measurements. It has to be noted that one of the most common type of print flaws (Lohweg, 2006) caused by the wiping unit was detected at a very early stage.

The following data are used for the model: machine speed - motor current - printing pressure side 1 (PPS1) - printing pressure side 2 (PPS2) - hydraulic pressure (drying blade) - wiping solution flow - drying blade side 1 (DBS1) - drying blade side 2 (DBS2) - acoustic signal (vertical side 1) - acoustic signal (horizontal side 1) - acoustic signal (vertical side 2) - acoustic signal (horizontal side 1).

It has been mentioned that it might be desirable to preprocess some of the signals output by the sensors which are used to monitor the behaviour of the machine. This is particularly true in connection with the sensing of noises and/or vibrations produced by the printing press, which signals a great number of frequency components. The classical approach to processing such signals is to perform a spectral transformation of the signals. The usual spectral transformation is the well-known Fourier transform (and derivatives thereof) which converts the signals from the time-domain into the frequency-domain. The processing of the signals is made simpler by working in the thus obtained spectrum as periodic signal components are readily identifiable in the frequency-domain as peaks in the spectrum. The drawbacks of the Fourier transform, however, reside in its inability to efficiently identify and isolate phase movements, shifts, drifts, echoes, noise, etc., in the signals. A more adequate "spectral" analysis is the so-called "cepstrum" analysis. "Cepstrum" is an anagram of "spectrum" and is the accepted terminology for the inverse Fourier transform of the logarithm of the spectrum of a signal. Cepstrum analysis is in particular used for analysing "sounds" instead of analysing frequencies (Bogert, 1963).

A test was performed by measuring twelve different parameters of the printing machine's condition while the machine was running (data collection) (Dyck, 2006). During this test the wiping pressure was decreased little by little, as long as the machine was printing only error sheets. The test was performed at a speed of 6500 sheets per hour and a sample frequency of

7 kHz. During this test 797 sheets were printed, that means, the set of data contained more than three million values per signal. In the first step before calculating the KLT of the raw data, the mean value per sheet was calculated to reduce the amount of data to 797 values per signal. As already mentioned, 12 signals were measured; therefore the four acoustical signals were divided by cepstrum analysis in *six new parameters*, so that all in all 14 parameters built up the new input vectors of matrix $\mathbf{X}$. As described above, at first the correlation matrix of the input data was calculated. Some parameters are highly correlated, e.g. PPS1 and PPS2 with a correlation factor 0.9183, DBS1 and DBS2 with a correlation factor 0.9421, and so forth. This fact already leads to the assumption that implementing the KLT seems to be effective in reducing the dimensions of the input data. The classifier model is shown in Fig. 4.

The KLT matrix is given by calculating the eigenvectors and eigenvalues of the correlation matrix, because the eigenvectors build up the transformation matrix. In Fig. 5 the calculated eigenvalues are presented. On the ordinate the variance contribution of several eigenvalues in percentage are plotted versus the number of eigenvalues on the abscissa axis. The first principal component has already a contribution of almost 60 % of the total variance. Looking at the first seven principal components, which cover nearly 95 % of the total variance, shows that this transformation allows a reduction of important parameters for further use in classification without relevant loss of information. The following implementations focussed only on the first principal component, which represents the machine condition state best.

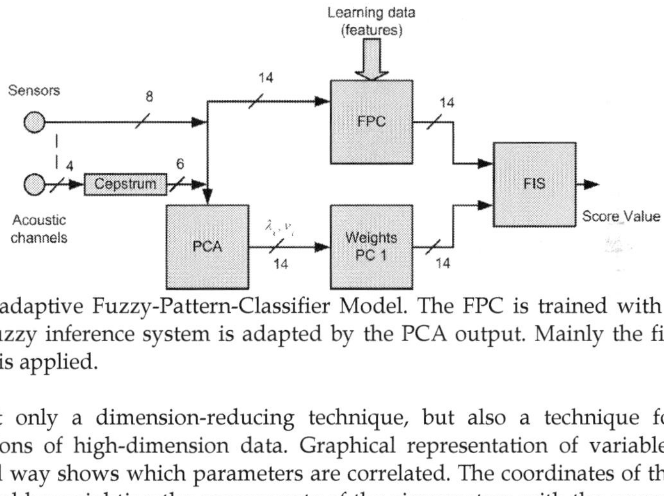

Fig. 4. The adaptive Fuzzy-Pattern-Classifier Model. The FPC is trained with 14 features, while the fuzzy inference system is adapted by the PCA output. Mainly the first principal component is applied.

PCA is not only a dimension-reducing technique, but also a technique for graphical representations of high-dimension data. Graphical representation of variables in a two-dimensional way shows which parameters are correlated. The coordinates of the parameter are calculated by weighting the components of the eigenvectors with the square root of the eigenvalues: the ith parameter is represented as the point ($\left|v_{1i}\sqrt{\lambda_1}\right|, \left|v_{2i}\sqrt{\lambda_2}\right|$). This weighting is executed for normalisation.

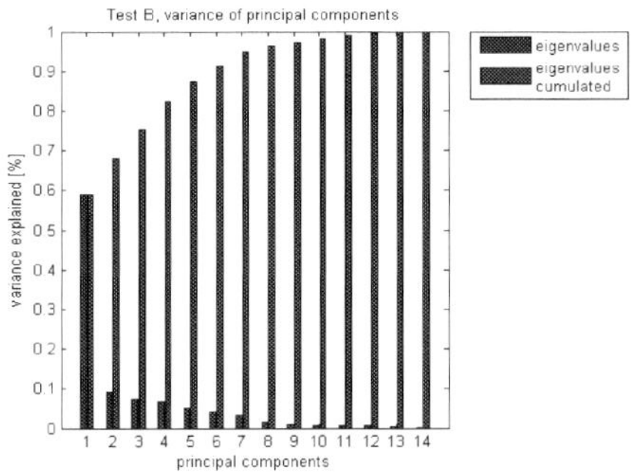

Fig. 5. Eigenvalues (blue) and cumulated eigenvalues (red). The first principal component has already a contribution of almost 60 % of the total normalized variance.

For the parameter "speed" of test B the coordinates are calculated as:

1. $(|v_{1,1}\sqrt{\lambda_1}|,|v_{2,1}\sqrt{\lambda_2}|) = (0.24\sqrt{7.8}, 0.14\sqrt{1.6}) = (0.67, 0.18)$, where

   $\mathbf{v}_1^T = (-0.24, -0.34, 0.19, 0.14, -0.02, -0.18, -0.34, ...)$, and

2. $\mathbf{v}_2^T = (0.14, -0.03, 0.65, 0.70, 0.10, 0.05, ...)$ and

   $\boldsymbol{\lambda}_i = \text{diag}(7.8, 1.6, 1.1, 0.96, 0.73, 0.57, ...)$.

All parameters calculated by this method are shown in Fig. 6. The figure shows different aspects of the input parameters. Parameters which are close to each other have high correlation coefficients. Parameters which build a right angle in dependence to the zero point have no correlation.

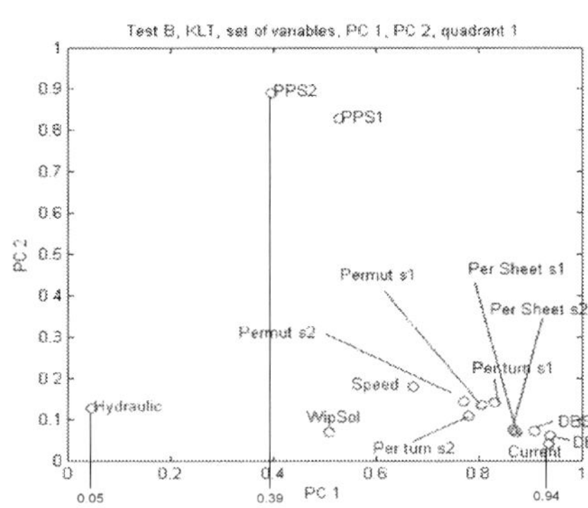

Fig. 6. Correlation dependency graph for PC1 and PC2.

The x-axis represents the first principal component (PC1) and the y-axis represents the second principal component (PC2). The values are always between zero and one. Zero means that the parameters' effect on the machine condition state is close to zero. On the other hand a value near one shows that the parameters have strong effects on the machine condition state. Therefore, a good choice for adaptation is the usage of normalized PC1 components.

The acoustical operational parameters sensed by the multiple-sensor arrangement are first analysed with the cepstrum analysis prior to doing the principal component analysis (PCA). The cepstrum analysis supplies the signal's representative of vibrations or noises produced by the printing press, such as the characteristic noises or vibrations patterns of intaglio printing presses. Thereafter the new acoustical parameters and the remaining operational parameters have to be fed into the PCA block to calculate corresponding eigenvalues and eigenvectors. As explained above, the weight-values of each parameter are taken as the weighted components of eigenvector one (PC1) times the square roots of the corresponding eigenvalues. Each weight-value is used for weighting the output of a rule in the fuzzy inference system (Fig. 4). E.g., the parameter "hydraulic pressure" receives the weight 0.05, the parameter "PPS2" receives the weight 0.39, the parameter "Current" receives the weight 0.94 and so forth (Fig. 6). The sum of all weights in this test is 9.87. All 14 weights are fed into the fuzzy inference system block (FIS).
Figure 7 shows the score value of test B. The threshold is set to 0.5, i.e. if the score value is equal to or larger than 0.5 the machine condition state is "good", otherwise the condition state of the machine is "bad" and it is predictable that error sheets will be printed. Figure 7 shows also that the score value passes the threshold earlier than the image signals. That means the machine runs in bad condition state before error sheets are printed.

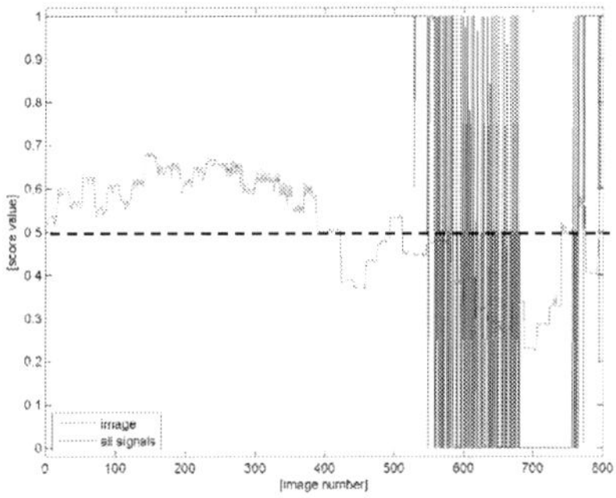

Fig. 7. Score value representation for 797 printed sheets. The green curve represents the classifier score value for wiping error detection, whilst the blue curve shows the results of an optical inspection system. The score value 0.5 defines the threshold between "good" and "bad" print.

6.2 Print Quality Check

As a second application example, an optical character recognition application is presented here. In an industrial production line, the correctness of dot-matrix printed digits are checked in real-time. This is done by recognizing the currently printed digit as a specific number and comparing it with what actually was to be printed. Therefore, an image is acquired from each digit, and 17 different features are extracted. Here, each feature can be interpreted as a single sensor, reacting on different characteristics (e.g., brightness, frequency content, etc.) of the signal (i.e. the image). Examples of the printed digits can be seen in Fig. 8. Actually, there exist also a slightly modified "4" and "7" in the application, thus twelve classes of digits must be distinguished.

Fig. 8. Examples of dot-matrix printed digits.

The incorporated classifier uses both the MFPC and PMFPC membership functions as introduced in section 5.3. Each membership function represents one of the 17 features obtained from the images. All membership functions are learned based on the dedicated training set consisting of 17 images per class. Their outputs, based on the respective feature values of each of the 746 objects which were investigated, are subsequently fused through aggregation using different averaging operators by using the classifier framework presented in (Mönks, 2009). Here, the incorporated aggregation operators are Yager's family of *Ordered Weighted Averaging (OWA)* (Yager, 1988) and Larsen's family of *Andness-directed Importance Weighting Averaging (AIWA)* (Larsen, 2003) operators (applied unweighted here)—which both can be adjusted in their andness degree—and additionally MFPC's original geometric mean (GM). We refer to (Yager, 1988) and (Larsen, 2003) for the definition of OWA and AIWA operators. As a reference, the data set is also classified using a *Support Vector Machine (SVM)* with a Gaussian radial basis function (RBF). Since SVMs are capable of distinguishing between only two classes, the classification procedure is adjusted to pairwise (or one-against-one) classification according to (Schölkopf, 2001). Our benchmarking measure is the classification rate $r_+ = \frac{n_+}{N}$, where n_+ is the number of correctly classified objects and N the total number of objects that were evaluated. The best classification rates at a given aggregation operator's andness ρ_g are summarised in the following Table 2, where the best classification rate per group is printed bold.

ρ_g	*Aggregation Operator*	PMFPC		MFPC D = 2		MFPC D = 4		MFPC D = 8		MFPC D = 16	
		P_{CE}	r_+	P_{CE}	r_+	P_{CE}	r_+	P_{CE}	r_+	P_{CE}	r_+
0.5000	AIWA	**0.255**	**93.70 %**	0.370	84.58 %	0.355	87.67 %	0.310	92.36 %	0.290	92.90 %
	OWA	**0.255**	**93.70 %**	0.370	84.58 %	0.355	87.67 %	0.310	92.36 %	0.290	92.90 %
0.6000	AIWA	**0.255**	**93.16 %**	0.175	87.13 %	0.205	91.02 %	0.225	92.36 %	0.255	92.23 %
	OWA	**0.255**	**93.57 %**	0.355	84.58 %	0.365	88.47 %	0.320	92.63 %	0.275	92.76 %
0.6368	GM	**0.950**	**84.45 %**	0.155	81.77 %	0.445	82.17 %	0.755	82.44 %	1.000	82.44 %
	AIWA	**0.245**	**91.42 %**	0.135	85.52 %	0.185	90.08 %	0.270	89.81 %	0.315	89.95 %
	OWA	**0.255**	**93.57 %**	0.355	84.72 %	0.355	88.74 %	0.305	92.63 %	0.275	92.76 %
0.7000	AIWA	**1.000**	**83.65 %**	0.420	82.71 %	0.790	82.57 %	0.990	82.31 %	1.000	79.22 %
	OWA	**0.280**	**93.57 %**	0.280	84.85 %	0.310	89.01 %	0.315	92.76 %	0.275	92.63 %

Table 2. "OCR" classification rates r_+ for each aggregation operator at andness degrees ρ_g with regard to membership function parameters D and P_{CE}.

The best classification rates for the "OCR" data set are achieved when the PMFPC membership function is incorporated, which are more than 11 % better than the best using the original MFPC. The Support Vector Machine achieved a best classification rate of $r_+ = 95.04\%$ by parameterising its RBF kernel with $\sigma = 5.640$, which is 1.34 % or 10 objects better than the best PMFPC approach.

7. Conclusion and Outlook

In this chapter we have reviewed fuzzy set theory based multi-sensor fusion built on Fuzzy-Pattern-Classification. In particular we emphasized the fact that many traps can occur in multi-sensor fusion. Furthermore, a new inspection and conditioning approach for securities and banknote printing was presented, based on modified versions of the FPC, which results in a robust and reliable detection of flaws. In particular, it was shown that this approach leads to reliable fusion results. The system model "observes" the various machine parameters and decides, using a classifier model with manually tuned or learned parameters, whether the information is as expected or not. A machine condition monitoring system based on an adaptive learning was presented, where the PCA is used for estimating significance weights for each sensor signal. An advantage of the concept is that not only data sets can be classified, but also the influence of input signals can be traced back. This classification model was applied to different tests and some results were presented. In the future we will mainly focus on classifier training with a low amount of samples, which is essential for many industrial applications. Furthermore, the classification results should be improved by the application of classifier nets.

8. References

Beyerer, J.; Punte León, F.; Sommer, K.-D. Informationsfusion in der Mess- und Sensortechnik (Information Fusion in measurement and sensing), Universitätsverlag Karlsruhe, 978-3-86644-053-1, 2006

Bezdek, J.C.; Keller, J.; Krisnapuram, R.; Pal, N. (2005). Fuzzy Models and Algorithms for Pattern Recognition and Image Processing, The Handbook of Fuzzy Sets, Vo. 4, Springer, 0-387-24515-4, New York

Bocklisch, S. F. & Priber, U. (1986). A parametric fuzzy classification concept, Proc. International Workshop on Fuzzy Sets Applications, pp. 147–156, Akademie-Verlag, Eisenach, Germany

Bocklisch, S.F. (1987). Prozeßanalyse mit unscharfen Verfahren, Verlag Technik, Berlin, Germany

Bogert et al. (1963). The Quefrency Alanysis of Time Series for Echoes: Cepstrum, Pseudo-autocovariance, Cross-Cepstrum, and Saphe Cracking, Proc. Symposium Time Series Analysis, M. Rosenblatt (Ed.), pp. 209-243, Wiley and Sons, New York

Bossé, É.; Roy, J.; Wark, S. (2007). Concepts, models, and tools for information fusion, Artech House, 1596930810, London, UK, Norwood, USA

Brown, S. (2004). Latest Developments in On and Off-line Inspection of Bank-Notes during Production, Proceedings, IS&T/SPIE 16th Annual Symposium on Electronic Imaging, Vol. 5310, pp. 46-51, 0277-786X, San Jose Convention Centre, CA, January 2004, SPIE, Bellingham, USA

Dujmović, J.J. & Larsen, H.L. (2007). Generalized conjunction/disjunction, In: International Journal of Approximate Reasoning 46(3), pp. 423–446

Dyck, W. (2006). Principal Component Analysis for Printing Machines, Internal lab report, Lemgo, 2006, private communications, unpublished

Eichhorn, K. (2000). Entwurf und Anwendung von ASICs für musterbasierte Fuzzy-Klassifikationsverfahren (Design and Application of ASICs for pattern-based Fuzzy-Classification), Ph.D. Thesis, Technical University Chemnitz, Germany

Hall, D. L. & Llinas, J. (2001). Multisensor Data Fusion, Second Edition - 2 Volume Set, CRC Press, 0849323797, Boca Raton, USA

Hall, D. L. & Steinberg, A. (2001a). Dirty Secrets in Multisensor Data Fusion, http://www.dtic.mil, last download 01/04/2010

Hempel, A.-J. & Bocklisch, S. F. (2008). , Hierarchical Modelling of Data Inherent Structures Using Networks of Fuzzy Classifiers, Tenth International Conference on Computer Modeling and Simulation, 2008. UKSIM 2008, pp. 230-235, April 2008, IEEE, Piscataway, USA

Hempel, A.-J. & Bocklisch, S. F. (2010). Fuzzy Pattern Modelling of Data Inherent Structures Based on Aggregation of Data with heterogeneous Fuzziness Modelling, Simulation and Optimization, 978-953-307-048-3, February 2010, SciYo.com

Herbst, G. & Bocklisch, S.F. (2008). Classification of keystroke dynamics - a case study of fuzzified discrete event handling, 9th International Workshop on Discrete Event Systems 2008, WODES 2008 , pp.394-399, 28-30 May 2008, IEEE Piscataway, USA

Jolliffe, I.T. (2002). Principal Component Analysis, Springer, 0-387-95442-2, New York

Larsen, H.L. (2003). Efficient Andness-Directed Importance Weighted Averaging Operators. International Journal of Uncertainty, Fuzziness and Knowledge-Based Systems, 11(Supplement-1) pp. 67–82

Liggins, M.E.; Hall, D. L.; Llinas, J. (2008). Handbook of Multisensor Data Fusion: Theory and Practice (Electrical Engineering & Applied Signal Processing), CRC Press, 1420053086, Boca Raton, USA

Lohweg, V.; Diederichs, C.; Müller, D. (2004). Algorithms for Hardware-Based Pattern Recognition, EURASIP Journal on Applied Signal Processing, Volume 2004 (January 2004) pp. 1912-1920, 1110-8657

Lohweg, V.; Dyck, W.; Schaede, J.; Türke, T. (2006a). Information Fusion Application On Security Printing With Parametrical Fuzzy Classification, Fusion 2006-9th International Conference on Information Fusion, Florence, Italy

Lohweg, V.; Li, R.; Türke, T.; Willeke, H.; Schaede, J. (2009). FPGA-based Multi-sensor Real Time Machine Vision for Banknote Printing, Proceedings, IS&T/SPIE 21th Annual Symposium on Electronic Imaging, Vol. 7251, No. 7251-28, 9780819475015, San Jose Convention Centre, CA, January 2009, SPIE, Bellingham, USA

Lohweg, V.; Schaede, J.; Türke, T. (2006). Robust and Reliable Banknote Authentication and Print Flaw Detection with Opto-Acoustical Sensor Fusion Methods, Proceedings, IS&T/SPIE 18th Annual Symposium on Electronic Imaging, Vol. 6075, No. 6075-02, 0277-786X, San Jose Convention Centre, CA, January 2006, SPIE, Bellingham, USA

Luo, R.C. & Kay, M.G. (1989). Multisensor integration and fusion in intelligent systems, Systems, IEEE Transactions on Man and Cybernetics, vol. 19, no. 5, pp. 901-931, Sep/Oct 1989, IEEE Piscataway, USA

Mönks, U.; Lohweg, V.; Larsen, H. L. (2009). Aggregation Operator Based Fuzzy Pattern Classifier Design, Workshop Machine Learning in Real-Time Applications (MLRTA 09), Artificial Intelligence 2009, Paderborn, Germany

Mönks, U.; Petker, D.; Lohweg, V. (2010). Fuzzy-Pattern-Classifier Training with Small Data Sets, In: Information Processing and Management of Uncertainty in Knowledge-Based Systems, E. Hüllermeier, R. Kruse and F. Hoffmann (Ed.), Vol. 80, pp. 426 – 435, Springer, 978-3-642-14054-9, Heidelberg

Niederhöfer, M. & Lohweg, V. (2008). Application-based approach for automatic texture defect recognition on synthetic surfaces, IEEE Int. Conference on Emerging Technologies and Factory Automation 19, pp. 229-232, Hamburg, IEEE Piscataway, USA

Polyanin, A.D. & Manzhirov, A.V. (2007). Handbook of mathematics for engineers and scienctists, Chapman & Hall/CRC, Boca Raton

Ross, A. & Jain, A. K. (2006). Multimodal Human Recognition Systems, In: Multi-Sensor Image Fusion and its Application, R. S. Blum and Z. Liu (Ed.), pp. 289-301, CRC Press, 0849-334-179, Boca Raton

Schlegel, M.; Herrmann, G.; Müller, D. (2004). Eine neue Hardware-Komponente zur Fuzzy-Pattern-Klassifikation (A New Hardware Component for Fuzzy-Pattern-Classification), Dresdener Arbeitstagung Schaltungs- und Systementwurf DASS'04, Dresden, April 2004, pp. 21-26

Schölkopf, B. & Smola, A.J. (2001). Learning with Kernels: Support Vector Machines, Regularization, Optimization, and Beyond, MIT Press

Wald. L. (2006). Some terms of reference in data fusion, IEEE Transactions on Geoscience and Remote Sensing, No. 37(3), pp. 1190-1193, IEEE, Piscataway, USA

Yager, R.R. (1988). On ordered weighted averaging aggregation operators in multicriteria decisionmaking, Systems, Man and Cybernetics, IEEE Transactions on 18(1) pp. 183–190

Zadeh, L. (1965). Fuzzy sets, Information Control, 8(3), pp. 338-353

15

Feature extraction: techniques for landmark based navigation system

Molaletsa Namoshe[1,2], Oduetse Matsebe[1,2] and Nkgatho Tlale[1]
[1]*Department of Mechatronics and Micro Manufacturing, Centre for Scientific and Industrial Research,*
[2]*Department of Mechanical Engineering, Tshwane University of Technology, Pretoria, South Africa*

1. Introduction

A robot is said to be fully autonomous if it is able to build a navigation map. The map is a representation of a robot surroundings modelled as 2D geometric features extracted from a proximity sensor like laser. It provides succinct space description that is convenient for environment mapping via data association. In most cases these environments are not known prior, hence maps needs to be generated automatically. This makes feature based SLAM algorithms attractive and a non trivial problems. These maps play a pivotal role in robotics since they support various tasks such as mission planning and localization. For decades, the latter has received intense scrutiny from the robotic community. The emergence of stochastic map proposed by seminal papers of (Smith et al., 1986; Moutarlier et al., 1989a; Moutarlier et al., 1989b & Smith et al., 1985), however, saw the birth of joint posterior estimation. This is a complex problem of jointly estimating the robot's pose and the map of the environment consistently (Williams S.B et al., 2000) and efficiently. The emergence of new sensors systems which can provide information at high rates such as wheel encoders, laser scanners and sometimes cameras made this possible. The problem has been research under the name Simultaneous Localization and Mapping (SLAM) (Durrant-Whyte, H et al. 2006 Part I and II) from its inception. That is, to localize a mobile robot, geometric features/ landmarks (2D) are generated from a laser scanner by measuring the depth to these obstacles. In office like set up, point (from table legs), line (walls) and corner (corner forming walls) features makes up a repeated recognisable pattern formed by a the laser data. These landmarks or features can be extracted and used for navigation purposes. A robot's perception of its position relative to these landmarks increases, improving its ability to accomplish a task. In SLAM, feature locations, robot pose estimates as well feature to robot pose correlations statistics are stochastically maintained inside an Extended Kalman filter increasing the complexity of the process (Thorpe & Durrant-Whyte, 2001). It is also important to note that, though a SLAM problem has the same attributes as estimation and tracking problems, it is not fully observable but detectable. This has a huge implication in the solution of SLAM problem. Therefore, it is important to develop robust extraction algorithms of geometric features from sensor data to aid a robot navigation system.

Accurate and reliable maps generated autonomously guarantees improved localization especially in GPS denied surroundings like indoor (Hough, P.V.C, 1959). The use of odometry is not sufficient for position estimation due unbounded position errors. Therefore, since office like environments consists of planar surfaces, a 2D space model is adequate to describe the robot surroundings because objects are predominantly straight line segments and right angle corners. Coincidentally, line segments and corner representation are the two most popular methods for indoor modelling from a laser rangefinder. The focus in this paper however is corner extraction methods. A number of line and corner extraction techniques first transform scan data into Cartesian space then a linear regression method or corner extraction algorithm is applied. Some algorithms employ Hugh transform (Hough, P.V.C, 1959). & (Duda, R. O, 1972) a popular tool for line detection from scan data due to its robustness to noise and missing data. It works in sensor measurement space. However, the computational cost associated to its voting mechanism renders real-time implementation impossible. On the other hand, an early work by (Crowley, J, 1989) paved the way to subsequent line extraction methods from a range sensor. In their work, a process for extracting line segments from adjacent co-linear range measurements was presented. The Kalman filter update equations were developed to permit the correspondence of a line segment to the model to be applied as a correction to estimated position. The approach was recently extended by (Pfister, S.T et al. 2003), first providing an accurate means to fit a line segment to a set of uncertain points via maximum likelihood formalism. Then weights were derived from sensor noise models such that each point's influence on the fit is according to its uncertainty. Another interesting work is one by (Roumeliotis & Bekey, 2000), where two Extended Kalman filters are used to extract lines from the scan data. In the algorithm, one Kalman filter is used to track the line segments while the other estimates line parameters. The combination of the two filters makes it possible to detect edges and straight line segments within the sensor field of view. There are many features types one can extract from a laser sensor, and are dependent on the obstacles found in the room. If the room has chair and table, one would be tempted to extract point features from their legs. Size, shape and texture of objects contribute to the type of feature to extract from the sensor. The use of generalised algorithms is not uncommon, i.e. algorithms which extract lines from wall, point features from table legs and arcs to categorise circular objects (Mendes, & Nunes, 2004). The parameters that distinguish each extracted feature makes up the map or state estimate.

The key to a successful robot pose estimation lies in its ability to effectively extract useful information about its location from observations (Li & Jilkov, 2003). Therefore we proposed an improved corner detection method to reduce computational cost and improved robustness.

The paper is structured as follows; section 2 deals with feature extraction, section 3 discuss the EKF-SLAM process. Section 4 is result and analysis, while section 5 covers conclusion and future work.

2. Feature Extraction

Feature extraction forms the lower part of the two layered procedure of feature detection. The top tier is the data segmentation process, which creates clusters of points deemed to originate from the same obstacle. It groups measurements of a scan into several clusters according to the distances between consecutive scans. These segments sectors then are fed to

the feature extraction algorithms, where features like corners or lines are considered. These features are well defined entities which are recognisable and can be repeatedly detected.
In this paper, real laser data from the sensor onboard a robot is processed to extract corner like features, common in most indoor environments. A robot used for this experiment is called Meer-Cat and was developed in house, depicted by Figure 1 below.

Fig. 1. Meer-Cat mobile platform equipped with Sick laser scanner. The robot has an upright board at the top used for tracking purposes via another laser sensor.

2.1 Corner Extraction

Most corner detection algorithms utilises a sliding window technique (Spinello, L, 2007) or picking out the ends points of a line segment as a corners, e.g. slight-and- Merge (Pfister, S.T et al. 2003). This is normally where two line segments meet. Although, an algorithm by (Einsele, T, 2001) is a Split and Merge procedure and it determine corners likewise, it has a slight variation in data processing. The following subsections discuses methods of corner extraction, to be used by an indoor navigation system.

2.1.1 Sliding window corner detector

The sliding window technique has three main parts; vectors determination from three points (Cartesian points), Angle check between the vectors, and the backward check when a corners angle is satisfied. Firstly the size of a window is determined by pre-setting a midpoint position. That is, a window sector size of 11 sample scans has midpoint at 6th sample data, 13 at 7th, and 15 at 8th and so on. The window is broken into two vectors (vi and vj), such that for an 11 sample size window, the first and the eleventh samples are terminal points of these vectors. Therefore, the algorithm assumes a corner if the vectors forms a triangular shape with the midpoint sample being one of its vertexes. An iterative search for a corner angle is carried out by sliding the window step by step over the entire scan. If conditions are met a corner is noted at midpoint. That is, an up bound for the angle between the vectors as well as the minimum allowable opposite distance c as shown in figure 2b below are set prior. A corner is normally described by angles less than 120 degrees, while the separation distance is tightly related to the angular resolution of the laser rangefinder. The distance c is set to very small values; computations greater than this value are passed as corners. If a corner is detected, an 'inward' search is conducted. This is done by checking for a corner angle violation/ existence between the 2nd and 10th, 3rd and 9th, and so on, for sample sector of 11 data points. This is from the assumption that a linear fit can be performed on the vectors. The searching routine of this method already demand high computation speed, therefore inward search will undoubtedly increase the complexity.

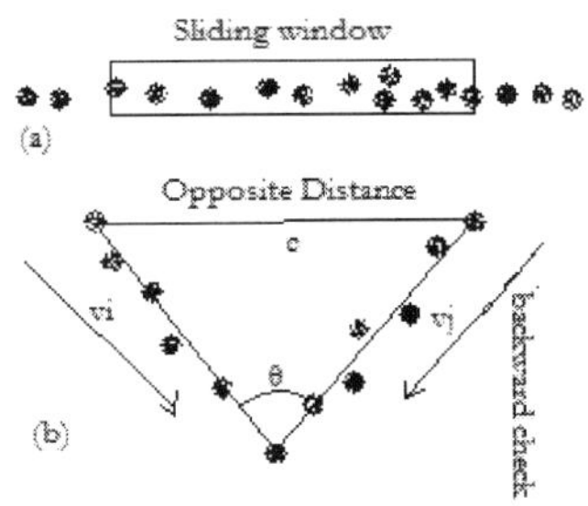

Fig. 2. (a), Sliding window technique. (b) Shows how two vectors centred at the midpoint are derived if a corner if found. The terminal points are at the first and the eleventh point given that the midpoint of the sector is 6.

The angle is calculated using cosine rule, that is,

$$\theta = \cos^{-1}(vi.vj / (\|vi\|\|vj\|)) . \tag{1}$$

Using the above methods one runs into the problem of mapping outliers as corners. This has huge implication in real time implementation because computation complexity of the SLAM process is quadratic the number of landmarks mapped. The outliers or 'ghost' landmarks corrupt the EKF SLAM process.

2.1.2 Split and Merge

Laser sensor produces range scans which describes a 2D slice of the environment. Each range point is specified in polar coordinates system whose origin is the location of the sensor on board the robot. Scan data from a laser range finder has almost negligible angular uncertainty, and the noise on range measurement is assumed to follow Gaussians distribution properties. Data segments originating from the same object can be represented by a line. And traditionally, straight lines are represented by the following parameters

$$y = mx + c \tag{2}$$

where c and m is the y -intercept and slope of a line respectively. The shortcoming with this representation is that vertical lines require infinite m (gradient).

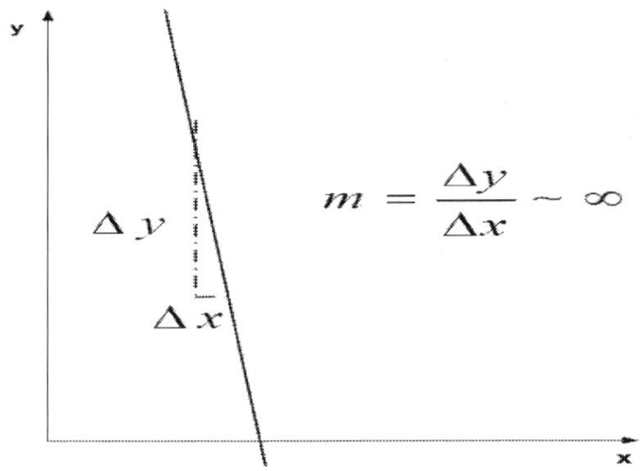

Fig. 3. As the line become vertical, the slope approaches infinity.

If objects in an environment can be represented by polygonal shapes, then line fitting is a suitable choice to approximate objects shapes. During data segmentation, clusters are formed, and a cluster can be represented by a set of lines, defined as follows:

$$C = \{l_i = [P_i, P_f, m, b]^T : 0 \le i < n\} \tag{3}$$

where P_i and P_f are respectively the Cartesian coordinates of the initial and the end of a line. While m and b are the parameters of an ith line. A method proposed by [14] is used to search for a breaking point of a cluster, which occurs at the maximum perpendicular distance to a line. The process starts by connecting the first and last data points of a cluster by a straight line ($Ax + By + C = 0$), where $A = y_f - y_i ; B = x_f - x_i ; C = -(By_f - Ax_f)$. Then for all data points between the extreme points, a perpendicular distance $d_\perp$ to the line is calculated. Such that

$$d_{\perp,k} = \frac{Ax_k + By_k + C}{\sqrt{A^2 + B^2}}. \tag{4}$$

If a tolerance value is violated by the $d_\perp$ then a break point is determined, this is done recursively until the point before last. The final step is to determine straight line parameters, i.e. an orthogonal regression method (Mathpages 2010-04-23) is applied to determine linear fit that minimizes quadratic error. The process is graphically represented by the figure below

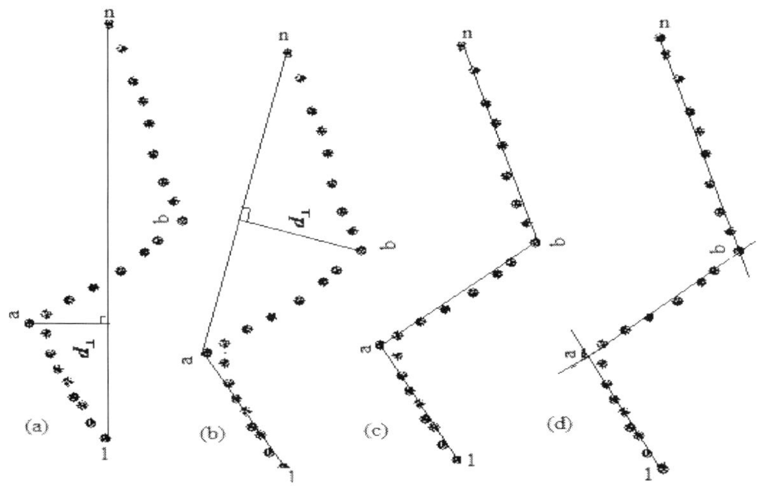

Fig. 4. Recursive line fitting

To mitigate the infinite slope problem, a polar representation or Hessen form is used. In the method, each point in the Cartesian coordinate space adds a sinusoid in the (ρ, θ) space. This is shown the figure 5 below.

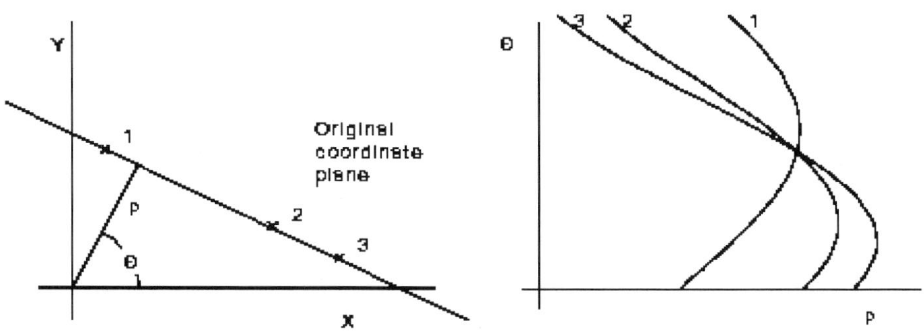

Fig. 5. Mapping between the Cartesian space and the polar Space.

The polar form used to represent lines is given as follows

$$\rho = x\cos(\theta) + y\sin(\theta) \tag{5}$$

where $\rho \geq 0$ is the perpendicular distance of the line to the origin. The angle θ is bounded by $-\pi < \theta \geq \pi$ and is the angle between the x axis and the normal of the line as shown in the figure 6 below.

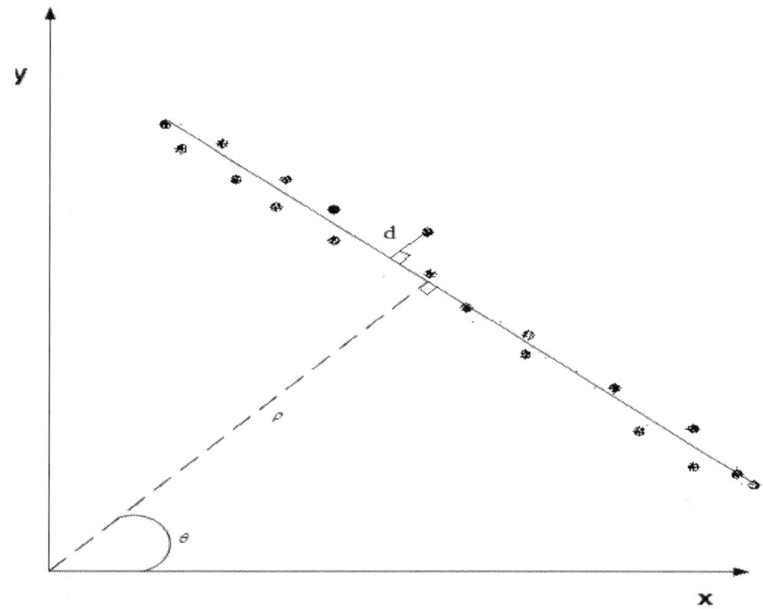

Fig. 6. Fitting line parameters. d is the fitting error we wish to minimize. A line is expressed in polar coordinates (ρ and θ). (x , y) is the Cartesian coordinates of a point on the line.

Using the above representation, the split-and-merge algorithm recursively subdivides scan data into sets of collinear points, approximated as lines in total least square sense. The algorithm determines corners by two main computations, the line extraction and collection of endpoints as corners. Initially, scanned data is clustered into sectors assumed to come from the same objects. The number of data points within a certain cluster as well as an identification of that cluster is stored. Clusters are then passed to a line fitting algorithm (Lu & Milios, 1994). When we perform a regression fit of a straight line to a set of (x , y) data points we typically minimize the sum of squares of the "vertical" distance between the data points and the line (Mathpages 2010-04-23).Therefore, the aim of the linear regression method is to minimize the mean squared error of

$$d^2 = \sum_i \left(\rho - \{x_i \cos(\theta) + y_i \sin(\theta)\}\right)^2 \quad (6)$$

such that (x_i, y_i) are the inputs points in Cartesian coordinates. The solution to the line parameters can be found by taking the first derivative of the equation 6 above with respect to ρ and θ respectively. We assume that

$$\frac{\partial d^2}{\partial \rho} = 0 \qquad and \qquad \frac{\partial d^2}{\partial \theta} = 0 \tag{7}$$

Line parameters can be determined by the following

$$\tan(2\theta) = \frac{-2\sum(y_m - y_i)(x_m - x_i)}{\sum[(y_m - y_i)^2 - (x_m - x_i)^2]}$$

$$\theta = 0.5a\tan 2\left(\frac{-2\sum(y_m - y_i)(x_m - x_i)}{\sum[(y_m - y_i)^2 - (x_m - x_i)^2]}\right) \tag{8}$$

if we assume that the Centroid is on the line then ρ can be computed using equation 4 as:

$$\rho = x_m \cos(\theta) + y_m \sin(\theta) \tag{9}$$

where

$$x_m = \frac{1}{N}\sum x_i \quad and \quad y_m = \frac{1}{N}\sum y_i \tag{10}$$

are (x_m , y_m) are Cartesian coordinates of the Centroid, and N is the number of points in the sector scan we wish to fit line parameter to.

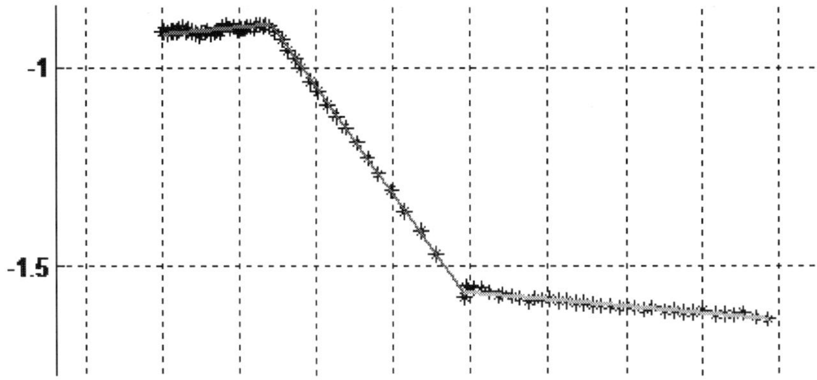

Fig. 7. Fitting lines to a laser scan. A line has more than four sample points.

During the line fitting process, further splitting positions within a cluster are determined by computing perpendicular distance of each point to the fitted line. As shown by figure 6. A point where the perpendicular distance is greater than the tolerance value is marked as a candidate splitting position. The process is iteratively done until the whole cluster scan is made up of linear sections as depicted by figure 7 above. The next procedure is collection of endpoints, which is joining points of lines closest to each other. This is how corner positions are determined from split and merge algorithm. The figure below shows extracted corners defined at positions where two line meet. These positions (corners) are marked in pink.

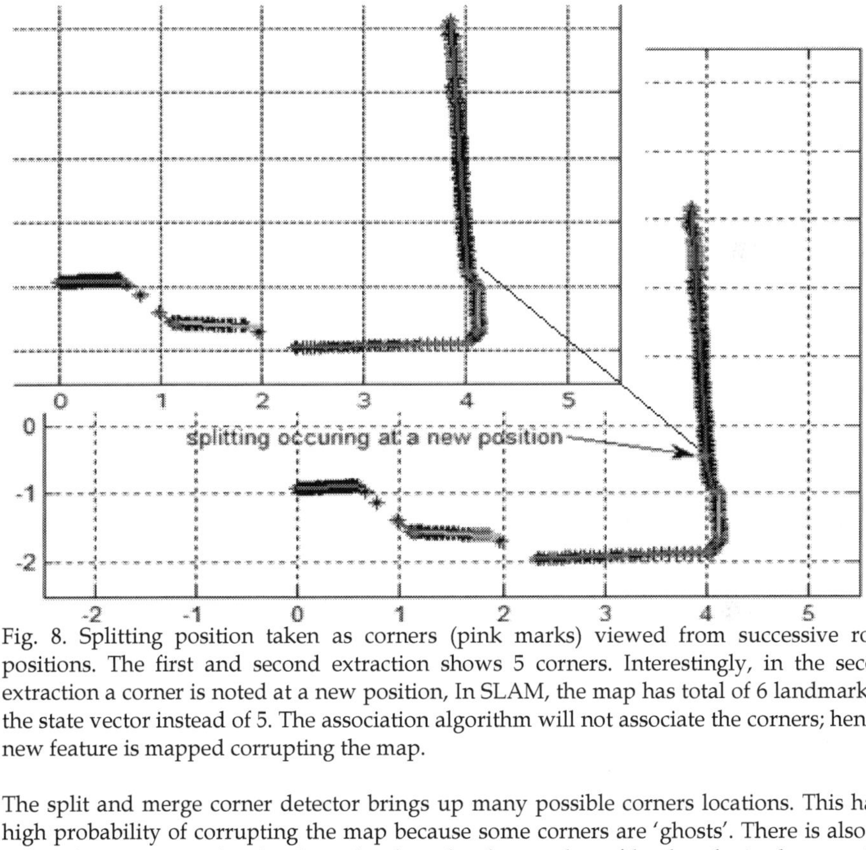

Fig. 8. Splitting position taken as corners (pink marks) viewed from successive robot positions. The first and second extraction shows 5 corners. Interestingly, in the second extraction a corner is noted at a new position, In SLAM, the map has total of 6 landmarks in the state vector instead of 5. The association algorithm will not associate the corners; hence a new feature is mapped corrupting the map.

The split and merge corner detector brings up many possible corners locations. This has a high probability of corrupting the map because some corners are 'ghosts'. There is also the issue of computation burden brought about by the number of landmarks in the map. The standard EKF-SLAM requires time quadratic in the number of features in the map (Thrun, S et al. 2002).This computational burden restricts EKF-SLAM to medium sized environments with no more than a few hundred features.

2.1.3 Proposed Method

We propose an extension to the sliding window technique, to solve the computational cost problem and improve the robustness of the algorithm. We start by defining the limiting bounds for both angle θ and the opposite distance c. The first assumption we make is that a corner is determined by angles between 70° to 110°. To determine the corresponding lower and upper bound of the opposite distance c we use the minus cosine rule. Following an explanation in section 2.1.1, lengths vectors of are determined by taking the modulus of vi and vj such that $a = \|v_i\|$ and $b = \|v_j\|$. Using the cosine rule, which is basically an extension of the Pythagoras rule as the angle increases/ decreases from the critical angle (90°), the minus cosine function is derived as:

$$c^2 = a^2 + b^2 + 2abf(\theta)$$
$$\text{where} \qquad (11)$$
$$f(\theta) = \frac{c^2 - (a^2 + b^2)}{2ab}$$

where $f(\theta)$ is minus cosine θ. The limits of operating bounds for c can be inferred from the output of $f(\theta)$ at corresponding bound angles. That is, θ is directly proportion to distance c. Acute angles give negative results because the square of c is less than the sum of squares of a and b. The figure 9 below shows the angle-to-sides association as well as the corresponding $f(\theta)$ results as the angle grows from acuteness to obtuseness.

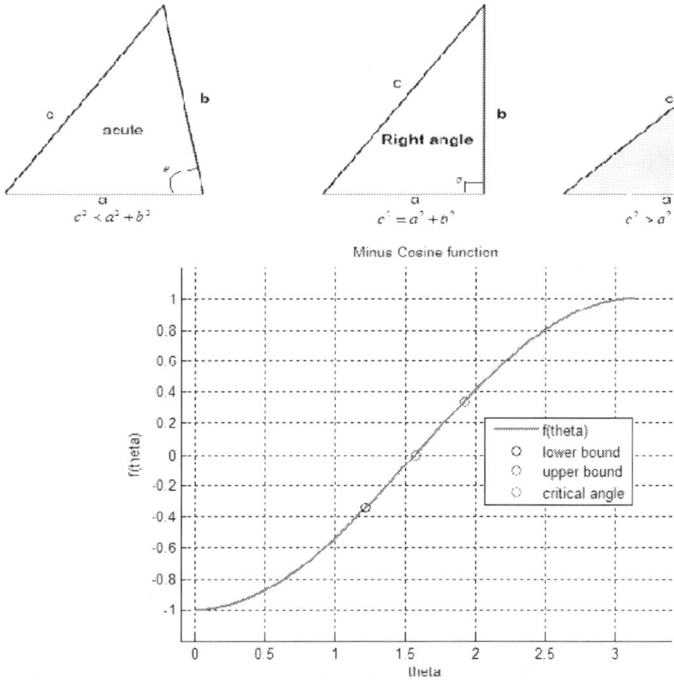

Fig. 9. The relation of the side lengths of a triangle as the angle increases. Using minus cosine function, an indirect relationship is deduced as the angle is increased from acute to obtuse.

The $f(\theta)$ function indirectly has information about the minimum and maximum allowable opposite distance. From experiment this was found to be within [-0.3436 0.3515]. That is, any output within this region was considered a corner. For example, at 90° angle $c^2 = a^2 + b^2$, outputting zero for $f(\theta)$ function. As the angle θ increases, acuteness ends and obtuseness starts, the relation between c^2 and $a^2 + b^2$ is reversed.

The main aim of this algorithm is to distinguish between legitimate corners and those that are not (outliers). Corner algorithms using sliding window technique are susceptible to mapping outlier as corners. This can be shown pictorial by the figure below

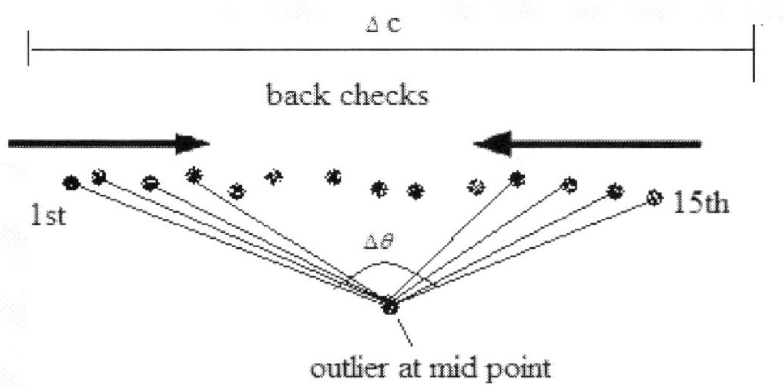

Fig. 10. Outlier corner mapping

where $\Delta\theta$ is the change in angle as the algorithm checks consecutively for a corner angle between points. That is, if there are 15 points in the window and corner conditions are met, corner check process will be done. The procedure checks for corner condition violation/ acceptance between the 2nd & 14th, 3rd & 13th, and lastly between the 4th & 12th data points as portrayed in figure 10 above. If $\Delta\theta$ does not violate the pre-set condition, i.e. (corner angles $\leq$ 120°) then a corner is noted. Δc is the opposite distance between checking points. Because this parameter is set to very small values, almost all outlier corner angle checks will pass the condition. This is because the distances are normally larger than the set tolerance, hence meeting the condition.
The algorithm we propose uses a simple and effect check, it shifts the midpoint and checks for the preset conditions. Figure 11 below shows how this is implemented

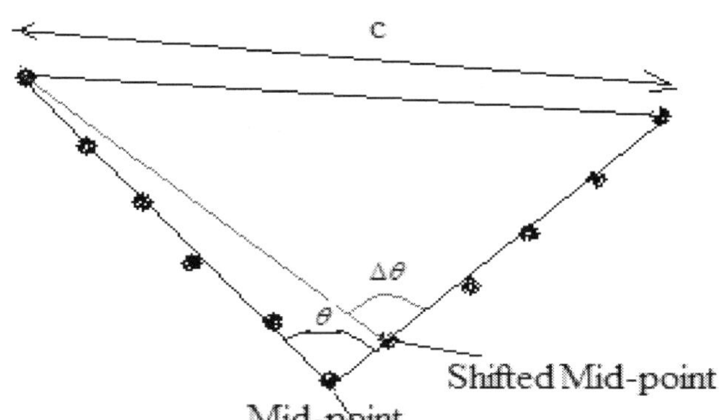

Fig. 11. Shifting the mid-point to a next sample point (e.g. the 7th position for a 11 sample size window) within the window

As depicted by figure 11 above, θ and $\Delta\theta$ angles are almost equal, because the angular resolution of the laser sensor is almost negligible. Hence, shifting the Mid-point will almost give the same corner angles, i.e. $\Delta\theta$ will fall with the $f(\theta)$ bounds. Likewise, if a Midpoint coincides with the outlier position, and corner conditions are met, i.e. θ and c (or $f(\theta)$ conditions) are satisfies evoking the check procedure. Shifting a midpoint gives a results depicted by figure 12 below.

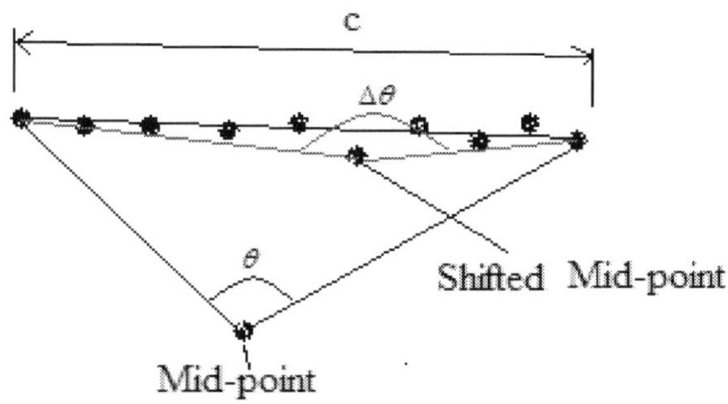

Fig. 12. If a Mid-point is shifted to the next consecutive position, the point will almost certainly be in-line with other point forming an obtuse triangle.

Evidently, the corner check procedure depicted above will violate the corner conditions. We expect $\Delta\theta$ angle to be close to 180° and the output of $f(\theta)$ function to be almost 1, which is outside the bounds set. Hence we disregard the corner findings at the Mid-point as ghost, i.e. the Mid-point coincide with an outlier point. The figure below shows an EKF SLAM process which uses the standard corner method, and mapping an outlier as corner.

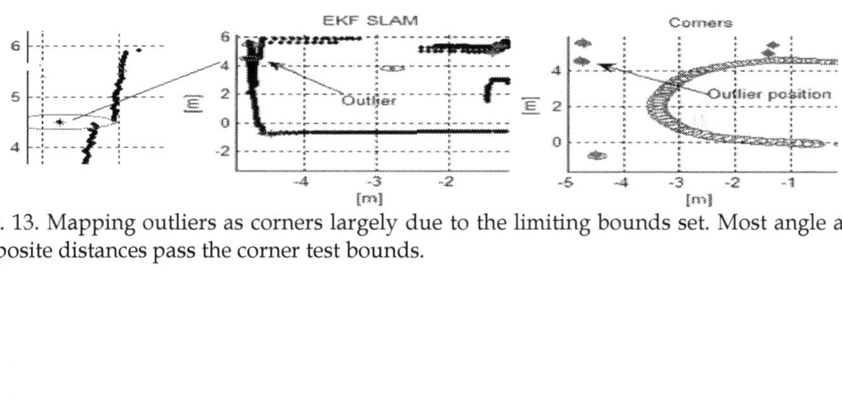

Fig. 13. Mapping outliers as corners largely due to the limiting bounds set. Most angle and opposite distances pass the corner test bounds.

```
[Rho, theta]= GetLaserMeasurements

lenMeasurements = length (Rho,2)  %Number of scan points

[x,y] = pol2cart (theta, Rho); % change to Cartesian coordinates

z = [ ]; % corner position in polar form

for i=1: lenMeasurements,
    if(isnan(Rho (i)) == 0)
      % check points
      corner = Corner_check ([x;y], i);

      if(corner)
         z = [z [Rho(i),theta(i)]]; %saving as z
      end
   end
end

function corner = Corner_check (XY, i)

FisrtTerminalPoint = i;
MidPoint = i +5;   % mid point position
SecondTerminalPoint = MidPoint +5;

[vi, vj] = calculate the two vectors

f(θ) = calculate the minus sign output from lengths of vectors

If ( f(θ) satisfies conditions)

        If (Δθ is acceptable)

        Corner = 1;
        else
          corner = 0;
      end

else
corner = 0;

end
```

Fig. 14. A pseudo code for the proposed corner extractor.

A pseudo code in the figure is able to distinguish outlier from legitimate corner positions. This is has a significant implication in real time implementation especially when one maps large environments. EKF-SLAM's complexity is quadratic the number of landmarks in the map. If there are outliers mapped, not only will they distort the map but increase the computational complexity. Using the proposed algorithm, outliers are identified and discarded as ghost corners. The figure below shows a mapping result when the two algorithms are used to map the same area

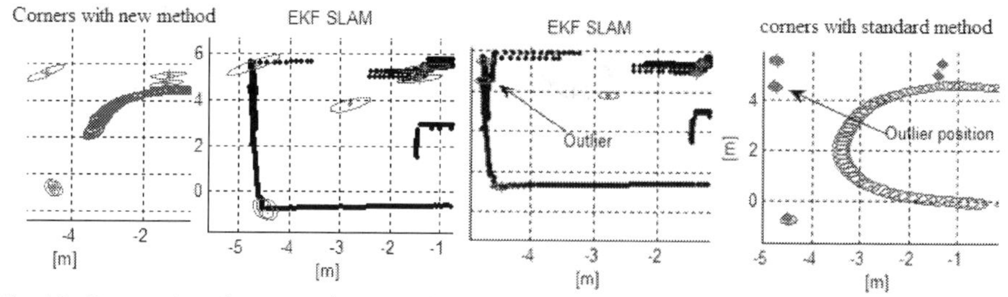

Fig. 15. Comparison between the two algorithms (mapping the same area)

3. EKF-SLAM

The algorithm developed in the previous chapter form part of the EKF-SLAM algorithms. In this section we discuss the main parts of this process. The EKF-SLAM process consists of a recursive, three-stage procedure comprising prediction, observation and update steps. The EKF estimates the pose of the robot made up of the position (x_r, y_r) and orientation ψ_r, together with the estimates of the positions of the N environmental features $\boldsymbol{x}_{f,i}$ where $i = 1 \cdots N$, using observations from a sensor onboard the robot (Williams, S.B et al. 2001).

SLAM considers that all landmarks are stationary; hence the state transition model for the ith feature is given by:

$$\boldsymbol{x}_{f,i}(k) = \boldsymbol{x}_{f,i}(k-1) = \boldsymbol{x}_{f,i} \tag{12}$$

It is important to note that the evolution model for features does have any uncertainty since the features are considered static.

3.1 Process Model

Implementation of EKF-SLAM requires that the underlying state and measurement models to be developed. This section describes the process models necessary for this purpose.

3.1.1 Dead-Reckoned Odometry Measurements

Sometimes a navigation system will be given a dead reckoned odometry position as input without recourse to the control signals that were involved. The dead reckoned positions can be converted into a control input for use in the core navigation system. It would be a bad idea to simply use a dead-reckoned odometry estimate as a direct measurement of state in a Kalman Filter (Newman, P, 2006).

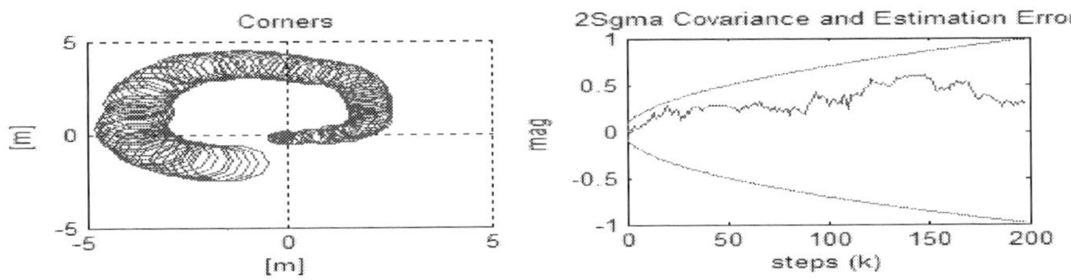

Fig. 16. Odometry alone is not ideal for position estimation because of accumulation of errors. The top left figure shows an ever increasing 2σ bound around the robot's position.

Given a sequence $\boldsymbol{x}_0(1), \boldsymbol{x}_0(2), \boldsymbol{x}_0(3), \cdots \boldsymbol{x}_0(k)$ of dead reckoned positions, we need to figure out a way in which these positions could be used to form a control input into a navigation system. This is given by:

$$\boldsymbol{u}_o(k) = \Theta \boldsymbol{x}_o(k-1) \oplus \boldsymbol{x}_o(k) \tag{13}$$

This is equivalent to going back along $\boldsymbol{x}_0(k-1)$ and forward along $\boldsymbol{x}_0(k)$. This gives a small control vector $\boldsymbol{u}_0(k)$ derived from two successive dead reckoned poses. Equation 13 subtracts out the common dead-reckoned gross error (Newman, P, 2006). The plant model for a robot using a dead reckoned position as a control input is thus given by:

$$\boldsymbol{X}_r(k) = \boldsymbol{f}(\boldsymbol{X}_r(k-1), \boldsymbol{u}(k)) \tag{14}$$

$$\boldsymbol{X}_r(k) = \boldsymbol{X}_r(k-1) \oplus \boldsymbol{u}_o(k) \tag{15}$$

Θ and $\oplus$ are composition transformations which allows us to express robot pose described in one coordinate frame, in another alternative coordinate frame. These composition transformations are given below:

$$\boldsymbol{x}_1 \oplus \boldsymbol{x}_2 = \begin{bmatrix} x_1 + x_2 \cos\theta_1 - y_2 \sin\theta_1 \\ y_1 + x_2 \sin\theta_1 + y_2 \cos\theta_1 \\ \theta_1 + \theta_2 \end{bmatrix} \tag{16}$$

$$\Theta \boldsymbol{x}_1 = \begin{bmatrix} -x_1 \cos\theta_1 - y_1 \sin\theta_1 \\ x_1 \sin\theta_1 - y_1 \cos\theta_1 \\ -\theta_1 \end{bmatrix} \tag{17}$$

3.2 Measurement Model

This section describes a sensor model used together with the above process models for the implementation of EKF-SLAM. Assume that the robot is equipped with an external sensor capable of measuring the range and bearing to static features in the environment. The measurement model is thus given by:

$$z(k) = \boldsymbol{h}(\boldsymbol{X}_r(k), x_i, y_i) + \gamma_h(k) = \begin{bmatrix} r_i(k) \\ \theta_i(k) \end{bmatrix} \tag{18}$$

$$r_i = \sqrt{(x_i - x_r)^2 + (y_i - y_r)^2} \tag{19}$$

$$\theta_i = \tan^{-1}\left[\frac{y_i - y_r}{x_i - x_r}\right] - \psi_r \tag{20}$$

(x_i, y_i) are the coordinates of the ith feature in the environment. $\boldsymbol{X}_r(k)$ is the (x, y) position of the robot at time k. $\gamma_h(k)$ is the sensor noise assumed to be temporally uncorrelated, zero mean and Gaussian with standard deviation σ. $r_i(k)$ and $\theta_i(k)$ are the range and bearing respectively to the ith feature in the environment relative to the vehicle pose.

$$\gamma_h(k) = \begin{bmatrix} \sigma_r \\ \sigma_\theta \end{bmatrix} \tag{21}$$

The strength (covariance) of the observation noise is denoted $\boldsymbol{R}$.

$$\boldsymbol{R} = diag\left(\sigma_r^2 \quad \sigma_\theta^2\right) \tag{22}$$

3.3 EKF-SLAM Steps

This section presents the three-stage recursive EKF-SLAM process comprising prediction, observation and update steps. Figure 17 below summarises the EKF - SLAM process described here.

$\boldsymbol{x}_{0|0} = 0; \boldsymbol{P}_{0|0} = 0$ Map initialization

$[z_0, R_0] = GetLaserSensorMeasuremet$

If (z_0 != 0)

$$\left[\boldsymbol{x}_{0|0}, \boldsymbol{P}_{0|0}\right] = AugmentMap(\boldsymbol{x}_{0|0}; \boldsymbol{P}_{0|0}, z_0, \boldsymbol{R}_0)$$

End

For k = 1: NumberSteps (=N)

$\left[\boldsymbol{x}_{R,kk-1}, \boldsymbol{Q}_k\right] = GetOdometryMeasurement$

$\left[\boldsymbol{x}_{k|k-1}, \boldsymbol{P}_{k|k-1}\right] = EKF\_\text{Pr}\,edict(\boldsymbol{x}_{k-1|k-1}; \boldsymbol{P}_{k-1|k-1}, \boldsymbol{x}_{Rk|k-1})$

$[z_k, R_k] = GetLaserSensorMeasuremet$

$H_k = DoDataAssociation(\boldsymbol{x}_{k|k-1}, \boldsymbol{P}_{k|k-1}, z_k, R_k)$

$\left[\boldsymbol{x}_{k|k}, \boldsymbol{P}_{k|k}\right] = EKF\_Update(\boldsymbol{x}_{k|k-1}; \boldsymbol{P}_{k|k-1}, z_k, R_k, H_k)$ {If a feature exists in the map}

$\left[\boldsymbol{x}_{k|k}, \boldsymbol{P}_{k|k}\right] = AugmentMap(\boldsymbol{x}_{k|k-1}; \boldsymbol{P}_{k|k-1}, z_k, R_k, H_k)$ {If it's a new feature}

If (z_k = =0)

$$\left[\boldsymbol{x}_{k|k}, \boldsymbol{P}_{k|k}\right] = \left[\boldsymbol{x}_{k|k-1}, \boldsymbol{P}_{k|k-1}\right]$$

end

end

Fig. 17. EKF- SLAM pseudo code

3.3.1 Map Initialization

The selection of a base reference B to initialise the stochastic map at time step 0 is important. One way is to select as base reference the robot's position at step 0. The advantage in choosing this base reference is that it permits initialising the map with perfect knowledge of the base location (Castellanos, J.A et al. 2006).

$$\boldsymbol{X}_0^B = \boldsymbol{X}_r^B = 0 \tag{23}$$

$$\boldsymbol{P}_0^B = \boldsymbol{P}_r^B = 0 \tag{24}$$

This avoids future states of the vehicle's uncertainty reaching values below its initial settings, since negative values make no sense. If at any time there is a need to compute the vehicle location or the map feature with respect to any other reference, the appropriate transformations can be applied. At any time, the map can also be transformed to use a feature as base reference, again using the appropriate transformations (Castellanos, J.A et al. 2006).

3.3.2 Prediction using Dead-Reckoned Odometry Measurement as inputs

The prediction stage is achieved by a composition transformation of the last estimate with a small control vector calculated from two successive dead reckoned poses.

$$X_r(k \mid k-1) = X_r(k-1 \mid k-1) \oplus u_o(k) \tag{25}$$

The state error covariance of the robot state $P_r(k \mid k-1)$ is computed as follows:

$$P_r(k \mid k-1) = J_1(X_r, u_o) P_r(k-1 \mid k-1) J_1(X_r, u_o)^T + J_2(X_r, u_o) U_O(k) J_1(X_r, u_o)^T \tag{26}$$

$J_1(X_r, u_o)$ is the Jacobian of equation (16) with respect to the robot pose, X_r and $J_2(X_r, u_o)$ is the Jacobian of equation (16) with respect to the control input, u_o. Based on equations (12), the above Jacobians are calculated as follows:

$$J_1(x_1, x_2) = \frac{\partial(x_1 \oplus x_2)}{\partial x_1} \tag{27}$$

$$J_1(x_1, x_2) = \begin{bmatrix} 1 & 0 & -x_2 \sin\theta_1 - y_2 \cos\theta_1 \\ 0 & 1 & -x_2 \cos\theta_1 - y_2 \sin\theta_1 \\ 0 & 0 & 1 \end{bmatrix} \tag{28}$$

$$J_2(x_1, x_2) = \frac{\partial(x_1 \oplus x_2)}{\partial x_2} \tag{29}$$

$$J_2(x_1, x_2) = \begin{bmatrix} \cos\theta_1 & -\sin\theta_1 & 0 \\ \sin\theta_1 & \cos\theta_1 & 0 \\ 0 & 0 & 1 \end{bmatrix} \tag{30}$$

3.3.3 Observation

Assume that at a certain time k an onboard sensor makes measurements (range and bearing) to m features in the environment. This can be represented as:

$$z_m(k) = [z_1 \quad . \quad . \quad z_m] \tag{31}$$

3.3.4 Update

The update process is carried out iteratively every k^{th} step of the filter. If at a given time step no observations are available then the best estimate at time k is simply the prediction $\boldsymbol{X}(k \mid k-1)$. If an observation is made of an existing feature in the map, the state estimate can now be updated using the optimal gain matrix $\boldsymbol{W}(k)$. This gain matrix provides a weighted sum of the prediction and observation. It is computed using the innovation covariance $\boldsymbol{S}(k)$, the state error covariance $\boldsymbol{P}(k \mid k-1)$ and the Jacobians of the observation model (equation 18), $\boldsymbol{H}(k)$.

$$\boldsymbol{W}(k) = \boldsymbol{P}(k \mid k-1)\boldsymbol{H}(k)\boldsymbol{S}^{-1}(k), \tag{32}$$

where $\boldsymbol{S}(k)$ is given by:

$$\boldsymbol{S}(k) = \boldsymbol{H}(k)\boldsymbol{P}(k \mid k-1)\boldsymbol{H}^{T}(k) + \boldsymbol{R}(k) \tag{33}$$

$\boldsymbol{R}(k)$ is the observation covariance.

This information is then used to compute the state update $\boldsymbol{X}(k \mid k)$ as well as the updated state error covariance $\boldsymbol{P}(k \mid k)$.

$$\boldsymbol{X}(k \mid k) = \boldsymbol{X}(k \mid k-1) + \boldsymbol{W}(k)\nu(k) \tag{34}$$

$$\boldsymbol{P}(k \mid k) = \boldsymbol{P}(k \mid k-1) - \boldsymbol{W}(k)\boldsymbol{S}(k)\boldsymbol{W}(k)^{T} \tag{35}$$

The innovation, $\boldsymbol{v}(k)$ is the discrepancy between the actual observation, $\boldsymbol{z}(k)$ and the predicted observation, $\boldsymbol{z}(k \mid k-1)$.

$$\boldsymbol{v}(k) = \boldsymbol{z}(k) - \boldsymbol{z}(k \mid k-1), \tag{36}$$

where $\boldsymbol{z}(k \mid k-1)$ is given as:

$$\boldsymbol{z}(k \mid k-1) = \boldsymbol{h}\left(\boldsymbol{X}_r(k \mid k-1), \boldsymbol{x}_i, \boldsymbol{y}_i\right) \tag{37}$$

$X_r(k \mid k-1)$ is the predicted pose of the robot and (x_i, y_i) is the position of the observed map feature.

3.4 Incorporating new features

Under SLAM the system detects new features at the beginning of the mission and when exploring new areas. Once these features become reliable and stable they are incorporated into the map becoming part of the state vector. A feature initialisation function $\boldsymbol{y}$ is used for this purpose. It takes the old state vector, $\boldsymbol{X}(k \mid k)$ and the observation to the new feature, $z(k)$ as arguments and returns a new, longer state vector with the new feature at its end (Newman 2006).

$$\boldsymbol{X}(k \mid k)^{*} = \boldsymbol{y}\left[\boldsymbol{X}(k \mid k), \quad \boldsymbol{z}(k)\right] \tag{338}$$

$$\boldsymbol{X}(k \mid k)^{*} = \begin{bmatrix} \boldsymbol{X}(k \mid k) \\ x_r + r\cos(\theta + \psi_r) \\ y_r + r\sin(\theta + \psi_r) \end{bmatrix} \tag{39}$$

Where the coordinates of the new feature are given by the function $\boldsymbol{g}$:

$$\boldsymbol{g} = \begin{bmatrix} x_r + r\cos(\theta + \psi_r) \\ y_r + r\sin(\theta + \psi_r) \end{bmatrix} = \begin{bmatrix} g_1 \\ g_2 \end{bmatrix} \tag{40}$$

r and θ are the range and bearing to the new feature respectively. (x_r, y_r) and ψ_r are the estimated position and orientation of the robot at time k.
The augmented state vector containing both the state of the vehicle and the state of all feature locations is denoted:

$$\boldsymbol{X}(k \mid k)^{*} = [\boldsymbol{X}_r^T(k) \quad \boldsymbol{x}_{f,1}^T \quad . \quad . \quad \boldsymbol{x}_{f,N}^T] \tag{41}$$

We also need to transform the covariance matrix $\boldsymbol{P}$ when adding a new feature. The gradient for the new feature transformation is used for this purpose:

$$\boldsymbol{g} = \begin{bmatrix} x_r + r\cos(\theta + \psi_r) \\ y_r + r\sin(\theta + \psi_r) \end{bmatrix} = \begin{bmatrix} g_1 \\ g_2 \end{bmatrix} \tag{42}$$

The complete augmented state covariance matrix is then given by:

$$\boldsymbol{P}(k \mid k)^{*} = \boldsymbol{Y}_{x,z} \begin{bmatrix} \boldsymbol{P}(k \mid k) & \boldsymbol{0} \\ \boldsymbol{0} & \boldsymbol{R} \end{bmatrix} \boldsymbol{Y}_{x,z}^T, \tag{43}$$

where $\boldsymbol{Y}_{x.z}$ is given by:

$$\boldsymbol{Y}_{x,z} = \begin{bmatrix} \boldsymbol{I}_{nxn} & \boldsymbol{0}_{nx2} \\ [\boldsymbol{G}_{x_r} \quad zeros(nstates - n)] & \boldsymbol{G}_z \end{bmatrix} \tag{44}$$

where *nstates* and n are the lengths of the state and robot state vectors respectively.

$$\boldsymbol{G}_{X_r} = \frac{\partial g}{\partial X_r} \tag{45}$$

$$\boldsymbol{G}_{X_r} = \begin{bmatrix} \frac{\partial g_1}{\partial x_r} & \frac{\partial g_1}{\partial y_r} & \frac{\partial g_1}{\partial \psi_r} \\ \frac{\partial g_2}{\partial x_r} & \frac{\partial g_2}{\partial y_r} & \frac{\partial g_2}{\partial \psi_r} \end{bmatrix} = \begin{bmatrix} 1 & 0 & -r\sin(\theta + \psi_r) \\ 0 & 1 & r\cos(\theta + \psi_r) \end{bmatrix} \tag{46}$$

$$\boldsymbol{G}_z = \partial g / \partial z \tag{47}$$

$$\boldsymbol{G}_z = \begin{bmatrix} \frac{\partial g_1}{\partial r} & \frac{\partial g_1}{\partial \theta} \\ \frac{\partial g_2}{\partial r} & \frac{\partial g_2}{\partial \theta} \end{bmatrix} = \begin{bmatrix} \cos(\theta + \psi_r) & -r\sin(\theta + \psi_r) \\ \sin(\theta + \psi_r) & r\cos(\theta + \psi_r) \end{bmatrix} \tag{48}$$

3.5 Data association

In practice, features have similar properties which make them good landmarks but often make them difficult to distinguish one from the other. When this happen the problem of data association has to be addressed. Assume that at time k, an onboard sensor obtains a set of measurements $z_i(k)$ of m environment features $\boldsymbol{E}_i (i = 1,...,m)$. Data Association consists of determining the origin of each measurement, in terms of map features $F_j, j = 1,...,n.$ The results is a hypothesis:

$$\boldsymbol{H}_k = [j_1 \quad j_2 \quad j_3 .....j_m], \tag{49}$$

matching each measurement $z_i(k)$ with its corresponding map feature. $F_{ji}(j_i = 0)$ indicates that the measurement $z_i(k)$ does not come from any feature in the map. Figure 2 below summarises the data association process described here. Several techniques have been proposed to address this issue and more information on some these techniques can be found in (Castellanos, J.A et al. 2006) and (Cooper, A.J, 2005).

Of interest in this chapter is the simple data association problem of finding the correspondence of each measurement to a map feature. Hence the Individual Compatibility Nearest Neighbour Method will be described.

3.5.1 Individual Compatibility

The IC considers individual compatibility between a measurement and map feature. This idea is based on a prediction of the measurement that we would expect each map feature to generate, and a measure of the discrepancy between a predicted measurement and an actual measurement made by the sensor. The predicted measurement is then given by:

$$\boldsymbol{z}_j(k \mid k-1) = \boldsymbol{h}(\boldsymbol{X}_r(k \mid k-1), x_j, y_j) \tag{50}$$

The discrepancy between the observation $\boldsymbol{z}_i(k)$ and the predicted measurement $\boldsymbol{z}_j(k \mid k-1)$ is given by the innovation term $\boldsymbol{v}_{ij}(k)$:

$$\boldsymbol{v}_{ij}(k) = \boldsymbol{z}_i(k) - \boldsymbol{z}_j(k \mid k-1) \tag{51}$$

The covariance of the innovation term is then given as:

$$\boldsymbol{S}_{ij}(k) = \boldsymbol{H}(k)\boldsymbol{P}(k \mid k-1)\boldsymbol{H}^T(k) + \boldsymbol{R}(k) \tag{52}$$

$\boldsymbol{H}(k)$ is made up of $\boldsymbol{H}_r$, which is the Jacobian of the observation model with respect to the robot states and $\boldsymbol{H}_{Fj}$, the gradient Jacobian of the observation model with respect to the observed map feature.

$$\boldsymbol{H}(k) = \begin{bmatrix} \boldsymbol{H}_r & 00 & 00 & \boldsymbol{H}_{Fj} & 00 \end{bmatrix} \tag{53}$$

Zeros in equation (53) above represents un-observed map features.

To deduce a correspondence between a measurement and a map feature, Mahalanobis distance is used to determine compatibility, and it is given by:

$$D_{ij}^2(k) = \boldsymbol{v}_{ij}^T(k)\boldsymbol{S}_{ij}^{-1}(k)\boldsymbol{v}_{ij}(k) \tag{54}$$

The measurement and a map feature can be considered compatible if the Mahalanobis distance satisfies:

$$D_{ij}^2(k) < \chi_{d,1-\alpha}^2 \tag{55}$$

Where $d = \dim(v_{ij})$ and $1-\alpha$ is the desired level of confidence usually taken to be 95%. The result of this exercise is a subset of map features that are compatible with a particular measurement. This is the basis of a popular data association algorithm termed Individual

Compatibility Nearest Neighbour. Of the map features that satisfy IC, ICNN chooses one with the smallest Mahalanobis distance (Castellanos, J.A et al. 2006).

3.6 Consistency of EKF-SLAM

EKF-SLAM consistency or lack of was discussed in (Castellanos, J.A et al. 2006), (Newman, P.M. (1999), (Cooper, A.J, 2005), and (Castellanos, J.A et al. 2006), It is a non-linear problem hence it is necessary to check if it is consistent or not. This can be done by analysing the errors. The filter is said to be unbiased if the Expectation of the actual state estimation error, $\tilde{\boldsymbol{X}}(k)$ satisfies the following equation:

$$E[\tilde{X}] = 0 \tag{56}$$

$$E\left[\left(\tilde{\boldsymbol{X}}(k)\right)\left(\tilde{\boldsymbol{X}}(k)\right)^T\right] \leq \boldsymbol{P}(k \mid k-1) \tag{57}$$

where the actual state estimation error is given by:

$$\tilde{\boldsymbol{X}}(k) = \boldsymbol{X}(k) - \boldsymbol{X}(k \mid k-1) \tag{58}$$

$\boldsymbol{P}(k \mid k-1)$ is the state error covariance. Equation (57) means that the actual mean square error matches the state covariance. When the ground truth solution for the state variables is available, a chi-squared test can be applied on the normalised estimation error squared to check for filter consistency.

$$\left(\tilde{\boldsymbol{X}}(k)\right)^T \left(\boldsymbol{P}(k \mid k-1)\right)^{-1} \left(\tilde{\boldsymbol{X}}(k)\right) \leq \chi^2_{d,1-\alpha} \tag{59}$$

where DOF is equal to the state dimension $d = \dim(x(k))$ and $1-\alpha$ is the desired confidence level. In most cases ground truth is not available, and consistency of the estimation is checked using only measurements that satisfy the innovation test:

$$\boldsymbol{v}_{ij}^T(k)\boldsymbol{S}_{ij}^{-1}\boldsymbol{v}_{ij}(k) < \chi^2_{d,1-\alpha} \tag{60}$$

Since the innovation term depends on the data association hypothesis, this process becomes critical in maintaining a consistent estimation of the environment map.

4. Result and Analysis

Figure 19 below shows offline EKF SLAM results using data logged by a robot. The experiment was conducted inside a room of 900 cm x 720cm dimension with a few obstacles. Using an EKF-SLAM algorithm which takes data information (corners locations & odometry); a map of the room was developed. Corner features were extracted from the laser data. To initialize the mapping process, the robot's starting position was taken reference. In figure 19 below, the top left corner is a map drawn using odometry; predictably the map is skewed because of accumulation of errors. The top middle picture is an environment drawn using EKF SLAM map (corners locations). The corners were extracted using an algorithm we proposed, aimed at solving the possibility of mapping false corners. When a corner is reobserved a Kalman filter update is done. This improves the overall position estimates of the robot as well as the landmark. Consequently, this causes the confidence ellipse drawn around the map (robot position and corners) to reduce in size (bottom left picture).

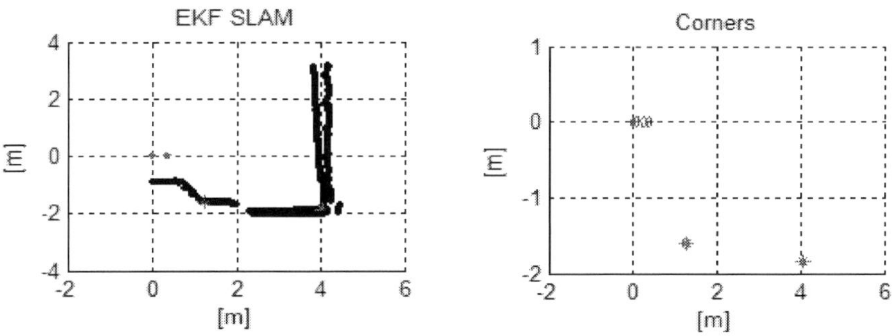

Fig. 18. In figure 8, two consecutive corner extraction process from the split and merge algorithm maps one corner wrongly, while in contrast our corner extraction algorithm picks out the same two corners and correctly associates them.

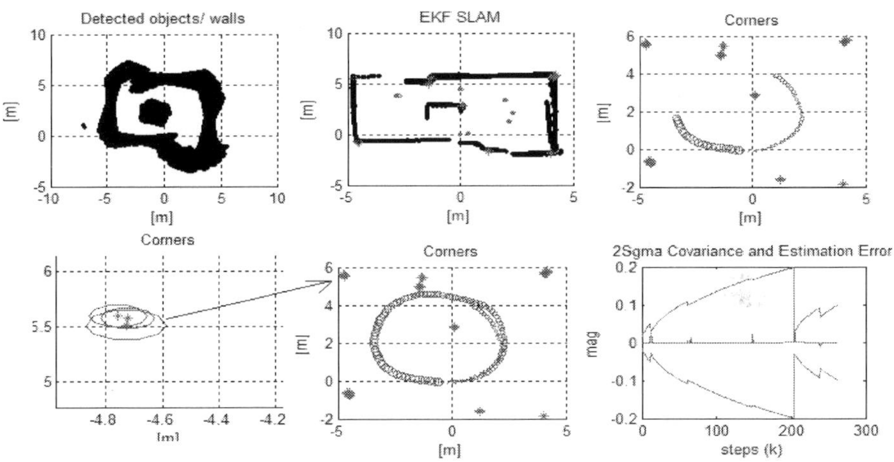

Fig. 19. EKF-SLAM simulation results showing map reconstruction (top right) of an office space drawn from sensor data logged by the Meer Cat. When a corner is detected, its position is mapped and a 2σ confidence ellipse is drawn around the feature position. As the number of observation of the same feature increase the confidence ellipse collapses (top right). The bottom right picture depict x coordinate estimation error (blue) between 2σ bounds (red). Perceptual inference

Expectedly, as the robot revisits its previous position, there is a major decrease in the ellipse, indicating robot's high perceptual inference of its position. The far top right picture shows a reduction in ellipses around robot position. The estimation error is with the 2σ, indicating consistent results, bottom right picture. During the experiment, an extra laser sensor was user to track the robot position, this provided absolute robot position. An initial scan of the environment (background) was taken prior by the external sensor. A simple matching is then carried out to determine the pose of the robot in the background after exploration. Figure 7 below shows that as the robot close the loop, the estimated path and the true are almost identical, improving the whole map in the process.

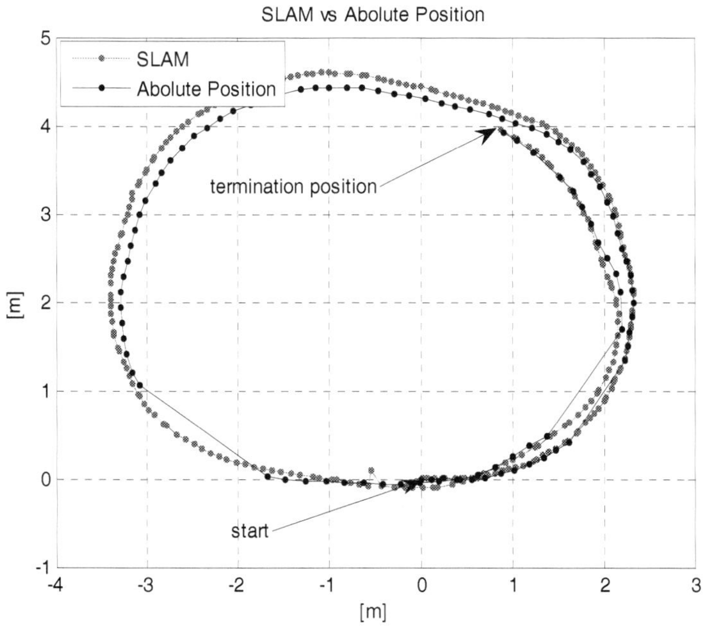

Fig. 20. The figure depicts that as the robot revisits its previous explored regions; its positional perception is high. This means improved localization and mapping, i.e. improved SLAM output.

5. Conclusion and future work

In this paper we discussed the results of an EKF SLAM using real data logged and computed offline. One of the most important parts of the SLAM process is to accurately map the environment the robot is exploring and localize in it. To achieve this however, is depended on the precise acquirement of features extracted from the external sensor. We looked at corner detection methods and we proposed an improved version of the method discussed in section 2.1.1. It transpired that methods found in the literature suffer from high computational cost. Additionally, there are susceptible to mapping 'ghost corners' because of underlying techniques, which allows many computations to pass as corners. This has a major implication on the solution of SLAM; it can lead to corrupted map and increase computational cost. This is because EKF-SLAM's computational complexity is quadratic the number of landmarks in the map, this increased computational burden can preclude real-time operation. The corner detector we developed reduces the chance of mapping dummy corners and has improved computation cost. This offline simulation with real data has allowed us to test and validate our algorithms. The next step will be to test algorithm performance in a real time. For large indoor environments, one would employ a try a regression method to fit line to scan data. This is because corridors will have numerous possible corners while it will take a few lines to describe the same space.

6. Reference

Bailey, T and Durrant-Whyte, H. (2006), Simultaneous Localisation and Mapping (SLAM): Part II State of the Art. Tim. *Robotics and Automation Magazine*, September.

Castellanos, J.A., Neira, J., and Tard´os, J.D. (2004) Limits to the consistency of EKF-based SLAM. In *IFAC Symposium on Intelligent Autonomous Vehicles.*

Castellanos, J.A.; Neira, J.; Tardos, J.D. (2006). Map Building and SLAM Algorithms, *Autonomous Mobile Robots: Sensing, Control, Decision Making and Applications*, Lewis, F.L. & Ge, S.S. (eds), 1st edn, pp 335-371, CRC, 0-8493-3748-8, New York, USA

Collier, J, Ramirez-Serrano, A (2009)., "Environment Classification for Indoor/Outdoor Robotic Mapping," *crv, Canadian Conference on Computer and Robot Vision* , pp.276-283.

Cooper, A.J. (2005). A Comparison of Data Association Techniques for Simultaneous Localisation and Mapping, Masters Thesis, Massachusets Institute of Technology

Crowley, J. (1989). World modeling and position estimation for a mobile robot using ultrasound ranging. In *Proc. of the IEEE Int. Conf. on Robotics & Automation (ICRA).*

Duda, R. O. and Hart, P. E. (1972) "Use of the Hough Transformation to Detect Lines and Curves in Pictures," *Comm. ACM, Vol. 15*, pp. 11–15 ,January.

Durrant-Whyte, H and Bailey, T. (2006). *Simultaneous Localization and Mapping (SLAM): Part I The Essential Algorithms,* Robotics and Automation Magazine.

Einsele, T. (2001) "Localization in indoor environments using a panoramic laser range finder," Ph.D. dissertation, Technical University of München, September.

Hough ,P.V.C., Machine Analysis of Bubble Chamber Pictures. (1959). *Proc. Int. Conf. High Energy Accelerators and Instrumentation.*

Li, X. R. and Jilkov, V. P. (2003). Survey of Maneuvering Target Tracking.Part I: Dynamic Models. *IEEE Trans. Aerospace and Electronic Systems*, AES-39(4):1333.1364, October.

Lu, F. and Milios, E.E..(1994). Robot pose estimation in unknown environments by matching 2D range scans. In *Proc. of the IEEE Computer Society Conf. on Computer Vision and Pattern Recognition (CVPR)*, pages 935–938.

Mathpages, "Perpendicular regression of a line" http://mathpages.com/home/kmath110.htm. *(2010-04-23)*

Mendes, A., and Nunes, U. (2004)"Situation-based multi-target detection and tracking with laser scanner in outdoor semi-structured environment", IEEE/RSJ Int. *Conf. on Systems and Robotics*, pp. 88-93.

Moutarlier, P. and Chatila, R. (1989a). An experimental system for incremental environment modelling by an autonomous mobile robot. In *ISER.*

Moutarlier, P. and Chatila, R. (1989b). Stochastic multisensory data fusion for mobile robot location and environment modelling. In *ISRR).*

Newman, P.M. (1999). On the structure and solution of the simultaneous localization and mapping problem. *PhD Thesis, University of Sydney.*

Newman, P. (2006) EKF Based Navigation and SLAM, *SLAM Summer School.*

Pfister, S.T., Roumeliotis, S.I., and Burdick, J.W. (2003). Weighted line fitting algorithms for mobile robot map building and efficient data representation. In *Proc. of the IEEE Int. Conf. on Robotics & Automation (ICRA).*

Roumeliotis S.I. and Bekey G.A. (2000). SEGMENTS: A Layered, Dual-Kalman filter Algorithm for Indoor Feature Extraction. In Proc. *IEEE/RSJ International Conference on Intelligent Robots and Systems,* Takamatsu, Japan, Oct. 30 - Nov. 5, pp.454-461.

Smith, R., Self, M. & Cheesman, P. (1985). On the representation and estimation of spatial uncertainty. SRI TR 4760 & 7239.

Smith, R., Self, M. & Cheesman, P. (1986). Estimating uncertain spatial relationships in robotics, *Proceedings of the 2nd Annual Conference on Uncertainty in Artificial Intelligence, (UAI-86),* pp. 435–461, Elsevier Science Publishing Company, Inc., New York, NY.

Spinello, L. (2007). Corner extractor, *Institute of Robotics and Intelligent Systems,* Autonomous Systems Lab, http://www.asl.ethz.ch/education/master/mobile_robotics/year2008/year2007, ETH Zürich

Thorpe, C. and Durrant-Whyte, H. (2001). Field robots. In *ISRR'.*

Thrun, S., Koller, D., Ghahmarani, Z., and Durrant-Whyte, H. (2002) Slam updates require constant time. Tech. rep., School of Computer Science, Carnegie Mellon University

Williams S.B., Newman P., Dissanayake, M.W.M.G., and Durrant-Whyte, H. (2000.). Autonomous underwater simultaneous localisation and map building. *Proceedings of IEEE International Conference on Robotics and Automation,* San Francisco, USA, pp. 1143-1150,

Williams, S.B.; Newman, P.; Rosenblatt, J.; Dissanayake, G. & Durrant-Whyte, H. (2001). Autonomous underwater navigation and control, *Robotica,* vol. 19, no. 5, pp. 481-496.

16

Sensor Data Fusion for Road Obstacle Detection: A Validation Framework

Raphaël Labayrade[1], Mathias Perrollaz[2], Dominique Gruyer[2] and Didier Aubert[2]
[1]ENTPE (University of Lyon)
France
[2]LIVIC (INRETS-LCPC)
France

1. Introduction

Obstacle detection is an essential task for autonomous robots. In particular, in the context of Intelligent Transportation Systems (ITS), vehicles (cars, trucks, buses, etc.) can be considered as robots; the development of Advance Driving Assistance Systems (ADAS), such as collision mitigation, collision avoidance, pre-crash or Automatic Cruise Control, requires that reliable road obstacle detection systems are available. To perform obstacle detection, various approaches have been proposed, depending on the sensor involved: telemeters like radar (Skutek et al., 2003) or laser scanner (Labayrade et al., 2005; Mendes et al., 2004), cooperative detection systems (Griffiths et al., 2001; Von Arnim et al., 2007), or vision systems. In this particular field, monocular vision generally exploits the detection of specific features like edges, symmetry (Bertozzi et al., 2000), color (Betke & Nguyen, 1998) (Yamaguchi et al., 2006) or even saliency maps (Michalke et al., 2007). Anyway, most monocular approaches suppose recognition of specific objects, like vehicles or pedestrians, and are therefore not generic. Stereovision is particularly suitable for obstacle detection (Bertozzi & Broggi, 1998; Labayrade et al., 2002; Nedevschi et al., 2004; Williamson, 1998), because it provides a tri-dimensional representation of the road scene. A critical point about obstacle detection for the aimed automotive applications is reliability: the detection rate must be high, while the false detection rate must remain extremely low. So far, experiments and assessments of already developed systems show that using a single sensor is not enough to meet these requirements: due to the high complexity of road scenes, no single sensor system can currently reach the expected 100% detection rate with no false positives. Thus, multi-sensor approaches and fusion of data from various sensors must be considered, in order to improve the performances. Various fusion strategies can be imagined, such as merging heterogeneous data from various sensors (Steux et al., 2002). More specifically, many authors proposed cooperation between an active sensor and a vision system, for instance a radar with mono-vision (Sugimoto et al., 2004), a laser scanner with a camera (Kaempchen et al., 2005), a stereovision rig (Labayrade et al., 2005), etc. Cooperation between mono and stereovision has also been investigated (Toulminet et al., 2006).

Our experiments in the automotive context showed that using specifically a sensor to validate the detections provided by another sensor is an efficient scheme that can lead to a very low false detection rate, while maintaining a high detection rate. The principle consists to tune the first sensor in order to provide overabundant detections (and not to miss any plausible obstacles), and to perform a post-process using the second sensor to confirm the existence of the previously detected obstacles. In this chapter, such a validation-based sensor data fusion strategy is proposed, illustrated and assessed.

The chapter is organized as follows: the validation framework is presented in Section 2. The next sections show how this framework can be implemented in the case of two specific sensors, i.e. a laser scanner aimed at providing hypothesis of detections, and a stereovision rig aimed at validating these detections. Section 3 deals with the laser scanner raw data processing: 1) clustering of lasers points into targets; and 2) tracking algorithm to estimate the dynamic state of the objects and to monitor their appearance and disappearance. Section 4 is dedicated to the presentation of the stereovision sensor and of the validation criteria. An experimental evaluation of the system is given. Eventually, section 5 shows how this framework can be implemented with other kinds of sensors; experimental results are also presented. Section 6 concludes.

2. Overview of the validation framework

Multi-sensor combination can be an efficient way to perform robust obstacle detection. The strategy proposed in this chapter is a collaborative approach illustrated in Fig. 1. A first sensor is supposed to provide hypotheses of detection, denoted 'targets' in the reminder of the chapter. The sensor is tuned to perform overabundant detection and to avoid missing plausible obstacles. Then a post process, based on a second sensor, is performed to confirm the existence of these targets. This second step is aimed at ensuring the reliability of the system by discarding false alarms, through a strict validation paradigm.

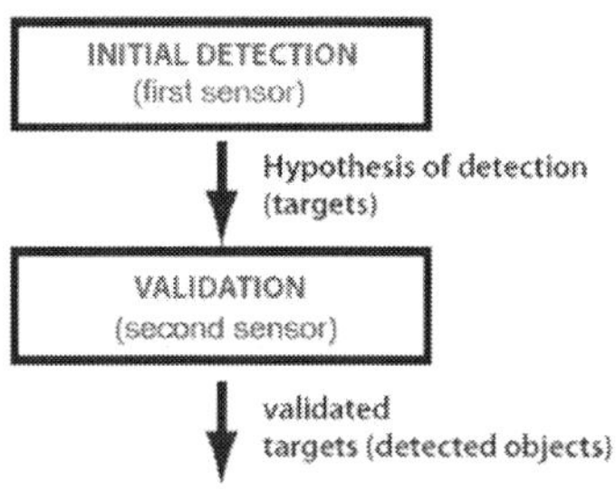

Fig. 1. Overview of the validation framework: a first sensor outputs hypothesis of detection. A second sensor validates those hypothesis.

The successive steps of the validation framework are as follows. First, a volume of interest (VOI) surrounding the targets is built in the 3D space in front of the equipped vehicle, for each target provided by the first sensor. Then, the second sensor focuses on each VOI, and evaluates criteria to validate the existence of the targets. The only requirement for the first sensor is to provide localized targets with respect to the second sensor, so that VOI can be computed.

In the next two sections, we will show how this framework can be implemented for two specific sensors, i.e. a laser scanner, and a stereovision rig; section 5 will study the case of an optical identification sensor as first sensor, along with a stereovision rig as second sensor. It is convenient to assume that all the sensors involved in the fusion scheme are rigidly linked to the vehicle frame, so that, after calibration, they can all refer to a common coordinate system. For instance, Fig. 2 presents the various sensors taken into account in this chapter, referring to the same coordinate system.

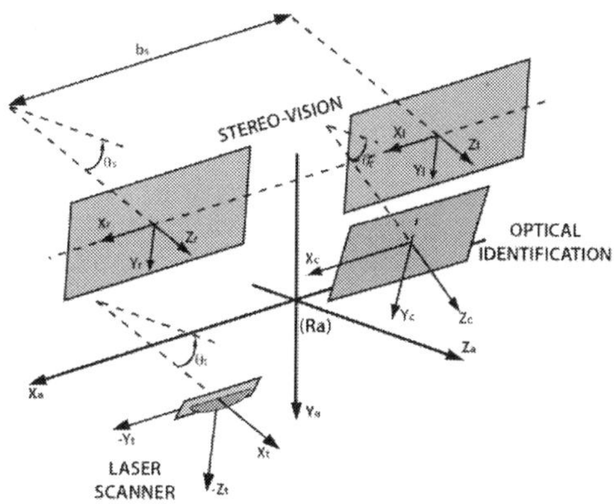

Fig. 2. The different sensors used located in the same coordinate system R_a.

3. Hypotheses of detection obtained from the first sensor: case of a 2D laser scanner

The laser scanner taken into account in this chapter is supposed to be mounted at the front of the equipped vehicle so that it can detect obstacles on its trajectory. This laser scanner provides a set of laser points on the scanned plane: each laser point is characterized by an incidence angle and a distance which corresponds to the distance of the nearest object in this direction. Fig. 4. shows a (X, -Y) projection of the laser points into the coordinate system linked to the laser scanner and illustrated in Fig. 2.

3.1 Dynamic clustering

From the raw data captured with the laser scanner, a set of clusters must be built, each cluster corresponding to an object in the observed scene (a so-called 'target'). Initially, the first laser point defines the first cluster. For all other laser points, the goal is to know whether they are a member of the existent cluster or whether they belong to a new cluster. In the literature, a large set of distance functions can be found for this purpose.

The chosen distance $D_{i,\mu}$ must comply with the following criteria (Gruyer et al., 2003):
- Firstly, this function $D_{i,\mu}$ must give a result scaled between 0 and 1 if the measurement has an intersection with the cluster μ. The value 0 indicates that the measurement i is the same object than the cluster μ with a complete confidence.
- Secondly, the result must be above 1 if the measurement i is out of the cluster μ,
- Finally, this distance must have the properties of distance functions.

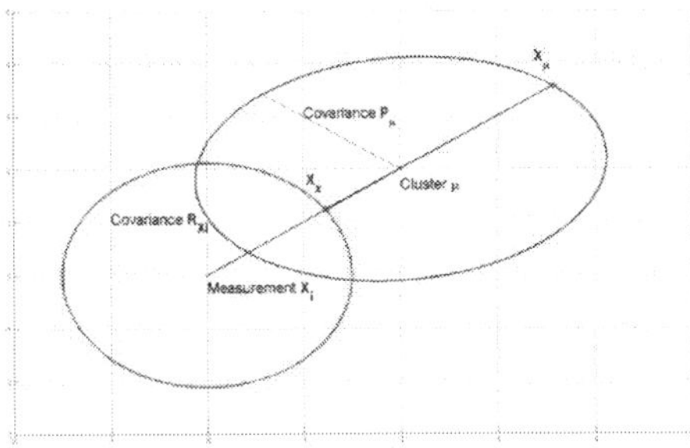

Fig. 3. Clustering of a measurement.

The distance function must also use both cluster and measurement covariance matrices. Basically, the chosen function computes an inner distance with a normalized part build from the sum of the outer distances of a cluster and a measurement. Only the outer distance uses the covariance matrix information:

$$D_{i,j} = \frac{\sqrt{(X_i - \mu)\cdot(X_i - \mu)^t}}{\sqrt{(X_\mu - \mu)} + \sqrt{(X_X - X_i)}} \tag{1}$$

In the normalizing part, the point X_μ represents the border point of a cluster μ (centre μ). This point is located on the straight line between the cluster μ (centre μ) and the measurement i (centre X_i). The same border measurement is used with the measurement. The computation of X_μ and X_X is made with the covariance matrices R_x and P_μ. P_μ and R_x are respectively the cluster covariance matrix and the measurement covariance matrix. The measurement covariance matrix is given from its polar covariance representation (Blackman & Popoli, 1999) with ρ_0 the distance and θ_0 the angle:

$$R_X = \begin{bmatrix} \sigma_{x_0}^2 & \sigma_{x_0 y_0}^2 \\ \sigma_{x_0 y_0}^2 & \sigma_{y_0}^2 \end{bmatrix} \tag{2}$$

where, using a first order expansion:

$$\begin{cases} \sigma_{x_0}^2 = \sigma_{\rho_0}^2 \cos^2\theta_0 + \sigma_{\theta_0}^2 \rho_0{}^2 \sin^2\theta_0 \\ \sigma_{y_0}^2 = \sigma_{\rho_0}^2 \sin^2\theta_0 + \sigma_{\theta_0}^2 \rho_0{}^2 \cos^2\theta_0 \\ \sigma_{x_0 y_0}^2 = \frac{1}{2}\sin 2\theta 0 \left[\sigma_{\rho_0}^2 - \sigma_{\theta_0}^2 \rho_0{}^2\right] \end{cases} \tag{3}$$

$\sigma_{\rho_0}^2$ and $\sigma_{\theta_0}^2$ are the variances in both distance and angle of each measurement provided by the laser scanner. From this covariance matrix, the eigenvalues σ and the eigenvectors V are extracted. A set of equations for ellipsoid cluster, measurement modeling and the line between the cluster centre μ and the laser measurement X is then deduced:

$$\begin{cases} x = V_{11}\sqrt{\sigma_1{}^2}\cos\Psi + V_{12}\sqrt{\sigma_2{}^2}\sin\Psi \\ y = V_{21}\sqrt{\sigma_1{}^2}\cos\Psi + V_{22}\sqrt{\sigma_2{}^2}\sin\Psi \\ y = ax + b \end{cases} \tag{4}$$

x and y give the position of a point on the ellipse and the position of a point in a line. If x and y are the same in the three equations then an intersection between the ellipse and the line exists. The solution of the set of equations (4) gives:

$$\Psi = \arctan\left(\frac{-\sqrt{\sigma_1{}^2}\left[V_{2,1} - aV_{1,1}\right]}{\sqrt{\sigma_2{}^2}\left[V_{2,2} - aV_{1,2}\right]}\right) \quad \text{with } \Psi \in \left[\frac{-\pi}{2}, \frac{\pi}{2}\right] \tag{5}$$

From (5), two solutions are possible:

$$X_\mu = P_\mu \sqrt{\sigma^2}\begin{bmatrix}\cos\Psi \\ \sin\Psi\end{bmatrix} \text{ and } X_\mu = P_\mu \sqrt{\sigma^2}\begin{bmatrix}\cos\Psi + \pi \\ \sin\Psi + \pi\end{bmatrix} \tag{6}$$

Then equation (1) is used with X_μ to know if a laser point belongs to a cluster. Fig. 3 gives a visual interpretation of the used distance for the clustering process. Fig. 4 gives an example of a result of autonomous clustering from laser scanner data. Each cluster is characterized by its position, its orientation, and its size along the two axes (standard deviations).

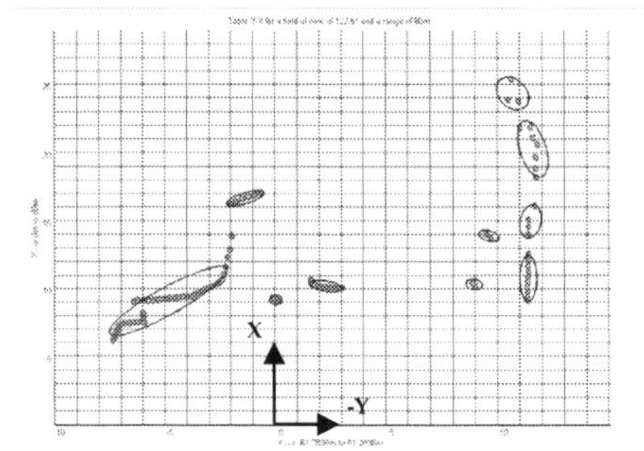

Fig. 4. Example of a result of autonomous clustering (a laser point is symbolized by a little circle, and a cluster is symbolized by a black ellipse).

3.2 Tracking algorithm

Once objects have been generated from laser scanner data, a multi-objects association algorithm is needed to estimate the dynamic state of the targets and to monitor appearances and disappearances of tracks. The position of previously perceived objects is predicted at the current time using Kalman Filtering. These predicted objects are already known objects and will be denoted in what follows by Y_j. Perceived objects at the current time will be denoted by X_i. The proposed multi-objects association algorithm is based on the belief theory introduced by Shafer (Shafer, 1976).

In a general framework, the problem consists to identify an object designated by a generic variable X among a set of hypotheses Yi. One of these hypotheses is supposed to be the solution. The current problem consists to associate perceived objects X_i to known objects Y_j. Belief theory allows assessing the veracity of P_i propositions representing the matching of the different objects.

A basic belief allowing the characterization of a proposition must be defined. This basic belief (mass $m_\Theta(\,)$) is defined in a [0,1] interval. This mass is very close to the one used in probabilistic approach, except that it is distributed on all the propositions of the referential of definition $2^\Omega = \{ A / A \subseteq \Omega \} = \{\emptyset, \{Y_1\}, \{Y_2\}, \ldots, \{Y_n\}, \{Y_1, Y_2\}, \ldots, \{\Omega\}\}$. This referential is the power set of $\Omega = \{Y_1, Y_2, \cdots, Y_n\}$ which includes all the admissible hypotheses. These hypotheses must also be exclusive $\left(Y_i \cap Y_j = \emptyset, \forall i \neq j\right)$. The masses thus defined are called *"basic belief assignment"* and denoted *"bba"* and verify:

$$\sum_{A \subseteq \Omega} m^\Omega(A) = 1 \quad A \in 2^\Omega, A \neq \emptyset \tag{7}$$

The sum of these masses is equal to 1 and the mass corresponding to the impossible case $m_{1..n}^\Omega\{X_i\}(\emptyset)$ must be equal to 0.

In order to succeed in generalizing the Dempster combination rule and thus reducing its combinatorial complexity, the reference frame of definition is limited with the constraint that a perceived object can be connected with one and only one known object.

For example, for a detected object, in order to associate among three known objects, the frame of discernment is:

$$\Omega = \{Y_1, Y_2, Y_3, Y_*\}$$

where Y_i means that "X and Y_i are supposed to be the same object"

In order to be sure that the frame of discernment is really exhaustive, a last hypothesis noted "Y_*" is added (Royere et al., 2000). This one can be interpreted as "a target has no association with any of the tracks". In fact each Y_j represents a local view of the world and the "Y_*" represents the rest of the world. In this context, "Y_*" means that *"an object is associated with nothing in the local knowledge set"*.

In our case, the definition of the *bba* is directly in relation with the data association applications. The mass distribution is a local view around a target X_i and of a track Y_j. The *bba* on the association between X_i and Y_j will be noted $m_j^{\Omega}\{X_i\}(\ )$. It is defined on the frame of discernment Ω = $\{Y_1, Y_2, \ldots Y_n, Y_*\}$ and more precisely on focal elements $\{Y, \overline{Y}, \Omega\}$ were $\overline{Y}$ means not Y.

Each one will respect the following meaning:

$m_j^{\Omega}\{X_i\}(Y_j)$: Degree of belief on the proposition « X_i is associated with Y_j »;

$m_j^{\Omega}\{X_i\}(\overline{Y}_j)$: Degree of belief on the proposition « X_i is not associated with Y_j »;

$m_j^{\Omega}\{X_i\}(\Omega)$: Degree on « the ignorance on the association between X_i and Y_j »;

$m_j^{\Omega}\{X_i\}(Y_*)$: mass representing the reject: X_i is in relation with nothing.

In fact, the complete notation of a belief function is: $m_{S,t}^{\Omega}\{X\}[BC_{S,t}](A) \quad A \in 2^{\Omega}$

With S the information source, t the time of the event, Ω the frame of discernment, X a parameter which takes value in Ω and BC the *evidential corpus* or *knowledge base*. This formulation represents the degree of belief allocated by the source S at the time t to the hypothesis that X belong to A (Denoeux & Smets, 2006).

In order to simplify this notation, we will use the following basic belief function notation $m_j^{\Omega}\{X\}(A)$. The t argument is removed because we process the current time without any links with the previous temporal data.

In this mass distribution, X denotes the processed perceived objects and the index j the known objects (track). If the index is replaced by a set of indices, then the mass is applied to all targets.

Moreover, if an iterative combination is used, the mass $m_j^{\Omega}\{X_i\}(Y_*)$ is not part of the initial mass set and appears only after the first combination. It replaces the conjunction of the combined masses $m_j^{\Omega}\{X_i\}(\overline{Y}_j)$. By observing the behaviour of the iterative combination with n mass sets, a general behaviour can be seen which enables to express the final mass set according to the initial mass sets. This enables to compute directly the final masses without s recurrent stage. For the construction of these combination rules, the work and a first formalism given in (Rombaut, 1998) is used. The use of a *basic belief assignment* generator using the strong hypothesis: *"an object cannot be in the same time associated and not associated to another object"* allows obtaining new rules. These rules firstly reduce the influence of the conflict (the combination of two identical mass sets will not produce a conflict) and, secondly the complexity of the combination (Gruyer & Berge-Cherfaoui 1999a; Gruyer & Berge-Cherfaoui 1999b). The rules become:

$$m_{1..n}^{\Omega}\{X_i\}(Y_j) = m_j^{\Omega}\{X_i\}(Y_j)\prod_{\substack{a=1\\a\neq j}}^{n}\left(1 - m_a^{\Omega}\{X_i\}(Y_a)\right) \tag{8}$$

$$m_{1..n}^{\Omega}\{X_i\}\left(\left\{Y_j, Y_*\right\}\right) = m_j^{\Omega}\{X_i\}(\Omega)\prod_{\substack{a=1\\a\neq j}}^{n} m_a^{\Omega}\{X_i\}(\bar{Y}_a) \tag{9}$$

$$m_{1..n}^{\Omega}\{X_i\}\left(\left\{Y_j, Y_k, Y_*\right\}\right) = m_j^{\Omega}\{X_i\}(\Omega).m_k^{\Omega}\{X_i\}(\Omega)\prod_{\substack{a=1\\a\neq j\\a\neq k}}^{n} m_a^{\Omega}\{X_i\}(\bar{Y}_a) \tag{10}$$

$$m_{1..n}^{\Omega}\{X_i\}\left(\left\{Y_j, Y_k, \ldots, Y_l, Y_*\right\}\right) = m_j^{\Omega}\{X_i\}(\Omega).m_k^{\Omega}\{X_i\}(\Omega)\ldots.m_l^{\Omega}\{X_i\}(\Omega)\prod_{\substack{a=1\\a\neq j\\a\neq k\\\ldots\ldots\\a\neq l}}^{n} m_a^{\Omega}\{X_i\}\left(\bar{Y}_a\right) \tag{11}$$

$$m_{1..n}^{\Omega}\{X_i\}\left(\bar{Y}_j\right) = m_j^{\Omega}\{X_i\}(\bar{Y}_j)\prod_{\substack{a=1\\a\neq j}}^{n} m_a^{\Omega}\{X_i\}(\Omega) \tag{12}$$

$$m_{1..n}^{\Omega}\{X_i\}(\Omega) = \prod_{a=1}^{n} m_a^{\Omega}\{X_i\}(\Omega) \tag{13}$$

$$m_{1..n}^{\Omega}\{X_i\}(Y_*) = \prod_{a=1}^{n} m_a^{\Omega}\{X_i\}(\bar{Y}_a) \tag{14}$$

$$m_{1..n}^{\Omega}\{X_i\}(\varnothing) = 1 - \left[\prod_{a=1}^{n}\left(1 - m_a^{\Omega}\{X_i\}(Y_a)\right) + \sum_{a=1}^{n} m_a^{\Omega}\{X_i\}(Y_a)\prod_{\substack{b=1\\b\neq a}}^{n}\left(1 - m_b^{\Omega}\{X_i\}(Y_b)\right)\right] \tag{15}$$

$m\{X_i\}(Y_*)$ is the result of the combination of all non association belief masses for X_i. Indeed, new target(s) apparition or loss of track(s) because of field of view limitation or objects occultation, leads to consider with attention the Y_* hypothesis which models these phenomena.
In fact, a specialized *bba* can be defined given a local view of X with Y association. In order to obtain a global view, it is necessary to combine the specialized *bbas*. The combination is possible when *bbas* are defined on the same frame of discernment and for the same parameter X.

In a first step, a combination of $m_j^{\Omega}\{X_i\}(\ )$ with $j \in [1..n]$ is done using equations (8) to (15). The result of the combination gives a mass $m_{1..n}^{\Omega}\{X_i\}(\ )$ defined on 2^{Ω}. We can repeat these operations for each X_i and to obtain a set of *p bbas*: $m_{1..n}^{\Omega}\{X_1\}(\ )$, $m_{1..n}^{\Omega}\{X_2\}(\ )$,.. $m_{1..n}^{\Omega}\{X_p\}(\ )$

p is the number of targets and Ω the frame including the *n* tracks corresponding to the *n* hypotheses for target-to-track association.

In order to get a decision, a pignistic transformation is applied for each $m_{1..n}^{\Omega_i}\{X_i\}(\ )$ with $i \in [1..p]$. The pignistic probabilities $BetP^{\Omega_i}\{X_i\}(Y_j)$ of each Y_j hypothesis are summarized in a matrix corresponding to the target point of view.
However, this first matrix gives the pignistic probabilities for each target without taking into consideration the other targets. Each column is independent from the others. A dual approach is proposed in order to consider the possible association of a track with the targets in order to have the tracks point of view.
The dual approach consists in using the same *bba* but combined for each track Y.

From the track point of view, the frame of discernment becomes $\Theta = \{X_1,\ldots,X_m,X_*\}$

The X_* hypothesis models the capability to manage either track disappearance or occultation. For one track Y_j, the *bbas* are then:

$m_i^{\Theta}\{Y_j\}(X_i) = m_j^{\Omega}\{X_i\}(Y_j)$: Degree of belief on the proposition « Y_j is associated with X_i »;

$m_i^{\Theta}\{Y_j\}(\overline{X}_i) = m_j^{\Omega}\{X_i\}(\overline{Y}_j)$: Degree of belief on the proposition « Y_j is not associated with X_i »;

$m_i^{\Theta}\{Y_j\}(\Theta) = m_j^{\Omega}\{X_i\}(\Omega)$: Degree of « the ignorance on the association between Y_j *and* X_i ».

The same combination -equations (8) to (15)- is applied and gives $m_{1..p}^{\Theta}\{Y_i\}(\ )$.
These operations can be repeated for each Y_j to obtain a set of *n bbas*:

$$m_{1..p}^{\Theta_1}\{Y_1\}(\ ),\ m_{1..p}^{\Theta_2}\{Y_2\}(\ ),..\ m_{1..p}^{\Theta_n}\{Y_n\}(\ )$$

n is the number of tracks and Θ_j is the frame based on association hypothesis for Y_j parameter. The index *j* in Θ_j is now useful in order to distinguish the frames based on association for one specific track Y_j for $j \in [1..n]$.
A second matrix is obtained involving the pignistic probabilities $BetP^{\Omega_i}\{Y_i\}(X_j)$ about the tracks.

The last stage of this algorithm consists to establish the best decision from the previously computed associations using the both pignistic probabilities matrices ($BetP^{\Omega_i}\{X_i\}(Y_j)$ and $BetP^{\Omega_i}\{Y_i\}(X_j)$). The decision stage is done with the maximum pignistic probability rule. This rule is applied on each column of both pignistic probabilities matrices.
With the first matrix, this rule answers to the question *"which track Y_j is associated with target X_i?"*:

$$X_i = d(Y_j) = \underset{i}{Max}\left[BetP^{\Omega_i}_{\{X_i\}(Y_j)} \right] \tag{16}$$

With the second matrix, this rule answers to the question *"which target X_i is associated to the track Y_j?"*:

$$Y_j = d(X_i) = \underset{j}{Max}\left[BetP^{\Theta_j}_{\{Y_j\}(X_i)} \right] \tag{17}$$

Unfortunately, a problem appears when the decision obtained from a pignistic matrix is ambiguous (this ambiguity quantifies the duality and the uncertainty of a relation) or when the decisions between the two pignistic matrices are in conflict (this conflict represents antagonism between two relations resulting each one from a different belief matrix). Both problems of conflicts and ambiguities are solved by using an assignment algorithm known under the name of the Hungarian algorithm (Kuhn, 1955; Ahuja et al., 1993). This algorithm has the advantage of ensuring that the decision taken is not *"good"* but *"the best"*. By the *"best"*, we mean that if a known object has defective or poor sensors perceiving it, then the sensor is unlikely to know what this object corresponds to, and therefore ensuring that the association is good is a difficult task. But among all the available possibilities, we must certify that the decision is the *"best"* of all possible decisions.
Once the multi-objects association has been performed, the Kalman filter associated to each target is updated using the new position of the target, and so the dynamic state of each target is estimated, i.e. both speed and angular speed.

4. Validation of the hypotheses of detection: case of a stereovision-based validation

In order to validate the existence of the targets detected by the laser scanner and tracked over time as describe above, a stereovision rig is used. The geometrical configuration of the stereoscopic sensor is presented in Fig. 5. The upcoming steps are as follows: building Volumes Of Interest (VOI) from laser scanner targets, validation criteria evaluation from 'obstacle measurement points'.

4.1 Stereovision sensor modeling

The epipolar geometry is rectified through calibration, so that the epipolar lines are parallel. Cameras are described by a *pinhole* model and characterized by (u_0, v_0) the position of the optical center in the image plane, and a = *focal length / pixel size* (pixels are supposed to be square). The extrinsic parameters of the stereoscopic sensor are (0, Y_s^0, Z_s^0) the position of the central point of the stereoscopic baseline, θ_s the pitch of the cameras and b_s the length of stereoscopic baseline. Given a point P (X_a, Y_a, Z_a) in the common coordinate system R_a, its position (u_r, Δ_s, v) and (u_l, Δ_s, v) in the stereoscopic images can be calculated as:

$$u_r = u_0 + \alpha \frac{X_a - b_s/2}{(Y_a - Y_S{}^0)\sin\theta_s + (Z_a - Z_S{}^0)\cos\theta_s} \tag{18}$$

$$u_l = u_0 + \alpha \frac{X_a + b_s/2}{(Y_a - Y_S{}^0)\sin\theta_s + (Z_a - Z_S{}^0)\cos\theta_s} \tag{19}$$

$$v = v_0 + \alpha \frac{(Y_a - Y_S{}^0)\cos\theta_s - (Z_a - Z_S{}^0)\sin\theta_s}{(Y_a - Y_S{}^0)\sin\theta_s + (Z_a - Z_S{}^0)\cos\theta_s} \tag{20}$$

$$\Delta_s = \alpha \frac{b_s}{(Y_a - Y_S{}^0)\sin\theta_s + (Z_a - Z_S{}^0)\cos\theta_s} \tag{21}$$

where $\Delta_s = u_l - u_r$ is the disparity value of a given pixel, $v = v_l = v_r$ its y-coordinate.

This transform is invertible, so the coordinates in R_a can be retrieved from images coordinates through:

$$X_a = b_s / 2 + \frac{b_s(u_r - u_0)}{\Delta_s} \tag{22}$$

$$Y_a = Y_S{}^0 + \frac{b_s((v - v_0)\cos\theta_s + \alpha\sin\theta_s)}{\Delta_s} \tag{23}$$

$$Z_a = Z_S{}^0 + \frac{b_s(\alpha\cos\theta_s - (v - v_0)\sin\theta_s)}{\Delta_s} \tag{24}$$

The coordinate system $R_\Delta = (\Omega, u_r, v, \Delta_s)$ defines a 3D space E_Δ, denoted disparity space.

4.2 Building Volumes Of Interest (VOI) from laser scanner

The first processing step of the validation algorithm is the conversion of targets obtained from laser scanner into VOI (Volumes Of Interest). The idea is to find where the system should focalize its upcoming processing stages. A VOI is defined as a rectangular parallelepiped in the disparity space, frontal to the image planes.

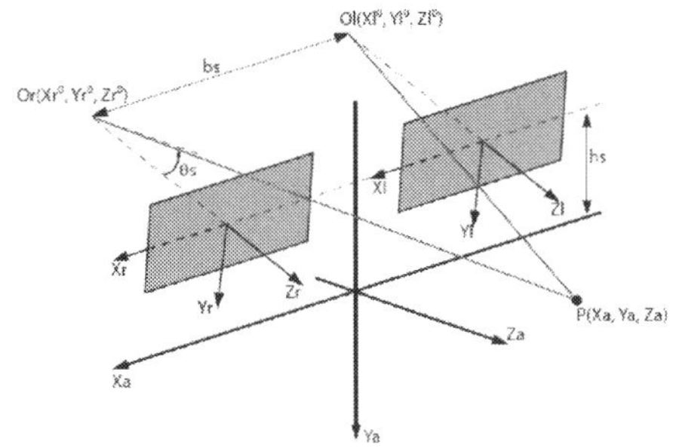

Fig. 5. Geometrical configuration of the stereoscopic sensor in R_a.

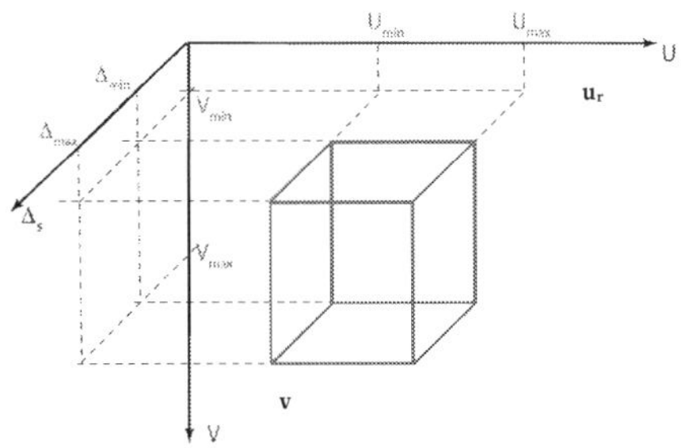

Fig. 6. Definition of the volume of interest (VOI).

Fig. 6 illustrates this definition. This is equivalent to a region of interest in the right image of the stereoscopic pair, associated to a disparity range. This definition is useful to distinguish objects that are connected in the images, but located at different longitudinal positions.
To build volumes of interest in the stereoscopic images, a bounding box V_o is constructed in R_a from the laser scanner targets as described in Fig. 7 (a). Z_{near} , X_{left} and X_{right} are computed from the ellipse parameters featuring the laser target. Z_{far} and Y_{high} are then constructed from an arbitrary knowledge of the size of the obstacles. Fig. 7 (b) shows how the VOI is projected in the right image of the stereoscopic pair. Equations (18-20) are used to this purpose.

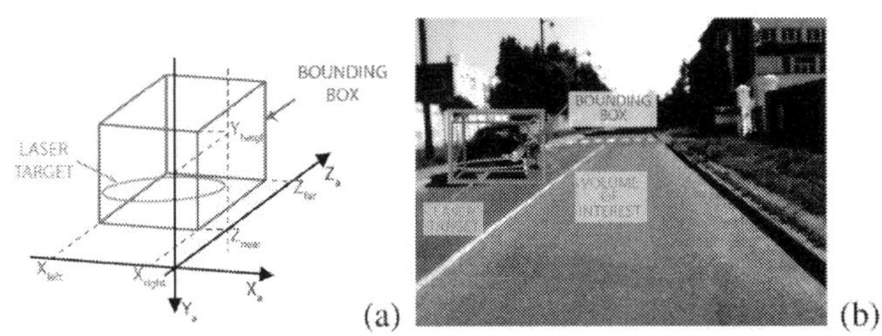

Fig. 7. (a): Conversion of a laser target into bounding box. (b): Projection of the bounding box (i.e. VOI) into the right image of the stereoscopic pair.

4.3 Computation of 'obstacle measurement points'

In each VOI, measurement points are computed, which will be used for the further validation stage of the data fusion strategy. This is performed through a local disparity map computation.

1) Local disparity map computation: The local disparity map for each VOI is computed using a classical Winner Take All (WTA) approach (Scharstein & Szeliski, 2002) based on Zero Sum of Square Difference (ZSSD) criterion. Use of a sparse disparity map is chosen to keep a low computation time. Thus, only high gradient pixels are considered in the process.

2) Filtering: Using directly raw data from the local disparity map could lead to a certain number of errors. Indeed, such maps could contain pixels belonging to the road surface, to targets located at higher distances or some noise due to matching errors. Several filtering operations are implemented to reduce such sources of errors: the cross-validation step helps to efficiently reject errors located in half-occluded areas (Egnal & Wildes, 2002), the double correlation method, using both rectangular and sheared correlation window provides instant classification of the pixels corresponding to obstacles or road surface (Perrolaz et al., 2007). Therefore only obstacle pixels are kept; it is required to take in consideration the disparity range of the VOI in order to reject pixels located further or closer than the processed volume; a median filter rejects impulse noise created by isolated matching errors.

3) Obstacle pixels: Once the local disparity map has been computed and filtered, the VOI contains an 'obstacle disparity map', corresponding to a set of measurement points. For better clarity, we will call *obstacle pixels* the measurement points present in the 'obstacle disparity map'.

We propose to exploit the *obstacle pixels* to reject false detections. It is necessary to highlight the major features of what we call 'obstacles', before defining the validation strategy. These features must be as little restrictive as possible, to ensure that the process of validation remains generic against the type of obstacles.

4.4 Stereovision-based validation criteria

In order to define validation criterion, hypotheses must be made to consider a target as an actual obstacle: 1) its size shall be significant; 2) it shall be almost vertical; 3) its bottom shall be close to the road surface.

The derived criteria assessed for a target are as follows:

1) The observed surface, which must be large enough;
2) The orientation, which must be almost vertical;
3) The bottom height, which must be small enough.

Starting from these three hypotheses, let us define three different validation criteria.

1) Number of obstacle pixels: To validate a target according to the first feature, the most natural method consists in checking that the volume of interest associated to the target actually contains *obstacle pixels*. Therefore, our validation criterion consists in counting the number of *obstacle pixels* in the volume, and comparing it to a threshold.

2) Prevailing alignment criterion: One can also exploit the almost verticality of obstacles, while the road is almost horizontal. We offer therefore to measure in which direction the *obstacle pixels* of the target are aligned. For this purpose, the local disparity map of the target is projected over the v-disparity plane (Labayrade & al., 2002). A linear regression is then computed to find the global orientation of the set of *obstacle pixels*. The parameters of the extracted straight line are used to confirm the detection.

3) Bottom height criterion: A specific type of false detections by stereovision appears in scenes with many repetitive structures. Highly correlated false matches can then appear as objects closer to the vehicle than their actual location. These false matches are very disturbing, because the validation criteria outlined above assume that matching errors are mainly uncorrelated. These criteria are irrelevant with respect to such false detections. Among these errors, the most problematic ones occur when the values of disparities are over-evaluated. In the case of an under-evaluation, the hypothesis of detection is located further than the actual object, and is therefore a case of detection failure. When the disparity is significantly over-evaluated, the height of the bottom of an obstacle can be high and may give the feeling that the target flies without ground support. So the validation test consists to measure the altitude of the lowest *obstacle pixel* in the VOI, and check that this altitude is low enough.

4.5 Detailed architecture for a laser scanner and a stereovision rig

The detailed architecture of the framework, showing how the above mentioned criteria are used, is presented in Fig. 8. As the first sensor of the architecture, the laser scanner produces fast and accurate targets, but with a large amount of false positives. Indeed, in case of strong vehicle pitch or non-plane road geometry, the intersection of the scanning plane with the road surface produces errors that can hardly be discriminated from actual obstacles. Thus, as the second sensor of the architecture, the stereovision rig is aimed at discarding false positives through the application of the above-mentioned confirmation criteria.

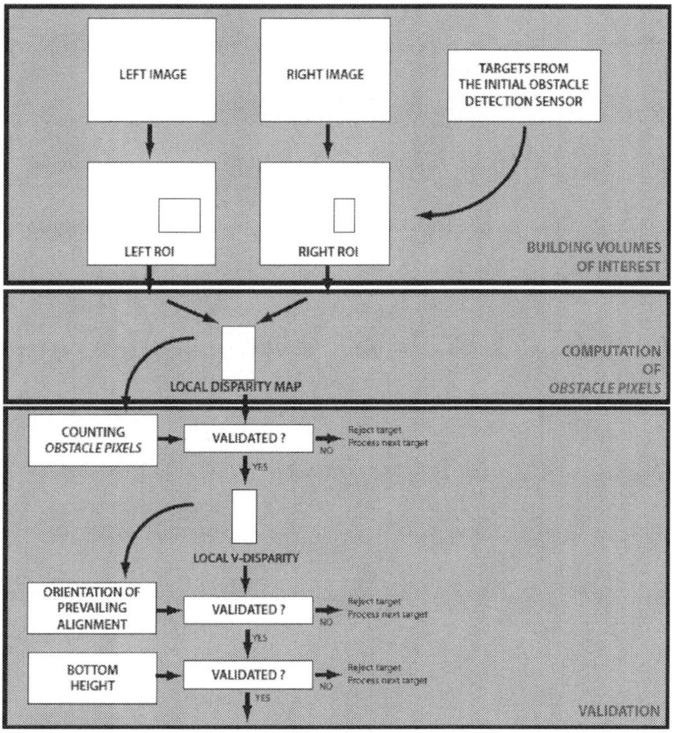

Fig. 8. Detailed architecture of the framework, using a laser scanner as the first sensor, and stereovision as validation sensor.

4.6 Experimental setup and results

The stereoscopic sensor is composed of two *SMaL*™ CMOS cameras, with 6 *mm* focal length. VGA 10 bits grayscale images are grabbed every 30 *ms*. The stereoscopic baseline is 30 *cm*. The height is 1,4 *m* and the pitch $\theta_s = 5°$.

The telemetric sensor is a *Sick*™ laser scanner which measures 201 points every 26 *ms*, with a scanning angular field of view of 100°. It is positioned horizontally 40 *cm* over the road surface. Fig. 9 shows the laser points projected in the right image of the stereoscopic sensor, as well as bounding boxes around obstacles, generated from the laser point clustering stage.

Fig. 10 presents examples of results obtained in real driving conditions. False positives are generated by the laser scanner, and are successfully discarded after the validation process. A quantitative evaluation was also performed. The test vehicle has been driven on a very bumpy and dent parking area to obtain a large number of false detections due to the intersection of the laser plane with the ground surface. 7032 images have been processed. The number of false alarms drops from 781 (without the validation step) to 3 (with the validation step). On its part, the detection rate is decreased by 2.6% showing that the validation step hardly affects it.

Fig. 9. Right image from stereoscopic pair with laser points projected (cross), and resulting targets (rectangles).

Fig. 10. Common sources of errors in detection using a laser scanner. (a): laser scanning plane intersects road surface. (b): non planar road is seen as an obstacle. (c): laser temporal tracking failed. All of these errors are correctly discarded by the stereovision-based validation step.

5. Implementation with other sensors

The validation framework presented in Fig. 1 is generic and can be used along with arbitrary sensors. Good results are likely to be obtained if the two sensors present complementary features, for instance distance assessment accuracy / obstacle 3D data. For instance, the first sensor providing hypotheses of detection can be a radar or optical identification. In this section we focalize on the latter sensor as the first sensor of the architecture, and keep using the stereovision rig as the second sensor.

5.1 Optical identification sensor

Optical identification is an example of cooperative detection, which is a recently explored way of research in the field of obstacle detection. With this approach, the different vehicles in the scene cooperate to enhance the global detection performance.

The cooperative sensor in this implementation is originally designed for cooperation between obstacle detection and vehicle to vehicle (V2V) telecommunications. It can as well be used for robust high range obstacle detection. The process is divided in two parts: an emitting near IR lamp on the back of an object, emitting binary messages (an unique ID code), and a high speed camera with a band pass filter centered around near IR, associated to an image processing algorithm to detect the sources, track them and decode the messages. This sensor is described more in details in (Von Arnim et al., 2007).

5.2 Building Volumes Of Interest (VOI) from optical identification

VOIs are built in a way similar to the method used for laser scanner. A bounding box around the target, with arbitrary dimensions, is projected into the disparity space. However, ID lamps are localized in decoding-camera's image plane, with only two coordinates. So, to obtain fully exploitable data, it is necessary to retrieve a tri-dimensional localization of the detection in *Ra*. Therefore, it has been decided to fix a parameter: the lamp height is considered as known. This constraint is not excessively restrictive because the lamp is fixed once and for all on the object to identify.

5.3 Experimental results with optical identification sensor

Fig. 11 (a) presents optical identification in action: a vehicle located about 100 m ahead is detected and identified. Fig. 11 (b) presents a common source of error of optical identification, due to the reflection of the IR lamp on the road separating wall. This error is correctly discarded by the stereovision-based validation process. In this implementation, the stereoscopic processing gives the opportunity to validate the existence of an actual obstacle, when a coherent IR source is observed. This is useful to reject false positives due to IR artifacts; another example is the reflection of an ID lamp onto a specular surface (another vehicle for instance).

Fig. 11. (a): Detection from optical identification system projected in the right image. (b): Error in detection: ID lamp reflected on the road separating wall. This error is correctly discarded by the stereovision-based validation step.

6. Conclusion

For the application of obstacle detection in the automotive domain, reliability is a major consideration. In this chapter, a sensor data fusion validation framework was proposed: an initial sensor provides hypothesis of detections that are validated by a second sensor. Experiments demonstrate the efficiency of this strategy, when using a stereovision rig as the validation sensor, which provide rich 3D information about the scene. The framework can be implemented for any initial devices providing hypothesis of detection (either single sensor or detection system), in order to drastically decrease the false alarm rate while having few influence on the detection rate.

One major improvement of this framework would be the addition of a multi-sensor combination stage, to obtain an efficient multi-sensor collaboration framework. The choice to insert this before or after validation is still open, and may have significant influence on performances.

7. References

Ahuja R. K.; Magnanti T. L. & Orlin J. B. (1993). *Network Flows, theory, algorithms, and applications*, Editions Prentice-Hall, 1993.

Bertozzi M. & Broggi, A. (1998). Gold: A parallel real-time stereo vision system for generic obstacle and lane detection, *IEEE Transactions on Image Processing*, 7(1), January 1998.

Bertozzi, M., Broggi, A., Fascioli, A. & Nichele, S. (2000). Stereo vision based vehicle detection, In *Proceedings of the IEEE Intelligent Vehicles Symposium*, Detroit, USA, October 2000.

Betke, M. & Nguyen, M. (1998). Highway scene analysis form a moving vehicle under reduced visibility conditions, *Proceedings of the IEEE International Conference on Intelligent Vehicles*, Stuttgart, Germany, October 1998.

Blackman S. & Popoli R. (1999). *Modern Tracking Systems*, Artech, 1999.

Denoeux, T. & Smets, P. (2006). Classification using Belief Functions: the Relationship between the Case-based and Model-based Approaches, *IEEE Transactions on Systems, Man and Cybernetics B*, Vol. 36, Issue 6, pp 1395-1406, 2006.

Egnal, G. & Wildes, R. P. (2002). Detecting binocular half-occlusions: Empirical comparisons of five approaches, *IEEE Transactions on Pattern Analysis and Machine Intelligence*, 24(8):1127–1133, 2002.

Griffiths, P., Langer, D., Misener, J. A., Siegel, M., Thorpe. C. (2001). Sensorfriendly vehicle and roadway systems, *Proceedings of the IEEE Instrumentation and Measurement Technology Conference*, Budapest, Hongrie, 2001.

Gruyer, D. & Berge-Cherfaoui V. (1999a). Matching and decision for Vehicle tracking in road situation, *IEEE/RSJ International Conference on Intelligent Robots and Systems*, Koera, 1999.

Gruyer, D., & Berge-Cherfaoui V. (1999b). Multi-objects association in perception of dynamical situation, *Fifteenth Conference on Uncertainty in Artificial Intelligence, UAI'99*, Stockholm, Sweden, 1999.

Gruyer, D. Royere, C., Labayrade, R., Aubert, D. (2003). Credibilistic multi-sensor fusion for real time application. Application to obstacle detection and tracking, *ICAR 2003*, Coimbra, Portugal, 2003.

Kaempchen, N.; Buehler, M. & Dietmayer, K. (2005). Feature-level fusion for free-form object tracking using laserscanner and video, *Proceedings of the IEEE Intelligent Vehicles Symposium*, Las Vegas, USA, June 2005.

Kuhn H. W. (1955), *The Hungarian method for assignment problem*, Nav. Res. Quart., 2, 1955.

Labayrade, R.; Aubert, D. & Tarel, J.P. (2002). Real time obstacle detection on non flat road geometry through 'v-disparity' representation, *Proceedings of the IEEE Intelligent Vehicles Symposium*, Versailles, France, June 2002.

Labayrade R.; Royere, C. & Aubert, D. (2005). A collision mitigation system using laser scanner and stereovision fusion and its assessment, *Proceedings of the IEEE Intelligent Vehicles Symposium*, pp 440– 446, Las Vegas, USA, June 2005.

Labayrade R.; Royere C.; Gruyer D. & Aubert D. (2005). Cooperative fusion for multi-obstacles detection with use of stereovision and laser scanner", *Autonomous Robots, special issue on Robotics Technologies for Intelligent Vehicles*, Vol. 19, N°2, September 2005, pp. 117 - 140.

Mendes, A.; Conde Bento, L. & Nunes U. (2004). Multi-target detection and tracking with a laserscanner, *Proceedings of the IEEE Intelligent Vehicles Symposium*, University of Parma, Italy, June 2004.

Michalke, T.; Gepperth, A.; Schneider, M.; Fritsch, J. & Goerick, C. (2007). Towards a human-like vision system for resource-constrained intelligent Cars, *Proceedings of the 5th International Conference on Computer Vision Systems*, 2007.

Nedevschi, S.; Danescu, R.; Frentiu, D.; Marita, T.; Oniga, F.; Pocol, C.; Graf, T. & Schmidt R. (2004). High accuracy stereovision approach for obstacle detection on non planar roads, *Proceedings of the IEEE Intelligent Engineering Systems*, Cluj Napoca, Romania, September 2004.

Perrollaz, M., Labayrade, R., Gallen, R. & Aubert, D. (2007). A three resolution framework for reliable road obstacle detection using stereovision, *Proceedings of the IAPR International Conference on Machine Vision and Applications*, Tokyo, Japan, 2007.

Rombaut M. (1998). *Decision in Multi-obstacle Matching Process using Theory of Belief*, AVCS'98, Amiens, France, 1998.

Royere, C., Gruyer, D., Cherfaoui V. (2000). Data association with believe theory, *FUSION'2000*, Paris, France, 2000.

Scharstein, D. & Szeliski, R. (2002). A taxonomy and evaluation of dense two-frame stereo correspondence algorithms, *International Journal of Computer Vision*, 47(1-3):7–42, 2002.

Shafer G. (1976). *A mathematical theory of evidence*, Princeton University Press, 1976.

Skutek, M.; Mekhaiel, M. & Wanielik, M. (2003). Precrash system based on radar for automotive applications, *Proceedings of the IEEE Intelligent Vehicles Symposium*, Columbus, USA, June 2003.

Steux, B.; Laurgeau, C.; Salesse, L. & Wautier, D. (2002). Fade: A vehicle detection and tracking system featuring monocular color vision and radar data fusion, *Proceedings of the IEEE Intelligent Vehicles Symposium*, Versailles, France, June 2002.

Sugimoto, S.; Tateda, H.; Takahashi, H. & Okutomi M. (2004). Obstacle detection using millimeter-wave radar and its visualization on image sequence, *Proceedings of the IAPR International Conference on Pattern Recognition*, Cambridge, UK, 2004.

Toulminet, G.; Bertozzi, V; Mousset, S.; Bensrhair, A. & Broggi. (2006). Vehicle detection by means of stereo vision-based obstacles features extraction and monocular pattern analysis, *IEEE Transactions on Image Processing*, 15(8):2364–2375, August 2006.

Von Arnim, A.; Perrollaz, M.; Bertrand, A. & Ehrlich, J. (2007). Vehicle identification using infrared vision and applications to cooperative perception, *Proceedings of the IEEE Intelligent Vehicles Symposium*, Istanbul, Turkey, June 2007.

Williamson, T. (1998). *A High-Performance Stereo Vision System for Obstacle Detection*. PhD thesis, Carnegie Mellon University, 1998.

Yamaguchi, K.; Kato, T. & Ninomiya, Y. (2006). Moving obstacle detection using monocular vision, *Proceedings of the IEEE Intelligent Vehicles Symposium*, Tokyo, Japan, June 2006.

17

Biometrics Sensor Fusion

Dakshina Ranjan Kisku, Ajita Rattani, Phalguni Gupta,
Jamuna Kanta Sing and Massimo Tistarelli
Dr. B. C. Roy Engineering College, Durgapur - 713206, India
University of Sassari, Alghero (SS), 07140, Italy
Indian Institute of Technology Kanpur, Kanpur - 208016, India
Jadavpur University, Kolkata - 700032, India
University of Sassari, Alghero (SS), 07140, Italy

1. Introduction

Performance of any biometric system entirely depends on the information that is acquired from biometrics characteristics (Jain et. al., 2004). Several biometrics systems are developed over the years in the last two decades, which are mostly considered as viable biometric tools used for human identification and verification. However, due to some negative constraints that are often associated with the biometrics templates are generally degraded the overall performance and accuracy of the biometric systems. In spite of that, many biometrics systems are developed and implemented over the years and deployed successfully for user authentication. Modality based categorization of the biometric systems are made on the basis of biometric traits are used. While single biometric systems are used for verification or identification of acquired biometrics characteristics/attributes, it is called uni-biometrics authentication systems and when more than one biometric technology are used in fused form for identification or verification, it is called multimodal biometrics. It has been seen that, depending on the application context, mono-modal or multimodal biometrics systems can be used for authentication.

In biometric, human identity verification systems seek considerable improvement in reliability and accuracy. Several biometric authentication traits are offering 'up-to-the-mark' and negotiable performance in respect of recognizing and identifying users. However, none of the biometrics is giving cent percent accuracy. Multibiometric systems remove some of the drawbacks of the uni-modal biometric systems by acquiring multiple sources of information together in an augmented group, which has richer details. Utilization of these biometric systems depends on more than one physiological or behavioral characteristic for enrollment and verification/ identification. There exist multimodal biometrics (Jain et. al., 2004) with various levels of fusion, namely, sensor level, feature level, matching score level and decision level. Further, fusion at low level / sensor level by biometric image fusion is an emerging area of research for biometric authentication.

A multisensor multimodal biometric system fuses information at low level or sensor level of processing is expected to produce more accurate results than the systems that integrate

information at a later stages, namely, feature level, matching score level, because of the availability of more richer and relevant information.
Face and palmprint biometrics have been considered and accepted as most widely used biometric traits, although the fusion of face and palmprint is not studied at sensor level/low level when it is compared with existing multimodal biometric fusion schemes. Due to incompatible characteristics of face and palmprint images, where a face image is processed as holistic texture features on a whole face or divided the face into local regions and palmprint consists of ridges and bifurcations along with three principal lines, difficult to integrate in different levels of fusion in biometric.
This chapter proposes a novel biometric sensor generated evidence fusion of face and palmprint images using wavelet decomposition and monotonic decreasing graph for user identity verification. Biometric image fusion at sensor level refers to a process that fuses multispectral images captured at different resolutions and by different biometric sensors to acquire richer and complementary information to produce a fused image in spatially enhanced form. SIFT operator is applied for invariant feature extraction from the fused image and the recognition of individuals is performed by adjustable structural graph matching between a pair of fused images by searching corresponding points using recursive descent tree traversal approach. The experimental results show that the proposed method with 98.19% accuracy is found to be better than the uni-modal face and palmprint authentication having recognition rates 89.04% and 92.17%, respectively if all methods are processed in the same feature space, i.e., in SIFT feature space.
The chapter is organized as follows. Next section introduces a few state-of-the-art biometrics sensor fusion methods for user authentication and recognition. Section 3 discusses the process of multisensor biometric evidence fusion using wavelet decomposition and transformation. Section 4 presents the overview of feature extraction by using SIFT features from fused image. Structural graph for corresponding points searching and matching is analyzed in Section 5. Experimental results are discussed in section 6 and conclusion is drawn in the last section.

2. State-of-the-art Biometrics Sensor Fusion Methods

In this section two robust multisensor biometrics methods are discussed briefly for user authentication. The first method (Raghavendra, et. al., 2010) has presented a novel biometric sensor fusion technique for face and palmprint images using Particle Swarm Optimisation (PSO). The method consists of the following steps. First the face and palmprint images obtained from different sensors are decomposed using wavelet transformation and then, PSO is employed to select the most discriminative wavelet coefficients from face and palmprint to produce a new fused image. Kernel Direct Discriminant Analysis (KDDA) has been applied for feature extraction and the decision about accept/reject is carried out using Nearest Neighbour Classifier. (NNC).
The second method (Singh, et. al., 2008) is a multispectral image fusion of visible and infrared face images and verification decision is made using match score fusion. The fusion of visible and long wave infrared face images is performed using 2vn-granular SVM which uses multiple SVMs to learn both the local and global properties of the multispectral face images at different granularity levels and resolution. The 2vn-GSVM performs accurate classification which is subsequently used to dynamically compute the weights of visible and

infrared images for generating a fused face image. 2D log polar Gabor transform and local binary pattern feature extraction algorithms are applied to the fused face image to extract global and local facial features, respectively. The corresponding matching scores are fused using Dezert Smarandache theory of fusion which is based on plausible and paradoxical reasoning. The efficacy of the proposed algorithm is validated using the Notre Dame and Equinox databases and is compared with existing statistical, learning, and evidence theory based fusion algorithms.

3. Multisensor Biometrics Evidence Fusion using Wavelet Decomposition

Multisensor image fusion is performed with one or more images; however the fused image is considered as a unique single pattern from where the invariant keypoint features are extracted. The fused image should have more useful and richer information together from individual images. The fusion of the two images can take place at the signal, pixel, or feature level.

The proposed method for evidence fusion is based on the face and palmprint images decomposition into multiple channels depending on their local frequency. The wavelet transform provides an integrated framework to decompose biometric images into a number of new images, each of them having a different degree of resolution. According to Fourier transform, the wave representation is an intermediate representation between Fourier and spatial representations. It has the capability to provide good optimal localization for both frequency and space domains.

3.1 Basic Structure for Image Fusion

The biometrics image fusion extracts information from each source image and obtains the effective representation in the final fused image. The aim of image fusion technique is to fuse the detailed information which obtains from both the source images. By convention, multi-resolutions images are used for image fusion, which are obtained from different sources. Multi-resolution analysis of images provides useful information for several computer vision and image analysis applications. The multi-resolution image used to represent the signals where decomposition is performed for obtaining finer detail. Multi-resolution image decomposition gives an approximation image and three other images viz., horizontal, vertical and diagonal images of coarse detail. The Multi-resolution techniques are mostly used for image fusion using wavelet transform and decomposition.

Our method proposes a scheme where we fuse biometrics face and palmprint images of the identical resolutions and the images are completely different in texture information. The face and palmprint images are obtained from different sources. More formally, these images are obtained from different sensors. After re-scaling and registration, the images are fused together by using wavelet transform and decomposition. Finally, we obtain a completely new fused image, where both the attributes of face and palmprint images are focused and reflected. The proposed method for image fusion opposes the multi-resolution image fusion approach where multi-resolution images of same the subject are collected from multiple sources. However, these multi-resolution images belong to the same subject rather than different subjects. In the proposed approach, face and palmprint images are acquired from two different sensors, i.e., from two different sources and to make alignment of the corresponding pixels, feature-based image registration algorithm has been used (Hsu, & Beuker, 2000).

Prior to image fusion, wavelet transforms are determined from face and palmprint images. The wavelet transform contains low-high bands, high-low bands and high-high bands of the face and palmprint images at different scales including the low-low bands of the images at coarse level. The low-low band has all the positive transform values and remaining bands have transform values which are fluctuating around zeros. The larger transform values in these bands respond to sharper brightness changes and thus to the changes of salient features in the image such as edges, lines, and boundaries. The proposed image fusion rule selects the larger absolute values of the two wavelet coefficients at each point. Therefore, a fused image is produced by performing an inverse wavelet transform based on integration of wavelet coefficients correspond to the decomposed face and palmprint images. More formally, wavelet transform decomposes an image recursively into several frequency levels and each level contains transform values. Let it be a gray-scale image, after wavelet decomposition, the first level would be

$$I = I_{LL_1} + I_{LH_1} + I_{HL_1} + I_{HH_1} \tag{1}$$

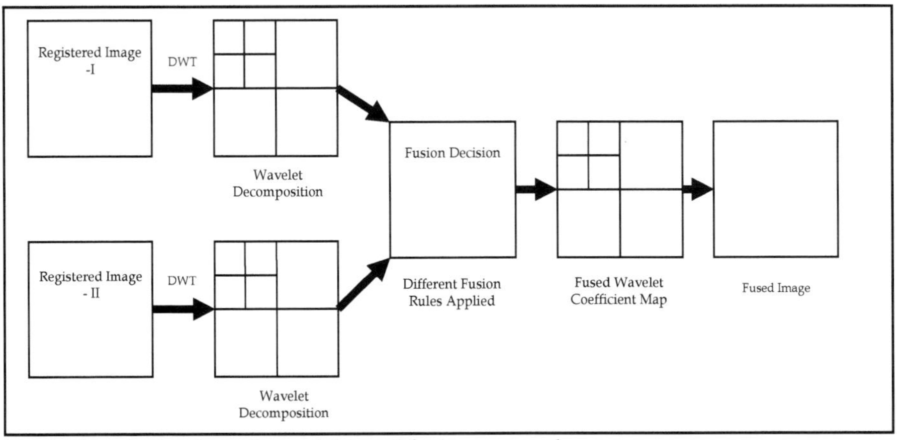

Fig. 1. Generic structure of wavelet based fusion approach.

Generally, I_{LL_1} represents the base image, which contains coarse detail of positive transform values and the other high frequency detail such as I_{LH_1}, I_{HL_1} and I_{HH_1} represent the vertical, horizontal and diagonal detail of transform values, respectively, and these details fluctuating transform values around zeros. After nth level decomposition of the base image in low frequency, the nth level would be the following:

$$I_{n-1} = I_{LL_n} + I_{LH_n} + I_{HL_n} + I_{HH_n} \tag{2}$$

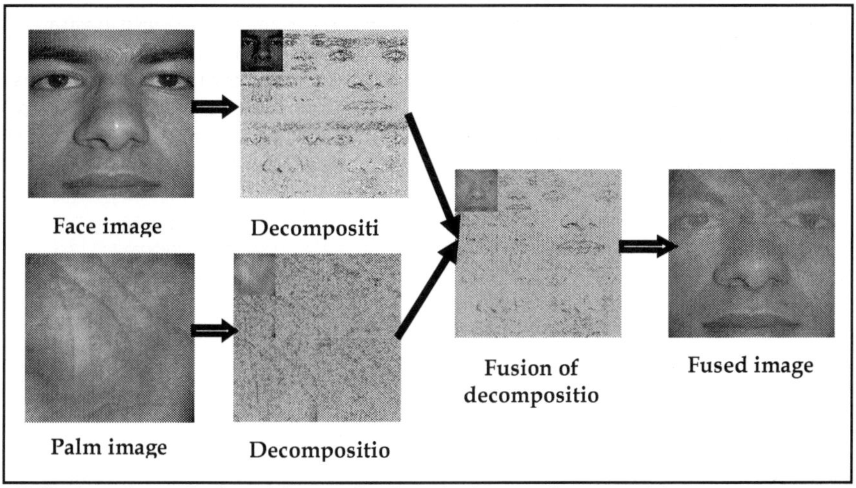

Fig. 2. Fusion of wavelet based face and palmprint images decompositions.

So, the nth level of decomposition will be consisting of 3n+1 sub-image sequences. The 3n+1 sub-image sequences are then fused by applying different wavelet fusion rules on the low and high frequency parts. Finally, inverse wavelet transformation is performed to restore the fused image. The fused image possesses good quality of relevant information for face and palm images. Generic wavelet-based decomposition and image fusion approach are shown in the Fig. 1 and Fig. 2 respectively.

4. SIFT Features Extraction

To recognize and classify objects efficiently, feature points from objects can be extracted to make a robust feature descriptor or representation of the objects. In this work the technique to extract features from images, which are called Scale Invariant Feature Transform (SIFT) (Lowe, 2004; Lowe, 1999) has been used. These features are invariant to scale, rotation, partial illumination and 3D projective transform and they are found to provide robust matching across a substantial range of affine distortion, change in 3D viewpoint, addition of noise, and change in illumination. SIFT image features provide a set of features of an object that are not affected by occlusion, clutter, and unwanted "noise" in the image. In addition, the SIFT features are highly distinctive in nature which have accomplished correct matching on several pair of feature points with high probability between a large database and a test sample. Following are the four major filtering stages of computation used to generate the set of image feature based on SIFT.

4.1 Scale-space Extrema Detection

This filtering approach attempts to identify image locations and scales that are identifiable from different views. Scale space and Difference of Gaussian (DoG) functions are used to detect stable keypoints. Difference of Gaussian is used for identifying key-points in scale-space and locating scale space extrema by taking difference between two images, one with scaled by some constant times of the other. To detect the local maxima and minima, each feature point is compared with its 8 neighbors at the same scale and in accordance with its 9 neighbors up and down by one scale. If this value is the minimum or maximum of all these points then this point is an extrema. More formally, if a DoG image is given as $D(x, y, \sigma)$, then

$$D(x, y, \sigma) = L(x, y, k_i\sigma) - L(x, y, k_j\sigma) \tag{3}$$

where $L(x, y, k\sigma)$ is the convolution of the original image $I(x, y)$ with the Gaussian blur $G(x, y, k\sigma)$ at scale $k\sigma$, i.e.,

$$L(x, y, k\sigma) = G(x, y, k\sigma) * I(x, y) \tag{4}$$

where * is the convolution operator in x and y, and

$$G(x, y, \sigma) = \frac{1}{2\pi\sigma^2} e^{-(x^2+y^2)/2\sigma^2}$$

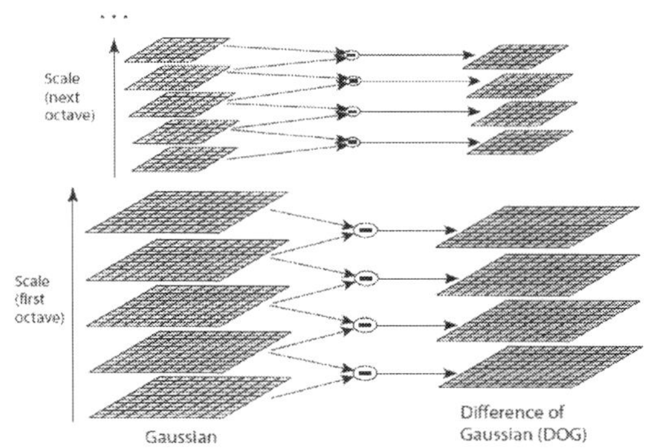

Fig. 3. Difference-of-Gaussian (DoG) octave (Lowe, 1999).

From Equations (3) and (4) it can be concluded that a *DoG* image between scales $k_i\sigma$ and $k_j\sigma$ is just the difference of the Gaussian-blurred images at scales $k_i\sigma$ and $k_j\sigma$. For scale-space extrema detection with the SIFT algorithm, the image is first convolved with Gaussian-blurs at different scales. The convolved images are grouped by octave (an octave corresponds to doubling the value of σ), and the value of k_i is selected so that we obtain a fixed number of convolved images per octave. Then the Difference-of-Gaussian images are taken from adjacent Gaussian-blurred images per octave. Fig. 3 shows difference-of-gaussian octave.

4.2 Keypoints Localization

To localize keypoints, a few points after detection of stable keypoint locations that have low contrast or are poorly localized on an edge are eliminated. This can be achieved by calculating the Laplacian space. After computing the location of extremum value, if the value of difference of Gaussian pyramids is less than a threshold value the point is excluded. If there is a case of large principle curvature across the edge but a small curvature in the perpendicular direction in the difference of Gaussian function, the poor extrema is localized and eliminated.

First, for each candidate keypoint, interpolation of nearby data is used to accurately determine its position. The initial approach is to just locate each keypoint at the location and scale of the candidate keypoint while the new approach calculates the interpolated location of the extremum, which substantially improves matching and stability. The interpolation is done using the quadratic expansion of the Difference-of-Gaussian scale-space function, $D(x, y, \sigma)$ with the candidate keypoint as the origin. This Taylor expansion is given by:

$$D(p) = D + \frac{\partial D^T}{\partial p} p + \frac{1}{2} p^T \frac{\partial^2 D}{\partial p^2} p \tag{5}$$

where D and its derivatives are evaluated at the sample point and $p = (x, y, \sigma)^T$ is the offset from this point. The location of the extremum, $\hat{p}$ is determined by taking the derivative of this function with respect to p and setting it to zero, giving

$$\hat{x} = -\frac{\partial^2 D^{-1}}{\partial x^2} \frac{\partial D}{\partial x} \tag{6}$$

If the offset p is larger than 0.5 in any dimension, then it is an indication that the extremum lies closer to another candidate keypoint. In this case, the candidate keypoint is changed and the interpolation performed instead about that point. Otherwise the offset is added to its candidate keypoint to get the interpolated estimate for the location of the extremum.

4.3 Assign Keypoints Orientation

This step aims to assign consistent orientation to the key-points based on local image characteristics. From the gradient orientations of sample points, an orientation histogram is formed within a region around the key-point. Orientation assignment is followed by key-point descriptor which can be represented relative to this orientation. A 16x16 window is chosen to generate histogram. The orientation histogram has 36 bins covering 360 degree range of orientations. The gradient magnitude and the orientation are pre-computed using pixel differences. Each sample is weighted by its gradient magnitude and by a Gaussian-weighted circular window.

Following experimentation with a number of approaches to assign a local orientation, the following approach has been found to give the most stable results. The scale of the keypoint is used to select the Gaussian smoothed image, L, with the closest scale, so that all computations are performed in a scale-invariant manner. For each image sample, $L(x, y)$, at this scale, the gradient magnitude, $m(x, y)$, and orientation, □(x, y), is precomputed using pixel differences:

$$m(x, y) = \sqrt{(L(x+1, y) - L(x-1, y))^2 + (L(x, y+1) - L(x, y-1))^2} \tag{7}$$

$$\Theta(x, y) = \tan^{-1} ((L(x, y+1) - L(x, y-1)) / (L(x+1, y) - L(x-1, y))) \quad (8)$$

An orientation histogram is formed from the gradient orientations of sample points within a region around the keypoint. The orientation histogram has 36 bins covering the 360 degree range of orientations. Each sample added to the histogram is weighted by its gradient magnitude and by a Gaussian-weighted circular window with a σ that is 1.5 times that of the scale of the keypoint.

4.4 Generation of Keypoints Descriptor

In the last step, the feature descriptors which represent local shape distortions and illumination changes are computed. After candidate locations have been found, a detailed fitting is performed to the nearby data for the location, edge response and peak magnitude. To achieve invariance to image rotation, a consistent orientation is assigned to each feature point based on local image properties. The histogram of orientations is formed from the gradient orientation at all sample points within a circular window of a feature point. Peaks in this histogram correspond to the dominant directions of each feature point. For illumination invariance, 8 orientation planes are defined. Finally, the gradient magnitude and the orientation are smoothened by applying a Gaussian filter and then are sampled over a 4 x 4 grid with 8 orientation planes. Keyppoint descriptor generation is shown in Fig. 4.

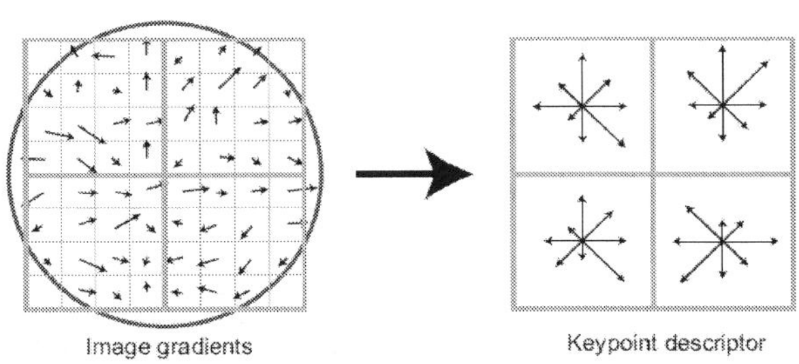

Fig. 4. A keypoint descriptor created by the gradient magnitude and the orientation at each point in a region around the keypoint location.

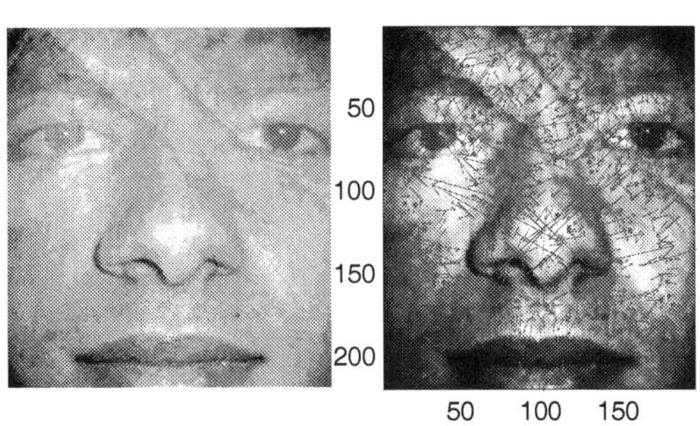

Fig. 5. Fig. 5(a) Fused Image, (b) Fused Image with extracted SIFT features.

In the proposed work, the fused image is normalized by histogram equalization and after normalization invariants SIFT features are extracted from the fused image. Each feature point is composed of four types of information - spatial location (*x*, *y*), scale (*S*), orientation (θ) and Keypoint descriptor (*K*). For the sake experiment, only keypoint descriptor information has been taken which consists of a vector of 128 elements representing neighborhood intensity changes of current points. More formally, local image gradients are measured at the selected scale in the region around each keypoint. The measured gradients information is then transformed into a vector representation that contains a vector of 128 elements for each keypoints calculated over extracted keypoints. These keypoint descriptor vectors represent local shape distortions and illumination changes. In Fig. 5, SIFT features extracted on the fused image are shown.

Next section discusses the matching technique by structural graph for establishing correspondence between a pair of fused biometric images by searching a pair of point sets using recursive descent tree traversal algorithm (Cheng, et. al., 1991).

5. Matching using Monotonic-Decreasing Graph

In order to establish a monotonic-decreasing graph based relation (Lin, et. al., 1986; Cheng, et. al., 1988) between a pair of fused images, a recursive approach based tree traversal algorithm is used for searching the feature points on the probe/query fused sample, which are corresponding to the points on the database/gallery fused sample. Verification is performed by computing of differences between a pair of edges that are members of original graph on gallery sample and graph on probe sample, respectively.

The basic assumption is that the moving features points are rigid. Let $\{g_1, g_2, \ldots, g_m\}$ and $\{p_1, p_2, \ldots, p_n\}$ be two sets of feature points at the two time instances where *m* and *n* may or may not be same. Generally, identical set of feature points are not available from a pair of instances of a same user or from different users. So, It is assumed that *m≠n*.

The method is based on the principle of invariance of distance measures under rigid body motion where deformation of objects does not occur. Using the strategy in [8], maximal matching points and minimum matching error obtained. First, we choose a set of three points, say g_1, g_2 and g_3 on a given fused gallery image which are uniquely determined. By connecting these points with each other we form a triangle $\Delta g_1 g_2 g_3$ and three distances, $d(g_1, g_2)$, $d(g_2, g_3)$ and $d(g_1, g_3)$ are computed. Now, we try to locate another set of three points, p_i, p_j and p_k on a given fused probe image that also form a triangle that would be best matching the triangle $\Delta g_1 g_2 g_3$. Best match would be possible when the edge (p_i, p_j) matches the edge (g_1, g_2), (p_j, p_k) matches (g_2, g_3) and (p_i, p_k) matches (g_1, g_3). This can be attained when these matches lie within a threshold ε . We can write,

$$\begin{cases} | d(p_i, p_j) - d(g_1, g_2) | \leq \varepsilon_1 \\ | d(p_j, p_k) - d(g_2, g_3) | \leq \varepsilon_2 \\ | d(p_i, p_k) - d(g_1, g_3) | \leq \varepsilon_3 \end{cases} \quad (9)$$

Equation (9) is used for making closeness between a pair of edges using edge threshold ε. Traversal would be possible when p_i correspond to g_1 and p_j corresponds to g_2 or conversely, p_j to g_1 and p_i to g_2. Traversal can be initiated from the first edge (p_i, p_j) and by visiting n feature points, we can generate a matching graph $P' = (p_1', p_2', p_3', \ldots, p_m')$ on the fused probe image which should be a corresponding candidate graph of G. In each recursive traversal, a new candidate graph P_i' is found. At the end of the traversal algorithm, a set of candidate graphs $P_i' = (p_{1i}', p_{2i}', p_{3i}', \ldots, p_{mi}')$ $i = 1,2,\ldots,m$ is found and all of which are having identical number of feature points.
For illustration, consider the minimal k^{th} order error from $G.$, the final optimal graph P'' can be found from the set of candidate graphs P_i' and we can write,

$$|P''-G|_k \leq |P_i'-G|_k, \forall i \tag{10}$$

The kth order error between P'' and G can be defined as

$$|P''-G|_k = \sum_{i=2}^{m} \sum_{j=1}^{\min(k,i-1)} |d(p_i', p_{i-j}') - d(g_i, g_{i-j})|, \tag{11}$$
$$\forall k, k = 1,2,3,\ldots, m$$

The Equation (11) denotes sum of all differences between a pair edges corresponding to a pair of graphs. This sum can be treated as final dissimilarity value for a pair of graphs and also for a pair of fused images. It is observed that, when k is large, the less error correspondence is found. This is not always true as long as we have a good choice of the edge threshold ϵ. Although for the larger k, more comparison is needed. For identity verification of a person, client-specific threshold has been determined heuristically for each user and the final dissimilarity value is then compared with client-specific threshold and decision is made.

6. Experiment Results

The experiment is carried out on multimodal database of face and palmprint images collected at IIT Kanpur which consists of 750 face images and 750 palmprint images of 150 individuals. Face images are captured under control environment with $\pm 20^0$ changes of head pose and with at most uniform lighting and illumination conditions and with almost consistent facial expressions. For the sake of experiment, cropped frontal view face has been taken covering face portion only. For the palmprint database, cropped palm portion has been taken from each palmprint image which contains three principal lines, ridges and bifurcations. The proposed multisensor biometric evidence fusion method is considered as a semi-sensor fusion approach with some minor adjustable corrections in terms of cropping and registration. Biometric sensors generated face and palmprint images are fused at low level by using wavelet decomposition and fusion of decompositions. After fusion of cropped face and palmprint images of 200×220 pixels, the resolution for fused image has been set to 72 dpi. The fused image is then pre-processed by using histogram equalization. Finally, the matching is performed between a pair of fused images by structural graphs drawn on both the gallery and the probe fused images using extracted SIFT keypoints.

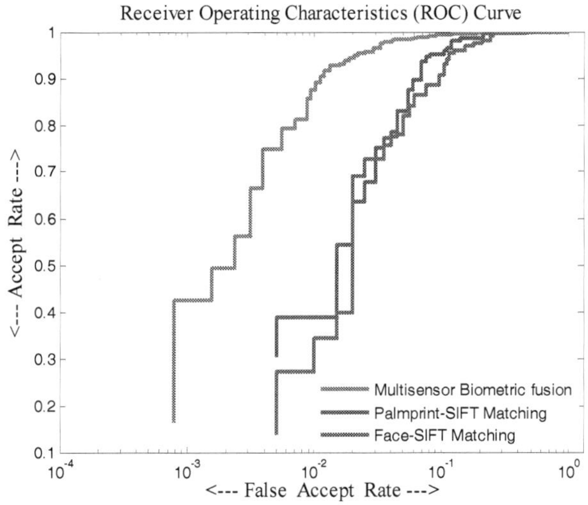

Fig. 6. ROC curves (in 'stairs' form) for the different methods.

The matching is accomplished for the method and the results show that fusion performance at the semi-sensor level / low level is found to be superior when it is compared with two monomodal methods, namely, palmprint verification and face recognition drawn on same feature space. Multisensor biometric fusion produces 98.19% accuracy while face recognition and palmprint recognition systems produce 89.04% accuracy and 92.17% accuracy respectively, as shown in the Fig. 6. ROC curves shown in Figure 6 illustrate the trade-off between accept rate and false accept rate. Further, it shows that the increase in accept rate accompanied by decrease in false accept rate happens in each modality, namely, multisensor biometric evidence fusion, palmprint matching and face matching.

7. Conclusion

A novel and efficient method of multisensor biometric image fusion of face and palmprint for personal authentication has been presented in this chapter. High-resolution multisensor face and palmprint images are fused using wavelet decomposition process and matching is performed by monotonic-decreasing graph drawn on invariant SIFT features. For matching, correspondence has been established by searching feature points on a pair of fused images using recursive approach based tree traversal algorithm. To verify the identity of a person, test has been performed with IITK multimodal database consisting of face and palmprint samples. The result shows that the proposed method initiated at the low level / semi-sensor level is robust, computationally efficient and less sensitive to unwanted noise confirming the validity and efficacy of the system, when it is compared with mono-modal biometric recognition systems.

8. References

Bicego, M., Lagorio, A., Grosso, E. & Tistarelli, M. (2006). On the use of SIFT features for face authentication. *Proceedings of International Workshop on Biometrics, in association with CVPR.*

Cheng, J-C. & Don, H-S. (1991). *A graph matching approach to 3-D point correspondences*

Cheng, J.C. & Dong Lee, H.S. (1988). A Structural Approach to finding the point correspondences between two frames. *Proceedings of International Conference on Robotics and Automation*, pp. 1810 -1815.

Hsu, C. & Beuker, R. (2000). Multiresolution feature-based image registration. *Proceedings of the Visual Communications and Image Processing*, pp. 1 - 9.

http://www.eecs.lehigh.edu/SPCRL/IF/image_fusion.htm

Jain, A.K. & Ross, A. (2004). Multibiometric systems. *Communications of the ACM*, vol. 47, no.1, pp. 34 - 40.

Jain, A.K., Ross, A. & Pankanti, S. (2006). Biometrics: A tool for information security. *IEEE Transactions on Information Forensics and Security*, vol. 1, no. 2, pp. 125 - 143.

Jain, A.K., Ross, A. & Prabhakar, S. (2004). An introduction to biometrics recognition. *IEEE Transactions on Circuits and Systems for Video Technology*, vol. 14, no. 1, pp. 4 - 20.

Lin, Z.C., Lee, H. & Huang, T.S. (1986). Finding 3-D point correspondences in motion estimation. *Proceeding of International Conference on Pattern Recognition*, pp.303 - 305.

Lowe, D. G. (2004). Distinctive image features from scale invariant keypoints. *International Journal of Computer Vision*, vol. 60, no. 2.

Lowe, D.G. (1999). Object recognition from localscale invariant features. *International Conference on Computer Vision*, pp. 1150 - 1157.

Park, U., Pankanti, S. & Jain, A.K. (2008). Fingerprint Verification Using SIFT Features. *Proceedings of SPIE Defense and Security Symposium.*

Poh, N., & Kittler, J. (2008). On Using Error Bounds to Optimize Cost-sensitive Multimodal Biometric Authentication. *17th International Conference on Pattern Recognition*, pp. 1 - 4.

Raghavendra, R., Rao, A. & Kumar, G.H. (2010). Multisensor biometric evidence fusion of face and palmprint for person authentication using Particle Swarm Optimization (PSO). *International Journal of Biometrics (IJBM)*, Vol. 2, No. 1.

Ross, A. & Govindarajan, R. (2005). Feature Level Fusion Using Hand and Face Biometrics. *Proceedings of SPIE Conference on Biometric Technology for Human Identification II*, pp. 196 - 204.

Ross, A. & Jain, A.K. (2003). Information Fusion in Biometrics. *Pattern Recognition Letters*, vol. 24, pp. 2115 - 2125.

Singh, R., Vatsa, M. & Noore, A. (2008). Integrated Multilevel Image Fusion and Match Score Fusion of Visible and Infrared Face Images for Robust Face Recognition. *Pattern Recognition - Special Issue on Multimodal Biometrics*, Vol. 41, No. 3, pp. 880-893.

Stathaki, T. (2008). *Image Fusion – Algorithms and Applications.* Academic Press, U.K.

18

Fusion of Odometry and Visual Datas to Localization a Mobile Robot

André M. Santana†, Anderson A. S. Souza‡, Luiz M. G. Gonçalves‡, Pablo J. Alsina‡, Adelardo A. D. Medeiros‡

† *Federal University of Piauí - UFPI*
Department of Informatics and Statistic - DIE
Teresina, Piauí, Brasil

‡ *Federal University of Rio Grande do Norte - UFRN*
Department of Computer Engineering and Automation - DCA
Natal, Rio Grande do Norte, Brasil

1. Introduction

Applications involving wheeled mobile robots have been growing significantly in recent years thanks to its ability to move freely through space work, limited only by obstacles. Moreover, the wheels allow for greater convenience of transportation in environments plans and give greater support to the static robot.

In the context of autonomous navigation of robots we highlight the localization problem. From an accumulated knowledge about the environment and using the current readings of the sensors, the robot must be able to determine and keep up its position and orientation in relation to this environment, even if the sensors have errors and / or noise. In other words, to localize a robot is necessary to determine its pose (position and orientation) in the workspace at a given time.

Borenstein et al. (1997) have classified the localization methods in two great categories: relative localization methods, which give the robot's pose relative to the initial one, and absolute localization methods, which indicate the global pose of the robot and do not need previously calculated poses.

As what concerns wheel robots, it is common the use of encoders linked to wheel rotation axes, a technique which is known as odometry. However, the basic idea of odometry is the integration of the mobile information in a determined period of time, what leads to the accumulation of errors (Park et al., 1998). The techniques of absolute localization use landmarks to locate the robot. These landmarks can be artificial ones, when introduced in the environment aiming at assisting at the localization of the robot, or natural ones, when they can be found in the proper environment.

It´s important to note that, even the absolute location techniques are inaccurate due to noise from the sensors used. Aiming to obtain the pose of the robot with the smallest error possible an efficient solution is to filter the information originated by its sensors. A mathematical tool to accomplish this task is the Kalman filter.

Still on autonomous robots, a key attribute is a reliable perception of the world. Besides the reliability for the general acceptance of applications, the technologies used must provide a solution at a reasonable cost, that is, the components must be inexpensive. A solution is to use optical sensors in the robots to solve environment perception problems.

Due to the wide use of personal digital cameras, cameras on computers and cell phones, the price of image sensors has decreased significantly, making them an attractive option. Furthermore, the cameras can be used to solve a series of key problems in robotics and in other automatized operations, as they provide a large variety of environmental information, use little energy, and are easily integrated into the robot hardware. The main challenges are to take advantage of this powerful and inexpensive sensor to create reliable and efficient algorithms that can extract the necessary information for the solution of problems in robotics.

The system that will be presented shows a localization technique equipped for flat and closed environments with floor lines. This is not a very limiting prerequisite, as many environments such as universities, shopping malls, museums, hospitals, homes and airports, for example, have lines as floor components.

The algorithm used is based on the Extended Kalman Filter (EKF), to allow the robot to navigate in an indoor environment using odometry and preexisting floor. The lines are identified using the Hough transform. The prediction phase of EKF is done using the geometric model of the robot. The update phase uses the parameters of the lines detected by the Hough transform directly in Kalman's equations without any intermediate calculation stage.

The use of lines is justified as follows: a) lines can be easily detected in images; b) floor lines are generally equally well spaced, reducing the possibility of confusion; c) a flat floor is a 2D surface and thus there is a constant and easy-to-calculate conversion matrix between the image plane and the floor plane, with uncertainties about 3D depth information; and d) after processing the number of pixels in the image that belong to the line is a good reliability measure of the landmark detected.

Literature shows works using distance measures to natural landmarks to locate the robot. Bezerra (2004) used in his work the lines of the floor composing the environment as natural landmarks. Kiriy and Buehler (2002) have used extended Kalman Filter to follow a number of artificial landmarks placed in a non-structured way. Launay et al. (2002) employed ceiling lamps of a corridor to locate the robot. Odakura et al. (2004) show the location of the robot using Kalman filter with partial observations. More recent studies show a tendency to solve the problem of simultaneous localization and mapping - SLAM. Examples of work in this area: Amarasinghe et al. (2009), Marzorati et al. (2009) and Wu et al. (2009).

2. Proposed System and Theoretical Background

The system proposed in this study presents an adequate technique to localization a mobile robot in flat and closed environments with pre-existing floor lines. The algorithm used is based on Extended Kalman Filter (EKF) to allow the robot to navigate in an indoor environment by fusing odometry information and image processing. The prediction phase of the EKF is done using the odometric model of the robot and the update phase uses the parameters of the lines detected by Hough directly in the Kalman equations without any intermediate calculation stage. Figure 1 shows the scheme of the proposed system.

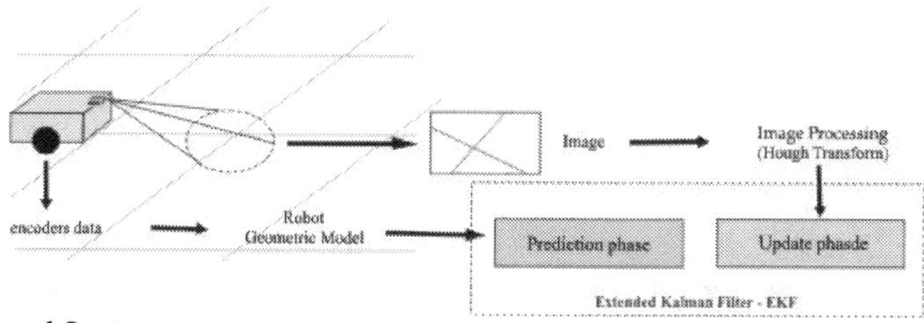

Fig. 1. Proposed System.

2.1 Kalman Filter

In 1960, Rudolph Emil Kalman published a famous paper describing a recursive process for solving problems related to linear discrete filtering (Kalman 1960). His research has provided significant contributions by helping to establish solid theoretical foundation in many areas of the engineering systems.

With the advance computing, the Kalman filter and its extensions to nonlinear problems represent a product widely used in a modern engineering. Next will be described in summary form, the Kalman filter applied to linear and nonlinear systems.

2.2 Discrete Kalman Filter - DKF

Aiube et al. (2006) define the Kalman filter as a set of mathematical equations that provides an efficient recursive process of estimation, since the square error of estimation is minimized. Through the observation of the variable named " observation variable" another variable, not observable, the "state variable" can be estimated efficiently The modeling of the Discrete Kalman Filter-DKF presupposes that the system is linear and described by the model of the equations of the System (1):

$$\begin{cases} s_t = \mathbf{A}_t s_{t-1} + \mathbf{B}_t u_{t-1} + \gamma_{t-1} \\ z_t = \mathbf{C}_t s_t + \delta_t \end{cases} \tag{1}$$

in which **s** ϵ R^n is the state vector; **u** ϵ $\mathbf{R}^l$ is the vector of input signals; **z** ϵ $\mathbf{R}^m$ is the vector of measurements; the matrix *n x n*, **A**, is the transition matrix of the states; **B**, *n x l*, is the coefficient matrix on entry; matrix **C**, *m x n*, is the observation matrix; γ ϵ $\mathbf{R}^n$ represents the vector of the noises to the process and δ ϵ $\mathbf{R}^m$ the vector of measurement errors. Indexes *t* and *t-1* represent the present and the previous instants of time.

The Filter operates in prediction-actualization mode, taking into account the statistical proprieties of noise. An internal model of the system is used to updating, while a retro-alimentation scheme accomplishes the measurements. The phases of prediction and actualization to DKF can be described by the Systems of Equations (2) and (3) respectively.

$$\begin{cases} \bar{\mu}_t = \mathbf{A}_t \, \mu_{t-1} + \mathbf{B}_t u_{t-1} \\ \bar{\Sigma}_t = \mathbf{A}_t \Sigma_{t-1} \mathbf{A}_t^T + \mathbf{R}_t \end{cases} \tag{2}$$

$$\begin{cases} \mathbf{K}_t = \bar{\Sigma}_t \mathbf{C}_t^T (\mathbf{C}_t \bar{\Sigma}_t \mathbf{C}_t^T + \mathbf{Q}_t)^{-1} \\ \mu_t = \bar{\mu}_t + \mathbf{K}_t(\boldsymbol{z}_t - \mathbf{C}_t \bar{\mu}_t) \\ \Sigma_t = (\mathbf{I} - \mathbf{K}_t \mathbf{C}_t)\bar{\Sigma}_t \end{cases} \tag{3}$$

The Kalman Filter represents the state vector $\mathbf{s}_t$ by its mean μ_t and co-variance Σ_t. Matrixes $\mathbf{R}$, $n \times n$, and $\mathbf{Q}$, $l \times l$, are the matrixes of the covariance of the noises of the process (γ) and measurement (δ) respectively, and matrix $\mathbf{K}$, $n \times m$, represents the gain of the system.

2.3 Extended Kalman Filter - EKF

The idea of the EKF is to linearize the functions around the current estimation using the partial derivatives of the process and of the measuring functions to calculate the estimations, even in the face of nonlinear relations. The model of the system to EKF is given by the System (4):

$$\begin{cases} \boldsymbol{s}_t = g(\boldsymbol{s}_{t-1}, \boldsymbol{u}_{t-1}) + \gamma_t \\ \boldsymbol{z}_t = h(\boldsymbol{s}_t) + \delta_t \end{cases} \tag{4}$$

in which $g(\mathbf{u}_{t-1}; \mathbf{s}_{t-1})$ is a non-linear function representing the model of the system, and $h(\mathbf{s}_t)$ is a nonlinear function representing the model of the measurements. Their prediction and actualization phases can be obtained by the Systems of Equations (5) and (6) respectively.

$$\begin{cases} \bar{\mu}_t = g(\mu_{t-1}, \boldsymbol{u}_{t-1}) \\ \bar{\Sigma}_t = \mathbf{G}_t \Sigma_{t-1} \mathbf{G}_t^T + \mathbf{R}_t \end{cases} \tag{5}$$

$$\begin{cases} \mathbf{K}_t = \bar{\Sigma}_t \mathbf{H}_t^T (\mathbf{H}_t \bar{\Sigma}_t \mathbf{H}_t^T + \mathbf{Q}_t)^{-1} \\ \mu_t = \bar{\mu}_t + \mathbf{K}_t(\boldsymbol{z}_t - h(\bar{\mu}_t)) \\ \Sigma_t = (\mathbf{I} - \mathbf{K}_t \mathbf{H}_t)\bar{\Sigma}_t \end{cases} \tag{6}$$

The matrix $\mathbf{G}$, $n \times n$, is the jacobian term linearizes the model and $\mathbf{H}$, $l \times n$, is the jacobian term linearizes the measuring vector. Such matrixes are defined by the Equations (7) e (8).

$$\mathbf{G}_t = \frac{\partial g(\mu_{t-1}, \boldsymbol{u}_{t-1})}{\partial \mathbf{s}_{t-1}} \tag{7}$$

$$\mathbf{H}_t = \frac{\partial h(\mathbf{s}_{t-1})}{\partial \mathbf{s}_t} \tag{8}$$

3. Modeling

3.1 Prediction phase: process model

Traditionally, the behavior of the robot motion is described by its dynamic model. Modeling this type of system is quite complex because there are many variables involved (masses and moments of inertia, friction, actuators, etc.). Even in the most elaborate systems cannot faithfully portray the behavior of the robot motion.

A classic method used to calculate the pose of a robot is the odometry. This method uses sensors, optical encoders, for example, which measure the rotation of the robot's wheels.

Using the cinematic model of the robot, its pose is calculated by means of the integration of its movements from a referential axis.
As encoders are sensors, normally their reading would be implemented in the actualization phase of the Kalman Filter, not in the prediction phase. Thrun et al. (2005) propose that odometer information does not function as sensorial measurements; rather they suggest incorporating them to the robot's model. In order that this proposal is implemented, one must use a robot's cinematic model considering the angular displacements of the wheels as signal that the system is entering in the prediction phase of the Kalman Filter.
Consider a robot with differential drive in which the control signals applied and its actuators are not tension, instead angular displacement, according to Figure 2.

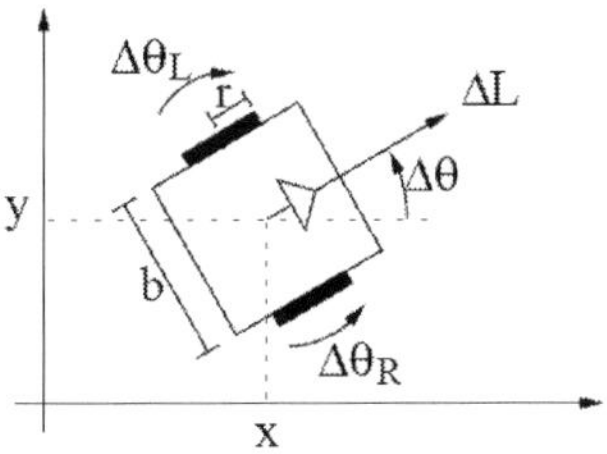

Fig. 2. Variables of the kinematic model.

With this idea, and supposing that speeds are constant in the sampling period, one can determine the geometric model of the robot's movement (System 9).

$$\begin{cases} x_t = x_{t-1} + \frac{\Delta L}{\Delta \theta}[\sin(\theta_{t-1} + \Delta\theta) - \sin(\theta_{t-1})] \\ y_t = y_{t-1} + \frac{\Delta L}{\Delta \theta}[\cos(\theta_{t-1} + \Delta\theta) - cos(\theta_{t-1})] \\ \theta_t = \theta_{t-1} + \Delta\theta \end{cases} \quad (9)$$

The turn easier the readability of the System (9) representing the odometry model of the robot, two auxiliary variables have been employed ΔL and Δθ.

$$\begin{cases} \Delta L = (\Delta\theta_R r_R + \Delta\theta_L r_L)/2 \\ \Delta\theta = (\Delta\theta_R r_R - \Delta\theta_L r_L)/b \end{cases} \quad (10)$$

in which $\Delta\theta_R$ is the reading of the right encoder and functions relatively the robot by means of the angular displacement of the right wheel; $\Delta\theta_L$ is the reading of the left encoder and functions as a displacement applied to the left wheel; b represents the distance from wheel to wheel of the robot; r_L and r_R are the spokes of the right and the left wheels respectively.
It is important to emphasize that in real applications the angular displacement effectively realized by the right wheel differs of that measured by the encoder. Besides that, the supposition that the speeds are constant in the sampling period, which has been used to obtain the model 9, is not always true. Hence, there are differences between the angular displacements of the wheels ($\Delta\hat{\theta}_R$ and $\Delta\hat{\theta}_L$) and those ones measured by the encoders ($\Delta\theta_R$ and $\Delta\theta_L$). This difference will be modeled by a Gaussian noise, according to System (11).

$$\begin{cases} \Delta\hat{\theta}_R = \Delta\theta_R + \varepsilon_R \\ \Delta\hat{\theta}_L = \Delta\theta_L + \varepsilon_L \end{cases} \tag{11}$$

It is known that odometry possesses accumulative error. Therefore, the noises ε_R and ε_L do not possess constant variance. It is presumed that these noises present a proportional standard deviation to the module of the measured displacement. With these new considerations, System (9) is now represented by System (12):

$$\begin{cases} x_t = x_{t-1} + \frac{\Delta\hat{L}}{\Delta\hat{\theta}}\left[\sin\left(\theta_{t-1} + \Delta\hat{\theta}\right) - \sin(\theta_{t-1})\right] \\ y_t = y_{t-1} + \frac{\Delta\hat{L}}{\Delta\hat{\theta}}\left[\cos\left(\theta_{t-1} + \Delta\hat{\theta}\right) - cos(\theta_{t-1})\right] \\ \theta_t = \theta_{t-1} + \Delta\hat{\theta} \end{cases} \tag{12}$$

in which:

$$\begin{cases} \Delta\hat{L} = (\Delta\hat{\theta}_R r_R + \Delta\hat{\theta}_L r_L)/2 \\ \Delta\hat{\theta} = (\Delta\hat{\theta}_R r_R - \Delta\hat{\theta}_L r_L)/b \end{cases} \tag{13}$$

One should observe that this model cannot be used when $\Delta\hat{\theta} = 0$. When it occurs, one uses an odometry module simpler than a robot (System 14), obtained from the limit of System (12) when $\Delta\hat{\theta} \rightarrow 0$.

$$\begin{cases} x_t = x_{t-1} + \Delta\hat{\theta}\cos(\theta_{t-1}) \\ y_t = y_{t-1} + \Delta\hat{\theta}\sin(\theta_{t-1}) \\ \theta_t = \theta_{t-1} \end{cases} \tag{14}$$

Thrun's idea implies a difference as what concerns System (4), because the noise is not audible; rather, it is incorporated to the function which describes the model, as System (15) shows:

$$\begin{cases} \boldsymbol{s}_t = p(\boldsymbol{s}_{t-1}, \boldsymbol{u}_{t-1}, \varepsilon_{t-1}) \\ \boldsymbol{z}_t = h(\boldsymbol{s}_t) + \delta_t \end{cases} \tag{15}$$

in which $\varepsilon_t = [\varepsilon_R \quad \varepsilon_L]^T$ is the noise vector connected to odometry.

It is necessary, however, to bring about a change in the prediction phase of the System (6) resulting in the System (16) equations:

$$\begin{cases} \bar{\mu}_t = \mu_{t-1} + p(\mathbf{u}_{t-1}, \mu_{t-1}, 0) \\ \bar{\Sigma}_t = \mathbf{G}_t \Sigma_{t-1} \mathbf{G}_t^T + \mathbf{V}_t \mathbf{M}_t \mathbf{V}_t^T \end{cases} \tag{16}$$

in which, $\mathbf{M}$, $l \times l$, is the co-variance matrix of the noise sensors (ε) and $\mathbf{V}$, $n \times m$, is the jacobian mapping the sensor noise to the space of state. Matrix $\mathbf{V}$ is defined by equation (17).

$$\mathbf{V}_t = \frac{\partial p(\mathbf{s}_{t-1}, \mathbf{u}_{t-1}, 0)}{\partial \mathbf{u}_{t-1}} \tag{17}$$

Making use of the odometry model of the robot described in this section and the definitions of the matrixes used by the Kalman Filter, we have:

$$\mathbf{G}_t = \begin{pmatrix} 1 & 0 & \frac{\Delta\hat{L}}{\Delta\hat{\theta}}\left[\cos\left(\theta_{t-1} + \Delta\hat{\theta}\right) - \cos(\theta_{t-1})\right] \\ 0 & 1 & \frac{\Delta\hat{L}}{\Delta\hat{\theta}}\left[\sin\left(\theta_{t-1} + \Delta\hat{\theta}\right) - \sin(\theta_{t-1})\right] \\ 0 & 0 & 1 \end{pmatrix} \tag{18}$$

$$\mathbf{V}_t = \begin{pmatrix} K_1\cos(K_2) - K_3[\sin(K_2) - \sin(\theta_{t-1})] & -K_1\cos(K_2) + K_3[\sin(K_2) - \sin(\theta_{t-1})] \\ K_1\sin(K_2) - K_3[-\cos(K_2) + \cos(\theta_{t-1})] & -K_1\sin(K_2) + K_3[-\cos(K_2) + \cos(\theta_{t-1})] \\ r_R/b & -r_L/b \end{pmatrix} \tag{19}$$

$$\mathbf{M}_t = \begin{pmatrix} \alpha_1|\Delta\hat{\theta}_R| & 0 \\ 0 & \alpha_1|\Delta\hat{\theta}_L| \end{pmatrix} \tag{20}$$

Elements m_{11} and m_{22} in the Equation (20) represent the fact that the standard deviations of ε_R and ε_L are proportional to the module of the angular displacement. The variables k_1, k_2 and k_3 are given by System (21), considering $rd = re = r$.

$$\begin{cases} K_1 = \frac{r(\Delta\hat{\theta}_R + \Delta\hat{\theta}_L)}{b(\Delta\hat{\theta}_R - \Delta\hat{\theta}_L)} \\ K_2 = \theta_{t-1} + \frac{r(\Delta\hat{\theta}_R - \Delta\hat{\theta}_L)}{b} \\ K_3 = \frac{b\Delta\hat{\theta}_L}{2[r(\Delta\hat{\theta}_R - \Delta\hat{\theta}_L)/b]^2} \end{cases} \tag{21}$$

3.2 Update phase: Sensor Model

The landmarks adopted in this work are lines formed by the grooves of the floor in the environment where the robot navigates. The system is based on a robot with differential drive and a fixed camera, as in Figure 3.

Fig. 3. Robotic System.

Due to the choice of the straight lines as landmarks, the technique adopted to identify them was the Hough transform [Hough, 1962]. This kind of transform is a method employed to

identify inside a digital image a class of geometric forms which can be represented by a parametric curve [Gonzales, 2007]. As what concerns the straight lines, a mapping is provided between the Cartesian space (X, Y) and the space of the parameters (ρ, α) where the straight line is defined.
Hough defines a straight line using its common representation, as Equation (22) shows, in which parameter (ρ) represents the length of the vector and (α) the angle this vector forms with axis X. Figure 4 shows the geometric representation of these parameters.

$$\rho = x.\cos(\alpha) + y.\sin(\alpha) \quad (22)$$

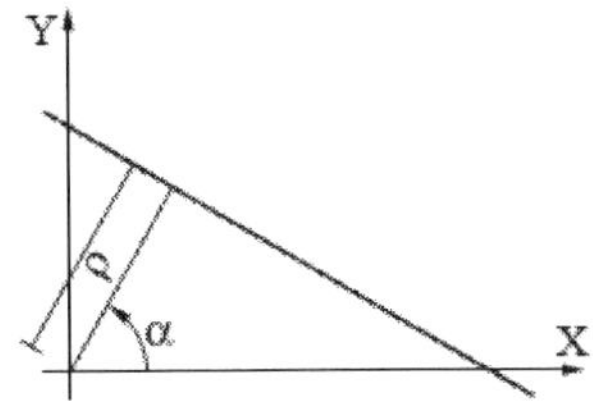

Fig. 4. Line parameters: ρ and α.

The robot navigates in an environment where the position of the lines in the world is known and every step identifies the descriptors of the lines contained in the image ρ^I e α^I. These descriptors are mapped to the plane of a moving coordinate system and obtaining ρ^M e α^M. This transformation is easy and relies only on the correct calibration of camera parameters. Figure 5 illustrates the coordinate systems used in mathematical deduction of the sensor model.

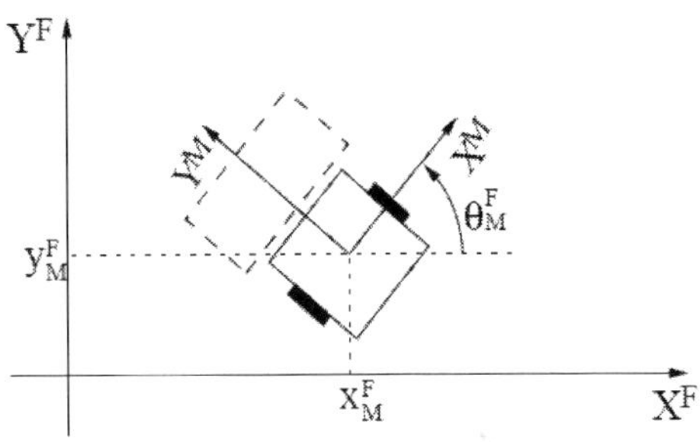

Fig. 5. Mobile (*M*) and Fixed (*F*) coordinate systems.

We define a fixed coordinate system (*F*) and a mobile one (*M*), attached to the robot, both illustrated in Figure 5. The origin of the mobile system has coordinates (x_M^F, y_M^F) in the fixed system. θ_M^F represents the rotation of the mobile system with respect to the fixed one. One should note that there is a straight relation among these variables $(X_M^F, Y_M^F, \theta_M^F)$ and the robot's pose (x_t, y_t, θ_t), which is given by Equations (23).

$$x_t = x_M^F \qquad y_t = y_M^F \qquad \theta_t = \theta_M^F + \pi/2 \tag{23}$$

We use the relation between coordinates in the *(M)* and *(F)* systems (System 24) and Equation (22) in both coordinate systems (Equations 25 and 26).

$$\begin{cases} x^F = \cos(\theta_M^F)\, x^M - \sin(\theta_M^F)\, y^M + x_M^F \\ y^F = \sin(\theta_M^F)\, x^M + \cos(\theta_M^F)\, y^M + y_M^F \end{cases} \tag{24}$$

$$\rho^F = x^F \cos(\alpha^F) + y^F \sin(\alpha^F) \tag{25}$$

$$\rho^M = x^M \cos(\alpha^M) + y^M \sin(\alpha^M) \tag{26}$$

By replacing Equations (24) in Equation (25), doing the necessary equivalences with Equation (26) and replacing some variables using Equations (23), we obtain the Systems (27) and (28), which represent two possible sensor models $h(.)$ to be used in the filter. To decide about which model to use, we calculate both values of α^M and use the model which generates the value closer to the measured value.

$$\begin{cases} \rho^M = \rho^F - x_t \cos(\alpha^F) - y_t \sin(\alpha^F) \\ \alpha^M = \alpha^F - \theta_t + \frac{\pi}{2} \end{cases} \tag{27}$$

$$\begin{cases} \rho^M = -\rho^F + x_t \cos(\alpha^F) + y_t \sin(\alpha^F) \\ \alpha^M = \alpha^F - \theta_t - \frac{\pi}{2} \end{cases} \tag{28}$$

The sensor model is incorporated into the EKF through the matrix H (Equation 8). Representation for **H** obtained from the System (27) is given by Equation (29) and, using the System (28), **H** is described by Equation (30).

$$\mathbf{H} = \begin{pmatrix} -\cos(\alpha^F) & -\sin(\alpha^F) & -x_t \sin(\alpha^F) + y_t \cos(\alpha^F) \\ 0 & 0 & -1 \end{pmatrix} \tag{29}$$

$$\mathbf{H} = \begin{pmatrix} \cos(\alpha^F) & \sin(\alpha^F) & x_t \sin(\alpha^F) - y_t \cos(\alpha^F) \\ 0 & 0 & -1 \end{pmatrix} \tag{30}$$

4. Image Processing

4.1 Detection of lines

Due to the choice of floor lines as landmarks, the technique adopted to identify them was the Hough transform [Hough, 1962]. The purpose of this technique is to find imperfect instances of objects within a certain class of shapes by a voting procedure. This voting procedure is carried out in a parameter space, from which object candidates are obtained as local maxima in an accumulator grid that is constructed by the algorithm for computing the Hough transform [Bradski and Kaehler, 2008].

In our case, the shapes are lines described by Equation (22) and the parameter space has coordinates (ρ,α). The images are captured in grayscale and converted to black and white using the edge detector Canny [Canny, 1986]. Figure 6.a shows a typical image of the floor,

Figure 6.b shows the image after applying the Canny detector and Figure 6.c shows lines detected by Hough.

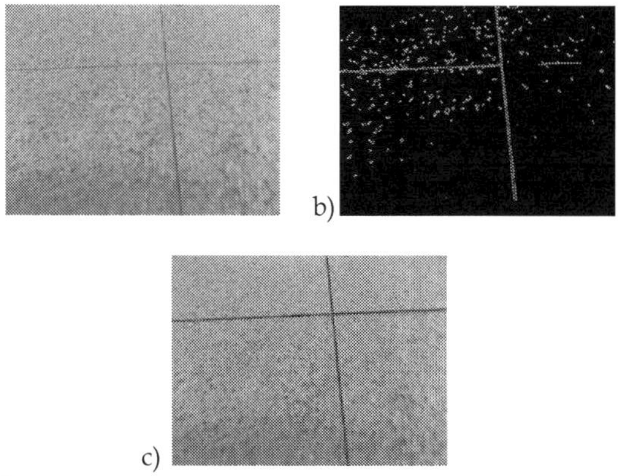

a) b) c)

Fig. 6. Image processing.

4.2 From images to the word

We assume that the floor is flat and that the camera is fixed. So, there is a constant relation (a homography **A**) between points in the floor plane (x, y) and points in the image plane (u, v):

$$s.\begin{pmatrix} u \\ v \\ 1 \end{pmatrix} = \mathbf{A}.\begin{pmatrix} x \\ y \\ 1 \end{pmatrix} \tag{31}$$

The scale factor s is determined for each point in such a way that the value of the third element of the vector is always 1. The homography can be calculated off-line by using a pattern containing 4 or more remarkable points with known coordinates (see Figure 7.a). After detecting the remarkable point in the image, we have several correspondences between point coordinates in the mobile coordinate system M and in the image. Replacing these points in Equation (31), we obtain a linear system with which we can determine the 8 elements of the homography matrix **A**.

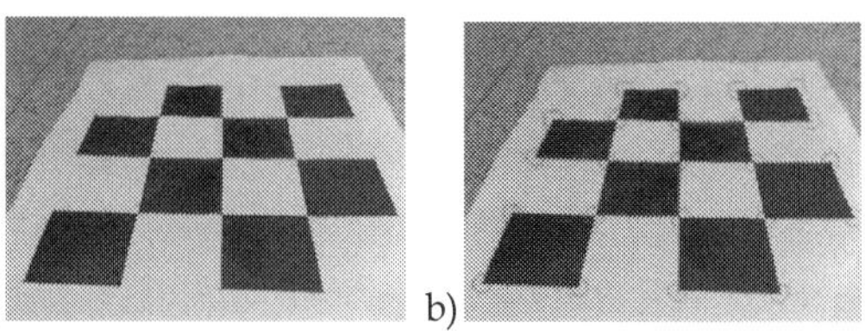

a) b)

Fig. 7. Calibration pattern.

Once calculated the homography, for each detected line we do the following: a) using the values of $(\tilde{\rho}, \tilde{\alpha})$ in the image obtained by the Hough transform, calculate two point belonging to the image line; b) convert the coordinates of these two points to the mobile

coordinate system M using **A**; c) determine $(\tilde{\rho}^M, \tilde{\alpha}^M)$ of the line that passes through these two points.
To verify the correctness of the homography found, we calculated the re-projection error using the points detected in the image and their counterparts worldwide. The average error was calculated at e = *1.5 cm*. To facilitate interpretation of this value, the figure shows a circle of e radius drawn on the pattern used.

4.3 Sensor noise

As it is showed in Figure 3, the camera position used in this work is not parallel to the floor, but at a slope. The resulting effect caused by the camera slope can be seen in Figures 6 and 7. From experimentation, one observed that existing information at the top of the image suffered higher noise if compared to the bottom area, what made us consider that noise variance must be proportional to the distance (ρ) of the straight line on the image. Besides, one noticed that quality of horizontal lines which appeared on the image was better than that of vertical ones, what allowed us to understand that noise variance was also related to the straight line angle (α) on the image.
If those aspects above are taken into consideration, then the sensor noise variance adopted in this work is in accordance with the Equation (22). The values of the constants a , b and c were calculated through experimentation and their values are: a = 0:004, b = 0:3 and c = 45.

$$\sigma(\rho, \alpha) = a + b.\sin(\alpha).(exp^{\frac{\rho}{c}} - 1) \tag{22}$$

In this equation, the term $[exp^{\frac{\rho}{c}} - 1]$ represents the distance proportionality, and the term $[sin(\alpha)]$, the angle influence. Figure 8 shows the behavior of the function described by Equation (22) using the values of a, b and c already submitted, and given ρ in meters and α in degrees.

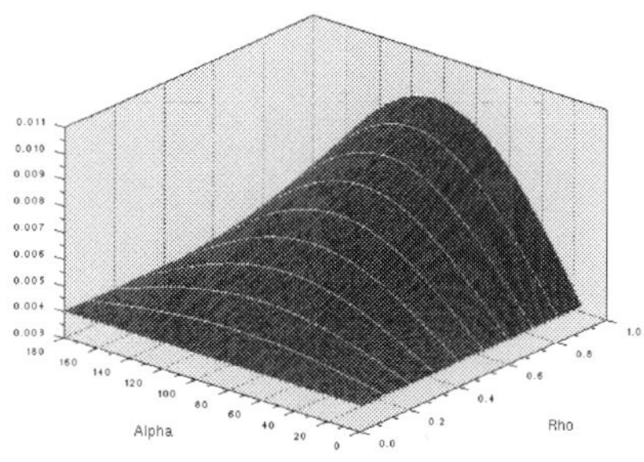

Fig. 8. Noise variance function.

5. Results

The experiments were carried out using the Karel robot, a reconfigurable mobile platform built in our laboratory that has coupled to the structure, a webcam and a laptop for information processing (Figure 3). The robot has two wheels that are driven by DC motors with differential steering. Each motor has an optical encoder and a dedicated card based on a PIC microcontroller that controls local velocity. The cards communicate with the computer through a CAN bus, receiving the desired wheel velocities and encoder data.

To validate the proposed system, results were obtained in two different environments: one containing only a pattern of lines and another containing two patterns of lines. The first experiment was carried out by making the robot navigate in an environment where there are vertical lines on the floor: (I) was command the robot to move forward by 25m, (II) rotate 90 degrees around its own axis (III) move forward 5m, (IV) 180 rotate around its own axis (V) move forward 5m, (VI) rotate 90 degrees around its axis and, finally, walking forward 25m. Figure 9 shows the map of the environment and the task commanded to the robot.

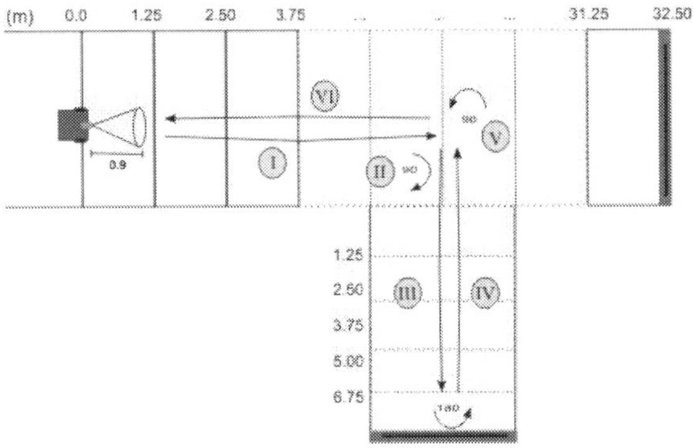

Fig. 9. Experience 01.

In this experiment, during the full navigation of the robot 1962 images were processed and the matching process was successful in 93% of cases. The average observation of each line was 23 times.

In this work the sensors used have different sampling rates. We decided to use the encoders reading in a coordinated manner with the image capture. The camera captures images 640 x 480 (Figure 6) and each image is processed, on average, 180 ms. Figure 10 shows the graphs of the acquisition time (image and encoder), processing time and total time of the system, including acquisition, processing and calculations of the localization algorithm. The average time of acquisition was 50 ms, the processing was 125 ms and the average total time the system was 180 ms. The peaks on the graph made themselves available after the first turning motion of the robot (II), or after it enters a new corridor with different lighting.

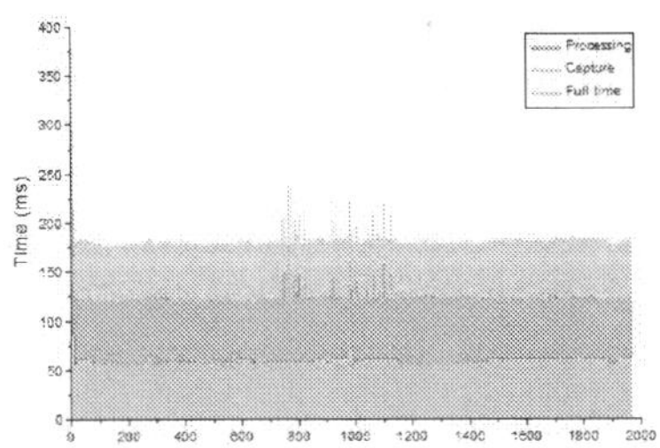

Fig. 10. Times of the system.

About the homography, Figure 7.a shows the pattern that was used at the beginning of the experiment to calculate it. The camera was positioned so that it was possible to have a viewing angle of about twice the size of the robot. It is important to remember that the camera position is such that the image plane is not parallel to the floor plan. Equation (23) shows the homography matrix used.

$$\mathbf{A} = \begin{pmatrix} 0.1417 & 0.0009 & -49.2065 \\ 0.0073 & -0.0761 & 98.6323 \\ 0.0001 & 0.0029 & 1 \end{pmatrix} \tag{23}$$

Besides the proposed system, another location system was also implemented: location system using geometric correction. In this system, every step, the lines are identified and used to calculate the robot pose using trigonometry. When there are no lines identified, the robot pose is calculated by odometry. Figure 11 shows the trajectories calculated using EKF, Geometric Correction and Odometry. It is easy to see that the behavior of the system based on Kalman filter (proposed system) was more satisfactory. The final error, measured *in-loco*, was 0.27m to the system using EKF, 0.46m using the geometric correction system and 0.93m using only odometry.

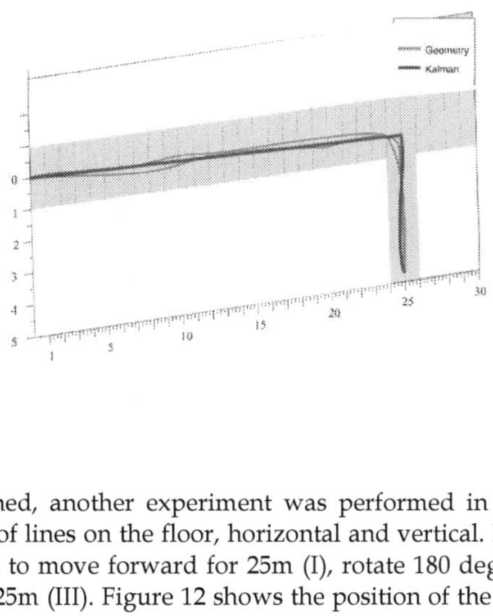

Fig. 11. Trajectories.

As previously mentioned, another experiment was performed in an environment where there are two patterns of lines on the floor, horizontal and vertical. In this environment, the robot was commanded to move forward for 25m (I), rotate 180 degrees around its axis (II) and move forward by 25m (III). Figure 12 shows the position of the lines and controlled the robot trajectory.

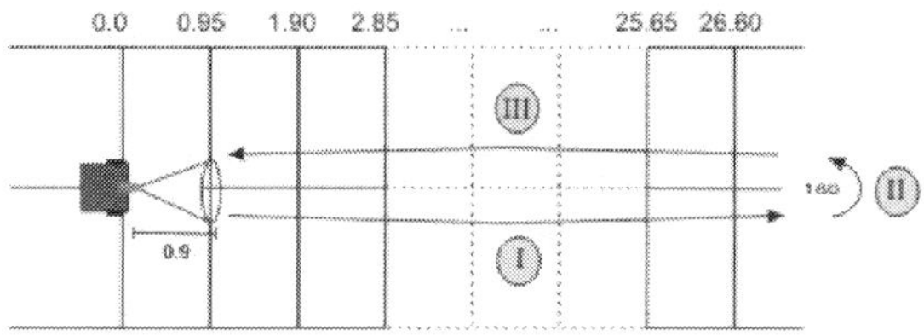

Fig. 12. Experience 02.

In this second experiment, the matching process was successful in 95% of cases. Considering the full navigation of the robot, 2220 images were processed and found that in 87% of step lines were observed (61% and 26% a line two lines). The final error, measured *in-loco* was lower than that found in Experiment 0.16m and allowed us to infer that for greater precision of the proposed system is not enough just a lot of lines in the environment, but rather, they are competitors.

6. Conclusions and Perspectives

This paper presented a localization system for mobile robots using fusion of visual data and odometer data. The main contribution is the modeling of the optical sensor made such a way that it permits using the parameters obtained in the image processing directly to equations of the Kalman Filter without intermediate stages of calculation of position or distance.

Our approach has no pretension to be general, as it requires a flat floor with lines. However, in the cases where can be used (malls, museums, hospitals, homes, airports, etc.) when compared with another approach using geometric correction was more efficient.

As future works, we intend: to improve the real-time properties of the image processing algorithm, by adopting some of the less time consuming variants of the Hough transform; Replace the Kalman Filter by a Filter of Particles, having in view that the latter incorporates more easily the nonlinearities of the problem, besides leading with non-Gaussian noises; Develop this strategy of localization to a proposal of SLAM (Simultaneous Localization and Mapping), so much that robot is able of doing its localization without a previous knowledge of the map and, simultaneously, mapping the environment it navigates.

7. References

Aiube, F. , Baidya T. and Tito, E. (2006), Processos estocásticos dos preços das commodities: uma abordagem através do filtro de partículas, *Brazilian Journal of Economics*, Vol.60, No.03, Rio de Janeiro, Brasil.

Amarasinghe, D., Mann, G. and Gosine, R. (2009), Landmark detection and localization for mobile robot applications: a multisensor approach, *Robotica Cambridge*.

Bezerra, C. G. (2004), Localização de um robô móvel usando odometria e marcos naturais. *Master Thesis*, Federal University of Rio Grande do Norte, Natal, RN, Brasil.

Borenstein, J., Everett, H., Feng, L., and Wehe, D. (1997), Mobile robot positioning: Sensors and techniques. *Journal of Robotic Systems*, pp. 231–249.

Bradski, G. and Kaehler, A. (2008), *Learning OpenCV: Computer Vision with the OpenCV Library*, O'Reilly Media.

Canny, J. (1986), A computational approach to edge detection, *IEEE Trans. Pattern Analysis and Machine Intelligence*, pp. 679 -698.

Gonzalez, R. C. and Woodes, R. E. (2007), *Digital Image Processing*. Prentice Hall.

Hough, P. V. C (1962), Method and means for recognizing complex patterns, *US Pattent 3069654*, Dec. 18.

Kalman, R. E. (1960), A new approach to linear filtering and predictive problems, *Transactions ASME, Journal of basic engineering*.

Kiriy, E. and Buehler, M. (2002), Three-state extended Kalman filter for mobile robot localization. *Report Centre for Intelligent Machines - CIM*, McGill University.

Launay, F., Ohya, A., and Yuta, S. (2002), A corridors lights based navigation system including path definition using a topologically corrected map for indoor mobile robots. *IEEE International Conference on Robotics and Automation*, pp.3918-3923.

Marzorati, D., Matteucci, M., Migliore, D. and Sorrenti, D. (2009), On the Use of Inverse Scaling in Monocular SLAM, *IEEE Int. Conference on Robotics and Automation*, pp. 2030-2036.

Odakura, V., Costa, A. and Lima, P. (2004), Localização de robôs móveis utilizando observações parciais, *Symposium of the Brazilian Computer Society*.

Park, K. C., Chung, D., Chung, H., and Lee, J. G. (1998), Dead reckoning navigation mobile robot using an indirect Kalman filter. *Conference on Multi-sensor fusion* and Integration for Intelliget Systems, pp. 107-118.

Thrun, S., Burgard, W., and Fox, D. (2005). *Probabilistic Robotics*. MIT Press.

Wu, E., Zhou, W., Dail, G. and Wang, Q. (2009), Monocular Vision SLAM for Large Scale Outdoor Environment, *IEEE Int. Conference on Mechatronics and Automation*, pp. 2037-2041, (2009).

19

Probabilistic Mapping by Fusion of Range-Finders Sensors and Odometry

Anderson Souza, Adelardo Medeiros and Luiz Gonçalves
Federal University of Rio Grande do Norte
Natal, RN, Brazil

André Santana
Federal University of Piauí
Teresina, PI, Brazil

1. Introduction

One of the main challenges faced by robotics scientists is to provide autonomy to robots. That is, according to Medeiros (Medeiros, 1998) a robot to be considered autonomous must present a series of abilities as reaction to environment changes, intelligent behavior, integration of data provided by sensors (sensor fusion), ability for solving multiple tasks, robustness, operation without failings, programmability, modularity, flexibility, expandability, adaptability and global reasoning. Yet in the context of autonomy, the navigation problem appears. As described in Fig. 1, sense, plan and act capabilities have to be previously given to a robot in order to start thinking on autonomous navigation. These capabilities can be divided into sub-problems abstracted hierarchically in five levels of autonomy: *Environment Mapping, Localization, Path Planning, Trajectory Generation,* and *Trajectory Execution* (Alsina et. al., 2002).

At the level of *Environment Mapping* the robot system has to generate a computational model containing the main structural characteristics of the environment. In other words, it is necessary to equip the robot with sensing devices that allow the robot to perceive its surrounds acquiring useful data to producing information for construction of the environment *map*. Further, in order to get a trustworthy mapping, the system needs to know the position and orientation of the robot with relation to some fixed world referential. This process that includes sensory data capture, position and orientation inferring, and subsequently processing with objective of construction of a computational structure representing the robot underlying space is simply known as *Robotic Mapping*.

In this work, we propose a mapping method based on probabilistic robotics, with the map being represented through a modified occupancy grid Elfes (1987). The main idea is to let the mobile robot construct its surroundings geometry in a systematic and incremental way in order to get the final, complete map of the environment. As a consequence, the robot can move in the environment in a safe mode based on a trustworthiness value, which is calculated by its perceptual system using sensory data. The map is represented in a form that is coherent

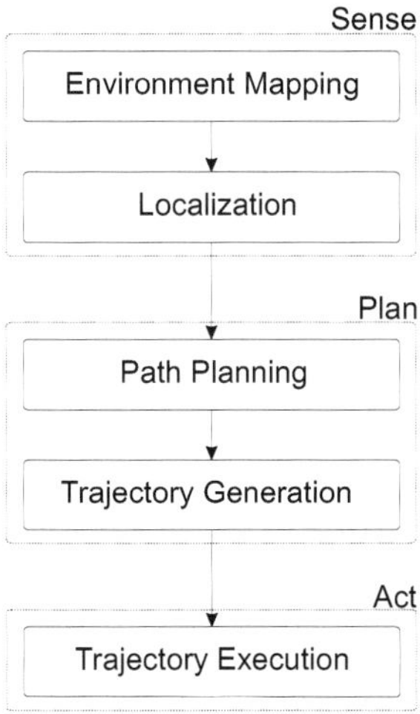

Fig. 1. Hierarchical levels for autonomous navigation.

with sensory data, noisy or not, coming from sensors. Characteristic noise incorporated to data is treated by probabilistic modeling in such a way that its effects can be visible in the final result of the mapping process. Experimental tests show the viability of this methodology and its direct applicability to autonomous robot tasks execution, being this the main contribution of this work.

In the folowing, the formal concepts related to robotics mapping through sensor fusion are presented. A brief discussion about the main challenges in environment mapping and their proposed solutions is presented as well the several manners of representing the mapped environments. Further, the mapping algorithm proposed in this work, based on a probabilistic modeling on occupancy grid. The proposed modeling of sensory information with fusing of sonar data that are used in this work and odometry data provided by the odometry system of the robot is described. Given that odometry is susceptible to different sources of noise (systematic and/or not), further efforts in modeling these kinds of noises in order to represent them in the constructed map are described. In this way, the mapping algorithm results in a representation that is consistent with sensory data acquired by the robot. Results of the proposed algorithm considering the robot in an indoor environment are presented and, finally, conclusions showing the main contributions and applications plus future directions are given.

2. Robotic Mapping

In order to formalize the robotics mapping problem, some basic hypotheses are established. The first is that the robot precisely knows its position and orientation inside the environment in relation to some fixed reference frame, that is, a global coordinate system. This process of inferring position and orientation of the robot in an environment is known as the localization problem. The second hypothesis is that the robot has a perceptual system, that is, sensors that makes possible acquisition of data, proper and of the environment, such as cameras, sonars and motor encoders, between others.

With these assumptions, robotics mapping can be defined as the problem of construction of a spatial model of an environment through a robotic system based on accurate knowledge of position and orientation of the robot in the environment and on data given by the robot perceptual system.

With respect to the model used for representing the map, Thrun (Thrun, 2002) proposes a classification following two main approaches, the *topological* and the *metric* maps. Topological maps are those computationally (or mathematically) represented by way of a graph, which is a well known entity in Math. In this representation, in general, the nodes correspond to spaces or places that are well defined (or known) and the links represent connectivity relations between these places. Metric maps (or metric representations) reproduce with certain degree of fidelity the environment geometry. Objects as walls, obstacles and doorway passages are easily identified in this approach because the map has a topographic relation very close to the real world. This proposed classification is the most used up to date, besides a subtle variation that adds a class of maps based on *features* appears in some works (Choset & Fox, 2004; Rocha, 2006). This category is treated sometimes as a sub-category of the metric representation due to the storage of certain notable objects or features as for example edges, corners, borders, circles and other geometric shapes that can be detected by any feature detector.

Fig. 2 illustrates the above mentioned ways of representing a mapped environment. Each one of these forms of representation have its own advantages and disadvantages. It is easier to construct and to maintain a map based on the metric approach. It allows to recognize places with simple processing and facilitates the computation of short paths in the map. However, it requires high computational efforts to be kept and needs to know the precise position and orientation of the robot at all time, what can be a problem. On its turn, the topological representation needs few computational efforts to be kept and can rely on approximated position and orientation, besides being a convenient way for solving several classes of high-level problems. However, it is computationally expensive to construct and maintain this representation and it makes it difficult the identification or recognition of places.

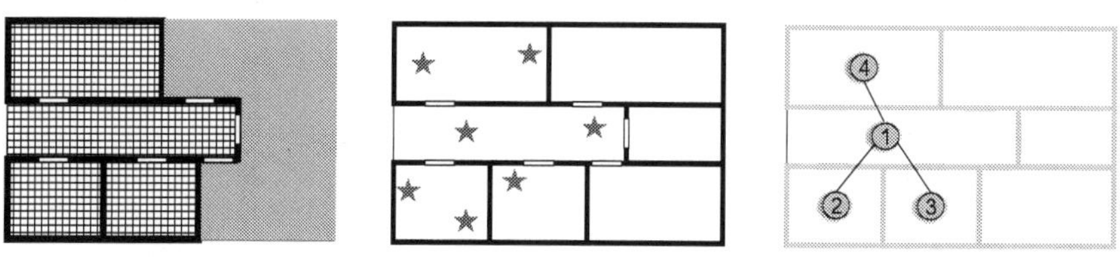

(a) (b) (c)

Fig. 2. (a) Metric map; (b) Feature-based map; (c) Topologic map.

Several challenges that can be found in the robotics mapping problem are enumerated by Thrun as (Thrun, 2002):

1. *Modeling sensor errors*

   There are several sources of errors causing different types or natures of noise in the sensory data. Error can be easy modeled for noises that are statistically independent in different measures. However, there is a random dependence that occurs because errors inherent to robot motion accumulate over time affecting the way that sensory measures are interpreted.

2. *Environment dimension*
   Besides the lack of precision in the robot system, a second challenge is the size of the environment to be mapped, that is, the map gets less precise and more expensive to built it as the environmnet gets bigger.
3. *Data association*
   This problem is also known as data correspondence (or matching). During the mapping, it is often current that the same object or obstacle is perceived several times by the robot system in different instants. So, it is desirable that an already seen object gets recognized and treated in a different manner that a not yet mapped object. Data association aims to determine the occurrence of this case in an efficient manner.
4. *Environment dynamics*
   Another challenge is related to the mapping of dynamic environments as for example places where people are constantly walking. The great majority of algorithms for mapping considers the process running in static environments.
5. *Exploration strategy*
   The mapping must incorporate a good exploration strategy, which should consider a partial model of the environment. This task appears as the fifth challenge for the robotics mapping problem.

Robots can be used to construct maps of indoor (Ouellette & Hirasawa, 2008; Santana & Medeiros, 2009; Thrun et. al., 2004), outdoor (Agrawal et. al., 2007; Triebel et. al., 2006; Wolf et. al., 2005), subterranean (Silver et. al., 2004; Thrun et. al., 2003), and underwater environments (Clark et. al., 2009; Hogue & Jenkin, 2006). With respect to its use, they can be employed in execution of tasks considered simple such as obstacle avoidance, path planning and localization. Map can also be used in tasks considered of more difficulty as exploration of galleries inside coal-mines, nuclear installations, toxic garbage cleanness, fire extinguishing, and rescue of victims in disasters, between others. It is important to note that these tasks can be extended to several classes of mobile robots, as aerial, terrestrial and aquatic (Krys & Najjaran, 2007; Santana & Medeiros, 2009; Steder et. al., 2008).

3. Probabilistic Occupancy Grid Mapping

Errors present after acquisition process may lead to a wrong interpretation of sensory data and the consequently construction of a not reliable (Thrun, 2002). So, a treatment of these errors should be done in order to eliminate or to have at least controlled these errors. Here we choose to explore the use of a probabilistic approach in order to model these errors. Note that by knowing the amount and type of errors of a robot system, one can rely on this to let it do tasks in a more efficient way.

3.1 Localization

As explained previously, localization, that is, inferring position and orientation of the robot inside its environment is an important requirement for map construction. Some researchers makes this assumption farther important stating that localization is the fundamental and main problem that should be treated in order to give autonomy to a robot (Cox, 1991). As well, Thrun (Thrun et. al., 2000) treats localization as the key problem for the success of an autonomous robot.

Localization methods generally fall in one of the following approaches: relative, absolute or using multisensor-fusion. Relative localization (or *dead reckoning*) is based on the integration of sensory data (generally from encoders) over time. The current localization of the robot is calculated after a time interval from the previous one plus the current displacement/rotation perceived in that time slot by the sensor. Several sources may generate errors between each time step, so, note that this approach also integrates errors. The calculated localizations are in reality estimations whose precision depends on the amount of accumulated error. In fact, the robot may be lost after some time. Absolute localization gives the actual localization of the robot at a given time. This actual localization is generally calculated based on the detection of objects or landmarks in the environment, with known localization, from which the position and orientation of the robot can be calculated by triangulation or some other methodology. Note that a GPS (and/or compassing) or similar method can also be used to get absolute position and orientation of the robot in the environment. Multi-sensor fusion combines relative and absolute localization. For example, a robot relying on its encoders may, after certain period of time, do absolute localization in order to rectify its actual localization from landmarks in the environment. In general Kalman filter and/or similar approaches are used in this situation to extend the maximum possible the amount of time necessary for absolute re-localization, since this is generally time consuming so the robot does anything while actually localizing itself. We consider using relative localization in this work since no information with respect to the environment is given to the robot previously.

One of the most used ways for estimating the robot position and orientation is by using *odometry*. Odometry gives an estimate of the current robot localization by integration of motion of the robot wheels. By counting pulses generated by encoders coupled to the wheels axes (actually, rotation sensors that count the amount of turns) the robot system can calculate the linear distance and orientation of the robot at the current instant. Odometry is most used because of its low cost, relative precision in small displacements and high rate of sampled data (Borenstein et. al., 1996). However, the disadvantage of this method is the accumulation of errors that increases proportionally to the displacement. Propagated error is systematic or not. Systematic errors are due to uncertainty in the parameters that are part of the kinematics modeling of the robot (different wheel diameters, axis lenght diffenent from its actual size, finite sample rate of the encoders, and others). Non systematic errors occur due to unexpected situations as unexpected obstacles or slipping of the wheels (Santana, 2007).

Particularly, with the objective of modeling the odometry of our robot, a methodology based on utilization of empirical data (Chenavier & Crowley, 1992) is used in this work. From experimental data collected in several samples it was possible to devise the function that approximates the odometry errors. This practical experiment is done in two phases. In the first one the angular and linear errors were modeled in a linear displacement (translation only) and in the second one the angular and linear errors were modeled in an angular displacement (rotation only). From these experiments, it was possible to stablish a fucntion that describes, in approximation, the behavior of systematic errors present at the odometry system. Equations 1 and 2 represents these funcions (linear and angular, respectively.

$$E_{lin}(\Delta l) = 0.09\Delta l + \sigma \tag{1}$$

$$E_{ang}(\Delta\theta) = 0.095\Delta\theta + \alpha \tag{2}$$

In the above Equations, Δl is the linear displacement estimated by odometry, $\Delta\theta$ is the angular displacement estimated by odometry, σ is the mean linear error due to a rotation and α is the mean angular error due to a linear displacement. In the performed experiments, σ and α have presented, approximately, constant values not varying proportionally with the linear and angular displacements. With the same empirical data and adopting, again, the methodology described above (Chenavier & Crowley, 1992), factors were estimated that multiplied by the linear and angular displacements gives an estimate of the variance of the non systematic errors. In this case, the errors are represented by normal distributions, or Gaussians with mean equals to zero and variance ε_{lin} for the linear case and ε_{ang} for the angular case. Equations 3 and 4 describe the computation of the variance of the linear and angular errors respectively.

$$\varepsilon_{lin} = \kappa_{ll}\Delta l + \kappa_{l\theta}\Delta\theta \tag{3}$$

$$\varepsilon_{ang} = \kappa_{\theta\theta}\Delta\theta + \kappa_{\theta l}\Delta l \tag{4}$$

κ_{ll} is the linear error coefficient in a linear displacement Δl, $\kappa_{l\theta}$ is the linear error coefficient caused by a rotation $\Delta\theta$, $\kappa_{\theta\theta}$ is the angular error coefficient in a rotation $\Delta\theta$, and $\kappa_{\theta l}$ is the angular error coefficient caused by a linear displacement Δl. These coefficients are calculated by Equations 5, 6, 7, and 8, respectively.

$$\kappa_{ll} = \frac{Var(e_{lin})}{\mu(\Delta l)} \tag{5}$$

$$\kappa_{l\theta} = \frac{Var(e_{lin})}{\mu(\Delta\theta)} \tag{6}$$

$$\kappa_{\theta\theta} = \frac{Var(e_{ang})}{\mu(\Delta\theta)} \tag{7}$$

$$\kappa_{\theta l} = \frac{Var(e_{ang})}{\mu(\Delta l)} \tag{8}$$

In Equations 5, 6, 7, and 8, parameter $Var(.)$ is the variance, $\mu(.)$ is the mean, e_{lin} and e_{ang} are the linear and angular errors, respectively that are obtained from the comparison between the real displacement values and the estimated given by the odometry system. By grouping the two error sources (systematic and not), a model for global error is obtained as given by Equations 9 and 10).

$$\mathbb{E}_{lin} = E_{lin}(\Delta l) + \mathcal{N}(0, \varepsilon_{lin}) \tag{9}$$

$$\mathbb{E}_{ang} = E_{ang}(\Delta\theta) + \mathcal{N}(0, \varepsilon_{ang}) \tag{10}$$

In the above Equations, $\mathcal{N}(0, \varepsilon_{lin})$ is a Gaussian noise with mean equals 0 and variance ε_{lin} to the linear case, and $\mathcal{N}(0, \varepsilon_{ang})$ is a Gaussian noise with mean equals 0 and variance ε_{ang} to the angular case. The modeling of these errors makes it possible to represent them in the environment map, resulting in a more coherent with the sensory data.

3.2 Occupancy Grid Mapping

The use of occupancy grid for mapping is proposed by Elfes and Moravec (Elfes, 1987) and is better formalized in the PhD thesis of the first author (Elfes, 1989). The objective is to construct consistent maps from sensory data under the hypothesis that the robot position and orientation is known. The basic idea is to represent the environment as a grid that is a multi-dimensional matrix (in general 2D or 3D) that contains cells of the same size. Each cell corresponds to a random variable that represents its occupancy probability. Fig. 3 shows an example of a occupancy grid of part of an environment using data provided by a sonar array.

Dark cells represent objects (or obstacles) detected by the sonar array, clear cells represent free regions, and gray cells are regions not yet mapped. Spatial model based on occupancy grid can be directly used in navigation tasks, as path planning with obstacle avoidance and position estimation (Elfes, 1989). The state values are estimated by way of interpretation of data coming from depth sensors probabilistic modeled using probabilistic function. It is possible to update each cell value through Bayesian probabilistic rules every time that new readings are done in different positions in the environment.

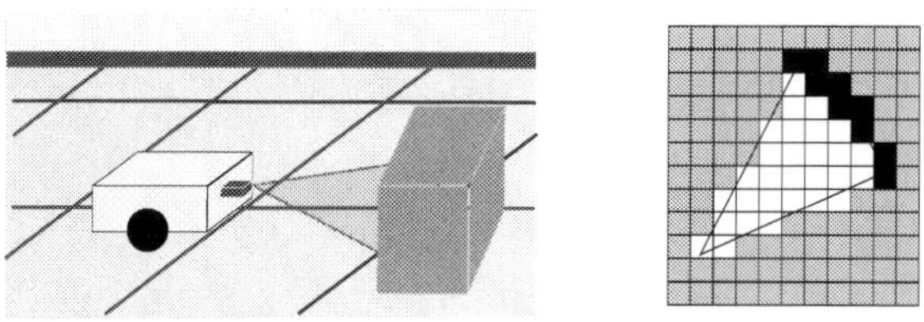

Fig. 3. Use of occupancy grid for representing sonar array data.

Most part of current researches related to environment mapping for robotics uses probabilistic techniques constructing probabilistic models for the robots, sensors and mapped environments. The reason for the popularity is of probabilistic techniques comes from the assumed existence of uncertainty present in sensory data. With probabilistic techniques, it is possible to treat this problem by explicitly modeling the several sources of noise and their influence in the measures (Thrun, 2002).

The standard algorithm formalized by Elfes (Elfes, 1989) aims to construct a map based on sensory data and knowing the robot position and orientation. In our work, we use the odometry system of the robot for calculating position and orientation. So the occupancy grid map construction is based on the fusion of data given by the sonars with data provided by the odometry system of the robot. Equation 11 presents the mathematical formulation that usually describes the occupancy grid mapping (Elfes, 1987; 1989; Thrun et. al., 2003; 2005).

$$P(\mathbf{m}|\mathbf{z}_{1:t}) \tag{11}$$

In the Equation 11, $\mathbf{m}$ represents the acquired map and $\mathbf{z}_{1:t}$ is the set of sensory measures realized up to time instant t. It is important to clear that the algorithm assumes that position and orientation of the robot are known. Continuous space is discretized in cells that, together, approximate the environment shape. This discretization corresponds to a plan cut of the 3D environment in the case of using a 2D grid or could be a 3D discretization in the case of a 3D grid. This depends of the sensors model and characteristics. For example, sonar allows a 2D sample of the environment, however stereo vision allows a 3D reconstruction. In this work, we use sonars.

Considering the discretization of the environment in cells, the map $\mathbf{m}$ can be defined as a finite set of cells $m_{x,y}$ where each cell has a value that corresponds to the probability of it being occupied. The cells can have values in the interval $[0,1]$ with 0 meaning empty and 1 meaning occupied. Being the map a set of cells, the mapping problem can be decomposed in several problems of estimation of the value of each cell in the map. Equation 12 represents an instance for the estimation of the value of a cell $m_{x,y}$, that is, the probability of cell $m_{x,y}$ being occupied when sensory measures $\mathbf{z}_{1:t}$ until the t instant.

$$P(m_{x,y}|\mathbf{z}_{1:t}) \tag{12}$$

Due to numerical instability, with probabilities close to 0 or 1 it is common to calculate the *log-odds* (or probability logarithm) of $P(m_{x,y}|\mathbf{z}_{1:t})$ instead of $P(m_{x,y}|\mathbf{z}_{1:t})$. The *log-odds* is defined by:

$$l_{x,y}^{t} = log\frac{P(m_{x,y}|\mathbf{z}_{1:t})}{1 - P(m_{x,y}|\mathbf{z}_{1:t})} \tag{13}$$

The probability occupancy value can be recovered through Equation 14.

$$P(m_{x,y}|\mathbf{z}_{1:t}) = 1 - \frac{1}{e^{l_{x,y}^{t}}} \tag{14}$$

The value of *log-odds* can be estimated recursively at any instant t by using the Bayes rule applied to $P(m_{x,y}|\mathbf{z}_{1:t})$ (see Equation 15).

$$P(m_{x,y}|\mathbf{z}_{1:t}) = \frac{P(z_t|\mathbf{z}_{1:t-1}, m_{x,y})P(m_{x,y}|\mathbf{z}_{1:t-1})}{P(z_t|\mathbf{z}_{1:t-1})} \tag{15}$$

in Equation 15, $P(z_t|\mathbf{z}_{1:t-1}, m_{x,y})$ represents the probabilistic modelo of the depth sensor, $P(m_{x,y}|\mathbf{z}_{1:t-1})$ is the value of cell $m_{x,y}$ at instant $t-1$ and $P(z_t|\mathbf{z}_{1:t-1})$ is the real value measured by the sensor. Assuming that the mapping is performed in random environments, the current measure of the sensor is independent of past measures, given the map $\mathbf{m}$ at any instant. This results in Equations 16 and 17.

$$P(z_t|\mathbf{z}_{1:t-1}, \mathbf{m}) = P(z_t|m) \tag{16}$$

$$P(z_t|\mathbf{z}_{1:t-1}) = P(z_t) \tag{17}$$

Given that the map is decomposed in cells, this suposition can be extended as shown in Equation 18.

$$P(z_t|\mathbf{z}_{1:t-1}, m_{x,y}) = P(z_t|m_{x,y}) \tag{18}$$

With basis on the above assumptions, Equation 15 can be simplified resulting in Equation 19.

$$P(m_{x,y}|\mathbf{z}_{1:t}) = \frac{P(z_t|m_{x,y})P(m_{x,y}|\mathbf{z}_{1:t-1})}{P(z_t)} \tag{19}$$

By applying the *total probability* rule to Equation 19, Equation 20 is obtained. The last calculates the probability of occupation for cell $m_{x,y}$ having as basis the probabilistic model of sensor $P(z_t|m_{x,y})$ and the occupancy value of the cell available previously $P(m_{x,y}|\mathbf{z}_{1:t-1})$.

$$P(m_{x,y}|\mathbf{z}_{1:t}) = \frac{P(z_t|m_{x,y})P(m_{x,y}|\mathbf{z}_{1:t-1})}{\sum_{m_{x,y}} P(z_t|m_{x,y})P(m_{x,y}|\mathbf{z}_{1:t-1})} \tag{20}$$

Computationally, the mapping using occupancy grid can be implemented by Algorithm 1 (Thrun et. al., 2005). The algorithm has as input variables a matrix with all occupancy values $\{l_{t-1,(x,y)}\}$ attributed to the occupancy grid constructed until instant $t-1$, a robot localization vector $\mathbf{x}_t = (x, y, \theta)'$ at instant t and the values of sensor readings z_t at instant t. If a cell $m_{x,y}$ of the occupancy grid is inside the field of view of the sensors (line 2), the occupancy grid value is updated taking into account the previous value of the cell $l_{t-1,(x,y)}$, the sensor model $inverse\_sensor\_model(m_{x,y}, \mathbf{x}_t, z_t)$ and the constant l_0 that is attributed to all cells at beginning indicating that they are not mapped (line 3). If the cell $m_{x,y}$ is out of the field of view, its value is kept (line 5).

Algorithm 1 occupancy_grid_mapping($\{l_{t-1,(x,y)}\}, \mathbf{x}_t, z_t$)

1: **for** all cells $m_{x,y}$ **do**
2:     **if** $m_{x,y}$ in perceptual field of z_t **then**
3:         $l_{t,(x,y)} = l_{t-1,x,y} + inverse\_sensor\_model(m_{x,y}, \mathbf{x}_t, z_t) - l_0$
4:     **else**
5:         $l_{t,(x,y)} = l_{t-1,(x,y)}$
6:     **end if**
7: **end for**
8: return $\{l_{t,(x,y)}\}$

It is important to emphasize that the occupancy values of the cells at Algorithm 1 are calculated through log-odd that is the logarithm of the probability of avoiding numerical instabilities. In order to recover the probability values Equation 14 can be used.

With basis on this algorithm, we implemented the method proposed in this work. The main difference is in the probabilistic modeling of the sensors. Our proposed model implements the *inverse_sensor_model* used in the algorithm.

3.3 Proposed Model

In this work, we use a sonar array as sensors measuring the distance of the robot with respect to some object. Sonar arrays are often used because of its fast response time, simplicity on its output (distance is directly given) and its low cost when compared to other sensor types (Lee et. al., 2006). In general, a setup as our (array of sonar) is mounted. The used setup has an uncertainty of about 1% of the measured value and an aperture that rotates around $+15^o$ to -15° in relation to the main axis (see Fig. 4). The distance returned by the sonar is the one to the closest object inside its sonar bean. The maximum returned distance depends on the sonar model.

Let consider three regions inside the working area of the sonar as seen in Fig. 4. Region I represents free area. Region II is associated to the sensor measure such that the object that has

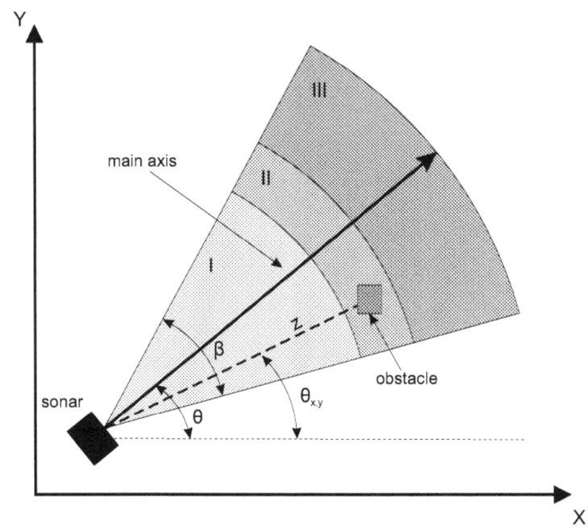

Fig. 4. Regiões significativas em feixe de sonar.

reflected the sound wave may be anywhere inside this region. Region III is the one covered, in theory, by the sonar bean. However it is not known if it is empty or occupied. Considering the above regions, the model adopted to represent the sonar is described as a Gaussian distribution as given by Equation 21.

$$P(z, \theta | d_{x,y}, \theta_{x,y}) = \frac{1}{2\pi\sigma_z\sigma_\theta} exp\left[-\frac{1}{2}\left(\frac{(z - d_{x,y})^2}{\sigma_z^2} + \frac{(\theta - \theta_{x,y})^2}{\sigma_\theta^2}\right)\right] \tag{21}$$

In the above Equation, θ is the orientation angle of the sensor with respect to the x axis of the global reference frame (see Fig. 4), $\theta_{x,y}$ is the angle between the vector with initial point at the sonar through cell $m_{x,y}$, that may be or not with obstacle, and to the global frame axis x (see Fig. 4), σ_z^2 and σ_θ^2 are the variance that gives uncertainty in the measured distance z and in the θ angle, respectively. Fig. 5 illustrates the function that estimates the occupancy for this model.

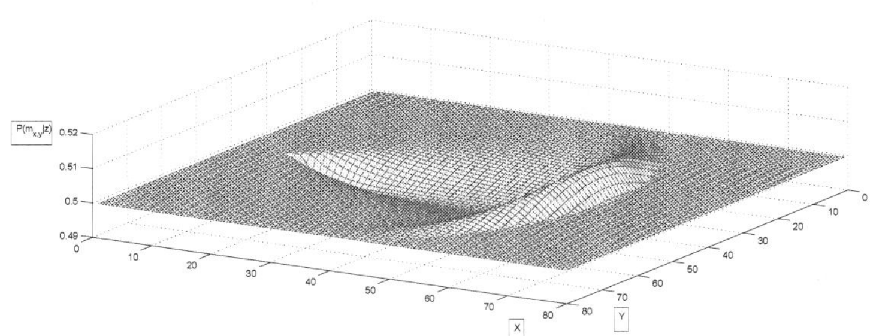

Fig. 5. Function of occupancy for a sensor modeled by a two-dimensional Gaussian distribution. Both uncertainties in the angle and in the distance being represented.

Having as basis a 2D Gaussian model in this work we also consider uncertainties that are inherent to the odometry system besides sonar uncertainties. Using odometry errors modele given in Section 3.1 of this text, described by Equations 9 and 10, it is possible to stablish a relation between the variances σ_z^2 and σ_θ^2 that (model sonar errors) with odometry errors as:

$$\sigma_z = z \times \eta + \mathbb{E}_{lin}$$

$$\sigma_\theta = \frac{\beta}{2} + \mathbb{E}_{ang}$$

or

$$\sigma_z = z \times \eta + E_{lin}(\Delta l) + \mathcal{N}(0, \varepsilon_{lin}) \tag{22}$$

$$\sigma_\theta = \frac{\beta}{2} + E_{ang}(\Delta\theta) + \mathcal{N}(0, \varepsilon_{ang}) \tag{23}$$

In the above Equations, z the measure given by the sonar, η is an error factor typical of the sonar in use (an error of about 1%) and β the aperture angle of the sonar bean (see Fig. 4). Variances σ_z^2 and σ_θ^2 can be calculated through Equations 22 and 23, now considering the influences caused by odometry. Equation 22 calculates uncertainty to a distance z and a linear displacement Δl. $E_{lin}(\Delta l)$ is the function used to compute systematic errors of odometry (Equation 1) and $\mathcal{N}(0, \varepsilon_{lin})$ is the normal distribution used to compute non systematic errors (Equation 3). Equation 23 gives uncertainty of the orientation angle of the sonar θ and an angular displacement $\Delta\theta$ performed by the robot. $E_{ang}(\Delta\theta)$ (Equation 2) describes the systematic error of an angular displacement and $\mathcal{N}(0, \varepsilon_{ang})$ (Equation 4) is the normal distribution that estimates non systematic errors for the same displacement.

Throgh this proposed modification, it is possible to represent degradation of the odometry errors in the map. The probability for a correct measure calculated by Equation 21 is now weighted by the errors of the odometry system. In this way, the final map is more coherent with the quality of sensors data (sonar and odometry). Fig. 5 illustrates a degraded measure mainly by angular errors in odometry. Fig. 6 illustrates a degraded measure mainly by linear errors of odometry.

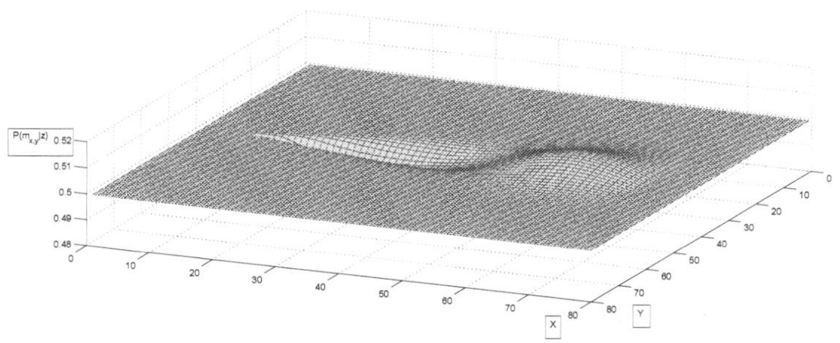

Fig. 6. Measurements degraded mainly by linear odometry errors.

3.4 Map Generation

The processing steps done in data coming from the sonars (Souza, 2008) are listed next.

- **Preprocessing:** Data coming from sonar goes through a filter that discards false readings. Distances measured below a minimum threshold and above a maximum threshold are eliminated due to its susceptibility to errors. These limits are 4 and 15 cm in this work, respectively.
- **Sensor position:** Position and orientation of the sensors with respect to the robot and also the robot with respect to the reference frame are calculated.
- **Interpretation by the probabilistic model:** Sonar data are interpreted by the proposed probabilistic model to form the *sonar view*.
- **Sonar map:** Each sonar generates its own local map from its *view* that is then added to the global map.

As exposed above, odometry errors accumulate over robot motion and degrades the quality of the map. At a certain time, the value attributed to a given cell does not have a substantial influence in the form used to define if it is occupied, empty or not mapped yet. At this instant, the mapping process is strongly corrupted and an absolute localization approach must be used to correct these errors in order for the robot to continue the mapping.

4. Experiments

The robot used in this work is a Pioneer-3AT, kindly named Galatea, which is projected for locomotion on all terrain (the AT meaning) (see Fig. 7).

Fig. 7. Galatea robotic platform.

The Pioneer family is fabricated by ActiveMedia Robotics designed to support several types of perception devices. The robot comes with an API (Application Program Interface) called ARIA (ActiveMedia Robotics Interface) that has libraries for C++, Java and Python languages (in this work we use C++ language.). The ARIA library makes possible to develop high-level programs to communicate with and control the several robot devices (sensors and actuators) allowing reading of data about the robot in execution time.

The software package comes with a robot simulator (MobileSim) that allows to test some functions without using the real robot. It is possible to construct environments of different shapes to serve as basis to experiments and tests. Galatea has an embedded computer, a PC104+ with a pentium III processor of 800MHz, 256Mb of RAM memory, a 20Gb hard disk, communication interface RS232, Ethernet connection and wireless network board 10/100. Galatea has 2 sonar arrays with 8 sonars in which one and encoders coupled to the 2 motor axes that comprises its odometry system. To control all of these, we use the RedHat 7.3 Linux operating system.

4.1 Initial Simulated Experiments

Preliminary tests of our proposed algorithm are done with the MobileSim. We have simulated environment using a CAD model that comes with the simulator describing one of the buildings of Columbia University at USA. Fig. 8 shows the geometry of this test environment.

Fig. 8. Simulated environment to be mapped.

The simulated robot has mapped part of this environment following the doted path at Fig. 8. The robot perform the maping process until the odometry errors degrade the quality of the final map. At this point, values of each cell do not define anymore whether a cell is occupied, empty or mapped yet. That is, the robot has no subsides to construct a trustable map due to odometry errors. Part (a) of Fig. 9 illustrates this this situation. Galatea is represented by the red point, white regions are empty, dark regions are occupied cells and gray regions are not mapped yet cells. As this situation occur, we simulated an absolut localization for Galatea correcting its odometry and consequently indicating that it can continue the mapping without considering past accumulated errors. Fig. 9 (b) shows the moment at which the robot localization is rectified and Fig. 9 (c) illustrates the mapping continuation after this moment.

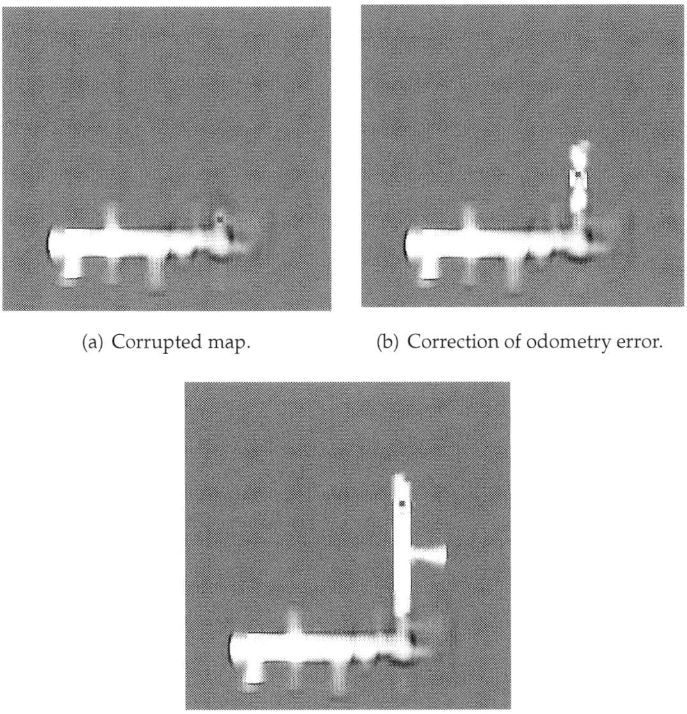

(a) Corrupted map. (b) Correction of odometry error.

(c) Mapping continuation.

Fig. 9. Sequences of steps in the mapping of a simulated environment.

4.2 Experiments with Galatea robot

We perfcormed several experiments at Computing Engineering Department (DCA) building at UFRN, Brazil. The building geometry is formed by corridors and rectangular rooms. Some initial experiments are shown in previous work (Souza et. al., 2008) using a simplified model for the depth sensors in order to verify the system behavior as a whole. From this initial simplified setup we could evaluate influency of problems that typical of sonars in the map quality, not possible in simulation. The main problem detected is the occurency of multiple reflections. Fig. 10 shows a map constructed for the corridors of DCA building. Dotted line indicates the real localization of the walls. It is easy to note that several measures indicate obstacles or empty areas behind the walls plan, e.g, in areas that could not be mapped. These false measures are typically caused by multiple reflections inside the environment.

Robots with a more complex shape as the one used in this work are more susceptible to false measures. This happens because the sensors, in general, have irregular distribution along the robot body facilitating occurency of false measures. On the opposite, robots with circular shape have a regular distribution, being easier to eliminate these false measures only by tunning the sensors characteristics (Ivanjko & Petrovic, 2005). In order to solve this problem, we have implemented a method for filtering false measures. This strategy represents the sonar

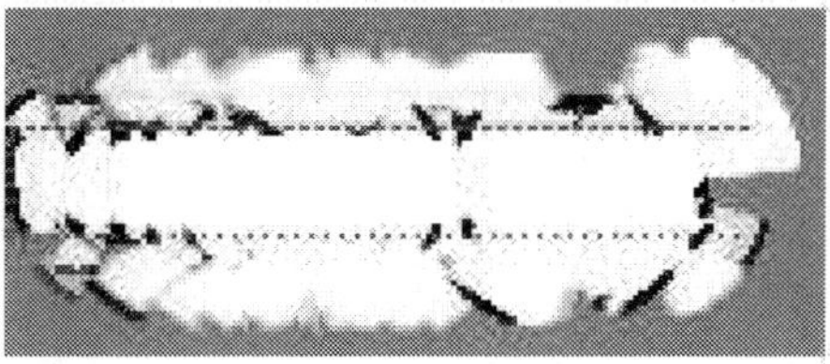

Fig. 10. Corrupted mapping due to wrong measures of the sonars.

measures by circles in such a way that if a given measure invades the circular region defined by another measure, the invaded region measure is eliminated. This technique is called Bubble Circle (BC) Threshold (Lee & Chung, 2006). Results for our work were not convincing thus other alternatives were studied.

After several experiments and observations, we could verify that in environments with rectangular shapes, as this one formed by strait corridors and not as big rooms, more consistent maps are constructed by using the side sonars. These comprise angles of 90° with the walls when the robot is parallel to the walls. The same for the rear and front sonars with smallest angles with respect to the robot main axis. So we discard the other sensors given that they produced false measures due to its disposition with respect to the walls. In fact we believe that these several other sensors with oblique angles were projected to be used when the robot is operating in outdoor environments. In fact, we could verify latter that the same consideration has been reported in the work of Ivanjko (Ivanjko & Petrovic, 2005), in this case working with the Pioneer-2DX robot.

Now, after solving the above mentioned problems, we have done another set of experiments using Algorithm 1, which is a modification of the one proposed by Thrun (Thrun et. al., 2005). The main differential of the algorithm proposed here is the inclusion of the probabilistic model of the sensor that represents the uncertainties inherent to to perceptionm in the occupancy grid map. Fig. 11 shows the mapping of the same corridor yet in the beginning of the process, however with degradation caused by the odometry error. The red dotted boundary indicates actual walls position. The red point at the white region indicates the localization of Galatea at the map and the point at the right extremity of the Fig. is the last point were the mapping should stop. Fig. 12 shows the evolution of the mapping. Observe the decreasing of quality in the mapping as the robot moves that, in its turn, increases the odometry errors. The map shown in Fig. 13 presents an enhancement in its quality. At this point, the absolute localization was done because the map was degraded. Odometry error goes to zero here, rectifying the robot position and orientation.

The mapping process goes up to the point shown in Fig. 14 where it is necessary another correction by using absolute localization, then going until the final point as shown in Fig. 15. By considering probabilistic modeling of odometry errors and sensor readings to try to diminish error effects at the mapping process, we could have a substantial enhancement in the mapping quality. However, we remark that at some time of the process the map gets eventually corrupted by the effects of non systematic errors. Fig. 16 shows the situation using modeling to attenuating the effect of these errors. In this case, the effect is very small because the errors become very little for the travelled distance.

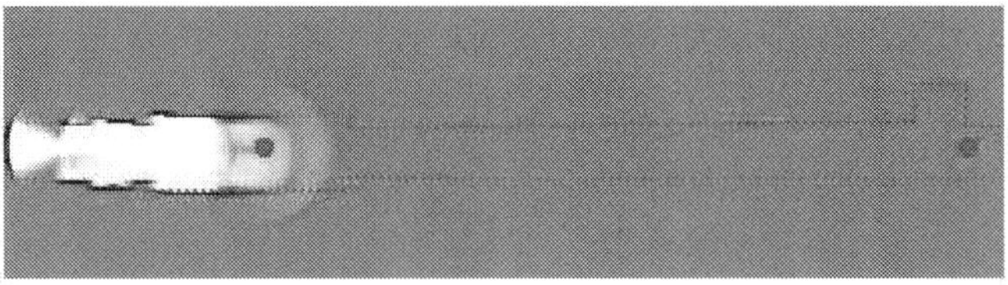

Fig. 11. Use of the proposed model considering representation of odometry errors in the mapping.

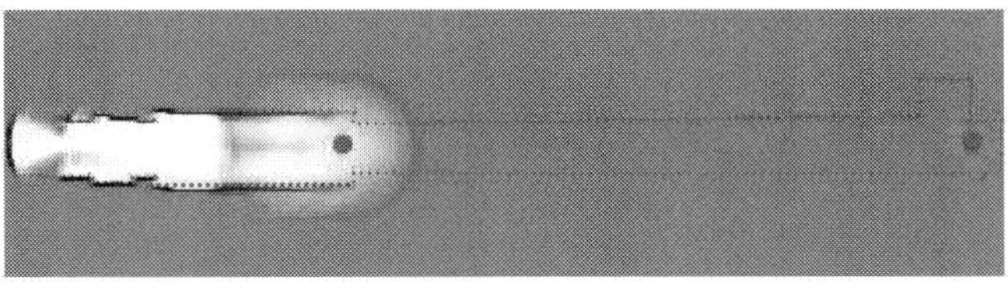

Fig. 12. Representation of odometry error in the map construction.

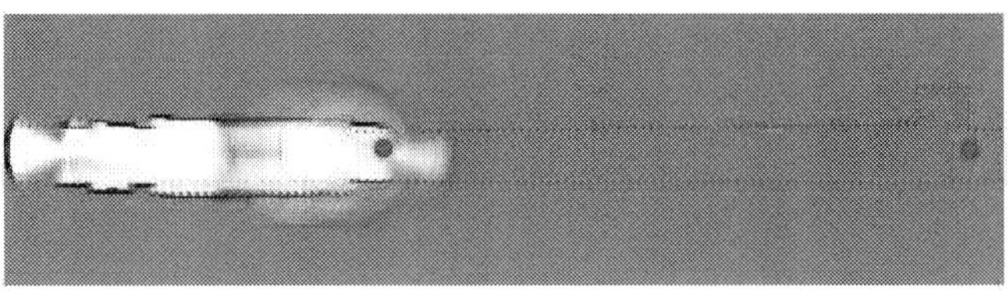

Fig. 13. Rectification of the robot localization (absolute localization).

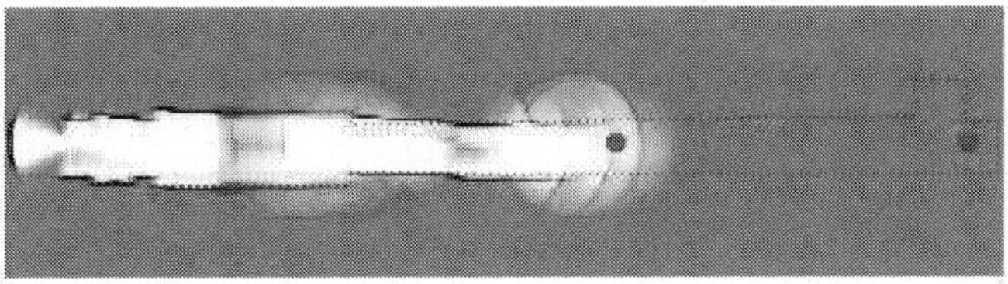

Fig. 14. Nova correção da localização.

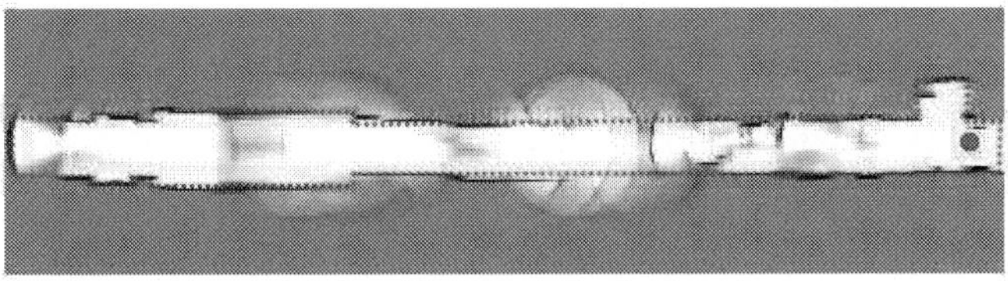

Fig. 15. Mapa final adquirido com o modelo proposto.

Fig. 16. Mapa construído com o modelo proposto e como correção dos erros sistemáticos de odometria.

5. Conclusion and Future Directions

In this work we propose a method for mapping with spatial representation of the environment based on occupancy grid. Our method incorporates a probabilistic model for sonar that consider the uncertainties inherent to this type of sensor as well as for the accumulative errors caused by odometry system of the robot. With this modeling, the quality of the map gets influenced by the uncertainty given by the odometry system indicating the actual trustworthiness of the sensory data collected by the robot system. Once a map gets constructed, the robot can use it to perform other high-level tasks as navigation, path planning, and decision taking, between others.

With basis on the results given by the performed experiments, we conclude that the algorithm proposed in this work gives a more realistic and actual manner for representing a mapped environment using the occupancy grid technique. This is becuse that now we know that the data provided by the sensors have errors and we know how much this error can grow, that is, we have an upper limit for the error, controlling its growing. Even with the difficulties given by the sonar limitations, our system presents satisfactory results. Other types of depth sensors can be added to this model or use a similar approach, as for example *lasers*, thus increasing map consistency.

As next work, we intend to study techniques and exploration heuristics in order for a robot to perform the mapping process in autonomous way. Besides, forms to enhance robot localization with incorporation of other sensors will also be studied that together can improve map quality. Future trials with emphasis in Localization and Simultaneous Mapping (SLAN) will also be done, having as basis the studies done in this work. Fusion of information with the ones provided by a visual system (stereo vision) will be further done. With this, we intend to explorate the construction of 3D maps allowing the use of robots in other higher level tasks, as for example, analysis of building structure.

6. References

Agrawal, M.; Konolige, K. & Bolles, R.C. (2007). Localization and Mapping for Autonomous Navigation in Outdoor Terrains : A Stereo Vision Approach. In: *IEEE Workshop on Applications of Computer Vision, WACV '07.*

Alsina, P. J.; Gonçalves, L. M. G.; Medeiros, A. A. D.; Pedrosa, D. P. F. & Vieira, F. C. V. (2002). Navegação e controle de robôs móveis. In: *Mini Curso - XIV Congresso Brasileiro de Automática*, Brazil.

Borenstein, J.; Everett, R. H. & Feng, L. (1996). *Where am I? Sensors and Methods for Mobile Robot Positionig*, University of Michigan, EUA.

Chenavier, F. & Crowley, J. L. (1992). Position estimation for a mobile robot using vision and odometry, In: *Proceeding of the 1992 IEEE International Conference on Robotics and Automation*, Nice, France.

Choset, H. & Fox, D. (2004). The World of Mapping. In: *Proceedings of WTEC Workshop on Review of United States Research in Robotics*, National Science Foundation (NSF), Arlington, Virginia, USA.

Clark, C. M.; Olstad, C. S.; Buhagiar, K. & Gambin, T. (2009). Archaeology via Underwater Robots: Mapping and Localization within Maltese Cistern Systems. In: *10th International Conf. on Control, Automation, Robotics and Vision*, pp.662 - 667, Hanoi, Vietnam.

Cox, I. J. (1991). Blanche - An Experiment in Guidance and Navigation of an Autonomous Robot Vehicle, In: *IEEE Transactions on Robotics and Automation*, Vol. 7, No. 2.

Elfes, A. (1987). Sonar-based real-world mapping and navigation, In: *IEEE Journal of Robotics and Automation*, Vol. 3, No. 3 , pp. 249-265.

Elfes, A. (1989). Occupancy Grid: A Probabilistic Framework for Robot Perception and Navigation, *PhD Thesis*, Carnegie Mellon University, Pittsburg, Pensylvania, USA.

Hogue, A. & Jenkin, M. (2006). Development of an Underwater Vision Sensor for 3D Reef Mapping, In: *Proceedings IEEE/RSJ International Conference on Intelligent Robots and Systems (IROS 2006)*, pp. 5351-5356.

Ivanjko, E. & Petrovic, I. (2005). Experimental Evaluation of Occupancy Grids Maps Improvement by Sonar Data Dorrection, In: *Proceedings of 13th Mediterranean Conference on Control and Automation*, Limassol, Cyprus.

Krys, D. & Najjaran, H. (2007). Development of Visual Simultaneous Localization and Mapping (VSLAM) for a Pipe Inspection Robot. In: *Proceedings of the 2007 International Symposium on Computational Intelligence in Robotics and Automation, CIRA 2007*. pp. 344-349.

Lee, K. & Chung, W. K. (2006). Filtering Out Specular Reflections of Sonar Sensor Readings, In: *The 3rd International Conference on Ubiquitous Robots and Ambient Intelligent (URAI)*.

Lee, Y.-C.; Nah, S.-I.; Ahn, H.-S. & Yu, W. (2006). Sonar Map Construction for a Mobile Robot Using a Tethered-robot Guiding System, In: *The 6rd International Conference on Ubiquitous Robots and Ambient Intelligent (URAI)*.

Medeiros, A. A. D. (1998). A Survey of Control Architectures for Autonomous Mobile Robots. In: *JBCS - Journal of the Brazilian Computer Society, Special Issue on Robotics*, ISSN 0104-650004/98, vol. 4, n. 3, Brazil.

Ouellette, R. & Hirasawa, K. (2008). Mayfly: A small mapping robot for Japanese office environments. In: *IEEE/ASME International Conference on Advanced Intelligent Mechatronics* ,pp. 880-885.

Rocha, R. P. P. (2006). Building Volumetric Maps whit Cooperative Mobile Robots and Useful Information Sharing: A Distributed Control Approach based on Entropy. *PhD Thesis*, FEUP - Faculdade de Engenharia da Universidade do Porto, Portugal.

Santana, A. M. (2007). Localização e Planejamento de Caminhos para um Robô Humanóide e um Robô Escravo com Rodas. *Master Tesis*, UFRN, Natal, RN. 2007.

Santana, A M. & Medeiros, A. A. D. (2009). Simultaneous Localization and Mapping (SLAM) of a Mobile Robot Based on Fusion of Odometry and Visual Data Using Extended Kalman Filter. In: *In Robotics, Automation and Control*, Editor: Vedran Kordic, pp. 1-10. ISBN 978-953-7619-39-8. In-Tech, Austria.

Silver, D.; Ferguson, D.; Morris, A. C. & Thayer, S. (2004). Features Extraction for Topological Mine Maps, In: *Proceedings of the IEEE/RSJ International Conference on Intelligent Robots and Systems (IROS 2004)*, Vol. 1, pp. 773-779.

Souza, A. A. S. (2008). Mapeamento com Grade de Ocupação Baseado em Modelagem Probabilística, *Master Thesis*, UFRN, Natal, Brazil.

Souza, A. A. S.; Santana, A. M.; Britto, R. S.; Gonçalves, L. M. G. & Medeiros, A. A. D. (2008). Representation of Odometry Errors on Occupancy Grids. In: *Proceeding of International Conference on Informatics in Control, Automation and Robotics (ICINCO2008)*, Funchal, Portugal.

Steder, B.; Grisetti, G.; Stachniss, C. & Burgard, W. (2008). Visual SLAM for Flying Vehicles, In: *IEEE Transactions on Robotics*, Vol. 24 , Issue 5, pp. 1088-1093.

Triebel, R.; Pfaff, P. & Burgard, W. (2006). Multi-Level Surface Maps for Outdoor Terrain Mapping and Loop Closing. In: *Proceedings of IEEE/RSJ International Conference on Intelligent Robots and Systems*, pp. 2276 - 2282.

Thrun, S. (2002). Robotic mapping: A survey. In: *Exploring Artificial Intelligence in the New Millenium*,Ed. Morgan Kaufmann, 2002.

Thrun, S.; Fox, D.; Burgard, W. & Dellaert, F. (2000). Robust Monte Carlo Localization for Mobile Robots, In: *Artificial Inteligence*, Vol. 128, No. 1-2, pp. 99-141.

Thrun, S.; Hähnel, D.; Fergusin, D.; Montermelo, M.; Riebwel, R.; Burgard,W.; Baker, C.; Omohundro, Z.; Thayer, S. & Whittaker, W. (2003). A system for volumetric mapping of underground mines. In: *Proceedings of the IEEE International Conference on Robotics an Automation (ICRA 2003)*, Vol. 3, pp. 4270-4275.

Thrun, S.; Martin, C.; Liu, Y.; Hähnel, D.; Emery-Montemerlo, R.; Chakrabarti, D. & Burgard, W. (2004). A Real-Time Expectation Maximization Algorithm for Acquiring Multi-Planar Maps of Indoor Environments with Mobile Robots, In: *IEEE Transactions on Robotics and Automation*, Vol. 20, No. 3, pp. 433-443.

Thrun, S.; Fox, D. & Burgard, W. (2005). *Probabilistic Robotics*, MIT Press, Cambridge.

Wolf, D.; Howard, A. & Sukhatme, G. S. (2005). Towards geometric 3D mapping of outdoor environments using mobile robots. In: *Proceedings of IEEE/RSJ International Conference on Intelligent Robots and Systems (IROS 2005)*, pp. 1507-1512.

20

Sensor fusion for electromagnetic stress measurement and material characterisation

John W Wilson[1], Gui Yun Tian[1,2,*], Maxim Morozov[1] and Abd Qubaa[1]

[1]*School of Electrical, Electronic and Computer Engineering, Newcastle University, UK +44 191 222 5639*

[2]*School of Automation, Nanjing University of Aeronautics and Astronautics, 29 Yudao St., Nanjing 210016, China*

**Corresponding author: g.y.tian@newcastle.ac.uk*

Abstract

Detrimental residual stresses and microstructure changes are the two major precursors for future sites of failure in ferrous steel engineering components and structures. Although numerous Non-Destructive Evaluation (NDE) techniques can be used for microstructure and stress assessment, currently there is no single technique which would have the capability to provide a comprehensive picture of these material changes. Therefore the fusion of data from a number of different sensors is required for early failure prediction Electromagnetic (EM) NDE is a prime candidate for this type of inspection, since the response to Electromagnetic excitation can be quantified in several different ways: e.g. eddy currents, Barkhausen emission, flux leakage, and a few others.

This chapter reviews the strengths of different electromagnetic NDE methods, provides an analysis of the different sensor fusion techniques such as sensor physical system fusion through different principles and detecting devices, and/or feature selection and fusion, and/or information fusion. Two sensor fusion case studies are presented: pulsed eddy current thermography at sensor level and integrative electromagnetic methods for stress and material characterisation at feature (parameters) level.

1. Introduction

In recent years, non-destructive testing and evaluation (NDT&E) techniques have been developed which allow quantitative analysis of the stresses acting on a material; either through direct measurement of displacement (strain measurement)(1) or measurement of material properties which interact with stress and can therefore be used to indicate the material stress state. The second category includes magnetic(2) and electromagnetic (induction) NDT&E inspection techniques which allow the quantification of material stresses through magnetic and electrical properties, including magnetic permeability μ, electrical conductivity σ and domain wall motion. Although magnetic and electromagnetic techniques are promising candidates for stress measurement, the fact that the stress measurement is performed indirectly, means the relationship between the measured signal and stress is complex and heavily dependent on material microstructure, thus material-specific calibration is almost always required.

Because of the complex nature of the mechanisms which contribute to cracking, degradation and material stresses, the use of more than one NDE methods is often required for comprehensive assessment of a given component. The development of fusion techniques to integrate signals from different sources has the potential to lead to a decrease in inspection time and also a reduction in cost. Gathering of data from multiple systems coupled with efficient processing of information can provide great advantages in terms of decision making, reduced signal uncertainty and increased overall performance. Depending on the different physical properties measured, fusion techniques have the benefit that each NDE modality reveals different aspects of the material under inspection. Therefore professional processing and integration of defect information is essential, in order to obtain a comprehensive diagnosis of structural health.

With research and development in NDE through a wide range of applications for engineering and medical sciences, conventional NDT&E techniques have illustrated different limitations, e.g. ultrasonic NDT&E needs media coupling, eddy current NDT&E can only be used to inspect surface or near surface defects in metallic or conductive objects, etc. As industrial applications require inspection and monitoring for large, complex safety critical components and subsystems, traditional off-line NDT and quantitative NDE for defect detection cannot meet these needs. On-line monitoring e.g. structural health monitoring (SHM) for defects, as well as precursors e.g. material abnormal status for life cycle assessment and intelligent health monitoring is required. Recent integrative NDE techniques and fusion methods have been developed to meet these requirements [(3)].

Information fusion can be achieved at any level of signal information representation. As a sensor system includes the sensing device itself, signal conditioning circuitry and feature extraction and characterisation algorithms for decision making, sensor fusion should include: sensor physical system fusion through different excitation and detecting devices [(4, 5)]; sensor data or image pixel-level fusion through arithmetic fusion algorithms e.g. adding, subtraction, multiplication etc[(6, 7)]; feature selection and combination from sensor data features[(8, 9, 10)]; information fusion through case studies[(10, 11)]. Signal level data fusion, represents fusion at the lowest level, where a number of raw input data signals are combined to produce a single fused signal. Feature level fusion, fuses feature and object labels and property descriptor information that have already been extracted from individual input sensors. Finally, the highest level, decision level fusion refers to the combination of decisions already taken by individual systems. The choice of the fusion level depends mainly upon the application and complexity of the system.

In this chapter, three different applications of electromagnetic NDE sensor fusion are discussed and the benefits of the amalgamation of different electromagnetic NDE techniques are examined. In section 2, three kinds of sensor fusion are reported: Section 2.1. introduces PEC thermography using integrative different modality NDE methods; Section 2.2 looks at

Magnetic Barkhausen Emission (MBE) and Magneto-Acoustic Emission (MAE) for microstructural determination using different sensing devices for material characterisation, and in section 2.3, the theoretical links between electromagnetic properties, stress and microstructural changes using features or parameters from PEC and MBE for the quantification of stresses and microstructure are examined. In section 3 a summary of sensor fusion in ENDE is given.

2. Integrative electromagnetic NDE techniques

In this section, experimental results are presented for three different integrative NDE techniques, offering potential solutions to the problems associated with the attempt to gain a full understanding of material status from the application of a single technique. Sensor electromagnetic NDE fusion at the sensor system level, feature extraction, modality features and information are discussed.

2.1 Pulsed eddy current thermography

Pulsed eddy current (PEC) thermography[(4, 5)] is a new technique which uses thermal camera technology to image the eddy current distribution in a component under inspection. In pulsed eddy current (a.k.a. induction) thermography, a short burst of electromagnetic excitation is applied to the material under inspection, inducing eddy currents to flow in the material. Where these eddy currents encounter a discontinuity, they are forced to divert, leading to areas of increased and decreased eddy current density. Areas where eddy current density is increased experience higher levels of Joule (Ohmic) heating, thus the defect can be identified from the IR image sequence, both during the heating period and during cooling. In contrast to flash lamp heating, in PEC thermography there is a direct interaction between the heating mechanism and the defect. This can result in a much greater change in heating around defects, especially for vertical, surface breaking defects. However, as with traditional eddy current inspection, the orientation of a particular defect with respect to induced currents has a strong impact; sensitivity decreases with defect depth under the surface and the technique is only applicable to materials with a considerable level of conductivity (ferrous and non-ferrous metals and some conductive non-metals, such as carbon fibre).

Figure 1a shows a typical PEC thermography test system. A copper coil is supplied with a current of several hundred amps at a frequency of 50kHz - 1MHz from an induction heating system for a period of 20ms - 1s. This induces eddy currents in the sample, which are diverted when they encounter a discontinuity leading to areas of increased or decreased heating. The resultant heating is measured using an IR camera and displayed on a PC.

Figure 1b shows a PEC thermography image of a section of railtrack, shown from above. It can be seen that the technique has the ability to provide a "snapshot" of the complex network of cracking, due to wear and rolling contact fatigue (RCF) in the part. It is well known that in the initial stages, RCF creates short cracks that grow at a shallow angle, but these can sometimes grow to a steep angle. This creates a characteristic surface heat distribution, with the majority of the heating on one side of the crack only. This is due to two factors, shown in figure 1c; a high eddy current density in the corner of the area bounded by the crack and an increase in heating, due to the small area available for diffusion.

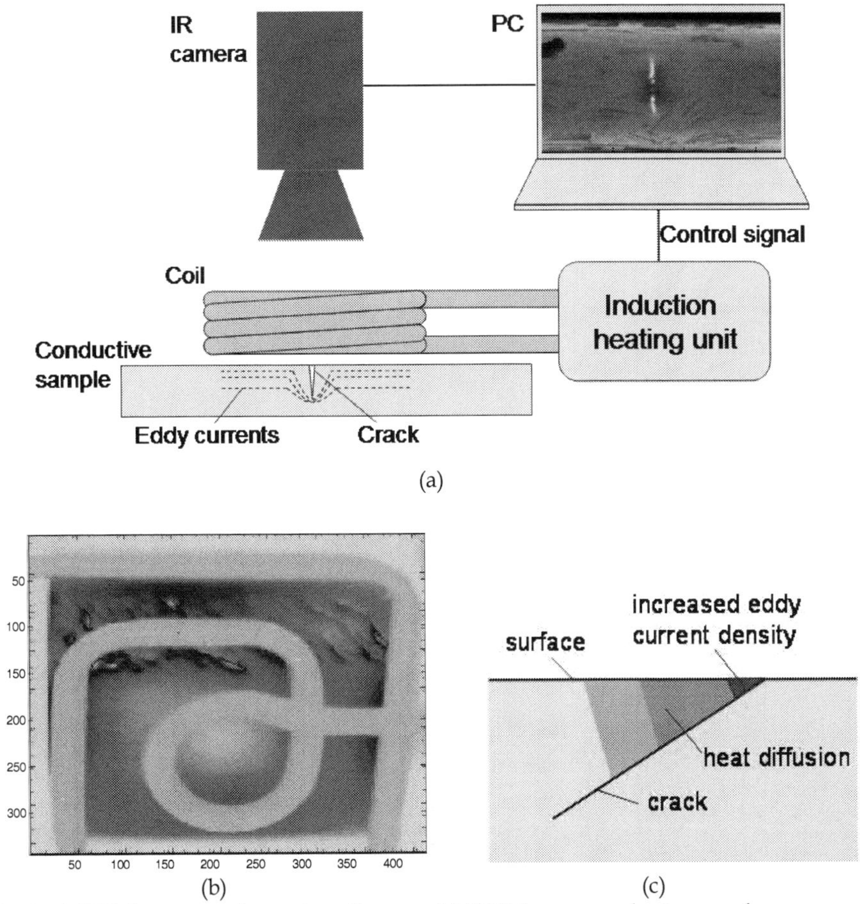

Fig. 1. a) PEC thermography system diagram, b) PEC thermography image of gauge corner cracking on a section of railtrack, c) Eddy current distribution and heat diffusion around angular crack

This ability to provide an instantaneous image of the test area and any defects which may be present is an obvious attraction of this technique, but further information can be gained through the transient analysis of the change in temperature in the material. The sample shown in figures 2a and 2b is made from titanium 6424 and contains a 9.25mm long semicircular (half-penny) defect with a maximum depth of around 4.62mm. The crack is formed by three point bending technique and the sample contains a 4mm deep indentation on the opposite side to the crack, to facilitate this process. Figure 2d shows the transient temperature change in five positions in the defect area, defined in figure 2c. It can be seen from the plot that different areas of the crack experience a very different transient response, corresponding to the combined effects of differing eddy current distributions around the crack and differing heat diffusion characteristics. This shows that the technique has the potential to offer both near-instantaneous qualitative defect images and quantitative information through transient analysis.

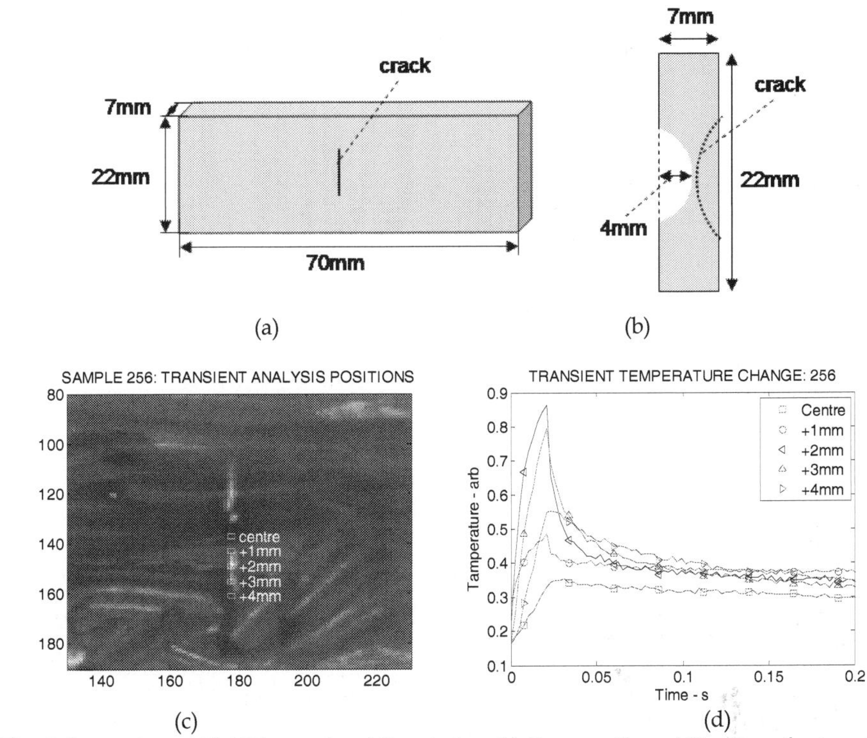

Fig. 2. Inspection of Ti 6424 sample; a) Front view, b) Cross section, c) Positions for transient analysis, d) Transient temperature change in different positions on the sample surface

2.2. Potential for fusion of MBE and MAE for microstructural characterisation

Although MBE and MAE are both based on the sensing of domain wall motion in ferromagnetic materials in response to a time varying applied magnetic field, the two techniques have important differences when applied to stress measurement and microstructural evaluation. Due to the skin effect, MBE is a surface measurement technique with a maximum measurement depth below 1mm and a strong reduction in sensitivity with increased depth. As MAE is essentially an acoustic signal, it does not suffer from the same restrictions as MBE and can be considered to be a bulk measurement technique. The interpretation of MAE can however, be complex, thus the implementation of a combination of the two techniques is advisable.

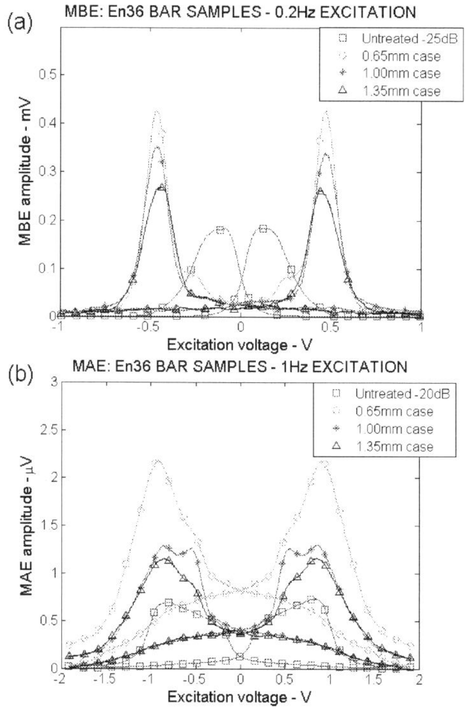

Fig. 3. MBE (a) and MAE (b) profiles measured on En36 gear steel samples of varying case depths

Figure 3 shows the results from a set of tests to quantify the case hardening depth in En36 gear steel. It can be seen from the plot that for case depths >0.64mm, the shape of the MBE profile remains the same, indicating that the case depth has exceeded the measurement depth, whereas for MAE, the profile shape continues to change up to the maximum depth of 1.35mm, indicating a greater measurement depth for this technique.

2.3. *Complementary features of PEC and MBE for stress measurement*

In this section selected results from a series of tests to quantify tensile stresses in mild steel are reported. Figures 4b and 5a show the change in the non-normalised PEC maximum ΔB_Z and the MBE_{ENERGY} respectively. Both results exhibit the greatest change within the first 100MPa of applied elastic tensile stress. This is due to a large initial change in permeability for the initial application of tensile stress. This is confirmed by examination of Figure 5c, where an initial shift in the peak 1 position towards a lower voltage and a corresponding increase in peak 1 amplitude indicates maximum domain activity at an earlier point in the applied field cycle, though this trend is reversed as stresses are increased. As the material under inspection is an anisotropic rolled steel this large initial permeability change is thought to be due to the rotation of the magnetic easy axis towards the applied load direction in the early stages of the test. The two peak activity which is observable in Figure

5c indicates that two different mechanisms are responsible for the change in MBE with stress. The peaks exhibit opposite behaviour; peak 1 increases with stress, whereas peak 2 decreases with stress. This indicates that each peak is associated with a different microstructural phase and / or domain configuration, active at a different point in the excitation cycle.

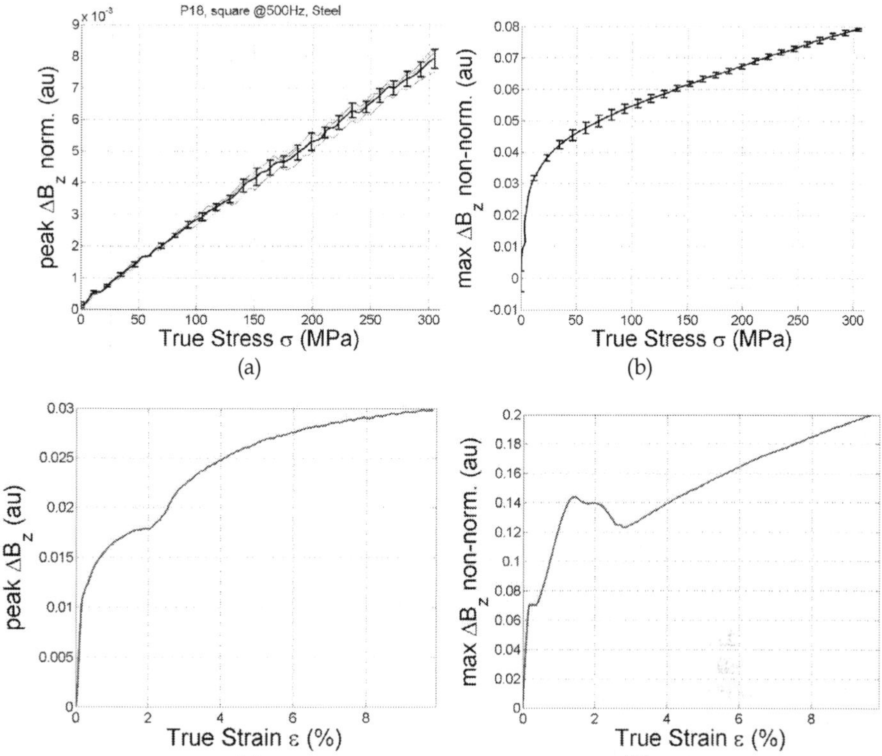

Fig. 4. Results of PEC measurements on steel under elastic and plastic deformation; a) Normalised PEC response *peak*(ΔB^{NORM}),under elastic stress; (b) Non-normalised PEC response *max*($\Delta B^{NON-NORM}$) under elastic stress, a) Normalised PEC response *peak*(ΔB^{NORM}) under plastic strain (b) Non-normalised PEC response *max*($\Delta B^{NON-NORM}$) under plastic strain

Figure 5b shows the change in MBE_{ENERGY} for plastic stress. The MBE_{ENERGY} exhibits a large increase in the early stages of plastic deformation indicating a change in the domain structure due to the development of domain wall pinning sites, followed by a slower increase in MBE_{ENERGY} as applied strain increases. Figure 5d shows the development of the MBE profile for an increase in plastic stress. It can be seen from the plot that as plastic deformation increases, the overall amplitude of the MBE profile increases, corresponding to the increase in MBE_{ENERGY}. It can also be seen that the increase in overall amplitude is coupled with a shift in peak position with respect to the excitation voltage. This change in the MBE profile is due to the development of material dislocations increasing domain wall pinning sites, leading to higher energy MBE activity later in the excitation cycle. Examination of this in peak position has shown that it has a strong correlation to the stress/strain curve in the plastic region.

The dependence of the MBE peak position qualitatively agrees with the dependence of $max(\Delta B^{NON\text{-}NORM})$ as a function of strain shown in Figure 4d. These dependencies decrease according to the tensile characteristics in the yielding region and therefore it has the same value for two different strains, which makes it difficult to quantify the PD. However the dependence of $peak(\Delta B^{NORM})$ as function of strain, shown in Figure 4c, increases in the same region which provides complimentary information and enables PD characterisation using two features proportional to the magnetic permeability and electrical conductivity respectively.

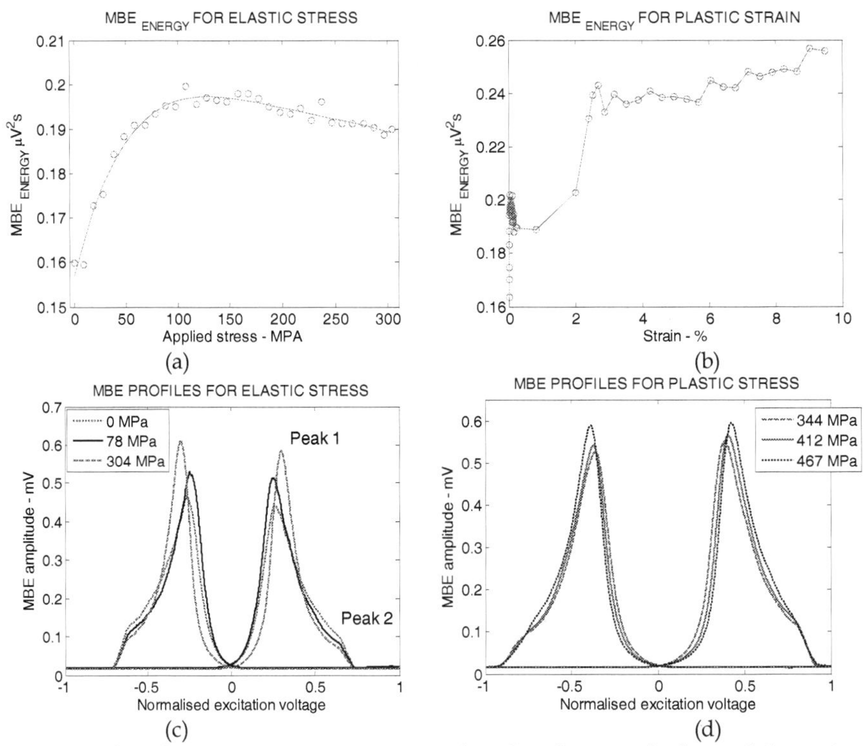

Fig. 5. Results of MBE measurements on steel under elastic and plastic deformation; a) MBE_{ENERGY} for elastic stress, b) MBE_{ENERGY} for plastic strain, c) MBE profiles for elastic stress, c) MBE profiles for plastic stress

These results illustrate the complementary nature of these two electromagnetic NDE techniques. PEC can be used for simple stress measurement, but to gain a full picture of the microstructural changes in the material, MBE profile analysis should be employed. Thus, fusion of PEC and MBE in a single system, with a common excitation device and a combined MBE/PEC pickup coil has the potential to provide comprehensive material assessment. This fusion technique has been used for the second Round Robin test organised by UNMNDE (*Universal Network for Magnetic Non-Destructive Evaluation*) for the characterisation of material degradation and ageing

3. Sensor fusion for electromagnetic NDE

Many attempts have been made at sensor and data fusion for NDE applications, with varying levels of success. Previous work[9] reports the development of a dual probe system containing an electromagnetic acoustic transducer (EMAT) and a pulsed eddy current (PEC) transducer. EMATs have excellent bulk inspection capabilities, but surface and near surface cracks can be problematic, whereas the PEC system can accurately characterise surface breaking cracks (as well as deep subsurface ones), thus PEC data was used to characterise near surface defects and EMAT data was used to characterise deep defects. The nature of PEC means that it also lends itself to the extraction of different features from the same signal. Hilbert transform and analytic representation are used to extract a variety of features from the PEC signal in order to characterise metal loss and subsurface defects in aluminium samples. Paper [12] reports the influence of duty cycle on the ability to detect holes and EDM notches beneath rivet heads in subsurface layers of stratified samples. The works highlight the gains that can be made from feature fusion if clear correlations are established between material / defect properties and signal features prior to fusion.

MBE has the capability to provide stress and microstructure information, but has a low measurement depth (up to 1 mm), a weak correlation with defects and the determination of exact correlations between signal features and material properties can be difficult without a full range of calibration samples; consequently the combination of MBE with other inspection techniques has received some attention in recent years. Quality Network, Inc. (QNET), the marketing and services affiliate of the Fraunhofer Institute for Non-Destructive Testing (IZFP) has introduced the multi-parameter micro-magnetic microstructure testing system (3MA)[13]. The 3MA system is optimised to measure surface and subsurface hardness, residual stress, case depth and machining defects through simultaneous measurement of MBE, incremental permeability, tangential magnetic field strength and eddy current impedance. As 3MA is a commercial system, exact details of the 3MA operational parameters are not available, but it is implied in the literature that variations in excitation field strength and frequency is used to control measurement depth and the measured parameters are combined using a multiple regression technique.

Chady et al. have assessed the comparative strengths of MBE, ECT, flux leakage and Hysteresis loop measurement for the characterisation of fatigue failure through cyclic dynamic loading of S355J2G3 structural steel [14]. Pixel level fusion of the scan results from the different inspection techniques was performed and it was found that fusion of all the signals creates opportunity to detect and evaluate quantitatively a level of material degradation.

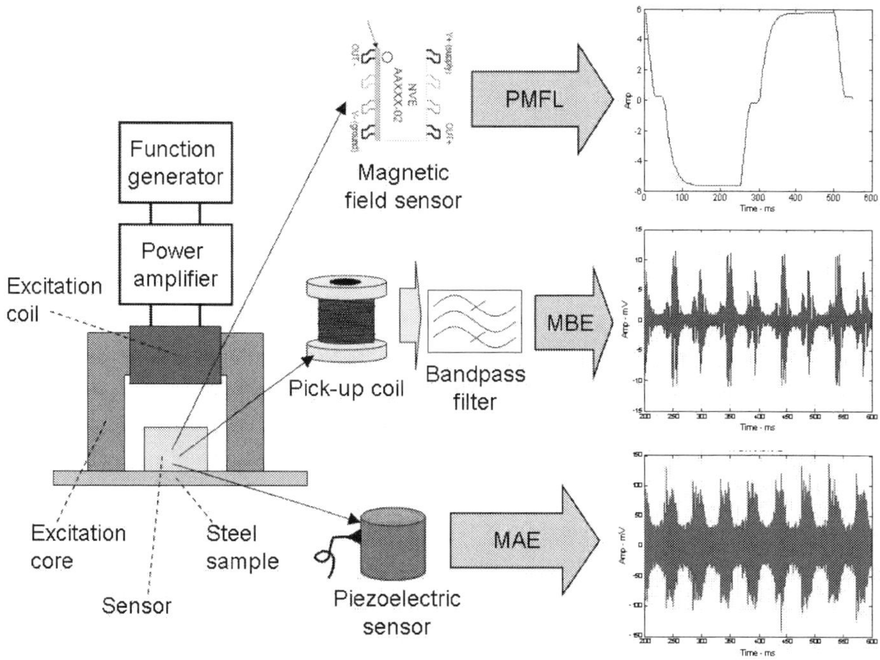

Fig. 6. Sensor fusion for comprehensive evaluation of defects and material properties

In addition to the sensor or data fusion above, Figure 6 shows an example of how sensor fusion can be used to implement a comprehensive material assessment system. A common excitation device is used to apply an electromagnetic field to the material under assessment and the response of the material is measured in several different ways. Firstly, a magnetic field sensor, operating as a pulsed magnetic flux leakage (PMFL)(15) sensing device, is used to measure the tangential magnetic field. This signal is analysed to extract information and quantify any surface, subsurface or opposite side defects which may be present. Secondly, the field at the surface of the material is measured using a coil, the measured signal is then band-pass filtered to reject the low frequency envelope and isolate the Barkhausen emission signal. This can then be used to characterise surface material changes, such as surface residual stresses and microstructural changes, i.e. degradation, corrosion, grinding burn. Using MBE, these changes can be quantified up to a depth of around 1mm. Bulk stress/microstructure changes are quantified using a piezoelectric sensor to measure magneto-acoustic emission, thus by comparing MBE and MAE measurements(16), bulk and surface changes can be separated and quantified.

The capability to simultaneously measure defects and surrounding stresses is especially useful where stress corrosion cracking (SCC) is expected. Residual stress concentrations, along with information on existing cracks and their surrounding stresses can be used to identify sites of potential future failure by identifying crack precursors.

4. Conclusions

Sensor fusion for electromagnetic NDE at different stages and levels has been discussed and three case studies for fusion at sensor and feature levels have been investigated. Instead of applying innovative mathematical techniques to utilise multiple sensors to improve the fidelity of defect and material characterisation, physics based sensor fusion is investigated. It has been shown that the three types of sensing system fusion, feature selection and integration and information combination for decision making in Quantitative NDE and material characterisation have different complementary strengths. Our future research efforts will explore the platform of features (parameters) of the signatures from the multimodal sensor data spaces using physical models and mathematic techniques for different engineering and medical challenges, including quantitative non-destructive evaluation, structural health monitoring, target detection and classification, and non-invasive diagnostics.

Acknowledgement

The Authors would like to thank the EPSRC for funding the work through EP/E005071/1 and EP/F023324/1, and the Royal Academy of Engineering (RAEng) for the Global Research Award "Global research and robin tests on magnetic non-destructive evaluation" awarded to Professor Gui Yun Tian.

5. References

1. P J Withers, M Turski, L Edwards, P J Bouchard and D J Buttle, 'Recent advances in residual stress measurement', Int. Journal of Pressure Vessels and Piping, Vol. 85, No. 3, pp. 118-127, 2008.
2. J W Wilson, G Y Tian and S Barrans, 'Residual magnetic field sensing for stress measurement', Sensors and Actuators A: Physical, Vol. 135, No. 2, pp. 381-387, 2007.
3. Gros X. Emanuel, Applications of NDT Data Fusion, Kluwer Academic Publishers, 2001.
4. J. Wilson, G.Y. Tian, I.Z. Abidin, Suixian Yang, D. Almond, Pulsed eddy current thermography: system development and evaluation, Insight - Non-Destructive Testing and Condition Monitoring, Volume: 52, Issue: 2 February 2010, 87-90
5. J. Wilson, G.Y. Tian, I.Z. Abidin, S. Yang, D. Almond, Modelling and evaluation of eddy current stimulated thermography, Nondestructive Testing and Evaluation, pp. 1 - 14, 2010.
6. V. Kaftandjian, Y. Min Zhu, O. Dupuis, and D. Babot, ' The Combined Use of the Evidence Theory and Fuzzy Logic for Improving Multimodal Nondestructive Testing Systems', IEEE Transaction on Instrumentation and Measurement , Vol. 54, No. 5, 2005.
7. X. Gros, Z. Liu, K. Tsukada, and K. Hanasaki, 'Experimenting with Pixel-Level NDT Data Fusion Techniques', IEEE Transaction on Instrumentation and Measurement, Vol. 49, No. 5, 2000.

8. Z. Liu, D. Forsyth, M. Safizadeh, and A. Fahr, 'A Data-Fusion Scheme for Quantitative Image Analysis by Using Locally Weighted Regression and Dempster-Shafer Theory', IEEE Transaction on Instrumentation and Measurement, Vol. 57, No. 11, 2008.
9. R.S. Edwards, A. Sophian, S. Dixon, G.Y. Tian, Data fusion for defect characterisation using a dual probe system, Sensors and Actuators, A: Physical 144 (1), 2008, pp. 222-228.
10. Tianlu Chen, Gui Yun Tian, Ali Sophian, Pei Wen Que, Feature extraction and selection for defect classification of pulsed eddy current NDT, NDT & E International, Volume 41, Issue 6, September 2008, Pages 467-476.
11. Y. Yin, G.Y. Tian, G.F. Yin, A.M. Luo, Defect identification and classification for digital X-ray images, Applied Mechanics and Materials 10-12, 2008, pp. 543-547.
12. Ilham Zainal Abidin, Catalin Mandache, Gui Yun Tian, Maxim Morozov, Pulsed eddy current testing with variable duty cycle on rivet joints, *NDT & E International, Volume 42, Issue 7, October 2009, Pages 599-605.*
13. Dobmann, G., Altpeter, I., Wolter, B. and Kern, R., 'Industrial Applications of 3MA - Micromagnetic Multiparameter Microstructure and Stress Analysis', 5th Int. Conference Structural Integrity of Welded Structures (ISCS2007), Timisora, Romania, 20-21 Nov 2007.
14. Chady, T., Psuj, G., Todaka, T. and Borkowski, B., 'Evaluation of fatigue-loaded steel samples using fusion of electromagnetic methods', Journal of Magnetism and Magnetic Materials, Vol. 310(2), Mar. 2007, pp. 2737-2739.
15. .W. Wilson and G.Y. Tian, Pulsed electromagnetic methods for defect detection and characterisation, NDT & E International, Vol. 40(4), Jun 2007, pp. 275-283.
16. J.W. Wilson, V. Moorthy, G.Y. Tian and B.A. Shaw, Magneto-acoustic emission and magnetic Barkhausen emission for case depth measurement in En36 gear steel, IEEE Transactions on Magnetics, Vol. 45(1), Jan 2009, pp. 177-183.

21

Iterative Multiscale Fusion and Night Vision Colorization of Multispectral Images

Yufeng Zheng
Alcorn State University
USA

1. Introduction

Multispectral images usually present complimentary information such as visual-band imagery and infrared imagery (near infrared or long wave infrared). There is strong evidence that the fused multispectral imagery increases the reliability of interpretation (Rogers & Wood, 1990; Essock et al., 2001); whereas the colorized multispectral imagery improves observer performance and reaction times (Toet et al. 1997; Varga, 1999; Waxman et al., 1996). A fused image in grayscale can be automatically analyzed by computers (for target recognition); while a colorized image in color can be easily interpreted by human users (for visual analysis).

Imagine a nighttime navigation task that may be executed by an aircraft equipped with a multisenor imaging system. Analyzing the combined or synthesized multisensory data will be more convenient and more efficient than simultaneously monitoring multispectral images such as visual-band imagery (e.g., image intensified, II), near infrared (NIR) imagery, and infrared (IR) imagery. In this chapter, we will discuss how to synthesize the multisensory data using image fusion and night vision colorization techniques in order to improve the effectiveness and utility of multisensor imagery. It is anticipated that the successful applications of such an image synthesis approach will lead to improved performance of remote sensing, nighttime navigation, target detection, and situational awareness. This image synthesis approach involves two main techniques, image fusion and night vision colorization, which is reviewed as follows, respectively.

Image fusion combines multiple-source imagery by integrating complementary data in order to enhance the information apparent in the respective source images, as well as to increase the reliability of interpretation. This results in more accurate data (Keys et al., 1990) and increased utility (Rogers & Wood, 1990; Essock et al., 1999). In addition, it has been reported that fused data provides far more robust aspects of operational performance such as increased confidence, reduced ambiguity, improved reliability and improved classification (Rogers & Wood, 1990; Essock et al., 2001). A general framework of image fusion can be found in Reference (Pohl & Genderen, 1998). In this chapter, our discussions focus on *pixel-level* image fusion. A quantitative evaluation of fused image quality is important for an objective comparison between the respective fusion algorithms, which measures the amount of useful information and the amount of artifacts introduced in the fused image.

Two common fusion methods are the discrete wavelet transform (DWT) (Pu & Ni, 2000; Nunez et al., 1999) and various pyramids (such as Laplacian, contrast, gradient, and morphological pyramids) (Jahard et al., 1997; Ajazzi et al., 1998), which both are *multiscale fusion* methods. Recently, an advanced wavelet transform (*a*DWT) method (Zheng et al., 2004) has been proposed, which incorporates principal component analysis (PCA) and morphological processing into a regular DWT fusion algorithm. The *a*DWT method can produce a better fused image in comparison with pyramid methods and regular DWT methods. Experiments also reveal an important relationship between the fused image quality and the wavelet properties. That is, a higher level of DWT decomposition (with smaller image resolution at a higher scale) or a lower order of wavelets (with a shorter length) usually results in a more sharpened fused image. This means that we can use the level of DWT decomposition and the length of a wavelet as the control parameters of an *iterative* DWT-based fusion algorithm.

So far, only a few metrics are available for quantitative evaluation of the quality of fused imagery. For example, the root mean square error (RMSE) may be the natural measure of image quality if a "ground truth" image is available. Unfortunately, for realistic image fusion applications there are no ground truths. Piella et al. (2003) presented an image fusion metric, the image quality index (IQI), which measures how similar the fused image is to both input images. More recently, Zheng et al. (2007) proposed an image quality metric, termed as "the ratio of SF error (rSFe)", which is a relative measurement regardless of the type of image being analyzed. The rSFe metric is defined upon "spatial frequency" (SF) (Eskicioglu & Fisher, 1995). In addition, the rSFe value can show the fusion status (i.e., under-fused or over-fused). Refer to Section 2.3 for a review of fusion metrics.

On the other hand, a *night vision colorization* technique can produce colorized imagery with a naturalistic and stable color appearance by processing multispectral night-vision imagery. Although appropriately false-colored imagery is often helpful for human observers in improving their performance on scene classification, and reaction time tasks (Essock et al., 1999; Waxman et al., 1996), inappropriate color mappings can also be detrimental to human performance (Toet & IJspeert, 2001; Varga, 1999). A possible reason is lack of physical color constancy (Varga, 1999). Another drawback with false coloring is that observers need specific training with each of the unnatural false color schemes so that they can correctly and quickly recognize objects; whereas with colorized nighttime imagery rendered with natural colors, users should be able to readily recognize and identify objects.

Toet (2003) proposed a night vision (NV) colorization method that transfers the natural color characteristics of daylight imagery into multispectral NV images. Essentially, Toet's natural color-mapping method matches the statistical properties (i.e., mean and standard deviation) of the NV imagery to that of a natural daylight color image (manually selected as the "target" color distribution). However, this color-mapping method colorizes the image regardless of scene content, and thus the accuracy of the coloring is very much dependent on how well the target and source images are matched. Specifically, Toet's method weights the local regions of the source image by the "global" color statistics of the target image, and thus will yield less naturalistic results (e.g., biased colors) for images containing regions that differ significantly in their colored content. Another concern of Toet's *"global-coloring"* method is that the scene matching between the source and target is performed manually. To address the aforementioned bias problem in global coloring, Zheng et al. (2005; 2008) presented a *"local coloring"* method that can colorize the NV images more like daylight imagery. The local-coloring method will render the multispectral images with natural colors segment by segment (also referred to as "segmentation-based"), and also provide automatic association between the source and target images (i.e., avoiding the manual scene-matching in global coloring).

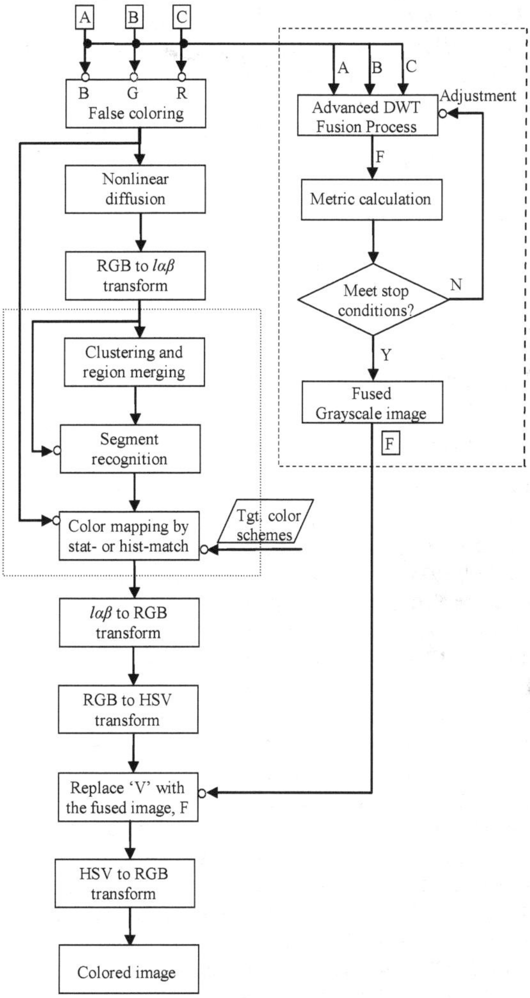

Fig. 1. The diagram of image fusion and night vision colorization. The *iterative image fusion* (shown within the right dashed box) takes multispectral images (A, B, C) as inputs, and fuses them into a grayscale image, F. The *night vision colorization* (shown in the left column) takes the same multispectral images (A, B, C) and also the fused image F as inputs, and generates a colored image. Three steps shown inside a dotted rectangle are performed in the *lαβ* color space.

In this chapter, a joint approach that incorporates image fusion and night vision colorization is presented to synthesize and enhance multisensor imagery. This joint approach provides two sets of synthesized images, fused image in grayscale and colored image in colors using the image fusion procedure and night vision colorization procedure. As shown in Fig. 1, the *image fusion* (shown in the right dashed box) takes multispectral images (A, B, C) as inputs and fuses them into a grayscale image (F). The *night vision colorization* (shown in the left column) takes the same multispectral images (A, B, C) and the fused image (F) as an input and eventually generates a colored image. The image fusion process can take more than three bands of images; whereas the night vision colorization can accept three (or less) bands of images. If there are more than three bands of images available, (e.g. II, NIR, MWIR (medium-wave IR) and LWIR (long-wave IR)), we may choose a visual band image (II) and two bands of IR images for the following colorization (refer to Section 4 for a detailed discussion). Two procedures are discussed respectively in Sections 2 and 3. Note that in this chapter, the term "multispectral" is used equivalently to "multisensory"; and by default the term "IR" means "LWIR" unless specified.

The remainder of this chapter is organized as follows: The multiscale image fusion methods are discussed in Section 2. Image quality metrics are also reviewed in this section. The night vision colorization methods are fully described in Section 3. The experiments and discussions are given in Section 4. Finally, conclusions are made in Section 5.

2. Multiscale image fusion

Image fusion serves to combine multiple-source imagery using advanced image processing techniques. In this section, Laplacian pyramid and DWT fusion methods are briefly reviewed, then an advanced discrete wavelet transform (*a*DWT) method is introduced. Next, several established fusion metrics are discussed. With an established fusion metric, an iterative *a*DWT fusion process (i.e., *a*DWTi) can be formed. Finally, a newly proposed orientation based fusion is described. The orientation based fusion is performed by using Gabor wavelet transforms, which may be considered a multiscale procedure in frequency domain.

2.1 Laplacian pyramid

The Laplacian pyramid was first introduced as a model for binocular fusion in human stereo vision (Burt & Adelson, 1985), where the implementation used a Laplacian pyramid and a maximum selection rule at each point of the pyramid transform. Essentially, the procedure involves a set of band-pass copies of an image is referred to as the Laplacian pyramid due to its similarity to a Laplacian operator. Each level of the Laplacian pyramid is recursively constructed from its lower level by applying the following four basic steps: blurring (low-pass filtering); sub-sampling (reduce size); interpolation (expand); and differencing (to subtract two images pixel by pixel) (Burt & Adelson, 1983). In the Laplacian pyramid, the lowest level of the pyramid is constructed from the original image.

2.2 The advanced DWT method

The regular DWT method is a multi-scale analysis method. In a regular DWT fusion process, DWT coefficients from two input images are fused pixel-by-pixel by choosing the average of the approximation coefficients (i.e., the low-pass filtered image) at the highest transform scale; and the larger absolute value of the detail coefficients (i.e., the high-pass filtered images) at each transform scale. Then, an inverse DWT is performed to obtain a fused image. At each DWT scale of a particular image, the DWT coefficients of a 2D image consist of four parts: approximation, horizontal detail, vertical detail, and diagonal detail. In the *advanced DWT* (*a*DWT) method (Zheng et al., 2004), we apply PCA to the two input images' approximation coefficients at the highest transform scale. That is, we fuse them using the principal eigenvector (corresponding to the larger eigenvalue) derived from the two original images, as described in Eq. (1) below:

$$C_F = (a_1 \cdot C_A + a_2 \cdot C_B)/(a_1 + a_2), \tag{1}$$

where C_A and C_B are approximation coefficients (image matrices) transformed from input images A and B. C_F represents the fused coefficients; a_1 and a_2 are the elements (scalars) of the principal eigenvector, which are computed by analyzing the original input images. Note that the denominator in Eq. (1) is used for normalization so that the fused image has the same energy distribution as the original input images.

For the detail coefficients (the other three quarters of the coefficients) at each transform scale, the larger absolute values are selected, followed by neighborhood morphological processing, which serves to verify the selected pixels using a "filling" and "cleaning" operation (i.e., the operation fills or removes isolated pixels locally). Such an operation (similar to smoothing) can increase the consistency of coefficient selection thereby reducing the distortion in the fused image.

2.3 Image quality metrics

2.3.1 Image quality index

The *image quality index* (IQI) was introduced by Wang and Bovik (2002). Given two sequences $x = (x_1, \ldots, x_n)$ and $y = (y_1, \ldots, y_n)$, let $\bar{x}$ denote the mean of x, and σ_x and σ_{xy} denote the variance of x and covariance of x and y, respectively. The global quality index of two vectors is defined as

$$Q_0(x,y) = \frac{\sigma_{xy}}{\sigma_x \sigma_y} \cdot \frac{2\overline{xy}}{(\bar{x}^2 + \bar{y}^2)} \cdot \frac{2\sigma_x \sigma_y}{(\sigma_x^2 + \sigma_y^2)} = \frac{4\sigma_{xy}\overline{xy}}{(\bar{x}^2 + \bar{y}^2)(\sigma_x^2 + \sigma_y^2)}, \tag{2}$$

Note that $Q_0 \in [0, 1]$ can reflect the correlation (similarity), luminance distortion, and contrast distortion between vectors x and y, which correspond to the three components (factors) in Eq. (2). Keep in mind that for the image quality evaluation with Q_0, the values x_i, y_i are positive grayscale values. The maximum value $Q_0 = 1$ is achieved when x and y are identical.

Then, the fused image quality metric (i.e., the image quality index) (Wang & Bovik, 2002; Piella & Heijmans, 2003) can be defined as

$$Q_w = \lambda Q_0(I_A, I_F) + (1-\lambda)\, Q_0(I_B, I_F), \tag{3}$$

where subscripts A, B, and F denote the input images (A, B) and the fused images (F); and weight $\lambda = S(I_A) \,/\, [S(I_A) + S(I_B)]$. $S(I_A)$ denotes the "saliency" of image A, which may be the local variance, $S(I_A) = \sigma_A$. Since image signals are generally non-stationary, it is more appropriate to measure the weighted image quality index Q_w over local regions (e.g., using a sliding window) and then combine the different results into a single measure.

2.3.2 Spatial frequency and the ratio of spatial frequency error

The metric "*spatial frequency*" (SF) (Eskicioglu & Fisher, 1995; Li et al., 2001) is used to measure the overall activity level of an image. The spatial frequency of an image is defined as

$$SF = \sqrt{[(RF)^2 + (CF)^2 + (MDF)^2 + (SDF)^2]/(4-1)}, \tag{4}$$

where RF and CF are row frequency and column frequency, respectively; and MDF and SDF represent the main diagonal SF and the secondary diagonal SF. Eq. (4) is a revision of the original definition (Zheng et al., 2007) for spatial frequency by introducing two diagonal SFs and also the normalization of the degree of freedom. Four directional spatial frequencies are defined as follows:

$$RF = \sqrt{\frac{1}{MN}\sum_{i=1}^{M}\sum_{j=2}^{N}[I(i,j) - I(i,j-1)]^2}, \tag{5a}$$

$$CF = \sqrt{\frac{1}{MN}\sum_{j=1}^{N}\sum_{i=2}^{M}[I(i,j) - I(i-1,j)]^2}; \tag{5b}$$

$$MDF = \sqrt{w_d \cdot \frac{1}{MN}\sum_{i=2}^{M}\sum_{j=2}^{N}[I(i,j) - I(i-1,j-1)]^2}, \tag{5c}$$

$$SDF = \sqrt{w_d \cdot \frac{1}{MN}\sum_{j=1}^{N-1}\sum_{i=2}^{M}[I(i,j) - I(i-1,j+1)]^2}; \tag{5d}$$

where $w_d = 1/\sqrt{2}$ in Eqs. (5c-d) is a distance weight; similarly, it can be considered that $w_d = 1$ in Eqs. (5a-b). M and N are the image size (in pixels). Notice that the term "spatial frequency" is computed in the spatial domain as defined in Eqs. (4-5), does not correspond with the Fourier transform where the spatial frequency is measured in frequency domain with the unit of "cycles per degree" or "cycles per millimeter".

With Eq. (4) we can calculate the SFs of input images (SF_A and SF_B) or of the fused image (SF_F). Now we determine how to calculate a reference SF (SF_R) with which the SF_F can be compared. The four differences (inside square brackets) defined in Eqs. (5a-d) are actually the four first-order gradients along four directions at that pixel, denoted as *Grad*[I(i,j)]. The four reference gradients can be obtained by taking the maximum of absolute gradient values between input image A and B along four directions:

$$Grad^D[I_R(i,j)] = \max\{|Grad^D[I_A(i,j)]|, |Grad^D[I_B(i,j)]|\},$$

for each of four directions, i.e., D = {H, V, MD, SD}, (6)

where 'D' denotes one of four directions (Horizontal, Vertical, Main Diagonal, and Secondary Diagonal). Substituting the differences (defined inside square brackets) in Eqs. (5a-d) with $Grad^D[I_R(i,j)]$, four directional reference SFs (i.e., RF_R, CF_R, MDF_R and SDF_R) can be calculated. For example, the reference row frequency, RF_R, can be calculated as follows:

$$RF_R = \sqrt{\frac{1}{MN}\sum_{i=1}^{M}\sum_{j=2}^{N}[Grad^H(I_R(i,j))]^2}. \tag{7}$$

Similar to Eq. (4), the overall *reference spatial frequency*, SF_R, can be computed by combining four directional reference SFs (SF_R is not formulated here). Note that the notation of

"*Grad*^{H}[I_R(i,j)]" is interpreted as "the horizontal reference gradient at point (i,j)", and no reference image is needed to compute the SF_R value.
Finally, the *ratio of SF error* (rSFe) is defined as follows:

$$rSFe = (SF_F - SF_R) / SF_R, \quad (8)$$

where SF_F is the spatial frequency of the fused image; whereas SF_R is the reference spatial frequency. Clearly, an ideal fusion has rSFe = 0; that is, the smaller the rSFe's absolute value, the better the fused image. Furthermore, rSFe > 0 means that an *over-fused* image, with some distortion or noise introduced, has resulted; rSFe < 0 denotes that an *under-fused* image, with some meaningful information lost, has been produced.

2.4 The iterative *a*DWT method

The IQI (Wang & Bovik, 2002; Piella & Heijmans, 2003) value is calculated to measure the fused image quality by the *a*DWT. It is then fed back to the fusion algorithm (*a*DWT) in order to achieve a better fusion by directing the parameter adjustment. Previous experiments (Zheng et al., 2004) showed that a higher level DWT decomposition (with lower image resolution at higher scale) or a lower order of wavelets (with shorter length) usually resulted in a more sharpened fused image. The IQI value usually tends to be larger for a fused image with a lower level decomposition or a higher order of wavelets. This means that we can use the level of DWT decomposition and the length of a wavelet as control parameters of an *iterative aDWT* (*a*DWTi) algorithm. With the definition of IQI, we know that it has an ideal value, 1, i.e., $0 < IQI \leq 1$. The level of DWT decomposition (L_d) is a more significant factor than the length of wavelet (L_w) in the sense of the amplitude of IQI changing. The iterative *a*DWT algorithm optimized by the IQI is denoted as *a*DWTi-IQI. Similarly, *a*DWTi-rSFe means an iterative *a*DWT optimized by rSFe metric.
Of course, some termination conditions are needed in order to stop the fusion iteration. The following conditions are demonstrated with IQI metric. For example, the fusion iteration stops when (1) it converges at the ideal value - the absolute value of (IQI-1) is smaller than a designated small tolerance error, i.e. $|IQI-1| < \varepsilon$; (2) there is no significant change of the IQI value between two consecutive iterations; (3) the IQI value is generally decreasing for subsequent iterations; or (4) the parameters' boundaries are reached. In implementing an iterative fusion procedure, appropriate parameters' initializations and boundaries' restrictions should be designated upon the definition of parameters and the context, which will help reduce the number of iterations (N_i). The details of implementation are described in Reference (Zheng et al., 2005).
The iterative *a*DWT algorithm hereby described can be combined with the rSFe metric (*a*DWTi-rSFe) (Zheng et al., 2007) or other fusion IQ metrics.

2.5 Orientation based fusion

Gabor wavelet transforms (GWT) have received considerable attentions because the characteristics of certain cells in the visual cortex of some mammals can be approximated by these filters. Further, biological research suggests that the primary visual cortex performs a similar orientational and Fourier space decomposition (Jones & Palmer, 1987), so they seem to be sensible for a technical vision or a recognition system. The details of GWT implementation are described elsewhere (Zheng & Agyepong, 2007).

In the *orientation-based fusion* algorithm, the Gabor wavelet transforms are performed with each input image at M spatial frequencies by N orientations, notated as $M \times N$. For a 16×16 GWT, a total of 256 pairs (magnitudes and phases) of filtered images are extracted with 256 Gabor wavelets (also called Gabor kernels, or Gabor filter bank) distributed along 16 bands (located from low to high frequencies) by 16 orientations (0.00°, 11.25°, 22.50°, ..., 157.50°, 168.75°). The size of each Gabor filter should match the image size being analyzed. If all input images are of the same size, then the set of 256 Gabor wavelets are only computed once. Instead of doing spatial convolution, the GWT can be accomplished in frequency domain by using fast Fourier transforms (FFT) that will significantly speed up the process.

Many GWT coefficients are produced, for example, 512 coefficients (256 magnitudes plus 256 phases) per pixel in an 16×16 GWT. Suppose a set of $M \times N$ GWT are performed with two input images (I_A and I_B). At each frequency band (b = 1, 2, …, M), the index of *maximal* GWT magnitude between two images is selected pixel by pixel; and then two index frequencies, $H_A(b)$ and $H_B(b)$, are calculated as its index accumulation along N orientations, respectively. The final H_A and H_B are the weighted summations through M bands, where the band weights (W_b) are given empirically. Eventually, the fused image (I_F) is computed as

$$I_F = (I_A .{*}\ H_A + I_B .{*}\ H_B)/(H_A + H_B), \quad (9)$$

where '.*' denotes element-by-element product of two arrays; and

$$H_A = \sum_{b=1}^{M} W_b H_A(b)', \quad (10a)$$

$$H_B = \sum_{b=1}^{M} W_b H_B(b)', \quad (10b)$$

where W_b are the band weights decided empirically. The middle frequency bands (Hollingsworth et al., 2009) in GWT (by suppressing the extreme low and extreme high frequency bands) usually give a better representation and consistency in image fusion, especially for noisy input images.

The orientation-based fusion algorithm can be further varied by either keeping DC (direct current) or suppressing DC in GWT. "Keeping DC" will produce a contrast-smooth image (suitable for contrast-unlike images); while "suppressing DC" (i.e., forcing DC = 0.0) will result a sharpened fusion (suitable for contrast-alike images). *Color fusion* can be achieved by replacing the red channel of a color image with the fused image of red channel and LWIR image, which is suitable for poorly illuminated color images.

3. Night vision colorization

The aim of *night vision colorization* is to give multispectral (NV) images (source) the appearance of normal daylight color images. The proposed "local coloring" method renders the multispectral images segment-by-segment with the statistical properties of natural scenes using the color mapping technique. The main steps of the *local coloring* procedure are given below: (1) A false-color image (source image) is first formed by assigning multispectral (two or three band) images to three RGB channels. The false-colored images usually have an unnatural color appearance. (2) Then, the false-colored image is segmented using the features of color properties, and the techniques of nonlinear diffusion, clustering, and region merging. (3) The averaged mean, standard deviation, and histogram of a large sample of natural color images are used as the target color properties for each color scheme.

The target color schemes are grouped by their contents and colors such as plants, mountain, roads, sky, water, buildings, people, etc. (4) The association between the source region segments and target color schemes is carried out automatically utilizing a classification algorithm such as the nearest neighbor paradigm. (5) The color mapping procedures (statistic-matching and histogram-matching) are carried out to render natural colors onto the false-colored image segment by segment. (6) The mapped image is then transformed back to the RGB space. (7) Finally, the mapped image is transformed into HSV (Hue-Saturation-Value) space and the "value" component of the mapped image is replaced with the "fused NV image" (a grayscale image). Note that this fused image replacement is necessary to allow the colorized image to have a proper and consistent contrast.

3.1 Color space transform

In this section, the RGB to *LMS* (long-wave, medium-wave and short-wave) transform is discussed first. Then, an *lαβ* space is introduced from which the resulting data representation is compact and *symmetrical*, and provides a higher *decorrelation* than the second order. The reason for the color space transform is to decorrelate three color components (i.e., *l*, *α* and *β*) so that the manipulation (such as statistic matching and histogram matching) on each color component can be performed independently. Inverse transforms (*lαβ* space to the ***LMS*** and *LMS* to RGB) are needed to complete the proposed segmentation-based colorization, which are given elsewhere (Zheng & Essock, 2008).
The actual conversion (matrix) from RGB tristimulus to device-independent XYZ tristimulus values depends on the characteristics of the display being used. Fairchild (1998) suggested a "general" device-independent conversion (while non-priori knowledge about the display device) that maps white in the chromaticity diagram to white in the RGB space and vice versa.

$$\begin{bmatrix} X \\ Y \\ Z \end{bmatrix} = \begin{bmatrix} 0.5141 & 0.3239 & 0.1604 \\ 0.2651 & 0.6702 & 0.0641 \\ 0.0241 & 0.1228 & 0.8444 \end{bmatrix} \begin{bmatrix} R \\ G \\ B \end{bmatrix}. \tag{11}$$

The XYZ values can be converted to the *LMS* space using the following equation

$$\begin{bmatrix} L \\ M \\ S \end{bmatrix} = \begin{bmatrix} 0.3897 & 0.6890 & -0.0787 \\ -0.2298 & 1.1834 & 0.0464 \\ 0.0000 & 0.0000 & 1.0000 \end{bmatrix} \begin{bmatrix} X \\ Y \\ Z \end{bmatrix}. \tag{12}$$

A logarithmic transform is employed here to reduce the data skew that existed in the above color space:

$$\boldsymbol{L} = \log L, \quad \boldsymbol{M} = \log M, \quad \boldsymbol{S} = \log S. \tag{13}$$

Ruderman et al. (1998) presented a color space, named *lαβ* (Luminance-Alpha-Beta), which can decorrelate the three axes in the ***LMS*** space:

$$\begin{bmatrix} l \\ \alpha \\ \beta \end{bmatrix} = \begin{bmatrix} 0.5774 & 0.5774 & 0.5774 \\ 0.4082 & 0.4082 & -0.8165 \\ 1.4142 & -1.4142 & 0 \end{bmatrix} \begin{bmatrix} \boldsymbol{L} \\ \boldsymbol{M} \\ \boldsymbol{S} \end{bmatrix}. \tag{14}$$

The three axes can be considered as an achromatic direction (*l*), a yellow-blue opponent direction (*α*), and a red-green opponent direction (*β*). The *lαβ* space has the characteristics of compact, symmetrical and decorrelation, which highly facilitate the subsequent process of color-mapping (see Section 3.4).

3.2 Image segmentation

The nonlinear diffusion procedure has proven to be equivalent to an adaptive smoothing process (Barash & Comaniciu, 2004). The diffusion is applied to the false-colored NV image here to obtain a smooth image, which significantly facilitates the subsequent segmentation process. The clustering process is performed separately on each color component in the *lαβ* color space to form a set of "clusters". The region merging process is used to merge the fragmental clusters into meaningful "segments" (based on a similarity metric defined in 3D *lαβ* color space) that will be used for the color-mapping process.

3.2.1 Adaptive smoothing with nonlinear diffusion

Nonlinear diffusion methods have been proven as powerful methods in the denoising and smoothing of image intensities while retaining and enhancing edges. Barash and Comaniciu (2004) have proven that nonlinear diffusion is equivalent to adaptive smoothing and bilateral filtering is obtained from an extended nonlinear diffusion. Nonlinear diffusion filtering was first introduced by Perona and Malik (1990). Basically, diffusion is a PDE (partial differential equation) method that involves two operators, smoothing and gradient, in 2D image space. The diffusion process smoothes the regions with lower gradients and stops the smoothing at region boundaries with higher gradients. Nonlinear diffusion means the smoothing operation depends on the region gradient distribution. For color image diffusion, three RGB components of a false-colored NV image are filtered separately (one by one). The number of colors in the diffused image will be significantly reduced and will benefit the subsequent image segmentation procedures - clustering and merging.

3.2.2 Image segmentation with clustering and region merging

The diffused false-colored image is transformed into the *lαβ* color space. Each component (l, α or β) of the diffused image is *clustered* in the *lαβ* space by individually analyzing its histogram. Specifically, for each intensity component (image) l, α or β, (i) normalize the intensity onto [0,1]; (ii) bin the normalized intensity to a certain number of levels N_{Bin} and perform the histogram analysis; (iii) with the histogram, locate local extreme values (i.e., peaks and valleys) and form a stepwise mapping function using the peaks and valleys; (iv) complete the clustering utilizing the stepwise mapping function.

The local extremes (peaks or valleys) are easily located by examining the crossover points of the first derivatives of histograms. Furthermore, "peaks" and "valleys" are expected to be interleaved (e.g., valley-peak-valley-…-peak-valley); otherwise, a new valley value can be calculated with the midpoint of two neighboring peaks. In addition, two-end boundaries are considered two special valleys. In summary, all intensities between two valleys in a histogram are squeezed in their peak intensity and the two end points in the histogram are treated as valleys (rather than peaks). If there are n peaks in a histogram, then an n-step mapping function is formed. If there are two or more valley values (including the special valley at the left end) at the left side of the leftmost peak, then use the special (extreme) valley intensity.

Clustering is done by separately analyzing three components (l, α & β) of the false-colored image, which may result in inconsistent clusters in the sense of colors. *Region merging* is necessary to incorporate the fragmental "clusters" into meaningful "segments" in the sense of colors, which will improve the color consistency in a colorized image. If two clusters are similar (i.e., $Q_w(x,y) > T_Q$ (a predefined threshold)), these two clusters will be merged. $Q_w(x,y)$ is a similarity metric (derived from the IQI metric described in Section 2.3.1) between two clusters, x and y, which is defined in the $l\alpha\beta$ color space as follows:

$$Q_w(x,y) = \sum_{k=\{l,\alpha,\beta\}} [w_k \cdot Q_k(x,y)], \tag{15a}$$

where w_k is a given weight for each color component. $Q_k(x,y)$ is formulated below:

$$Q_k(x,y) = \frac{2\overline{x}\overline{y}}{(\overline{x}^2 + \overline{y}^2)} \cdot \frac{2\sigma_x \sigma_y}{(\sigma_x^2 + \sigma_y^2)}, \tag{15b}$$

where $\overline{x}$ and σ_x are the mean and the standard deviation of cluster x in a particular component, respectively. Similar definitions are applied to cluster y. The sizes (i.e., areas) of two clusters (x and y) are usually unequal. Notice that $Q_k(x,y)$ is computed with regard to the diffused false-color image.

3.3 Automatic segment recognition

A *nearest neighbor* (NN) paradigm (Keysers et al., 2002) is demonstrated to classify the segments obtained from the preceding procedure (described in Section 3.2). To use the NN algorithm, a distance measure between two segments is needed. The similarity metric $Q_w(x,y)$ (as defined in Eqs. (15)) between two segments, x and y, is used as the distance measure. Thus, the closer two segments in $l\alpha\beta$ space, the larger their similarity.
Similar to a training process, a look up table (LUT) has to be built under supervision to classify a given segment ($\mathbf{s}_j$) into a known color group (C_i), i.e., $C_i = T(\mathbf{s}_j)$, ($i \leq j$), where $\mathbf{s}_j$ is a feature vector that distinguishingly describes each segment; C_i stands for a known color scheme (e.g., sky, clouds, plants, water, ground, roads, etc.); and T is a classification function (i.e., a trained classifier). We use segment color statistics (e.g., mean and deviation of each channel) as features (of six statistical variables). The statistical features ($\mathbf{s}_j$) are computed using the diffused false-color images and the color mapping process is carried out between a false-color segment and a daylight color scheme. The reason for using the diffused false-color images here is because the diffused images are less sensitive to noise. In a training stage, a set of multispectral NV images are analyzed and segmented such that a sequence of feature vectors, $\{\mathbf{s}_j\}$ can be computed and the LUT (mapping) between $\{\mathbf{s}_j\}$ and $\{C_i\}$ can be manually set up upon the experimental results. In a classifying (testing) stage, all $Q_w(\mathbf{x}_k, \mathbf{s}_j)$ values (for j = 1, 2, 3, …) are calculated, where x_k means the classifying segment and sj represents one of the existing segments from the training stage. Certainly, $\mathbf{x}_k$ is automatically classified into the color group of the largest Q_w (similarity). For example, if $Q_w(\mathbf{x}_1, \mathbf{s}_5)$ is the maximum, then the segment of $\mathbf{x}_1$ will be colorized using the color scheme $T(\mathbf{s}_5)$ that is the color used to render the segment of $\mathbf{s}_5$ in the training stage.

3.4 Color mapping

3.4.1 Statistic matching

A *"statistic matching"* is used to transfer the color characteristics from natural daylight imagery to false color night-vision imagery, which is formulated as:

$$I_C^k = (I_S^k - \mu_S^k) \cdot \frac{\sigma_T^k}{\sigma_S^k} + \mu_T^k, \qquad \text{for } k = \{\, l, \alpha, \beta \,\}, \tag{16}$$

where $\mathbf{I}_C$ is the colored image, $\mathbf{I}_S$ is the source (false-color) image in *lαβ* space; **μ** denotes the mean and **σ** denotes the standard deviation; the subscripts 'S' and 'T' refer to the source and target images, respectively; and the superscript '*k*' is one of the color components: { *l, α, β*}. After this transformation, the pixels comprising the multispectral source image have means and standard deviations that conform to the target daylight color image in *lαβ* space. The color-mapped image is transformed back to the RGB space through the inverse transforms (*lαβ* space to the ***LMS***, exponential transform from ***LMS*** to *LMS*, and *LMS* to RGB, refer to Eqs. (11-14)) (Zheng & Essock, 2008).

3.4.2 Histogram matching

Histogram matching (also referred to as histogram specification) is usually used to enhance an image when histogram equalization fails (Gonzalez & Woods, 2002). Given the shape of the histogram that we want the enhanced image to have, histogram matching can generate a processed image that has the specified histogram. In particular, by specifying the histogram of a target image (with daylight natural colors), a source image (with false colors) resembles the target image in terms of histogram distribution after histogram matching. Similar to statistic matching, histogram matching also serves for color mapping and is performed component-by-component in *lαβ* space. Histogram matching and statistic matching can be applied separately or jointly.

4. Experimental results and discussions

One pair of off-focal images (two clocks) captured at different focal planes (Fig. 2) and five pairs of multispectral images (Figs. 3-6 and Fig. 10) were tested and compared by using the presented multiscale image fusion algorithms and night vision colorization algorithm. Two-band images are image intensified (II) versus infrared (IR) as shown in Figs. 3-5, or visible versus IR image as shown in Fig. 6 and Fig. 10. Note that there was no post-processing imposed on the fused images. The fusion process illustrated here was accepting two input images. In fact, the fusion procedure can accept more than two input images (e.g., three or more images) that will go through the same fusion rules to yield a fused image.

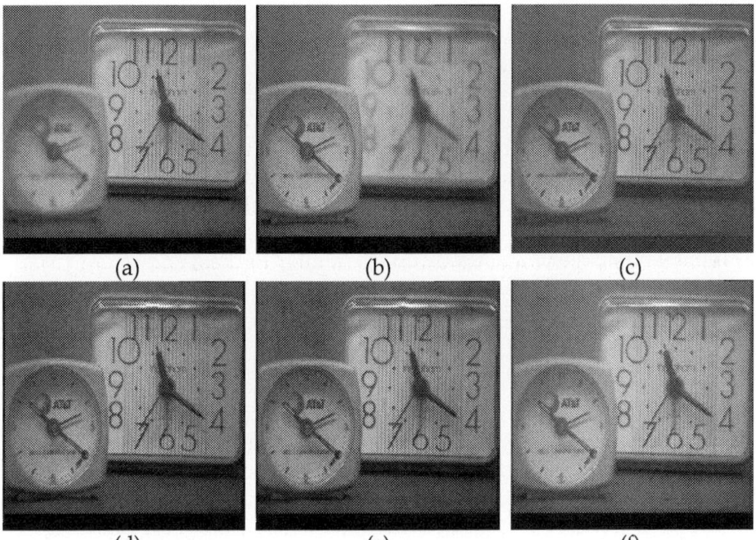

Fig. 2. Image fusion with off-focal image pair (512×512 pixels): (a) and (b) are the input images; (c) Fused image by Laplacian pyramid; (d) Fused image by *a*DWTi-IQI; (e) Fused image by *a*DWTi-rSFe; (f) Orientation-based fusion (16×16) without DC (i.e., suppressing DC). The IQI values of four fused images shown in (c, d, e, f) are 0.8887, 0.9272, 0.9222, *0.9391*.

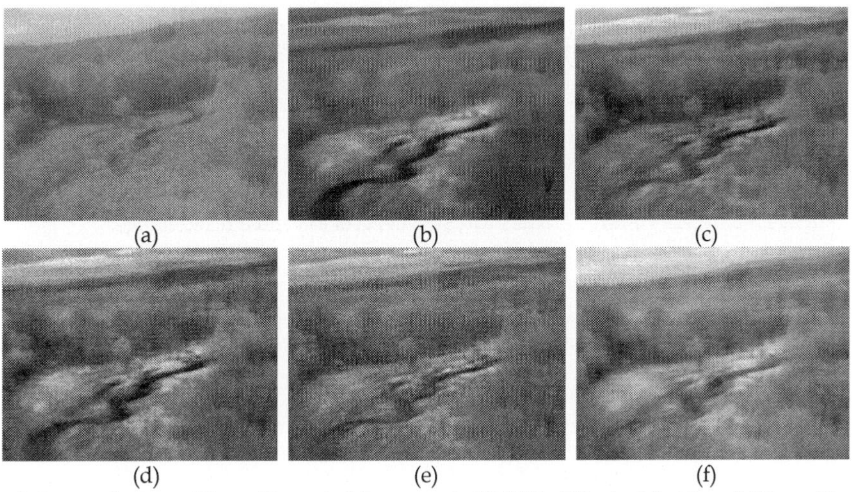

Fig. 3. Image fusion with multispectral image pair #1 (531×401 pixels): (a) and (b) are II and IR images; (c) Fused image by Laplacian pyramid; (d) Fused image by *a*DWTi-IQI; (e) Fused image by *a*DWTi-rSFe; (f) Orientation-based fusion (16×16). The IQI values of four fused images shown in (c, d, e, f) are 0.7680, *0.7768*, 0.7132, 0.7087.

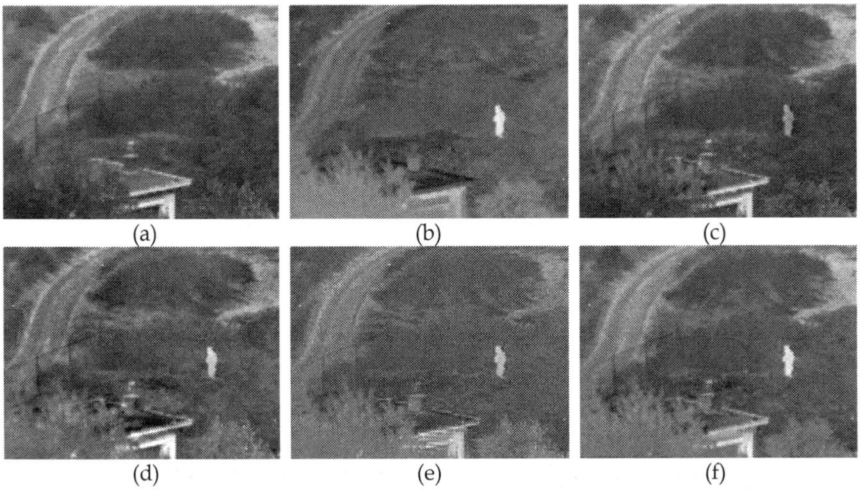

Fig. 4. Image fusion with multispectral image pair #2 (360×270 pixels): (a) and (b) are II and IR images; (c) Fused image by Laplacian pyramid; (d) Fused image by *a*DWTi-IQI; (e) Fused image by *a*DWTi-rSFe; (f) Orientation-based fusion (16×16). The IQI values of four fused images shown in (c, d, e, f) are 0.7335, 0.7089, 0.6107, *0.7421*.

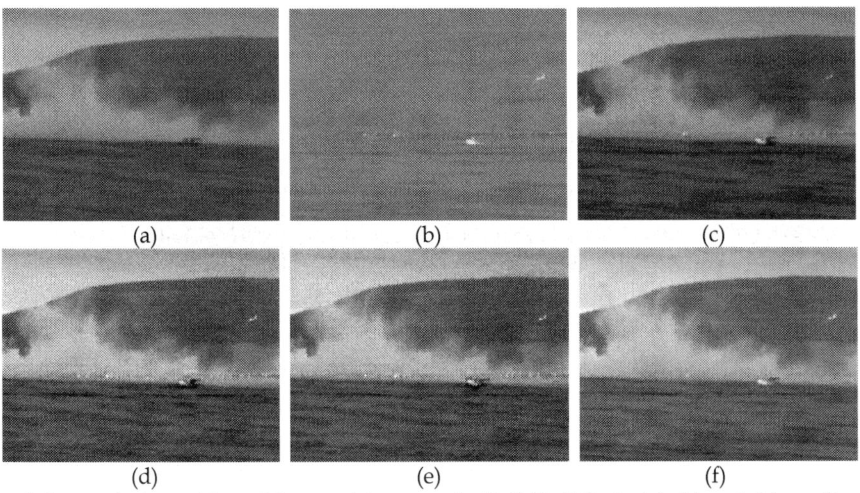

Fig. 5. Image fusion with multispectral image pair #3 (360×270 pixels): (a) and (b) are II and IR images; (c) Fused image by Laplacian pyramid; (d) Fused image by *a*DWTi-IQI; (e) Fused image by *a*DWTi-rSFe; (f) Orientation-based fusion (16×16). The IQI values of four fused images shown in (c, d, e, f) are 0.8160, *0.8347*, 0.8309, 0.8249.

For each case as demonstrated in Figs. 2-6, the IQI values of four fusions are shown in the figure captions. Actually, there were no iterations in Laplacian pyramid fusion and orientation based fusion. For the Laplacian pyramid algorithm, a pair of fixed parameters,

$(L_d, L_w) = (4, 4)$ as typically used in literature, were used in all pyramid fusions (shown in Figs. 2-6). In general, the *a*DWTi-IQI algorithm converges at larger numbers of N_i and L_w but a smaller number of L_d; whereas the *a*DWTi-rSFe algorithm converges at a larger number of L_d but smaller numbers of N_i and L_w. Furthermore, the *a*DWTi-IQI algorithm produces a smooth image, which is especially suitable for noisy images such as multispectral NV images; whereas the *a*DWTi-rSFe algorithm yields a sharpened image, which is ideal for well exposed daylight pictures (like the two-clock image pair). On the other hand, the orientation-based fusion using Gabor wavelet transform is good for the fusion between contrast-unlike images such as visible versus IR (thermal) images.
The IQI values (the higher the better) of four fusions, as shown in the figure captions of Figs. 2-6, are used for quantitative evaluations. The IQI results showed that, the orientation-based fusion is the best in Figs. 2, 4, & 6, while the *a*DWTi-IQI fusion is the best in Figs. 3 & 5. Visual perceptions provide the same rank of fused images as the quantitative evaluations.

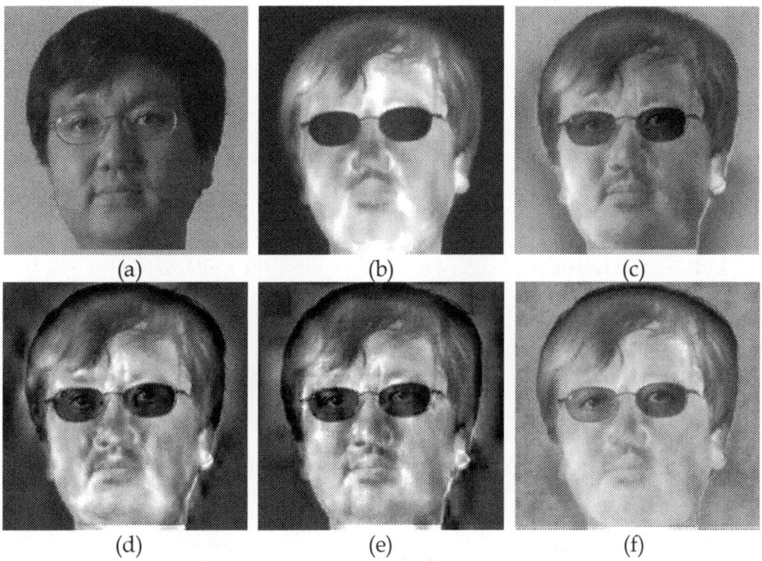

Fig. 6. Image fusion with visible and IR images (taken at daytime; 259×258 pixels). (a) Visible image; (b) IR image; (c) Fused image by Laplacian pyramid; (d) Fused image by *a*DWTi-IQI; (e) Fused image by *a*DWTi-rSFe; (f) Orientation-based fusion (16×16). The IQI values of four fused images shown in (c, d, e, f) are 0.6088, 0.6267, 0.6065, *0.6635*.

As shown in Fig. 6, Laplacian fusion (Fig. 6c) is pretty good but the eyes behind the glasses are not as clear as shown in the orientation fusion (Fig. 6f). Notice that eyes are the most important facial features in face recognition systems and applications. The iterative fusions of *a*DWTi-IQI and *a*DWTi-rSFe show overshot effect especially around the head boundary. The IQI values reveal the same rank of different fusions. The 16×16 orientation fusion (16 bands by 16 orientations, Fig. 6f) presents more details and better contrast than other multiscale fusions (Figs. 6c-e). In an $M \times N$ orientation-based fusion, a larger M (number of bands) is usually beneficial to the detailed images like Fig. 6.

The tree pairs of multispectral images were completely analyzed by the presented night vision colorization algorithm; and the results using *local coloring* algorithm are illustrated in Figs. 7-9. The original input images and the fused images used in the coloring process are shown in Figs. 3-5a, Figs. 3-5b and Figs. 3-5d, respectively. The smooth images (Figs. 3-5d) fused by the *a*DWTi-IQI algorithm were used in night vision colorization because they show better contrast and less sensitive to noises. The false colored images are shown in Figs. 7-9a, which were obtained by assigning image intensified (II) images to blue channels, infrared (IR) images to red channels, and providing averaged II and IR images to green channels. The rationale of forming a false-color image is to assign a long-wavelength NV image to the red channel and to assign a short-wavelength NV to the blue channel. The number of false colors were reduced with the nonlinear diffusion algorithm with AOS (additive operator splitting for fast computation) implementation that facilitated the subsequent segmentation. The segmentation was done in *lαβ* space through clustering and merging operations (see Figs. 7-9b). The parameter values used in clustering and merging are N_{Bin} = [24 24 24], w_{k} = [0.25 0.35 0.40] and T_{Q} = 0.90. To emphasize two chromatic channels (due to more distinguishable among segments) in *lαβ* space, relatively larger weights were assigned in w_{k}. With the segment map, the histogram-matching and statistic-matching could be performed segment by segment (i.e., locally) in *lαβ* space. The source region segments were automatically recognized and associated with proper target color schemes (after the training process is done). The locally colored images (segment-by-segment) are shown in Figs. 7-9c. From a visual examination, the colored images (Figs. 7-9c) appear very natural, realistic, and colorful. The comparable colorization results by using *global coloring* algorithm are presented in Reference (Zheng & Essock, 2008). This segmentation-based *local coloring* process is fully automatic and well adaptive to different types of multisensor images. The input images are not necessary to be multispectral NV images although the illustrations given here use NV images.

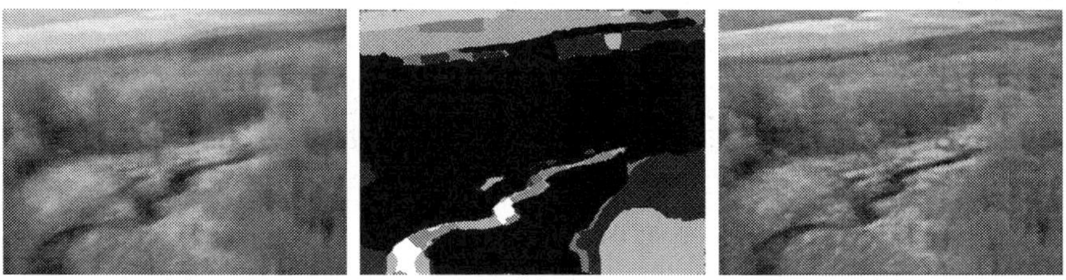

(a) (b) (c)

Fig. 7. Night vision colorization with multispectral image pair #1 (531×401 pixels): Original multispectral images are shown in Figs. 3a-b, and the fused image used in colorization is shown in Fig. 3d. (a) is the false-colored image using Figs. 3a-b; (b) is the segmented image from image (a), where 16 segments were merged from 36 clusters; (c) is the colored image, where six auto-classified color schemes (sky, clouds, plants, water, ground and others) were mapped by jointly using histogram-matching and statistic-matching.

(a) (b) (c)

Fig. 8. Night vision colorization with multispectral image pair #2 (360×270 pixels): Refer to Figs. 4a,b,d for the original multispectral images and the fused image used in colorization. (a) is the false-colored image using Figs. 4a-b; (b) is the segmented image of 12 segments merged from 21 clusters; (c) is the colored image with five auto-classified color schemes (plants, roads, ground, building and others).

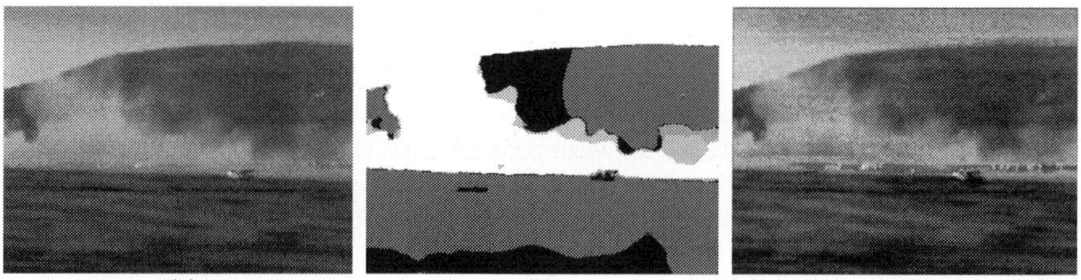

(a) (b) (c)

Fig. 9. Night vision colorization with multispectral image pair #3 (360×270 pixels): Refer to Figs. 5a,b,d for the original multispectral images and the fused image used in colorization. (a) is the false-colored image using Figs. 5a-b; (b) is the segmented image of 14 segments merged from 28 clusters; (c) is the colored image with three auto-classified color schemes (plants, smoke and others).

A different *color fusion* is illustrated in Fig. 10f by replacing the red channel image in Fig. 10a with the orientation fused images in Fig. 10e (IQI = 0.7849). The orientation-based fusion (Fig. 10e) was formed by combining the red channel image of Fig. 10a (visible band) and a IR (thermal) image (Fig. 10b), which shows a better result than Figs. 10c-d. The colors in Fig. 10f is not as natural as daylight colors but useful for human perception especially for those poorly illuminated images. For example, Fig. 10f shows a better contrast and more details than Fig. 10a and Figs. 10c-e. Note that non-uniform band weights (W_b = [0.0250 0.0250 0.0500 0.0500 0.0875 0.0875 0.0875 0.0875 0.0875 0.0875 0.0875 0.0875 0.0500 0.0500 0.0250 0.0250]) were applied to the noisy input images in order to emphasize the contents at medium frequencies meanwhile suppress the noise at high-frequencies.

The night vision colorization process demonstrated here took two-band multispectral NV images as inputs. Actually, the local-coloring procedure can accept two or three input images. If there are more than three bands of images available, we may choose the low-light intensified (visual band) image and two bands of IR images. As far how to choose two bands of IR images, we may use the image fusion algorithm as a screening process. The two selected IR images for colorization should be the two images that can produce the most (maximum) informative fused image among all possible fusions. For example, given three IR images, IR_1, IR_2, IR_3, the two chosen images for colorization, I_{C1}, I_{C2}, should satisfy the following equation: $Fus(I_{C1}, I_{C2}) = max\{Fus(IR_1, IR_2), Fus(IR_1, IR_3), Fus(IR_2, IR_3)\}$, where *Fus* stands for the fusion process and *max* means selecting the fusion of maximum information.

Fig. 10. Color fusion with visible color image and IR image (taken outdoors at dusk; 400×282 pixels). (a) Color image; (b) IR image; (c) Fused image by Laplacian pyramid (IQI = 0.7666); (d) Fused image by *a*DWTi-IQI (IQI = 0.7809); (e) Orientation-based fusion (16×16; IQI = *0.7849*) between of the red channel of (a) and LWIR image; (f) Color fusion by replacing the red channel of Image (a) with Image (e).

5. Conclusions

The multispectral image fusion and night vision colorization approaches presented in this chapter can be performed automatically and adaptively regardless of the image contents. Experimental results with multispectral imagery showed that the fused image is informative and clear, and the colorized image appears realistic and natural. We anticipate that the presented fusion and colorization approaches for multispectral imagery will help improve target recognition and visual analysis, especially for nighttime operations.

Specifically, the proposed approaches can produce two versions of synthesized imagery, a grayscale image and a color image. The image fusion procedure is based on multiscale analysis, and the fused image is suitable to machine analysis (e.g., target recognition). The night vision colorization procedure is based on image segmentation, pattern recognition, and color mapping. The colorized image is good for visual analysis (e.g., pilot navigation). The synthesized multispectral imagery with proposed approaches will eventually lead to improved performance of remote sensing, nighttime navigation, and situational awareness.

6. Acknowledgements

This research is supported by the U. S. Army Research Office under grant number W911NF-08-1-0404.

7. References

Ajazzi, B.; Alparone, L.; Baronti, S.; & Carla, R.; (1998). Assessment of pyramid-based multisensor image data fusion, in *Proc. SPIE 3500*, 237–248.

Barash, D. & Comaniciu, D. (2004). A common framework for nonlinear diffusion, adaptive smoothing, bilateral filtering and mean shift, *Image Vision Computing* **22**(1), 73-81.

Burt, P. J. & Adelson, E. H. (1983). The Laplacian pyramid as a compact image code, *IEEE Trans. Commun.* Com-31 (4), 532-540.

Burt, P. J. & Adelson, E. H. (1985). Merging images through pattern decomposition, *Proc. SPIE* 575, 173–182.

Eskicioglu, A. M. & Fisher, P. S. (1995). Image quality measure and their performance, *IEEE Trans. Commun.* **43**(12), 2959–2965.

Essock, E. A.; McCarley, J. S.; Sinai, M. J. & DeFord, J. K. (2001). Human perception of sensor-fused imagery, in *Interpreting Remote Sensing Imagery: Human Factors*, R. R. Hoffman and A. B. Markman, Eds., Lewis Publishers, Boca Raton, Florida.

Essock, E. A.; Sinai, M. J. & et al. (1999). Perceptual ability with real-world nighttime scenes: imageintensified, infrared, and fused-color imagery, *Hum. Factors* **41**(3), 438–452.

Fairchild, M. D. (1998). *Color Appearance Models*, Addison Wesley Longman Inc., ISBN: 0-201-63464-3, Reading, MA.

Gonzalez, R. C. & Woods, R. E. (2002). *Digital Image Processing* (Second Edition), Prentice Hall, ISBN: 0201180758, Upper Saddle River, NJ.

Hollingsworth, K. P.; Bowyer, K. W.; Flynn, P. J. (2009). The Best Bits in an Iris Code, *IEEE Trans. on Pattern Analysis and Machine Intelligence*, vol. 31, no. 6, pp. 964-973.

Jahard, F.; Fish, D. A.; Rio, A. A. & Thompson C. P. (1997). Far/near infrared adapted pyramid-based fusion for automotive night vision, in *IEEE Proc. 6th Int. Conf. on Image Processing and its Applications* (IPA97), pp. 886–890.

Jones J. P. & Palmer, L. A. (1987). The two-dimensional spectral structure of simple receptive fields in cat striate cortex, Journal of Neurophysiology, vol.58 (6), pp. 1187–1211.

Keys, L. D.; Schmidt, N. J.; & Phillips, B. E. (1990). A prototype example of sensor fusion used for a siting analysis, in Technical Papers 1990, ACSM-ASPRS Annual Conf. *Image Processing and Remote Sensing* **4**, pp. 238–249.

Keysers, D.; Paredes, R.; Ney, H. & Vidal, E. (2002). Combination of tangent vectors and local representations for handwritten digit recognition, Int. Workshop on Statistical Pattern Recognition, Lecture Notes in Computer Science, Vol. 2396, pp. 538-547, Windsor, Ontario, Canada.

Li, S.; Kwok, J. T. & Wang, Y. (2001). Combination of images with diverse focuses using the spatial frequency, *Information Fusion* **2**(3), 169–176.

Nunez, J.; Otazu, X.; & et al. (1999). Image fusion with additive multiresolution wavelet decomposition; applications to spot1landsat images, *J. Opt. Soc. Am. A* **16**, 467–474.

Perona, P. & Malik, J. (1990). Scale space and edge detection using anisotropic diffusion, *IEEE Transactions on Pattern Analysis and Machine Intelligence* **12**, 629–639.

Piella, G. & Heijmans, H. (2003). A new quality metric for image fusion, in *Proc. 2003 Int. Conf. on Image Processing*, Barcelona, Spain.

Pohl C. & Genderen J. L. V. (1998). Review article: multisensor image fusion in remote sensing: concepts, methods and applications, *Int. J. Remote Sens.* **19**(5), 823–854.

Pu T. & Ni, G. (2000). Contrast-based image fusion using the discrete wavelet transform, *Opt. Eng.* **39**(8), 2075–2082.

Rogers, R. H. & Wood, L (1990). The history and status of merging multiple sensor data: an overview, in Technical Papers 1990, ACSMASPRS Annual Conf. *Image Processing and Remote Sensing* **4**, pp. 352–360.

Ruderman, D. L.; Cronin, T. W. & Chiao, C. C. (1998). Statistics of cone responses to natural images: implications for visual coding, *Journal of the Optical Society of America A* **15** (8), 2036–2045.

Toet, A. (2003). Natural colour mapping for multiband nightvision imagery, *Information Fusion* **4**, 155-166.

Toet, A. & IJspeert, J. K. (2001). Perceptual evaluation of different image fusion schemes, in: I. Kadar (Ed.), *Signal Processing, Sensor Fusion, and Target Recognition X*, The International Society for Optical Engineering, Bellingham, WA, pp.436–441.

Toet, A.; IJspeert, J.K.; Waxman, A. M. & Aguilar, M. (1997). Fusion of visible and thermal imagery improves situational awareness, in: J.G. Verly (Ed.), *Enhanced and Synthetic Vision 1997*, International Society for Optical Engineering, Bellingham, WA, pp.177–188.

Varga, J. T. (1999). Evaluation of operator performance using true color and artificial color in natural scene perception (Report ADA363036), Naval Postgraduate School, Monterey, CA.

Wang, Z. & Bovik, A. C. (2002). A universal image quality index, *IEEE Signal Processing Letters* **9**(3), 81–84.

Waxman, A.M.; Gove, A. N. & et al. (1996). Progress on color night vision: visible/IR fusion, perception and search, and low-light CCD imaging, *Proc. SPIE Vol. 2736*, pp. 96-107, Enhanced and Synthetic Vision 1996, Jacques G. Verly; Ed.

Zheng, Y. & Agyepong, K. (2007). Mass Detection with Digitized Screening Mammograms by Using Gabor Features, Proceedings of the SPIE, Vol. 6514, pp. 651402-1-12.

Zheng, Y. & Essock, E. A. (2008). A local-coloring method for night-vision colorization utilizing image analysis and image fusion, *Information Fusion* **9**, 186-199.

Zheng, Y.; Essock, E. A. & Hansen, B. C. (2005). An advanced DWT fusion algorithm and its optimization by using the metric of image quality index, *Optical Engineering* **44** (3), 037003-1-12.

Zheng, Y.; Essock, E. A. & Hansen, B. C. (2004). An advanced image fusion algorithm based on wavelet transform—incorporation with PCA and morphological processing, *Proc. SPIE 5298*, 177–187.

Zheng, Y.; Essock, E. A.; Hansen, B. C. & Haun, A. M. (2007). A new metric based on extended spatial frequency and its application to DWT based fusion algorithms, *Information Fusion* **8**(2), 177-192.

Zheng, Y.; Hansen, B. C. & Haun, A. M. & Essock, E. A. (2005). Coloring Night-vision Imagery with Statistical Properties of Natural Colors by Using Image Segmentation and Histogram Matching, *Proceedings of the SPIE*, Vol. 5667, pp. 107-117.

22

Super-Resolution Reconstruction by Image Fusion and Application to Surveillance Videos Captured by Small Unmanned Aircraft Systems

Qiang He[1] and Richard R. Schultz[2]

[1]*Department of Mathematics, Computer and Information Sciences*
Mississippi Valley State University, Itta Bena, MS 38941
QiangHe@mvsu.edu
[2]*Department of Electrical Engineering*
University of North Dakota, Grand Forks, ND 58202-7165
RichardSchultz@mail.und.edu

1. Introduction

In practice, surveillance video captured by a small Unmanned Aircraft System (UAS) digital imaging payload is almost always blurred and degraded because of limits of the imaging equipment and less than ideal atmospheric conditions. Small UAS vehicles typically have wingspans of less than four meters and payload carrying capacities of less than 50 kilograms, which results in a high vibration environment due to winds buffeting the aircraft and thus poorly stabilized video that is not necessarily pointed at a target of interest. Super-resolution image reconstruction can reconstruct a highly-resolved image of a scene from either a single image or a time series of low-resolution images based on image registration and fusion between different video frames [1, 6, 8, 18, 20, 27]. By fusing several subpixel-registered, low-resolution video frames, we can reconstruct a high-resolution panoramic image and thus improve imaging system performance. There are four primary applications for super-resolution image reconstruction:

1. *Automatic Target Recognition:* The interesting target is hard to identify and recognize under degraded videos and images. For a series of low-resolution images captured by a small UAS vehicle flown over an area under surveillance, we need to perform super-resolution to enhance image quality and automatically recognize targets of interest.
2. *Remote Sensing:* Remote sensing observes the Earth and helps monitor vegetation health, bodies of water, and climate change based on image data gathered by wireless equipments over time. We can gather additional information on a given area by increasing the spatial image resolution.
3. *Environmental Monitoring:* Related to remote sensing, environmental monitoring helps determine if an event is unusual or extreme, and to assist in the development of an appropriate experimental design for monitoring a region over time. With the

development of green industry, the related requirements become more and more important.

4. *Medical Imaging:* In medical imaging, several images of the same area may be blurred and/or degraded because of imaging acquisition limitations (e.g., human respiration during image acquisition). We can recover and improve the medical image quality through super-resolution techniques.

An Unmanned Aircraft System is an aircraft/ground station that can either be remote-controlled manually or is capable of flying autonomously under the guidance of pre-programmed GPS waypoint flight plans or more complex onboard intelligent systems. UAS aircrafts have recently been found a wide variety of military and civilian applications, particularly in intelligence, surveillance, and reconnaissance as well as remote sensing. Through surveillance videos captured by a UAS digital imaging payload over the same general area, we can improve the image quality of pictures around an area of interest. Super-resolution image reconstruction is capable of generating a high-resolution image from a sequence of low-resolution images based on image registration and fusion between different image frames, which is directly applicable to reconnaissance and surveillance videos captured by small UAS aircraft payloads.

Super-resolution image reconstruction can be realized from either a single image or from a time series of multiple video frames. In general, multiframe super-resolution image reconstruction is more useful and more accurate, since multiple frames can provide much more information for reconstruction than a single picture. Multiframe super-resolution image reconstruction algorithms can be divided into essentially two categories: super-resolution from the spatial domain [3, 5, 11, 14, 26, 31] and super-resolution from the frequency domain [27, 29], based on between-frame motion estimation from either the spatial or the frequency domains.

Frequency-domain super-resolution assumes that the between-frame motion is global in nature. Hence, we can register a sequence of images through phase differences in the frequency domain, in which the phase shift can be estimated by computing the correlation. The frequency-domain technique is effective in making use of low-frequency components to register a series of images containing aliasing artifacts. However, frequency-domain approaches are highly sensitive to motion errors. For spatial-domain super-resolution methods, between-frame image registration is computed from the feature correspondences in the spatial domain. The motion models can be global for the whole image or local for a set of corresponding feature vectors [2]. Zomet *et al.* [31] developed a robust super-resolution method. Their approach uses the median filter in the sequence of image gradients to iteratively update the super-resolution results. This method is robust to outliers, but computationally expensive. Keren *et al.* [14] developed an algorithm using a Taylor series expansion on the motion model extension, and then simplified the parameter computation. Irani *et al.* [11] applied local motion models in the spatial domain and computed multiple object motions by estimating the optical flow between frames.

Our goal here is to develop an efficient (i.e., real-time or near-real-time) and robust super-resolution image reconstruction algorithm to recover high-resolution video captured from a low-resolution UAS digital imaging payload. Because of the time constraints on processing video data in near-real-time, optimal performance is not expected, although we still anticipate obtaining satisfactory visual results.

This paper proceeds as follows. Section 2 describes the basic modeling of super-resolution image reconstruction. Our proposed super-resolution algorithm is presented in Section 3, with experimental results presented in Section 4. We draw conclusions from this research in Section 5.

2. Modeling of Super-Resolution Image Reconstruction

Following the descriptions in [4, 7], we extend the images column-wise and represent them as column vectors. We then build the linear relationship between the original high-resolution image $\vec{X}$ and each measured low-resolution image $\vec{Y}_k$ through matrix representation. Given a sequence of low resolution images $i_1, i_2, \cdots, i_n$ (where n is the number of images), the relationship between a low-resolved image $\vec{Y}_k$ and the corresponding highly-resolved image $\vec{X}$ can be formulated as a linear system,

$$\vec{Y}_k = D_k C_k F_k \vec{X} + \vec{E}_k \text{, for } k = 1, \cdots, n \tag{1}$$

where $\vec{X}$ is the vector representation for the original highly-resolved image, $\vec{Y}_k$ is the vector representation for each measured low-resolution image, $\vec{E}_k$ is the Gaussian white noise vector for the measured low-resolution image i_k, F_k is the geometric warping matrix, C_k is the blurring matrix, and D_k is the down-sampling matrix. Assume that the original highly-resolved image has a dimension of $p \times p$, and every low-resolution image has a dimension of $q \times q$. Therefore, $\vec{X}$ is a $p^2 \times 1$ vector and $\vec{Y}_k$ is a $q^2 \times 1$ vector. In general, $q << p$, so equation (1) is an underdetermined linear system. If we group all n equations together, it is possible to generate an overdetermined linear system with $nq^2 \geq p^2$:

$$\begin{bmatrix} \vec{Y}_1 \\ \vdots \\ \vec{Y}_n \end{bmatrix} = \begin{bmatrix} D_1 C_1 F_1 \\ \vdots \\ D_n C_n F_n \end{bmatrix} \vec{X} + \begin{bmatrix} \vec{E}_1 \\ \vdots \\ \vec{E}_n \end{bmatrix} \tag{2}$$

Equivalently, we can express this system as

$$\mathbf{Y} = \mathbf{H}\vec{X} + \mathbf{E}, \tag{3}$$

where

$$\mathbf{Y} = \begin{bmatrix} \vec{Y}_1 \\ \vdots \\ \vec{Y}_n \end{bmatrix}, \ \mathbf{H} = \begin{bmatrix} D_1 C_1 F_1 \\ \vdots \\ D_n C_n F_n \end{bmatrix}, \ \mathbf{E} = \begin{bmatrix} \vec{E}_1 \\ \vdots \\ \vec{E}_n \end{bmatrix}.$$

In general, the solution to super-resolution reconstruction is an ill-posed inverse problem. The accurate analytic mathematical solution can not be reached. There are three practical estimation algorithms used to solve this (typically) ill-posed inverse problem [4], that is, (1) maximum likelihood (ML) estimation, (2) maximum *a posteriori* (MAP) estimation, and (3) projection onto convex sets (POCS).

Different from these three approaches, Zomet *et al.* [31] developed a robust super-resolution method. The approach uses a median filter in the sequence of image gradients to iteratively update the super-resolution results. From equation (1), the total error for super-resolution reconstruction in the L_2-norm can be represented as

$$L_2(\vec{X}) = \frac{1}{2}\sum_{k=1}^{n}\left\|\vec{Y}_k - D_k C_k F_k \vec{X}\right\|_2^2 . \tag{4}$$

Differentiating $L_2(\vec{X})$ with respect to $\vec{X}$, we have the gradient $\nabla L_2(\vec{X})$ of $L_2(\vec{X})$ as the sum of derivatives over the low-resolution input images:

$$\nabla L_2(\vec{X}) = \sum_{k=1}^{n} F_k^T C_k^T D_k^T \left(D_k C_k F_k \vec{X} - \vec{Y}_k\right) \tag{5}$$

We can then implement an iterative gradient-based optimization technique to reach the minimum value of $L_2(\vec{X})$, such that

$$\vec{X}^{t+1} = \vec{X}^t + \lambda \nabla L_2(\vec{X}) , \tag{6}$$

where λ is a scalar that defines the step size of each iteration in the direction of the gradient $\nabla L_2(\vec{X})$.

Instead of a summation of gradients over the input images, Zomet [31] calculated n times the scaled pixel-wise median of the gradient sequence in $\nabla L_2(\vec{X})$. That is,

$$\vec{X}^{t+1} = \vec{X}^t + \lambda \cdot n \cdot median\left\{F_1^T C_1^T D_1^T \left(D_1 C_1 F_1 \vec{X} - \vec{Y}_1\right), \cdots, F_n^T C_n^T D_n^T \left(D_n C_n F_n \vec{X} - \vec{Y}_n\right)\right\} , \tag{7}$$

where t is the iteration step number. It is well-known that the median filter is robust to outliers. Additionally, the median can agree well with the mean value under a sufficient number of samples for a symmetric distribution. Through the median operation in equation (7), we supposedly have a robust super-resolution solution. However, we need to execute many computations to implement this technique. We not only need to compute the gradient map for every input image, but we also need to implement a large number of comparisons to compute the median. Hence, this is not truly an efficient super-resolution approach.

3. Efficient and Robust Super-Resolution Image Reconstruction

In order to improve the efficiency of super-resolution, we do not compute the median over the gradient sequence for every iteration. We have developed an efficient and robust super-resolution algorithm for application to small UAS surveillance video that is based on a coarse-to-fine strategy. The coarse step builds a coarsely super-resolved image sequence from the original video data by piece-wise registration and bicubic interpolation between every additional frame and a fixed reference frame. If we calculate pixel-wise medians in the coarsely super-resolved image sequence, we can reconstruct a refined super-resolved image. This is the fine step for our super-resolution image reconstruction algorithm. The advantage of our algorithm is that there are no iterations within our implementation, which is unlike traditional approaches based on highly-computational iterative algorithms [15]. Thus, our algorithm is very efficient, and it provides an acceptable level of visual performance.

3.1 Up-sampling process between additional frame and the reference frame

Without loss of generality, we assume that i_1 is the reference frame. For every additional frame i_k $(1 < k \le n)$ in the video sequence, we transform it into the coordinate system of the reference frame through image registration. Thus, we can create a warped image

$i_k w = \text{Regis}(i_1, i_k)$ of i_k in the coordinate system of the reference frame i_1. We can then generate an up-sampled image $i_k u$ through bicubic interpolation between $i_k w$ and i_1,

$$i_k u = \text{Interpolation}(i_k w, i_1, factor), \tag{8}$$

where $factor$ is the up-sampling scale.

3.2 Motion estimation

As required in multiframe super-resolution approaches, the most important step is image registration between the reference frame and any additional frames. Here, we apply subpixel motion estimation [14, 23] to estimate between-frame motion. If the between-frame motion is represented primarily by translation and rotation (i.e., the affine model), then the Keren motion estimation method [14] provides a good performance. Generally, the motion between aerial images observed from an aircraft or a satellite can be well approximated by this model. Mathematically, the Keren motion model is represented as

$$\begin{pmatrix} x' \\ y' \end{pmatrix} = s \begin{pmatrix} \cos(\theta) & -\sin(\theta) \\ \sin(\theta) & \cos(\theta) \end{pmatrix} \begin{pmatrix} x \\ y \end{pmatrix} + \begin{pmatrix} a \\ b \end{pmatrix}, \tag{9}$$

where θ is the rotation angle, and a and b are translations along directions x and y, respectively. In this expression, s is the scaling factor, and x' and y' are registered coordinates of x and y in the reference coordinate system.

3.3 Proposed algorithm for efficient and robust super-resolution

Our algorithm for efficient and robust super-resolution image reconstruction consists of the following steps:

1. Choose frame i_1 as the reference frame.
2. For every additional frame i_k:
   - Estimate the motion between the additional frame i_k and the reference frame i_1.
   - Register additional frame i_k to the reference frame i_1 using the $i_k w = \text{Regis}(i_1, i_k)$ operator.
   - Create the coarsely-resolved image $i_k u = \text{Interpolation}(i_k w, i_1, factor)$ through bicubic interpolation between the registered frame $i_k w$ and the reference frame i_1.
3. Compute the median of the coarsely resolved up-sampled image sequence $\{i_2 u, \ \cdots, \ i_n u\}$ as the updated super-resolved image.
4. Enhance the super-resolved image if necessary by sharpening edges, increasing contrast, etc.

4. Experimental Results

The proposed efficient and robust super-resolution image reconstruction algorithm was tested on two sets of real video data captured by an experimental small UAS operated by

Lockheed Martin Corporation flying a custom-built electro-optical (EO) and uncooled thermal infrared (IR) imager. The time series of images are extracted from videos with low-resolution 60 x 80. In comparison with five well-known super-resolution algorithms in real UAS video tests, namely the robust super-resolution algorithm [31], the bicubic interpolation, the iterated back projection algorithm [10], the projection onto convex sets (POCS) [24], and the Papoulis-Gerchberg algorithm [8, 19], our proposed algorithm gave both good efficiency and robustness as well as acceptable visual performance. For low-resolution 60 x 80 pixel frames with five frames in every image sequence, super-resolution image reconstruction with up-sampling factors of 2 and 4 can be implemented very efficiently (approximately in real-time). Our algorithm was developed using MATLAB 7.4.0. We implemented our algorithm on a Dell 8250 workstation with a Pentium 4 CPU running at 3.06GHz with 1.0GB of RAM. If we ported the algorithm into the C programming language, the algorithm would execute much more quickly.

Test data taken from small UAS aircraft are highly susceptible to vibrations and sensor pointing movements. As a result, the related video data are blurred and the interesting targets are hard to be identified and recognized. The experimental results for the first data set are given in Figures 1, 2, and 3. The experimental results for the second data set are provided in Figures 4, 5, and 6.

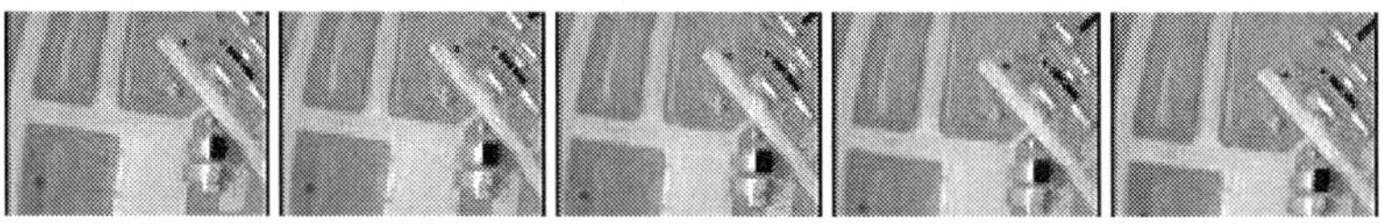

(a) (b) (c) (d) (e)

Fig. 1. Test Set #1 low-resolution uncooled thermal infrared (IR) image sequence captured by a small UAS digital imaging payload. Five typical frames are shown in (a), (b), (c), (d), and (e), with a frame size of 60 x 80 pixels.

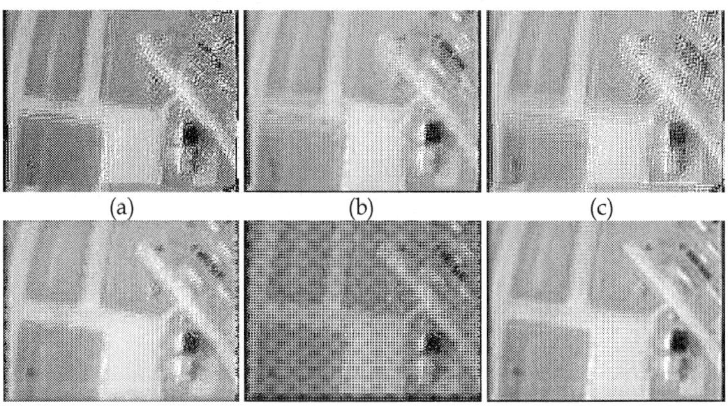

(a) (b) (c)

(d) (e) (f)

Fig. 2. Test Set #1 super-resolved images, factor 2 (reduced to 80% of original size for display). Results were computed as follows: (a) Robust super-resolution [31]. (b) Bicubic interpolation. (c) Iterated back projection [10]. (d) Projection onto convex sets (POCS) [24]. (e) Papoulis-Gerchberg algorithm [8, 19]. (f) Proposed method.

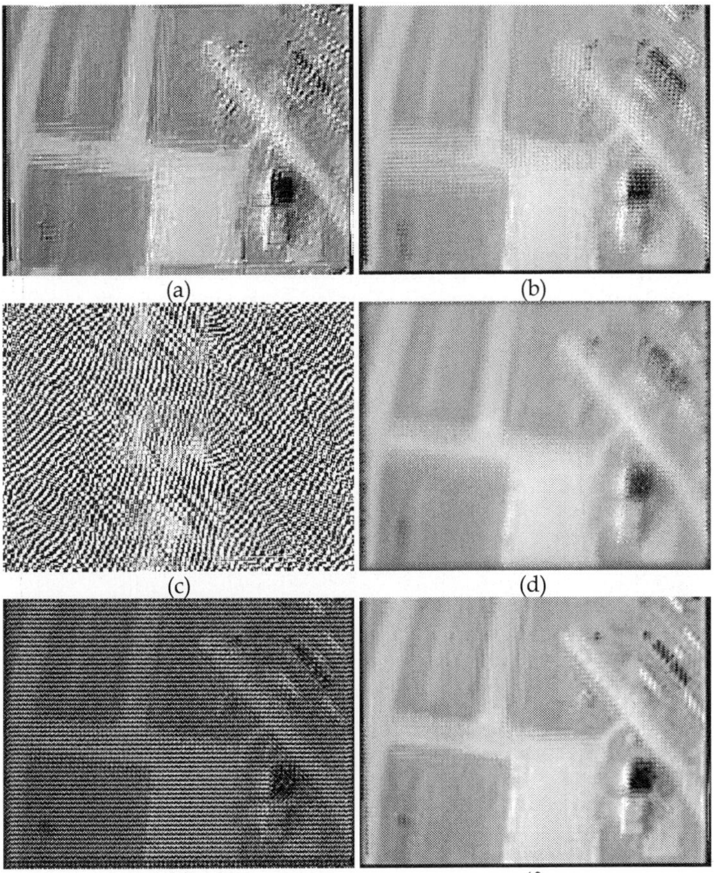

(a) (b) (c) (d) (e) (f)

Fig. 3. Test Set #1 super-resolved images, factor 4 (reduced to 60% of original size for display). Results were computed as follows: (a) Robust super-resolution [31]. (b) Bicubic interpolation. (c) Iterated back projection [10]. (d) Projection onto convex sets (POCS) [24]. (e) Papoulis-Gerchberg algorithm [8, 19]. (f) Proposed method.

(a) (b) (c) (d) (e)

Fig. 4. Test Set #2 low-resolution uncooled thermal infrared (IR) image sequence captured by a small UAS digital imaging payload. Five typical frames are shown in (a), (b), (c), (d), and (e), with a frame size of 60 x 80 pixels.

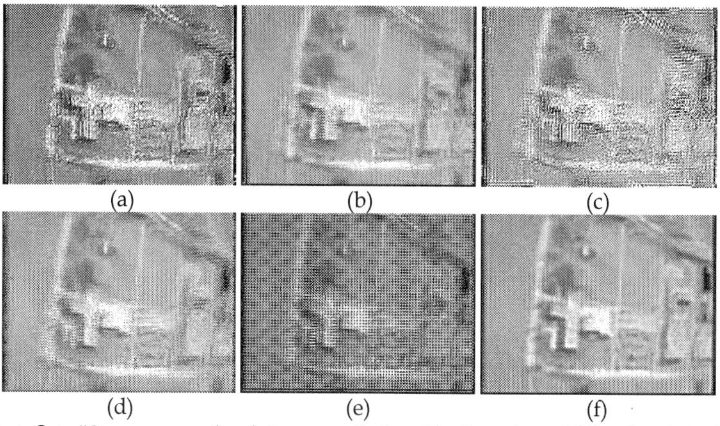

Fig. 5. Test Set #2 super-resolved images, factor 2(reduced to 80% of original size for display). Results were computed as follows: (a) Robust super-resolution [31]. (b) Bicubic interpolation. (c) Iterated back projection [10]. (d) Projection onto convex sets (POCS) [24]. (e) Papoulis-Gerchberg algorithm [8, 19]. (f) Proposed method.

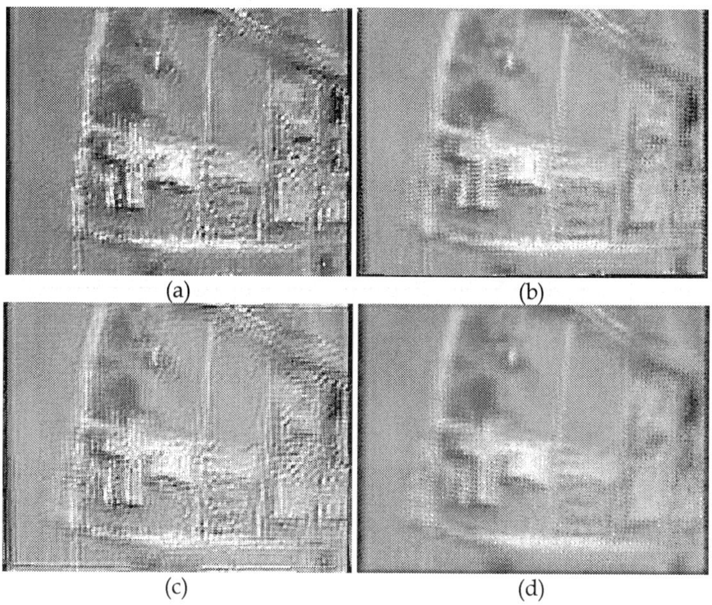

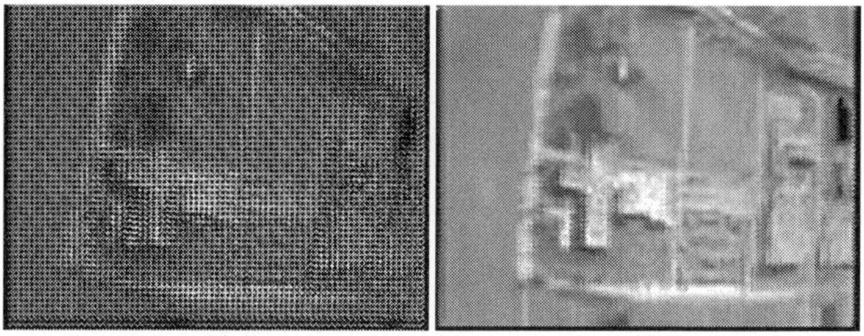

(e) (f)

Fig. 6. Test Set #2 super-resolved images, factor 4(reduced to 60% of original size for display). Results were computed as follows: (a) Robust super-resolution [31]. (b) Bicubic interpolation. (c) Iterated back projection [10]. (d) Projection onto convex sets (POCS) [24]. (e) Papoulis-Gerchberg algorithm [8, 19]. (f) Proposed method.

Tables 1, 2, 3, and 4 show the CPU running times in seconds for five established super-resolution algorithms and our proposed algorithm with up-sampling factors of 2 and 4. Here, the robust super-resolution algorithm is abbreviated as RobustSR, the bicubic interpolation algorithm is abbreviated as Interp, the iterated back projection algorithm is abbreviated as IBP, the projection onto convex sets algorithm is abbreviated as POCS, the Papoulis-Gerchberg algorithm is abbreviated as PG, and the proposed efficient super-resolution algorithm is abbreviated as MedianESR. From these tables, we can see that bicubic interpolation gives the fastest computation time, but its visual performance is rather poor. The robust super-resolution algorithm using the longest running time is computationally expensive, while the proposed algorithm is comparatively efficient and presents good visual performance. In experiments, all of these super-resolution algorithms were implemented using the same estimated motion parameters.

Algorithms	RobustSR	Interp	IBP	POCS	PG	MedianESR
CPU Time (s)	9.7657	3.6574	5.5575	2.1997	0.3713	5.2387

Table 1. CPU running time for Test Set #1 with scale factor 2.

Algorithms	RobustSR	Interp	IBP	POCS	PG	MedianESR
CPU Time (s)	17.7110	2.5735	146.7134	11.8985	16.7603	6.3339

Table 2. CPU running time for Test Set #1 with scale factor 4.

Algorithms	RobustSR	Interp	IBP	POCS	PG	MedianESR
CPU Time (s)	8.2377	2.8793	9.6826	1.7034	0.5003	5.2687

Table 3. CPU running time for Test Set #2 with scale factor 2.

Algorithms	RobustSR	Interp	IBP	POCS	PG	MedianESR
CPU Time (s)	25.4105	2.7463	18.3672	11.0448	22.1578	8.2099

Table 4. CPU running time for Test Set #2 with scale factor 4.

5. Summary

We have presented an efficient and robust super-resolution restoration method by computing the median on a coarsely-resolved up-sampled image sequence. In comparison with other established super-resolution image reconstruction approaches, our algorithm is not only efficient with respect to the number of computations required, but it also has an acceptable level of visual performance. This algorithm should provide a movement in the right direction with respect to real-time super-resolution image reconstruction. In future research, we plan to try other motion models such as planar homography and multi-model motion in order to determine whether or not we can achieve better performance. In addition, we will explore to incorporate the natural image characteristics to set up the criterion of super-resolution algorithms such that the super-resolved images provide high visual performance under natural image properties.

6. References

1. S. Borman and R. L. Stevenson, "Spatial Resolution Enhancement of Low-Resolution Image Sequences - A Comprehensive Review with Directions for Future Research." University of Notre Dame, Technical Report, 1998.
2. D. Capel and A. Zisserman, "Computer Vision Applied to Super Resolution." *IEEE Signal Processing Magazine*, vol. 20, no. 3, pp. 75-86, May 2003.
3. M. C. Chiang and T. E. Boulte, "Efficient Super-Resolution via Image Warping." *Image Vis. Comput.*, vol. 18, no. 10, pp. 761-771, July 2000.
4. M. Elad and A. Feuer, "Restoration of a Single Super-Resolution Image from Several Blurred, Noisy and Down-Sampled Measured Images." *IEEE Trans. Image Processing*, vol. 6, pp. 1646-1658, Dec. 1997.
5. M. Elad and Y. Hel-Or, "A Fast Super-Resolution Reconstruction Algorithm for Pure Translational Motion and Common Space Invariant Blur." *IEEE Trans. Image Processing*, vol. 10, pp. 1187-1193, Aug. 2001.
6. S. Farsiu, D. Robinson, M. Elad, and P. Milanfar, "Advances and Challenges in Super-Resolution." *International Journal of Imaging Systems and Technology*, Special Issue on High Resolution Image Reconstruction, vol. 14, no. 2, pp. 47-57, Aug. 2004.
7. S. Farsiu, D. Robinson, M. Elad, and P. Milanfar, "Fast and Robust Multi-Frame Super-resolution." *IEEE Transactions on Image Processing*, vol. 13, no. 10, pp. 1327-1344, Oct. 2004.
8. R.W. Gerchberg, "Super-Resolution through Error Energy Reduction." *Optica Acta*, vol. 21, no. 9, pp. 709-720, 1974.
9. R. C. Gonzalez and P. Wintz, *Digital Image Processing*. New York: Addison-Wesley, 1987.
10. M. Irani and S. Peleg, "Super Resolution from Image Sequences." *International Conference on Pattern Recognition*, vol. 2, pp. 115-120, June 1990.
11. M. Irani, B. Rousso, and S. Peleg, "Computing Occluding and Transparent Motions." *International Journal of Computer Vision*, vol. 12, no. 1, pp. 5-16, Feb. 1994.
12. M. Irani and S. Peleg, "Improving Resolution by Image Registration." *CVGIP: Graph. Models Image Processing*, vol. 53, pp. 231-239, 1991.
13. A. K. Jain, *Fundamentals in Digital Image Processing*. Englewood Cliffs, NJ: Prentice-Hall, 1989.

14. D. Keren, S. Peleg, and R. Brada, "Image Sequence Enhancement Using Sub-Pixel Displacements." In *Proceedings of IEEE Computer Society Conference on Computer Vision and Pattern Recognition (CVPR '88)*, pp. 742-746, Ann Arbor, Michigan, June 1988.
15. S. P. Kim and W.-Y. Su, "Subpixel Accuracy Image Registration by Spectrum Cancellation." In *Proceedings IEEE International Conference on Acoustics, Speech and Signal Processing*, vol. 5, pp. 153-156, April 1993.
16. R. L. Lagendijk and J. Biemond. *Iterative Identification and Restoration of Images*. Boston, MA: Kluwer, 1991.
17. L. Lucchese and G. M. Cortelazzo, "A Noise-Robust Frequency Domain Technique for Estimating Planar Roto-Translations." *IEEE Transactions on Signal Processing*, vol. 48, no. 6, pp. 1769–1786, June 2000.
18. N. Nguyen, P. Milanfar, and G. H. Golub, "A Computationally Efficient Image Superresolution Algorithm." *IEEE Trans. Image Processing*, vol. 10, pp. 573-583, April 2001.
19. A. Papoulis, "A New Algorithm in Spectral Analysis and Band-Limited Extrapolation." *IEEE Transactions on Circuits and Systems*, vol. 22, no. 9, pp. 735-742, 1975.
20. S. C. Park, M. K. Park, and M. G. Kang, "Super-Resolution Image Reconstruction: A Technical Overview." *IEEE Signal Processing Magazine*, vol. 20, no. 3, pp. 21-36, May 2003.
21. S. Peleg, D. Keren, and L. Schweitzer, "Improving Image Resolution Using Subpixel Motion." *CVGIP: Graph. Models Image Processing*, vol. 54, pp. 181-186, March 1992.
22. W. K. Pratt, *Digital Image Processing*. New York: Wiley, 1991.
23. R. R. Schultz, L. Meng, and R. L. Stevenson, "Subpixel Motion Estimation for Super-Resolution Image Sequence Enhancement." *Journal of Visual Communication and Image Representation*, vol. 9, no. 1, pp. 38-50, 1998.
24. H. Stark and P. Oskoui, "High-Resolution Image Recovery from Image-Plane Arrays Using Convex Projections." *Journal of the Optical Society of America, Series A*, vol. 6, pp. 1715-1726, Nov. 1989.
25. H. S. Stone, M. T. Orchard, E.-C. Chang, and S. A. Martucci, "A Fast Direct Fourier-Based Algorithm for Sub-Pixel Registration of Images." *IEEE Transactions on Geoscience and Remote Sensing*, vol. 39, no. 10, pp. 2235-2243, Oct. 2001.
26. L. Teodosio and W. Bender, "Salient Video Stills: Content and Context Preserved." In *Proc. 1st ACM Int. Conf. Multimedia*, vol. 10, pp. 39-46, Anaheim, California, Aug. 1993.
27. R. Y. Tsai and T. S. Huang, "Multiframe Image Restoration and Registration." In *Advances in Computer Vision and Image Processing*, vol. 1, chapter 7, pp. 317-339, JAI Press, Greenwich, Connecticut, 1984.
28. H. Ur and D. Gross, "Improved Resolution from Sub-Pixel Shifted Pictures." *CVGIP: Graph. Models Image Processing*, vol. 54, no. 181-186, March 1992.
29. P. Vandewalle, S. Susstrunk, and M. Vetterli, "A Frequency Domain Approach to Registration of Aliased Images with Application to Super-Resolution." *EURASIP Journal on Applied Signal Processing*, vol. 2006, pp. 1-14, Article ID 71459.
30. B. Zitova and J. Flusser, "Image Registration Methods: A Survey." *Image and Vision Computing*, vol. 21, no. 11, pp. 977-1000, 2003.
31. A. Zomet, A. Rav-Acha, and S. Peleg, "Robust Superresolution." In *Proceedings of IEEE Computer Society Conference on Computer Vision and Pattern Recognition (CVPR '01)*, vol. 1, pp. 645-650, Kauai, Hawaii, Dec. 2001.